# Music, Movies, Meanings, and Markets:
# Cinemajazzamatazz

**Routledge Interpretive Marketing Research**
Edited by Stephen Brown *University of Ulster,*
*Northern Ireland*

Recent years have witnessed an "interpretive turn" in marketing and consumer research. Methodologies from the humanities are taking their place alongside those drawn from the traditional social sciences.

Qualitative and literary modes of marketing discourse are growing in popularity. Art and aesthetics are increasingly firing the marketing imagination.

This series brings together the most innovative work in the burgeoning interpretive marketing research tradition. It ranges across the methodological spectrum from grounded theory to personal introspection, covers all aspects of the postmodern marketing 'mix', from advertising to product development, and embraces marketing's principal sub-disciplines.

1. **The Why of Consumption**
   *Edited by S. Ratneshwar, David Glen Mick and Cynthia Huffman*

2. **Imagining Marketing**
   Art, Aesthetics and the Avant-garde
   *Edited by Stephen Brown and Anthony Patterson*

3. **Marketing and Social Construction**
   Exploring the Rhetorics of Managed Consumption
   *Chris Hackley*

4. **Visual Consumption**
   *Jonathan Schroeder*

5. **Consuming Books**
   The Marketing and Consumption of Literature
   *Edited by Stephen Brown*

6. **The Undermining of Beliefs in the Autonomy and Rationality of Consumers**
   *John O'Shaughnessy and Nicholas Jackson O'Shaughnessy*

7. **Marketing Discourse**
A Critical Perspective
*Per Skålén, Markus Fellesson and Martin Fougère*

8. **Explorations in Consumer Culture Theory**
*Edited by John F. Sherry Jr. and Eileen Fischer*

9. **Interpretation in Social Life, Social Science, and Marketing**
*John O'Shaughnessy*

10. **Interpreting Consumer Choice**
The Behavioral Perspective Model
*Gordon R. Foxall*

11. **Managing Service Firms**
The Power of Managerial Marketing
*Per Skålén*

12. **Interactive Marketing**
Revolution or Rhetoric?
*Christopher Miles*

13. **Beyond the Consumption Bubble?**
*Karin M. Ekström and Kay Glans*

14. **Music, Movies, Meanings, and Markets: Cinemajazzamatazz**
*Morris B. Holbrook*

*Also available in the Routledge Interpretive Marketing Research series:*

**Representing Consumers: Voices, views and visions**
*Edited by Barbara B. Stern*

**Romancing the Market**
*Edited by Stephen Brown, Anne Marie Doherty and Bill Clarke*

**Consumer Value: A framework for analysis and research**
*Edited by Morris B. Holbrook*

**Marketing and Feminism: Current issues and research**
*Edited by Miriam Catterall, Pauline Maclaran and Lorna Stevens*

# Music, Movies, Meanings, and Markets: Cinemajazzamatazz

Morris B. Holbrook

Routledge
Taylor & Francis Group

LONDON AND NEW YORK

First published 2011 by Routledge

2 Park Square, Milton Park, Abingdon, Oxon OX14 4RN
711 Third Avenue, New York, NY 10017, USA

*Routledge is an imprint of the Taylor & Francis Group, an informa business*

First issued in paperback 2016

*Library of Congress Cataloging in Publication Data*
Holbrook, Morris B.
 Music, movies, meanings, and markets : cinemajazzamatazz / by
Morris B. Holbrook.
  p. cm. — (Routledge interpretive marketing research ; 14)
  Includes bibliographical references. (alk. paper)
 1. Motion picture music—United States—History and criticism.
 2. Jazz in motion pictures. I. Title.
 ML2075.H635 2011
 781.5′420973—dc22                                    2010048880

ISBN: 978–0–415–89313–8 (hbk)
ISBN: 978–1–138–20300–6 (pbk)

Typeset in Sabon by
Keystroke, Station Road, Wolverhampton

For Sally and Chris,
With Love

# Contents

*Preface*                                                          xiii
*Acknowledgments*                                                 xxiii

**PART I**
**Introduction: Ambi-Diegetic Music in Motion Pictures**            1

  1 The Role of Ambi-Diegetic Film Music in the Product
    Design of Hollywood Movies: Macromarketing in
    La-La-Land                                                      3

**PART II**
**Ambi-Diegetic Jazz and the Development of Character**            55

Introduction to Part II                                            56

  2 Ambi-Diegetic Film Music as a Product-Design and
    -Placement Strategy: The Crosby Duets in *High
    Society* (1956)                                                63

  3 The Cinemusical Role of "My Funny Valentine" in
    *The Fabulous Baker Boys* (1989) and *The Talented
    Mr. Ripley* (1999)                                             98

**PART III**
**The Plot Thickens: Cinemusical Meanings in the
Crime-Plus-Jazz Genre**                                           143

Introduction to Part III                                          144

  4 *Pete Kelly's Blues* (1955)                                    149

  5  *The Cotton Club* (1984)                                      157

  6  *Kansas City* (1996)                                          162


**PART IV**
**Jazz, Films, and Macromarketing Themes: Art versus**
**Commerce in the Young Man-with-a-Horn Genre**          **171**

Introduction to Part IV                                          172

  7  *Young Man with a Horn* (1950)                               179

  8  *Paris Blues* (1961)                                         188

  9  *Mo' Better Blues* (1990)                                    200


**PART V**
**Ambi-Diegetic, Nondiegetic, and Diegetic Cinemusical**
**Meanings in Motion Pictures: Commerce, Art, and**
**Brando Loyalty . . . or . . . De Niro, My God, to Thee**     **213**

Introduction to Part V                                          214

 10  Commerce and *New York, New York* (1977): He's
     Delightful; He's Delicious; He's . . . De Niro              219

 11  Art and *Heart Beat* (1980): Stars Fell on Algolagnia       229

 12  Brando Loyalty and *The Score* (2001): How Do You
     Keep the Music Paying?                                      234


**PART VI**
**God Is in the Details**                                      **241**

Introduction to Part VI                                         242

 13  His Eye Is on the Sparrow: Small-but-Significant
     Cinemusical Moments in Jazz Film Scores by
     Miles Davis and John Lewis                                 247

 14  Small-but-Significant Implications of the Man Who
     Isn't There in *Sweet Smell of Success* (1957)            262

PART VII
**Jazz Biopics as Tragedy and Comedy: Pivotal Ambi-
Diegetic Cinemusical Moments in Tragedepictions and
Comedepictions of Jazz Heroes**                                   271

Introduction to Part VII                                          272

15  When Bad Things Happen to Great Musicians: The
    Troubled Role of Ambi-Diegetic Jazz in Three
    Tragedepictions of Artistic Genius on the Silver Screen       275

16  A Cinemusicaliterary Analysis of the American Dream
    as Represented by Biographical Jazz Comedepictions in
    the Golden Age of Hollywood Biopics: Blow, Horatio,
    Blow; O, Jakie, O; Go, Tommy, Go; No, Artie, No               296

    *References*                                                  361

# Preface

Born in 1943, I grew up in Milwaukee, surrounded by jazz (a father who collected old swing recordings and played piano transcriptions of solos by Teddy Wilson, Fats Waller, and other great artists) and other kinds of music (most conspicuously, a grandfather who sang ancient ditties to his own self-accompaniment on the guitar and two grandmothers who specialized in piano renditions of the classical warhorses). By the age of six, I had started piano lessons and had begun studying the usual simplistic stuff—finger exercises and easy pieces by Bach and Mozart. At age ten or eleven—frustrated by my inability *ever* to play the opening allegro from Mozart's Sonata in A minor through *even once* as written—I had transferred to a jazz-oriented teacher named Tommy Sheridan, who changed my whole *life* by introducing me, over the next seven or eight years, to the essentials of jazz harmony and improvisation.

With this as a foundation, during my high-school years, I played in a small jazz group—a piano-guitar-bass-drums combo called the Baywood Jazz Quartet—that performed for dances and parties with a few very rare chances to appear in concert or on television. At the start of my senior year, I attended the Lenox School of Jazz in the Berkshire Mountains of Massachusetts (near Tanglewood), where the august members of the Modern Jazz Quartet (John Lewis, Milt Jackson, Percy Heath, and Connie Kay)—with plenty of help from the likes of Gunther Schuller, George Russell, J. J. Johnson, and other education-minded jazz luminaries (such as Max Roach and Dizzy Gillespie, but not in the year I attended)—held court in a manner too informal to be called academic but too serious to be considered fun-and-games. These gentlemen, especially John Lewis and Gunther Schuller, did me the great service of impressing upon me at the tender age of 16 that I did not stand *any* chance for success as a professional jazz musician (a verdict that I can well appreciate when I consider that some of them—far, far more talented and accomplished than I—did not manage to achieve much material success from their own jazz careers).

Thus chastened, I let my jazz activities go into eclipse during my college days—confining myself mostly to compulsive record buying and obsessive listening—but saw them emerge from hiding after settling down in New York City, where I played for several years during the 1970s in a small jazz band that performed the music for services at our local Episcopal church. These quasi-professional duties came to an end in the 1980s when my wife Sally, son Chris, and I began to spend more and more time out of town on weekends, making it impossible to play in church on Sundays. But my deep love for jazz persevered as a major source of continuity in my life—fueled mostly by the reading, auditioning, and viewing of thousands upon thousands of books, magazines, records, CDs, videos, and DVDs with which I have surrounded myself via a collection that rivals the Library of Congress in its space-consuming completeness. Finally, in the last couple of years, I have begun playing again with others, with some colleagues at Columbia University in general, and with Nancy Morgan—a wonderful singer of songs from the Great American Songbook—in particular.

I am, in short, the proverbially fanatic jazz aficionado.

Meanwhile, my work as a member of the academic community began at Harvard College with a concentration in English, took a right turn in the direction of Marketing via the MBA program at Columbia University, centered in Consumer Behavior while earning a doctorate at Columbia, and has since gravitated in the direction of research on what I call Commercial Communication in the Culture of Consumption—namely, studies of the audiences for advertising, the media, entertainment, and the arts. In the latter connection, I have published numerous studies in an area of experimental psychology that I call Consumer Esthetics; have used quantitative techniques applied to empirical data to investigate the determinants of Consumer Tastes for films, music, books, and other cultural offerings; have helped to introduce the study of Consumption Symbolism in movies, television programs, novels, plays, songs, and other works of art and pop culture; and have worked toward developing the consumption-relevant interpretation of cultural artifacts based on approaches drawn from Semiotics, Hermeneutics, and what I call Subjective Personal Introspection. Readers interested in this previous research will find plentiful examples in my books entitled *Daytime Television Game Shows and the Celebration of Merchandise: The Price Is Right* (Holbrook 1993), *Consumer Research: Introspective Essays on the Study of Consumption* (Holbrook 1995a), and *Playing the Changes on the Jazz Metaphor: An Expanded Conceptualization of Music-, Management-, and Marketing-Related Themes*, (Holbrook 2007b), as well as in my work co-authored with Beth Hirschman on *Postmodern Consumer Research: The Study of Consumption as Text* (Hirschman and Holbrook 1992) and *The Semiotics of Consumption: Interpreting Symbolic Consumer Behavior in Popular Culture and Works of Art* (Holbrook and Hirschman 1993). All these volumes contain extensive bibliographical references that point the way to studies by myself and many others of topics related to the themes just mentioned.

I am also, then, something of a scholar in the area of interpreting works of art and entertainment.

These two sides of my personality—jazz aficionado and communications scholar—flow together in the present effort to study and understand the uses and meanings of jazz in motion pictures, referred to by my subtitle as *cinemajazzamatazz*. For me, the study of jazz as one form of film music seems to represent an obvious and likely confluence of interests. But, for the rest of the world, this alignment of themes has not always proven so propitious.

(1) First—by general agreement (but cf. Dickinson 2003a; Flinn 1992)— we have a shortage of studies devoted to the topic of *film music in general* in that, historically, only a few scholars (reviewed later) have chosen to delve deeply into this area of investigation (Atkins 1983; Brown 1994; Burt 1994; Chion 1994; Flinn 1992; Gorbman 1987; Hagen 1971; Kalinak 1992; Karlin 1994; Kassabian 2001; Prendergast 1992; Schelle 1999; Smith 1998) with the occasional anthology of collected studies beginning to emerge at a less-than-moderate pace (Buhler, Flinn, and Neumeyer ed. 2000; Dickinson ed. 2003; Donnelly ed. 2001; Goldmark, Kramer, and Leppert ed. 2007; Lannin and Caley ed. 2005; Romney and Wootton ed. 1995; Wojcik and Knight ed. 2001). As Flinn (1992) admits, "In fact most studies of film music introduce themselves with a comment on just how little has been done in the field" (p. 3). So Dickinson (2003a) begins by suggesting that "For a long while, there seemed to exist a custom for starting any book on film music with a complaint about the degree to which academics had overlooked the topic" (p. 1). In this connection, note the title *Unheard Melodies* chosen by Gorbman (1987) for her book on *Narrative Film Music* and the subtitle of the work by Prendergast (1992) on *Film Music* as a *Neglected Art*. Neumeyer and Buhler (2001) start with the comment that "The literature of cinema is large," followed immediately by the reservation that "Within this broad expanse of literature, film music remains at best a niche market" (p. 16). Donnelly (2001a) agrees that "writers and scholars have paid it [film music] . . . scant attention" (p. 1). Indeed, reviewing the past couple of decades, Donnelly (2001a) laments that "little has changed in film studies. . . . The discipline has roundly failed to incorporate the study of film music into its schemes" (p. 4). Extending this point to the role of sound itself (music, dialogue, sound effects), Stilwell (2001) notes "an extraordinary thing about the film soundtrack"—namely, "the gap between its importance to the cinematic experience and . . . its relative neglect in the reception and study of cinema" (p. 167). Recently, Goldmark, Kramer, and Leppert (2007) introduce their edited volume on *Music in Cinema* with the admission that this area is "still a marginal part of the much larger field of study focused on . . . film": "The film music literature . . . has tended to accept without serious challenge the status hierarchy that puts music on the bottom and treats film as above all a visual medium" (p. 2).

(2) Second, even fewer have bravely ventured into the troubled waters of studies on the *film musical* (Altman 1987; Feuer 1993)—again, with the occasional anthology beginning sporadically to appear (Cohan ed. 2002; Marshall and Stilwell ed. 2000). Face it: Musicals pose some rather impenetrable puzzles. Actors suddenly begin singing and dancing in very unrealistic ways. From out of nowhere, unseen orchestras provide accompaniment to

on-screen musical performances. For no apparent reason, beautiful women form kaleidoscopic patterns that could never occur in the real world. Traditional film and music scholars appear to find all this quite confusing and even alarming. Better to leave it alone and to study something else.

(3) Third, only rarely have researchers devoted sustained attention to *popular music in films* (as opposed to the classically-oriented serious music that normally provides the backgrounds for conventional motion pictures). As Altman (1987) puts it, "Film music scholarship has concentrated almost exclusively on 'classical' music" (p. 26). Scorsese (1995) adds that, surprisingly, "The subject of popular music in motion pictures has been largely neglected in film studies" (p. 1). Knight and Wojcik (2001) agree that "Until recently, film music criticism has largely ignored popular music in favor of analyzing the classical nondiegetic film score" (p. 5). Also unfortunately, as noted by Garner (2000) under what he calls "the curse of lyrical centricity," those few studies that do consider pop songs in cinema typically focus on the words or titles and ignore the music itself (p. 14).

(4) And, fourth, only the most sparsely populated paucity of musically concerned cinemaphiles have addressed issues related to the more specialized area of *jazz in film* (Gabbard 1996; Meeker 1981; Yanow 2004).

Among the latter intrepid investigators, under the title *Jazz in the Movies*, David Meeker (1981) offers an encyclopedic compilation of every motion picture released up to the time he wrote that contains substantial jazz content, with details concerning the identities of relevant artists, the names of tunes performed, and some scattered comments on how the music serves the film's dramatic content. Unfortunately, he omits many musicians, singers, or composers that would seem essential to such a project—for example, Bing Crosby, Billie Holiday, Fred Astaire, Frank Sinatra, Henry Mancini, and André Previn (to name just a few of the jazz-oriented contributors who are missing from Meeker's index). Most seriously, Meeker's volume—published in 1981—is, by now, over a quarter-century old and badly in need of updating.

Some of this updating appears in the excellent book by Krin Gabbard (1996) entitled *Jammin' at the Margins: Jazz and the American Cinema*. In this well-conceived work, Gabbard—a professor of comparative literature—applies his knowledge of jazz to a survey of jazz in motion pictures, beginning with *The Jazz Singer* (1927) and extending right up to Spike Lee's *Mo' Better Blues* (1990) and Robert Altman's *Short Cuts* (1993). Again, the author inevitably omits the most recent jazz-related films. But, more importantly, we find a specialized focus—namely, an emphasis on issues related to gender and race—that sometimes distracts us from other matters of more concern to the music itself. Thus—however interesting, worthwhile, and laudable in its own right—Gabbard's insistent search for racist implications and gender biases often bypasses questions of substance related to the nature of the actual musical performances that appear in the context of the films under investigation. Examples of this tendency abound and will reappear in what follows; so I shall let just one illustration suffice for the time being—namely, some comments related to the night when Hoagy Carmichael (composer of such illustrious standards as "Stardust" and "Skylark") asked to sit in with the band led by King Oliver featuring Louis Armstrong. Oliver's pianist at the time was Lil Hardin (Armstrong's second wife). So Gabbard (1996) asks whether Carmichael was "feminized" by his desire "to sit in a woman's chair" and concludes that Hoagy was "sufficiently secure about his own masculinity to feel neither fear nor shame at taking the place of a woman" (p. 259). But does anybody seriously believe that this is what was going through Hoagy Carmichael's mind—consciously or unconsciously—at a time like this? More likely, I think, he was worrying about the key in which he would need to play "Royal Garden Blues"; whether he could negotiate the correct chord changes at a suitable up-tempo pace; whether he would manage a convincing solo when his turn came around; the nonpareil beauty of Louis Armstrong's playing. Stuff like that. Very often, Gabbard ignores such musical substance in favor of playing the race and gender cards.

The most recent volume about *Jazz on Film*, subtitled *The Complete Story of the Musicians & Music Onscreen*, comes from Scott Yanow (2004) and makes good on its claims of completeness—for example, including coverage of the "test list" mentioned earlier (Crosby, Holiday, Astaire, Sinatra, Mancini, and Previn). In addition to the usual concern for jazz in Hollywood films, Yanow (2004) covers jazz videos (VHS and DVD) as well as shorts, television specials, and documentaries devoted to jazz. With all this going for it, Yanow's book necessarily confines itself to relatively brief coverage of each film—providing a short capsule; a rating from 1 ("either the jazz is irrelevant or the movie stinks") to 10 ("essential"); and a few relatively skimpy critical insights; but very little sustained interpretation of how jazz contributes to cinemusical ends. Though it bears only indirectly on our present concerns with jazz in film, Yanow's 122-page section on "Videos and DVDs" provides a valuable listing of interest to any self-respecting lover of jazz. Unfortunately, Yanow (2004) includes many errors of the sort that tend to afflict projects of this type. For example, it is *not* correct to characterize "Three Windows" from the MJQ's soundtrack to *No Sun in Venice* (1957) as a "medley" (p. 55). In describing an hour-long show called *Reed Royalty* and hosted by Branford Marsalis—which apparently included a number of fine musicians but omitted Zoot Sims, Al Cohn, Art Pepper, Paul Desmond, Stan Getz, Jimmy Giuffre, and Sonny Rollins, among many others—Yanow (2004) comments, without justification, that "The key missing players are Buddy DeFranco, Jackie McLean and Pepper Adams, but nearly all of the other significant musicians are here" (p. 114). On her Snader Telescription, June Christy sings with Claude Williamson and *not* with Claude Williams (p. 121). With all due respect, Yanow's assessments that Forest Whitaker did an "excellent" (p. 146) or "impeccable" (p. 147) job of miming Charlie Parker's solos in *Bird* (1988) are absolute nonsense, as I shall argue at some length in a later chapter. In *The Cotton Club* (1984)—also discussed later—Richard Gere does much more than merely "hint" at Bix Beiderbecke (p. 154); he flawlessly plays Bix's cornet solo on "Singin' the Blues" note for note. A scene from *Paris Blues* (1961)—described later—prompts Yanow (2004) to see Louis Armstrong and Paul Newman as "battling it out" (p. 188) in what would be more accurately portrayed as a celebratory Satchmo love fest. And, confusingly, Yanow (2004) refers to Harold Arlen and Ted Koehler's "Ill Wind" as "I'll Wind" (p. 228). On the other hand, with considerable justification, Yanow (2004) complains at frequent intervals that, in these videos and films, jazz performances typically appear in fragmented form, with major portions omitted and other material submerged below intrusive voiceovers. For example, when reporting on the much-maligned nineteen-hour *Jazz—A Film by Ken Burns* (2000), Yanow (2004) correctly notes that "the flaws are huge" and that "Relatively little music is actually heard except brief excerpts with the talking heads chitchatting virtually nonstop" (p. 68). Indeed, few dedicated jazz listeners could have watched this disappointing series without constant annoyance when magnificent musical passages disappear beneath the incessant palaver of commentators such as Wynton Marsalis, Stanley Crouch, and Albert Murray—talented folks who should have known better than to entrust Ken Burns with the nearly sacred task of documenting the history of America's one truly original contribution to the arts. (On a similar theme, see Wootton 1995, p. 101.)

   In what follows, especially when commenting on the insightful work by Gabbard (1996, 2000, 2001, 2003, 2004, 2007, 2008), I shall have frequent occasion to mention issues related to race and gender. But mostly, I wish to focus on the uses and meanings of jazz in motion pictures *as film music*. From this perspective, I shall pay particular attention to exemplars of a type that I refer to as *ambi-diegetic film music*. This focus differs from the vast majority of earlier work in that most previous studies have dealt *either* with diegetic (on-screen or source) music *or* with nondiegetic (off-screen or background) music.

   As I shall argue at greater length in what follows, the first category—namely, *diegetic music* (also called *source music*)—refers to on-screen music produced inside the context of the film as an aspect of its realistic depiction of a scene or setting and usually not in the service of its dramatic development. Sometimes this music emanates from an off-camera source but is nonetheless audible to the film's characters—as when they hear an orchestra while dancing or music over a PA system in a cocktail lounge. For example, when the heroine enters a shopping mall with Muzak playing in the background, we have a case of diegetic or source music as a routine and inconsequential part of the *mise-en-scène*. By contrast, the second category—namely, *nondiegetic music* (also called *background music*, *extradiegetic music*, or the *underscore*)—refers to off-screen music produced outside the film as a means to the dramatic development of its plot lines, characterizations, or key themes. For example, when a comical leitmotif accompanies the appearance of a frivolous character or a sinister musical passage announces the presence of a hidden danger, we have a case of nondiegetic or background music used in the service of dramatic development.

But, as I shall argue, the conventional distinction between these two categories of diegetic and nondiegetic music—so often explored in the literature in a manner that implicitly assumes them to be mutually exclusive and exhaustive—ignores the existence of other possibilities in general and of an additional type of film scoring on which I shall focus in particular. Specifically, this third category—namely, what we shall call *ambi-diegetic music*—refers to *on-screen music* produced inside the film (like diegetic music) that plays a role in furthering the movie's *dramatic development* (as is typical of nondiegetic music). When on-screen performers play a jazz piece in a manner that advances the plot, comments on the nature of a character's persona, or reinforces a key theme, we have a case of *ambi-diegesis in music, movies, meanings, and markets*.

In short, because diegetic music and nondiegetic music have received the lion's share of attention in the relevant literature and because jazz has tended to be neglected in that literature, the present book focuses primarily on *the uses and meanings of ambi-diegetic jazz in motion pictures*. You know what I mean. You've seen it all a hundred times. The hero of a film we're watching walks into a dark, crowded, smoke-filled nightclub with a horn case tucked under his arm. On a small stage at one end of the dingy room, a quartet—piano, bass, drums, and tenor sax—performs a furiously fast rendition of "Cherokee." When they come to a screeching halt, our hero—a trumpet player named Mose—asks if he can sit in. The bandleader kicks off a speedy tempo and—without consulting about song titles or solo ordering or key signatures or chord changes—the horns fall in with a perfectly synchronized two-part arrangement of a never-before-heard blues piece, later identified in the closing credits as "Cinemajazzamatazz After Dark." The horns take turns soloing brilliantly and then trade sixteen-, eight-, four-, and two-bar phrases at a blistering pace. They end to thunderous applause and congratulations all around. Mose has proven his merit. He has earned new respect in the local jazz community and—we see from across the room—from his date for the evening, Moxy, who has begun to look at him with bedroom eyes. So we have learned something about the character of Mose. He is accomplished, brave, tough, and sexy. He's just the guy to solve the mystery and catch the vicious murderer who has been terrorizing the community's children after school. Moxy's nine-year-old aphasic daughter—Perphonia, who cannot talk but who sings like an angel (occasionally performing accomplished ad lib renditions of songs from the Duke Ellington repertoire)—is safe now that Mose has arrived on the scene. All that remains is to unfold the happy ending implied by this cinemusically propitious jam session.

So let me now develop the implications of this brief example in the chapters that follow. I shall begin with an "Introduction" that highlights the positions adopted by students of film music in the recent literature in general and that relates such projects to our primary focus on ambi-diegetic jazz in particular. From there, we shall move to a series of chapters that pursue various illustrations bearing on the uses and meanings of ambi-diegetic jazz in films, with a special focus on aspects of these meanings that pertain to my own field of marketing and consumer behavior. We shall see cases where, as a form of symbolic consumption, the ambi-diegetic performance of a jazz piece develops the character of a hero (heroine) in ways that render him (her) a suitable love object for his leading lady (her leading man). We shall examine jazz-related films that develop the theme of art-versus-commerce, most often taking the side of anti-commercialism. We shall observe examples where—as part of the film's design as a cultural offering—jazz represents a difficult life choice to be painfully accepted or wisely avoided. As an aspect of product design, we shall even encounter a case in which watered-down jazz expresses the watered-down character of a likeable-but-bland hero. And in a series of biographical movies that contradict and support the familiar rags-to-riches success-story paradigm—that is, tragedepictions and comedepictions—we shall assess the market-driven viability of the American Dream in the lives of great jazz musicians.

Please note that virtually all of the films and soundtracks mentioned herein are available in VHS, DVD, or CD formats from on-line sources such as amazon.com or netflix.com and from bricks-and-mortar dealers like Blockbuster or Walmart. Further, many or even most of the cinemusical illustrations can be found on such sites as apple.com/itunes/ or youtube.com. Examples of the latter (from various chapters) can be accessed by visiting youtube.com and searching for the keywords shown in quotes:

Chapter 1—"Casablanca, As Time Goes By"; "Breakfast at Tiffany's, Moon River"; "Gold Diggers of 1933, Busby Berkeley"; "Gigi, Louis Jordan"; "State Fair, It Might As Well Be Spring"; "Umbrellas of Cherbourg, I Will Wait for You"; "Man Who Knew Too Much, Que Sera"; "Maytime, Will You Remember?"

Chapter 2—"High Society, Now You Has Jazz"; "High Society, Well Did You Evah"

Chapter 3—"Pal Joey, Lady Is a Tramp"; "Pal Joey, My Funny Valentine"; "My Funny Valentine, Chet Baker, Tokyo"; "Fabulous Baker Boys, Makin' Whoopee"; "Talented Mr. Ripley, My Funny Valentine"

Chapter 4—"Pete Kelly's Blues, He Needs Me"; "Pete Kelly's Blues, Hard Hearted Hannah"

Chapter 5—"Cotton Club, Minnie the Moocher"

Chapter 6—"Kansas City, Robert Altman"

Chapter 7—"Young Man with a Horn, Doris Day"

Chapter 8—"Paris Blues, 10of10"

Chapter 9—"Mo' Better Blues, Spike Lee, Terence Blanchard"

Chapter 10—"New York, New York, Liza Minnelli"

Chapter 11—"Art Pepper, You'd Be So Nice to Come Home To"

Chapter 12—"The Score, Theatrical Trailer"

Chapter 13—"Golden Striker, Modern Jazz Quartet"; "Ascenseur, Miles Davis"; "Skating in Central Park, Modern Jazz Quartet"; "Odds Against Tomorrow, Club Scene"

Chapter 14—"Sweet Smell of Success, Jazz Club"; "Jim Hall, I'm Getting Sentimental Over You"

Chapter 15—"Lady Sings the Blues, Diana Ross"; "'Round Midnight, Body and Soul"; "Sweet Love Bitter"; "Bird, Scene from Movie"

Chapter 16—"Jazz Singer, Toot Toot Tootsie"; "Fabulous Dorseys, Art Tatum"; "Glenn Miller Story, Moonlight Serenade"; "Benny Goodman Story, Let's Dance"; "Five Pennies, Danny Kaye, Battle Hymn"; "Gene Krupa, Sal Mineo, Lesson"; "Second Chorus, Artie Shaw, Concerto for Clarinet"

The discussions that follow will reveal the power of ambi-diegetic jazz in contributing to the dramatic development of plot lines, characterizations, and thematic ideas through the design of appropriate film music. With luck, in the future, the reader-as-viewer will never watch jazz-related cinemusical moments in the same way again. In this, I hope to make the market-directed role of music in the movies more clear or at least more susceptible to interpretation. For such enhanced insights will reward the interpretive efforts of audience members who come to films with a curiosity about, an appreciation of, and a love for cinemajazzamatazz.

# Acknowledgments

Please address correspondence to: Morris B. Holbrook, Professor Emeritus, Columbia University @ Apartment 5H, 140 Riverside Drive, New York, NY 10024 (212-873-7324; mbh3@columbia.edu). I must begin by gratefully acknowledging the support of the Columbia Business School's Faculty Research Fund. I further appreciate the friendly-and-insightful editorial advice of series editor Stephen Brown and of the kind folks at Routledge—especially Laura Stearns, Stacy Noto, K. E. Priyamvada, and Meesha Nehru. Huge debts of gratitude extend to the marvelously supportive Dougie Brownlie and to the heroically helpful Alan Bradshaw for their wonderfully generous encouragement. Additional beneficence has come from many journal and book editors to whom I am grateful—Alan Bradshaw, Matthew Caley, Andrea Davies, Rog Dickinson, Fuat Firat, James Fitchett, Steve Lannin, Pauline Maclaran, Catherine Pasonage, Lisa Peñalosa, Jonathan Schroeder, Avi Shankar, Cliff Shultz, Barb Stern, Alladi Venkatesh, and Tony Whyton. Indeed, material from various chapters borrows from previously published journal articles that have been enlarged for broader coverage, extended to provide fuller details, updated to maintain accuracy, revised to eliminate repetitions, adjusted to ensure consistency throughout the book, edited for stylistic uniformity, and so forth. Accordingly, I wish to thank the following publishers and publications for permissions to include revised-and-expanded versions of the following articles in the present volume (with the relevant chapters indicated parenthetically).

## Taylor & Francis / Routledge

(Chapter 1) Holbrook, Morris B. (2003a), "A Book-Review Essay on the Role of Ambi-Diegetic Film Music in the Product Design of Hollywood Movies: Macromarketing in La-La-Land," *Consumption, Markets & Culture*, 6 (3, September), 207–230.

(Chapter 2) Holbrook, Morris B. (2005), "Ambi-Diegetic Music in the Movies: The Crosby Duets in *High Society*," *Consumption, Markets & Culture*, 8 (2, June), 153–182.

(Chapters 4, 5, and 6) Holbrook, Morris B. (2008), "Musical Meanings in Movies: The Case of the Crime-Plus-Jazz Genre," *Consumption, Markets & Culture*, 11 (4, December), 307–327.

## Sage Publications

(Chapter 3) Bradshaw, Alan and Morris B. Holbrook (2007), "Remembering Chet: Theorising the Mythology of the Self-Destructive Bohemian Artist as Self-Producer and Self-Consumer in the Market for Romanticism," *Marketing Theory*, 7 (2, June), 115–136.

(Chapters 7, 8, and 9) Holbrook, Morris B. (2005), "Art versus Commerce as a Macromarketing Theme in Three Films from the Young-Man-with-a-Horn Genre," *Journal of Macromarketing*, 25 (1, June), 22–31.

(Chapter 8) Holbrook, Morris B. (2006), "Reply to Bradshaw, McDonagh, and Marshall: Turn off the Bubble Machine," *Journal of Macromarketing*, 26 (1, June), 84–87.

(Chapter 14) Holbrook, Morris B. (2004), "Ambi-Diegetic Music in Films as a Product-Design and -Placement Strategy: The *Sweet Smell of Success*," *Marketing Theory*, 4 (3, September), 171–185.

(Chapter 16) Holbrook, Morris B. (2009), "A Cinemusicaliterary Analysis of the American Dream as Represented by Biographical Jazz Comedepictions in the Golden Age of Hollywood Biopics: Blow, Horatio, Blow; O, Jakie, O; Go, Tommy, Go; No, Artie, No," *Marketing Theory*, 9 (3, September), 259–313.

## Intellect

(Chapter 3) Holbrook, Morris B. (2005), "The Ambi-Diegesis of 'My Funny Valentine,'" in *Pop Fiction—The Song in Cinema*, ed. Steve Lannin and Matthew Caley, Bristol, UK: Intellect, 48–62.

## Wiley-Blackwell

(Chapters 10, 11, and 12) Holbrook, Morris B. (2007), "Cinemusical Meanings in Motion Pictures: Commerce, Art, and Brando Loyalty . . . Or . . . De Niro, My God, To Thee," *Journal of Consumer Behaviour*, 6 (November–December), 398–418.

## Equinox Publishing

(Chapter 15) Holbrook, Morris B. (2007), "When Bad Things Happen to Great Musicians: The Role of Ambi-Diegetic Jazz in Three Tragedepictions of Artistic Genius on the Silver Screen," *Jazz Research Journal*, 1 (1, May), 99–128.

Most of all, the book would not have happened without the love and encouragement of Sally and Chris Holbrook, to whom it is affectionately dedicated.

Part I

# Introduction: Ambi-Diegetic Music in Motion Pictures

# 1 The Role of Ambi-Diegetic Film Music in the Product Design of Hollywood Movies

## Macromarketing in La-La-Land

As detailed in the Preface and despite the obvious importance of film music to (macro)marketing-related questions about designing a popular form of entertainment, sometimes with aspirations to the stature of artistic creation, the use of music in motion pictures has inspired only a smattering of serious scholarly attention—though the occasional anthology has slowly begun to appear, often enough to suggest that this area of inquiry enjoys growing vitality. Studies of the film musical are even more sparse—again, with a few scattered collections beginning to emerge. And work on our particular area of interest—namely, jazz in films—remains scarcer than teenagers at a Benny Goodman memorial concert.

Among the few who have studied aspects of product design related to film music, most have devoted primary attention to the classic Hollywood musical score intended to reinforce the dramatic development of plot and character while remaining largely in the background without attracting the conscious awareness of the movie audience. For example, borrowing from the tradition of Nineteenth Century Romantic music (Wagner in particular), a *leitmotif* (that is, a short musical phrase) might be associated with a particular narrative object (character, setting, theme, or event) in such a way that playing that motivic phrase might serve to indicate the presence or immanence of the relevant referent while altering the phrase might signal changes in its meaning (e.g., Adorno and Eisler 2003, p. 27; Altman 2007, p. 219; Brown 1994, p. 98; Karlin 1994, p. 73; Neumeyer and Buhler 2001, p. 28; Prendergast 1992, pp. 40, 73, 232).

Such uses of externally-generated music as part of a film's background score are considered *nondiegetic*. By contrast, those uses in which internally-generated music is foregrounded as part of the on-screen action are *diegetic* in nature. Before proceeding, these terms deserve a bit of clarification.

## CONVENTIONAL WISDOM ON DIEGETIC AND NONDIEGETIC MUSIC IN MOTION PICTURES

The noun *diegesis* and the adjective *diegetic* fail to appear in my *Merriam-Webster's Collegiate Dictionary* and, I would assume, are therefore likely to fall outside the purview of the typical (macro)marketing-oriented reader.

Bordwell (1985) traces the term *diegesis* back to Plato's *Republic* where—in a usage retained by Aristotle in the *Poetics*—it referred to "a story or narration" (Gabbard 1996, p. 300). As described by Gorbman (1987), the term *diegesis* had its murky reawakening within the context of film criticism in work by the French *filmologues* during the 1950s. Thus, in some rather obscure publications that we won't be finding at our local Barnes & Noble, Gérard Genette defined *diegesis* as "the spatiotemporal universe referred to by the primary narration" (quoted by Gorbman 1987, pp. 20–21), while Etienne Souriau offered a definition of *diegesis, diegetic* as "all that belongs, 'by inference,' to the narrated story, to the world supposed or proposed by the film's fiction" (Gorbman 1987, p. 21). Picking up the definition proposed by Souriau, Metz (1974) regarded *diegesis* as "the denotative material of a film" (p. xi) or, expanding a bit, as "the narration itself, but also the . . . characters, the landscapes, the events, and other narrative elements, in so far as they are considered in their denoted aspect" (p. 98). In his book on *How to Read a Film*, Monaco (1981) preserves this connection between *diegesis* and *denotation* (p. 144). To this, Gorbman (1987) adds her own definition of *diegesis* as the "narratively implied spatiotemporal world of the actions and characters" (p. 21). Drawing on the work of Burch (1979), Tan (1996) conceptualizes the *diegetic effect* as "the illusion of being present in the fictional world" or, in Burch's terms, the "experience of the fictional world as the environment" (p. 52) where "the events appear to be real, concrete, and taking place in the here and now" (p. 53). With respect to the sound-track, as explained by Gabbard (1996), "diegetic sound refers to what the characters might actually hear" (p. 300).

By common agreement, *diegetic music*—also called *source music*—is produced *within the film* as part of the on-screen action or *mise-en-scène* (even if the music itself comes from off-screen but is still audible to the on-screen characters). As defined by Gorbman (1987), "Diegetic music" is "music that (apparently) issues from a source within the narrative" (p. 22). Referring to this "distinction that has long been noted" in the applications of such names as "diegetic," "actual," and "objective," Chion (1994) proposes the term *screen music* to designate "music arising from a source located directly in the space and time of the action, even if this source is a radio or an offscreen musician" (p. 80). Such music attracts the attention of the viewer and serves to reinforce the realism of a particular scene or to establish the ambience of a setting—much in the manner of costumes, décor, scenery, landscaping, or other props. Thus, if a character switches on a radio, we will most likely hear a piece of pop music. If the two young lovers attend a fancy dress ball, they will whirl to the sounds of a waltz played by the dance orchestra. If the heroine's kid brother joins a grunge band, we will experience its unsavory sounds when she opens the garage door. According to the critical consensus, such diegetic uses of music in film enhance the verisimilitude of the *mise-en-scène*—augmenting its realistic depiction without adding much to the film's depth of meaning, narrative significance, connotative richness, or dramatic development.

By contrast, ***nondiegetic music***—or ***background music***—is produced from ***outside the film*** and provides an underscore to the events unfolding on the screen. Gorbman (1987) defines the ***nondiegetic*** as "narrative intrusion upon the diegesis" (p. 22) via what Gabbard (1996) calls "extradiegetic music . . . that the characters do not hear" (p. 300). Noting the correspondence of such names as "nondiegetic," "commemorative," and "subjective," Chion (1994) adopts the term *pit music* to designate "music that accompanies the image from a nondiegetic position, outside the space and time of the action" (p. 80). Such music remains largely in the background, generally goes unnoticed at the conscious level, and serves to enrich the meaning of the film's plot, the subtleties of its characterizations, the connotations of its events, and/or the significance of its narrative themes. As a classic example, noted by Gorbman (1987), "the menacing 'shark' theme, heard even before the camera in *Jaws* reveals the deadly shark closing in on the unsuspecting swimmers, gives the viewer advance knowledge of the narrative threat" (p. 58). Thus, whenever the heroine approaches, we may hear a haunting love ballad associated with her sweet innocence, her virginal purity, and her tremulous sensitivity. Or an appearance of the villain may prompt the rehearsal of a nasty electronic wail that serves to represent his evil intent, his callous scurrility, and his maleficent machinations. Such nondiegetic uses, they say, establish associations and identifications that further the dramatic development of the plot, flesh out the persona of a particular character, or add depth to key story-related themes.

In sum, the conventional wisdom has suggested that ***diegetic music*** adds to a film's ***realism***, whereas ***nondiegetic music*** contributes to the ***dramatic development*** of plot, characters, and other themes. Think, for example, of the difference between (say) Bernard Herrmann (nondiegeticist supreme) and (say) Henry Mancini (master of the commercially accessible diegetic filler song). Until the relatively recent revelations by Smith (1998), the former type of approach had received the lion's share of attention from those writing about film music. Indeed, rather imperiously, Rosar (2002) actually defines *film music* as including *only* the nondiegetic type of background scoring. Notice, then, the set of *implicit homologies* that underlie such contrasts— with the last three entries recapitulating the terms stressed by Chion (1994):

| | |
|---:|:---|
| Diegesis | Nondiegesis |
| Source Music | Background Music |
| From Within | From Without |
| Realistic Depiction | Dramatic Development |
| Mancini | Herrmann |
| Neglected | Given Precedence |
| Screen Music | Pit Music |
| Actual | Commemorative |
| Objective | Subjective |

As we shall see, such parallel binary oppositions permeate the writings of many whose work we shall consider in what follows.

## AMPLIFICATIONS

### Work That Focuses on Purely Diegetic or Nondiegetic Uses of Film Music

Studies that maintain the traditional diegetic/nondiegetic, source/background, realistic/dramatic, and related parallel binary distinctions—that is, the familiar homologies just described—are not hard to find. These would include the following examples.

Atkins (1983) suggests that "The categories of background scoring and source music are logical ones into which all film music can be divided" (p. 14). For example, in *Casablanca* (1943), the song "As Time Goes By" begins as source music played by Sam (Dooley Wilson) in the nightclub owned by Rick (Humphrey Bogart) but then migrates to Max Steiner's background score where it serves "in lushly orchestrated music cues behind many of the most dramatic and romantic scenes in the film" (p. 14; see also Neumeyer and Buhler 2001, p. 33).

In describing music from the Hollywood films of the 1930s and 1940s, Flinn (1992) emphasizes what she calls "the 'classical' understanding of film music"—namely, "that the [nondiegetic background] score" (such as uses of the aforementioned *leitmotif*) "supports the development of the film's story line, that it exists to reinforce the narrational information already provided by the image" (p. 14). Examples include Max Steiner's music for *Gone with the Wind* (1939), where we find "leitmotivs for Scarlet O'Hara, Rhett Butler, and the other characters within the film" and where "'Tara's Theme' works in much the same way, although it identifies a place and not a character" (p. 108).

As described by Prendergast (1992), Leonard Rosenman's nondiegetic background score for *The Cobweb* (1955) uses Schoenbergian atonal compositional techniques to probe the mental states of residents at an insane asylum (p. 119). Thus, Rosenman explained his choice of twelve-tone or serial forms as an attempt "to show what was going on inside characters' heads" (p. 119), as when dissonant music indicates that "two individuals have troublesome problems within themselves" (p. 123). Later, Prendergast (1992) discusses the score by Bernard Herrmann for Alfred Hitchcock's *Psycho* (1960), remarkable for its use of a strings-only orchestra in an effort to complement the film's black-and-white photography with a "black and white sound" (p. 133). In the famous shower scene, the brutality of the murder is reflected by the violently strident music with its widely spaced diminished chords and major sevenths (p. 144). Still later—speaking mostly of nondiegetic (background) music and drawing on a discussion by Aaron Copland—Prendergast (1992) mentions some key ways in which the musical score helps to realize "the meaning of a film" (p. 213). These include its powers to create an "*atmosphere of time and place*" (p. 213); "*psychological refinements*" such as "*the unspoken thoughts of a* character" (p. 216); or an "*underpinning for the theatrical buildup of a scene*" (p. 222). Such nondiegetic musical functions are beautifully illustrated in Prendergast's analysis of David Raksin's score for William Wyler's *Carrie* (1952) where "an elegant waltz tune . . . is used . . . to recall those times between Hurstwood and Carrie when their problems did not involve mere survival" (p. 228).

Brown (1994) staunchly maintains the diegetic/nondiegetic, source/ background, realistic/dramatic contrast(s) as a basis for his work (p. 67) and considers this distinction to be one of "the cinematic givens"—namely, "(a) that there will almost always be an invisible nondiegetic score to boost the affective impact at key moments, and (b) that source music . . . is being or can be heard by the characters in the narrative" (p. 68). In preserving, this diegetic/nondiegetic distinction, Brown (1994) makes it quite clear that he intends to focus primarily on the latter: "Film music, in its 'pure' state is nondiegetic . . . , and it is this type of music that will serve as the principal object of discussion" (p. 22). Toward this end, Brown (1994) provides an excellent example of dramatic meanings in nondiegetic background music drawn from Miklós Rózsa's score for Alfred Hitchcock's *Spellbound* (1945), wherein similar-but-different love and suspense themes help us anticipate such events as an embrace between Gregory Peck and Ingrid Bergman (strings playing the love theme in a major mode) or physical violence (the suspense theme played by a somewhat weird-sounding theremin in a heavily chromatic minor mode) and wherein "The interrelatedness of the two themes [especially in their rhythmic structures] suggests that love and madness are two sides of the same coin" (p. 7). Elsewhere, Karlin (1994) agrees that "what Rózsa did with the theremin in *Spellbound* . . . immediately summarized the psychotic condition of the hero" (p. 34) so as "to emphasize [his] psychological disturbance" (p. 105). Later, Brown (1994) describes Erich Wolfgang Korngold's score for *The Sea Hawk* (1940) in terms that leave no doubts concerning his nondiegetic focus on "the association of the heroism abstractly evoked by the fanfare theme with the character of Thorpe" (p. 103). Further, Brown (1994) explains quite perceptively how certain harmonic practices create certain emotional effects or other meanings, as in Bernard Herrmann's use of the "Hitchcock chord," otherwise known as a "minor major-seventh chord" (p. 153)—for example, reading upwards in the key of C minor, C-E♭-G-B. Brown points out that "this type of chord frequently appears in modern jazz, an idiom that has often been heard by traditional musical ears as definitely belonging to the domain of the irrational" (p. 153). Thus, "What characterizes the Herrmann/Hitchcock sound are the ways in which . . . novel harmonic colorations make descent into the irrational felt as an ever-lurking potential" (p. 153) where—in films such as *Vertigo* (1958) and *Psycho* (1960)— "the 'Hitchcock chord' . . . immediately throws the viewer/listener off the rationalized center of normal Western tonality into a more irrational, mythic domain" (pp. 159–160). This level of musicological detail goes far toward making Brown's analyses of nondiegetic film scores all the more convincing. Later, when explicitly discussing the use of jazz in films, Brown (1994) focuses especially on two nondiegetic background scores—one by John Lewis for Robert Wise's *Odds Against Tomorrow* (1959) and another by

Miles Davis for Louis Malle's *Ascenseur Pour L'Échafaud* (1958)—both discussed at length in Chapter 13. In Brown's view, Lewis provides "a consistently moody interplay of timbres and dissonant harmonies that strikingly parallel the coldness and loneliness of the film's winter settings . . . and the bitterness of its narrative" (p. 185), while Davis "communicates" via "a set of minor-mode improvisations, filled with tritones and minor thirds, with Davis's trumpet wailing softly over a slow, grim accompaniment" in a way that "bleakly creates most of the film's musical affect" (p. 185) to convey a mood of desolation and despair.

Karlin (1994) also carefully preserves the traditional diegetic/nondiegetic, source/score, or on-screen/background distinction where "Source music can be well used to give the flavor of a particular period in time" (p. 69) and where "The *score*, also called 'underscoring' or the 'background score'" (p. 68) will serve "all the emotional and other dramatic needs of the film" (p. 41) insofar as it reflects "the film's dramatic theme(s), its characters, its rhythms and textures, and most important, its dramatic requirements" (p. 86). Quoting composer Jerry Goldsmith, Karlin (1994) sees "the real function of scoring" as "to support the film's impact on the mind and the emotions of the audience" (p. 87). Further, Karlin (1994) suggests, "The specific sound of a particular instrument or group of instruments can characterize or represent a major dramatic element"—as when Karlin himself used recorders as appropriate instruments to capture "the personality (nonassertive and wispy) and background (medieval literature)" of Sandy Dennis (as a school teacher) in *Up the Down Staircase* (1967) (p. 34). Later, Karlin (1994) describes Franz Waxman's nondiegetic score for Billy Wilder's *The Spirit of St. Louis* (1957) as "an indispensable element . . . pulling the scenes along, getting inside Lindbergh's mind as he reminisces, and dramatizing his struggle to stay awake during his long trip over the Atlantic" (p. 116). Thus, "*The characters in the story* are perhaps the most typical motivation for [background] melodies and other [nondiegetic] musical material" (p. 71).

Commenting on the films by Woody Allen, Garner (2000) distinguishes explicitly between diegetic music (e.g., Dick Hyman and various cohorts appearing on-screen to bolster the realism of scenes at Elaine's restaurant or at a reception for the Museum of Modern Art in *Manhattan* [1979]) and nondiegetic music (e.g., the off-screen presentation of Gershwin's songs or his *Rhapsody in Blue* to accompany character-revealing voiceovers in the same film) (p. 15).

Buhler (2001) provides a nice summary of and commentary on the traditional diegetic/nondiegetic and source/background distinctions (p. 40). Paraphrasing his discussion, diegetic (source) music helps to tell the story in a realistic manner in the sense (say) that an orchestra should perform at a dance party, whereas nondiegetic (background) music comments on the story in a way that adds dramatic meaning (as when a lush romantic theme in a major key enters the underscore just as the hero declares his everlasting love for the heroine). Here, Buhler (2001) makes implicit reference to the distinctions or homologies (parallel binary oppositions) noted earlier—referring to these as "a linked set of binary oppositions that inscribe a hierarchy of covert cultural values in the practice and interpretation of film music" (p. 43). As an example of this traditional view in action, consider Buhler's analysis of Max Steiner's score for *The Informer* (1935) in which the music "grants insight into what must otherwise remain unseen and unsaid"—"psychology, mood, motivation . . . the deepest well of inner life within the character" (p. 47). Similarly, in *Amistad* (1997), the background score by John Williams does much to support the side of John Quincy Adams when opposing Senator Calhoun in the debate on slavery, brightening noticeably when Adams says the word "freedom" (p. 50).

Garwood (2003) preserves the traditional view of nondiegetic music in discussing the compilation score for *Sleepless in Seattle* (1993)—with the usual emphasis on how background music shapes the dramatic development of plot, character, and other themes "as a key to understanding what a *character* may be feeling at a particular moment" (p. 109). For example, "Stardust" and "In the Wee Small Hours of the Morning"—performed by Nat Cole and Carly Simon, respectively—accompany "matching scenes of lonely reverie" (p. 113) in which these songs provide "a suitable setting for the characters' sleepless pondering [and] are attuned to the 'real' emotions of the characters . . . when they are alone" (p. 114).

Lannin (2005) describes how the transformation of "Unchained Melody" in *Ghost* (1990)—via its movement from the diegetic to the nondiegetic score—mirrors the transition of Sam (Patrick Swayze) from life to death, appearing diegetically when Sam is alive and then nondiegetically with Sam as a ghost (p. 77). Similarly, but in the opposite direction, Smith (2005) analyzes the manner in which Paul McCartney's "Live or Let Die" migrates from the nondiegetic background to the diegetic score during one crucial scene in George Armitage's *Grosse Point Blank* (1997). Specifically, when the leading character Martin Blank (John Cusack) enters a convenience store, the Ultimart, the music switches from nondiegetic "anger and confusion" in a heavy-rock version by Guns N' Roses (p. 131) to a diegetic expression of "commodity culture and competition within corporate capitalism" in an easy-listing rendition by Adam Fields (p. 130). Thus, the music negotiates a nondiegetic/diegetic transformation both in its score/source origins and in its dramatic meanings: "The shift from the bombastic style of Guns N' Roses to the homogenized, sweet instrumental sounds of Adam Fields parallels the hero's experience in which the site of his nostalgia has been converted to a shrine for commodity culture" (p. 132).

Even such a savvy commentator as Gabbard (2007) tends to draw on the traditional concept of nondiegetic music in his discussion of Louis Malle's *Ascenseur Pour L'Échafaud* (1958), to which we shall return in Chapter 13. Here, the music—supplied by Miles Davis and a jazz quintet—stays mostly in the background and underscores the film's various characters, themes, and plot development in ways that emerge most clearly in one critical scene, described at length by Gabbard (2007), wherein "the film's female protagonist, Florence (Jeanne Moreau), slowly walks through the Paris night while Davis and his quintet read her mind with their improvisations" (p. 263) so that "We can celebrate a few nearly perfect minutes when jazz and the cinema elegantly complement each other" (pp. 264–265). Later, Gabbard (2007) interprets a nondiegetic performance of "Nature Boy" by Miles Davis in *The Talented Mr. Ripley* (1999), a movie to which we shall return in Chapter 3, as the embodiment of "sexual tension" in a "deeply homoerotic scene" in which Tom Ripley (Matt Damon) plays chess with a naked Dickie Greenleaf (Jude Law) (p. 269). Thus, focusing on the cine-musical role of jazz, Gabbard (2007) maintains an emphasis on the traditional role of nondiegetic music in the dramatic development of plot and character.

## Conventional Perspectives in Music and Cinema (Buhler, Flinn, and Neumeyer)

If we focus our attention on just one representative source, we find that variations on the traditional contrasts just described appear at length and often with insightful embellishments in the collection of essays edited by Buhler, Flinn, and Neumeyer (ed. 2000) under the title *Music and Cinema*. This volume compiles work by scholars from a number of academic disciplines ranging from music theory to film criticism, from comparative literature to psychology, and from media to cultural studies. In other words, the approach is interdisciplinary, pandisciplinary, or what Kalinak (2000) calls *non*disciplinary. For the purposes at hand, I shall focus primarily on ways in which the essays presented by Buhler and Co. bear on the diegetic/nondiegetic distinction just elaborated. In this respect, I believe that the Buhler-and-Co. book is well worth studying because it offers, in microcosm, a fine sampling of current thought on the subject of film music in general and the respective role(s) of diegetic/nondiegetic music in particular.

In their "Introduction," Neumeyer, Flinn, and Buhler (2000) comment on the stature of film music as a "neglected art" based on an "unheard melody"—that is, as an aspect of motion-picture design that has prompted only limited scholarly attention—partly because it exists mostly in the background, eludes conscious awareness, and gets "folded into" the narrative work of the film's story line (p. 1) and partly because it falls between the cracks of various relevant disciplines such as film studies, musicology, or other academic specialties with something to say on the topic (p. 2). One virtue of the collection by Buhler and Co. (ed. 2000) is that it brings together work from a diverse range of scholarly perspectives—mostly consistent with the diegetic/nondiegetic exegesis already adumbrated. Neumeyer, Flinn, and Buhler (2000) review the work of earlier theorists such as Carroll (1988) and Doane (1987), who agree that "what music adds to the image is a specificity of emotion" (Neumeyer, Flinn, and Buhler 2000, p. 12). More broadly, "it can reflect emotion or create atmosphere, it can evoke social or ethnic stereotypes or localize time or place . . . , and it can closely imitate screen action" (p. 13)—all this according to what Buhler (2001) calls the "synchronization" theory of the nondiegetic score (p. 44). When exaggerated, the latter practice is labeled *mickey-mousing* because it involves a case of musical form imitating action movements (fast, slow, jerky, stopping-and-starting, rising, falling, etc.) in the manner that one might find in an animated cartoon (Neumeyer, Flinn, and Buhler 2000, p. 13). As further connoted by this epithet and as elaborated by other chapters to follow, mickey-mousing entails a level of simple-mindedness—a slavish matching of music to action—that leaves much to be desired in terms of aesthetic profundity. Far more profound are the nondiegetic uses envisioned by Copland (1957) in which background music conveys "the unspoken thoughts of a character or the unseen implications of a situation" (quoted by Neumeyer, Flinn, and Buhler 2000, pp. 13–14). True to the classic vision developed by Gorbman (1987), such nondiegetic music remains "inaudible" (Neumeyer, Flinn, and Buhler 2000, p. 14) in the sense that we don't notice it—at least not until the level of mickey-mousing becomes so blatant as to seem obtrusive in the manner deprecated by Adorno and Eisler (1947, ed. 1994). (For further discussions of the aesthetically discredited aspects of mickey-mousing, see Brown 1994, pp. 16, 107–110; Buhler 2001, p. 45; Dyer 2007, p. 250; Goldmark 2007, pp. 226, 241; Karlin 1994, pp. 79–80, 165; Prendergast 1992, pp. 45, 80; Romney and Wootton ed. 1995, p. 136; and Sinker 1995, p. 114.) In sum, overall, Neumeyer, Flinn, and Buhler (2000) emphasize the diegetic/nondiegetic or source/background distinction that we have already noted as a key axis in the traditional analysis of film music as "one of the more durable polarities in film-music theory and practice" (p. 17). These authors comment further that "in nearly every case writers on film music have to date given precedence to nondiegetic orchestral music and to the dramatic feature film" (p. 18).

In his chapter on "*Star Wars*, Music, and Myth," Buhler (2000) pursues the aforementioned classic focus on the (quasi-Wagnerian) *leitmotif*, finding in the score by John Williams the Wagnerian manner of mythologizing—for example, in the way that the film's music is "fundamental" to representing "the Force" via "leitmotivic deployment" (p. 44). I shall leave it to *Star Wars* aficionados (among whom I do not number myself) to work out the subtleties of Buhler's detailed analysis of Force- and Darkside-related musical themes, as well as the cinemusical connections between John Williams and Richard Wagner.

Indeed, Paulin (2000) follows Buhler (2000) by addressing "Richard Wagner and the Fantasy of Cinematic Unity" in an essay questioning the Nineteenth-Century master's relevance to film-scoring practices—suggesting that many theorists have tended to "overstate" Wagner's influence and have actually elevated the German composer to the status of a "fetish object" whose wish-fulfilling invocation helps to disguise or cover up "the stain of cinema's status as nonauratic, mechanically (re-)produced, low-cultural mass medium" (p. 59). Paulin (2000) finds inconsistency in Wagner's own definitions of purpose concerning such concepts as the *Gesamtkunstwerk* ("total work of art") and, therefore, detects a sort of misguided pretentiousness in attempts to link film music to such Wagnerian practices as the *leitmotif*. In Paulin's view, the cinematic use of "nondiegetic music (defined as having no source within the 'real' world as filmed)" (p. 63) tends to "follow" the film or strive to "fit" it in a way that effaces Wagner's emphasis on the "dominant role of music" (p. 66). Paulin reminds us that the excessive subservience of background music to on-screen action—as practiced, at times, by such otherwise estimable film composers as Max Steiner and Erich Wolfgang Korngold—has evoked the aforementioned deprecatory term *mickey-mousing* by virtue of "its cartoonish mimicry of the image" (p. 69). Such practices—as earlier critiqued by Arnheim (1957)—appear desirable only as long as they avoid excessive "redundancy" of the "mickey-mouse" variety (Paulin 2000, p. 71). (Again, note that further critiques of mickey-mousing have appeared in the aforementioned work by Brown, Buhler, Dyer, Goldmark, Karlin, Prendergast, Romney and Wootton, and Sinker.) As special antagonists to excessive redundancy, Paulin (2000) cites Adorno and Eisler (1947, ed. 1994; Adorno and Eisler 2003), whose work—targeted at film composers in general and at leitmotifs in particular—Paulin (2000) summarizes as suggesting that "in linking itself too closely to the image, music becomes an empty supplement that reinforces an already explicit message but adds nothing unique in its own voice" (p. 72). Indeed, Paulin (2000) concludes that—as long as music is "subjugated" to the larger purposes of a film (which is almost always)—anything resembling the Wagnerian *Gesamtkunstwerk* constitutes an *impossibility* (p. 74), little more than a marketing gimmick to give a little respectability to an otherwise degradingly commodified form of commerce (p. 79).

This cinematic "impossibility theorem" strikes me as less telling, however, than the trenchant philosophical analysis by London (2000) of "Leitmotifs and Musical Reference in the Classical Film Score"—namely, his account of how motivic musical elements may "refer" to "characters or actions that may (or may not) be present on the imagetrack" (p. 85). In this connection, London develops a philosophically grounded analogy between the role of the leitmotif in music and that of the proper name in language (p. 85). Here, he follows the work of Kripke (1980), who (à la John Stuart Mill) sees proper names as purely denotative—that is, as "semantically empty or meaningless" in the sense that they point to a referent but do not suggest additional descriptive properties that the referent may possess (p. 86). We might question this opinion, of course, on the grounds that (say) "Paul Desmond" carries connotations very different from "Paul Emil Breitenfeld" (the saxophonist's real name). Ditto the contrast between "Marilyn Monroe" and "Norma Jean Mortenson." Nonetheless, London (2000) suggests that—like proper names in language—leitmotifs in music can become associated with particular places, objects, or characters and can thereby indicate the actual, physical, or psychological presence of various objects (p. 89). At this point—somewhat surprisingly, but I believe correctly—London (2000) pushes beyond Kripke to suggest that leitmotifs differ from proper names by also accomplishing an important expressive purpose insofar as, beyond merely designating, "they also contain ... the capacity for signifying or expressing emotion" (p. 89). Here, London offers an especially clear explication of the manner in which a musical motif can advance an emotive theme, can play a role in plot development, or (most importantly) can deepen a characterization. This view encapsulates much of the logic that underlies the nondiegetic role of music in film and—because it is highly relevant, philosophically grounded, and cogently expressed—deserves our careful attention. Briefly, (1) a certain leitmotif L is established as a referent to an object or character X. But (2) L also has certain expressive properties. Thus, (3) we conclude that these expressive properties of L also characterize X. Further, (4) transformation of the leitmotif L (e.g., reorchestration, modulation, shifting from major to minor in tonality or from 4/4 to 3/4 in meter) suggests a corresponding change in X so that "X's leitmotif can serve as a cue to character development and transformation" (p. 90). London (2000) goes on to demonstrate how these principles apply to Max Steiner's score for *Mildred Pierce* (1945)—an analysis that is beautifully done but not central to our present purposes. More essential is the manner in which London has nailed down a key aspect of the role traditionally ascribed to nondiegetic music—namely, its power to establish "the essential identity of each character" (p. 94) and even to develop this identity via shifting subtleties of musical characterization that reveal depths of emotional travails (e.g., happy to sad), awakenings (e.g., sleepy to alert), or personal transformations (e.g., young and vigorous to old and feeble). In this, London (2000) adopts a philosophical perspective. Had he been a psychologist, he might have called on post-Pavlovian classical learning theory to describe how the frequent pairing of a character with a musical motif can establish an association that may operate, perhaps below the level of conscious awareness, to enrich that character's identity. Or he might have invoked cognitive consistency theory, as in Heider's balance model, to show how a positive link between A and B plus a connection between B and C exerts pressure toward a consistency-preserving identification of C with A. Such Pavlovian learning or Heiderian balance serves, for example, as the bulwark on which marketers have erected the advertising edifice of celebrity endorsements according to the logic (say) that (1) Roger Federer is awesome; (2) Roger wears a Rolex watch; therefore, (3) Rolex watches are awesome. Psychologically, the nondiegetic musical leitmotif works according to a closely related mechanism: (1) Mildred is associated with Theme M; (2) Theme M never changes; therefore, (3) Mildred is steadfast.

As it moves beyond an emphasis on the nondiegetic use of music in the classic Hollywood film scores, the collection by Buhler and Co. (ed. 2000) begins to pursue various newer focuses in general and those devoting more attention to diegetic music in particular, while still mostly adhering to the traditional homologies or parallel binary oppositions mentioned earlier. In this connection, Flinn (2000) offers a chapter on "Music and History in the New German Cinema" that spreads its focus among diegetic and nondiegetic exemplars in ways that show how even the same music (Beethoven's Ninth Symphony) can support different meanings in different cinematic applications (by Alexander Kluge, Rainer Werner Fassbinder, and Hans-Jürgen Syberberg). But in considering the diegetic uses of popular songs in post-War German cinema, typical of the analyses discussed thus far, Flinn (2000) adopts an implicit view of diegetic/nondiegetic music as useless/useful in the development of a character's identity. Specifically, she claims that—when a recording such as "The Great Pretender" is played diegetically on a phonograph—the "borrowed" nature of such performances works against their clear association with a cinematic character (p. 131). I believe that this argument greatly underestimates the power of diegetic music—say, a pop song dropped into the context of a film's action as part of the events unfolding on the screen—to evoke associations or identifications that deepen the development of a character, that advance various aspects of a plot, or that reflect other important dramatic themes. Someone—usually the director—has *chosen* the diegetic song for its *capacity to convey some relevant thought or feeling*. We shall return to this point later. For now, suffice it to say that Flinn's explicit perspective mirrors the classic homologies reviewed earlier as part of the conventional wisdom.

A similar exercise in playing around the edges of the familiar homologies appears in the essay by Gabbard (2000) on "Robert Altman's History Lesson" in *Kansas City* (1996). While focusing sensitively on various details of Altman's use of jazz, Gabbard (2000) does mostly preserve the traditional distinction between "diegetic and extradiegetic registers" (p. 146). For example, though he comments on a scene in which Carolyn (Miranda Richardson) and Blondie (Jennifer Jason Leigh) converse to the accompaniment of music that *later* turns out to be performed by a female jazz pianist (Geri Allen) playing the role of Mary Lou Williams so that "the music allows an emotional aspect of one scene to carry over into another that would otherwise seem entirely unrelated" (p. 147), Gabbard (2000) seems eager to reassure us that "In many ways this is standard Hollywood practice—what Claudia Gorbman [godmother of the diegetic/nondiegetic distinction] has called 'narrative cuing'" (p. 147).

The same traditional homologous mentality based on parallel bipolar oppositions structures the discussion by Marks (2000) of "Music, Drama, Warner Brothers" in the cases of *Casablanca* (1941) and *The Maltese Falcon* (1942). Produced virtually simultaneously, both films feature the same star (Humphrey Bogart). Both have achieved "cult status" as legendary masterpieces (p. 162). Yet the two motion pictures differ markedly in their use of music. In *Casablanca*, much of the music interspersed within Max Steiner's limited background score consists of diegetic source material (familiar tunes and songs heard in performance at Rick's café). By contrast, in *The Maltese Falcon*, Adolph Deutsch's score remains nondiegetic all the way. In *Casablanca*, for about a half-hour during a long scene at the café, we hear familiar pop tunes from the 1920s and 1930s that fall outside the Steiner score (p. 173)—"As Time Goes By" being only the most memorably famous in a list that includes "If I Could Be With You," "You Must Have Been a Beautiful Baby," "It Had to Be You," and "The Very Thought of You" (practically a Hit-Parade-styled review of the top-40 songs of the day). In sharp contrast, the music by Adolph Deutsch for *The Maltese Falcon* consists entirely of background scoring with no use of diegetic material: "No character ever turns on a radio, plays a record, or goes to a club like Rick's, where music is to be sung, listened to, or ignored" (p. 178). Thus, Deutsch keeps the nondiegetic music below the level of consciousness where, as traditionally envisioned, it "speaks to our emotions without our awareness of it" (p. 179). In short, the analytic framework pursued by Marks (2000) rests on an extrapolation of the diegetic/nondiegetic distinction as exemplified by two classic-but-contrasting films.

Further reliance on the conventional diegetic/nondiegetic homologies appears in a contribution by Smith (2000) on "the Film Music of Henry Mancini." Mostly, Smith pursues a focus on the changes in scoring practices wrought by the commercialization of the Hollywood soundtrack as the film studios moved into the marketing of musical recordings. Here, describing the commercial imbrication of Hollywood and the recording industry via the soundtrack album, the author adds further in-depth comments to those found in his earlier book on the same topic (Smith 1998; see also Smith 2003). Mancini—with 20 Grammy Awards to his credit (Smith 2000, p. 247)—was a (maybe *the*) master of this emerging soundtrack genre. Depending on your viewpoint, Mancini either helped to broaden the audience for jazz or pandered to his listeners via the popularization of formerly hip music so as to symbolize the decline of film music into "crass commercialism" (p. 248). Smith's appraisal adopts a more sympathetic stance based on an awareness of how Mancini's oeuvre responded to the economic pressures brought to bear by the film studios' commercial impetus toward the marketing of soundtrack recordings (p. 249). These motion-picture albums served as agents of "cross-promotion" whereby a hit record of film music lured people to the theaters to see the movie, while a popular movie generated demand for its soundtrack recording (p. 250). For additional discussions of cross-promotion, see Altman (1987, p. 353; 2001, p. 26); Brown (1994, p. 172); Cohan (2002b, p. 6); Creekmur (2001, pp. 383, 399); Dickinson (2003a, p. 6; 2003b, pp. 145, 150); Donnelly (2001b, p. 161); Flinn (1992, p. 152); Garner (2001, pp. 191, 196); Gorbman (2007, p. 151); Grossberg (2003, p. 84); Karlin (1994, pp. 68, 87, 221, 242, 245); Kermode (1995, p. 17); Knight and Wojcik (2001, pp. 3, 13); Majumdar (2001, p. 161); Prendergast (1992, p. 146); Ramaeker (2001, p. 85); Romney and Wootton (1995, p. 4; ed. 1995, p. 130); Smith (2001, p. 410); Sinker (1995, p. 111); Stilwell (2005, p. 140); and Toop (1995, p. 75). Smith (1998) provides an excellent historical overview of such synergies in general and of the post-1950s soundtrack bonanza in particular. Meanwhile, reaching back to the familiar diegetic/nondiegetic homologies, Smith (2000) views this commercial exploitation of soundtrack recordings as encouraging a growing reliance on diegetic source music. To put it mildly, Mancini excelled in the creation of such diegetic material—for example, a big-band number heard on the radio or a jazz blues played by the quintet in a dark, smoky nightclub. Think of Audrey Hepburn winsomely singing "Moon River" in *Breakfast at Tiffany's* (1961) or recall the delicious role of Lola Albright and her accompanists in the late-1950s TV series *Peter Gunn* (unsuccessfully revived as film versions in 1967 and 1989 with Laura Devon and Barbara Williams, respectively, replacing the essential Ms. Albright). Mancini developed the habit of inserting such musical material ubiquitously and then re-recording the various themes as separate tunes to fill out a commercially viable film- or television-music recording, as in the cases of *Hatari!* (1962) or *The Pink Panther* (1964, plus sequels). Given this perspective, Smith (2000) logically emphasizes the diegetic/nondiegetic split wherein Mancini provides limited background scoring for the usual nondiegetic purposes while tossing in various commercially viable diegetic tunes that—anticipatory of what today we call "product placement"—are more or less irrelevant to the film's dramatic motivation. Thus, reflecting a dichotomy that runs deep in music-related film criticism, Smith concludes that, in general, "Mancini used only two or three themes as the basis of a film's nondiegetic underscore" and that the remaining themes "typically appear only once and are largely included to flesh the score into a satisfying album" (p. 252): "With so little dramatic function, spotting for source music adheres much more closely to the practices of product placement, and, like other tie-ins, the absence of the music at such moments would have little effect on the film" (pp. 253). Here, we find the familiar homologous dichotomizations ringing through Smith's analysis, as a foundation for its many penetrating insights—especially those related to his discussion of Mancini's use of orchestration for dramatic purposes, as when two pianists became physically nauseous while perform-ing on two out-of-tune pianos intended to evoke "the heroine's psycho-logical sense of dislocation" in *Wait Until Dark* (1967) (p. 257) or when a change in orchestration suggests that a character in *Experiment in Terror* (1962) has been *mis*-recognized (p. 266). In the end, Smith (2000) continues to hammer away at the familiar either/or dichotomies of the traditional diegetic/nondiegetic homologies where "On the one hand, he [Mancini] exploited diegetic music as an opportunity to introduce fully fleshed-out tunes, songs that could be excerpted and included in the film's accompanying soundtrack album" and "On the other hand, Mancini's nondiegetic music was typically organized around a small number of themes, each of which could be varied and developed to serve the specific narrative functions of classical Hollywood underscore" (p. 267). Further, Smith (2000) sees Mancini's approach as a "precursor" to the more recent trend toward compilation soundtracks in which already-available pop recordings supply the diegetic source music, subject to the same sort of commercially-inspired compartmentalization pioneered by Mancini, so that "In several recent film scores . . . , we see a division of labor that mirrors Mancini's division between source music and nondiegetic underscore" (p. 267; see also Smith 1998). Additional studies of pop-oriented film music suitable for compilations or composite scores have appeared in the work of Altman (2001, p. 28); Bergfelder (2000, p. 85); Creekmur (2001, p. 375); Donnelly (2001b, p. 152); Garner (2000, p. 14; 2001, p. 188); Garwood (2003, p. 109); Gorbman (2007, p. 149); Grossberg (2003, pp. 83, 91); Karlin (1994, p. 225); Keightley (2003, p. 165); Kermode (1995, p. 12); Knight and Wojcik (2001, p. 1); Prendergast (1992, p. 146); Romney and Wootton (1995, p. 4; ed. 1995, p. 130); Sinker (1995, p. 113); Smith (2001, p. 407); Stilwell (2005, p. 140); and Wood (2002, p. 217).

A remaining question concerns the nature of the psychological process(es) whereby music plays out its nondiegetic role as a continuous source of "commentary" and "identifications"—that is, as an agent for registering emotive overtones and significant dramatic meanings of events, characters, and other key themes. We have already noted the obvious relevance of psychological phenomena related to classical conditioning (the formation of associations between X and Z) and cognitive consistency (the inference of a link between X and Z based on common links of X to Y and Y to Z). The essay by Cohen (2000) on "Perspectives from Cognitive Psychology" pushes further into the heart of such psychological phenomena to provide a useful tutorial and to offer an insightful theoretic scheme. Focusing primarily on nondiegetic music, Cohen describes how, intuitively, "music selections produce associations that add meaning to the film" (p. 361). However, from a neopositivistic perspective, Cohen wants empirical evidence to bolster this intuition. This she finds in a review of her own work—her experimental findings, for example, showing that different sounds (fast/slow, high/low) attached to different visual stimuli (computer-generated bouncing balls) prompt different associations (happy/sad) (p. 362); that different background music (A or B) matched with different geometric characters (triangles or circles) produce different impressions (level of perceived activity) (p. 363); that an ambiguous male-female chase scene (danger/romance) varies in interpretation with different background music (p. 363); and that judgments of filmed interactions among wolves (playing/fighting) also depend on the musical background (p. 364). Based on this bedrock of neopositivistic empiricism, Cohen (2000) concludes—plausibly enough—that nondiegetic music "helps define the meaning of a scene" and that this effect "is most pronounced when the scene is depicted as ambiguous" (p. 364).

## KASSABIAN ON HEARING FILM AND THE ELUSIVE "IN BETWEEN"

The references cited earlier together with the contributions collected by Buhler and Co. (ed. 2000) open up a conceptual gap or void that needs filling. Specifically, conventional work on film music that compartmentalizes this terrain into dichotomized homologous extremes (diegetic/nondiegetic, source/

background, ambient/meaningful, realistic/dramatic, actual/commemorative, objective/subjective, etc.) has neglected the gray areas of musical meaning that lie *between* the poles of these parallel binary oppositions *and/or* that involve hitherto unexplored *combinations* of (say) diegetic source music with meaningful associations and identifications related to the dramatic development of plot, character, key themes, and so forth. An awareness of and partial correction for this problem of oversight or neglect surfaces in a treatise by Kassabian (2001) entitled *Hearing Film: Tracking Identifications in Contemporary Hollywood Film Music.*

Kassabian (2001) begins with a dichotomy of her own—arguing for a distinction between "two main approaches to film music in contemporary Hollywood" (p. 2). The first involves the *composed score*—in the manner of the classical nondiegetic music described earlier—which produces *assimilating identifications* (that is, associations that draw the viewer into the world of the film). The second involves the *compiled score* (based on pre-existing songs and recordings)—in the manner documented by Smith (1998, 2000), inspired by the post-Mancinian vogue of soundtrack albums, and further described by many other authorities (cited earlier)—which produces *affiliating identifications* (that is, associations that draw on experiences from outside the world of the film). In pursuing the composed/compiled and assimilating/affiliating homologies (p. 5), Kassabian (2001) regards film music as a "meaning-making system" (p. 7) or "a semiotic system" (p. 11). To summarize, she isolates "two distinct models of contemporary Hollywood musical practice" based on the "ties between assimilating identifications and composed scores on the one hand, and affiliating identifications and compiled scores on the other" (p. 13). Kassabian's two-path formulation has proven influential and appears to have encouraged an emerging stream of research based on the "compiled score" that draws on pre-existing songs and recordings. (In this connection, see the references, cited earlier, to Altman, Bergfelder, Creekmur, Donnelly, Garner, Garwood, Gorbman, Grossberg, Karlin, Keightley, Kermode, Knight and Wojcik, Prendergast, Romney and Wootton, Sinker, Smith, Stilwell, and Wood.)

Meanwhile, Kassabian (2001) is concerned with the process whereby film music evokes meanings and moods—that is, with how viewers *receive* film music (p. 18). In this connection, she cites empirical work by Tagg and Clarida that "describes in detail how film music communicates certain meanings" (p. 18)—for example, a mood, a feeling, a gender. In her view, audience members possess a degree of *competence* that facilitates the decoding of musically encoded meanings, associations, or identifications so as to achieve a "correspondence between producer's intention and consumer's reading, between transmission and reception" (p. 20). This competence is "based on decipherable codes learned through experience" (p. 23), as when "we learn through exposure what a given tempo, series of notes, key, time signature, rhythm, volume, and orchestration are meant to signify" (p. 23). Low, ominous notes played by tubas, for example, signal impending danger (p. 24). Via such shared competence, music serves as a "communicative system" (p. 24). In this connection, Kassabian's own studies have shown certain gender-based musical associations such as those between female/male, nature/culture, green plants/concrete sidewalks, private/public, home/workplace, legato/staccato, regular/syncopated, euphonious/discordant, and so forth (pp. 30–31).

Addressing the diegetic/nondiegetic distinction that we have already found to be ubiquitous in the work of traditional film theorists, Kassabian (2001) begins in the usual way by contrasting "diegetic versus nondiegetic music" where "Diegetic music is . . . produced within the implied world of the film" and "Nondiegetic music is produced from some unspecified external source" (p. 42). Further, Kassabian revisits the sort of traditional homologies that we enumerated earlier—in particular, that which aligns *diegetic* versus *non-diegetic* music with *realistic depiction* versus *dramatic development*, respectively, according to what Kassabian describes as a principle of "inverse proportionality in which the more identifiably within the narrative the music is produced, the less liable it is to take its cues from the events of the narrative" (p. 49). (The reverential force of the traditional homology appears to enable Kassabian to offer such a patently illogical statement without the inclusion of a qualifier such as "paradoxically" or "ironically.")

However, it soon transpires that Kassabian (2001) wishes to problematize this facile dichotomization on the grounds that "it institutes some troubling ideas about film music" (p. 42). First, she says, it obscures the role played by music in establishing the diegesis itself (p. 42). Second and most important to our present concerns, by suggesting that film music lies "either 'in' (diegetic) or 'out' (nondiegetic) of the narrative world of the film" (p. 42), the traditional dichotomy fails to describe "music that seems to fall 'in between'" (p. 42).

Developing this point farther, Kassabian (2001) borrows from Hagen (1971) to elaborate on the familiar homologies discussed earlier. Hagen's categorization scheme retains the two familiar polar extremes: *source music* (i.e., diegetic music) and *dramatic scoring* (i.e., nondiegetic music). But Hagen adds a third possibility—*source scoring*—which falls "between diegetic and nondiegetic music" (Kassabian 2001, p. 45). According to Hagen (1971, p. 190), when compared with source music, "source scoring takes on a much closer relationship to the film": "It follows the framework of the scene more critically and matches the nuances of the scene musically" (quoted by Kassabian 2001, p. 45). In other words, for Kassabian (2001), "Source scoring combines aspects of source music [diegetic] and dramatic scoring [nondiegetic] in terms of both its relationship to the film's narrative world and its coincidence with the onscreen events" (p. 45). For example, when Loretta (Cher Bono) turns on the radio in *Moonstruck* (1987), we hear some (diegetic) light jazz that then carries over to successive scenes as time passes (thereby becoming part of the nondiegetic background) (p. 46). Kassabian gives several comparable examples before concluding that "The inside/outside, diegetic/nondiegetic dichotomy has difficulty with all these musical events; they belong to a third 'in between' category" (p. 47).

Besides emphasizing an *in-between* level of musical diegesis, Kassabian (2001) proposes three essential purposes served by music in film: *identification* of some character, place, event, or theme (as when music signals the presence of the shark in *Jaws* or of Darth Vader in *The Empire Strikes Back*, p. 57); *mood* as a reflection of the affective state of one or more character(s) (as when the opening theme in a western evokes a sense of the wide-open spaces, p. 59); and *commentary* as an indication of how viewers should construe some particular scene or event (as when the music tells us that an otherwise romantic situation is actually funny or that an apparently innocent setting will soon be the occasion for horror, p. 59). All this positions film music as a "semiotic system" (p. 60) with rich possibilities for shaping identifications, establishing moods, and suggesting commentaries that help to delineate characters, advance the plot, and develop key themes as the drama unfolds.

After enunciating the preliminary and all-important concepts just described, Kassabian (2001) proceeds to two chapters that contrast the aforementioned processes of *assimilation* and *affiliation*. The former, *assimilation*, appears in the classical Hollywood scores by such film composers as John Williams or Danny Elfman (p. 92). Illustratively, Kassabian addresses the theme of *nationalism*—reminiscent of what Fiske (1982) would call a *dominant* reading—and its emergence in such musical scores as those for *The Hunt for Red October* (1990), *Lethal Weapon 2* (1989), or *Indiana Jones and the Temple of Doom* (1984). In Kassabian's view, such examples of background music work, via audience competences based on past listening experience, to assimilate viewers into identifying with one or another of the film's available subject positions—with (say) the perspectives of the Alec Baldwin, Mel Gibson, or Harrison Ford characters in the films just mentioned. By contrast, the logic of *affiliation* depends on a different kind of process (p. 117)—reminiscent of a Fiskean *resistant reading*—in which identifications stem from various *subcultural* or *individualistic* connections based on (say) "race, class, education, age, [or] gender" (p. 119). For example, in *Dangerous Minds* (1995), rap music becomes a vehicle for establishing an affiliation between LouAnn (Michele Pfeiffer) and her (primarily nonwhite) students (p. 121). Similarly, *Corrina, Corrina* (1994) bolsters the theme of an interracial romance by showing that Corrina (Whoopi Goldberg) and Manny (Ray Liotta) share the same musical tastes—namely, a liking for Eric Satie, Bill Evans, Louis Armstrong, Billie Holiday, and "You Go to My Head" (p. 131)—preferences that some viewers happen to share, helping to form an affiliative bond between these viewers and the central characters.

In short, the contrasts that Kassabian (2001) draws between assimilating and affiliating identifications tend to parallel the distinctions maintained by Fiske (1982) and others between dominant and resistant readings, closed and open texts, or readerly and writerly interpretations (for a review, see Holbrook 1993). The key issue concerns the degree of identificatory freedom allowed or encouraged by a film's musical materials. The classic Hollywood film draws viewers toward assimilating identifications that support dominant ideologies. By contrast, compilation scores in the more contemporary style encourage affiliating identifications consistent with various forms of resistance. In sum, "assimilating identifications narrow or tighten possibilities, while affiliating identifications open outward" (p. 141). Kassabian (2001) makes it clear that she herself tends to prefer the latter (affiliating) to the former (assimilating) types of film music because "affiliating identifications . . . offer more possibilities for perceivers' historically constituted subjectivities than assimilating identifications do" (p. 143). And, to repeat, Kassabian's influence appears to have mirrored and/or encouraged a burgeoning stream of research focused on the role of the compilation or composite score (as in the aforementioned work by Altman, Bergfelder, Creekmur, and many others).

Thus, at bottom, the main argument of Kassabian's book depends on a *descriptive claim* (based on the homology between classical/compilation scores and assimilating/affiliating identifications) conjoined with a *normative prescription* (the evaluative superiority of the affiliative compilation-oriented approach, based on largely ideological considerations). The former claim sounds plausible but rests on an empirical assertion that Kassabian (2001) does not and probably cannot substantiate. The latter prescription seems attractive but hinges on politically oriented personal tastes. However, neither of these potential difficulties concerns me as much as what I would regard as a *missed opportunity* associated with the *in-between aspects* of the diegetic/nondiegetic split that Kassabian mentions early in the book but then pretty much ignores during its subsequent chapters. Let us therefore turn our attention to this *missed opportunity* found in the *in-between*.

## CRITIQUE AND PROPOSAL: THE CASE OF AMBI-DIEGETIC FILM MUSIC

In short, I believe that—in addressing a level *in between* the diegetic/nondiegetic extremes—Kassabian (2001) has located an important but neglected aspect of film music that clearly deserves our attention, *but* that her "in-between" description misstates the true nature of the relevant phenomenon. Specifically, Kassabian seems to envision a single *diegetic-nondiegetic axis* that—in accord with traditional thinking, resting on the homologies mentioned earlier—aligns with an axis between *realistic depiction* (tied to the physical location of a scene or the ambience of a setting) as opposed to *dramatic development* (tied to nuances of characterization, the unfolding of plot structure, the significance of thematic ideas, or other important meanings carried by the semiotic system). Usefully, she posits an intermediate position—a fuzzy area—at middling locations along these two concordant continua. Schematically, recalling our earlier depiction of the traditional homologies:

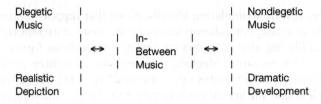

| Diegetic | | | | Nondiegetic |
|----------|---|---|---|-------------|
| Music | | | | Music |
| | | In- | | |
| | ↔ | Between | ↔ | |
| | | Music | | |
| Realistic | | | | Dramatic |
| Depiction | | | | Development |

A comparable tendency to look for an **additional category** and beyond appears in the work of Chion (1994). Though Chion deals with cinematic sound in general—extending well past our primary focus on music—he does emphasize a contrast between what he calls *on-screen sound, off-screen sound*, and *nondiegetic sound* (p. 73). This tripartite contrast hinges on Chion's distinction between *acousmatic sound* and *visualized sound*. Following Schaeffer (1967, p. 91), *acousmatic sound* or *acousmatic music* refers to sounds or music whose sources are absent from the cinematic image—that is, "sounds one hears without seeing their originating cause" (Chion 1994, p. 71). By contrast, *visualized sound* or *visualized music* is "accompanied by the sight of its source or cause" (p. 72). Within the acousmatic/visualized distinction, Chion (1994) employs a second but less clearly articulated contrast—namely, that between sound or music that is *internal* as opposed to *external* to the *reality* of the film's *story world* (p. 73). This distinction resembles those by Chion that we have earlier discussed under the headings objective vs. subjective; actual vs. commemorative; and screen music vs. pit music (Chion 1994, p. 80).

Combining these two key distinctions, Chion (1994) proposes *three major types* of cinematic sound or music: *on-screen* (visualized and internal); *off-screen* (acousmatic and internal); and *nondiegetic* (acousmatic and external). With this as a basis, Chion makes *three arguments*. First, Chion (1994) suggests that, historically, on-screen or visualized sound has tended to be neglected by film scholars in that "offscreen sound has long dominated an entire field of . . . theorizing about film sound" (p. 73). Second, in a manner akin to that of Kassabian (2001), Chion (1994) suggests the importance of various "exceptions" that must be woven into the scheme (p. 73) such as *ambient sound* (e.g., birds singing or church bells ringing), *internal sound* (e.g., a character's mental voices), and *on-the-air sound* (e.g., a telephone or radio broadcast) (p. 78). Third and most important to our purposes here, Chion (1994) hints that "music . . . inscribed in the action can of course be just as 'commemorative' as a nondiegetic music cue" (p. 80). This is a point crucial to our present concerns because it corresponds implicitly to what I shall label *ambi-diegetic music*. Though Chion fails to develop this key insight, I take it to be essential to the revelation of *another important type of film music*.

Specifically, I believe that Kassabian's sketchy focus on *in-between-ness* and Chion's restricted emphasis on *exceptions* overlook the possibility of *another important type of film music*. Rather than assuming an intermediate position in the manner of Kassabian (2001) or fancier ways of elaborating key distinctions in the manner of Chion (1994), this *additional type* works by *combining the opposite ends of two traditional continua*. Specifically, the additional type of film music is produced *inside* the film's stream of events in the manner conventionally associated with *diegetic music* (what Chion would call "visualized") *but* contributes to the film's *dramatic development* of character, plot, or themes in the manner conventionally associated with *nondiegetic music* (what Chion would call "commemorative" or "subjective"). I shall assign this *combination* of musical categories, typically construed as opposites by most writers, a new terminological designation—namely, *Ambi-Diegetic Film Music.*

This additional type of film music can be conceptualized according to a two-by-two cross-classification of the key axes of interest—previously viewed as conjoint but now recognized as orthogonal—where I shall combine the terminology variously favored by **Chion** (1994, shown in <u>**bold underlined letters**</u>) and by *Kassabian* (2001, shown in *bold italics*) to produce an <u>**ADDITIONAL TYPE**</u> (shown in <u>***BOLD ITALICIZED UNDERLINED CAPITAL LETTERS***</u>), as follows:

*Table 1* Typology of Music in Films

| | <u>Internal to Story World</u><br>(Objective; Actual)<br>(Screen Music) | <u>External to Story World</u><br>(Subjective;<br>Commemorative) |
|---|---|---|
| | *Realistic Depiction* | *Dramatic Development* |
| <u>Acousmatic Zone</u><br>(Source Absent from Image)<br><br>*Produced Outside* | <u>Off-Screen Music</u><br><br>*In-Between Music* | <u>Nondiegetic Pit Music</u><br><br>*Nondiegetic Music* |
| *Visualized Zone*<br>(Source Present in Image)<br><br>*Produced Inside* | <u>On-Screen Music</u><br><br>*Diegetic Music* | <u>**AMBI-DIEGETIC FILM MUSIC**</u> |

As indicated by this typology, *ambi-diegetic film music* includes those types of film music that are produced within the *visualized zone* that lies *inside* the film's imaged action (as when a character performs a song on-screen) but that play an important role in the *external* subjective or commemorative aspects of the film's *dramatic development* (as when this musical performance sheds light on a character's motivations or persona, provides associations that identify important aspects of the plot or setting, or reflects key thematic ideas or other important meanings).

In what follows, I shall have frequent occasion to refer to this conceptualization of *ambi-diegetic film music*. For this reason, it may be useful to provide a Streamlined Typology of Music in Films that highlights the three types of cinemusical moments most central to our present concerns.

*Table 2* Streamlined Typology of Music in Films

|  | *Realistic Depiction* | *Dramatic Development* |
| --- | --- | --- |
| *Produced Off-Screen* | *In-Between Music* | *Nondiegetic Music* |
| *Produced On-Screen* | *Diegetic Music* | <u>AMBI-DIEGETIC FILM MUSIC</u> |

## CLEAR BUT NEGLECTED EXAMPLES OF AMBI-DIEGETIC FILM MUSIC

### The Musical: Some Preliminary Considerations

The most obvious examples of ambi-diegetic film music appear in the traditional Hollywood musical, a genre of film music that—with such rare exceptions as Altman (1987) or Feuer (1993), plus the occasional musicals-oriented anthology devoted to film (Cohan ed. 2002; Marshall and Stilwell ed. 2000) or theatrical productions (Everett and Laird 2002, ed. 2002)—has been neglected by those working in this area of film criticism, perhaps partly because ambi-diegesis has represented a type of cinemusical functioning that most film critics, distracted by their traditional dichotomized homologies, have failed to recognize. (For especially clear comments on this neglect of film musicals, see Altman 1987, pp. 28, 365; Chion 1994, p. 73; Conrich 2000, p. 47; Donnelly 2001a, p. 4; Feuer 1993, pp. ix, xi; MacKinnon 2000, p. 43; Marshall and Stilwell 2000, p. 2; Rodman 2000, p. 188; Smith 1998, p. 21.)

Altman (1987) makes it clear that the problem of defining the nature of a musical is quite complex but, nonetheless, that it tends to hinge on the presence of diegetic (on-screen) musical performances where "The musical, according to the industry, is a film with music ... that emanates from ... the diegesis, the fictional world created by the film" (p. 12). Of course, this definition neglects the presence of diegetic music in *non*musicals and therefore requires considerable complication and revision—which Altman (1987) provides by means of a six-step program toward carving out a workable conceptualization. In the process, he begins with a "preliminary corpus" in which "every conceivable film with diegetic music is at first accepted and treated as a musical" (p. 13). However, he acknowledges that "the presence of diegetic music alone is simply not enough to produce a musical" but, rather, that "it is the tendency to transform diegetic music into supra-diegetic music—with a consequent reversal of the traditional image/sound hierarchy—that distinguishes the musical as a genre" (p. 71). In other words, musicals typically incorporate scenes in which the on-screen action supra-diegetically reflects music coming from off-screen in ways that render the on-screen action unrealistic, idealized, or fantastic so that "The musical does not just oppose reality to dreams, it merges the two" (p. 77). As noted by Cohan (2002b), one aspect of the musical's tendency to blend reality with fantasy stems from its (supra-diegetic) hallmark tendency to show diegetic singers or dancers on-screen accompanied by heard-but-not-seen orchestras off-screen, as when a character bursts into song or dance with the aid of an "inexplicable orchestral accompaniment" (p. 1). Indeed, Rubin (2002) finds that this tendency toward the "impossible" serves as a defining characteristic of the musical where "a musical is a film containing a significant proportion of musical numbers that are impossible—i.e., persistently contradictory in relation to the realistic discourse of the narrative" (p. 57).

Altman (1987) continues to worry and tug at the problem of defining the musical genre and its subgenres until, in Chapter V on "Genre History," he finally gets around to a list of defining characteristics (pp. 102–119). Here, as intimated earlier, "the presence of diegetic music alone is insufficient to classify a film as a musical" (p. 103). Rather, to qualify as a member of the musical genre, a feature-length film must tell a story (i.e., qualify as a narrative) about a romantic couple (i.e., a courtship model that excludes, for example, *The Wizard of Oz* [1939]) portrayed via dual-focus binary oppositions (ultimately reconciled) but with some degree of realism (albeit combined with inherently unrealistic aspects of formal patterning) and bound for some type of success (most typically a wedding) where musical sounds coexist with ordinary sound effects and dialog (thereby disqualifying, say, the jazz-opera *Umbrellas of Cherbourg* [1964]) in ways that contribute to the film's meaning (as when signifying the romantic triumph of marriage) but that also permit dissolves between narrative- and number-oriented productions (in the manner of, say, Busby Berkeley), sometimes in ways that privilege (musical) sound over the (narrative) image (pp. 102–110; see also Altman 2002; Cohan 2002a). Notice that, as Altman (1987) insists repeatedly, this conceptualization combines aspects of semantics and syntax wherein "generic status" is achieved "only when characteristic semantic elements [e.g., a romantic couple] are built into a stable syntax [e.g., binary oppositions]" (p. 117). With this as a basis, as already mentioned, Altman (1987) identifies "three subgenres which together make up the near totality of the musical genre as a whole" (p. 121)—namely, *the fairy tale musical* (set in a locale frequented by aristocrats with an emphasis on the need to restore order to this imaginary realm); *the show musical* (set in the world of the theater or other entertainment media with an emphasis on the creation of an artwork by a romantic couple from the stage or screen); and *the folk musical* (set in the America of yesteryear with an emphasis on achieving a nostalgic form of community through marriage).

To repeat a point emphasized many times in the present work, *I shall be less concerned with the distinctions between Altman's three types or with his comments on supra-diegetic music than with the **ambi-diegetic ways in which on-screen musical performances**—whether in musicals or **non-musicals**—can contribute to a film's **dramatic development**.* In this spirit, Marshall and Stilwell (2000) broaden the "definition of the musical" to include "any film in which music is an integral part of the narrative" (p. 1) so that—for example—the films by Woody Allen (along with most of the films discussed in the present work) would qualify as musicals under this expanded definition (p. 1), as would (say) *The Wizard of Oz* or *The Umbrellas of Cherbourg* (p. 3; see also Lindeperg and Marshall 2000). And Wood (2002) concludes that the hallmark of the musical is that "the primary entertainment value" of a film or play hinges on the musical performances themselves (p. 215).

As clearly indicated in the classic works by Altman (1987) and Feuer (1993), many of the performances found in a typical musical are "diegetic" in the sense that they appear on-screen but—unlike ordinary source music—incorporate off-screen orchestras, come from the realm of fantasy, and/or do little to advance the realism of the *mise en scène*. Here, one thinks of the production numbers famously concocted by Busby Berkeley; the swimming scenes mounted by Esther Williams and Co.; or some (but not all) of the brilliant song-and-dance routines perfected by Fred Astaire, Gene Kelly, and their various partners in terpsichore. Thus—in movie musicals, true to their essence, as identified by Wood (2002, p. 215)—many spectacular singing-and-dancing productions fall under the heading of "numbers" as opposed to "narrative" and serve the purpose of *pure entertainment* in ways that contribute *neither* to nondiegetic dramatic development *nor* to realistic diegesis and certainly *not* to any ambi-diegetic combination of the two (Altman 1987, p. 62; Cohan 2002b, pp. 2, 7; Conrich 2000, p. 48; Dyer 2002a, p. 23; Flinn 1992, p. 105; Karlin 1994, p. 170; Rubin 2002, p. 53). For example, when Fred Astaire shows off his miraculously virtuosic dancing ability or when Busby Berkeley creates his monumental kaleidoscopes of female body parts, movie music enters the realm of exciting or imaginative but narratively irrelevant fantasy. As described by Altman (1987), "Busby Berkeley . . . liberates the picture plane of all diegetic responsibilities . . . the simultaneous movement of the dancers produces a kaleidoscope effect . . . as if the screen were transformed into an electronically generated visual accompaniment to the music" (p. 71).

Karlin (1994) refers to the numbers-versus-narrative contrast as "nonorganic" versus "organic" and again mentions Busby Berkeley as the paragon of *non*organic spectacles when "setting up elaborate and dazzling production numbers that deliberately stopped the story cold" because "his staging was far more interesting than the plot" (p. 170). In this, Wood (2002) sees Berkeley as the ultimate exemplar of abstraction as opposed to realism where, as "cogs in a larger visual machine," dehumanized dancers become "the voyeuristic subject of a visual spectacle" in which "Having choreographed the large-scale production numbers, Berkeley's camera then becomes a roving eye that reduces the multiple body parts of chorines into geometric shapes seen from all possible angles" (p. 221). As Rubin (2002) puts it, the "Berkeleyesque" entails "elements of spectacle . . . such as large-scale chorus formations, geometric patterns, and giant props" (p. 54). Interpreting Berkeley's work in *Gold Diggers of 1933*, Mellencamp (2002) notes the connection between the Berkeleyesque dance routines and the modernist aspects of mass production on the assembly line where "factory principles of standardization . . . operate in Berkeley's female formations of assembly-line symmetry, harmony, anonymity, perfection" (p. 68). To repeat, as described by Rubin (2002), the "spectacular production number" typical of the "Berkeleyesque spectacle on the screen" (p. 54) departs from narrative concerns in ways that render it "impossible"—that is, "impossible from the standpoint of the realistic discourse of the narrative" (p. 57): "In terms of effects, the numbers create configurations that are feasible only with a movie camera . . . and that would be either impossible or incomprehensible on a theatrical stage" (p. 58). Cohan (2002b) agrees that "those extravagant, eye-popping Busby Berkeley numbers . . . become increasingly longer and more impossible in their size, scope and temporality . . . often appearing to set up a parallel universe of pure spectacle" (pp. 7–9).

As described by Robertson (2002), "Berkeley abandons all pretense to theatrical verisimilitude and instead offers a 'stage' spectacle" (p. 129) so that "the film spectator's experience is one of sheer astonishment . . . as . . . Berkeley transforms live action into . . . amazing and impossible abstractions" (p. 131). In a similar vein, Tinkcom (2002) mentions the numbers-over-narrative aspects of the Berkeley style (p. 121) and, ultimately, privileges "the camp pleasures of texture, masquerade, and performance" (p. 126) over any more ambi-diegetic senses in which on-screen song-and-dance routines further the development of plot, character, and other themes in the manner of primary interest to the present work. In the same spirit, Robertson (2002) finds anything-but-ambi-diegetic meaning in the Berkeley productions associated with the manner in which they create "an overall abstract design" that packages and commodifies female body parts for mass consumption and in which "women in the Berkeley musical function as both fetishized image and fetishized commodity (p. 133). However, Robertson (2002) does allow for "potentially oppositional ways in which female spectators might be able to negotiate their experience of these texts" (p. 134)—for example, with regard to their potential lesbian-inflected meanings or their interpretation as feminist camp that mirrors and mocks the commodification of women. In *this* sense, aspects of the narrative—for example, a story about gold diggers (women who offer themselves in exchange for financial rewards)—find what we would call ambi-diegetic echoes in the spectacular woman-commodifying dance numbers: "Her masquerade entails a camp recognition of herself as a stereotype and her manipulation of that stereotype for her own ends" (p. 140). (For similarly resistant ways of reading the outrageously excessive performances of Carmen Miranda, see Roberts 2002.) Indeed, Mizejewski (2002) offers the usual description of Berkeley's staging style wherein "Berkeley's chorus girl numbers . . . amplify previous, accumulated meanings of the chorus girl's body as a product suitable for show" (p. 187) but—like Robertson (2002), Roberts (2002), and others—emphasizes the diverse opportunities for oppositional readings that such cinemusical conventions tend to invite, as when "commodified chorus girls are literalized as currency, doppled with gold coins" so that "the woman-as-currency visual metaphor" suggests "readings that tend to veer in extreme directions, from misogyny to feminist camp" (p. 188).

On a smaller scale, returning to the contrast between numbers and narrative, Krämer (2000) describes the song-and-dance performances by Fred Astaire and Audrey Hepburn (trained in ballet) in *Funny Face* (1957) as taking "the numbers principle, stylistic excess and self-referentiality of the Hollywood musical to such extremes that the integrity and coherence of the film's diegetic world and the causal logic of its narrative are seriously undermined" (p. 66). Thus—though Cohan (2002b) recognizes that Astaire often achieved an "*integrated* form" of "song, dance, and story" in a manner that we would call ambi-diegetic, one clear example being "Dancing in the Dark" from *The Band Wagon* (1953) in which the relationship between Fred and Cyd Charisse (also trained in ballet) advances as they dance so that "their duet resolves the conflict in ages and musical styles . . . and . . . moves them on to the next segment of the narrative action" (Cohan 2002a, p. 89)— he nonetheless suggests that, in general, "Impossible song and dance numbers [Busby Berkeley, Esther Williams, Betty Grable] occur in studio-era musicals all the time" (2002b, p. 2). Thus, in general and as described by Cohan (2002a), Astaire dances in ways that often privilege numbers over narrative and that sacrifice story to spectacle: "Astaire's solo numbers . . . do more than simply texture a characterization or advance a story's linear movement . . . since they interfere with the narrative economy of his films by foregrounding the value of his performance as spectacle" (p. 88). For example, in "I Left My Hat in Haiti" from *Royal Wedding* (1951), "this big production number . . . overblown, incoherent, and terrific to watch . . . fills no apparent plot function whatsoever" (p. 91).

In sum, the numbers-versus-narrative distinction has recognized that much of the music in musicals provides sheer entertainment with very little contribution to the realistic depiction of the story or to the film's dramatic development. However, just as obviously, the typical musical also contains what we would call ambi-diegetic performances in which characters sing, dance, or play instruments on-screen (perhaps supported by off-screen orchestral accompaniments) and in which these diegetic performances serve to advance the dramatic development of plot, character, and other narrative themes. Familiar illustrations of such ambi-diegetic cinemusical performances in movie musicals would cover the entire gamut from Al Jolson belting out "My Mammy" in *The Jazz Singer* (1927) to Robert Preston singing "Seventy-Six Trombones" in *The Music Man* (1962) to Ewan MacGregor and Nicole Kidman performing "Come What May" in *Moulin Rouge* (2001). Put simply, when Fred Astaire, Bing Crosby, Gene Kelly, Elvis Presley, or Michael Jackson sing and dance, they furnish us with multiple associations based on body language, song lyrics, costumes, props, and other cues that tell us something about their characters as well as about the direction of plot movement, story lines, or other key thematic concerns. Just recall the meanings that Fred Astaire could generate by dancing with a broomstick; that Cyd Charisse could express by cavorting with a pair of nylon stockings; or that Gene Kelly could generate by galumphing in a rainstorm. Or remember the significance of Frank Sinatra singing to Rita

Hayworth and Grace Kelly. Who could deny the dramatic importance of such on-screen musical performances?

We must note, again, that many such ambi-diegetic cinemusical moments contain "mixed" aspects in the sense that—while the key singer, dancer, or instrumentalist appears diegetically on-screen—various components of the musical fabric often emanate from the off-camera background region normally associated with nondiegetic music. For example, after the on-screen characters begin to sing a love song to each other (perhaps accompanied by a diegetic pianist or a small band of supporting musicians), a more complex accompaniment often joins them from the off-screen realm (played perhaps by an unseen orchestra, an invisible instrumental soloist, or a heavenly choir of backup singers who are never visible to the viewer). Nonetheless, we would often classify such examples as *ambi-diegetic* in the sense that the *key performers*—say, the hero and heroine—appear *on-screen* and pour their hearts out in ways that advance the *dramatic development* of plot, character, or other themes.

## Examples of Ambi-Diegetic Performances in Musicals

When we contemplate the traditional distinction between a diegetic "track" (realistic on-screen source music) as opposed to a nondiegetic "track" (off-screen background music that works toward dramatic development), it becomes clear that—though Altman (1987) exaggerates the case a bit and, of course, does not use our term "ambi-diegetic"—the musical provides one conspicuous instance of "crossing-over" in which what we would call ambi-diegetic cinemusical moments (wherein on-screen music carries dramatic meanings) frequently occur: "This intermixing is at the very heart of the style characteristic of the American film musical" (p. 63). The essence of this "crossing-over" or "intermixing" corresponds to what we would call *ambi-diegetic film music*—the point being that Altman (1987) clearly recognizes the ubiquity of such ambi-diegetic effects in Hollywood musicals, even while glossing over the fact that similar ambi-diegetic cinemusical moments also occur in innumerable films that might not qualify as members of the musical genre.

As noted earlier, many of the productions found in musicals consist of "numbers" as opposed to "narratives" insofar as they aim at mere entertainment value (or worse) without much regard to (diegetic) cinematic realism or (nondiegetic) dramatic development—Busby Berkeley extravanganzas being the most conspicuous examples of such tendencies (Altman 1987, p. 71; Cohan 2002b, p. 7; Flinn 1992, p. 105; Karlin 1994, p. 170; Mellencamp 2002, p. 68; Mizejewski 2002, p. 187; Previn 1991, p. 58; Robertson 2002, p. 129; Rubin 2002, p. 54; Tinkcom 2002, p. 121; Wood 2002, p. 221). Nonetheless—even after ignoring such purely entertaining musical numbers that lack any dramatic significance—we find innumerable cases of what we would call ambi-diegetic performances in Hollywood musicals. Let us consider a few salient illustrations.

Atkins (1983) distinguishes between two types of film musicals—namely, the "backstage musical" and the "book show" (p. 15). The book show resembles operetta in that no attempt is made to justify orchestral accompaniments that seem to come from nowhere. But in the backstage musical, "all musical numbers fit into the definition of source music" (p. 15). Indeed—in such backstage musicals as *Cabaret* (1972), *A Star Is Born* (1976), or *Nashville* (1975)—"the film audience sees some sort of show within a show" (p. 15). Obviously, such shows-within-shows work toward the dramatic development of plot, themes, and characterizations—where, very often, leading characters are themselves on-screen performers who reveal their personalities through the ways in which they perform.

Altman (1987; 2002) emphasizes the structure based on key parallels via which the meanings of diegetic performances in musicals often operate. One example comes from *New Moon* (1940) in which Marianne (Jeanette MacDonald) and Charles (Nelson Eddy) sing on-screen in ways that evince a set of clear binary oppositions: on-deck/below-deck; entertainment/social purpose; free/imprisoned (Altman 1987, p. 17); female/male; rich/poor; cultured/practical; restrained/energetic; easily offended/tenacious; proper/rebellious (p. 19). This "dual focus" characterizes the structure of many or even most Hollywood musicals as a basis for the development of dramatic meanings "built around parallel stars of opposite sex and radically divergent values" (p. 19). In such a situation—musically and dramatically—"the plot of *New Moon* depends on . . . the resolution of their differences" (p. 20). From this perspective, ambi-diegetic music serves to underline the key contrasts premised on the male/female comparisons central to the love story: *"Each segment must be understood . . . by comparison to the segment which it parallels"* (p. 20).

A further example, dissected by Altman (1987, 2002) in some detail, comes from Vincente Minnelli's *Gigi* (1958) with songs by Alan Jay Lerner and Fritz Loewe. Here, Gigi (Leslie Caron) and Gaston (Louis Jourdan) negotiate a set of parallel on-screen musical performances that comprise a full dramatic organization based on the dual-focus structure where "Each scene involving only one of the lovers is invariably matched by a parallel scene (song, shot, event) featuring the other lover" and where "the musical uses one character's actions to establish the context of the other character's parallel activities" (1987, p. 22). And, of course, the actions or activities in question very often involve on-screen musical performances of the type that we would call ambi-diegetic. Thus, for example, Gaston walks through a park singing about how he doesn't understand "Gigi" and sits down on the very same bench where Gigi sang "I Don't Understand the Parisians" (p. 22). Meanwhile, Honoré (Maurice Chevalier) mirrors one age-based aspect of the opposition between Gaston (older) and Gigi (younger) when he sings the pair of songs entitled "Not Young Any More" and "Thank Heaven for Little Girls." In sum—partly via its on-screen musical performances—"*Gigi* appears as a series of paired segments built around a fundamental duality, that of sexual differentiation, and two minor oppositions, beauty/riches and child/adult" (p. 26). In the case of *Gigi*—as in so many musicals—such oppositions are resolved through marriage. Indeed, this basic structure—the reconciliation of opposites—provides a prototype for the Hollywood musical and something close to a working definition of the genre, where musical numbers serve to portray a set of oppositions in need of resolution: "By reconciling terms previously seen as mutually exclusive, the musical succeeds in reducing an unsatisfactory paradox to a more workable configuration, a concordance of opposites" (p. 27).

Altman (1987) next presents a masterful account of how the dual structure of binary oppositions just described unfolds via what we would call ambi-diegetic musical performances in a number of films. As we would quickly agree (Holbrook and Hirschman 1993), Altman (1987) emphasizes that *every* aspect of the musical typically reflects the relevant, dramatically parallel, binary oppositions—for example, costumes, settings, scenery, and so forth (p. 33). Here, we focus primarily on music as embodied in songs and dances—where, as elsewhere, we find striking homologies between parallel binary oppositions. For example, in *The Pirate* (1948), Gene Kelly's "Niña" (celebrating the woman of his dreams) parallels Judy Garland's "Mack the Black" (honoring her ideal man). Elsewhere, in the "echo duet," lovers alternate verses ("People Will Say We're in Love" from *Oklahoma!*; "If I Loved You" from *Carousel*; "Every Little Moment" from *Presenting Lily Mars*; "Make Believe," "Why Do I Love you?," and "You Are Love" from *Showboat*) or even lines to a song ("Anything You Can Do" from *Annie Get Your Gun*; "No Two People" from *Hans Christian Anderson*; "I Love You More" from *Pajama Game*; "Paris Loves Lovers" from *Silk Stockings*; "I Remember It Well" from *Gigi*; and "Bess You Is My Woman Now" from *Porgy and Bess*) (p. 38). The latter piece switches between Porgy (male, slower tempo, regular beat, diatonic, consonant) and Bess (female, faster pace, syncopated, chromatic, dissonant) in ways that anticipate later developments: "That Bess should run off and leave Porgy in the final sequence comes as no surprise to those who have listened carefully to the music along the way" (p. 40). Embracing a wide variety of musical films, Altman (1987) shows how contrasts in singing-and-dancing styles serve to highlight the parallel oppositions at the heart of his analyses—Chevalier (rasping, natural, carefree) versus MacDonald (mellifluous, trained, sophisticated) or Kelly-Astaire-and-Travolta (tap-dance or ballroom styles) versus Caron-Charisse-and-Gorney (ballet routines of high art). Further, the resolution of such differences often appears in the form of a musical performance that combines or reconciles the lovers' contrasting styles—as in "Swing Me an Old Fashioned Song" from *Little Miss Broadway* (1938), "Swing Trot" from *The Barkleys of Broadway* (1949), or "Girl Hunt" from *The Band Wagon* (1953)—where we find "a combination of old and new, of classical and modern" (p. 52).

In agreement with Altman, Feuer (1993) suggests that "the narrative resolution of every musical involves bringing together the forces of entertainment with forces opposed to entertainment": "The synthesis achieved through the union of the romantic couple" entails a reconciliation of the reality principle ("values associated with rational cognitive thought") and the pleasure principle ("the world of the imagination . . . and entertainment") (p. 71). Extending this view of *The Band Wagon*, Babington (2000) provides a psychoanalytic interpretation in which—as for Oedipus—"the son (Entertainment) defeats the father (Art) and possesses the mother (the Musical)" (p. 32). More generally, Cohan (2002b) suggests, "Musicals repeatedly quote from show business . . . institutions (minstrelsy, vaudeville, Tin Pan Alley, jazz, swing) and then as often valorize them as a refreshing, vital contrast with the stuffier, more elitist world of 'high art' (opera, ballet, classical music and theater)" (p. 14). Something comparable, as described by Altman (1987), happens in the contrasted dancing styles explored by Fred Astaire (as the ballet dancer Petrov and also as the tap dancer Pete Peters) and Ginger Rogers (as a tap dancer who aspires to something "higher") in *Shall We Dance* (1937): "Their marriage is hailed in the press as a merger of jazz and ballet, and on the stage by a dance ('They All Laughed') which fades balletic pirouettes into tap breaks through the intermediary of ballroom steps and swings" so that "the couple as a unit achieves balance, permanent in its symmetry" (p. 82; see also Wood 2002, p. 228).

Among the *fairy tale musicals* that Altman (1987) describes, we find various RKO productions featuring Fred Astaire and (often) Ginger Rogers, as when their dancing reflects the quarrelsome nature of their relationship. In *Roberta* (1935), "it is the challenge dance that constitutes the Astaire/Rogers trademark" (p. 163). After commenting on the proliferation of challenge dances in a number of subsequent Fred-and-Ginger films, Altman (1987) praises the extent to which what we would call ambi-diegetic song-and-dance routines tend to present on-screen performances in ways that advance the dramatic development of plot and character in these motion pictures. In his words, the Astaire/Rogers dances achieve "a trim sense of integration, a reduction of distance between narrative and number . . . to the point where the dance and song numbers *are* narrative" (p. 167).

Turning to various *show musicals*, Altman (1987) suggests that this subgenre—which includes various backstage films—generally deals with situations in which the success (bliss) of a romantic couple (marriage) depends on the creation of a show (play, revue, magazine, or whatever). Very often, such films depict not only music but also the audience for that music on-screen. And—here, via what we would call ambi-diegetic cinemusical moments—source music serves to parallel and reinforce relevant aspects of the inevitable love story. Thus, "Borrowing its formula from the well known metaphor, show musical syntax depends on couples who 'make beautiful music together'" (p. 212). In such show musicals, a "bridge" occurs between narrative and numbers when an actor performs a song as part of a show or during a rehearsal such that "the actor represents both his character within the narrative . . . and his character within the show" (p. 231). Obviously, this situation creates opportunities for the creation of what we would call ambi-diegetic cinemusical meanings. For example, Altman

(1987) comments on the thematic counterpoint between the old and the new in *The Band Wagon* (1953), where Astaire's affinity for familiar songs ("Dancing in the Dark," "You and the Night and the Music," "Something to Remember You By") builds "a watertight case for the values of yester-year" (p. 260).

As a *folk musical* of interest to Altman (1987)—exhibiting the charac-teristic tendency of folk musicals to "glorify the past" (p. 272) and to cele-brate the small-town or rural values of the community and the extended family (p. 274)—consider the music by Jerome Kern and Oscar Hammerstein II for *Show Boat* (1929, 1936, 1951), which in Altman's description achieves something close to the quintessence of what we are calling ambi-diegetic cinemusical meaning where songs "grow directly out of and further the plot" and serve as "expressions of heartfelt personal emotion" (pp. 285–286; but cf. Stanfield 2000). Clearly, in the folk musical, what we would call the ambi-diegetic development of plot and character infuses the on-screen singing of such "folk musical stars" as Judy Garland, Gene Kelly, and Frank Sinatra— all of whom perform in ways that evoke "the expression of personal emotion" (p. 287). Much of this expressive effect depends on the familiarity of the songs incorporated into the typical folk musical—as when they have received previous wide exposure via Broadway show-tune albums—where the music by Rodgers and Hammerstein for *Oklahoma!* (1943) serves as the prototype and where audience recognition of every song builds a sense of shared community as part of a national folk culture (p. 321).

As further described by Sears (2002), *Oklahoma!* ushered in a new era wherein "songs grow . . . seamlessly out of the plot and characters" (p. 127) in a manner that, when transferred to film, we would call ambi-diegetic. For example "The Surrey with the Fringe on Top" initiates the relationship between Laurey and Curly: "As Curly begins to describe the beautiful surrey in which he will take Laurey to the dance that night, he is really telling her how much he wants to spend a romantic evening with her" (p. 124). In the film musical *State Fair* (1945), Rodgers and Hammerstein contributed tunes that continued their "strategy of using songs to move the plot and explicate character" (p. 127): "The soliloquy 'It Might as Well Be Spring' provides the most personal, intimate observation of any character in this film, as we see a young girl learning about love between men and women" (p. 128). Indeed, Riis and Sears with Everett (2002) suggest that the Rodgers-and-Hammerstein approach proved foundational for subsequent musicals on stage and in films in so far as their song lyrics "built story lines and, most crucially, . . . developed characters" (p. 138).

As indicated by Feuer (1993), one classic case in which the musical offers what we would call ambi-diegetic cinemusical meaning appears when—as so often happens—the entertaining show, with quintessential Hollywood reflexivity, celebrates the value of entertainment itself. In other words, as its dramatic rationale, the on-screen music tells us about . . . what else? . . . the virtues of on-screen music. We find such moments, most conspicuously, in such productions as "Dames" from *Dames* (1934); "Be a Clown" from *The*

*Pirate* (1948); "There's No Business Like Show Business" from *Annie Get Your Gun* (1950); "You Wonderful You" from *Summer Stock* (1950); "Make 'Em Laugh" from *Singin' in the Rain* (1952); "Applause, Applause" from *Give a Girl a Break* (1953); "There's No Business Like Show Business" (again) from *There's No Business Like Show Business* (1954); "Stereophonic Sound" from *Silk Stockings* (1954); and "That's Entertainment" from *The Band Wagon* (1953)—the latter of which eventually served as the title for a whole series of films commemorating the glories of the Hollywood musical: "The ode to entertainment almost always occupies the finale position, coming at the summit of the show, the culmination of all the narrative energy the film possesses . . . including us in the celebration of another entertainment triumph" (pp. 36–37).

A further example from Feuer (1993; see also Feuer 2002) of what we would call ambi-diegetic musical meaning appears in the sorts of reflexive song lyrics or self-reflecting dances that support their own narrative texts with the appropriate singing or dancing routines—for example, telling a girl you love her or tap dancing in a happy way to indicate that you feel amorous or joyous: "Numbers in which a performer sings and dances *as* she sings about singing and dancing abound in the musical film" (p. 50). In analyzing this phenomenon, Feuer (1993) gives particular attention to those musicals in which serious music (e.g., opera) contrasts with jazz (e.g., swing): "In the Hollywood musical, the war between elite and popular art came to be represented by a standard plot which I will call the 'opera *vs* swing' narrative" (p. 54) where "The particular syntax opposing popular and elite elements arises out of the genre's overall rhetoric of affirming itself by applauding popular forms" (pp. 55–56). A clear example—one that hinges firmly on what we would call ambi-diegetic cinemusical meanings—appears in the (ambi-diegetic) comparisons between Peter Lawford (classically trained) and Frank Sinatra (swing oriented) in *It Happened in Brooklyn* (1947):

> European music [associated with Lawford] is seen as decrepit, cold, out of touch with the needs of the people; whereas swing [associated with Sinatra], as the music of the folk in Brooklyn, represents youth, community, warmth, personal expression and spontaneity.
>
> (Feuer 1993, p. 57)

A similar ambi-diegetic theme returns in *Babes in Arms* (1939) when Betty Jaynes (operatic style) and Judy Garland (popular style) team up for a duet on "Opera Vs. Jazz" in which Betty proclaims her liking for opera while Judy voices a preference for swing. As the film continues, Garland's viewpoint tends to triumph when "The strategy . . . consists in strongly implying that a difference in musical idiom is *significant*, then demonstrating swing's superiority": "Swing is contagious and Jaynes catches it" (p. 59). As two additional carefully constructed examples of what we would call ambi-diegetic cinemusical meanings, "Almost every popular musical performance in **The Band Wagon** is matched up with a segment which parodies the lack of spontaneity and pretentiousness of the high-art world" (p. 62), while "The entire sub-plot of **Silk Stockings** ridicules elite art through a farcical contrast between modern serious music and modern popular music" (p. 64). As Feuer (1993) puts it—with implications for what follows in the present jazz-oriented volume—"The Hollywood musical is uniquely equipped to blow its own horn": "A film like **Silk Stockings** makes sure we recognize that horn as a jazz instrument" (p. 65). Later, Feuer (1993) singles out the (ambi-diegetic) significance of Cyd Charisse's sexy dance with the lacey under-garments in which Charisse as Ninotchka (rigid, rational, militaristic) adopts the values espoused by Fred Astaire (spontaneous, effortless, free) in a "sensuous dance" that "trades her military garb for silk and satin" (p. 116; see also Holbrook 1985).

Reaching back to an earlier era, Karlin (1994) praises Rouben Mamoulian's use of Rodgers-and-Hart's songs for *Love Me Tonight* (1932), where source music serves a clear dramatic purpose:

> In that one film, he demonstrated how entertaining and dramatically effective it could be to listen to a song being sung while the plot actually continued to develop . . . one of the best being the Rodgers and Hart song, "Isn't It Romantic?"
>
> (Karlin 1994, p. 169)

With special reference to the example of Joe (Gene Kelly) and Jane (Judy Garland) in *Summer Stock* (1950), Laing (2000) describes the use of what we would call ambi-diegetic music to express the thoughts and feelings of characters through the use of on-screen singing wherein "What is particularly striking about this type of number is the way in which the character appears to be the actual site of the music's production": "So when ... Joe sings 'You Wonderful You' to Jane, it is not a song, as such, that he is singing, but a musically-embodied version of his feelings towards her" (p. 7).

Echoing Altman (1987, p. 63), the fact that diegetic singing (by a character on-screen) is often supported in the musical by nondiegetic accompaniment (by an orchestra performing off-screen) inspires Laing (2000) to suggest the importance of an in-between or mixed area that we would call ambi-diegetic and that entails "a collapsing of the conventional divisions between the sources of music": "Music which comes from the diegetic space, through, for example, the character beginning to sing, becomes accompanied by music on the nondiegetic track" to produce "a state of music which seems to belong exclusively to neither level but instead occupies an entirely new space" (p. 8).

Lindeperg and Marshall (2000) manage to discuss Jacques Demy's *Les Parapluies de Cherbourg* or *The Umbrellas of Cherbourg* (1964) with amazingly little attention to the remarkable music by Michel Legrand that transfuses this full-length jazz opera. Further, they denigrate the musical themes associated with Mme Emery (Anne Vernon), the mother of Geneviève

(Catherine Deneuve), as "fragmented"—claiming that they "fail to cohere into a strong melodic line" (p. 104). This seems surprising when we consider that Vernon (miming the singing voice of Christiane Legrand, Michel's sister and a much-admired charter member of the Swingle Singers) performs the most magnificently Baroque-like musical passage in the entire film—namely, her songful plea when seeking financial help from the local jeweler—and that this beautifully-crafted cinemusically-significant ambi-diegetic theme resurfaces while Mme Emery tells the wealthy Roland Cassard (Marc Michel) that Geneviève will become his bride (in an unfortunate marriage of economic convenience), continues as the young girl picks out a wedding dress (with heavily ironic implications), and then transforms into spine-chilling organ music at the church where Geneviève leaves her true lover Guy (Nino Castelnuovo, whose baby she is carrying) pretty much in the lurch. Anyway, despite missing the beauty of the ambi-diegetic cinemusical passages provided by Emery/Vernon/Legrand, Lindeperg and Marshall (2000) do correctly notice the heart-rending manner in which the movie's main theme—"I Will Wait For You"—circulates through the film as a poignant statement of "Geneviève and Guy's love and the obstacles to it" (p. 104).

On an even darker note, Killick (2001) gives specific illustrations of what we would call ambi-diegetic songs used to develop plot and character via "insidious" ways of perpetuating and reinforcing a "stereotype" of Jews as (say) "obsessed with money and unscrupulous in acquiring it" (p. 186). One example comes from Fagin's song entitled "Pick a Pocket or Two" in *Oliver!* (1968). Here, even without explicitly identifying Fagin as Jewish in the text of the screenplay itself, the musical aspects of the tune strongly convey that impression via harmonic and melodic elements conventionally associated with Jewish music. Similar comments pertain to the on-screen (ambi-diegetic) performances by Sally Bowles (Liza Minnelli) in *Cabaret* (1972) where—though the characters themselves are not Jewish—the song in question evokes something of the aforementioned ugly stereotype by virtue of repeating the word "money" (recalling Tevye's "All day long I'd biddy-biddy-bum" in *Fiddler on the Roof*) in a minor key ("the usual 'Jewish' mode"): "The use of 'Jewish' music . . . makes sense only as a hint that the cynical money-grubbing philosophy expressed in the song is typical of Jews" (p. 196). Killick (2001) even attributes similar connections between musical style and stereotyping to the hit song by ABBA from 1976, also entitled "Money, Money, Money," where "the music, which differs from their other hit songs precisely in those features I have been identifying as 'Jewish,' . . . adds . . . an association between Jewish-sounding music and themes of avarice" (p. 197).

Speaking of otherwise lost or undercover meanings in racial or ethnic stereotypes, as conveyed by subtle ambi-diegetic on-screen cinemusical cues (songs and lyrics), Gill (2001) presents a rather fascinating discussion of Jewish influences on music by the Gershwins for *Porgy and Bess*. Pointing to the minstrelsy-oriented work in blackface by many Jewish entertainers— most conspicuously, Al Jolson, Eddie Cantor, and Sophie Tucker (see also

Rogin 2002)—and suggesting that "the most obvious context in which to view and hear *Porgy and Bess* is . . . blackface minstrelsy" (p. 356), Gill (2001) insists on "the constitutive role that Yiddishkeit plays in the Gershwins' music, and in many of Hollywood's representations of African American culture" (p. 349). For example, in the song "It Ain't Necessarily So," Gill finds that "the words Ira Gershwin used to express . . . Methuselah's quality of life at age nine hundred deserve special attention" (p. 349)—namely, the phrase about a man "what's" nine hundred years old, where "to mistake an adjectival subordinate clause, requiring introduction by 'that' or 'who,' for a noun clause, which requires an introductory 'what,' is less a feature of black English than the Yiddish English that was the native tongue of the Gershwins" (p. 349).

Though primarily concerned with the Broadway production, McClung and Laird (2002) offer a description of Kurt Weill and Ira Gershwin's music for *Lady in the Dark*—later made into a TV video starring Ann Sothern in 1954—that, for once, clearly articulates the musical subtleties that contribute to the ambi-diegetic potential for a song such as "My Ship," which begins by "arpeggiating a complex of notes whose constituents are D minor and F major triads": "Weill worked out this musical riddle over the course of the drama . . . the 'incorrect' minor submediant giving way to the 'correct' major tonic to parallel the heroine's psychoanalytic treatment" (p. 170).

It goes without saying that the movie versions of Broadway shows often depart significantly from the scores for the original stage productions. For example, the film version of *On the Town* (1949) omits two Bernstein-Comden-and-Green masterpieces—"Lucky To Be Me" and "Some Other Time"—in ways that miss vibrant opportunities for dramatic development. Wood (2002) comments insightfully on how often-distorted stage-to-screen transformations or adaptations of Broadway productions reappear as movie musicals. Here, he notes the importance of diegesis—that is, "the extent to which music featured on the soundtrack could plausibly emanate from a source within the visual frame or the narrative as a performance, a rehearsal, or some other likely musical activity" (p. 213). Moving toward a recognition of what we are calling ambi-diegetic music, Wood (2002) suggests that "The basic component of the musical, the song, can be understood as a very flexible template, whose lyrics may provide narrative thrust, insight into a character's psyche or reflection on an external object" (p. 223). For example, Wood (2002) compares the reappearances of Irving Berlin's "Blue Skies" (first found on-stage in *Betsy* from 1926) in ways that create four different meanings in four different films via performances by Al Jolson in *The Jazz Singer* (1927, "charismatic style and optimistic mood"); by Ethel Merman in *Alexander's Ragtime Band* (1938, "tinged with melancholy"); by Bing Crosby in *Blue Skies* (1946, projecting "reassurance and optimism"); and by Crosby with Danny Kaye in *White Christmas* (1954, "upbeat . . . charismatic") (p. 227).

Perhaps mercifully, the musicals by Stephen Sondheim have generally escaped conversion to the motion-picture realm—one striking exception being *Sweeney Todd: The Demon Barber of Fleet Street* (2007), starring

Johnny Depp as the haircutter who eats his clients for lunch—but, of relevance to our present cinemusical concerns, Lovensheimer (2002) quotes Gordon (1990) regarding the degree to which Sondheim strives for a total integration of music, lyrics, and text as "his means of creating characters for a given show" (Lovensheimer 2002, p. 183): "Sondheim's music and lyrics grow out of the dramatic idea inherent in the show's concept and themselves become part of the drama" (Gordon 1990, p. 7; quoted by Lovensheimer 2002, p. 183). Of special note, Sondheim focuses *Assassins* on characters who attempted or succeeded in killing American presidents in ways that create "a troubling work that perplexed and even angered some critics and still has the power to disturb American audiences" (Lovensheimer 2002, p. 189): "*Assassins* allows each character to have his or her appropriate turn, or specialty number [where the] unrelated styles also allow the distinctness of each character from the others" (p. 190). But Lovensheimer adds that "The initial and nervous critical reception of *Assassins* in the United States perhaps suggests that Sondheim revealed too much too clearly" (p. 195). I saw *Assassins* off-Broadway at Playwrights Horizons when I believe it was still in previews during early December of 1990. Especially at this early stage, I found the spectacle of essentially evil terrorists happily singing in cheerful ways about heinous crimes to be deeply disturbing. As explained by Lovensheimer (2002), I was suitably shocked. Dare we hope that this profoundly troubling musical will find its way to the silver screen?

Meanwhile, Warfield (2002) describes Jonathan Larson's *Rent*—the retelling of Puccini's *La Bohéme*, set in New York's East Village—in terms that suggest considerable potential for the role of ambi-diegetic music in the 2005 stage-to-screen adaptation: "Remarkably, virtually all of the show's songs contribute to plot or character development with a realistic text that includes justifiable use of common vulgarities" (p. 244). Clearly, Broadway shows continue to supply material that Hollywood musicals can borrow as the basis for ambi-diegetic meaning.

## Other Examples of Ambi-Diegetic Film Music

Though neglected—perhaps even more egregiously than the musicals themselves—and not systematically treated as an explicit (ambi-diegetic) category, the central role of what we would call ambi-diegesis in film music from *non*-musicals has prompted implicit recognition from a number of perceptive but scattered commentators. Thus, ambi-diegetic uses of songs show up in all sorts of films that fall outside the "musical" genre and that are typically classified as dramas, comedies, mysteries, action adventures, sci-fi fantasies, westerns, or whatever—as when one or more film character(s) often pause(s) to perform a song or otherwise to engage in some form of music making or listening that is produced *inside* the movie in the *visualized zone* that appears *on-screen* but that also serves the film's purposes of *dramatic development*. Let us consider some specific examples of *ambi-diegetic film music* in *non*-musicals.

Atkins (1983) defines "source music" as "music that, whether emanating from a source visible on the screen (such as a musical instrument or ensemble, a vocalist, a radio, a record player, or a television receiver) or not, is assumed to be audible to the characters in the film" and suggests that this source or diegetic music "is a type of motion picture music that has been heard in countless films, and has enhanced the dramatic and emotional content of many of them" (p. 13). In sympathy with our earlier observations, Atkins (1983) adds that "In the wealth of literature about film music, however, there has been little discussion of this type of music" (p. 13). From a viewpoint that closely parallels our discussion of ambi-diegetic film music, Atkins (1983) proposes "To show the way in which source music can enhance the dramatic elements in a film" (p. 17). For example, *Lights of New York* (1928)—the first all-talking feature film—"demonstrates how effective the source music could be in conveying not only the feeling of realism, but also the mood of honky-tonk sordidness that pervaded the era of bootleggers and gangsters" (p. 33). Speaking of sordidness, in *The Blue Angel* (1930), the chief protagonist is a performer played by Marlene Dietrich, for whom Sammy Lerner and Frederick Hollander's "Falling in Love Again" serves as "the perfect vehicle for the character she portrays" so as "to reveal and establish a character" (p. 39). Meanwhile, in *Song of Love* (1947) Katharine Hepburn plays the role of Clara Schumann and performs "highly emotional" music dubbed by Artur Rubinstein in ways that "add . . . dramatic . . . value" (p. 23). In *Citizen Kane* (1941), the musical ineptitude of Kane's wife Susan Alexander (Dorothy Comingore) is crucial to the story, where "the failure of the musical performance conveys a development of plot and characterization" (p. 22). A similar development appears in *Annie Hall* (1977) when Annie (Diane Keaton) sings "It Had to Be You" to general indifference from a nightclub crowd—prompting "outraged annoyance" from Alvy (Woody Allen) and "wistful reactions" from Annie/Diane in ways that "tell the audience . . . how she and Woody Allen relate to each other" (p. 24). During *Brothers* (1977), a character modeled on Angela Davis plays a recording of Mozart to imply that "this lady has a spiritual (or 'highbrow') side to her nature" (p. 25). *Save the Tiger* (1973) features a character played by Jack Lemmon, who—as a symptom of his mental derangement—transports himself into the past by playing tapes of old records such as Bunny Berigan's performance of Duke-and-Gershwin's "I Can't Get Started" to reflect his "impending psychosis" (p. 57). Johnny Green's choices of source music for *They Shoot Horses, Don't They?* (1969) contribute powerfully to the film's dramatic effect by reinforcing "the dreary, existential mood of the picture" (p. 65). When source music appears as "the creation of one of the protagonists in a film"—as in *Four Daughters* (1938), *Four Wives* (1939), *Suicide Squadron* (1942), *The Constant Nymph* (1943), *Escape Me Never* (1947), *Between Two Worlds* (1944), *Deception* (1946), or *Humoresque* (1947) (all relatively forgotten films in which the musician-as-hero theme achieved something of a temporary vogue)—the relevant "symphony, concerto, or rhapsody" helps to convey "the personality of the imaginary composer" (p. 89). It should be clear from all this that Atkins (1983) insists on the important role played by what we would call ambi-diegetic music in films.

According to Atkins (1983), when performing Henry Mancini's "Moon River" as Holly Golightly in *Breakfast at Tiffany's* (1961), Audrey Hepburn "expressed something of her philosophy of life" (p. 49). Similarly, the manner in which Prendergast (1992) describes this use of "Moon River" gives implicit recognition to what we would call its ambi-diegetic role. Recall that the song appears conspicuously in an on-screen version sung by Holly/Audrey, self-accompanied on guitar while sitting on her fire escape. Prendergast interprets this performance as "a kind of gentle character sketch for the film's main character"—a mix of "city sophistication" and "the simpleness of the country girl" (p. 147). Further, in a nondiegetic deployment at the film's conclusion, this theme "adds substantially to the film's dramatic climax" (p. 146) when Audrey rescues her cat (Cat) to the strains of a heavenly choir singing "Moon River" (Holbrook 1998c, 2008d).

In her analysis of the music from *Penny Serenade* (1941), Flinn (1992) interprets the meanings of on-screen source music in a manner that we would call ambi-diegetic. Thus, the playing of old 78-rpm recordings gives expression to the characters' deepest feelings in ways that "suggest an emotional state": "'My Blue Heaven' initiates the sense of Julie and Roger's early happiness [while] 'Happy Birthday' [suggests] a feeling of festivity and family togetherness" (p. 139).

Even while insisting that he intends to focus primarily on nondiegetic film music, Brown (1994) acknowledges that—via what we would call ambi-diegetic meanings—"it is quite possible for diegetic, or source, music to create the same effect and affect in the viewer that nondiegetic music does" (p. 22). He presents an example from *The Black Cat* (1934) in which "an apparently diegetic cue takes off on its own and functions nondiegetically" (p. 60). Specifically, at one point, Boris Karloff turns on a radio that plays Schubert's Unfinished Symphony just as Bela Lugosi kills a cat (whose soul passes to the heroine). In this, "The Schubert symphony, although played on a phonograph, provides exactly the kind of affective backing traditionally expected of the nondiegetic score" (p. 61). Brown (1994) gives a few more examples of what we would call ambi-diegesis (dramatic development via diegetic music) in a chapter subtitled "The Source Beyond the Source." One such illustration concerns Hitchcock's *Rope* (1948), in which Phillip (Farley Granger) is a concert pianist who has partnered with Brandon (John Dall) to commit a ghoulish murder and in which—while performing Poulenc's "*Mouvement Perpétuel* Number 1"—the criminals' "symbolic undoing" occurs when a college professor named Rupert (James Stewart) "sets a metronome at an ever increasing pace, ultimately making it impossible for Phillip to continue playing" (p. 75). Similarly, Thomas (2007) interprets this cinemusical moment from *Rope* as a "key scene" in which "detective/mentor Rupert stands in an imperious, effeminizing gesture over Phillip, subjecting . . . both Phillip and Poulenc's music to the rigors of the metronome"

(p. 284). As noted by Brown (1994), in Fritz Lang's *M* (1931), the serial killer played by Peter Lorre whistles a snatch from Grieg's "In the Hall of the Mountain King" just before he kills another child victim. At one point, as Lorre follows his next intended prey, the child's mother appears and Lorre stops whistling so that the symbolic inevitability of the crime has been replaced by "a return to the natural order of things" (p. 78). Instead of our term "ambi-diegetic," Brown (1994) coins the (somewhat more awkward) name "quasi-nondiegetic" to describe this musical situation: "It is as if the villain uses diegetic music to create a quasi-nondiegetic score to accompany the narrative he or she is trying to control" (pp. 84–85). Another example comes from Hitchcock's *Vertigo* (1958) when Midge (Barbara Bel Geddes) plays a selection from Johann Christian Bach's "Sinfonia in E-flat" on her phonograph and Scottie (James Stewart) asks her to turn it off. Because Bach's piece represents "the very embodiment of rationalized art,", "this gesture is "symptomatic of Scottie's refusal to accept the normal world" (p. 82). Later, at the sanatorium, Midge tries to coax Scottie out of his depression by playing a record of Mozart's Symphony No. 34, but "Again, Scottie rejects Midge's music, remaining totally impassive and unresponding"—thereby abandoning "her entire, ordered, real universe" (p. 83). Turning to the case of jazz as film music, Brown (1994) comments briefly on the use by Orson Welles of Henry Mancini's score for *Touch of Evil* (1958) in which the composer supplied "a series of Latin-flavored (to suit the Mexican setting) cues written in an even dirtier, grittier jazz idiom than previously heard in the movies" and where Welles "made it a point of keeping most of the musical cues within the diegetic framework, thus emphasizing the association between the score and the film's seedy settings" (p. 184). And in describing Michel Legrand's music for Jean-Luc Godard's *Vivre Sa Vie* (1962), he finds the director "tampering with the diegetic music in such a way that it functions somewhat nondiegetically" (p. 197) so that "Godard ... treats even his diegetic music as a raw material carefully integrated into both the film's aesthetic and narrative structures" (p. 198). Ultimately, Brown (1994) sees the use of diegetic music (on-screen realism) for nondiegetic purposes (dramatic development) as an aspect of postmodernism or what he calls "the postmodern breakdown of the classic distinction between music as nondiegetic affect and music as diegetic action" (p. 247). This "postmodernization" allows music "to wander indiscriminately between the ... domains of the diegetic and the nondiegetic" (p. 249). Indeed, in an "Appendix" that begins by presenting the familiar diegetic/nondiegetic distinction (p. 349), Brown (1994) adds a third type that he now calls "narrative" music and that bears considerable resemblance to our ambi-diegetic category insofar as it entails "music that plays an active role in the film's narrative ... structure and is performed ... by character(s) contained within that structure" (p. 350).

From a closely related point of view, Karlin (1994) comments on how diegetic or source music can migrate into the nondiegetic background, where its overt on-screen meanings are transferred to the implicit behind-the-scenes realm—as in the case of *Casablanca* (1942) and its much-celebrated use of "As Time Goes By," first diegetically and later nondiegetically, thereby illustrating that "Source music can be effectively integrated into the dramatic underscoring . . . to achieve additional unity and emotional power" (p. 69). Similarly, in *The Magnificent Seven* (1960), Elmer Bernstein "segues . . . from source music . . . played by the villagers . . . to orchestral score near the end of the scene" (p. 128). Further, in Erich Wolfgang Korngold's score for *The Adventures of Robin Hood* (1938), "the few moments of visual on-screen source music are treated as part of the score rather than as a separate element" (p. 99).

Biancorosso (2001) provides a specific illustration of dramatically meaningful diegetic music, drawn from Alfred Hitchcock's *Vertigo* (1958), in which the bells of a mission tower sound the death knell for the Kim Novak character: "On the one hand, the music seems like a component of the diegetic soundscape; on the other, the sound of the bells comments upon the scene nondiegetically as well as being a realistic element of it" (p.51).

Moving from the sublime to the not-so-sublime, Knight and Wojcik (2001) consider *Wayne's World* (1992)—which deploys 30 different songs drawn from sources ranging from Tchaikovsky to Alice Cooper—as the embodiment of cases in which diegetic source music plays a key role in dramatic development: "Often, songs cue us to characters' subjectivity, as when we hear Tchaikovsky as an internal diegetic soundover for Garth's fantasy girl, Donna Dixon" (pp. 1–2).

Turning to Hitchcock's remake of *The Man Who Knew Too Much* (1956), Pomerance (2001) regards Doris Day's on-screen performance(s) of "Que Sera, Sera (What Will Be, Will Be)"—regarded by Doris herself as "for children"; deemed by the film's musical director Bernard Herrmann to be "a piece of junk"; and prompting one commentator to dub Doris the "woman who sang too much" (p. 56)—as central to the meanings of the motion picture. Pomerance (2001) insists that "this deceptively simple and very popular little song plays a role of the most profound significance in a very complex film" (p. 56). Thus, Pomerance treats "a piece of music that has been received . . . in a derogatory, much lighter spirit" as worthy of "straightforward serious-ness" insofar as "Whatever will be, will be what some people determine should be" (p. 64). In his view, "One can see this logic as a dictum for compre-hending not only this film but all films": "'Whatever it is that must happen *will in fact happen*' [so that] the future's not ours to see, but it will come" (p. 70).

Focusing on French films from the 1930s, Conway (2001) suggests that "The incorporation of songs and singers in French films of this era . . . invites us to explore the meanings they create within the narratives" (pp. 134–135). In particular, as exemplified by a *chanteuse réaliste* such as Edith Piaf, "The realist song is almost always about loss and tends to be intensely cynical about the possibility of romantic love and domestic stability": "It typically chronicles the plight of a woman facing heartbreak and poverty" (p. 135). Conway (2001) proceeds to give examples in which such on-screen per-formances mirror aspects of a film's dramatic development of plot and character so that the relevant song becomes "a shorthand for female transgression . . . and for the intense emotions of sexual desire, melancholy, and despair" (p. 137). Though the songs Conway mentions differ in the degree to which they appear as source rather than background music, often blurring the distinction between the two, her main point aligns closely with our conception of ambi-diegetic music—namely that "songs are important . . . in terms of the meanings they create within narratives" (p. 155).

Returning to Henry Mancini's source music for *Touch of Evil* (1958), Leeper (2001) discusses what we would call the ambi-diegetic use by Orson Welles of on-screen performances to advance the dramatic development of plot and character. Thus, Mancini's score pursues a "reliance upon diegetic cues . . . especially rock and jazz idioms" to provide "a thematic analogue of border crossings that structures the score in a direct relationship to the film's narrative organization" (p. 226). Put more simply, this means that most of the music emanates from car radios, juke boxes, nightclubs, and other diegetic sources. This "diegetic source music" (p. 231) embodies "Welles's intention to maintain only diegetic music in the film" (p. 232) and to emphasize ethnicity-related aspects of the dramatic characterizations: "His innovative decision was to use primarily diegetic sources for the film's music" (p. 237) where "a musical cacophony of styles and rhythms [empha-sizes] the variety of cultures, races, and classes of people listening to them" (p. 232). Examples include Charlton Heston as Ramon Miguel Vargas (Mexican—mariachi music); a teenage gang (young, wild, dangerous—rock and roll music); and Janet Leigh as Suzy Vargas (white suburbanite—fluffy, sanitized, easy-listening music) (p. 234).

Further exploring aspects of ethnicity, Knee (2001) shows how *Broken Strings* (1940) uses diegetic jazz performances (in a manner that we would call ambi-diegetic) to advance the dramatic development of plot and character—arguing that "although *Broken Strings*'s swing performances are generally very brief, they are also of considerable importance to the narrative [and are] pivotal in the film's conceptual development, its themes, its character motivations" (p. 278). Specifically, in this film, violinist Johnny Williams (William Washington) turns from classical music to swing in order to earn money that will help his injured father Arthur Williams (Clarence Muse). Though his classically trained father disapproves of jazz and despite playing with two broken strings, the son's evident skills as a jazz violinist eventually win the day:

> The breaking of the strings in effect 'blackens' the violin, transforming it from an instrument of servitude under a white idiom [classical music] to an instrument of free(d) black expression [jazz], an instrument damaged but paradoxically also reinvested with lost strength and vitality.
>
> (Knee 2001, p. 281)

(For another African American violinist with two broken strings, see *The Soloist* [2009] in which Jamie Foxx as Nathaniel Ayers gives ambi-diegetic performances on a two-stringed violin and later on a top-notch cello that clearly reflect the depths of his underlying emotions.)

As described by Gabbard (2001), during various phases of the romance between Robert Kincaid (Clint Eastwood) and Francesca Johnson (Meryl Streep), director Eastwood's *The Bridges of Madison County* (1995) makes what we would call ambi-diegetic use of compilation-score source music from a radio in Francesca's kitchen (as well as dance music at a roadhouse) to mirror Kincaid's masculinity by means of associating his persona with performances by the legendary African-American singer Johnny Hartman. Esteemed especially for his classic recording with John Coltrane entitled *John Coltrane and Johnny Hartman* (1963), Hartman possessed a fine deep baritone reminiscent of Billy Eckstine and unequivocally masculine in the image it projected. According to Gabbard (2001), via source music from the radio and roadhouse band, Eastwood taps these associations with Hartman to convey "nonthreatening . . . phallic masculinity at its most unproblem-atic" (p. 296): "In *Bridges*, Eastwood has gone farther than ever before in expropriating black masculinity and sexuality for one of his own characters" (p. 302). For example, while Robert and Francesca chat in her kitchen, Johnny sings "Easy Living" on the radio in a manner that "endows Clint Eastwood's actions with real masculine authority at the same time that it heightens the film's romanticism" (p. 306). When they dance in the kitchen to Johnny's "I See Your Face Before Me," Gabbard (2001) suggests, "Hartman's music can . . . make us feel what the characters are feeling and somehow connect these feelings to our own experiences" (p. 307).

Smith (2001) also focuses on compilation scores in which popular tunes often serve as source music that emanates "from boom boxes, jukeboxes, radios, and stereos . . . within the diegesis" but that produces a "frisson of pleasure" due to the fact that "the song . . . is also a perfectly apt or ironic comment on the action depicted within the film" (p. 419). Thus, speaking of source music in what we would call its ambi-diegetic role, Smith notes that this "use of pop music conforms to the same sorts of dramatic functions served by orchestral scores": "It underlines character traits, suggests elements of character development or point of view, reinforces aspects of the film's setting, and supports the film's structure (p. 414).

In his analysis of the music chosen by Quentin Tarantino for his films, Garner (2001) points to what we would call the ambi-diegetic manner in which (diegetic) source music reveals aspects of character (dramatic development) in that "The process of music selection is foregrounded": "It is the choice of this-music or that-music . . . which is made indicative of character or situation" (p. 189). One could hardly hope for a more per-suasive case of ambi-diegetic music in action: "Clearly what matters most about much of the music in Tarantino's films—all of it culled from exist-ing records and movies—is the situational use his characters make of it" (p. 190). For example, in *Jackie Brown* (1997), "the music in the opening credits . . . is drawn from the diegesis, and is used to say something about character" (p. 196) so that—as the film progresses—"The music's datedness

... serves to authenticate her identity" and "lays the foundation stone of Jackie's character" (p. 193). *Pulp Fiction* (1994) achieves what Garner (2001) regards as "two of the most striking, memorable uses of music by characters in Tarantino's work" (p. 199) when Mia (Uma Thurman) listens to Dusty Springfield's "Son of a Preacher Man" and then dances to Urge Overkill's rendition of Neil Diamond's "Girl, You'll Be a Woman Soon": "Both scenes . . . foreground the central female character's music selection" where the first suggests "illicit sexual relations, in both its lyrics and performative style" (p. 200) and the second "lyrically promises female maturity and fulfillment" (p. 201).

Further reflecting an implicit recognition of the ambi-diegetic role played by film music, Dickinson (2003a) makes room in her anthology for work that deals with a "largely younger set of ideas" relating to "the role of music and musicians within film narratives," where "music . . . is a prominent bearer of far-reaching cultural propositions" so as to inspire "exciting areas where new writing is just beginning to trickle through and where more research would be greatly welcomed" (p. 7). Here, she refers primarily to compilation scores, filmed concerts, music documentaries, and biopics before recommending "studies of musicians within movie narratives" (pp. 8–9) and concluding, "It is hoped that more books and articles . . . which help create a much broader picture of how music and film cultures overlap and influence each other will be forthcoming in the near future" (p. 9). Certainly, her broadened scope would include aspects of what we are calling ambi-diegetic uses of music in film where, among other roles, "Music . . . is . . . a lifestyle choice through which we delineate our social identities" (p. 11).

Without relying on an explicit vocabulary to capture the essence of his departure from traditional thinking, Biancorosso (2004) emphasizes the role of what we would call ambi-diegetic film music in contributing to cinemusical meanings. Thus, he examines ways in which diegetic on-screen music or "mundane" music such as "café music" or "muzak playing in lobbies or shopping malls" carries significance for the dramatic development of plot, characters, and other themes when "the music is either heard or sung by one or more characters" as "diegetic" music that is "understood to be taking place within the fictional world of the film" (p. 192): "For the spectator, . . . even the most perfunctory incidental music is . . . potentially imbued with a function, a meaning in relation to the whole [to become] a vehicle of great narrative import" (p. 193). For example, in Michelangelo Antonioni's *Zabriskie Point* (1969), we encounter a scene in which Patti Page's "Tennessee Waltz"—played on the jukebox of a down-and-out bar in the California desert—serves to provide a "nuanced characterization of a milieu" and to represent "the perceivable element of an isolated, economically depressed outpost with an aging population, in stark contrast to urban, trend-setting L.A." (p. 196). Again, in Bertrand Tavernier's *A Sunday in the Country* (1984), we find an example where, while a father and daughter meet in a café, a local band plays a waltz that supports the deep melancholy of their conversation to convey "a layer of unspoken—perhaps, unspeakable—feelings" that include "regret and resignation on his part and profound empathy for him, as well as anger toward her mother, on hers" (p. 201). In other words, Biancorosso (2004) emphasizes ways in which what we would call ambi-diegetic film music "switches status" between its conventional diegetic and nondiegetic roles: "Now it is apprehended as anchored, realistically motivated sound, now as non-diegetic inflection" (p. 202). As one more example, consider the singing of the theme song from the "Mickey Mouse Club" by the military platoon depicted in Stanley Kubrick's *Full Metal Jacket* (1987): "Numbed by murder, their repetitious, almost compulsive music making is symbolic of a collective, mental unraveling" (p. 207).

As recently as 2007, Goldmark, Kramer, and Leppert (2007) also mention the traditional diegetic/nondiegetic distinction between "source music" and "dramatic scoring" (p. 3). However, their purpose centers on disputing the value of this easy distinction in ways that uncover possibilities for what we would call ambi-diegetic cinemusical moments wherein "The music of a film . . . tends to take on a life or identity of its own" and wherein, as for ambi-diegetic music, "It is not difficult to show that linking music and image produces a reciprocity of representation in which each responds to the forces and values inscribed in the other" (p. 4).

In this spirit, McClary (2007) finds a vivid example of what we would call ambi-diegetic music in Jane Campion's *The Piano* (1992) when the mute pianist Ada (Holly Hunter) reveals her deepest emotions via on-screen performances in which "Michael Nyman's score . . . blurs the distinction between the diegetic and nondiegetic": "Ada's music . . . serves as her only expressive outlet, and it hints at the passionate interiority that seethes behind her impassive face" (p. 54).

After doing much to popularize the diegetic/nondiegetic distinction (Gorbman 1987), Gorbman (2007) now undercuts its legitimacy by giving several examples of what we would call ambi-diegetic music in films. Specifically, she discusses the work of various "*mélomanes*"—that is, *auteur* directors who control all aspects of their films, *including* the choice and placement of music. These include Quentin Tarantino, Jean-Luc Godard, Stanley Kubrick, Martin Scorsese, Woody Allen, Alain Resnais, Sally Potter, Jim Jarmusch, Wim Wenders, and Aki Kaurismäki (p. 151). As Gorbman (2007) implicitly recognizes, such music often plays a role that we would call ambi-diegetic and "where it is on-screen characters who choose a song" (p. 152). For example, in Tarantino's *Jackie Brown* (1997), "Didn't I Blow Your Mind This Time" by the Delfonics takes on "a special kind of diegetic resonance involving characters' knowledge or lack of knowledge, and characters' openness (or not) to 'hearing' one another" (p. 152). Something similar happens in the films by Kubrick, who "often uses popular songs . . . to provide apt or ironic commentary"—as when, in *Eyes Wide Shut* (1999), Tom Cruise "walks through a ballroom populated by anonymous, masked couples, some nude and others clothed" while "they dance to 'Strangers in the Night'" (p. 153). Again, in Godard's *Prénom Carmen* (1983), we see a string quartet on-screen, playing music from Beethoven: "When the male violinist comments about the violence of the musical passage at hand, . . . we link that musical violence with the physical violence of the bank robbery scene with which it is interwoven" (p. 157).

Returning to a familiar illustration, Hoeckner (2007) emphasizes what we would call the ambi-diegetic role of on-screen source music in *Casablanca* (1942) in general and of "As Time Goes By" in particular. When Ilsa (Ingrid Bergman) first asks Sam (Dooley Wilson) to play the song, in "perhaps the most beautiful shot of a woman's face ever," we see "gleams of tears in her eyes" (p. 170). Later, when Rick (Humphrey Bogart) asks Sam to play the song for him again, "Now we see in an extended flashback what the music makes Rick see and made Ilsa see before" (p. 171): "Moreover, the lyrics do not just comment on the dramatic situation; they also communicate the essence of the film" (p. 171).

After referring to the diegetic/nondiegetic contrast as "one of the most basic distinctions in film music" (p. 184) where diegetic music contributes to cinematic "realism" as in "backstage musicals and nightclub-centered gangster films" (p. 188) and where nondiegetic music supports "meanings" that include "the delineation of emotional or narrative content by musical accompaniment" (p. 188), Stilwell (2007) hastens to add that "there are quite a lot of cases that do not seem so easy to label as diegetic or nondiegetic"— that is, where "the border between diegetic and nondiegetic is crossed" (p. 184) to close what she calls a "fantastical gap" (p. 186). Especially clear illustrations of "the transition between one diegetic/nondiegetic state to the other" include those in which we "negotiate that gap" (p. 187) in ways that add significant meanings to the unfolding dramatic development. Thus, Stilwell (2007) begins by maintaining the usual "disjunction" between the "empathetic underscore" and various kinds of "anempathetic source music" (p. 190) where "The alliance of empathy with the underscore and anempathy with source music is certainly prevalent in the classical Hollywood aesthetic, and it is still a dominant mode of scoring" (p. 190). "Still," she quickly adds, "it is only an alliance, not an unbreakable bond" (p. 190)—as, for example, when the source music from *Casablanca* triggers and reflects romantic memories and we find "Rick wallowing in diegetic nostalgia" (p. 190). As I have insisted rather strenuously, one such case of breaking the bond (among others) pertains to what we would call ambi-diegetic film music. Stilwell (2007) recognizes this phenomenon implicitly in situations where diegetic music mirrors a character's feelings—for example, the use of source music in *The Killing Fields* (1984) when "the first time Sydney Schanberg puts 'Nessum dorma' on his stereo as a backdrop for news footage from Cambodia . . . the swelling of the music . . . empathetically mimics Schanberg's feelings" (p. 194). As another illustration, Stilwell (2007) describes how Jane Campion's *Holy Smoke* (1999) begins with nondiegetic music—Neil Diamond's "Holly Holy" under the opening credits—that transitions into diegetic music when Ruth (Kate Winslet) follows some women to a scene in which they engage in a cult-like dance, thereby creating "a sense of arrival, of the completion that Ruth will find here" as she becomes "transformed" and "rises to a new state" (p. 198). In situations such as these, Stilwell (2007) finds the diegetic/nondiegetic distinction useful for what it suggests about cases in which the boundary is crossed (including those, I would argue, that we refer to by the term ambi-diegetic) and in which "the border region . . . takes on great narrative and experiential import": "These moments . . . are important moments of revelation, of symbolism, and of emotional engagement within the film and without" (p. 200).

## Reading Between the Lines in Smith's Essay on Marketing Popular Film Music

At greater length and of considerable relevance to the field of (macro)-marketing, though he generally clings pretty close to the traditional diegetic/ nondiegetic distinction, Smith (1998) also offers illustrations of what we would call *ambi-diegetic film music* that, though not labeled as such, might have served in his work to elucidate this category, had he chosen to move in this direction. Specifically, Smith (1998) wrote *The Sounds of Commerce*— subtitled *Marketing Popular Film Music*—primarily to trace the influences on film music that resulted from Hollywood's entry into the business of producing soundtrack albums. However, aspects of Smith's book could and should be read as illustrations of cinemusical ambi-diegesis. For the present purposes, I shall briefly renegotiate Smith's treatise from that perspective.

In this light, as noted earlier, Henry Mancini's "Moon River"—sung on-screen by Audrey Hepburn in *Breakfast at Tiffany's* (1961)—falls clearly into the ambi-diegetic classification in that it "functions within the film's larger systems of signification, particularly those that bear on the construction of Holly Golightly's character" (p. 72). Indeed—reminiscent of Atkins (1983) and Prendergast (1992)—Smith (1998) elaborates a view of "Moon River" and similar songs as "oblique statements of their films' over-arching themes" that serve "to connote both a nostalgic rural past and a utopian future for the film's heroine" but that also convey "a cynical reminder of . . . the repressed sexual wish that motivates her actions" (p. 82). It takes Smith (1998) three full pages of text to elaborate these interpretive meanings—during which, he characterizes Holly via the use of such moon- and river-related terms as "romantic allure," "emotionally distant, cold, and unattainable," "drifter," "broken dreams and heartache," "dreaminess," "style," "desire for glamour and social status," "freedom, open possi-bilities," "a complex and contradictory mix of romantic fantasy and sexual predation" (pp. 91–94). Whether we do or don't agree with this character-ization of Holly's persona, we must acknowledge that—as advertised— "Moon River" works toward forming multiple associations with her complex identity (Holbrook 1998c, 2008d).

Comparably, in portraying Frank Sinatra as a co-dependent heroin addict, Elmer Bernstein's jazz-flavored score for *The Man with the Golden Arm*

(1955) uses jazz performances within nightclubs and other music-related settings to serve as "a prototype of how jazz might be dramatically motivated as diegetic music" (Smith 1998, p. 73)—thereby providing another illustration of how film music might play what we would call an ambi-diegetic role.

Later, Smith (1998) recognizes that the compilation-based approach to film music constitutes something of a "hybrid of the musical and the traditional classical Hollywood score" (p. 155). By this, he means that the songs often function to foster dramatic development in that "Songs . . . may perform any or all of the classical score's traditional functions . . . as a way of establishing mood and setting, and as a commentary on the film's characters and action" (p. 155). What Smith (1998) fails to emphasize or at times even implicitly denies (pp. 160–161) is that often such cases fall into our ambi-diegetic category insofar as the origins of the music emanate from inside the film. As an example, consider the oft-mentioned case of *American Graffiti* (1973), where "the close connection between music and setting was expressed through the comprehensive motivation of the music within the diegesis" to a point where "the radio is virtually a character in the film" (p. 165). Here, the diegetic radio music—courtesy of Wolfman Jack—allows filmmaker George Lucas to limn "a particular sociocultural milieu" and to establish "a sense of subcultural identity" (pp. 165–166).

In such situations, "musical allusion . . . serves as an expressive device to either comment on the action or suggest the director's attitude toward the characters, settings, and themes of the film" (pp. 167–168). Clearly, these comments anticipate the discussion by Kassabian (2001) of affiliative identification—as well as many of the ambi-diegetic examples mentioned heretofore. (For a broader review of the semiotic role played by cinematic consumption symbolism, see Holbrook and Hirschman 1993.)

Often such associative identifications stem from compilation scores used *non*diegetically—as in *The Graduate* (1967), *Easy Rider* (1969), or *The Last Picture Show* (1971). But in *American Graffiti* (1973)—which Smith (1998) regards as "a contemporary prototype of the compilation score" and "a perfect synthesis of the compilation score's narrational possibilities" (p. 171)—we find a clear case of what we would call ambi-diegesis. Indeed, as a paragon of musical nostalgia, the movie epitomizes the essence of ambi-diegetic film music. On one hand, as Smith (1998) indicates, "By structuring the soundtrack as a radio show, the film consistently motivates the music as part of the diegesis" (p. 177) so as to serve "a realistic motivation" with Wolfman Jack as "the source of much of the film's music" (p. 183). On the other, discussing "the music's narrational functions" for the length of nine pages (pp. 176–184), Smith stresses that "the allusiveness of the music opens up a number of interpretive possibilities" related to "setting, character, and authorial commentary" (p. 176). In this interpretation, seen from the present perspective, the film emerges as a paradigm instance of ambi-diegesis where "a common function of all film music involves underscoring character traits, signifying points of view, and expressing emotional states" and where

"*American Graffiti* merely magnifies that function in its roughly one-song-per-scene format" (p. 182). Thus, typical of *ambi-diegesis*, this film utilizes *diegetic* music produced *inside* the movie for purposes of *dramatic development* in ways that "reinforce aspects of setting, characterization, and theme" (p. 231).

## Concluding Examples of Ambi-Diegesis: Buhler and Co. Revisited

Finally, let us return to the anthology on *Music and Cinema* by Buhler and Co. (ed. 2000) to highlight some examples that depart from the general tenor of the book insofar as they *do* go beyond the traditional homologies listed earlier to focus on illustrations of what we would call *ambi-diegetic film music*. A few of these departures from tradition are relatively minor and fleeting in their brevity. For example, speaking again of the source music composed by Henry Mancini, Smith (2000) does acknowledge that "this is the music to which the characters of the film listen" so that "the music either gives the characters dramatic nuance or it suggests something about their milieu" (p. 253). In a similar spirit, Neumeyer, Flinn, and Buhler (2000) describe the source/background diegetic/nondiegetic homology but then allow that "the polarity of source and background music . . . , isolated in their respective diegetic or extradiegetic spheres, is an extreme case; in practice, music can and does routinely cross the membrane that separates them" (p. 17). Along the same lines, in his analysis of Robert Altman's *Kansas City* (1996), Gabbard (2000) describes an on-screen "tenor battle" between two saxophonists (Craig Handy and Joshua Redman playing the parts of Coleman Hawkins and Lester Young), which occurs simultaneously with some violent action behind a nightclub where some gangsters assault a petty crook and stab him repeatedly, while the film is edited to jump back and forth between these two events. Rather ingeniously (Altman for doing it) and insightfully (Gabbard for noticing it), three types of *cutting* are combined here: first, what jazz musicians call a *cutting contest* between the two tenor saxophonists; second, the literal *cutting* (stabbing and slashing) of the unfortunate knifing victim; third, the *cinematic cutting* between the two scenes in the way the film is edited. Each type of cutting comments on the others in mutual reciprocity. Comparably, again referring to *Casablanca*, Marks (2000) suggests that diegetic music at the café (songs performed in-situ) is "used to make narrative points, sometimes obvious, sometimes subtle, through association of melodies and lyrics with the story unfolding on-screen" (p. 173).

Besides these brief examples from Buhler and Co. (ed. 2000), we must note three more extended exegeses that implicitly acknowledge how music produced *inside* a film so as to be visible *on-screen* can and often does serve the purpose of *dramatic development* in the manner that we would refer to as *ambi-diegetic*.

First, Everett (2000) addresses the use of "Songlines" (p. 99) in auto-biographical or first-person narrative films, emphasizing what we would call their ambi-diegetic role: "The songs tend to be foregrounded within the films' inevitably ironic and self-conscious discourse, where their essentially ambiguous status, simultaneously intra- and extradiegetic, private and public, mirrors that of autobiography itself, and draws the spectator directly into the remembering process" (p. 101). In this connection, Everett disputes the classical doctrine (Gorbman 1987) that diegetic film music should remain "inaudible," "unnoticed," or "unheard"—the notion that "while music powerfully influences our emotional response . . . , its fundamental role is to support and protect the narrative without drawing attention to itself" (p. 103). Rather, Everett (2000) stresses that songs used to evoke associations, identifications, nostalgic recollections, or historical connections are often "firmly anchored into the diegesis by some identifiable source, such as a gramophone, radio, or jukebox" (p. 106). As an example, Everett cites the work by Dennis Potter in *The Singing Detective*, wherein the characters frequently burst into lip-synched performances of popular songs that provide autobiographical commentary on "the meaning of the emotional and physical surround" (p. 114). David Kelly's *Ali McBeal* would provide a more recent illustration.

Second, Rodman (2000) tackles the "Tonal Design and the Aesthetic of Pastiche in Herbert Stothart's *Maytime*." Obviously, as with other members of the musical genre, the relevant music is produced *inside* the film's action and yet, as Rodman strongly emphasizes, serves the purpose of *dramatic development* (p. 188). Indeed, Rodman concerns himself with an in-depth analysis of how Stothart organized the music in *Maytime* (1937) to bolster the film's narrative plan. As sung by Jeanette MacDonald and Nelson Eddy, Rodman claims, the "musical numbers" help to "delineate character" (p. 189) and to "add meaning to the narrative" (p. 190). To condense considerably, Rodman sees the film as achieving a rapprochement between MacDonald's "highbrow" character Marcia (associated with opera in the key of D) and Eddy's "lowbrow" character Paul (associated with popular music in the key of C). Rodman diagrams this opposition and discusses the musical progress compellingly—viewing the operetta style as the mediating ground between Marcia's operatic and Paul's populist tendencies, as represented by "Will You Remember?" (the one song retained from Sigmund Romberg's original score), which becomes "the structural centerpiece of the film" (p. 197). In this, recalling the analysis of the "dual-focus" structure by Altman (1987), Rodman (2000) outlines a clear dialectic in which "Because operetta represents a middle ground between the highbrow of opera and the lowbrow of popular song, in a sense combining aspects of both styles, it serves as a point of synthesis" (p. 198). This synthesis is consummated in a beyond-the-grave love match during the film's concluding moments when the two characters achieve a "ghostly union" (p. 198) mirrored by the dialectic pattern of musical modulation (from D or C to D-flat or D♭):

> In life, Marcia and Paul's keys were C and D [so that] D♭ signifies the meeting of the two characters (by half-step), and ultimately the literal

"elevation" of Paul (up a half-step), and Marcia's renunciation of opera (descending a half-step) for Paul.

(Rodman 2000, p. 202)

At the tonal level, this structure parallels that of the typical dual-focus narrative: "The D♭ tonal area achieves its synthesis by opening new ground . . . in which two key constellations [C and D] are assimilated within a new key of synthesis [D♭]" (pp. 203–204). Thus, Rodman (2000) provides an admirably insightful explication of how ambi-diegetic film music can support the most profound aspects of characterization and plot development.

Third, Pomerance (2000) foregrounds the dramatic musical meanings of a performance piece—that is, what we would call its ambi-diegesis—in his meticulous reading of "'Storm Clouds' and *The Man Who Knew Too Much*." Specifically, in far more detail than we have space to recount here, Pomerance takes us on a measure-by-measure (sometimes even a beat-by-beat) guided tour of Alfred Hitchcock's "ways of marrying image and sound" (p. 207)—as evidenced in the great scene at the end of his 1959 masterpiece whose score, at the climactic moment, features a full-length cantata entitled "Storm Clouds" (composed by Arthur Benjamin and conducted on-screen by the film's musical director Bernard Herrmann) that is "performed . . . diegetically" in the Albert Hall *and* that stands "at the dramatic center of the film" (p. 208). To summarize with painful brevity, the highly suspenseful action involves a plot by a would-be assassin to shoot the Prime Minister at the precise moment near the end of this piece when the loud crash of two cymbals will obscure the sound of the gun's firing. Doris Day (whose son has been kidnapped) watches in horror while her husband Jimmy Stewart runs around helplessly trying to avert the pending doom until finally, at the critical moment, the political leader is saved by the terrified mother's scream. It takes just a couple of sentences to convey the broad outlines of this dramatic scene, yet the cantata stretches on for over nine minutes, with us watching those cymbals in dread, while the suspense builds and builds until the shattering climax. Pomerance devotes 30 pages to a second-by-second account of how—with its complex imbrication of music and drama—this scene unfolds. The musically annotated action of the man with the cymbals presciently parallels the meticulously planned machinations of the intended killer. Finally, at measure 154, "the cymbalist raises the cymbals near his face": "The cymbals are the storm clouds, and they are about to clap together . . . to make a sound" (p. 235). This crash symbolizes or, I suppose, "cymbalizes" the crisis of conflict between the Doris Day character's roles as a professional singer and mother. Beyond its relevance to the foiled assassination attempt, it therefore encapsulates various themes that have threaded through the film. It also emblematizes the ambi-diegetic manner in which performed music (Doris Day's "Que Sera, Sera," hymns sung in a chapel service, and music in the marketplace, not to mention "Storm Clouds") is used to reinforce the dramatic development: "There is never a moment in this film when the sung material, or musical ground of any kind, is either extraneous or marginal to the central meaning of the shot and the sequence in which we experience it" (p. 242). In this sense, Hitchcock pushes the role of musical dramatization to a sort of ambi-diegetic apotheosis: "Here Hitchcock advances a step further than any other filmmaker has done, dramaturgically shifting the music on occasion to a foregrounded role as important as any other roles in the film" (p. 243).

One could not sum up the essence of ambi-diegesis much more compactly than that; nor make a much more convincing case for its importance to the potential meaning of music in motion pictures; nor end on a more affirmative note concerning the value of further work on the interpretive analysis of the role played by ambi-diegetic film music in general and by jazz in particular in the product design of Hollywood movies, a project to which we now turn.

# Part II

# Ambi-Diegetic Jazz and the Development of Character

# Introduction to Part II

Recent work on the semiotics and hermeneutics of film music, reviewed in Chapter 1, has implied that—as one key element of cinematic composition or, from a marketing-related perspective, as one key aspect of the product design of a motion picture—ambi-diegetic film music plays a key role in shaping the meanings conveyed to a movie audience. Here, *ambi-diegetic film music* refers to cinemusical material that (like *diegetic* music) appears *on-screen* as performed by one or more actors but that (like *nondiegetic* music) advances the *dramatic development* of character, plot, or other important cinematic themes. Also, as previously discussed from a (macro)-marketing-related perspective, we might regard ambi-diegetic film music as a kind of product placement, in which the director, writers, or other individuals who create a motion picture insert a particular offering—namely, a musical performance—into the movie in a manner intended to structure its meaning. In this sense, ambi-diegetic film music resembles other sorts of cinematic consumption symbolism such as clothing, fashion accessories, automobiles, houses, gardens, pets, and other significant possessions or meaningful facets of consumer behavior that guide our understanding of a film's characters, plotlines, and other thematic aspects of potential social significance (Holbrook and Hirschman 1993). Before proceeding, let us briefly review the latter point in a bit more detail.

## RELEVANCE TO CONSUMPTION, MARKETS, AND THE CULTURE OF MUSIC IN FILMS

The relevance of ambi-diegetic film music to (macro)marketing-related considerations appears in at least four aspects of the ways in which movie music serves to shape the cinematic experience. Overall, it appears that—as part of the cinematic consumption experience—film music performs services in the co-creation of value by producers and consumers (Vargo and Lusch 2004), whereby value emerges as an interactive relativistic preference experience (Holbrook 1999b; Holbrook 2006d). In this connection, the broad relevance of film music for issues of concern to (macro)marketing and consumer researchers emerges in four main ways whereby cinemusical meanings relate to important aspects of consumption, markets, and the consumer culture (Holbrook 2003a, 2004, 2005a, 2005b, 2005e, 2006c, 2007a, 2007f, 2008a, 2008b, 2008c, 2009). Before proceeding, in anticipation of discussions to follow, let us review these four aspects briefly.

## (1) Product Placement

First, as already mentioned, we might regard ambi-diegetic film music as an example of *product placement* wherein a symbolic market offering is inserted into an artistic vehicle or entertainment medium in a way that structures its interpretation by members of the market, audience, or consuming public. Recently, much attention has focused on the meanings that stem from the insertion of branded products into entertainment vehicles— Reece's Pieces in *ET the Extra-Terrestrial* (1982), Aston Martins in James Bond's *Die Another Day* (2002), or Mini Coopers in *The Italian Job* (2003). In a similar way, the appearance of music in a movie represents a form of product placement in which the tune, song, or performance itself constitutes a viable cultural offering that competes for patronage in the marketplace. For example, in an age when the sales of many types of recordings (LPs, cassette tapes, CDs) have declined to an alarming degree, soundtrack albums from films such as *The Bodyguard* (1992), *Titanic* (1997), *O Brother, Where Art Thou?* (2000), and *High School Musical* (2006) have held high positions in the *Billboard* bestseller lists. From this perspective, placing music in a film serves as a promotional tool to enhance the success of its soundtrack-album profits. (For further discussion of such cross-promotions, see the aforementioned work by Altman, Brown, Cohan, Creekmur, Dickinson, Donnelly, Flinn, Garner, Gorbman, Grossberg, Karlin, Kermode, Knight and Wojcik, Majumdar, Prendergast, Ramaeker, Romney and Wootton, Smith, Sinker, Stilwell, and Toop.)

## (2) Product Design

Second, ambi-diegetic cinemusical moments constitute key aspects of *product design* in constructing the creative offering. Like any strategic problem in product management, the choice of music as one key design element (its style, its composition, its instrumentation, its orchestration, its vocal performance) plays an important role in shaping the consumption experiences of the relevant market of consumers (who, in this case, comprise members of the viewing audience watching the motion picture of interest). As in other cases of marketing strategy, the film's producers (director, writers, actors, composer, conductor, musicians, and so on) will do everything possible to design and execute the offering in a way that communicates the intended meaning to the market by delivering the intended consumption experience to the target audience.

## (3) Symbolic Consumer Behavior

Third, to the extent that the characters in a movie engage in music-related consumption experiences, we may view the contribution of the relevant ambi-diegetic cinemusical meanings as one more aspect of *symbolic consumer behavior* by means of which acts of cinematic consumption help to convey various associations, connotations, or interpretations that further the dramatic development of plot, character, and other important cinematic themes (Holbrook and Grayson 1986; Holbrook and Hirschman 1993; see also Garner 2001). In this—like other aspects of props (a Rolex wristwatch or Ferrari automobile), costumes (Prada shoes or a Vuitton handbag), décor (a Victorian living room or a sleek contemporary kitchen), scenery (a well-manicured lawn or the view of a dingy back-alley scene from a tenement window), and so forth—the music that film characters choose for playing, singing, listening, and/or dancing sheds light on their personalities, moves the plot forward, and conveys other important cinemusical meanings. For this reason, as reflected in the present work, interpretive studies from the viewpoint of marketing and consumer research explore the role of ambi-diegetic film music in developing significant themes associated with playing-singing-listening-and-dancing as a form of symbolic consumer behavior.

## (4) Themes of Social Significance

Fourth, the deployment of film music in general and of ambi-diegetic cinemusical meanings in particular may reflect, embody, and convey *themes of social significance* of the type that interest students of (macro)marketing and consumer-culture studies. In this connection, Part II of the present volume focuses most explicitly on themes related to relations of a romantic nature and to ways of developing characters or plotlines from that perspective. Later, Parts III, IV, and V address the uses of film music to develop the theme of art-versus-commerce as it applies to the tension between creative integrity and popular appeal in the work of professional jazz musicians (see also Bradshaw, McDonagh, and Marshall 2006a). Part VII depicts the dark versus light sides of celebrity by tracing the meanings of ambi-diegetic cinemusical moments in tragedepictions of heroic failures as opposed to comedepictions of success stories worthy of the American Dream. Meanwhile, a number of commentators have focused energetically on various race-, gender-, and status-related themes of social significance (Aaron 2000; Arbuthnot and Seneca 2002; Arroyo 2000; Clover 2002; Cohan 2002a; Conway 2001; Dyer 2000; Feuer 1993; Fowler 2000; Gabbard 1996, 2000, 2001, 2003, 2004, 2007; Gill 2001; Kalinak 2000; Knee 2001; Knight 2001; MacKinnon 2000; McCracken 2001; Mellencamp 2002; Mizejewski 2002; Osgerby 2000; Roberts 2002; Robertson 2002; Rogin 2002; Stanfield 2000; Stilwell 2001; Thomas 2007; Tinkcom 2002; Wojcik 2001; Wood 2002). For example, consider the masterful analysis by Knight (2001) of the gender- and race-related concerns surrounding the recordings by Louis Armstrong/Ella Fitzgerald and by Miles Davis/Gil Evans of the music from *Porgy and Bess*—emerging just before the commercial 1959 release of Otto Preminger's film with musical direction by André Previn. Though somewhat distanced from the details of the film itself, Knight's reading of Miles and Gil's record cover—on which a well-dressed Davis holds a trumpet in his lap and sits next to a light-skinned woman whose knee shows below her skirt line—presents a *tour de force* of race- and gender-oriented interpretive insights to conclude that "it ain't necessarily so" that "love and romance and sex adhere to the lines enforced by the dominant social order" (p. 338). Also, consider the profoundly insightful analysis by Clover (2002) of the manner in which *Singin' in the Rain* (1952) satirizes Hollywood's habit of leaving certain talented contributors unacknowledged in the film's credits even while committing exactly the same sin itself via its unacknowledged plundering of African-American dance routines:

> What *Singin' in the Rain* doesn't-but-does know is that the real art of the film musical is dance, that a crucial talent source for that art is African-American performance, and that, relative to its contribution, this talent source is undercredited and underpaid.
>
> (Clover 2002, p. 164)

## ILLUSTRATIONS

As discussed in Chapter 1, the most obvious examples of ambi-diegetic film music appear in the traditional Hollywood musical, a genre of film music that—until the recent successes of *Moulin Rouge!* (2001), *Chicago* (2002), *Rent* (2005), *Hairspray* (2007), *Sweeney Todd* (2007), and *Mamma Mia!* (2008)—had faded from public prominence and that (with rare exceptions such the aforementioned work by Altman, Cohan, Feuer, or Marshall and Stilwell) has been neglected by those working in this area of film criticism (as noted in our earlier references to Altman, Chion, Conrich, Donnelly, Feuer, MacKinnon, Marshall and Stilwell, Rodman, and Smith). With songs by Cole Porter, as featured in Chapter 2, the music performed by Bing Crosby in *High Society* (1956) plays a crucial role in fleshing out Bing's persona and in developing his rekindled relationship with the Grace Kelly character.

Elsewhere and even more frequently, comparable ambi-diegetic uses of songs show up in all sorts of films that fall outside the "musical" genre and that are typically classified as dramas, comedies, mysteries, action adventures, sci-fi fantasies, westerns, or whatever. Think, for example, of the incidental music used to develop various aspects of character, plot, and other dramatic themes in such motion pictures as *The Fabulous Baker Boys* (1989) and *The Talented Mr. Ripley* (1999). While noting numerous such performances in these two films, Chapter 3 focuses special attention on the role in both films played by Rodgers and Hart's "My Funny Valentine" (1937)—first, in developing the image of Susie Diamond (Michelle Pfeiffer) as a steamy, sultry, seductively sexy saloon singer in *The Fabulous Baker Boys*; second and by contrast, in portraying the character of Tom Ripley (Matt Damon) as a self-absorbed, sociopathic, sexually ambivalent wastrel in *The Talented Mr. Ripley*. Other examples, discussed in Part III, concern the use of ambi-diegetic music in such crime-and-jazz films as *Pete Kelly's Blues* (1955), *The Cotton Club* (1984), and *Kansas City* (1996). Further illustrations, described in Part IV, appear in three films from the young-man-with-a-horn genre—namely, *Young Man With a Horn* (1949), *Paris Blues* (1961), and *Mo' Better Blues* (1990)—where ambi-diegetic music reflects the manner in which jazz has moved over time from a commercial form of enter-tainment to a more esoteric species of art-for-art's-sake elitism. Additional jazz-oriented illustrations permeate the many motion pictures discussed in Parts V, VI, and VII. Elsewhere, beyond the scope of the jazz-oriented focus that will concern us for the remainder of the present volume, comparable cases of cinemusical ambi-diegesis abound—as in the many non-jazz exam-ples enumerated and reviewed, with plentiful illustrations, in Chapter 1.

The case pursued at some length in Chapter 2 harks back to the golden age of movie musicals in general and to the remarkable but critically neglected film *High Society* (1956) in particular. Specifically, from a perspective that draws on the tradition of semiotic analysis or hermeneutic interpretation of motion pictures (Holbrook and Hirschman 1993) and that admittedly reflects a large degree of subjective personal introspec-tion (Holbrook 1995a), we shall examine the role of three duets sung by Bing Crosby—with Grace Kelly, Louis Armstrong, and Frank Sinatra, respectively—and shall inquire how these duets, especially the pivotal duet between Bing and Louis on "Now You Has Jazz," shape the experience of viewing the film and structure the meanings contributed by its ambi-diegetic music. Then, pursuing a similar perspective in Chapter 3, we shall focus on the role of "My Funny Valentine" (as earlier performed by Frank Sinatra, Kim Novak, and Chet Baker) in reflecting the characters played by Michelle Pfeiffer in *The Fabulous Baker Boys* (1989) and by Matt Damon in *The Talented Mr. Ripley* (1999).

## NOTE ON METHOD

As elsewhere in the present work, the approach pursued here stems from the interpretivistic tradition (Hirschman ed. 1989) or postpositivistic ethos (Sherry 1991) that has recently emerged as an alternative perspective on the study of consumer behavior in general or audience experiences in particular (Hirschman and Holbrook 1992). Insights drawn from this turn toward interpretation have often taken the form of autoethnography (Holbrook 1996, 1998a, 1998c, 2005c, 2006a, 2006b) or subjective personal intro-spection (aka SPI; Holbrook 1995a, 2005c, 2006a, 2006b; see also Wohlfeil and Whelan 2006). This is not the place to defend such approaches at length—beyond noting that, over the past 20 years, semiotic or hermeneutic analyses (Holbrook and O'Shaughnessy 1988) and autoethnographic or SPI approaches (Holbrook 1995a) have received detailed justifications in the literature via arguments that continue to surface in periodic updates (Holbrook 2005c, 2006a, 2006b) and that apply with special appropriateness to the case of consumption-related aspects of film (Holbrook and Hirschman 1993). The output of such postpositivistic approaches typically appears in a form such as that evinced by my essays for the present volume in general and by those for Part II in particular.

# 2 Ambi-Diegetic Film Music As a Product-Design and -Placement Strategy
## The Crosby Duets in *High Society* (1956)

## INTRODUCTION

As one illustration of ambi-diegetic film music in action—and, therefore, as an example of how cinematic product design shapes the consumption experiences of motion-picture audiences and of how ambi-diegetic music as a form of product placement influences the meaning of a film's consumption symbolism—the present chapter examines the role of a pivotal cinemusical duet ("Now You Has Jazz") by two stellar performers (Bing Crosby and Louis Armstrong) in an under-appreciated MGM musical (*High Society*) made at mid-century (1956) under the musical direction of a gifted composer ("Body and Soul," "Out of Nowhere," "I Cover the Waterfront") and multiple Oscar winner (Johnny Green) with tunes and lyrics written by one of our greatest songwriters (Cole Porter).

Based on Philip Barry's play *The Philadelphia Story* (1939)—later a movie of the same name starring Cary Grant, James Stewart, and Katharine Hepburn (1940)—Charles Walters' *High Society* (1956) subscribes to the demonstrably valid premise, common in the 1950s and still alive today, that old guys (Humphrey Bogart, Fred Astaire, Sean Connery, Harrison Ford, Michael Douglas) can win the hearts of young gals (Audrey Hepburn, Leslie Caron, Catherine Zeta-Jones, Julia Ormond, Gwyneth Paltrow). But in pairing off Bing Crosby as Dexter (53 years old at the time) with Grace Kelly as Tracy (28), Porter and Co. faced a challenge intensified by some of the film's own structural elements but resolved via its use of ambi-diegetic music.

Specifically, the romantic sailing song "True Love," performed as a duet by Dexter/Bing and Tracy/Grace, makes the Crosby character seem at least as venerable and almost as creaky as the Ancient Mariner (albeit minus the albatross). Meanwhile, the scene presenting "You're Sensational" shows the Grace Kelly character smitten by the sexy charms of the hypnotically blue-eyed and more-or-less age-appropriate Frank Sinatra as Mike Connor (41). How can the film rehabilitate the image of Dexter/Bing in time to let him plausibly win the hand of Tracy/Grace in the end?

The answer lies in the symbolically central cinemusical role played by the ambi-diegetic Crosby-Armstrong duet entitled "Now You Has Jazz." In this masterpiece of cinemusical ambi-diegesis—via his visual, musical, and historical connection with Armstrong and thereby with a walking embodiment of jazz iconography—Crosby as Dexter attains a rejuvenated insouciance, an awakened vitality, a revivified breath of virile creativity that make the years melt away. Figuratively, Dexter/Bing emerges from this ambi-diegetic performance ready to do battle with his younger romantic rival Mike/Frank.

In a subsequent dueling duet with Connor/Sinatra on "Well, Did You Evah?"—almost as satisfying as the earlier one with Satchmo—the old crooner matches or perhaps *out*matches the young swinger in every cinemusical nuance. In this, Dexter/Bing slays the Dragon of Advancing Age to emerge from the cinemusical Fountain of Youth as Tracy/Grace's viable suitor of choice.

For the chronologically challenged (including yours truly, who is more than a decade older than both Bing Crosby and Louis Armstrong in *High Society*), the fate of Tracy/Grace and Dexter/Bing—transformed by the rejuvenating powers of ambi-diegetic jazz—provides a happy ending, indeed.

## THE CASE OF HIGH SOCIETY

Every now and then, when I'm feeling blue, I go back and revisit the old MGM musical from my youth entitled *High Society* (1956). Directed by Charles Walters, this film brought together the rather sizeable talents of Bing Crosby, Frank Sinatra, Louis Armstrong, Celeste Holm, and Grace Kelly to perform songs by the nonpareil Cole Porter under the musical direction of Johnny Green (himself a noted composer and a major force at the MGM Studios) in a remake of Phillip Barry's play *The Philadelphia Story* (1939), set to music. On the surface, this sounds like a winning combination. It never fails to brighten my day. But over the years, though it was the top Hollywood moneymaker of 1956, *High Society* has met with something less than enthusiastic critical acclaim.

### High Society Versus The Philadelphia Story

Partly, *High Society* (1956) suffers from inevitable comparisons with the movie version of *The Philadelphia Story* (1940)—featuring Katharine Hepburn as the aristocratic Tracy Samantha Lord; Cary Grant as her former husband C. K. Dexter-Haven; James Stewart as the intrusive newspaper writer Mike Connor; and Ruth Hussey as Connor's photographer companion Liz Imbrie—that is, four thespian superstars in the roles later recreated musically by Grace Kelly, Bing Crosby, Frank Sinatra, and Celeste Holm (with a little help from Louis Armstrong as an extra added attraction, appearing as a sort of narrator who sometimes thinks he's a Greek chorus). The script for *High Society* by John Patrick actually sticks fairly close to that for *The Philadelphia Story*, as adapted from Philip Barry's original play. The problem is that Hepburn, Grant, Stewart, and Hussey are just so damned good—so charming, so insouciant, so believable—in their respective roles that I can easily imagine how a viewer who had watched and admired *The Philadelphia Story* in 1940 could see little reason to remake this film . . . *ever*. Kate Hepburn—who had also played the role of Tracy Lord on Broadway, in a part specially written for her—triumphs as the brilliant but bossy, clever but threatening, beautiful but aloof heroine. James Stewart, as the inadvertently intrusive but powerfully attractive newspaperman Mike Connor, does his typically convincing Jimmy-Stewart thing to perfection. Further, as a love interest for Mike/Jimmy, Ruth Hussey as Liz Imbrie strikes me as a lot more plausible than Celeste Holm in the same role opposite Frank Sinatra. Liz/Ruth conveys an aura of hip sex appeal aimed in the direction of Mike/Jimmy, whereas Liz/Celeste treats Mike/Frank more in a manner that comes across as motherly.

However, from the perspective of one who saw *High Society* first (back when it came out in 1956 when I was 12 or 13 years old and hormone-primed to appreciate the wonders of Grace Kelly) and found *The Philadelphia Story* only much later (as an adult with a near reverence for Katharine Hepburn, especially in her films with Cary Grant), I can report that there is at least one respect in which the former enjoys an advantage over the latter. Specifically, having encountered Dexter/Bing before I met up with Dexter/Cary, I cannot shake the feeling that Cary Grant appears uncharacteristically noninvolved in his part—delightfully insouciant and flippantly droll, yes, but rather casual or even uncaring in his oblique and almost half-hearted pursuit of Tracy/Katharine. In *High Society*, Dexter/Bing leaves no such doubt about his amorous intentions toward Tracy/Grace, whom he plainly and passionately adores. Crosby manages to convey much of Dexter/Cary's merry charm while also positioning himself as a bastion of sincerity. The latter virtue, by contrast, cannot be found in the character of Dexter/Cary in *The Philadelphia Story*.

## The Chronologically-Challenged R(ev)ival

Nonetheless, to my eyes, *High Society* did suffer at the time of its appearance from the impression that some of its key role players—Cole Porter, Bing Crosby, and Louis Armstrong, for starters—were, to put it politely, past their peak, stylistically if not biologically. This problem of chronological fit did not afflict *The Philadelphia Story* circa 1940 in anything like the same way. Katharine Hepburn and Co. were then youthful (30-ish), in vogue, and very "with it." Further, Kate and Crew did not need to worry about the vintage of their ambi-diegetic music, which plays a comparatively minor part in their film via the on-screen performances of "Lydia, the Tattooed Lady" (played and sung by Tracy/Katharine's younger sister in a purposely inept version intended to shock the intruding newspaper people) and "Over the Rainbow" (shakily intoned by Mike/James to convey his inebriated condition in a drunken late-night rendezvous with Tracy/Katharine at her swimming pool).

By contrast, when *High Society* was released in 1956, the heyday of the big Hollywood musical and the ascendancy of its typical cast of characters were rapidly drawing to a close. Elvis Presley had invaded the scene at the start of a soon-to-be-burgeoning career. Others such as Little Richard, Fats Domino, Ray Charles, Chuck Berry, Buddy Holly, Jerry Lee Lewis, and the rest were poised in the wings on the brink of utterly transforming the music business. These rock-'n'-rollers would soon be followed by the British Invasion bringing us the Beatles, the Rolling Stones, the Who, and those compatriot rock stars who pretty much took over the music scene for the remainder of the twentieth century and beyond.

Though he had recently experienced the miraculous revival of a troubled career—winning an Oscar for his non-singing role as Maggio in *From Here to Eternity* (1953)—even the comparatively young Frank Sinatra was starting to sound more and more like the about-to-emerge Leader of the Rat Pack or the Chairman of the Board who would all-too-quickly segue into Ol' Blue Eyes. After all, Frank grew up in the age of the big bands—first, with the Harry James Orchestra; then, with Tommy Dorsey; next, under his own steam at Columbia Records, often with lush backgrounds by Axel Stordahl; later, in hundreds of superb recordings for Capitol Records under the batons not only of Stordahl but also of arrangers like Nelson Riddle, Billy May, and Gordon Jenkins; ultimately, in summer-to-autumnal performances for his own label Reprise Records with arrangements by those already mentioned, plus the likes of Johnny Mandel, Neil Hefti, Don Costa, and Quincy Jones. In other words—documented at length by such biographers as Frank (1978), Friedwald (1995), Petkov and Mustazza (ed. 1995), Rockwell (1984), Shaw (1968), Sinatra (1985), or Wilson (1976); portrayed in such presentations as his daughter Tina's CBS biopic *Sinatra* (1992); and discussed in more detail by yours truly in Chapter 3 of the present volume (see also Holbrook 2005e)—Frank Sinatra, that old self-described "saloon singer," was a child of the Swing Era. Thus, circa 1956, Sinatra could be considered "new" or "young" only by comparison with the likes of Bing Crosby, Louis Armstrong, or Cole Porter themselves—who, collectively, seemed so indisputably . . . old.

## The Age-Related Structural Problem: Old Guy, Young Gal

The structural challenge faced by *High Society* is to rehabilitate the 53-year-old Bing Crosby as Dexter enough to make him seem a plausible love object for the 28-year-old Grace Kelly as Tracy or, as Dexter/Bing affectionately calls her, "Sam" (short for her middle name, Samantha). Admittedly, films during the 1950s were propitious places and times for old guys hitting on young gals. The cinema brought us romantic possibilities for, among others, Humphrey Bogart (age 55) and Audrey Hepburn (age 25) in *Sabrina* (1954); Bing Crosby (51) and Grace Kelly (26) in *The Country Girl* (1954); Fred Astaire (56) and Leslie Caron (24) in *Daddy Long Legs* (1955); Cary Grant

(51) and Grace Kelly (27) in *To Catch a Thief* (1955); Fred Astaire (58) and Audrey Hepburn (28) in *Funny Face* (1957); James Stewart (50) and Kim Novak (25) in *Vertigo* (1958); or Cary Grant (59) and Audrey Hepburn (34) in *Charade* (1963). Indeed, if we look at the love objects selected for, say, Harrison Ford (e.g., Julia Ormond) or Sean Connery (e.g., Catherine Zeta-Jones) or Michael Douglas (e.g., Gwyneth Paltrow), we can see that this trend toward sacrificing young maidens on the altar of aging priapicity has continued to the present day.

With such rare exceptions as *Harold and Maude* (1972), *Class* (1983), or *White Palace* (1990) plus the recent television series on CBS entitled *Accidentally on Purpose*—which feature older women with younger men—age discrepancies hardly ever appear in the gender-opposite direction (that is, Woman > Man as opposed to Man > Woman). Hence, my earlier comments on the appropriateness of Celeste/Liz as the love object for Mike/Frank. (Note, by the way, that Celeste Holm only *looks* older than Frank Sinatra. She was actually four years his junior and had been paired romantically with him in *The Tender Trap* [1955].) Hence, also, the much-publicized shortage of roles for mature actresses—as opposed to mature actors—in Hollywood productions. Here, the point is simply that—in Hollywood, as elsewhere—the old, rich guy quite frequently gets the young, beautiful gal. Or as the great jazz saxophonist Paul Desmond—watching a youthful chorus-line dancer on parade with a wealthy business tycoon and recalling T. S. Eliot—put it: "This is the way the world ends, not with a whim but a banker."

Incidentally, in real life at around the time they made *High Society*, Bing Crosby and Grace Kelly are reported to have done some serious real-life romancing (Shepherd and Slatzer 1981, p. 225). Further, shortly after the film's release, Bing married Kathryn Grant, who was five years younger than Grace. Hence, for those interested in an accuracy check, Bing Crosby's real-world persona does appear to fit the typical Hollywood scenario rather comfortably.

## Old Bing

But still—even if we maintain the most charitable attitudes toward the elderly—we have to admit that Bing Crosby circa 1956 carries a load of symbolic associations and iconographic meanings that render him symbolically at odds with the youth culture of his time as embodied by the young and lovely Grace Kelly. As recounted at length in the excellent half-life biography of *Bing Crosby* by Giddins (2001), Bing's recording efforts began rather inauspiciously, back in the late 1920s, with his performances as part of the often-schlocky or -corny Paul Whiteman Orchestra and with the Rhythm Boys on such unfortunate and way-politically-incorrect tunes as "Mississippi Mud" in 1927. After re-recording "Mud" with Frank Trumbauer in 1928, in a version that featured a famous cornet solo by Bix Beiderbecke, Bing went on to a star-quality singing career of the highest magnitude.

Among the first to perfect the use of the then-new microphone for singing *to* people (a la Frank Sinatra with the bobby soxers in later years) instead of *at* them (a la Al Jolson with his down-on-one-knee belting or Rudy Vallee with his megaphone) (Giddins 2001, pp. 7, 118, 232; McCracken 2001, p. 111; Pleasants 1974, p. 142), Crosby developed a dependably jaunty, effortlessly lilting, buoyantly carefree, casually patrician style of vocalizing that set the standard during the 1930s and 1940s, producing immensely popular recordings well into the 1950s. In these regards, Henry Pleasants (1974) suggests that—amidst *The Great American Popular Singers*—Crosby ranks as "among the most profoundly and decisively influential" (p. 127). But his innovations tend to take the form of laid-back understatement rather than in-your-face overkill. Thus, Pleasants (1974) adopts the following sort of vocabulary to describe the Crosby style: "easy," "free of artistic pretension," "mellow richness of voice" (p. 127); "jaunty and debonair," "relaxed, casual, effortless" (p. 129); "conversational," "stopped singing *at* you . . . and began singing *to* you" (p. 142). In *Jazz Singing*, Friedwald (1990) adds that "Crosby . . . was the one who came up with the kind of 'natural' that worked": "There's a sense of just plain rightness to everything he does" (p. 34). In a gender-inflected account, McCracken (2001) sees Crosby as performing a crucial break from the more feminized approach of Rudy Vallee toward the conventional masculinized role of the new crooner who "sought to legitimize crooning by connecting it to traditional tropes of masculinity [such as] a good work ethic, patriarchy, religious belief, whiteness, and contained emotions" (p. 127). Perhaps the definitive analysis of Crosby as a singer appears in *Pocketful of Dreams* wherein Giddins (2001) offers an appraisal that, across hundreds of pages, deploys the following rhetoric to describe Bing's formidable gifts: "the most influential and successful popular performer in the first half of the twentieth century," "the voice of the nation," "friendly, unassuming, melodious, irrefutably American" (p. 4); "preternatural calm" (p. 6); "the first to render the lyrics of a modern ballad with purpose," (p. 7); "America's troubadour" (p. 8); "a masterly, innovative musician" (p. 10); "polished timbre and flawless enunciation" (p. 172); "the era's first great interpreter" (p. 174); "regal nonchalance," "cool yet approachable" (p. 198); "expansive repertoire, expressive intimacy, and spotless timbre," "rich, strong, masculine, and clean" (p. 231)"; "aggressive yet gentle, heartfelt yet humorous" (p. 232); "an aristocrat of the people," "a North Star of stability, decency, and optimism" (p. 298); "liked and trusted," "credible to all" (p. 299); "unschooled, artless quality" (p. 324); "rhythmic," "discriminating aplomb" (p. 377); "modest, playful, intelligent, and appealingly aloof" (p. 402); "disarmingly, almost nakedly, artless," "smooth," "a style beyond style" (p. 512); "a genius for popularity," "a central style of universal appeal" (p. 517). I could go on. Pleasants (1974), Friedwald (1990), Giddins (2001), and others *do* go on . . . and on. But the point, Dear Reader, is that—besides his skills in acting, hosting radio shows, raising horses, and playing golf—*Bing Crosby could SING*.

Bing Crosby's stylistic orientation came not so much from the swing bands of the 1930s as from the earlier New Orleans jazz style of the 1920s or Dixieland as this approach is often called (sometimes with unflattering connotations)—namely, "two-beat jazz à la King Oliver and Jelly Roll Morton" (Friedwald 1990, p. 45). In this vein, Bing had big hits with such household-name songs as (just to mention a few because the list is literally endless) "My Blue Heaven" (1927), "Great Day" (1929), "Dinah" (1931), "You're Getting to be a Habit with Me" (1933), "June in January" (1934), "Pennies from Heaven" (1936), "Too Marvelous for Words" (1937), "Alexander's Ragtime Band" (1938), "Swinging on a Star" (1944), and "Don't Fence Me In" (1944). (This last—in a 78-rpm shellac version from Bing's cowboy album on Decca—was a constant feature on my record player when I was about six years old. Who, of course, but Cole Porter could have written such a classic?)

Many contemporary fans of (say) Eminem or 'N Sync or Lady Gaga—for whom greatness is more or less synonymous with a half-time slot at the Super Bowl—do not remotely realize the extent to which Bing Crosby was *the* twentieth-century musical megastar with far more blockbuster hit songs than anybody else: "During his career Bing placed more records (368) and number one hit singles (42) on the general pop charts in the United States than any other artist" (www.kcmetro.cc.mo.us/pennvalley/biology/lewis/crosby/charthits.htm). Bing Crosby also carried his strangely comforting devil-may-care persona into any number of successful films—such as the series of "Road" movies with Bob Hope during the 1940s and other classics like *King of Jazz* (1930), *Pennies from Heaven* (1936), *Birth of the Blues* (1941), *Holiday Inn* (1942), *Going My Way* (1944), *Blue Skies* (1946), and *White Christmas* (1954)—where he could be counted on to supply a happy brand of vocalizing loaded with *joie de vivre*. We might contemplate the enormity of Crosby's market success by regarding the appeal of his work through the prism provided by Giddins (2001), who lists the following achievements (among many others): (1) an audience of 50 million people for Bing's weekly *Kraft Music Hall* radio show (1935–1946) (p. 6); (2) winning a national poll in the late 1940s as "the most admired man alive" (p. 6); (3) releasing 396 charted recordings—compared with 209 for Sinatra, 149 for Elvis, and 68 for the Beatles (p. 9); (4) the most-ever number-one hits—38—compared with 24 for the Beatles and 18 for Elvis (p. 9); (5) the introduction of 14 Oscar-nominated songs in motion pictures—compared with eight each for Astaire and Sinatra (p. 354); (6) placing in the Quigley poll in 14 of 20 years during the 1930s and 1940s (p. 364).

Today, with all the time that has passed since the height of the Crosby Era, it is too easy to forget the greatness of Bing's contribution. One reminder appears in the autobiographical *My Singing Teachers* by the masterful Mel Tormé (1994), himself a post-Crosby singing legend. At a time during the 1990s when he probably ranked as the world's most respected pop-jazz singer, Tormé (1994) leaves little doubt concerning his admiration for Bing—commenting appreciatively on Crosby's "charm," his "ease" (p. 17);

his "off-the-elbow approach to life," his "human, accessible, and un-affected" qualities (p. 18); his "unmatched resonance and control" (p. 19)—and concluding: "If there is anyone I have modeled myself after over the years, I would have to say it is Bing Crosby" (pp. 19–20).

As a young boy during Bing Crosby's peak years, I listened for countless hours to my all-time personal favorite—"South Rampart Street Parade" (1952) by Bing with the Andrews Sisters backed by Matty Matlock's Orchestra (including Red Nichols and Charlie Teagarden on trumpets). That 78-rpm recording of "South Rampart"—my second copy, held in reserve for when the first one wore out, which it definitively did circa 1953—is the only shellac record from this period that I have kept in my collection, even though it is no longer playable (by me) for lack of the appropriate equipment and has (finally) been reissued on compact disc (MCA/Decca MCAD2-11503). Meanwhile, as a kid, I literally memorized the vocal parts on a scintillating series of duets by Bing with his teenage son Gary, billed as "Gary Crosby and Friend": "Play a Simple Melody" (1950), "Sam's Song" (1950), "Moonlight Bay" (1951), "When You and I Were Young, Maggie, Blues" (1951), "Cornbelt Symphony" (1953), and "Call of the South" (1953). (The "Simple Melody"/"Sam's Song" coupling became the first double-sided pairing of gold records in history.) Three more that I did not own—and, indeed, had never heard until some recent exploits on the World Wide Web brought them into my collection at last—included "Fatherly Advice" (1952), "What a Little Moonlight Can Do" (1953), and "Down by the Riverside" (1953). I would, of course, have paid practically any price to obtain copies of these latter three duet performances. But just try to find them at any price. Until very recently—thanks to the benighted folks who preside over the lackluster Crosby reissue program at Decca-MCA-Seagram-Vivendi-Whatever—the Bing-and-Gary duets have not existed on CD (Friedwald 1990, p. 441), though they have now begun to trickle out in a five-volume series of reissues on Sepia Recordings entitled *Through the Years* (Sepia 1111, 1122, 1129, 1139, 1146). At any rate, when I say that I memorized these pieces, I mean that my friend Johnny and I spend hundreds if not thousands of hours on the telephone learning to sing the Crosby-duet parts to "Simple Melody," "Moonlight Bay," and (the profoundly great) "Maggie Blues." Still today, over 50 years later, I can—if asked (which, alas, I seldom am)—rattle off the Gary Crosby obbligatos to "Maggie." And today—when I listen to that miraculous evocation of gleeful bounciness, complete with the scorching Dixieland effusions of the Matlock Band—I get goose bumps bordering on hives (Holbrook 1986, 1995a).

Imagine my surprise, years later, when I learned that the then-50-year-old Gary (who died in 1995 at age 62 after a long history of alcohol and drug abuse) had written what purported to be a venomously vituperative attack on his father called *Going My Own Way* (Crosby and Firestone 1983). Positioning this book as a kind of "*Daddy Dearest*," the cover to the paperback edition claims that "Christina Crawford's movie star parent [Joan Crawford] was, by comparison, a Mary Poppins." In this literary mis-adventure, it appears, son Gary accuses the elder Crosby of injurious harshness, excessive disciplinarianism, and unloving neglect bordering on child abuse. For example, Crosby and Firestone (1983) claim that, because Gary was considered too chubby, Bing would weigh him periodically and, if he had gained weight, would beat him with a metal studded belt until he bled. At a minimum, this accusation gives us reason to question the apparent *joie de vivre* found in "Simple Melody," "Sam's Song," "Maggie," and the rest of the father-son duets.

The Crosby-and-Firestone treatise appeared a couple of years after a veritable character assassination authored by Shepherd and Slatzer (1981) under the title *Bing Crosby: The Hollow Man*. Put simply, Shepherd and Slazter (1981) portray Bing Crosby as essentially petty, cold, irresponsible, lazy, hypocritical, enigmatic, and hollow by writing an essentially petty, cold, irresponsible, lazy, hypocritical, enigmatic, and hollow book. During the course of their relentless attack, they charge that Crosby (1) abandoned Al Rinker and Harry Barris, his friends and colleagues in the Rhythm Boys; (2) double-crossed his way to the top; (3) stole credit for other people's songs; (4) made people who had helped him "disappear" from his life; (5) found it impossible to express love, affection, gratitude, or other sentiments reflecting the milk of human kindness; (6) mercilessly neglected his first wife Dixie; (7) disciplined his four sons with Dixie in a manner bordering on child abuse; (8) pursued innumerable adulterous affairs on the side; (9) left Dixie on her death bed to go play golf and make a movie in Europe; (10) treated his second wife Kathryn in much the same way (probably minus the extramarital affairs); (11) dissed his first four sons publicly (by saying that he had failed them as a father); and (12) used his last will and testament to cheat his family members out of their rightful inheritances. In short, Shepherd and Slatzer (1981) present Bing Crosby as a sort of real-world one-man twelve-step program in moral turpitude.

Reading Shepherd-and-Slatzer's exposé with agonizing attention to every lurid detail, I am tempted to reply that . . . well . . . nobody's perfect. The main shock value of their jeremiad stems from the rampant disparity between Bing Crosby's carefully cultivated public image as a quasi-saintly family man and his real-life human failings as a rather withdrawn or even reclusive fellow with feet of clay. They itemize each and every departure from sainthood in exhaustive depth without managing to find one nice thing to say about the man beyond the obvious fact that he could sing like an angel. But most of Crosby's sins, chronicled so painstakingly by Shepherd and Slatzer, amount to sins of omission rather than commission. Apparently, revisiting the twelve-step program just described with slightly less opprobrious intent, Bing (1) did not sustain long-lasting friendships with people important to him early in his career; (2) could not be trusted to repay favors or kindnesses in an openly grateful way; (3) found it hard to share the credit for his success; (4) wasn't always around when you needed him; (5) withheld expressions of emotions of all kinds; (6) left Dixie alone with her friends a lot while he ran around with his own cronies, played golf, and visited the racetrack; (7) couldn't stand to be disobeyed by his children; (8) couldn't restrain his libido (during periods when his marriage to a reclusive alcoholic wife was in a shambles); (9) failed to cancel contractual obligations and stay at home in moments of crisis; (10) might have had similar difficulties with his second wife (who publicly minimized their import); (11) blamed himself for the fact that his first four sons had substantial problems resembling his own; and (12) didn't leave everybody what they wanted when he died. Frankly, I've seen much worse things written about . . . say . . . Jack Kennedy, Bill Clinton, Dwight Eisenhower, Michael Jackson, Benny Goodman, Johnny Carson, David Letterman, Martha Stewart, Alex Rodriguez, and Tiger Woods. Read in a slightly different light, much of the kvetching about Bing Crosby sounds a lot like resentment that he never invited us to his house for lunch.

In Web-posted quotations drawn from such marginally reliable sources as the *National Enquirer,* two of Gary Crosby's siblings—Lindsay and Dennis (both of whom committed suicide, in 1989 and 1991, respectively)—tended to concur with the complaints attributed to their older brother. For example, after his suicide at Christmastime, Lindsay was portrayed by the self-appointed family biographer Robert Slatzer as a miserable creature who had been beaten and terrorized by his father, especially at Christmas: "Lindsay hated his father with a passion . . . . Instead of being a time of joy and love and peace, Bing had made Christmas a time of pain and suffering for Lindsay and his three brothers" (Robert Slatzer, quoted at www.kcmetro.cc.mo.us/pennvalley/biology/lewis/crosby/lindsay.htm). However—considerably problematizing the project of Bing bashing—Phillip (the twin of Dennis) tends to side with his father and claims that "Gary is a whining, bitching crybaby, walking around with a two-by-four on his shoulder and just daring people to nudge it off" (www.kcmetro.cc.mo.us/pennvalley/biology/lewis/crosby/bingboys.htm): "I'm positive there isn't a word of truth in it (the book) because I don't think Gary can separate truth from fiction. For as long as I've known my brother he's told lies" (www.kcmetro.cc.mo.us/pennvalley/biology/lewis/crosby/garybook.htm). Phillip adds that "If anything, he [son Gary] wasn't abused enough or he wouldn't be the complete dud he is": "My parents were strict but they weren't overstrict" (www.kcmetro.cc.mo.us/pennvalley/biology/lewis/crosby/garybook.htm). Elsewhere, Phillip reiterates and expands this assessment: "My dad . . . was strict, but my father never beat us black and blue and my brother Gary was a vicious, no-good liar for saying so." To Phillip, "My dad was my hero. I loved him very much. And he loved all of us too, including Gary. He was a great father" (quoted by Neil Blincow at www.kcmetro.cc.mo.us/pennvalley/biology/lewis/crosby/quotes.htm#pa1). Bing's second wife Kathryn Grant Crosby concurs, describing Gary's book as "a piece of trash" and explaining that she (not Bing) had to do the spanking in their family because "Bing became physically ill at unpleasantness": "If Gary was beaten, he wasn't beaten enough because he didn't learn anything" (www.kcmetro.cc.mo.us/pennvalley/biology/lewis/crosby/garybook.htm).

Gary himself later recanted somewhat, admitting that his characterization of Bing had gotten "out of hand" (www.kcmetro.cc.mo.us/pennvalley/biology/lewis/crosby/garyobit.htm).

About the time I finished reading all this unsavory stuff on the Web, it occurred to me that I might benefit from taking a close look at the Crosby-and-Firestone book and examining in detail *what Gary Crosby actually said* about his father. This endeavor provides something of an eye-opening experience. Once we get past the daddy-dearest promotions on the cover, it turns out that Gary's account differs rather dramatically from the impression conveyed by the muckrakers who have publicized his story for its sensationalistic Bing-bashing value.

Specifically, Gary Crosby begins in a clearly conciliatory tone. The very first sentence in *Going My Own Way* encapsulates the major theme of the book: "*A couple of years before my father died I found out he really did love me*" (Crosby and Firestone 1983, p. 1). The dramatic tension in Crosby-and-Firestone's account stems from Gary's slow progress toward this realization. It is a sad story, especially from the viewpoint of anyone identifying with Gary, but a story worth telling.

Admittedly, if one reads Gary Crosby's autobiography with anti-paternal malice aforethought, one can find plenty of ammunition for the project of trashing his famous father. Yes, Bing comes across as very strict, bordering on abusive, toward the children of his first marriage—not to mention cold, distant, demanding, self-centered, and often absent. But Gary's book, on closer reading, recounts the spectacularly painful self-revelatory tale of a soul-baring reformed alcoholic in all its sordid glory. To be sure, Gary paints his father, mother, and brothers in a less than flattering light. But, at bottom, he mostly attacks himself—giving us an amazingly honest portrait of his own transgressions prior to the ultimate conquest of his personal demons.

Nobody, including Bing, escapes unscathed. But neither does Bing emerge as the moral monster that, by some accounts, he is cracked up to be. Rather, the trajectory of Gary's tale moves toward reconciliation and forgiveness. Near the end of the Crosby-and-Firestone book, we find passages focused on understanding and moving toward a resolution of differences in which Gary realizes that Bing "wasn't to blame because his fans found it inconceivable that such a wonderful man could father such horrible, rotten, ungrateful children" and admits that "He wasn't any tougher than a lot of fathers of his generation" (Crosby and Firestone 1983, p. 285): "At least he was trying to bring us up the best way he knew how. At least he tried. And that's more than can be said for a lot of fathers" (p. 286). After gaining these hard-won insights, Gary concludes, "I'm happy we made some kind of peace before he went": "We were able to give some kind of love to each other before it was too late" (Crosby and Firestone 1983, p. 291).

So it looks as if Bing Crosby was not quite the abomination that the attention-deficit-disordered speed-reading skimmers of Crosby and Firestone (1983) have carelessly inferred. But this consoling realization still begs the question of how we can enjoy the aforementioned Gary-and-Bing duets, knowing that they were recorded during a period of such trauma in young Gary's life. Thankfully, the answer seems to be that making these duet recordings provided something of a respite from Gary's other cares and woes. Indeed, Gary's account of the circumstances surrounding the recording of the mega-hits "Sam's Song" and "Play a Simple Melody" gives us some reason for rejoicing in our ability to detect happiness, expressed musically, when Gary suggests that "The hour and a half it took to record the two sides were one of the best times we ever had together": "We were working together as a team, and . . . he seemed to like what I was doing and we both had fun" (pp. 136–137). Happily, it seems that the enthusiasm of my youth was not wasted. This really is wonderful music. The power of Bing Crosby's dueting skills triumphs over everything, including familial squabbles. And it shows.

The authoritative Giddins (2001) tends to dismiss the flap over Bing Crosby's family life as "irresponsible" and "unfounded rumors" (p. 5): "Neither saint nor monster, Crosby survives his debunkers along with his hagiographers because the facts are so much more impressive than the prejudices and myths on either side" (p. 12). To me, based on Gary Crosby's book and the wayward comments of at least two of Gary's brothers, it appears that the elder Crosby represents something of a latter-day gender-reversed King-Lear-like figure—complete with three way-less-than-grateful sons and with Phillip playing the role of Cordelia. The key point, however, is that all this family bickering really does not matter much to the central issue at stake—namely, the nature of Bing Crosby's public persona at the time of making *High Society* and continuing until after his death at age 73 in 1977. In this connection, it would be fair to say that Crosby was widely regarded as the family man par excellence, the ideal father, the perfect husband, and Mr. Nice Guy (Giddins 2001, pp. 241, 457). For example, consider the description by Scot Haller and Maria Wilhelm—celebrating Bing as "not only a renowned performer but one of the nation's most beloved father figures"; "incontestably the No. 1 Big Family Man of Hollywood"; "Hollywood's Most Typical Father"; and "a wise, warm, Irish Catholic patriarch" (quoted at www.kcmetro.cc.mo.us/pennvalley/biology/lewis/crosby/bingboys.htm).

With his laid-back, song-crooning, pipe-smoking, bababa-bumming style and his suaver-than-suave beyond-relaxed mannerisms, Bing Crosby had achieved an image that was as patrician as it was paternal. People viewed him as a sincere and sympathetic mature man. Whether veridical or not, these attributed qualities represent commendable aspects of a carefully cultivated public persona. But they do not necessarily jibe with the prospectively romantic role played by Bing Crosby as Dexter opposite Grace Kelly as Tracy in *High Society*.

# Young Grace

Even in a motion-picture era when older guys routinely won younger gals, the romantic combination of Bing Crosby (whose career harks back to the days of singing with the Rhythm Boys in the Paul Whiteman Band of 1927) and Grace Kelly (who burst on the scene in 1952 as the ingénue in *High Noon* and who, quite literally, could have passed for Der Bingle's grand-daughter) begins as something of a stretch. Oh, sure, the two may have dated in real life, and Crosby may have subsequently married a woman five years younger than Kelly. But just take a cold, hard look at Bing and Grace, and you'll see what I mean. More importantly, this stretch grows into a percep-tible gap because, structurally, the film places at least two gigantic audio-visual barriers—that is, two huge ambi-diegetic cinemusical obstacles—in the way of our taking the Crosby–Kelly romance seriously.

## Ambi-Diegetic Cinemusical Obstacle Number One: The Ancient Mariner

Obstacle One appears in the form of the ambi-diegetic song called "True Love," a flashback in which we reminisce about the good old days when Dexter/Bing and Tracy/Grace were happily married and used to enjoy floating around the harbor at Newport on their fabulously expensive and oh-so-yare sailboat, also named the *True Love*. Now, be honest. Have you ever in your life heard anybody use the term "yare" before or since? Probably not, especially if you don't happen to inhabit one of the grand chateaus neighboring that of Tracy/Grace at Newport in *High Society* or one of the stately mansions near Tracy/Katharine on the Main Line in *The Philadelphia Story* (where the same arcane expression is used—not once, but twice). After I finally figured out how to spell the word—no easy lexicographical challenge—I gleaned that, according to Merriam-Webster (2001), it means "characterized by speed and agility . . . NIMBLE, LIVELY" (p. 1366), qualities that clearly describe both Grace Kelly and Katharine Hepburn far better than anything so comparatively mundane as a sailboat (let alone the rapidly-aging Bing Crosby). At any rate, the term "yare" seems to capture the tender feelings that Tracy/Grace still holds for the *True Love* and for her experiences with Dexter/Bing thereupon.

Here, in a nautical flashback, we see Tracy/Grace (looking adorably cute and about 15 years old) cuddling with Dexter/Bing (looking about 80), who wears an echt-Bingle captain's hat and sucks on his inevitable pipe while pumping away on a concertina, crooning the sappy-bordering-on-saprogenic lyrics, and waiting for you-figured-she-couldn't-sing-but-were-afraid-to-ask Kelly to join him in one of the film's three pivotal cinemusical duets. When she does, it turns out that Tracy/Grace can actually carry a tune . . . a little bit . . . in an unschooled but nonetheless melodious voice.

In his book on *Cole Porter*, McBrien (1998) describes "True Love" as a "simple . . . old-fashioned number" (p. 373) and as "a song whose cadence and lyrics are often banal" (p. 374), suggesting that "Cole himself was astonished when . . . the public embraced 'True Love'" (pp. 373–374). Indeed, "True Love" was nominated for an Oscar and, based on its sales figures, won Crosby and Kelly a gold record. In a rather paradoxical moment during a subsequent live concert by Frank Sinatra at the Royal Festival Hall (later issued on videotape), Princess Grace teases Frank that, unlike Sinatra, she had won a gold record. Frank did not go gold until a decade after *High Society* with "Strangers in the Night" (1966). All of which teaches us something, perhaps, about how bad music must become before the non-discerning public chooses to reward it with mass popularity. In a live recording of a concert at Carnegie Hall in 1984—included on a five-disk set entitled *Frank Sinatra: New York* (Reprise R2 520602)—Sinatra introduces his performance of "Strangers in the Night" with an acerbic comment to the effect that "I *hated* this G—D——song the first time I heard it. And I *still* hate it." As the orchestra begins its all-too-familiar intro-duction, the apparently inattentive audience cheers wildly.

Honesty compels me to report that Citron (1992) takes a somewhat different view of "True Love," claiming that Cole Porter blamed its soggy impression on "the way Bing Crosby sang his song" (p. 247) and insisting that Porter's publisher regarded it as "truly a simple, beautiful, tasteful composition worthy of Franz Schubert" (p. 247). In this connection, I will concede that "True Love" does feature one piece of harmonic ingenuity in its bridge, which "wanders freshly in and amazingly out of a new key" (p. 247). Specifically, from G major, it modulates to Bb major and then back to G major again—a rather nice harmonic turn of phrase, worthy of Cole Porter as the most sophisticated of composers.

OK, I'll confess. After writing the preceding paragraph, I went over to the piano and played the melody and chords to "True Love." Even with my own limited pianistic technique, I can see that—stripped of Bing Crosby's old-man-and-the-sea mannerisms—the piece is flat-out . . . wonderful.

At any rate, as an ambi-diegetic cinemusical portrait of connubial bliss, "True Love" makes the case for some deeply-ingrained cuddly-snuggly feelings between Dexter/Bing and Tracy/Grace. The impression we get here is incredibly . . . sweet. But the scene resembles more a father-figure relationship than a passionate love tryst—looks more like an old guy who bears a strong resemblance to the Ancient Mariner hitting on a young girl who really should be off playing with her dolls or maybe, in the case of Newport, her sports cars.

Hence, at this point in the film, I retain some doubts whether Dexter/ Bing—who soon thereafter expresses his continued undying devotion to Tracy/Grace (aka "Sam") via a plaintive song called "I Love You, Samantha" (accompanied by Louis Armstrong and His Band) in which he attests to his monogamous intentions—has the *cojones* to pull off his planned matrimonial coup. After wading knee-deep in schmaltz through "True Love," as Dexter/Bing fastidiously dons his tuxedo and croons softly with Louis and Co. piping from afar in the background, he more resembles a sartorially correct uncle than a dashing suitor—especially given that the song "Samantha" is (let's face it) one of the dreariest things Cole Porter ever wrote. OK, I admit, two authorities insist that Porter himself regarded this as the best song in the movie (Citron 1992, p. 246; McBrien 1998, p. 374). But I had to learn it once to play for the first-birthday party of a friend's daughter named Samantha. And—trust me, Dear Reader—it lies like a lead weight under your fingertips and drags its cumbersome tail heavily as you struggle to pull it along.

## Ambi-Diegetic Cinemusical Obstacle Number Two: Young Frank

Further damage to Dexter/Bing's stature as Tracy/Grace's potentially revived love interest appears in the ambi-diegetic song sung by Mike/Frank to Grace entitled "You're Sensational," in which the beguilingly blue-eyed Sinatra—heartthrob of many a bobby soxer from the 1940s, now poised to flaunt his resurgent post-Maggio, post-Oscar, post-Ava-Gardner, post-Capitol-Records popularity as a sadder-but-wiser swinger during the mid-1950s—practically charms the panties off his young blonde hostess. Further details on Frank Sinatra's celebrated charisma appear in Chapter 3 (see also Holbrook 2005e). McBrien (1998) reports that Cole Porter personally thought that "You're Sensational" had greater hit potential than the anemic "True Love" (p. 373) and that the composer felt that Frank Sinatra was "the only person singing today with passion" (p. 171). Suffice it here to comment that, to post-adolescent female members of the audience for this film, Frank was one of the biggest sex symbols of his era—especially when he leaned his slim body into a song, twitched that lower lip, batted those famous baby blues, and sang long breath-free lines with a look on his face of such deep sincerity that even a heterosexual guy could not help but feel spellbound. The Mike/Frank character who croons to Grace Kelly in *High Society* has animal magnetism to burn, as mirrored by Tracy/Grace's own reciprocal body language.

Watching such an erotic musical ambi-diegetic performance, we can forget all about the tough-guy mafia-connected barroom-brawl imagery that surrounds Frank Sinatra's private life. Hearing him sing these long sinuous lines with those celebrated Sinatra hallmarks—total breath control, immaculate intonation, perfect phrasing—we cannot fail to be captivated by the force of his erotic appeal. Whether all this was purely an act or not is—cinemusically speaking—beside the point.

The point is that—while singing "You're Sensational" in his typical vocally impeccable manner, complete with bewitching facial expressions and other compelling physiognomic gestures—Sinatra looks at Kelly (who earnestly returns his gaze) in a way that says, "You're mine. I know it. You know it. Two hundred million fans out there in movie land know it. And poor old doddering Dexter/Bing doesn't stand a chance. Does he? No, he does not!" For the moment, the viewer cannot help but become a believer.

This might be a suitable place to comment on the number-one magical ingredient in Frank Sinatra's arsenal of erotic come-ons—namely, his celebrated blue eyes. Like Paul Newman, Sinatra—seemingly, at will—could mount a spectacular ocular fireworks display. Incidentally, Bing Crosby also had nice blue eyes, but people tended not to notice because most of his films were in black and white (Giddins 2001, p. 483). So let us pause to consider a list of some (among many others) who have commented on the captivating impact of Frank Sinatra's aquamarine gaze. In rough chronological order, as samples of infatuation with Sinatra's jeepers-creepers periwinkle peepers, unabashed tributes to the awesome power of his cerulean charms have come from Gay Talese (1966, ed. 1995, p. 101); Arnold Shaw (1968, p. 51); Rosalind Russell (quoted by Thompson 1971, p. 146); Jacqueline Bisset (quoted by Frank 1978, p. 127); Pete Hamill (1980, p. 228); Whitney Balliett (1982, ed. 1995, pp. 185–186); Producer George Schlatter (quoted by Sinatra 1985, p. 247); Jonathan Schwartz (1989, ed. 1995, p. 246); and Johnny Mandel (quoted by Friedwald 1995, p. 372). OK, so the verdict is in. At least nine members of the jury—not to mention countless others not represented in my brief survey—agree that Mr. Frank Sinatra has one hell of a powerful ocular aura. He turns this organ of optokinetic omnipotence with full force on Tracy/Grace while singing "You're Sensational." And, powerless in the face of his nearly nuclear ambi-diegetic cinemusical attack, she experiences an emotional meltdown.

Later in *High Society*, Mike/Frank flashes a little more ambi-diegetic cinemusical magnetism in the direction of Tracy/Grace when he sings "Mind If I Make Love to You?" while dancing the rumba with her at a private Champagne-enriched pool party. Tracy/Grace gets all dreamy-eyed and caresses Mike/Frank. They foolishly speak of romance before she impetuously jumps fully-clothed into the pool for a drunken late-night swim. When Mike/Frank carries Tracy/Grace from the pool—dripping wet and gaily singing "True Love" in an inebriated caricature of her earlier performance of this piece with Dexter/Bing—she has reached the brink of adulterous indiscretion.

Mike/Frank redeems himself by refusing to take advantage of Tracy/Grace's inebriated hospitality. Interestingly, this demonstration of chivalry anticipates a comparable abstemious moment in a scene between Frank Sinatra and a tipsy Kim Novak in *Pal Joey* (1957), described in Chapter 3 (see also Holbrook 2005e). The cinematic Sinatra (unlike his real-life counterpart) keeps missing out on getting laid by the world's most beautiful women because of his no-doubt-fictitious sexual scruples. But the point is that—partly due to the irresistible magic of his ocularly amplified ambi-diegetic cinemusical spells—Frank in *High Society* could have had Grace if he had wanted to. There is that much palpable chemistry between Sinatra and Kelly. This poses quite an uphill battle for poor old Dexter/Bing to negotiate.

RECUPERATING BING

So how, as it stands midway through *High Society*, do we recuperate Bing Crosby's image enough to make him a suitable target for the romantic affections of Grace Kelly at the end?

## Contrast Effect: George Kittredge

Part of the answer lies in the *contrast effect*. Specifically, we make Tracy/Grace's intended marriage partner (the man whose wedding to Tracy/Grace all these people have ostensibly convened to celebrate) as big a drip as it is possible to imagine. Played to obnoxious perfection by John Lund in what seems to have been his only noteworthy movie assignment—perhaps because he so definitively enacted the self-destruction of his own screen image—the character of Tracy/Grace's fiancé George Kittredge emerges as an old fogey, a stuffed shirt, a grim businessman, a self-important jerk, a socially privileged bore, a pompous ass. Predictably, he drives . . . a station wagon. He self-righteously censures his prospective bride's playful late-night shenanigans. In short, he appears to be as a first-class loser. Significantly, George/John does not sing. And when he clumsily dances, his movements are stiff as a board. Obviously, he is far too concerned about propriety to deserve a liberated spirit such as Tracy/Grace.

By comparison—with his droll sense of humor, his charmingly casual mannerisms, and his lilting speech patterns—Dexter/Bing comes across as a knight in shining armor. Bing Crosby manages to convey a sort of suave charisma that in this film gives new meaning to the expression "to the manner born." His "manor" is not so shabby either—qualifying as a place that should be a luxury hotel were it not occupied by one quintessentially relaxed and delightfully musical gentleman. Dexter/Bing takes nothing seriously—with the possible exception of . . . jazz. Specifically, to the extent that he does any work at all, he is a successful composer of jazzy popular songs. An upbeat individual. A cheerful guy. A happy man. Exactly the qualities he needs to bollix the unappealing George/John and to win back the hand of the radiant Tracy/Grace.

## Similarity Effect: Two Pivotal Duets

But much if not most of the rehabilitation of Dexter/Bing's image arises from a *similarity effect* at work in two remaining pivotal duets. In the first ("Now You Has Jazz"), toward which I shall direct my primary attention, the iconographically antiquated and symbolically debilitated Dexter/Bing of "True Love" (re)emerges—via his visual and musical connection with the effervescent Louis Armstrong—as a strong, creative, virile force to be reckoned with. In the second ("Well, Did You Evah?"), which follows the duet with Armstrong, Dexter/Bing demonstrates his revived masculine vigor—now forging an audiovisual link with Frank Sinatra—by matching the performance of the younger sex symbol gesture for gesture, wisecrack for wisecrack, dance step for dance step, and note for note. Musically and cinematically, the first of these pivotal duets sets up the second, and the second corroborates Dexter/Bing's viable credentials as a suitable surreptitious suitor worthy of Tracy/Grace's renewed affection. Soon, we shall examine each pivotal ambi-diegetic cinemusical duet in more detail. But, first, let us pause to contemplate a bit of background on Bing Crosby's credentials as a singer of duets.

### The Master of Ambi-Diegetic Cinemusical Duets

Consider, first, the fact that Bing Crosby is perhaps *the* all-time master of the ambi-diegetic cinemusical duet. Probably more than any other singer-actor, Bing had a flare for timing in general and, in particular, for timing that made his interactions with other singers—his asides, his harmony parts, his ingenious obbligatos—seem as effortlessly spontaneous, as prototypically hip, and as utterly cool as possible. Giddins (2001) suggests that "of all the manifestations of his art, duets best exemplify the real Bing": "Bing was never more honestly and affably himself than in duets" (p. 513). Perhaps most famously, such tandem contributions surfaced in the *Road* movies—with Bob Hope, Dorothy Lamour, and so forth—but they also appeared in countless musical recordings with (among many others) Louis Jordan, Connee Boswell, Jack Teagarden, Lionel Hampton, Lee Wiley, Louis Armstrong, Gary Crosby, Fred Astaire, Rosemary Clooney, and—especially—the Andrews Sisters (Giddins 2001, p. 568). Hear, for example, the CD compilations on Decca (GRD-603), MCA/Decca (MCAD2-11503), and Sepia Recordings (1111, 1122, 1129, 1139, 1146). As much as anywhere, in these supernally cool duets, Bing Crosby lays claim to his stature as what Artie Shaw perceptively called "the first hip white person born in the United States" (quoted by Giddins 2001, p. 259).

   As just one among countless possible illustrations of this point, consider the ambi-diegetic cinemusical performance by Bing Crosby with Mary Martin of "Wait 'Til the Sun Shines, Nellie"—the chestnut from 1905 by Andrew Sterling and Harry Von Tilzer—in Victor Schertzinger's *Birth of the Blues* (1941). In this film—as Jeff Lambert, the leader of a group resembling the Original Dixieland Jazz Band—Crosby mimes brilliant clarinet parts played by Danny Polo with more aplomb than attention to such details as holding his instrument at an angle that might conceivably permit a correct embouchure or wiggling his fingers in a way that might vaguely correspond to the appropriate scales and arpeggios that we hear on the soundtrack. (On the foolish-to-ignore importance of visual realism in such miming-and-dubbing efforts, see Karlin 1994, pp. 42–45.) Meanwhile, Brian Donlevy plays the cornetist Memphis—ironically, with considerably more veridicality in miming the horn parts dubbed by "Porky" Carriere. Jack Teagarden plays a trombonist named Pepper, who strongly resembles his real-life bone-playing self. And Mary Martin—looking more incandescently beautiful than those of us who grew up on *Peter Pan* (1954) and *South Pacific* (1958) would have any reason to recall—plays Lambert/Crosby's love interest, Betty Lou Cobb.

Cobb/Martin performs Otto Harbach and Karl Hoschna's "Cuddle Up a Little Closer, Lovey Mine" (1908) in an audition for a job at a nightclub called the Black Tie Café run by a shady character named Blackie (J. Carrol Naish), where she appears more than fetching enough to get the gig (if ineffably corny in her singing style, as judged by our contemporary eyes and ears). That evening, after receiving some coaching from Jeff/Bing and Crew, Betty/Mary returns to do her act, with Lambert/Crosby's Basin Street Hot Shots in tow as her supporting accompaniment. Together Crosby, Martin, and Co. deliver a five-minute seven-chorus ambi-diegetic version of "Wait 'Til the Sun Shines, Nellie" that demonstrates Bing's ambi-diegetic cine-musical dueting talents about as well as any performance ever could.

On the first chorus, just warming up, Jeff/Bing mimes Danny Polo's great clarinet obbligatos—obliviously holding his horn at an impossible angle and carelessly forgetting to move his fingers. (This kind of sloppy miming of ambi-diegetic source music in films was common before the more recent days when careful synching has become the norm.) During the second chorus, Betty/Mary enters the club and teaches some of Blackie's confused customers how to dance the Dixieland Two-Step while the Hot Shots wail in the background. Chorus number three features a trombone solo by Pepper/Jack, during which he clowns with his dress-shirt cuff before the focus switches to the bassist, who breaks the hair ribbon on his bow and, in desperation, begins slapping the bass with spectacular results (a harmlessly misrepresentative revisionist history of what was actually an important musical innovation). In appreciation, Jeff/Bing—ultra hip, ultra cool—breaks the bow over his knee and throws it away.

On the fourth chorus, Cobb/Martin begins to sing. At first, Lambert/Crosby watches approvingly at very close range, with a wonderfully curious expression on his face, smirking and fluttering his eyelids. When the time comes for Betty/Mary to execute a little syncopation, he nudges her in the ribs with his elbow to produce the desired delay on the word "drifting"—sort of on-the-job Dixieland training, I guess. Jeff/Bing's own entrance—propitiously ending with a low note on the word "down"—is so perfectly timed and so charmingly rendered that members of the crowd, many of whom have stopped dancing and started watching in rapt enthusiasm, emit ecstatic gestures of approval. Lambert/Crosby continues with wonderful harmony and obbligato parts, occasionally nodding his head in what—if I were he—would be sublime self-satisfaction. In chorus five, the singing gets more jazzy still. Chorus six features both Lambert/Crosby and Cobb/Martin whistling improvisational passages—first trading fours, next twos—before returning to some even jazzier vocalizing.

Then, in the seventh chorus, Lambert/Crosby and Cobb/Martin pull out all the ambi-diegetic cinemusical stops. Jeff/Bing begins with some trombone-like bum-a-bum-bumming, facing the audience with his back turned to the band. Directly behind Lambert/Crosby, Memphis/Brian grabs Jeff/Bing's hat and softly tosses it past him, whereupon Lambert/Crosby nonchalantly reaches out, catches it effortlessly as it flies by, and pops it onto his head. I do not think that even the most impressive alley-oop dunk by (say) Michael Jordan has ever been executed more gracefully or with more finesse. The choreography for the rest of this chorus—complete with intricately synchronized knee-slapping flourishes and a delightfully humorous hog-calling parody—is so delicious that I nominate it as the single most dazzling 32 bars of male-female dueting I have ever seen.

The point of all this, of course, is that it establishes Bing Crosby as the reigning master of the ambi-diegetic cinemusical duet. Fifteen years later, in *High Society*, he gets a chance to show off these skills for all they are worth.

### "Now You Has Jazz"

Structurally, "Now You Has Jazz" is positioned as the centerpiece of *High Society*—the turning point, the musical watershed, the *Coup de Grace Kelly*. Here, the history of Newport as the long-time home of the famous Jazz Festival, the role of Dexter/Bing as a participant in organizing the festival, the legend of Louis Armstrong (vividly revived in the recent documentary by Ken Burns but perhaps at its zenith during the mid-1950s), and the tradition of many previous duets by Armstrong and Crosby (frequent musical partners over the years preceding this particular film) come together in a scintillating ambi-diegetic performance that transforms the image of Dexter/Bing from an older to a younger, from a more tired to a more energized, from a defeated to a triumphant character. It is a cinemusical moment—in its own way—as lively and vibrant as a tap dance by Fred Astaire, a Bach fugue played by Glenn Gould, a gazelle-like leap by Mikhail Baryshnikov, a slam dunk by Julius Erving, a basket catch by Willie Mays, or a double front somersault with a half twist by Nastia Liukin. It recaptures and presents for our delectation the vivacious joy of New Orleans or Dixieland jazz, as proffered by two of its instrumental and vocal masters—Armstrong and Crosby, named by Friedwald (1990) in *Jazz Singing* as "the two most important figures in jazz-derived popular singing" (p. 25)—two musical geniuses who originally shaped the development of this music and who appear together in *High Society*, three decades later, to demonstrate for all to see that they've still got what it takes.

It might be that I identify with this performance in an unusually strong way because, as I (re)write this (at age 66), I happen to be 13 years older than Bing Crosby (53) and 11 years older than Louis Armstrong (55) when they made *High Society*. When I first saw this film (at age 12 or 13), I thought that both Crosby and Armstrong seemed ancient—more or less synonymous, at that time, with "even older than my own parents" (though not by much). Today, my own son (40) is considerably older than Grace Kelly in the film (28). Currently, aspects of my own life are clearly old-fashioned or out-of-date or dinosaur-like. I don't own a GPS, a PDA, a DVR, an e-book reader, a cell phone, or even a fax machine. But I would like to imagine that, like Dexter/Bing in *High Society*, there is still some sort of creative energy, inventive spirit, or intellectual force lurking below the aging exterior surface. In "Now You Has Jazz," Bing Crosby and Louis Armstrong hold out hope.

## *Issues of Gender Asymmetry, Racial Stereotyping, and Ethnocentrism*

To appreciate "Now You Has Jazz," we have to get past a certain amount of gender asymmetry, racial stereotyping, and ethnocentric bias that were inevitably built into this particular ambi-diegetic cinemusical occasion.

First, as noted earlier, Dexter/Bing and friends inhabit a world in which an older guy routinely wins the heart of a younger gal, but the opposite hardly ever happens. This asymmetric aspect of gender relations in the real world has long been a mainstay of Hollywood casting—to the point where actresses over (say) 40 years old search in vain for romantic parts to play. To hear a gifted artist such as Faye Dunaway or Jacqueline Bisset expound on this topic is to receive a crash course in gender politics, Hollywood style. Beyond that, *High Society* tends to perpetuate the inherently sexist silver-screen tradition in which beautiful young women such as Tracy/Grace often come across as a bit empty-headed or, worse, as embodiments of the "dizzy blonde" stereotype. Dexter/Bing treats Tracy/Grace adoringly but somewhat in the manner of a beautiful trophy whom he places on a pedestal. Unlike Dexter/Bing, Tracy/Grace has little to offer in the way of (say) opinions, ideas, or talent—much less knowledge, wisdom, or artistic abilities. She seems refined, cool, and somewhat savvy only because she mostly keeps her mouth shut on topics more complicated than cocktails and sailboats.

Second, with respect to racial stereotyping, there's the obvious fact that this film is set in Newport, RI—the very bastion of elite WASP respectability. The year is 1956, and *Guess Who's Coming to Dinner* (1967) hasn't happened yet—not for America in general and especially not for Newport in particular. So, ineluctably, it's the white guys who are living in fancy houses, wearing elegant clothes, throwing posh parties, and planning elaborate wedding ceremonies. And it's the black guys who are playing ambi-diegetically in the jazz band—in this case, Louis Armstrong's All Stars (Satchmo himself on trumpet, of course, plus Edmond Hall on clarinet, Trummy Young on trombone, Billy Kyle on piano, Arvell Shaw on bass, and Barrett Deems on drums). Regrettably—except for when they are briefly playing their instruments on such tunes as "High Society Calypso" (which, if you listen carefully, spells out the whole plot of the film in advance), "Little One" (a wonderfully avuncular tune sung by Dexter/Bing to Tracy/Grace's little sister), or "I Love You, Samantha" (the aforementioned laborious declaration of Dexter/Bing's monogamous devotion)—the band members get to appear on-screen only briefly. Louis Armstrong does serve as a sort of one-man Greek chorus—offering sideline commentary on the film's dramatic developments throughout. But—except for the fact that they are obviously tight with their host and hang out with Dexter/Bing on various occasions— the cats in the band do not have an opportunity to rap with the parents of the bride, chat with the guests, dance to the orchestra, or develop intriguing subplots.

Well, OK. What else would you expect at this locale on this occasion? Presumably, all this reflects a clear-eyed view of how social relations were conducted in Newport, RI circa the mid-1950s. Rather than liberated politics, the film presents . . . historical accuracy. It makes little sense to fault it for that.

Indeed, some of the exaggerated political correctness that currently surrounds the jazz scene has gotten to be something of a nuisance. I am thinking, for example, of radio disk jockeys who seem constitutionally incapable of introducing (say) a tune by Charlie Parker without referring to it as a "composition" by "Mr. Charles Parker." When the "composition" in question is nothing more than a 12-bar blues based on a repeated riff such as that found in (say) "Now's the Time," Charlie Parker—a great admirer of such real composers as Stravinsky, Prokofiev, Bartok, and the rest— would have found attempts to dignify his tune in this manner to be screamingly funny. John Birks "Dizzy" Gillespie wanted people to call him "Diz" or (preferably) "Birks"—not "Mr. Gillespie." All this reaches the height of absurdity in the recent fetish of pronouncing Louis Armstrong's name as "Lou-isss" instead of "Lou-eeee"—apparently, forgetting the French influence in this hero's native New Orleans, on the misguided grounds that the former Anglicized pronunciation somehow sounds more respectful. When I was a kid, everybody called the guy "Lou-eeee" or "Satchelmouth" or "Satchmo" or "Satch" or "Pops" or all sorts of other things—all of them inherently approbatory or even worshipful. And Mr. Armstrong was perfectly happy with that. It was a sign of admiration and affection. Thus, for the benefit of history in widely available recordings, Ms. Ella Fitzgerald calls him "Lou-eeee." Mr. Bing Crosby pronounces his name "Lou-eeee." And Mr. Arvell Shaw, for many years the bassist in Armstrong's All-Stars, also refers to him as "Lou-eeee." And so do a lot of other characters who were close to this great man. So what's good enough for them is plenty good enough for me. And you. In short, let's not overindulge in political correctness for fear of missing the glories of a particularly wonderful piece of music.

Third, the musical structure of "Now You Has Jazz" betrays a definite Eurocentric bias—at least up to a point—with a certain degree of apparently ethnocentric musical schizophrenia. Cole Porter's biographer McBrien (1998) tells us that Porter admired few jazz artists, Louis Armstrong being one of the rare exceptions (p. 370)—a fact that, on the surface, seems propitious for their collaboration as composer and performer in *High Society*. After a witty and ironically erudite introduction—promising us some "shimmering sharps and flats" by these "cozy virtuosi" in Dexter/Bing's suavest manner—the tune starts off sounding as if it will be a straightforward

12-bar blues of the type central to the New Orleans tradition. But nothing could be farther from the truth. To the best of my knowledge, throughout his long career (nearing its end when he penned the music for *High Society*), Cole Porter wrote only three songs with "Blues" in their titles: "The Blue Boy Blues" from *Mayfair and Montmartre* (1922); "The Lost Liberty Blues" from *La Revue Des Ambassadeurs* (1928); and "The Red Blues" from *Silk Stockings* (1957). But, as far as I know, these were all Broadway-type show tunes or musical comedy numbers—not real blues songs. For example, in *Noel and Cole*, Citron (1992) describes "The Blue Boy Blues" as "a charming number sung by the subject of the famous Gainsborough painting who wonders what will become of him now that he has been sold to an American collector and is being moved to the Wild West" (p. 58). "The Lost Liberty Blues," performed by an actress dressed as the Statue of Liberty, is a kitsch "diatribe against . . . the prohibition of alcohol" (p. 74). And "The Red Blues" from *Silk Stockings* (1957) begins as an Eisenhower-Era parody of political repression in the Soviet Union and then segues into a rousing opportunity for Cyd Charisse as Ninotchka to show off her formidable jitterbug skills. Amusing, no doubt, but not exactly "Things Ain't What They Used To Be," "Now's the Time," "Bags' Groove," or "Straight, No Chaser."

Apparently, then, Porter never wrote an ordinary 12-bar blues, and—as appropriate as it might have been under the circumstances—he certainly did not do so in the case of "Now You Has Jazz." Even a non-musician will notice that this piece departs from the familiar 12-bar structure that one might associate with (say) Billie Holiday, Jimmy Rushing, Bill Haley, Little Richard, Ray Charles, Elvis Presley, or the Beatles. Thus, at the end of the first chorus—seemingly unable to wean himself from the Eurocentric tradition—Porter adds a four-bar tag, converting the piece to an apparent $(12 + 4) \times 2 = 32$-bar structure. To complicate the picture further, on the first time through the piece but not thereafter, he tacks on a two-bar trumpet break—thereby creating, just once, an unusual and very non-Dixie-sounding 18-bar phrase. Porter follows this with the 16-bar version, sans tag. But, next time, he leaves out two measures, giving us 14 bars of instrumental ensemble playing. Then, we hear two straightforward 12-bar improvisational choruses divided into four-bar segments (clarinet, trombone, clarinet-plus-trombone and piano, bass, piano-plus-bass), succeeded by an eight-bar drum break. After that, a solo by Armstrong plus a tag reverts to the 16-bar format— which is repeated two more times. Finally—following a wonderful key change from B-flat to C, flawlessly executed by Dexter/Bing—the piece ends with a chorus consisting of 16 bars plus a tag of about eight bars or so, giving us roughly 24 in all, depending on how you count the concluding flourish. Maybe there is a clear pattern here: 18, 16, 14, 12, 12, 16, 16, 16, and 24. But I certainly don't see it. Well, I suppose that if you add up all the measures, you get $144 = 12 \times 12$ in some sense. But this convoluted structure is certainly opaque to the casual listener. And it clearly departs drastically from the normal repetition of 12-bar choruses typical of blues pieces played by jazz musicians. Hence, despite its earthy overtones, "Now You Has Jazz" manages to retain a high degree of structural complexity characteristic of Western European music.

That Cole Porter would combine earthy overtones with structural complexity should come as no surprise, for the songwriter was a man of many contradictions. As just one example, though gay and inclined to have overt homosexual affairs whenever it suited him, Porter maintained a 35-year marriage to a somewhat older woman judged in her younger days to be "the most beautiful woman in America" and "one of the most beautiful women in the world" (Citron 1992, p. 50). Ashley Judd—playing opposite Kevin Kline in the Porter biopic *De-Lovely* (2004)—makes a convincing case for this assessment; and if their rendition of "So In Love" doesn't tear your heart out, it's probably because you haven't got one. However, in my view, we should take such fashion-related propaganda with a grain of salt. I have seen photographs of Cole's real-world wife Linda and find, in my own personal opinion, that she was nowhere near as beautiful as (say) my own grand-mothers—Kate and Bertha—on both sides of the family. And doubtless, Dear Reader, the same could be said for *your* grandmothers as well.

Fourth, somewhat more problematically, there's the embarrassing recourse by Cole Porter throughout the song to hints of some sort of mis-begotten ethnic dialect—evident in the title ("Now You Has Jazz") and scattered repeatedly along the way (as amplified, no doubt, via various impromptu insertions by Bing and/or Louis). Some of this is just plain annoying—*especially* the oft-repeated titular phrase, which can be excused only by the prosodic explanation that *has* rhymes with *jazz* and thereby provides an added touch of *asso*nance. Porter, perhaps with some thespian help from Crosby, gives us "da greatest" instead of "the greatest" and "evahbody" rather than "everybody." Also "fixin'" substitutes for "getting ready to." Here, actually, the typical Southern slang—which I spoke myself as a child—was "fidnin'"; mercifully, showing a little restraint, Porter and Crosby stopped short of going all the way in this direction. Further, some of the quaint verbiage found in this song can be explained as a simulation of "jazz argot" (rather than faux-black dialect). People are "cats"; snare drums are "skins"; the piano is a "box," one that "rocks"; the clarinet is a "stick," with a "lick"; the trombone is a "bone," rhymes with "phone." I used to talk this sort of jazz lingo myself with my musical buddies and still do sometimes when I renew some of the acquaintances from my youth. So I can attest that Crosby's and Armstrong's verbal mannerisms are not all just figments of Porter's imagination and are not really racist in tone.

Fifth, we know that Bing Crosby and Louis Armstrong were great friends and working colleagues from way back (Giddins 2001, pp. 151, 230, 234, 419, 431, 493). Together, among other tunes, they recorded "Pennies From Heaven" (1936, with the Jimmy Dorsey Orchestra); "Gone Fishin'" (1951, with the John Scott Trotter Orchestra); and 12 songs for an album called *Bing and Satchmo* that included "Sugar," "Way Down Yonder in New Orleans," "Muskrat Ramble," "Dardanella," "Lazy River," and "At the

Jazz Band Ball" (1960, with the Billy May Orchestra). They often appeared together on the airwaves—first on radio, later on television. And, of course, they starred together in motion pictures—starting with *Pennies From Heaven* (1936), continuing with *Here Comes the Groom* (1951), and culminating with *High Society* (1956). In short, their musical paths crossed on innumerable occasions and they had an obviously deep appreciation, admiration, and affection for one another—not to mention respect, reverence, and rapport. Indeed, Friedwald (1990) devotes four full pages to this topic, commenting that "The friendship of Armstrong and Crosby probably goes back to the late twenties" (p. 46). Still, as noted by Friedwald (1990), there's the lurking suspicion that—despite the bravado of their buddy duet in *High Society* and despite their long history of friendship and of working together—Armstrong and Crosby probably did not really hang out in each other's company on the same dinner- and cocktail-party circuit. Louis was much too busy smoking grass on his back porch in Queens. And Bing—if we believe everything we read—was way too preoccupied with psychologically traumatizing the unfortunate members of his immediate family circle in California. At any rate, as Friedwald (1990) explains: "It was said that Crosby never invited Armstrong (and hardly anyone else) to his house, but . . . their relationship and their empathy transcended that consideration (p. 48)." Here, the operative words are "and hardly anyone else." Apparently, Bing was not such a sociable sort of guy. But even the refractory Gary Crosby—one of Bing's aforementioned ungrateful children—reports positively on the Armstrong-Crosby relationship: "Louis loved my father [and] Louis was always one of [Bing's] favorites" (Crosby and Firestone 1983, pp. 219–220). As quoted by Giddins (2001), Armstrong called Crosby "a Natural Genius the day he was born" (p. 181): "Here's paying tribute to one of the finest Guys in this musical and wonderful world. With a heart as big" (p. 420). Again, as quoted by Giddins (2001), Bing reciprocated by acknowledging his "debt to the Reverend Satchelmouth . . . He is the beginning and the end of music in America. And long may he reign" (p. 152). When Louis Armstrong died in 1971, Bing Crosby (who died in 1977) served as a pallbearer at Armstrong's funeral. And Bing left this statement to encapsulate his feelings about his friend: "No question about it, the happiest times in my recording career were the days I worked with Louis Armstrong" (quoted by Friedwald 1990, p. 49). Clearly, the humanity of these two guys shines forth in their music—never more than when they play and sing together in "Now You Has Jazz."

### Ambi-Diegetic Cinemusical Meanings in the Crosby–Armstrong Duet

In a rather cute metaphoric device, "Now You Has Jazz" is positioned as a sort of tutorial wherein Dexter/Bing as teacher explains jazz to the assembled wedding guests at Uncle Willie's palatial house in Newport. In this capacity, Dexter/Bing plays a dual role—on one hand, as one of them, integrated into the upper echelons of the Newport social scene; on the other, as a quintes-sentially comfortable compatriot of the formidable jazz musicians who are set to play their hearts out. On one hand, knowledgeable about "shim-mering" flats and sharps; on the other, savvy about "exactly" or at least "approximately" how ambi-diegetic jazz music is "made." This boundary-crossing *comfort zone*, allowing Dexter/Bing to move with ease between the two worlds of jazz and high society, serves as the key to his symbolic rejuvenation via this performance.

By establishing a clear visual and aural link with the effervescent Louis Armstrong and with the tradition of New Orleans jazz, the Bing Crosby character figuratively takes a gulp from the Fountain of Youth, from the mainspring of creative genius, from the tradition of America's one true indigenous art form in which Armstrong himself undeniably played *the* seminal role. Today, partly thanks to the influence of the epic PBS docu-mentary on jazz by Ken Burns, few would doubt that Louis Armstrong is arguably *the* musical genius of the Twentieth Century. You can talk about your Igor Stravinsky or Arnold Schoenberg, your Bartok or Prokofiev, your Billie Holiday or Lester Young, your Ellington or Coltrane, your Miles or Thelonious, your Elvis or Madonna, your P. Diddy or Britney. I, too, happen to admire all (well, almost all) those artists. But—truth be told—*nobody* changed the face of music on the planet to the extent accomplished by Louis (aka Louie, aka Satchmo, aka Pops) Armstrong. When I first heard Satchmo's music, I thought, "Well, he's good, but why does he keep playing all those overly familiar clichés?" Only later did I realize that it was because he had *invented* all those phrases that *later* became the well-worn licks endlessly recycled by musical imitators.

So here's Louis Armstrong—playing and singing in that inimitably shining way of his—lending credence to Dexter/Bing and reminding us that Crosby, too, has paid his musical dues and has labored in the vineyards of N'Orleans-styled jazz since its earliest days on record. As already mentioned, Louis and Bing have performed together previously. But neither this pair nor anyone else who comes to mind has ever before achieved the ebulliently energizing *joie de vivre* expressed for all to behold in "Now You Has Jazz." Through this magic ambi-diegetic cinemusical moment, the Crosby character is imaginatively reborn.

To elaborate a bit, the essence of Dexter/Bing's rebirth lies *not* in any ability displayed by Bing Crosby to "get it up" or to "boogie" with the rock-'n'-rollers (though the anachronistic term "rock-'n'-roll" does appear in the song, for reasons that I have never been able to fathom, other than the fact that it rhymes with "pole"). *Rather* the essence of this rebirth lies in the total relaxation and apparent effortlessness with which Crosby blends his style with that of Armstrong. In the most understated manner possible, Dexter/Bing's performance is really a stunning masterpiece of subdued choreog-raphy.

It's all there in what Crosby does with his shoulders and arms and hands and face. When he holds up an arm, his wrist is (not limp but) relaxed. His eyebrows are serene. His lips are loose and limber. His cheeks puff out endearingly. His whole physiognomy conveys comfort and ease—a sense of standing on this stage in front of this joyfully blaring Dixieland group and knowing that this is exactly where he belongs. His image blends with that of jazz—the most spontaneous, the most original, the most innovative, the most free of all art forms. By virtue of ambi-diegetic cinemusical association, Dexter/Bing also becomes spontaneous, original, innovative, free—epitomized by what Corliss (2001) in *Time* refers to as his "patented airplane arm-swing" and what Giddins (2001) calls his "vaudeville shtick—jerky short-arm movements, tap dancing, torso wiggling" (p. 417).

Crosby's and Armstrong's moves on "Now You Has Jazz" would, in and of themselves, merit a book-length treatise. Multiple chapters could be devoted to the way Bing tilts his head back and closes his eyes when he says "jazz," "one that rocks," "aah," "oh-oh," or "jazz, jazz, jazz." As for Louis, someone should write a dissertation on the way he rolls his eyes heavenward during his blues chorus on trumpet or on the exquisitely comical body language with which he accompanies his little joke about the French loving "*le jazz hot.*" And, as the essence of synchrony, notice how Crosby's gaze follows Armstrong's arm as it pantomimes a plane taking off or how Bing matches his own hand gestures to the concluding drum bombs before triumphantly proclaiming, "That's Jazz!"

Are you watching Samantha? Are you primed for your *Coup de Grace Kelly*? After Crosby and Armstrong finish their marvelous duet, as the dance orchestra launches into Cole Porter's romantic "Easy to Love," Tracy/Grace tells Dexter/Bing that she liked the "cute" song he sang and asks him why he doesn't write "cute" songs like that. Significantly, he announces to her with pride that he *did* write that one. So much for her erstwhile disapproval of his lackluster career in music. At the moment, he looks like a triumphantly virile success, an invigorated musical winner.

Atop the ambi-diegetic cinemusical virtues just observed—once we get past the little problems with political correctness noted earlier—we find that "Now You Has Jazz" also carries what we might now regard as a refreshingly postmodern message. Specifically, in the spirit of multiculturalism, it proclaims the global appeal of jazz—widely regarded as America's one original contribution to the arts and surely one of our country's most successful cultural exports. As the song cheerfully points out, jazz—which, via its emphasis on spontaneity and improvisation, embodies the spirit of freedom—has achieved near universal popularity. In Bangkok, they rock 'round the clock. In Siam, they all like to jam. In Paris, they all love *le jazz hot.* "Now You Has Jazz" reminds us that—from the Equator to the Pole, from the East to the West Coast—Jazz is King, the thing that people dig most. Thus, we find a touchingly ecumenical spirit in the way this song embraces an international global consciousness and in the way Cole Porter's duet places a white icon and a black genius on a steamy stage in Newport, RI to proclaim the virtues of America's home-spun version of World Music.

The chic, ritzy, and patrician social setting notwithstanding, nobody is patronizing anybody here. Louis Armstrong, it happens, could not be bought or sold. (If you doubt this, recall Satchmo's stance against school segregation during the Eisenhower Era or his subsequent activities on behalf of civil rights.) And Bing Crosby sings the music he grew up with and cherishes beyond compare, accompanied by a favorite musical sidekick. For reasons that I cannot quite explain given its happy nature, this scene featuring "Now You Has Jazz" always brings tears to my eyes. Perhaps they are tears of joy. Perhaps they reflect a nostalgic awareness that we shall not see the likes of Louis Armstrong and Bing Crosby again. Not ever. Or maybe this scene moves me because—long before the days of flower power and in a very different social milieu—it is a genuine and spiritually elevating love fest.

Later, I shall address the manner in which ambi-diegetic performances by Louis Armstrong have played a role in establishing the masculinity and sexual potency of other cinematic characters (see also Gabbard 1996, 2001, 2008). For now, let us savor the incomparable ambi-diegetic cinemusical moments in "Now You Has Jazz" and move on to Stage Two in the recuperation of Bing.

### *"Well, Did You Evah?"*

Figuratively, Dexter/Bing emerges from his Armstrong duet, ready to do battle with Mike/Frank in an effort to slay the Dragon of Advancing Age. This second dramatic cinemusical encounter occurs in the form of one more key ambi-diegetic duet—this one called "Well, Did You Evah?"—borrowed with various topical updates from an earlier show by Cole Porter entitled *DuBarry Was a Lady* (1939), where it had been sung by a man (Charles Walters, who later directed *High Society*) and a woman (Betty Grable) (Citron 1992, p. 183). The performance in *High Society* pairs Bing Crosby with Frank Sinatra in a sort of inebriated comedic *pas de deux*—a drunken matching of verbal wits, musical sophistication, and physical agility.

The duet takes place in the elegant library at Uncle Willie's mansion while everybody else is dancing to the orchestra and enjoying a prenuptial party outside. Dexter/Bing sits quietly in a chair, casually thumbing through a magazine, *Touring Topics*. Mike/Frank shows up in search of some more of the champagne that he has earlier enjoyed while singing "You're Sensational" to Tracy/Grace. Sinatra comments that champagne is the "great leveler" and that it will make Crosby his "equal"—to which Bing replies, with deep irony, that he wouldn't say *that*. And *that*, ladies and gentleman, that social and musical challenge is exactly the point of this piece, precisely what this scene is all about. There follows an amazing cinemusical encounter—an exuberant exercise in voice-to-voice combat—a memorably significant stylistic sparring contest that no student of jazz in film should neglect.

It makes sense to contemplate the contextual setting for this historic pairing between Bing Crosby and Frank Sinatra. As every biographer of Frank Sinatra has pointed out, the younger singer considered Bing Crosby his "idol" (Frank 1978, p. 19; Friedwald 1995, p. 92; Pleasants 1974, p. 192; Rockwell 1984, p. 31): "Sometime in 1931 or 1932, Sinatra . . . made up his mind that he was going to be the next Bing Crosby (Friedwald 1995, p. 62). In this spirit, Sinatra regarded Crosby as "the father of his career" (Friedwald 1995, p. 150) or more fully, in Frank's own words, "the father of my career . . . the idol of my youth . . . and the dear, dear friend of my maturity" (quoted by Sinatra 1985, p. 133). When a boy, to the great consternation of his mother Dolly, Frank kept a picture of Bing on his wall at home (Frank 1978, p. 19; Pleasants 1974, p. 192; Talese 1966, p. 114). The youthful Sinatra dressed like Crosby (Frank 1978, p. 19). And early photographs show young Frank with his hair parted like Bing, clutching a very Crosby-like pipe in his hand (Frank 1978, p. 21; Rockwell 1984, p. 21).

More important musically, Frank studied Bing's recordings, emulated his style, and learned valuable lessons from Crosby's relaxed manner and from the intimacy of his technique with the microphone (Friedwald 1995, pp. 21, 64; Rockwell 1984, p. 51). Thus, commentators regard Sinatra as Crosby's "greatest disciple" (Friedwald 1995, p. 25). However, where Bing's approach stemmed from that of traditional New Orleans or Dixieland jazz—that is, a two-beat syncopated rhythm—Frank leaned more toward the smoother four-four sound of the swing-oriented dance bands. By eliminating the syncope, Sinatra forged a new style of singing (Friedwald 1990, p. 313). Indeed, Friedwald (1990) opines that "Sinatra is not a good blues singer" and that "when he trie[s] his hand at Dixieland jazz . . . he just can't make his voice fit into that old-time two-beat pattern" (p. 316). In this connection, it seems almost bizarre to acknowledge the fact that Frank could not have sung "Now You Has Jazz" with anything like the definitive authority and effortless aplomb that Bing bestowed on it. Strange, but true, because—according to Friedwald (1995)

> Sinatra . . . differs primarily from Crosby in that he favors the smooth, even lines of dance music from the mid-1930s, as opposed to the choppier, syncopated sound that Crosby grew up in and forever kept to some degree in his work.
>
> (Friedwald 1995, p. 146)

Moreover, Frank tended purposely to push Bing's approach in a rather different direction—namely, toward the *bel canto* manner for which he is justly famous and in which "Sinatra developed a hybrid style that represented a modification of the crooner's intimacy in the direction of more forthright, innately Italian lyricism—a folkish tunefulness . . . that would separate himself from Crosby" (Rockwell 1984, p. 62).

In his career, Sinatra took Crosby's advice that a pop singer should work with many different arrangers (Friedwald 1995, p. 371). Also, the two singers shared a direct connection with the great songwriter Jimmy Van Heusen—musical composer of innumerable pop-standard masterpieces such as "All the Way," "Aren't You Glad You're You," "But Beautiful," "Call

Me Irresponsible," "Darn That Dream," "Deep in a Dream," "Going My Way," "Here's That Rainy Day," "High Hopes," "How Are You Fixed For Love?," "I Could Have Told You," "I'll Only Miss Her When I Think of Her," "I Thought About You," "Imagination," "It Could Happen To You," "It's Always You," "Like Someone In Love," "Love and Marriage," "Moonlight Becomes You," "My Kind of Town," "Nancy," "Oh, You Crazy Moon," "Only the Lonely," "Personality," "Pocketful of Miracles," "Polka Dots and Moonbeams," "September of My Years," "Swinging on a Star," and "The Second Time Around," just to name a few. Specifically, Crosby introduced many of the classic songs that Van Heusen wrote with the lyricist Johnny Burke, as did Sinatra (Giddins 2001, p. 589); later, Frank worked extensively with songs featuring music by Van Heusen and words by Sammy Cahn (Friedwald 1995, p. 27). Indeed, Jimmy Van Heusen was "probably Sinatra's closest friend" (Friedwald 1995, p. 88). Further, besides the fact that they both sang a lot of Van Heusen songs, Sinatra borrowed many other tunes from the Crosby repertoire. For example, Frank's album *Moonlight Sinatra* (1966) is considered something of a tribute to Bing in that it contains several tunes associated with Crosby—"Moonlight Becomes You," "I Wished on the Moon," "The Moon Got in My Eyes," "The Moon Was Yellow," and "Reaching for the Moon" (Friedwald 1995, p. 263).

It is even possible that Frank's pet phrase "ring-a-ding-ding"—first documented, according to Friedwald (1995, pp. 231, 373), in the song "I Won't Dance" on the 1957 album *A Swingin' Affair*—was a verbal invention that Sinatra borrowed from Crosby. Specifically, more than Frank and much earlier, Bing was well known for coining charmingly idiosyncratic linguistic expressions such as "a dinger (a honey)" or "a whingdinger (superlative)" (Giddins 2001, p. 404). Crosby uses the expression "ring-ding-ding-a-linging" to replace "swinging" in his performance of "Now You Has Jazz" on a live television show (described later) that was broadcast in 1957 and on which Sinatra also appeared (Shaw 1968, p. 232). The question of who copped the phrase from whom therefore remains somewhat in doubt. Petkov and Mustazza (ed. 1995) believe it was "one of the many hipsterisms the singer [Sinatra] has coined over the years" (p. 87). But I'm not so sure. In the TV special, it seems to emanate so naturally from Crosby when, as if spontaneously, he unexpectedly rhymes "winging" with "ring-ding-ding-a-linging." At a minimum, it seems fair to say that Sinatra himself never achieved such a supremely cool use of his slightly modified pet phrase.

When Sinatra's career began to take off in the early 1940s, Crosby remained "the big star of that time" (Friedwald 1995, p. 92) or, in marketing terms, "the industry leader" (p. 132)—dominating the pop charts, especially with the adult population, and racking up more top-selling hits than any other singer in history. In those days, Frank(ie) appealed more to teenagers, Bing more to mature listeners (Friedwald 1995, p. 125): "Crosby appealed to an adult crowd; Frankie got the kids" (Rockwell 1984, p. 82).

Though Bing Crosby and Frank Sinatra had first met in 1943 (Rockwell 1984, p. 32) and would again work together many times on various projects during the years following "Well, Did You Evah?" (Friedwald 1995; Rockwell 1984), their collaboration in *High Society* (1956) is their first joint appearance on film and records. Reviewing their respective positions at this moment in time, it seems fair to suggest that Crosby's career had peaked circa 1950 and, at the time of *High Society*, had embarked on a long downhill trajectory. Meanwhile, Sinatra's fortunes had hit bottom in the early 1950s, had begun to rebound with his Oscar-winning performance as Maggio in *From Here to Eternity* (1953), and had gained even greater upward momentum with the appearance of such popular record albums for Capitol as *Swing Easy* (1953), *Songs for Young Lovers* (1954), and *In the Wee Small Hours of the Morning* (1955). According to Mel Tormé (1994), "Bing . . . was . . . the paramount singer among all the other singers of his time, and he held that exalted position for a long time, until Sinatra came along and unseated him" (p. 184). Thus, at the time of their duet on "Well, Did You Evah" in 1956, Bing was something of an incipient *ringard*, Frank something of an emerging *enfant terrible*. In this spirit, Nancy Sinatra (1985) reports that "On the set of *High Society*, Frank and Bing were nicknamed 'Dexedrine' and 'Nembutal'": "'Dexedrine' because of Pop's high energy level, and 'Nembutal' because of Bing's laid-back approach" (p. 322; see also Rockwell 1984, p. 121). Indeed, Sinatra had begun to usurp some of the market previously dominated by Crosby (Giddins 2001, pp. 8, 297, 365). In this connection, fully recognizing Sinatra's supreme excellence as a songster, Bing quipped: "A talent like that comes along once in a lifetime. . . . Why in *my* lifetime"? (quoted by Sinatra 1985, p. 133; see also Brennan 1990, ed. 1995, p. 213).

Nonetheless, both performers retained tremendous followings among music and movie fans. And Sinatra's daughter Nancy points out that "there was a tangible feeling of affection and mutual respect in all their scenes," concluding that "The Bing–Frank duet 'Well, Did You Evah?' was the highlight of the movie" (Sinatra 1985, p. 322). Frank (1978) agrees that Crosby and Sinatra "were both first-rate in their duet on 'Well, Did You Evah'" (p. 102).

Thus, viewed in context, this ambi-diegetic duet is charged with all sorts of extra-cinemusical associations and presents something like an Historic Battle of the Baritones. In this, the two singing warriors offer characteristic witticisms—Mike/Frank referring to Dexter/Bing as a "forgotten man"; Dexter/Bing serving Mike/Frank some champagne, calling it "a bit of the bubbly," and later telling him not to eat his glass; Mike/Frank praising the "French Champagne" and Dexter/Bing correcting him by pointing out that it is "domestic"; Dexter/Bing joking about poor Blanche being run down by an avalanche; Mike/Frank cracking wise about Mimsie Starr getting "pinched" (triple meaning) in the "Assss-tor Bar." Dexter/Bing calls a dress a "frock"; Mike/Frank calls a lady a "broad." Describing a drunk, Bing says "sauced"; Frank says "stoned." They compare singing styles—Sinatra objecting that he and his generation don't "dig" Crosby's kind of "croonin'"; Bing retorting that Frank must be one of those "newer fellas." Musically, they pair their voices flawlessly in an intricately arranged vocal passage—a little two-part harmony here, some tricky counterpoint there. In these passages, the Crosby and Sinatra voices—which ordinarily could be characterized as a low resonant baritone and a high clear baritone, respectively—cross over in a couple of places, with Bing singing the higher notes and Frank covering the lower range. Symbolically, this musical role-reversal tends to put Dexter/Bing "on top" of Mike/Frank, giving Bing the appearance of having a wider vocal range. Near the end, the smile that the two give each other on "collide with Mars" speaks volumes concerning their mutual admiration. And, as they exit the library where the scene has occurred, Crosby and Sinatra (who, after all, has danced with Gene Kelly in *On the Town* [1949]) execute an impressive flourish of dance steps that places them on an equal terpsichorean footing. Indeed, with regard to the old soft shoe, the shuffle step, and some samba rhythms, Dexter/Bing appears—if anything—even more adept than does Mike/Frank. Overall, as judged by Corliss (2001)—note carefully—"Crosby . . . beats Sinatra in their duet-duel 'Well, Did You Evah'." No wonder Bing later proclaimed his victorious duet with Frank as "his favorite scene from any of his movies" (Giddins 2001, p. 513). (Inexplicably, Yanow [2004]—forever under the wayward sway of his own unpredictable tastes—regards the Crosby–Sinatra duet as "a bit of a disappointment" [p. 169].)

As the vocalizing combatants sing, it *is* a "swell party." And, by the end of this priceless musical encounter, this dueling duet, Crosby and Sinatra are positioned—age-based (in)credulity notwithstanding—as imaginatively appropriate rivals on a now-level amorous playing field. Dexter/Bing's image is fully rehabilitated. His ultimate romantic triumph in winning the hand of Tracy/Grace over Mike/Frank (who must, in the last analysis, settle for Liz/Celeste as his final partner) has become, if not inevitable, at least highly plausible.

### The Missing Duet: Louis and Frank

You might be wondering why—for the sake of symmetry—*High Society* did not also include a rousing duet by Louis Armstrong and Frank Sinatra. The answer appears, quite vividly, on the aforementioned currently circulating videotape of an old television special—originally aired on October 13, 1957 under the sponsorship of (you guessed it) the 1958 Edsel—featuring Bing Crosby, Frank Sinatra, Louis Armstrong, and Rosemary Clooney (Shaw 1968, p. 232). This show offers a priceless slice of mid-1950s nostalgia with fast-stepping dancers doing the jitterbug and the cha-cha, dreamy eyed co-eds swooning to "Sweetheart of Sigma Chi," Bing's son Lindsay bravely trying to sound like his father, and a Frank-Rosie-Bing trio wading through an endless medley of pointlessly strung-together chestnuts.

Prior to a brief recap of "True Love" (still recognizably hit material during the year following the release of the movie), Crosby and Armstrong plus his All-Stars do a complete recreation of "Now You Has Jazz." Looser than the film version and with less tricky camera work, this rendition nonetheless produces a similar effect. Bing sings, Louis swings, and the band generates a marvelous feeling of relaxed spontaneity. At one point, in his impression of utter relaxation, Bing does a sort of dance shuffle that—I swear—vividly anticipates the "moon walk." As in the movie, the years seem to melt away while these two musicians clown their way through a masterfully comfortable performance.

But then, about 40 minutes into the show, Sinatra shows up with Armstrong on a bare stage to perform a duet on "Birth of the Blues." Written in 1926 by De Sylva-Brown-and-Henderson and recorded by Bing Crosby with Jack Teagarden for Decca in 1941, this song addresses a theme very similar to that which motivates "Now You Has Jazz"—namely, a list of the ingredients that go into making a great jazz performance or, in this case, a great blues rendition—"weird melodies," "wail," "new note," "blue note," . . . and . . . you know the drill. Why they didn't let Bing demonstrate his expertise with this material on the Edsel show makes about as much sense as why they thought that anybody would buy an Edsel.

At any rate, there they stand—Sinatra and Armstrong, all alone in the spotlight—singing a big-band arrangement of this swinging anthem, with Frank puffing away on a Chesterfield, Louis hamming it up all over the place, and Frank beaming his graciously undisguised approval. But wait. The student has obviously learned from the master because here, in a sense, Sinatra out-Crosbies Crosby. Bing's studied relaxation becomes Frank's smoke-blowing nonchalance. Bing's rapport with Louis becomes Frank's open-mouthed admiration. Bing's choppy Dixieland rhythm becomes Frank's classic big-band swing. Bing's light-hearted musicality becomes Frank's high-polished musicianship.

And, once again, that Satchmo-inspired rejuvenating magic starts to happen. Sinatra and Armstrong seem caught in a time warp, with the clock spinning backwards and with the two artists growing younger and younger as the retrograde seconds tick by. At the end of this riveting performance—in what I believe is the first televised occasion on which I've seen this gesture captured for the public record—Louis and Frank joyfully give each other "some skin" in lieu of a handshake.

Obviously, nothing like this could possibly have appeared ambi-diegetically in *High Society* without ruining the carefully devised structure of the film. If Sinatra had been allowed to drink from Armstrong's cinemusical Fountain of Youth, he would have maintained his amorous edge over Crosby. The playing field would have tipped dramatically in Mike/Frank's favor, and Dexter/Bing would have slid, slipped, and skidded back toward his own end zone.

## CODA

And so, to return to our main theme, the ambi-diegetic music in *High Society*—specifically, two love ballads and three central duets capped by "Now You Has Jazz" as the pivotal cinemusical moment (but omitting the fourth potentially ruinous duet that I have just imagined and dismissed)—has done all the work. Dexter/Bing's image has been threatened by "True Love"; fleshed out by "I Love You, Samantha"; further questioned by "You're Sensational"; refurbished by "Now You Has Jazz"; and vindicated by "Well, Did You Evah?" After this, Tracy/Grace is metaphorically washed in the cleansing waters of the guest-house swimming pool. Mike/Frank magnanimously resists the adulterous temptations of his hostess' drunken advances and settles for a future with his comical sidekick Liz/Celeste (with whom he has earlier sung his own unintentionally prescient ambi-diegetic duet on the delightful "Who Wants to Be a Millionaire?"). And a well-rested, reinvigorated Dexter/Bing awaits the new morn to pick up the pieces and remarry the woman of his dreams, for whom he has felt mawkish but nonetheless sincere "True Love" ever since the good old days when they used to go sailing together on his yacht—so very big; so very white; so very expensive; and so very, very yare. In the end, nothing wins a fair maiden divorcée's hand like a receding hairline, a rejuvenated image, and a whole lot of money. Go, Bing. Or is that Bingo? Clearly, there is nothing left for Grace Kelly (after what turned out to be her last acting appearance) but to abdicate her Hollywood throne in favor of her new regal role as a royal housewife in Monaco.

## EPILOGUE

In December/January of 1956/1957—shortly after *High Society*'s release, when I was 13 years old—my Mom and Dad took me to California to attend my half-sister's wedding. While in Los Angeles, we stopped by the MGM Studios and dropped in for a visit at the office of Johnny Green, my father's old classmate and friend from college. Johnny Green served as musical director for countless MGM movies, receiving Academy Award nominations for 14 and winning Oscars for *Easter Parade* (1948), *American in Paris* (1951), *West Side Story* (1961), and *Oliver!* (1968). His work on *High Society* was nominated in 1956/1957 but lost to *The King and I*.

Johnny Green also composed the music for, among other pop-jazz standards, "Body and Soul," "Coquette," "I Cover the Waterfront," and "Out of Nowhere." The former—though Bing Crosby never sang it on records—is "one of the most recorded songs of all time" (Giddins 2001, p. 244). The latter served as the vehicle for the first top-selling hit record released under Crosby's own name on Brunswick in 1931 (Giddins 2001, p. 244).

At the MGM Studios in 1957, Mr. Green—who must have just finished work on *High Society* at about this time, though I can't recall his mentioning it—took us for lunch in the company commissary. While we were eating, he pointed to a man standing at a nearby table and said, "Oh, there's Bing Crosby."

I was awestruck. But I was also astonished. Crosby was sporting some ordinary trousers and one of those short zippered jackets that old guys wear when they play golf. And Bing was just a shrimp. Just a small-sized little runt of a man. Without his elevator shoes and toupee, I now know, Crosby stood about five feet and seven inches tall (Giddins 2001, p. 317). Hmn. I guess it was the movies and all those glorious ambi-diegetic cinemusical duets that made him seem like such an immense giant.


## REPRISE

After writing the preceding paragraphs—while working on the umpteenth draft of the essay in this chapter—I took a little break to get some exercise. The particular ordeal in question—a dreaded part of my daily regimen—involves stepping up and down on a piano bench for an extended period of time. It sounds easy; but, pretty soon, it goes beyond tedium and starts to hurt.

To relieve the boredom and distract myself from the pain as much as possible, I usually watch television while climbing to nowhere, flipping channels in a frantic effort to draw my attention away from all the physical torture. On this particular occasion, I discovered that the Black Educational Television (BET) jazz channel was showing a documentary on the life of Louis Armstrong. And before I could say "ring-ding-ding-a-linging," there were Louis and . . . you guessed it . . . Bing Crosby on the TV screen in a replay of their aforementioned performance on the old Edsel show from 1957.

It is obvious to me, Dear Reader, that God Himself planned this little surprise. He wanted us to pay careful attention to the ways in which the ambi-diegetic Crosby–Armstrong version of "Now You Has Jazz" functions as a key design element in a great motion picture. He wanted us to recall how this brilliant duet shapes our cinemusical experience. He wanted us to remember how this piece serves definitively as a pivotal moment of consumption symbolism that structures the meaning of the film. In short, He wanted to remind us how ambi-diegetic film music—as a product-design and -placement strategy with resonantly significant overtones—reaches its epitome of excellence via the Crosby duets in *High Society*.

# 3 The Cinemusical Role of "My Funny Valentine" in *The Fabulous Baker Boys* (1989) and *The Talented Mr. Ripley* (1999)

## INTRODUCTION

The present chapter continues our focus on film music in general and on cinematic jazz in particular as an element of motion-picture design that advances the dramatic development of a movie's characterizations, plot, themes, and other meanings. Recall that we have defined *ambi-diegetic film music* as a type that occurs when music produced *on-screen* plays a role in a film's *dramatic development* by fleshing out a character, advancing the plot, reflecting a key theme, or representing some other significant meaning (Chapter 1). As earlier, this focus on *ambi-diegesis* results from examining a type of film music that is produced *inside* the film's stream of events in the manner traditionally associated with *diegetic music* but that contributes to the film's *significant meanings* in the manner traditionally associated with *nondiegetic music*. In the present chapter, we shall have occasion to examine *both* nondiegetic *and* ambi-diegetic aspects of cinemusical design.

The primary illustrations pursued here involve cinemusical performances in two fairly recent motion pictures—first, by Michelle Pfeiffer in *The Fabulous Baker Boys* (1989); second, by Matt Damon in *The Talented Mr. Ripley* (1999). In particular, beyond the various ambi-diegetic and non-diegetic cinemusical material discussed in what follows, the song "My Funny Valentine" plays key roles in both films—serving to mirror the character of Pfeiffer as a steamy, sultry, seductively sexy saloon singer and, by contrast, to develop the image of Damon as a self-absorbed, sociopathic, sexually stymied scoundrel.

Such contrasting deployments of one song depend on various relevant associations and identifications that we bring to each film from our previous experience with the relevant context and music involved. These include the tradition of screen actors performing in their own true voices (as opposed to lip-synching the dubbed singing of others). Beyond that, the song "My Funny Valentine" carries connotations associated with its long history of appearances in a wide variety of entertainment venues—the original Rodgers-and-Hart show *Babes In Arms* (1937); duty as a signature piece for certain jazz luminaries (Gerry Mulligan, Miles Davis, and—especially—Chet Baker); an aura-shaping trademark of various pop icons (Ella Fitzgerald,

Sarah Vaughan, and—especially—Frank Sinatra); performances on records by a host of artists ranging from Kenny Rogers to Miranda Sex Garden (with over 600 such versions currently available on CD); and inclusion in a variety of films such as *Gentlemen Marry Brunettes* (1955), *Sharky's Machine* (1981), *Waiting to Exhale* (1995), and—especially—*Pal Joey* (1957). Clearly, "My Funny Valentine" comes to its recent performances by Pfeiffer and Damon with a great deal of imaginative baggage attached, where such identifications inform our experience of hearing Michelle Pfeiffer (non-diegetically) and watching Matt Damon (ambi-diegetically) sing the song in *The Fabulous Baker Boys* (1989) and *The Talented Mr. Ripley* (1999).

Specifically, with accompaniment provided by Dave Grusin dubbing the piano parts for Jeff Bridges, Michelle Pfeiffer draws on the tradition of "My Funny Valentine" as a torch song—as previously lip-synched by Kim Novak in *Pal Joey* (1957), where Kim plays the chorus girl with a heart of gold competing with Rita Hayworth for the affections of . . . none other than . . . Frank Sinatra (whose background associations with the song also come into play). This Novak-related saloon-singer nexus rises to the fore in the performance by Michelle, whose own-voice singing of "Valentine" conveys an assertive, soft, extroverted, self-confident, feminine image (complemented by the role played by Jeff Bridges as an aspiring jazz pianist).

Meanwhile, drawing on another side of the "Valentine" iconography, Matt Damon does his best to emulate the anguished singing style of Chet Baker, whose vulnerable, fragile, introverted, self-destructive, androgynous vocal qualities transfer to the character played by Damon and prove proleptic of the developments in that character still to come in subsequent portions of the film.

In sum, via a structurally-anchored and historically-rooted account, this chapter explores the meanings in two recent cinemusical performances of "My Funny Valentine"—drawing out differences between the song stylings of Michelle Pfeiffer and Matt Damon, recalling Novak-plus-Sinatra and Chet Baker—as keys to the essence of these cinemusical experiences in which, in one way or another, every day is Valentine's Day.

## ANTECEDENT ASSOCIATIONS AND IDENTIFICATIONS

To repeat, in examining the cinemusical performances by Michelle Pfeiffer in *The Fabulous Baker Boys* (1989, directed by Steve Kloves with music by Dave Grusin) and by Matt Damon in *The Talented Mr. Ripley* (1999, directed by Anthony Minghella with music by Gabriel Yared), I shall focus special attention on the role in both films played by Rodgers-and-Hart's "My Funny Valentine" (1937) in mirroring the image of Susie Diamond as a steamy, sultry, seductively sexy saloon singer and, by contrast, in developing the character of Tom Ripley as a self-absorbed, sociopathic, sexually stymied scoundrel. Such contrasting uses of a song for purposes of characterization in the manner explored here depend on a variety of relevant

associations and identifications that we bring to each scene from our previous experience of the music involved and its motivating context. These
include aspects of acting tradition; past appearances of the musical piece in
various entertainment venues in general or prior cinemusical uses of the
material in particular; and associations, identifications, or other connections
with certain iconic performers from earlier times.

## Acting Tradition

Face it: Many or most actors and actresses cannot carry a tune, much less
sing with distinction. Thus, dubbing in the voices of accomplished singers is
an age-old practice that has made Hollywood institutions out of numerous
talented-but-invisible performers. Mel Tormé (1994) is particularly
resourceful in providing a list of such stand-in singers (pp. 185-188). Sticking
just with the females, they include: India Adams, Adele Addison, Marion
Doenges, Dorothy Ellers, Anita Ellis, Trudy Ewen, Pat Friday, Anita
Gordon, Jo Ann Greer, Louanne Hogan, Helen Kane, Lisa Kirk, Martha
Mears, Marni Nixon, Carol Richards, Joan Small, Trudy Stevens, Carol
Stewart, Jeri Sullivan, Sally Sweetland, Betty Wand, Annette Warren, Eileen
Wilson, and Nan Wynn—most of them not exactly household names—
which, of course, is exactly the point. They did their jobs to perfection by
remaining completely anonymous.

Yet some movie stars—including Michelle Pfeiffer in *The Fabulous Baker
Boys* and Matt Damon in *The Talented Mr. Ripley*—nonetheless dig deep
within their wells of creativity and give their singing opportunities the old
college try. This tradition of screen actors performing in their own true
voices has met with varying degrees of success ranging from exalted triumph
(Meryl Streep in *Postcards from the Edge* [1990] or Jeff Bridges in *Crazy
Heart* [2009]) to shaky mediocrity (Marilyn Monroe in *Gentlemen Prefer
Blondes* [1953]) to abysmal failure (Marlon Brando in *Guys and Dolls*
[1955]). In the cases of primary interest here, Pfeiffer establishes her credentials as a viable real-life torch singer with considerable dramatic credibility,
while Damon manages a commendably sincere evocation of an enigmatically
effete but undeniably compelling vocal stylist.

## History of the Song's Past Appearances

Beyond these issues of thespian authenticity, the song "My Funny Valentine"
carries connotations associated with its long history of appearances in a
wide variety of entertainment venues. Written in 1937 by Richard Rodgers
and Lorenz Hart for their Broadway show entitled *Babes In Arms* (but
inexplicably omitted from the 1939 screen version starring Mickey Rooney
and Judy Garland), the song reappeared to widespread attention in the revival
of *Babes in Arms* on Broadway in 1999. Originally, "My Funny Valentine"
limned the foibles of a slightly "dopey" individual named Valentine or Val
(Friedwald 2002, p. 354; Hyland 1995, p. 238). In his definitive biography

on *Lorenz Hart: A Poet on Broadway*, Nolan (1994) calls the song "a lament to a lame-duck February 14 lover" but notes that it was "so clearly destined for success [that] the name of one of the characters in the show was changed to match it" (p. 217). Meanwhile, "My Funny Valentine" has since come to serve as a generic bittersweet love call to anyone seen as an admittedly less-than-perfect but nonetheless suitable target for one's romantic affections.

In his classic work on *American Popular Song*, Alec Wilder (1972) reports on the iconic stature of "My Funny Valentine" as a favorite late-night cocktail-lounge torch song—one so popular with night-club singers that "the owner of a formerly famous East Side New York club inserted in all contracts with vocalists a clause which stated that they were forbidden to sing it" (p. 205). Here, the sly Wilder (1972) manages to imply that this benighted club owner mismanaged a "formerly famous" enterprise that has subsequently failed because of its refusal to give the people what they want—namely, "My Funny Valentine." He then proceeds to devote a full page and a half to a note-by-note dissection of the piece, ending on the resoundingly affirmative proclamation that "This is as finely distilled a theater song as I have ever heard" (p. 207).

Meanwhile, in his comprehensive work on *The Poets of Tin Pan Alley: A History of America's Great Lyricists*, Furia (1992) finds the song's lyrics to be a masterpiece of "unobtrusive" rhyming," "skewed flattery," "dispropor-tions," and "imbalance" in the service of dispensing "affectionately mock-ing" compliments to a "slightly dopey" character with a less-than-Greek figure and a somewhat-weak mouth (p. 119). Here, Furia evokes a dialectic tension between thesis and antithesis that yields to a resolving synthesis in the song's concluding lines (cf. Holbrook 1997a, 2003b).

More recently—in his *Biography of Twelve . . . Popular Songs*—Friedwald (2002) singles out "My Funny Valentine" as one of the 12 most-luminous masterpieces: "If there ever was an American *lied*, or art song, this is it" (p. 371). Friedwald especially succeeds in showing how this song achieves the ideal of "matching text to music" (p. 358) in such a way that—to paraphrase Alexander Pope—the sound convincingly echoes the sense. In this connection, three highlights appear particularly striking. First—throughout the song—"the major/minor nature of the music" (shifting twice between C minor and Eb major) brilliantly mirrors "the happy/sad nature of the lyric" (p. 360). Second—in the bridge, as the speaker rattles off a list of Valentine's defi-ciencies (less-than-statuesque figure, not too bright)—we arrive at the word "open" (referring to Valentine's weak mouth), accompanied by a startling leap in the melodic line that (taking only minor liberties with the actual musical notation), Friedwald describes as follows: "When we go from the high D down a whole octave to the middle D, the jump occurs on the word 'open,' and it goes without saying that this is a very 'open' interval indeed" (pp. 358). Third—even more powerfully, as the song reaches its climax—the speaker invites Valentine to "stay," as illustrated by a high note that lingers poignantly for a full two measures on a high E-flat, encouraging a musical gesture that Friedwald describes as "holding an especially long fermata to dramatically emphasize the second 'stay'" (p. 362). Elsewhere, Friedwald seems to slip a bit in his poetic and musical acumen. For example, he asks, "who but Hart would have come up with a musical comedy love song in which the declaration of love is conveyed as a list of the other person's faults?" Here, Friedwald almost willfully ignores the obvious answer—namely, Shakespeare in his Sonnet #130 on a very similar theme: "My Mistress' Eyes Are Nothing Like the Sun," which contains the delicious lines "And in some perfumes is there more delight / Than in the breath that from my mistress reeks." Then Friedwald announces that the second "stay" on a high E-flat is "backed by a *minor* chord" (p. 361)—namely, C minor—an observation that (though literally true) neglects how this minor chord immediately resolves (through the circle of fifths—Cm7, F7, B♭m7, E♭7) to a great big, fat, affirmative A♭ major and, from there (Gm7, C7, Fm7, B♭7), to E♭ major.

On a personal note, I cannot resist adding that, in 1957 at the tender age of 13 years, I once had the thrill of visiting a small smoke-filled restaurant-row supper club on La Cienega Boulevard in Los Angeles with my parents to hear the great Matt Dennis singing some of his own marvelous songs to his own very hip piano accompaniments—songs, mostly with lyrics by Tom Adair, like "Will You Still Be Mine," "Let's Get Away From It All," "Everything Happens To Me," "The Night We Called It a Day," "Violets For Your Furs," and (with Earl Brent) "Angel Eyes." At one point, Dennis asked if anyone had a request. With the unrepentant innocence of a 13-year-old, I stupidly spoke up and asked for a couple of my ill-considered favorites, to which Matt sadly shook his head: "No, I don't do that one. No, sorry, not that one either." Finally, feeling totally out-of-it, I had an inspiration: "My Funny Valentine." The great songwriter Matt Dennis smiled and nodded: "Now, *that's* more down my alley." He then played and sang his brilliant version of the tune, which can still be heard today on an album called *Play Melancholy Baby* (BMG Victor R25J-1008), originally recorded for RCA in . . . believe it or not . . . 1956. (For those intrepid record collectors who would like to recreate the magic of Matt Dennis singing and playing his own songs live in the mid-1950s, just as I heard them on La Cienega's restaurant row, a reissued import version of his *Plays & Sings* album on Kapp is available from amazon.com for a mere $25.95.)

While listening to the remarkably sensitive, finely tuned lyrics to "My Funny Valentine," we might gain some further perspective on the meanings packed into its poetry by contemplating the poignantly sad nature of the incredibly gifted man who wrote them—Lorenz (aka Larry) Hart, the man whom no less an authority than writer/director Joshua Logan described as "one of the great milestone geniuses in the history of our American musical theatre":

> He had color, a tone, a sort of bitter beauty that no one else had or ever will have, the most sensitive, the most touching, almost Chaplinesque ability to get laughs and make you cry at the very same time.
>
> (quoted by Nolan 1994, p. 316)

Larry Hart happened to be a five-foot, homosexual, alcoholic, cigar-smoking, chubby, bald-headed, misshapen, disheveled, mirror-avoiding dwarf in a less-than-liberated age when those kinds of nonconformity did not go unpunished. In the movie reel of your mind, imagine Danny DeVito playing a manic-depressive gay tobacco-beclouded lush before the days of political correctness—no doubt, the potential premise for a sure-fire Hollywood smash-hit biopic—and you've got the picture. Nolan (1994) tells the story that, when asked by a magazine reporter about his love life shortly after completing *Babes in Arms*, the great lyricist—whom everybody seemed to like enormously—replied, "I haven't any," and added, "Nobody would want *me*" (p. 219). Whether true or—more probably, judging from the constant whirl of his social life—not true, this deprecatory self-assessment seems painfully unfortunate coming from one of the most gifted wordsmiths of our time. Nolan (1994) finds it "strange" and "sad" to see

> one of the most successful writers on Broadway, poised this very moment on the brink of creating the most remarkable run of shows and songs ever produced by a single songwriting team, wealthy, famous, a man with a thousand friends, advertising to the world at large [that] he considers himself totally undesirable.
>
> (Nolan 1994, p. 219)

Tormented by such demons and a prisoner of his own despondent alcoholism, Larry Hart—arguably the greatest lyricist who has ever lived—died, officially of pneumonia but basically of self-neglect, before the end of seven more years at the age of 48. The cruelest blow came when Richard Rodgers—presumably, with regrets—decided to begin working with Oscar Hammerstein on what turned out to be *Oklahoma!*, a decision to which Hart gave his blessings with the dismally self-annihilating words, "Sure . . . you ought to get Hammerstein as your collaborator. I don't know why you've put up with me all these years" (Nolan 1994, p. 299). Joshua Logan's description of *Oklahoma!*'s opening night—with Hart sitting in a box and "applauding, howling with laughter, yelling bravos"—is enough to tear your heart out: "Larry . . . had taken his mother and he had to sit there with her, this sensitive, sensitive little man, seeing a revolutionary development in the theatre, brought about by his partner but without his own participation" (quoted by Nolan 1994, p. 304). Most disturbingly—perhaps recalling his shattered reaction to a tepid review of *Pal Joey* by Brooks Atkinson for the *New York Times* in 1940 (Nolan 1994, p. 281) and not surviving long enough to witness Atkinson's apologetic about-face when the show was triumphantly revived on Broadway in 1952 (Nolan 1994, p. 282)—Lorenz Hart's last words as he lay dying in the cold, rainy November of 1943 were, "What have I lived for?" (Nolan 1994, p. 312). Clearly, the challenge to a singer or other musician performing a Rodgers-and-Hart ballad in general or tackling "My Funny Valentine" in particular is to capture the essence of the tragedy that lurks below its wry surface.

Over the years—despite the fact that, as expressed in "I Like to Recognize the Tune," both Rodgers and Hart disliked jazzy treatments of their songs (Nolan 1994, p. 240)—"My Funny Valentine" has helped to shape the aura of various musically sophisticated pop icons (Ella Fitzgerald, Sarah Vaughan, and—especially—Frank Sinatra) and has done duty as a signature piece for various luminary jazz artists (Gerry Mulligan, Art Farmer, Jim Hall, Bill Evans, Miles Davis, and—especially—Chet Baker in both instrumental and vocal versions). Indeed, on records, the piece has been performed by a staggeringly diverse spectrum of performers ranging from Kenny Rogers to Jerry Garcia, from André Previn to Liberace, from Ethel Merman to Barbra Streisand, from Tony Bennett to Elvis Costello, from Linda Ronstadt to Nico, and from Van Morrison to Miranda Sex Garden (Holbrook, Lacher, and LaTour 2006; see also Friedwald 2002, pp. 349–373.) Over 600 such versions currently exist on compact disc (not even counting the innumerable 78-, 45-, and 33-rpm recordings that have become long-since out-of-print collector's items).

In addition to its prominence in strictly musical circles, "My Funny Valentine" has appeared in a variety of films. In *Gentlemen Marry Brunettes* (1955), starring Jane Russell, it was performed by Alan Young and Jeanne Crain in a voice supplied by Anita Ellis. As part of a voluptuously come-hither dance number in *Pal Joey* (1957), Kim Novak lip-synched the song to real-life singing by Trudi Ewen. *Sharky's Machine* (1981) used a version sung in the background by the inimitable Julie London. And *Waiting to Exhale* (1995) included a stylistically-updated, soul-inflected, disco-flavored rendition by Chaka Khan.

## Associations and Identifications with Earlier Iconic Performers

Central to the fundamental structure of the present essay, we must further emphasize three major musical connections that appear especially salient to the identifications associated with "My Funny Valentine." As already implied, these involve strong imaginative links of this song with the careers and personalities of three key performers—namely, those of (1) Frank Sinatra, as pushed in two different directions by (2) Kim Novak and by (3) Chet Baker.

### (1) Frank Sinatra

In reviewing the talents and accomplishments of Frank Sinatra with respect to American popular music in general and his encounters with a piece such as "My Funny Valentine" in particular, we find that Sinatra and "My Funny Valentine" are indelibly connected in the minds of music fans everywhere. And that the connotations of one are inextricably linked to those of the other.

To put it mildly—via his universally familiar "persona," his "image," his "legend"—Frank Sinatra has assumed "the iconic character of an American cultural institution" (Petkov and Mustazza ed. 1995, p. 156). Our widely shared associations and identifications with the Sinatra style and myth have developed collectively during the 60-year span of his career covering more than the last half of the Twentieth Century. Many variegated and often conflicting components of the Sinatra image have emerged over the years— family man, womanizer, barroom brawler, media hater, political campaigner, Democrat for Kennedy, Republican for Reagan, buddy of Peter Lawford, pal of Spiro Agnew, quasi-mobster, diplomat, movie actor, Las Vegas carouser, Oscar winner, entertainment bonanza, Atlantic City marketing tool, extraordinarily loyal and generous friend, astute businessman, Head of The Clan, Grammy-award honoree, practitioner of a religion called "My Way," proud Italian, patriotic American, gentleman, ruffian, humanitarian, egomaniac, powerful, humble, Hoboken, Palm Springs, Hollywood, celebrity, recluse, champ, chump, puppet, poet, pauper, pirate, pawn, king, pop schlock, art song, saloon singer, superstar, spontaneous improviser, consummate professional, Dodger fan, fixture at Yankee games via "New York, New York," young lion, elder statesman, charity donor, casino owner, tough guy, manic depressive, sorrowful, elated, up, down, hip, stodgy, hero, scoundrel, pensive balladeer, swaggering swinger, youthful brashness, sadder-but-wiser *savoir faire*, and . . . maybe most of all . . . *survivor* (Petkov and Mustazza ed. 1995, pp. 151–268). But—whether viewing this cultural icon through the eyes of our millennial sensibilities or regarding him from the vantage point of his musical reputation in the 1950s—virtually all Sinatraphiles of any age would agree in celebrating his skills as the reigning authority on the definitive interpretation of popular and jazz-oriented songs such as "My Funny Valentine." A sophisticated jazz musician once told me that the way to learn a pop standard is to listen to Sinatra's version and to transcribe it from the recording—no questions asked. On the subject of Sinatra's unparalleled popularity with jazz musicians, see Shaw (1968, pp. 172, 216, 237), Rockwell (1984, pp. 191, 201), and Lees (1987, p. 113). On the theme of his tendency to render definitive interpretations, see Wilder (1972, p. 147), Rockwell (1984, p. 81), and Petkov (1995, p. 79). Indeed, in *Jazz Singing*, Friedwald (1990) credits Sinatra with more or less *defining* "the basic repertoire of adult popular music" (p. 320) in general and its emphatic incorporation of "My Funny Valentine" in particular: "After Sinatra, singers did 'The Song Is You,' 'Night and Day,' 'Come Rain or Come Shine,' and maybe a few dozen others over and over until it got to the point where, as June Christy once discovered, customers were coming into record stores in search of albums that *didn't* have 'My Funny Valentine'" (pp. 318–319). In *Sinatra!*, Friedwald (1995) expands further on this point to the effect that "Sinatra's influence in determining what singers after him sang is immeasurable . . . No performer turned more songs into standards than Sinatra" (p. 157).

With Sinatra's re-emergence in the 1950s after the career crisis that had followed the inevitable waning of his earlier teen-idol days—during which, when Frank had sung to his adoring bobby-soxer fans at the Paramount

Theater, there was literally not a dry seat in the house (Rockwell 1984, p. 91)—he recorded one of *the* classic versions of "My Funny Valentine" with Nelson Riddle in 1953, as the opening tune on his *Songs For Young Lovers* album for Capitol Records, in an arrangement that was probably actually written by George Siravo (Friedwald 1995, p. 220; 2002, p. 362). As noted by Lees (1985), "The exquisite *My Funny Valentine* . . . remained comparatively unknown, a favorite of obscure cabaret singers, until Sinatra made this recording of it." According to Friedwald (2002), "My Funny Valentine" had been heard (e.g., Mabel Mercer) and recorded (e.g., Margaret Whiting) only very sporadically—lost in the shuffle of other great Rodgers-and-Hart standards (p. 355)—until "Sinatra made it into a classic" (p. 356): "It's only a slight exaggeration to say that 'My Funny Valentine' was really born when Frank Sinatra recorded it in November 1953" (p. 356). Sinatra's version set the standard—widely appreciated by other singers and musicians—for an emotively appropriate performance by the ultimate master of soft dreamy ballads tinged with fervent eroticism, deep melancholy, or romantic despair.

By the end of 1954, *Songs For Young Lovers* had become a bestseller, and Frank had—as on numerous other occasions—won both the *Metronome* and *DownBeat* popularity polls (Frank 1978, p. 91). Sinatra appeared on the cover of *Time* in 1955 (August 29). In 1956, he "was voted Musician's Musician in a poll carried out by *Metronome*, with the number of votes cast for him larger than the total of all the votes received by all the other poll nominees" (Frank 1978, p. 95).

The distinguished *New York Times* critic John Rockwell (1984) describes Sinatra's singing from this period in the following terms: "potent, mature sexual allure"; "punch and swagger"; "irresistible energy"; "ballad singing [with] vulnerability that mirrored the cocky aggression of his upbeat material"; "the most direct expression of emotion"; "a personality that [transforms] songs by others into the most immediate of individual statements" (p. 141). Writing in *The Atlantic* while praising Sinatra's work for Capitol in the 1950s in general and his recordings with Nelson Riddle in particular, another esteemed *New York Times* critic Stephen Holden (1984, ed. 1995) waxes similarly enthusiastic about Frank's "outpourings of emotion" (p. 67), his "balance between toughness and angst" (p. 68), and his "ability to lay bare the emotional facts" (p. 69): "With his rounded baritone, suggestive of the trombone at its most purringly lyrical, he conjured a fantasy world of tender rapture, at once virile and delicate [and] erotic" (p. 67). Petkov (1995)—an editor of *The Frank Sinatra Reader*—explicitly notes the affinity of Sinatra's style for the words of "Valentine"-lyricist Lorenz Hart (p. 77). Commenting on Frank's years at Capitol with the inimitable arranger Nelson Riddle—not to mention the impressive Gordon Jenkins and the magnificent Billy May—Petkov (1995) cannot contain his ardent admiration for the artist that he considers "the greatest of all American popular singers, in a class by himself" (p. 74): "He appears to be artless, and yet his creative ingenuity in finding ways to broaden and transform the emotional impact of . . . a popular song may well approach genius" (p. 82).

Amazingly enough, Richard Rodgers himself appears not to have appreciated stylistic virtues of the type just extolled. Listening to Mel Tormé perform the Rodgers-and-Hart classic "Blue Moon," Rodgers tried unsuccessfully to insist that Mel phrase "prayer . . . for someone" as "prayer for . . . someone"—the better to rhyme with "care for" (Petkov 1995, p. 78). Subsequently, the composer pettily punished Tormé's refusal to commit this phrasing atrocity by refusing to invite Mel and other singers of his ilk—including Sinatra!—to participate in a television special celebrating his career (Tormé 1990, p. 164). (This gives us a clue concerning the pressures probably felt by Larry Hart in working with a man like that.)

A few years after *Songs For Young Lovers*, Frank Sinatra participated as Kim Novak's and Rita Hayworth's love interest(s) in George Sidney's film version of *Pal Joey* (1957). Herein, he offers beautifully staged renditions—loaded with the famous Sinatra charisma—of "I Didn't Know What Time It Was" and "I Could Write a Book" from the original Broadway show. Rita Hayworth (miming vocals dubbed by Jo Ann Greer) provides an impressively racy rendition of the show's stripper anthem "Zip" and an appropriately erotic version of "Bewitched, Bothered, and Bewildered." Further, three songs from elsewhere in the Rodgers-and-Hart canon were added to the stage version—"There's a Small Hotel," "The Lady Is a Tramp," and "My Funny Valentine"—for purposes of rounding out the film, which was also retrofitted with a much-sanitized book and a vastly-happier ending to pander to the Hollywood-movie audience (Nolan 1994, p. 282).

In the motion picture, Sinatra does not get to sing "My Funny Valentine," but he does get to sit there on-screen while Hayworth watches him watching Novak (lip-synching Trudi Ewen) perform it in spot-lit splendor—exuding a highly inviting, sweeter-than-honey charm, amidst all the indelible emotional experiences associated with that moment. Further, famously, Sinatra does perform "There's a Small Hotel" and "The Lady Is a Tramp"—as potent come-ons to Rita's *femme fatale* character—helping to reinforce his hard-won image of aggressively self-protective toughness, swinging swagger, and secure or even egocentric masculinity. In this connection, Nolan (1994) appraises "The Lady Is a Tramp" as reflecting Rodgers-and-Hart's "best form": "Larry [Hart] joyfully thumbed his nose at the pretensions of 'society' ladies who went up to Harlem in ermine, ringsided at prizefights, patronized—the exact word—the opera" (p. 218). Of course, in the film *Pal Joey*, the gender roles are reversed—that is, "I" becomes "she"—when the Sinatra character gets to aim these comments in the direction of the Hayworth character. The womanizing tendencies of Frank's character in *Pal Joey* mirrored his real-life escapades with—among others, according to *Newsweek* (1965, ed. 1995)—Ava Gardner, Lana Turner, Marilyn Maxwell, Gloria Vanderbilt, Lauren Bacall, Shirley MacLaine, Lady Adelle Beatty, Juliet Prowse, Dorothy Provine, Jill St. John, Mia Farrow, and . . . early on . . . *Kim Novak* herself (p. 94). "The Lady Is a Tramp," in particular, went on to become one of Sinatra's signature songs—a number he "made his own" (Newquist 1968, ed. 1995, p. 131); still sang late in his career at Madison Square Garden (Rockwell 1974, ed. 1995, p. 166) or later at Radio City Music Hall (Holden 1990, ed. 1995, p. 189) or latest of all at the Garden State Arts Center in New Jersey (Kerrison 1993, ed. 1995, p. 192); and included at the very end in a performance with Luther Vandross on his all-time largest-selling platinum-shipping *Duets* album for Capitol (1993). Friedwald (1995) insists on this point: "It's almost as if Sinatra and Riddle wanted to summarize—in a single track—everything they had accomplished on the three [preceding] swing albums [to create] a Sinatra classic, performed thousands of times over succeeding decades" (p. 236). Even late in Frank's career, when sung in concert, "The Lady Is a Tramp" would still generate a "tumult" of applause (p. 447)—especially in a "newly minted . . . hard swinging" arrangement created by Billy Byers in the 1970s (p. 472).

Instinctively, Frank knew that he was truly right for this particular part in *Pal Joey*, agreeing to play second fiddle to Rita in a Hayworth/Sinatra/Novak billing and quipping that he did not mind being in the middle of that particular "sandwich" (Shaw 1968, p. 217) between what his daughter Nancy later called "Hollywood's most beautiful bookends" (Sinatra 1985, p. 323). Sinatra had long "dreamed" of playing the role of Joey (Frank 1978, p. 103), for which author John O'Hara joked that he (John) had "invented" him (Frank) (Shaw 1968, p. 229)—that is, a role that clearly resonates with Sinatra's own personal aura. Thus, Shaw (1968) comments that Joey/Frank emerges as "a first-rate singer, fast with the chicks, flip with the con, but tender of heart underneath" (p. 229). A review in *Look* praised Frank's performance as played with "all the brass the role demands . . . a gleam in his eye and a chip on his shoulder, as he portrays this unsavory character who could be so charming" (quoted by Frank 1978, p. 103). Other reviews characterized Sinatra's rendering of Joey as "Almost a one-man show"; "nothing short of terrific"; "as exciting a job of acting as of singing"; and "full of clever trinkets": "He brings vividly alive the glib, egotistical, raffish opportunism of John O'Hara's well-known story, and invests the part with such tremendous charm that he simply wraps up the picture" (quoted by Shaw 1968, p. 234).

Also, we should note that *Pal Joey* (1957) contributed powerfully to a revival of widespread interest in the songs by Rodgers-and-Hart. On this point, in his work on *The Golden Age of Popular Song*, Green (1989) comments that "Frank Sinatra . . . in . . . *Pal Joey* . . . made Rodgers-and-Hart world-famous all over again" (pp. 207–208). Apparently, ironically enough, Rodgers found this renewed appreciation of his work with Hart vexing because he felt that it detracted from the acclaim for his then-current collaborations with Hammerstein. For example, about that time, the critic Kenneth Tynan sounded the death knell for Rodgers-and-Hammerstein's *Flower Drum Song* when he dubbed it—with truly delicious wit—"The World of Woozy Song" (quoted by Green 1989, p. 208).

Then, during his President-of-the-Rat-Pack / Leader-of-the-Clan / Peak-of-the-Summit / Chairman-of-the-Board days circa 1962 and around the time that Talese (1966 [1993], ed. 1995) dubbed him *Il Padrone* (p. 104), Sinatra recorded two live versions of "My Funny Valentine"—both with small jazz groups featuring vibes and flute, unearthed and reissued by Bravura (DC2-104) and Reprise (9 45487-2), respectively. The latter—taped in Paris at the end of a long and tiring world tour—finds Frank in something less than peak vocal condition (Friedwald 1995, p. 390), but the Sinatra magic still shines through a small-group setting that is looser and jazzier than usual. Toward the conclusion of his career, as an aging Ol' Blues Eyes, Frank returned to the recording studio for one last version of this signature song—this time, a duet with Sinatra performing "My Funny Valentine" while Lorrie Morgan sings "How Do You Keep the Music Playing," recorded for his old label Capitol in 1994. This offering carries great sentimental value, though some might question the rationale for pairing these two rather disparate artists in song, especially since Sinatra's voice is once again below par (Friedwald 1995, p. 509). At the very end—approaching 80 years of age—Sinatra still included "My Funny Valentine" (without the Lorrie Morgan part) in his concert appearances, apparently to telling effect (Friedwald 1995, p. 515).

In sum, for the second half of the Twentieth Century, Frank Sinatra virtually *owned* one very viable approach to singing "My Funny Valentine"— an approach associated with the finely crafted art of the popular ballad, featuring detailed attention to the minute nuances of the lyrics, impeccable intonation, precise articulation, carefully controlled breathing, masculine integrity—that is, an approach reflecting vocal musicianship of the highest order dedicated to the purpose of creating a warmly glowing romantic bond with the listener. Mustazza (1995) sums up these qualities as follows:

> His . . . unmatched phrasing and breath control; the emotional readings of American popular song; the work with the finest arrangers, conductors, and musicians in the country; the untiring musical perfectionism . . . are . . . the embodiment of the popular American songs that he has made famous.
>
> (Mustazza 1995, p. 5)

In-depth coverage of Frank Sinatra's extraordinary capabilities as a singer, actor, entertainer, and businessman appears in a detailed biography by Shaw (1968) entitled *Sinatra: Twentieth-Century Romantic*. In an on-going commentary that extends throughout the book, Shaw (1968) proves particularly adept at explaining the basis for Frank's excellence as a singer with such phrases as "unique and unsurpassed singing" (p. 1); "popular singing as an art" (p. 2); "this constant counterpoint of toughness and tenderness," "a magnetic and enigmatic personality," "the master singer of our time" (p. 3); "a man sharing his innermost feelings with his listeners" (p. 37); "an experience to which audiences were compelled to respond . . . with their hearts" (p. 52); "intensity, immediacy, and involvement, all earmarks of jazz singing" (p. 368); "sincerity . . . as the . . . greatest pop singer of our time" (p. 369).

At the opposite end of the loquaciousness continuum, in a brevity-as-the-soul-of-wit tribute, *My Singing Teachers* by none other than the great Mel Tormé (1994) describes Frank as "The Voice of Our Time" (p. 86). Along similar lines, Steve Allen calls him "the best popular singer of them all" (quoted by Lees 1998, p. 91). Rosalind Russell (1973, ed. 1995) christens him "An American Classic" (p. 147). Marlene Dietrich—reflecting her native culture—describes him as "the Mercedes-Benz of men" (quoted by Russell 1973, ed. 1995, p. 149). Pete Hamill comes up with "a full-blown American legend" (quoted by Mustazza 1995, p. 4). Composer Alec Wilder dubs him "The Master" (quoted by Friedwald 1995, p. 175). Director Billy Wilder pronounces him "beyond talent" (quoted by Friedwald 1995, p. 497). Opera star Robert Merrill names him "a fine artist, a great American interpreter of our music" (quoted by Petkov 1995, p. 84). No less a personage than the great Lester Young calls Frank "my main man" (quoted by Friedwald 1995, p. 405). Friedwald (1995) himself goes even further: "Our culture's greatest popular artist" (p. 11), "indisputedly a great artist . . . the definitive voice of the American experience" (p. 516). Bing Crosby proclaims: "There is only one guy that's the greatest singer in the whole world. His name is Sinatra. And nobody else" (quoted by Sinatra 1985, p. 31). The marvelous jazz singer, Annie Ross, adds that "Sinatra reads a lyric so beautifully, and the way he phrases a song . . . makes you feel as if you personally are the one he's singing to" (quoted by Frank 1978, p. 127). Young Harry Connick, Jr. (1990, ed. 1995) labels Frank "A Perfect Singer . . . the greatest male singer of American popular song" (p. 253). The composer Cy Coleman calls the privilege of having Frank sing one of his songs "a badge of honor" (Friedwald 1995, p. 414).

The arranger Nelson Riddle—architect of the quintessential Sinatra sound at Capitol Records during the 1950s—characterizes the singer as "a giant": "After all these years, there is no one who can approach him" (quoted by Frank 1978, p. 91). Joshua Logan—the writer/director of Broadway and Hollywood musical productions, as quoted by Wilson (1976)—praises Frank as "the greatest performer of a song we've ever had": "To hear this man . . . convinces you he is a genius" (p. 334). Wilson (1976) himself agrees that "he sang songs in a personalized way, in an unbroken flow, almost coddling the lyrics" so that he "made the listeners feel that he was singing to them" (p. 62): "He confesses his own agony in his love songs, and the women in the audience want to take him right to bed with them" (p. 350).

Rockwell (1984) calls Sinatra "the preeminent popular singer of our time" (p. 52). Commenting on Frank's mastery of the microphone and his cultivation of the *bel canto* approach to singing, Rockwell (1984) traces the roots of the Sinatra style to "a creative reliance on amplification to encourage a more conversational vocal idiom, combined with a determination to invest his declamation with a flowing, melodic grace": "The ultimate effect of Sinatra's style . . . is of an utter naturalness, but a naturalness attained through the devices of art" (p. 71). To this, Rockwell (1984) adds that

"Sinatra . . . has validated an entire vernacular tradition and forced people to recognize its claims to classic status" (p. 243).

To appraise Frank Sinatra in *Singers and the Song*, the admirably informed and articulate Gene Lees (1987)—in my book, the best writer on jazz we have ever had—must push his elocutionary powers to the limit to come up with such descriptively adequate phrases as "exquisite enunciation" (p. 104), "an overwhelming persuasive immediacy" (p. 104), "remarkable breath control" (p. 105), "seamlessness" (p. 106), "naturalistic phrasing" (p. 107), "intimacy" (p. 108), "insouciant swing" (p. 111), "emotional depth" (p. 111), "perfect control" (p. 112), "musicianship" (p. 113), "art form" (p. 115), and "national treasure" (p. 115): "He was the best singer we had ever heard" (p. 103). Similar language surfaces in the review of Sinatra's 1982 Carnegie Hall concert by *The New Yorker*'s Whitney Balliett (1982, ed. 1995)—probably our all-time second-greatest writer on jazz—proclaiming that Frank's voice "has taken on timbre and resilience . . . can growl and sound hoarse . . . can shout . . . is tight and controlled": "The early Sinatra sang with veiled emotion; the present one was clearly moved by much of what he did at Carnegie Hall, and his transports were passed on to the audience (p. 185). Yes, they were. I know. We were there.

Even the drummer Buddy Rich—known as an uncompromisingly tough cynic who, according to Friedwald (1995), "prided himself on being hypermasculine and downright antisentimental" (p. 95)—got all misty-eyed when listening to his band mate in the Tommy Dorsey Orchestra: "You know, when Sinatra sings 'Star Dust,' I have to turn away from the audience so they won't see the tears rolling down my cheeks" (quoted by Tormé 1994, p. 154). Another tribute from a musician who worked often with Sinatra, vibraphonist Emile Richards, strikes a particular chord with me personally because it happens to coincide almost exactly with my own reactions to a piece of vocal wizardry—the incredible breath control—that Frank exhibits in his performances of "Ol' Man River" at the end of the bridge or release (the part about landing in jail) and the return to the main section of the chorus (the part about getting weary): "Frank . . . did it with one breath, and it was so effective, it gave me chills or made me cry every time" (quoted by Friedwald 1995, p. 23).

And then, of course, there are the fans. In the best-ever fan-appreciation chronicle, following her idolization of Frank Sinatra from her days as a bobby soxer in the early 1940s to her more mature fascination with his Madison Square Garden Concerts in 1974, Lear (1974, ed. 1995) takes issue with sociological speculations about "how his yearning vulnerability appealed to our mother instincts" and insists instead on "the deeply sexual undertones of the star's attractive power. . . . Whatever he stirred beneath our barely budding breasts . . . was sexy . . . exciting . . . terrific" (p. 48). But even heterosexual males felt the pull of Frank Sinatra's charismatic power. Thus, after proclaiming his own virility, Jewell (1985, ed. 1995) reports his lifelong devotion to Frank's singing style:

Even then, he was better than any of his rivals, more open, lighter and less mannered of tone, giving a personal stamp to a song like no one else I'd ever heard, making you feel he was singing only to you even if you weren't female.

(Jewell 1985, ed. 1995, p. 53)

As an expert on opera as well as pop singing, Henry Pleasants (1974) considers Sinatra "a musical genius who arrived at a moment predestined for that genius" (p. 190) and devotes part of his classic book on *The Great American Popular Singers* to praising Frank's "subtleties and refinements of phrase and enunciation," "variety of vocal coloration," "seamless legato," "intuitive grasp of phrasing," "feeling for the meaning and music of words," and "warmth and intimacy . . . , conveying a sense of sympathy and sincerity" (p. 187):

For one who has spent as much time with singers and singing as I have, for one who has thought so much about singing, who has read so much and written so much, it is difficult to preserve a seemly detachment when it comes to Sinatra. . . . with him I cannot restrain myself from saying that I rate him . . . well above any other American popular singer.

(Pleasants 1974, p. 196)

Along similar lines, Pleasants (1974) quotes with approval the words of tribute from Benny Green:

What few people, apart from musicians, have ever seemed to grasp is that he is not simply the best popular singer of his generation . . . but the culminating point is an evolutionary process which has refined the art of interpreting words set to music.

(Pleasants 1974, p. 197)

Friedwald (1995) begins his lovingly detailed tome on Frank Sinatra's musical artistry—*Sinatra!*—with a long chapter devoted to explicating "The Sinatra Style," from which we might excerpt the following appreciative language referring to "Sinatra's . . . capacity for emotional expressiveness" (p. 18); "exalted rapture," "unique rhythmic idiom" (p. 20); "fundamental mission . . . to tell a story in the most expressive way possible" (p. 22); "a multilayered process involving dynamics, shading, accenting, twisting of pitch and vocal color, all within a single long-breath phrase" (p. 23); "total credibility" (p. 24); "a consciously artistic attitude," "a sound expressly tailored to the acoustic requirements of microphones" (p. 26); "the long phrasing—often eight or even 16 bars to a breath—the tenuous, breathlessly romantic sound, and the deeply felt and communicated recital of the lyrics" (p. 45); "the acknowledged leader of the movement to win recognition for this music as an art form" (p. 54); "a body of work that . . . completely fulfills the potential of twentieth-century popular music" (p. 55).

There is some debate concerning the perfection of Sinatra's intonation during his great years at Capitol Records in the 1950s. Friedwald (1995) argues that "Sinatra never sang flat in the '40s, but occasionally, in the classic Capitol period, The Voice was a little under pitch" (p. 238). I would suggest that this author's admittedly keen ears have missed out on a phenomenon that resembles the note-bending proclivities of a blues singer, who shades certain tones downward so that they fall between a major and a minor third—sometimes called a "blue note." Frank sometimes does something comparable, often adding a downward-bending huskiness to his voice that makes it sound as if it were cracking with depth of feeling. Contra Friedwald (1995), who hints that "it may be overgenerous to claim that it was always deliberate" (p. 238), I believe that such expressions of emotion were entirely intentional and under Frank's total control. How else can we explain the tendency for his occasional flatness to occur only at those exact moments where it exerts the maximum dramatic impact? Indeed, Friedwald (1995) ultimately admits that, "in all contexts and all degrees of either agony or ecstasy, even if Sinatra falls short of the occasional note tonally, he always hits precisely the right tone emotionally" (p. 239).

If I might be permitted to inject my own two-cents worth of critical opinion, I would concede that other singers have sometimes excelled Frank Sinatra on single dimensions of the vocalist's art. For historical influence, I would pick Louis Armstrong. For nonchalance and comedic flair, Bing Crosby. For emotive readings of tragic lyrics, Billie Holiday. For utter hipness, Nat Cole. For total gracefulness, Johnny Mercer. For preternatural suaveness, Fred Astaire. For sheer inventiveness, Ray Charles. For vocal equipment and a ferocious sense of swing, Ella Fitzgerald. For technical mastery, Mel Tormé. For jazz credentials, Jon Hendricks, Dave Frishberg, or Bob Dorough. For breath control, nobody except maybe Carmen McRae during the mid-1950s. For a beautiful sound, Nancy LaMott. For disciplined diction and perfect intonation, Marlene VerPlanck. For fidelity to the composition, Meredith D'Ambrosio. For charismatic wholesomeness, John Pizzarelli. For blatant chutzpah, Judy Garland—followed closely or even surpassed by her daughter Liza Minnelli. But Frank alone combined *all* these qualities to a degree *never* matched by *any* other singer. In the end, Frank triumphed by virtue of his *well-roundedness* in the sense that he *had it all*. He was a one-man multi-dimensional *ideal point* in the market space of pop and jazz singers.

To be sure, as chronicled at length in lovingly painful detail by Friedwald (1995), Frank Sinatra occasionally had his sub-par, not-up-to-snuff, commercially-inspired, pandering-to-the-lowest-common-denominator moments —especially earlier in his career when he reluctantly operated under the misguided direction of Mitch Miller at Columbia Records and, then, later in his career at Reprise Records when he made a bid for the pop charts by giving us such dismal crowd pleasers as "Strangers In the Night," "The Impossible Dream," "Tie a Yellow Ribbon Round the Ole Oak Tree," "Something" (which, unfathomably, Frank himself claimed to admire but which strikes me as one of the most vapid songs ever written), and "Somethin' Stupid" (which the proud father sang as a hapless duet with his daughter Nancy "Boots For Walking" Sinatra). As Friedwald (1995) implies, Frank singing Peter-Paul-and-Mary's "Leaving on a Jet Plane" is not exactly "Come Fly with Me" (p. 436). And, in Friedwald's view, Sinatra's duet with Bono from U2 on "I've Got You Under My Skin" is "the bottom of the barrel, the all-time worst thing Sinatra has ever been involved with" (p. 508). Thus, Friedwald (1995) sums up the late-period Sinatra recordings with matter-of-fact derision: "Nearly nothing that Sinatra put down on tape during these years had any lasting substance" (p. 461). But, surely, when Frank recorded disco-style versions of "Night and Day" and "All or Nothing at All" in the mid-1970s, he reached "the nadir" of his recording career (p. 468).

During the 1980s—even while failing to consummate various abortive recording projects—Sinatra continued to show flashes of brilliance on-stage in his live concert outings. In the videotape of the *Concert for the Americas*, for example, Frank delivers a stellar performance with the Buddy Rich Orchestra. It is, for me personally, something of a shocker to watch the moon face of tenor saxophonist Steve Marcus—my old classmate from the Lenox School of Jazz in 1960—sitting directly behind Frank and wailing away in Buddy's sax section while Sinatra, in his late sixties, cooks his ass off in front (Friedwald 1995, p. 490). When a critic as inept as Ralph J. Gleason (1974, ed. 1995) has the bad sense to badmouth Sinatra with phrases such as "glossed up like a wax dummy" and "a self-conscious hood-lum hustle" (p. 225)—even after writing the surpassingly sycophantic liner notes for Frank's *Ring-A-Ding-Ding* album on Reprise, in which he clumsily coins the term "transilience" (presumably, a journalistic combination of "transcendence" and "resilience")—we come away with the impression that poor-old tongue-tied tin-eared Ralph has done a great deal more damage to himself than to Frank. Personally, with regard to Sinatra's late-career activities, my own response echoes that of Kennedy (1993, ed. 1995): "How can anybody be so good for so long?" (p. 257).

In his work on *Jazz Singing* in general, searching for words to capture the career-long phenomenon of Sinatra-As-Great-Singer, Friedwald (1990) concludes that "Sinatra was the first to consciously think of himself as an artist": "More important than even his conception and perfection of the swingin' lover style, the dominant idiom of nonrock pop singing since the fifties, Sinatra sang and thought in long form, deliberately seeking to create music that would outlive him" (p. 326). In this, of course, Frank succeeded brilliantly. After all, we're still talking about him.

Frank's work with such arrangers as Sy Oliver, Billy May, Nelson Riddle, Johnny Mandel, Neil Hefti, and Quincy Jones perfected the "hard-swinging, heterosexual approach" (Friedwald 1995, p. 285) loaded with aggressively animated "charismatic Sinatra virility" (p. 312). Elsewhere—especially with arrangements by the likes of Axel Stordahl, Nelson Riddle (again), Gordon Jenkins, Robert Farnon, and Don Costa—he achieved the essence of what, especially in a female singer, we would call the "torch song." The latter approach identifies Sinatra's excellence in his self-described category of "saloon singer" (Lees 1987, p. 113)—a tender, wistful, forlorn style of singing (Friedwald 1995, p. 312) that burns with arduous ardor presented in a compellingly personal delivery in which the singer's gender-specific characteristics appear with the fullest possible force as quintessentially masculine for a male singer such as Sinatra or as quintessentially feminine for a female lip-syncher such as Kim Novak.

## (2) Kim Novak

Playing the role of the "nice" chorus girl Linda English in *Pal Joey*, Kim Novak performs "My Funny Valentine" in a manner that positions her, appropriately enough, as firmly occupying the distaff side of the image associated with Frank Sinatra as the eponymous Joey Evans, boy-toy to Rita Hayworth as the stinking-rich socialite Vera Simpson. In this featured number—as when performing with the chorus line in "That Terrific Rainbow" and when half-completing an aborted striptease to "I Could Write a Book"—Kim's chorine-like stage presence is assertively extroverted and kittenishly self-confident, yet alluringly soft and coquettishly feminine. Though she does not actually sing the notes to "My Funny Valentine" in her own voice, she acts the part with utter conviction and lip-synchs to perfection, achieving a verisimilitude exceeding that often accomplished by real singers miming their own voices (including, by the way, Sinatra himself in this particular film). The chemistry between Linda/Kim and Joey/Frank practically jumps off the screen and bolsters rumors that the two were having a real-life affair at about this time (*Newsweek* 1965, ed. 1995, p. 94). Certainly, the sexual tension between these two characters is abundantly obvious to the voyeuristic inspection of Vera/Rita.

Linda/Kim shows no signs of substance abuse. But, in one scene, she indicates some affinity to the obvious fondness of Sinatra—whom Rockwell (1984) characterizes as "the self-described 'saloon singer'" and as "the archetypal balladeer of what might be called the 'booze sensibility'" (p. 162)—for alcohol rather than hard drugs as his intoxicant of choice. Specifically, after an apparent rejection by Joey/Frank, Linda/Kim gets drunk at the bar of Chez Joey and then goes in an inebriated state to look for him on Vera/Rita's yacht.

Instead of taking advantage of her spectacular but defenseless charms, Joey/Frank treats Linda/Kim with admirably restrained paws-off gallantry (comparable to that with which, as described Chapter 2, Sinatra's character treats Grace Kelly in *High Society*). Like a delicate sparrow, English/Novak evokes the discerning Evans/Sinatra's sense of protectiveness—with Joey/Frank seen as something of a clear-sighted eagle, capable of soaring with keen vision to the most elevated musical and romantic heights.

*(3) Chet Baker*

Meanwhile—from the depths of a tortured soul—an alternative approach to singing in general and to performing "My Funny Valentine" in particular appeared in the roughly contemporaneous work of the trumpeter and vocalist Chet Baker. Baker first recorded two uniquely personal versions of the piece on trumpet for Fantasy and Pacific Jazz while playing with the Gerry Mulligan Quartet in 1952 and 1953, respectively, just slightly earlier than Sinatra got around to recording the song. Inexplicably, Friedwald (2002) downplays Baker and Mulligan's justifiable claim to primogeniture in this respect (p. 363). According to Gavin (2002), the then-obscure tune was discovered and recommended by the Quartet's bassist, Carson Smith (p. 58). Baker's work on the horn is dark, somber, brooding, gently sad, and wistfully tentative. He had a flair for seeming constantly on the brink of losing his place or hitting a clinker, but somehow—magically—always managing to come up with the perfect note instead. Musically, on "My Funny Valentine" as in much of his playing, Chet sounds like a man on the verge of a nervous breakdown (Bradshaw and Holbrook 2007).

These suspicions intensified when Baker recorded a vocal version of the song with his own quartet featuring Russ Freeman on piano for Pacific Jazz in 1954. Here, he sings in a high effeminate voice that strikes almost everyone who hears it for the first time as very strange indeed—clearly, the antithesis of Sinatra's macho singing style—vulnerable, fragile, introverted, epicene in the extreme, yet deeply penetrating and compelling in a disturbing sort of way. As described by Lannin and Caley (2005), Baker's melancholy vocalizations project the animus/anima of "a feminized voice . . . within a masculine housing" to convey intense "feelings of loss" (p. 12). Roberts (2005) provides a similar assessment of Chet's early-career vocal qualities during the mid-1950s, finding his singing to be "feeble," "winsome," and "effeminate" (p. 122); "restrained," "melancholic," "sentimental," "depressing," and "wounded" (p. 123). On a personal note, after a few weeks of listening to Chet's "My Funny Valentine" and various other tracks from the early Baker-Freeman sessions (especially "Look For the Silver Lining"), I was hooked on Chet's voice and have been a hopeless Baker fan ever since. Believe me, if you relax and let it happen, this fascination grows on you.

On trumpet—though largely autodidactic, primarily intuitive, barely able to read music, harmonically illiterate, loathe to practice, and limited in technique to the middle register of the horn—Baker was nonetheless a superb musician with a completely distinct, intensely concentrated, clean, crisp, cliché-free sound all his own, crackling on up-tempo tunes and sweetly pure on slower ballads. In the words of Chet's friend Russ Freeman—the pianist, arranger, and composer for the mid-1950s Baker Quartet—"Chet struck me as a giant player": "You know, he didn't have any idea what key he was playing in or what the chords were—he knew nothing from a technical standpoint—it's all just by ear. . . . But there would be certain nights . . . when it was absolutely *staggering*" (quoted by Claxton 1993, pp. 41–42). In an interview with Betty Little, the USA Editor for *Chet's*

*Choice*, the great Dave Brubeck remembers that Chet did not read music well and "didn't think in terms of key or think in terms of the way most other musicians thought": "He was just totally natural . . . the most natural musician I have ever been around" (*Chet's Choice*, Volume 1, Special, on-line @ home.ica.net/~blooms/vol1special.htm). Another musician whom I admire enormously—namely, the magnificent bassist Niels-Henning Ørsted Pedersen, who played with Baker during his later European days—regarded Baker as "one of the major artists" of the 1950s–1970s and as "one of the most melodic players, one of the most sensitive players . . . very adventurous and imaginative . . . Any superlative I can come up with belongs to him" (quoted by Wulff 1993, p. 52).

And, I promise, Baker exhibited a uniquely insightful, mesmerizingly poignant singing style—soft but pure, effete but honest, delicate but clear as a bell, well-crafted in breath control, and always-always-always deadly accurate in his pitch-perfect intonation. As described by Valk (1989), Chet's singing was "innocent" but "sad," his trumpet solos "intense" but "precisely calibrated" (pp. 229–230). In the words of Zwerin (1981), "He reaches the same pure part of us as Beethoven's last quartets." Similarly, Friedwald (1990) extols Baker's passionate profundity—"profound in that Baker is strongest when he's weakest": (p. 367): "You keep wondering how Baker can possibly do so much with so little" (p. 368). Friedwald adds that Chet "also makes the most effective use of gender blur in all singing" (p. 368). Not surprisingly, as noted by Roberts (2005), Chet's mystique appealed powerfully to members of the gay audience:

> His self-mortification and ghostly pacification on record, coupled with William Claxton's glamorous photographs of him in the recording studio, created a palpable world of gay desire and loss . . . particularly during the mid-fifties when magazine editors, record producers and film producers were keen to identify Baker with the new "feminized" anti-hero in Hollywood-cinema (James Dean, Marlon Brando).
>
> (Roberts 2005, p. 123)

Summing up these qualities, Carr, Case, and Dellar (1986) explain how Chet created "the definitive 'My Funny Valentine'": "His melancholy tone and simple lyricism seemed to linger in the nerve endings long after the last note had sounded. . . . And his voice cast the same forlorn, little-boy-lost shadow" (p. 80).

In this connection, many listeners' reactions are doubtless reflected in an uncommonly well-expressed tribute written by an ordinary Italian jazz fan named Maurizio Po, who movingly recalls his reactions on first hearing the old Pacific Jazz album entitled *Chet Baker Sings*, falling under "Chet's magical spell," and finding this "a sort of revelation":

> I felt the sincere voice of a true poet, who was able to play out his melodically inventive and gentle introversion [and] who laid his heart

bare and made me feel the pure, natural caressing, tender voice . . . of an individual experience turning into a universal one.

(*Chet's Choice*, Volume 2, Number 3, on-line
@ home.ica.net/~blooms/vol2no3.htm)

In his book on *West Coast Jazz*, the noted jazz historian Ted Gioia (1992) offers a highly favorable appraisal of Chet Baker as "one of the finest soloists jazz has produced": "True, his range was limited, but . . . In the middle register, Baker always remained nonpareil" (pp. 167–168). Gioia (1992) credits Baker with an unsurpassed "unity of vision and clarity of intent," with distinctive "phrasing and use of space," and with an "airy tone . . . especially pure for a jazz musician" (p. 169). As "an antivirtuoso," Chet conveyed "a feeling too deeply felt to be betrayed by superficial frills or mere technique" (p. 181). Thus, "Baker's early recordings on the Pacific label are among the lasting masterpieces of postwar jazz" (p. 194). In an interview with Betty Little for *Chet's Choice* in 1994, Gioia classifies Chet Baker (like the alto saxophonist Paul Desmond) as a neoclassicist of the highest order, whose "playing exemplifies . . . restraint, continuity, sensitivity to form, the channeling of intense emotions into a cool focal point" as well as "musicality, melody, structure, harmonic inspiration, authenticity and style": "Chet is one of only a handful of artists from that period—Nat Cole is another that comes to mind—to exhibit these qualities so fully" (quoted in *Chet's Choice*, Volume 4, Number 3, on-line @ home.ica.net/~blooms/vol4 no3.htm).

In contrast to Gioia (1992), not every listener has perceived the excellence of the Chet Baker trumpet and vocal styles. In this connection, consider the astonishingly obtuse—not to mention male-chauvinistic—remarks by Gordon (1986) in his book on *Jazz West Coast* when considering the album *Chet Baker Sings*, which he labels "an unmitigated disaster": "The very worst faults of Baker's trumpet style—a tendency towards introspection, a limited emotional and dynamic range—are multiplied tenfold by his soft, quavering voice" (p. 83).

Overall, a more appreciatively well-balanced assessment of Baker's contribution comes from the critic Doug Ramsey, who plainly states that "When you look only at his music, it's clear that he had one of the greatest lyrical conceptions of any jazz artist." Ramsey adds, "Let me re-emphasize that—ANY" (interviewed by Betty Little for *Chet's Choice*, Volume 5, Number 1, on-line @ home.ica.net/~blooms/vol5no1.htm).

Chet Baker recorded "My Funny Valentine" on countless occasions during his long career. In my collection, I have at least 30 different versions of Chet playing and/or singing this song on CDs (not counting the dozens gathered over the years on 33-rpm albums), and there may well exist other available recordings that I have not yet managed to find. According to Friedwald (2002), "At least a hundred recordings of 'Valentine' are listed in Chet Baker's discography" (p. 364). Shortly before his untimely demise, in 1988 for Enja, Baker recorded a last performance of "My Funny Valentine" with a large orchestra in Hannover, Germany. His playing on this vale-dictory track—the last tune in Baker's last concert (p. 364)—manifests the same gorgeously sensitive lyricism that had characterized his many performances of this piece during the 35 years that had intervened since his earliest version with the Mulligan Quartet. Each rendition over the years revealed Chet's defining sense of vulnerable wistfulness, introverted fragility, ambivalent longing, and androgynous openness.

Baker's highly unconventional musical persona may have presaged various psychological traits that led this artist down a tragic path of self-destruction (Bradshaw and Holbrook 2007). For example, Gioia (1992) comments on Chet's susceptibility to the pleasure principle: "Immediate gratification was Baker's way almost from the start" (p. 191). Speaking from long experience, Russ Freeman dubs him "the world's oldest juvenile delinquent" (interview in *Chet's Choice*, Volume 1, Number 2, on-line @ home. ica.net/~blooms/vol1no2.htm). Another pianist, Frank Strazzeri, calls him "the biggest goof there ever was" (interview in *Chet's Choice*, Volume 5, Number 1, on-line @ home.ica.net/~blooms/vol5no1.htm).

Beginning in the mid-1950s while at the height of his recently achieved fame and fortune, as recounted with self-revealing candor in his auto-biographical fragment entitled *As Though I Had Wings: The Lost Memoir* (Baker 1997), Chet developed a heroin addiction that haunted him for the rest of his life. He fled this country to live and work in Europe, but never escaped his drug-related demons. Further, to the annoyance of some, Baker was a rather unrepentant junky. As recounted by his frequent collaborator, the pianist Harold Danko, when an intrusive interviewer once asked Chet to name "the worst thing about drugs," he responded, "The cost" (quoted by Betty Little in *Chet's Choice*, Volume 3, Number 1, on-line @ home.ica.net/~blooms/vol3no1.htm).

Aspects of Baker's life abroad are documented in *Chet Baker in Concert* and *Chet Baker in Europe: 1975-1988* by Wulff (1989, 1993). Chet spent time here and there, in and out of jail for drug possessions and prescription forgeries, as painfully chronicled in excruciating detail by Gavin (2002). Ultimately, Baker died in 1988 after a plunge from his hotel window in Amsterdam. Given his proven skills as a survivor, many doubt that Chet would have fallen accidentally or jumped purposely, strongly suspecting that he was probably pushed by an angry drug dealer to whom he owed money (more or less the story of his life). As reported by Valk (1989), however, the facts that Baker's lifeless body was full of cocaine and heroin when they found it, that his hotel door was locked from the inside, that markings from his pants indicated he had been sitting on the window sill, and that a small fortune worth of drugs was found on a table in his room pretty much shoot down the revenge-by-an-angry-drug-dealer theory. Gavin (2002) is exas-peratingly vague on this topic, suggesting that Chet "committed a sort of passive-aggressive suicide—opening a window and letting death come to him": "Baker, it seemed, had died willfully of a broken heart" (p. 369). We are left to hope that maybe—after consuming a heroin-and-cocaine "speedball"—Chet dozed off on the window ledge and somehow managed simply to fall out the window without awakening or, perhaps, while hallucinating. Meanwhile, the mysterious circumstances of his demise provide material for a novel by Bill Moody (2002) entitled *Looking For Chet Baker: An Evan Horne Mystery*, which probes further but still inconclusively into the context of the late trumpeter's life and times.

During his lifetime, Chet Baker appeared in a number of motion pictures—as both musician and actor—many of them produced in Italy or other parts of Europe. These include usually small acting roles in such obscure films as *Hell's Horizon* (1955), *Urlatori alla sbarra* (aka, *Howlers of the Dock*, 1959), and *Stolen Hours* (1963); participation as a trumpet soloist in *The Fast and the Furious* (1954), *The James Dean Story* (1957), *Urlatori alla sbarra* (1959), *Audace colpo dei soliti ignoti* (aka *Big Deal on Madonna Street*, 1959), *Smog* (1962), *Flic ou voyou* (aka *Cop or Hood*, 1979), *Le Jumeau* (aka *The Twin*, 1984), and *'Round Midnight* (1986); and credit as composer for *La concerto de la peur* (aka *Night of Lust*, 1962), *La nuit la plus longue* (aka *Sexus*, 1964), and *Man Outside* (1965). Unfortunately, most of these films have failed to appear on VHS or DVD and therefore elude our ability to document Baker's cinematic career in full detail. Selections from four Italian films scored by Piero Umiliani do surface on a compilation CD issued by Liuto Records in Rome, where we hear the familiar Baker qualities of delicate lyricism and brooding intensity. But perhaps most fittingly, Robert Altman's *The James Dean Story* (1957)—with music composed by Leith Stevens and arranged by Johnny Mandel and Bill Holman—featured haunting solos by Chet Baker on trumpet and by Bud Shank on alto. Parts of the soundtrack album originally issued by World Pacific Records appear on the compilation CD entitled *Chet Baker: The Pacific Jazz Years*. Chet sounds especially moody and mournful on a background piece called "Let Me Be Loved." If there is such a thing as crying through the horn, this is it. Here, the legendary iconographic link, based on their physical appearances, between the Chet Baker and James Dean mystiques is made concrete . . . in music.

These qualities also appear with painful clarity in a depressing photo-documentary made by the sometime fashion photographer Bruce Weber under the title *Let's Get Lost* (1989). Herein, Baker—whose handsome looks, photogenic star quality, and physical charisma had once inspired flattering comparisons with the likes of James Dean—emerges as a haunted shadow of his former self, a hopeless junky, a man devoid of self-respect who has alienated almost everyone who ever cared about him (including even his own mother, not to mention his wife and his semi-estranged children). Weber specializes in juxtaposing photos of the once-beautiful 24-year-old trumpeter—especially those taken by the brilliant West Coast photographer William Claxton and collected in Claxton's own book entitled *Young Chet* (1993)—with shots of the wrinkled and tormented visage of Baker as a 58-year-old, frail, denture-wearing lifetime drug addict. Somehow, Roberts (2005) manages to put a semi-positive spin on this documentation of Chet's transformation from "bittersweet icon of homoerotic and adolescent desire" to "haunted junkie": "Let's Get Lost is as much about the continuing resonance of William Claxton's images—which are a constitutive part of the film and its retrospective pleasures—as it is about the memory of what Baker's music meant for Weber and those non-conformist, lovelorn audiences of the 1950s and 1960s" (p. 124).

Indeed, the early Chet was good-looking enough to become an icon of hipness—as prominently featured on the cover of the book by Carr, Case, and Dellar (1986) documenting *The Hip: Hipsters, Jazz and the Beat Generation*. In his "Preface" to Claxton (1993), Christian Caujolle describes Baker's "look" as "the face of an angel" with, like that of James Dean, "a kind of palpable, genuinely physical beauty": "Chet himself is an image. . . . Too handsome. Too seductive. Too desirable. Ultimately, too Chet" (pp. 7–10). Claxton (1993) himself tells the story of how he discovered Baker's photogenic qualities: "As the latent images began to appear in the developing tray through the pale red darkroom illumination, it was Chet's face that came through like magic—a photographer's dream—a photogenic face ... what that mysterious term, photogenic, truly meant" (pp. 19–20).

By contrast, the older Baker who appears in Weber's film looks in every way as if he already has one foot in the grave—which, as it happens, he does (Bradshaw and Holbrook 2007). In a rather testy review of *Let's Get Lost* (1989) for *The New Yorker*, Pauline Kael (1989) describes Baker's appearance in the film as that of "a beauty who had turned into a sunken-eyed death's head." Gioia (1992) suggests that "in *Let's Get Lost* . . . he was no material for a romantic lead, just a burnt-out addict who interested his audience through his decadence as much as through his music" (p. 192).

I would have characterized Chet's appearance in this film, more charitably, as sadder-but-wiser. Nonetheless, one cannot deny that the trumpeter looks a bit the worse for wear, especially in connection with the formidable embouchure problems resulting from the loss of all his upper teeth after a drug-related attack by some hoodlums in L.A. According to Valk (1989), when Baker heroically taught himself to blow the trumpet while wearing dentures, only one brand of adhesive would hold his false teeth in place well enough for him to play with them. What a great missed opportunity for a television commercial! I can hear it now: "My career was over until I found . . . Fasteeth . . . the stickier-than-sticky denture cream."

On a personal note, I must report that I feel a sort of eerie frisson in watching Bruce Weber's film and in contemplating the many ways in which my own life has intersected that of the star-crossed trumpeter. Chet Baker was first arrested for heroin possession in the late-1950s while traveling from Chicago to a gig in Milwaukee, the hometown where I grew up and lived at the time (Baker 1997; Gavin 2002, p. 144). When Chet was deported from Germany in the spring of 1964, he returned to the USA and played a job at the Jazz Workshop in Boston, where I took a break from college studies to hear him perform on two magical evenings when he sounded the best I have ever heard him—fast and harmonically secure, showing a sustained power not normally associated with his work and barely hinted at in the five-album set of recordings that he made shortly thereafter for the Prestige label. In 1973—when a denture-wearing Chet rebounded from his woes and appeared for a historic two-week stand at the Half Note in New York, sounding weak and looking pathetic in his red-and-burgundy outfit with cowboy boots—we were there. And when Chet played a reunion concert with Gerry Mulligan at Carnegie Hall in 1974 (recorded by CTI and reissued on CD by CBS)—from which some of Gerry's introductory remarks and Chet's playing on "My Funny Valentine" can be heard in Weber's documentary—we were there, again. As mentioned in the film, Chet's subsequent nine-month engagement in NYC took place at Stryker's—a small now-defunct nightclub on 86th Street, three and a half blocks from our apartment—where we never heard him play, though we did travel all the way downtown to the Village Vanguard to hear him during this same period. Why didn't we walk the short distance to see Chet at Stryker's? The simple fact is that his demeanor and condition at this time were so obviously filled with physical pain and psychic anguish that, good as he actually sounded, we could not bear to witness such public deterioration and debilitation in someone whose music we loved so much. Randi Hultin—a lady friend from Norway—expressed a similar feeling quite eloquently: "I loved to listen to his playing but, tender and sorrowful as he often looked, I felt . . . we were stealing all the power from him" (quoted by Wulff 1993, p. 74). A few years after Chet's death, we visited the Prins Hendrik Hotel in Amsterdam from whose window he had taken his fatal plunge. We found it hard to evaluate the plausibility of an accidental fall because, when asked to identify his third-floor room, two different hotel employees pointed to two different windows. And when recently reviewing Weber's film, we noticed that—listing a cast of West Coast cronies from the 1950s—Baker refers to the arranger-tenor-bandleader Bill Holman as Bill *Holbrook*. Further, we discovered that much of the documentary was shot at and around the Shangri-La Hotel in Santa Monica—believe it or not, in the exact room where we have stayed on two or three occasions while visiting our son in L.A. and enjoying the same view out the window of the street, ocean, and palm trees. In short, the number of Chet's connections with my own life strike me as somewhat spooky.

After suffering through *Let's Get Lost* (1989), Baker fans probably thought or, at least, hoped they had witnessed the last desecration of this jazz icon's memory that they would be asked to endure. But such optimists had not counted on the relentlessly nasty journalistic instincts displayed at suffocating length by James Gavin (2002) in his merciless biography published 15 years after Baker's death and revealingly entitled *Deep in a Dream: The Long Night of Chet Baker*. In an appalling display of lust for character assassination, Gavin (2002) has combed through all available Baker-related material and memorabilia, has collected self-servingly jaundiced interviews of his own with various embittered individuals only too anxious to heap verbal abuse on Chet's corpse, and has meticulously edited out the very large number of complimentary comments from knowledgeable friends and fellow musicians available in the public record to produce a book that drags the great trumpeter and singer through the dirt from beginning to end. In Gavin's version, Baker emerges as one of the most worthless individuals ever to set foot on the planet—selfish; manipulative; irresponsible; deceitful; lazy; disloyal; abusive; violent; sociopathic; musically incompetent; unrepentant; bigoted; male chauvinistic; and in love only with drugs, his music, his own pretty image, and his passionless sexual exploits—roughly in that order.

A partial list of the verbiage deployed by Gavin (2002) to describe Baker—much of it selectively quoted or pointedly paraphrased from the often more balanced accounts provided by Chet's acquaintances and colleagues—would include "feminine" (p. 18); "not that intelligent" (p. 18); "devious" (p. 20); "juvenile delinquent" (p. 20); "compulsion to self-destruct" (p. 27); "marijuana fetish" (p. 40); "homophobic outbursts . . . as evidence of repressed gay tendencies" (p. 46); "ability to manipulate through charm while giving an impression of utter innocence" (p. 46); "kind of a freak talent" (p. 56); "a talented imbecile" (p. 71); "a spoiled little boy" (p. 76); "a barely literate hipster, brainless but . . . gifted" (p. 81); "a spoiled brat" (pp. 104-105); "struggling just to stay in tune" (p. 108); "impeccably shaped, but short on feeling" (p. 133); "deceitful" (p. 135); "an evil junkie and a whining, devious young man" (p. 146); "a lost soul" (p. 154); "a snake" (p. 162); "the snake-pit of human degradation" (p. 187); "paranoia . . . beneath his bravado" (p. 188); "known for spurting blood all over an Italian gas station toilet" (p. 199); "a burnout trying to salvage his wasted talent" (p. 208); "a career police informant" (p. 215); "about women . . . violently ambivalent" (p. 227); "knew the marketability of his addiction, and supplied writers with a treasure trove of scandal" (p. 240); "insanely jealous" (p. 249); "didn't bother to bathe" (p. 254); "could kill anybody . . . had that anger in him" (p. 270); "relied on drugs to escape every problem" (p. 279); "trampled on good people" (p. 292); "devil incarnate" (p. 293); "a coldhearted, almost demonic figure" (p. 297); "couldn't stand women . . . hated them all" (p. 298); "a brat and a nuisance" (p. 306); "hair . . . in greasy strands . . . needed a shave" (p. 308); "matted gray hairs . . . unclipped toenails protruding from his sandals" (p. 312); "often doused himself with Paco Rabanne cologne in lieu of bathing" (p. 312); "was committing suicide little by little" (p. 321); "a ghastly vision of death in progress" (p. 323); "would sing the tenderest songs of romance, then beat up the woman he professed to love" (p. 325); "a hooker to the end" (p. 346); "a walking corpse . . . only living for the stuff" (p. 362); "liar, cheater, son of a bitch" (p. 379). Not a pretty picture, especially when compared with the iconic mythologizing that had characterized the trumpeter's youth.

True, Gavin (2002) supplies some useful details not available elsewhere. For example, thanks to his painstaking research, we learn that in support of his drug habit Chet committed crimes ranging from cat burglary to arson and that he specialized in the forgery of checks and prescriptions—having perpetrated such fraudulent identity thefts in New York City (p. 148), Italy (p. 166), Germany (p. 184), Switzerland (p. 185), France (p. 194), California (pp. 214, 222, 224), and again New York City (p. 291). Faced with such accounts, we begin to view Gavin as more of a crime reporter than a musical biographer.

It seems amazing that anyone would have spent years in lavishing his formidable efforts on traveling, interviewing, reading, and collecting voluminous materials on a subject for whom he obviously feels such contempt (p. 381). Even more astonishingly, Gavin (2002) betrays not one iota of appreciation for the beauties of Chet Baker's musical gifts. He routinely chronicles the exact nature of Baker's drug intake prior to, during, and after studio-recording sessions or recorded-live club appearances but steadfastly refrains from conveying a scintilla of the music captured and immortalized on those occasions. In this, he fails spectacularly to portray the essence of this great musician's legacy. His work is pharmacologically informative but musicologically bankrupt.

Though Gavin (2002) bombards us with often trivial narcotics-related details, he fills his book with annoying musical inaccuracies. For example, he mistakenly tells us that "My Funny Valentine" has "thirty-five bars" rather than thirty-six (p. 58). He incorrectly attributes the role of Kirk Douglas' wife in *Young Man With a Horn* (1950) to Doris Day rather than to Lauren Bacall (p. 92). He misleadingly blames Clifford Brown rather than the pianist Richie Powell's wife as the driver in the car crash that ended the lives of all three (p. 96). He erroneously suggests that "The Music Goes Round and Round" was "a swing-era hit about the trombone"—apparently forgetting that, though Tommy Dorsey did play the (slide) trombone, he also played the trumpet, on which it is possible to "push the middle valve down" (p. 290).

Rather than compiling a long list of such inaccuracies, I shall content myself with just one dismal example of the musical neglect that pervades Gavin's book from start to finish. Specifically, in commenting on Bruce Weber's *Let's Get Lost* (1989), Gavin (2002) describes a relatively inconsequential scene involving "an interview at the Shangri-La" in which Baker wearily recalls the lyrics to a song called "Deep in a Dream" in a way that Gavin regards as symptomatic of his "lust for escape": "Jimmy Van Heusen's words tell of the nirvana a man enters when he settles into his armchair, cigarette in hand, and drifts off to sleep" (pp. 334–335). On the surface, as exploited by Gavin (2002), this story seems to provide an apt metaphor for the trumpeter's many failings—smoke, addiction, dissolution, endangerment, whatever. But, in fact, it illustrates the manner in which Gavin consistently shortchanges his readers. Specifically, the words to "Deep in a Dream" were *not* written by the great Jimmy Van Heusen (musical composer not only of "Deep in a Dream" but, as noted earlier, of innumerable classic standards recorded by Chet Baker and other jazz instrumentalists or singers of his generation). The "nice words" to "Deep in a Dream" were created by the lyricist Eddie DeLange (no slouch in his own right, with such credits as "Darn That Dream," "Do You Know What It Means to Miss New Orleans," and "Solitude"). Far from an inconsequential slip, this gaff embodies Gavin's characteristic musicological indifference to even a matter so central as the authors of the song whose lyrics provide *the title for his own book*!

Chet Baker emerges from all this as a heart-breakingly tragic loser in the game of life (Bradshaw and Holbrook 2007). That so much musical beauty could spring from such a physically tormented and psychically wounded soul almost defies belief. But there it is. And it shows up, once again, in Baker's posthumous contributions to two films with which we must deal briefly—namely, *L.A. Confidential* (1997) and *Playing By Heart* (1998).

## L.A. Confidential (1997)

Curtis Hanson's critically-acclaimed and multiple-award-winning *L.A. Confidential* (1997) takes place in Los Angeles in the mid-1950s and, with a background score composed by Jerry Goldsmith, uses ambi-diegetic jazz to provide a musical context that—as explicitly explained by the director in a promotional piece that introduces the VHS videotape—serves the goal of delineating key characters in the motion picture. Call me paranoid, but it strikes me that Hanson consciously deploys ambi-diegetic music by Chet Baker to limn the corruption, seediness, and depravity embodied by some rather unsavory central figures.

First, when tough-but-honest Officer Bud White (Russell Crowe) meets the nefarious Captain Dudley Smith (James Cromwell) in a bar to negotiate some police-department politics involving the return of White/Crowe's badge and gun in exchange for his promise to serve as a strong-arm guy (torturing gangsters and other crime suspects so that they will leave town in a manner secretly intended to help Smith/Cromwell take over organized crime in the area), over the tavern's PA system we hear Chet Baker's innocently sweet recording with Russ Freeman of "Look For the Silver Lining" as heavily ironic ambi-diegetic cocktail-lounge cinemusical commentary.

Second, when Sergeant Jack Vincennes (Kevin Spacey) and gossip columnist Sid Hudgens (Danny DeVito) stand aside at a political rally hosted by the corrupt, cowardly, and sexually deviant District Attorney Ellis Loew (Ron Rifkin)—plotting a nasty scheme to entrap Loew/Rifkin in a homosexual tryst with a youthful out-of-work gay actor, a plan that later backfires and results in the young man's grizzly death—we hear an announcement of the Gerry Mulligan Quartet with Chet Baker; see four actors directly behind Loew/Rifkin's head, miming the trumpet, baritone, bass, and drum parts; listen and watch as the band launches into Gerry and Chet's immortal version of "Makin' Whoopee." Following this, the Mulligan Quartet with Baker plays "The Lady Is a Tramp" while Vincennes (Spacey) receives a 50-dollar payoff from Hudgens (DeVito). Figuratively, this illicit bribe does indeed support some tramp-like whoopee.

Third, when White/Crowe visits the seedy Formosa Bar to elicit information from a reluctant snitch—first, with a 20-dollar bill, then by literally grabbing the poor fellow by the balls—the pathetic informant's symbolic emasculation is accompanied by the ambi-diegetic sounds on the music system of Chet Baker with the Lighthouse All-Stars tenderly performing "At Last." Again, ambi-diegetic jazz by the world's greatest down-and-out oft-imprisoned androgynous-sounding trumpet-playing junky carries clear connotations of sexual indiscretions, insidious blackmails, and larcenous felonies soon to follow.

## Playing By Heart (1998)

Meanwhile, further ambi-diegetic jazz played or influenced by Chet Baker appears in John Barry's music for Willard Carroll's *Playing By Heart* (1998)—which features three soundtrack appearances by Chet ("I'm Glad There Is You," "Everything Happens to Me," and "Lucius Lu") as well as various highly effective evocations of the Baker instrumental style by Chris Botti on trumpet. Interestingly, the two different soundtrack albums issued for this film contain four recordings by Baker, only one of which ("Everything Happens to Me") actually appears in the movie itself. The others ("Tenderly," "You Go to My Head," and "These Foolish Things," all from Baker's 1956 Paris recordings for the Barclay label) were apparently just added to the *Playing By Heart* album for their appropriateness to its tone and flavor. At any rate, in the film itself, the most important Baker-related contributions occur in two pivotal ambi-diegetic cinemusical moments involving a couple composed of Joan (Angelina Jolie) and Keenan (Ryan Phillippe).

In the first, at a nightclub/disco called The Blue Room in which Joan/ Angelina tries to engage Keenan/Ryan in the sort of soul-baring conversation that she hopes will further their romantic relationship, the latter character bears an unmistakable physical and psychological resemblance to Chet in his young-and-beautiful-but-troubled days. To reinforce this associative connection—as the couple begins to converse, over the club's sound system, we hear Chris Botti's Baker-like horn playing a bluesy 6/8 theme in D-flat minor: D♭-↑E; ↑Ab^^^-↓G♭-↓E; ↑Gb^^^-↓E-↓Db; ↑E^-↓D♭-↓B^-↑D♭. . . . (In this notation—used throughout the present volume—"D♭," "E," "A♭," etc. refer to the names of notes; "↑" and "↓" indicate upward and downward movement, respectively; "^" indicates the passage of one additional beat; and ";" or "." indicates the end of a measure.) This Baker-inspired cinemusical moment does not seem to appear on either of the two soundtrack albums, but it ambi-diegetically underscores what is arguably the most important piece of dialogue in the film. And the story that Keenan/Ryan unfolds therein is as dark, gloomy, and disturbing as one might have feared from the surrounding Chet-connected musical vibes, from observing Keenan/Ryan's Baker-like expressions of angst prior to this point in the movie, and from Joan/Angelina's assertion that he is suicidally depressed.

This dialogue—shocking in terms of where it is headed as Keenan/Ryan's revelation unfolds—has special relevance to the story that Joan/Angelina tells in order to coax Keenan/Ryan to open up to her. Her story (which echoes a segment included at the film's opening) involves a jazz-trumpeter friend who likes to play an old tune by (who else?) Chet Baker (thereby mirroring the Chet-inspired Botti horn that adds ambience to the club scene) and who says that talking about music . . . or love . . . is like dancing about architecture (a phrase that, speaking of suicidal depressives, was apparently borrowed from the sayings of none other than the pianist Clara Schumann, whose husband Robert the composer attempted to kill himself by jumping off a bridge into the Rhine River). Joan/Angelina says that this won't stop her from trying, and the momentum for this part of the story depends on the patient and loving manner in which she wins Keenan/Ryan to her point of view. No doubt, if Chet Baker had had someone like Joan/Angelina on his side, he would today be alive, well, and playing on Hollywood soundtrack albums in place of his smoothjazz- or chill-oriented quasi-clone Chris Botti.

The second pivotal ambi-diegetic cinemusical moment occurs at the movie's conclusion when four couples—scattered in a fragmentary way, both geographically and temporally, through earlier parts of the film—come together in one Altmanesque reconciliatory family reunion. The *mise-en-scène* places these pairs on a dance floor, swaying to the sounds of Joan/Angelina's old philosophically-inclined trumpet-playing pal, who begins with Chet's own recorded version of "Lucius Lu" and then segues into a haunting ballad, the movie's theme song entitled "Playing By Heart"—written by John Barry and performed by Chris Botti in the Baker style. While Keenan/Ryan (with blue hair) and Joan/Angelina (looking radiant) dance, we see the horn player behind them as Ryan tells Angelina that—with respect to the saying about dancing and architecture—they should try to prove the trumpeter wrong.

As the last verbal exchange in the movie, this ambi-diegetic cinemusical moment provides a powerful ending to a rather sweet film and continues to demonstrate the symbolic meaning of the Baker iconography. Here, a man who looks exactly like Chet dances a couple of feet in front of a trumpet player who sounds exactly like Chet and voices the very Chet-like opinion that communicating one's feelings—whatever they may be—is more important than anything, more important even than his own former tendencies toward what the new love of his life has described as suicidal depression.

So the tortured, pained, enigmatically effete cinemusical approach of Chet Baker just won't die. It returns, phoenix-like, to haunt us from the grave. Indeed—to this day—in bars, cafés, nightclubs, and other venues around cities like New York and Los Angeles, Baker remains the number-one source of jazz-related ambient music of choice. I have heard Chet's recordings played as background music at Birdland in the Big Apple. And, in a drama about a singularly desolate trumpet player (superbly enacted by the late John Spencer) produced at both the Mark Taper Forum in Los Angeles and the Manhattan Theatre Club in New York City—namely, *Glimmer, Glimmer and Shine* (2001) by Warren Leight, who had recently won the Tony Award for his Broadway play *Side Man* about another trumpet player who idolizes Clifford Brown—incidental music between the scenes and acts deployed several tunes played by Chet. Apparently, as a source of music intended for atmospheric enhancement or dramatic development, the Chet Baker mystique is . . . inextinguishable.

## SUMMARY

The comparisons just suggested at some length follow from a consideration of three different approaches to music in general and to performing "My Funny Valentine" in particular. They may be construed as suggesting that Kim Novak takes the Frank Sinatra approach in one direction (toward a wholesome and healthy distaff side), whereas Chet Baker pushes the Sinatra model along another path (toward a disturbing androgynous edge that hovers on the brink of expiration). Roberts (2005) encapsulates this contrast via a telling comparison of Frank and Chet in which he describes how "Baker's 'feminized' intonation removes from the delivery of the song all those qualities of vocal attack and swagger . . . sexual predatoriness and physical presence of . . . Frank Sinatra" (p. 125): "At the heart of the voice's softness we also hear death . . . in the delivery of the songs with the voice of someone who knows death, and more to the point, knows how close he himself is daily to its clutches" (p. 126). By way of summary, this pattern of homologous relationships appears as follows:

| Kim Novak | ← | Frank Sinatra | → | Chet Baker |
|---|---|---|---|---|
| Assertive | | Aggressive | | Vulnerable |
| Soft | | Tough | | Fragile |
| Extroverted | | Egocentric | | Introverted |
| Self-Confident | | Self-Protective | | Self-Destructive |
| Feminine | | Masculine | | Androgynous |
| No Drugs, But... | | Booze | | Hard Drugs |
| Hope | | Arrogance | | Despair |
| Life | | Worldliness | | Death |
| Sparrow-Like | | Eagle-Like | | Phoenix-Like |
| I | | | | I |
| Michelle Pfeiffer | | | | Matt Damon |
| I | | | | I |
| *The Fabulous Baker Boys* | | | | *The Talented Mr. Ripley* |

## THE FABULOUS BAKER BOYS (1989) AND THE TALENTED MR. RIPLEY (1999)

Clearly, then, "My Funny Valentine" comes to its recent use in performances by Michelle Pfeiffer and Matt Damon with a great deal of imaginative baggage attached. Such associations and identifications inform our experience of hearing Pfeiffer nondiegetically as she performs "My Funny Valentine" in

*The Fabulous Baker Boys* (1989) and watching Damon ambi-diegetically sing the song in *The Talented Mr. Ripley* (1999). Let us now consider these two illustrations of pivotal cinemusical moments involving jazz.

## Michelle Pfeiffer in *The Fabulous Baker Boys* (1989)

As noted earlier, Michelle Pfeiffer draws on the tradition of "My Funny Valentine" as a torch song, lip-synched by Kim Novak in *Pal Joey* (where Novak plays the chorine with a heart of gold competing with playgirl Rita Hayworth for the affections of Frank Sinatra). This Novak-related saloon-singer axis comes to the fore in the rendition by Pfeiffer, who reports on a *Fabulous Baker Boys* website (fabulousbakers.tripod.com) that she listened to performances by Billie Holiday, Dinah Washington, Sarah Vaughan, and Helen Merrill in preparing for her role as the world-weary ex-escort-service bombshell Susie Diamond. Michelle's own-voice rendition of "My Funny Valentine"—especially as vividly reinforced by the recollected imagery of her other singing performances, including her strikingly erotic piano-top choreography on "Makin' Whoopee," earlier in the film—reflects her carefully cultivated persona as a sexy-sultry-steamy-slithery-slinky-spicy-smart-seductive showgirl with the assertive-yet-soft, extroverted, self-confidently feminine qualities earlier associated with the "Valentine"-related Kim Novak persona. In this connection, Yanow (2004) finds Michelle's singing performances "surprisingly effective" (p. 158).

On the aforementioned website, Pfeiffer further describes her Oscar-nominated multiple-award-winning role in the character of ex-hooker Susie Diamond as "trashy, cocky and real smart." The film's writer/director Steve Kloves adds that "These songs were chosen because they're accurate for the lounges as they are today [and] also reflect the characters." It is this character-reflecting aspect of ambi-diegetic film music that I wish to emphasize in the present discussion. Indeed, Dave Grusin's nondiegetic underscore is used very sparingly in the film and appears mostly in the form of a Miles-Davis-like refrain on muted trumpet that tends to surface whenever the leading characters are feeling confused, lonely, unhappy, or otherwise sorry for themselves.

Besides Susie/Michelle, the relevant participants include the real-life brothers Jeff and Beau Bridges as Jack and Frank Baker—a pair of fraternal partners in a dual-piano lounge act, who have been playing together for 31 years, 15 of these professionally, and who specialize in such cocktail-circuit favorites as "People" (performed to dismal effect at the Starfire Lounge); "The Girl from Ipanema" (played wearing Hawaiian shirts on a two-day gig for which they are paid *not* to appear on the second night), and "You're Sixteen (You're Beautiful and You're Mine)" (an awful song that serves as their signature number and that resurfaces rather touchingly at a moment of reconciliation late in the film).

The ambi-diegetic tunes just mentioned capture the essence of the musical personality evinced by the older brother Frank/Beau (dubbed by John F.

Hammond on piano), whose limitations as a musician are exceeded only by his burdensome sense of responsibility as a family man devoted to making a decent income to support his beautiful wife and two wonderful kids, sincerely dedicated to the reality principle, and therefore subservient in every respect to the commercial, entertaining, audience-pandering, money-grubbing side of the lounge-act business. By contrast, "little brother" Jack/Jeff (dubbed on piano by the film's talented music director Dave Grusin and meticulously hand-synched by Jeff Bridges throughout) expresses his musical personality in two scenes when he retreats, first, to a piano in an abandoned restaurant and, second, to a collaboration with bass-and-drums accompaniment at a Seattle jazz club called Henry's. In these ambi-diegetic moments, Jack/Jeff plays a form of highly sophisticated, lyrically cerebral jazz of the type most closely associated with the influence of Bill Evans (as further refined by Dave Grusin). We sense his intense but lonely absorption in this music and feel the enormity of the loss implicit in his submission to the aesthetically vapid duties of a schlock-pandering cocktail-lounge pianist.

On both occasions, Susie/Michelle overhears Jack/Jeff's agonized pianistic *cri de coeur* and finds ways to let him know that she feels his pain. But, at least temporarily, Jack/Jeff remains trapped by his brotherly contract with Frank/Beau—knowing that his older brother could not sustain a decent livelihood without him and therefore submitting to this painful arrangement, even at the cost of sacrificing his own artistic creativity. Meanwhile, he adopts a cynical posture and, subservient to the pleasure principle, evinces a strong propensity toward womanizing, redeemed only by his heartfelt kindness to a little girl from the upstairs apartment and his concerned treatment of an aging black Labrador (strongly recalling Frank Sinatra's similar ministrations to his expressive pooch Snuffy in *Pal Joey*).

In short, the Fabulous Baker Boys embody a clearly structured series of parallel binary oppositions, reflected in summary form by the following set of homologous comparisons:

| **Frank/Beau** | **Jack/Jeff** |
| --- | --- |
| Business | Aesthetics |
| Entertainment | Creativity |
| Commerce | Art |
| Reality Principle | Pleasure Principle |
| Responsibility | Freedom |
| Sincere | Cynical |
| Family Man | Loner |
| Faithful | Womanizing |
| Head | Heart |
| Money | Love |
| Schlock Pop | Jazz |

This precarious balancing act begins to crumble when the Baker Brothers realize that, to bolster their flagging popular appeal, they need to supplement their act with the added attraction of a girl singer. The hilarious montage in which they audition 37 young women for this position—none of whom can carry a tune, as epitomized by the wonderfully over-the-top clowning of Jennifer Tilly on "The Candy Man"—culminates when the 38th applicant turns out to be Susie/Michelle, who arrives an hour-and-a-half late and who cheerfully admits that she has had *no* previous experience as a singer but has worked for a couple of years as a call girl at the Triple A Escort Service. After thus revealing her tough, outspoken, sarcastic, funny, irreverent, cynical, wisecracking, independent character, Susie/Michelle proceeds to perform a deeply felt version of "More Than You Know" (even instructing Jack/Jeff on how fast or, in this case, slow to set the tempo). Her rendition of this tune is a bit unpolished—compared to those of (say) Rosemary Clooney, Meredith D'Ambrosio, Blossom Dearie, Dena DeRose, Ella Fitzgerald, Billie Holiday, Shirley Horn, Carmen McRae, Jane Monheit, Frank Sinatra, Mel Tormé, Sarah Vaughan, and Dinah Washington—who stand tall among the countless performers lending their voices to this wonderful song. And, perhaps with the implicit excuse that this is only an audition, Susie/Michelle does omit the all-important bridge (which contains one of the most ardent climactic moments in all of popular music on the line about love being all one can give). But the compelling ambi-diegetic cinemusical performance of "More Than You Know" by Susie/Michelle is more than promising enough to land her the job of girl singer in this or virtually any other cabaret or lounge act.

Note the subtle distinction between "cabaret" and "lounge." The first implies taste and refinement. The second suggests schlock and sleaziness. Indeed, with the addition of Susie/Michelle and the careful polishing of her rough edges by Brother Frank/Beau (who buys her a slinky new black dress, misfits her with too-tight high heels, and coaches her not to say "fuck" on the open microphone), the Fabulous Baker Boys plus Susie Diamond transmogrify from the lowly status of a lounge act to the more exalted stature of a cabaret attraction. We watch Susie/Michelle deliver a moving ambi-diegetic performance of "Ten Cents a Dance"—looking stylish and sounding about as down-and-out as it is possible to sound (especially considering her own somewhat seedy background). A beautifully constructed cinemusical montage shows her singing "I Love You, Baby" (something of a saloon-oriented throwback, I would say) in a number of venues with various costume changes, growing more and more self-possessed from one film cut to the next, and culminating in the appearance of a greatly enlarged Susie/Michelle picture on the Baker Boys poster. At a posh resort, the lounge-pop and cabaret-jazz sides of the homologies visited earlier reach a sort of ambi-diegetic rapprochement when the piano-piano-vocal trio performs Bacharach and David's "The Look of Love"—one of the comparatively few songs that have strong support on both the vulgar saloon and elite nightclub circuits.

When Frank/Beau must leave the posh resort and return home for a family emergency (left significantly vague in the film's diegesis), Jack/Jeff and Susie/Michelle make love after she has delivered a stunning and much-celebrated ambi-diegetic cinemusical version of "Makin' Whoopee." The love scene—which, Dear Reader, I shall leave it up to your own febrile sensibilities to imagine—must surely rank as one of the hottest moments ever captured on film without the aid of full frontal nudity (indeed, perhaps all the *more* impassioned by virtue of its *lack* of blatant nakedness). However, the real seduction appears in the ambi-diegetic cinemusical performance of "Makin' Whoopee" wherein Susie/Michelle wears a sexy red dress that rides up to just ever so slightly below her crotch as she sprawls atop the Steinway grand and slithers around suggestively in the most sensual manner possible while Jack/Jeff supplies an inspired gospel-tinged accompaniment hand-synched to perfection by Bridges miming Grusin in case anyone is watching (which, given the visual fireworks of Susie/Michelle's explosive piano-lid dance, most probably anyone isn't). This sampling of ambi-diegetic jazz—so powerful in conveying the assertively sexy, extroverted-yet-soft, self-confidently feminine character of Susie/Michelle and the emerging power of her appeal to Jack/Jeff—has become something of a cult classic. Few of the many critics and other commentators whom I have read on the subject of *The Fabulous Baker Boys* fail to mention "Makin' Whoopee" as a bona fide cinemusical triumph.

Other ambi-diegetic music in *The Fabulous Baker Boys* involves the ubiquitous presence of pieces performed by and associated with Duke Ellington. Thus, when Susie/Michelle displays her boisterous character by disrupting the peace and quiet of the aforementioned posh resort, Duke's recording of "Perdido"—conspicuously featuring Clark Terry in a characteristically pungent trumpet solo—serves as the vehicle for her sonic bombardment (which Frank/Beau incorrectly identifies as Harry James, only to be routinely corrected by his more musically astute brother Jack/Jeff). Later—on the same portable boom box, still typical of her extroverted qualities—Susie/Michelle plays Ellington's "Do Nothin' Till You Hear from Me" (with its verbally unstated but provocatively implicit line about paying no attention to what's said). Toward the end, when Jack/Jeff visits the predictably bourgeois home of Brother Frank/Beau to attempt a fraternal reconciliation in league with his decision to break up the act and go his own separate way, we hear Tony Bennett's rendition of De Lange, Mills, and Ellington's "Solitude" playing ambi-diegetically as significantly prophetic ambient music in the Frank Baker household. Meanwhile, another prominent swing musician—namely, Benny Goodman and his Quartet featuring Teddy Wilson, Lionel Hampton, and Gene Krupa—supplies "Moonglow" as ambi-diegetic music for a dancing-and-falling-in-love scene between Jack/Jeff and Susie/Michelle, with a little interference from Frank/Beau, on the moonlit balcony that they share at the posh resort.

Most meaningful in pointing to the immanent dissolution of the formerly-duo now-trio act is a discussion by the three major protagonists of "Feelings"—that much-despised warhorse of the cocktail-bar circuit, hated by jazz aficionados but beloved to lounge lizards everywhere. In a scene that is nastily but deliciously funny to anyone with a finely honed set of jazz-oriented sensibilities, Susie/Michelle voices the case for aesthetically grounded artistic integrity by declaring that it is *not fun* to sing "Feelings" and wondering aloud whether anyone really needs to hear this trite piece ever again. Frank/Beau replies defensively that "Feelings" is a key part of their act and that they have a fiduciary responsibility to perform it for the audiences who have paid good money to hear it. Tellingly (in view of what comes later), Susie/Michelle replies that, to her, "Feelings" is like parsley—indeed, *less* than parsley.

This musical insight apparently motivates the lackluster manner in which Susie/Michelle ambi-diegetically delivers "Feelings" in the next scene, the only time when she (purposely) sings really badly on-screen with sloppy phrasing and pointed body language that vividly convey her complete lack of involvement with the piece and its performance. After this telling ambi-diegetic cinemusical episode, Susie/Michelle announces her intention to quit the group immediately and, however implausibly if comically, to pursue an alternative opportunity to make cat-food commercials. Her departure precipitates a monumental lovers' quarrel with Jack/Jeff and prepares the way for some shockingly violent hand-to-hand combat between the Baker Brothers—partly in response to a cruel but accurate insult from Jack/Jeff to the effect that if a customer asked Frank/Beau to play chopsticks, he would need the sheet music. This near-lethal fistfight between the brothers leads ultimately to their aforementioned reconciliation to the strains of "You're Sixteen." So far, so good. But still in doubt is the fate of the relationship between Jack/Jeff and Susie/Michelle.

In the movie's final scene—after Jack/Jeff has returned one more time to Henry's for some more ambi-diegetic Bill-Evans-inspired Dave-Grusin-executed solo piano (which, this time, prompts an offer from the club manager to take a steady gig on Tuesdays and Thursdays)—the more talented, jazz-oriented brother pays a visit to Susie/Michelle. What next transpires has prompted several critics and commentators to opine that the future of the couple's relationship is left hanging by the film's conclusion and remains in doubt. Such an interpretation depends on clinging to the literal meaning of the verbal exchange that occurs between the hero and heroine while ignoring the dramatic development conveyed by the film's music.

Specifically, both Susie/Michelle and Jack/Jeff apologize for their past insensitivities. Rather poignantly, Susie/Michelle admits that she has moved beyond cat-food jingles to doing promotions for vegetables—specifically, carrots and peas but, significantly, not much more elevated in the spectrum of living things than the parsley that she earlier associated with "Feelings." Indeed, Susie/Michelle makes this connection explicit, except that she substitutes the much-despised "Strangers in the Night" for "Feelings." (Somewhere in Musical Heaven, Frank Sinatra is smiling as he knowingly acknowledges the perils of commercialism. With consummate irony, as previously mentioned, the quintessentially unworthy "Strangers" was his biggest-selling record.) Meanwhile, Susie/Michelle says that she has to go or she'll be late (perhaps some indication of a dawning sense of punctuality). Jack/Jeff inquires whether he'll see her again. Susie/Michelle replies by asking what he thinks. He answers that he thinks he will, based on . . . tapping his head . . . intuition. She gives a little nod, followed by an almost imperceptible smile. Then, with a fetching backward glance, she turns and walks away.

If we attend to nothing but the literal meaning in this snatch of verbal dialog, we might possibly entertain doubts about whether this couple will reunite. But, Dear Reader, we would be very foolish to do that. For—beyond the little facial nuances and body gestures so beautifully conveyed by Susie/Michelle and Jack/Jeff in this concluding scene—what happens next gives the clearest possible signal of an impending romantic reconciliation. Specifically, as Susie/Michelle walks away, a new kind of nondiegetic background begins to play. One lone piano (unmistakably, Jack/Jeff via Dave Grusin) accompanies some humming (obviously, Susie/Michelle). As we, the camera, and Jack/Jeff watch Susie/Michelle strolling down the street, she begins her sensitively gentle nondiegetic rendition of . . . "My Funny Valentine." While Susie/Michelle continues to sing to the piano accompaniment by Jack/Jeff, an orchestra joins in as the film fades to black and the credits begin to roll. We cannot conceivably doubt that we are privileged to eavesdrop on a nondiegetic preview of the renewed relationship that will soon reunite this couple in song. And, when Susie/Michelle works her way toward the powerful concluding phrase in which she implores her lover Jack/Jeff to "stay . . . stay," the film credits reach the moment at which they announce the role of Dave Grusin in dubbing the piano performances by Jeff Bridges, and we are left with the prescient reminder that—as Richard Rodgers and Lorenz Hart have been insisting for over six decades—*every* day is Valentine's Day.

## Matt Damon in *The Talented Mr. Ripley* (1999)

Meanwhile, drawing on another side of the "My Funny Valentine" iconography and playing the title role of Tom Ripley in Anthony "English Patient" Minghella's *The Talented Mr. Ripley* (1999), Matt Damon does his best at one crucial juncture in the film to emulate the enigmatically effete style of Chet Baker singing "My Funny Valentine," an ambi-diegetic cinemusical venture in which Damon receives valuably convincing assistance from some lyrically cool Baker-like trumpet work by Guy Barker. We noted earlier that the appearance of Chet's music in soundtracks has recently become something of a Hollywood cliché—as in L.A. *Confidential* (1997) with the aid of Baker's 1950s recordings or in *Playing By Heart* (1998) via original performances by Chet and additional clone-like trumpet solos by Chris Botti—and that the definitive Baker symbology appears with its most starkly depressing glory in Bruce Weber's *Let's Get Lost* (1989), where the physically debilitated and psychically wasted jazz icon seems clearly to have ended up on the losing end of life's painful struggles. Baker's qualities of sensitive sadness, stubborn self-destructiveness, and sexual ambiguity transfer to the character played by Damon and prove proleptic of the developments in that character still to come in subsequent portions of the motion picture. Indeed, the film's full title—which flashes by very quickly, almost subliminally, during its opening credits (so much so that, if you blink, you'll miss it)— captures the Chet Baker persona as accurately as it does that of the Ripley/ Damon character: *The Mysterious Yearning Secretive Sad Lonely Troubled Confused Loving Musical Gifted Intelligent Beautiful Tender Sensitive Haunted Passionate Talented Mr. Ripley.*

Shot in parts of Italy frequented by Chet Baker himself during the 1950s as he tried to outdistance the long arm of the law (the narcotics police hounding him at every turn) by flitting from one European country to another (occasionally stopping to do serious jail time in various locales), the film makes explicit connections between Ripley/Damon and the troubled jazz musician. At one point, Tom/Matt drops a stack of records and Chet's classic *Chet Baker Sings* album on Pacific Jazz comes out on top. As noted by Gavin (2002), Baker has become "a world-wide myth": "The original *Chet Baker Sings* album held a mystique for all generations" (p. 378).

Relying in part on Damon-the-actor's physiognomic resemblance to the pretty-boy image of Baker-the-musician during the 1950s, director Minghella stages Tom/Matt's ambi-diegetic cinemusical performance of "My Funny Valentine" at a crowded, smoke-filled, neon-enhanced, slightly-seedy nightclub in Naples called "Hot Jazz Vesuvio," where the Ripley/ Damon sings the song "very much in the mood of Chet Baker." Quoted on the film's official website, Minghella explains that—like Chet Baker in the 1950s—"Ripley is the one who can genuinely, almost pathologically improvise": "Ripley is a master at it, the real anarchist and subverter" (www.talentedmrripley.com; see also www.sonyclassical.com/music/51337/ multimedia.html). For his part, on the same website, Matt Damon confesses modestly that it took him "two months of playing a couple of hours a day" to learn the piano and, describing his "Valentine"-related vocal style, discloses that "Basically, I just imitated Chet Baker['s] singing as best I could."

Using these cinemusical associations as an imaginative basis, Minghella builds up Ripley/Damon's homosexual inclinations and sociopathic tendencies beyond those found in the original Patricia Highsmith novel. Much as I happen to admire Chet Baker's introverted, vulnerable, fragile, androgynous singing persona and much as I therefore hate to admit it, the connective link between Tom/Matt and Chet works powerfully to advance the developing relationship—first homoerotic, then lethal—between Tom Ripley (Matt Damon) and Dickie Greenleaf (Jude Law). Via this associative connection, tragedy or at least pathology is identified with the 50-year-old image of a jazz icon ("the apparent androgyny of Chet Baker") and maybe even with the doomed lyricist ("Lorenz Hart's omni-directional sexual preferences") who penned Baker's most celebrated song (the "sexually ambiguous" overtones of Chet singing "My Funny Valentine") (Friedwald 2002, p. 371).

The expressive use of ambi-diegetic music in *The Talented Mr. Ripley* supports the main outlines of its exceedingly intricate plot. At the film's beginning, we find Tom Ripley (Matt Damon) playing piano accompaniment for an operatic singer (performing a piece composed by the film's music director Gabriel Yared) at a recital on the terrace of a Fifth Avenue penthouse overlooking Central Park in New York City. Ripley/Damon works as a men's room attendant, but dabbles in classical piano on the side—mostly playing works like J. S. Bach's "Italian Concerto." Because he is wearing a stolen jacket from Princeton, the party's filthy-rich host—Herbert Richard Greenleaf (James Rebhorn)—mistakes him for a friend of his picaresque playboy Princetonian son Dickie (Jude Law) and employs Tom/Matt to travel to Italy for the purpose of convincing the wayward Dickie/Jude to return home.

Realizing that he will need to charm young Greenleaf/Law and knowing that Dickie/Jude loves jazz, Ripley/Damon studies up on this alien artform by buying several jazz albums and giving himself blindfold tests in an effort to assimilate an understanding of the relevant jazz stylists of the day. Thus, we see him at his shabby apartment in the meatpacking district listening to "The Champ" by Dizzy Gillespie on Savoy and "KoKo" by Charlie Parker on the same label. As a classical aficionado—like the elder Greenleaf/Rebhorn—Ripley/Damon *hates* this music. He especially dislikes "My Funny Valentine" by Chet Baker and comments that he can't even tell if it is sung by a man or a woman.

Arriving in Italy and showing a Baker-like tendency toward forgery, Tom/Matt immediately poses as Dickie/Jude when he meets the wealthy but disillusioned Meredith Logue (Cate Blanchett)—who identifies, she says later, with people who have money but despise it. Meredith/Cate buys his fishy impersonation—hook, line, and sinker. And speaking of fish, Tom/Matt is soon spying on Dickie/Jude and his fiancée Marge Sherwood (Gwyneth Paltrow) as they cavort on Dickie's sailboat—significantly named *Bird* (after Charlie Parker). Gradually, Tom/Matt arranges to meet the young couple and insinuates himself into their good graces.

Ironically enough and further reminiscent of Chet Baker, Ripley/Damon openly admits that he is a fraud—expert in forging signatures and imitating others—which he proves by performing a dead-on vocal impression of the elder Greenleaf/Rebhorn. In private, he also accurately mimics Marge/Gwyneth and Dickie/Jude talking about himself. But nowhere does his flair for imitation exceed that which he invests in duplicitously pretending to be a jazz fan—his strategy for charming Dickie/Jude. Thus, on the point of being forced to leave the company of Marge and Dickie, Tom/Matt "accidentally" drops the contents of his briefcase, which include several jazz albums by the likes of Sonny Rollins and John Coltrane plus—coming out on top of the stack—*Chet Baker Sings*. Dickie/Jude becomes especially excited to see the Baker recording and announces with pride that he has named his sailboat . . . *Bird*. To show his enthusiasm, Dickie/Jude takes Tom/Matt to his favorite jazz club, Hot Jazz Vesuvio, in Naples—where Tom joins Dickie (on alto saxophone) and the rest of the Italian musicians on-stage for a rousing, impromptu, and totally faked version of "Tu Vuo'

Fa l'Americano." Besides enhancing the impression of Dickie/Jude as a good-time party boy, this episode is most notable for illustrating the effortless naturalness with which Ripley/Damon can blend seamlessly into virtually any environment, musical or otherwise.

Soon, Tom/Matt gets an opportunity to impress Dickie/Jude even further by virtue of his striking emulation of Chet Baker on "My Funny Valentine." Interestingly, though this cinemusical performance ends ambi-diegetically, it begins as a nondiegetic part of the musical score. Specifically, over what at first sounds like Chet Baker's muted trumpet in the background, we watch Marge/Gwyneth and Tom/Matt walk together through a village street while Marge/Gwyneth describes how she first met Dickie/Jude when he used to play "My Funny Valentine" on his alto sax at a small café in Paris. At this exact moment in the dialogue, we hear what sounds like Chet Baker enter vocally with the first words of the song's lyrics. Marge/Gwyneth says she later discovered that Dickie/Jude only knows about six songs. While the music proceeds, Marge/Gwyneth and Tom/Matt buy some fruit from Silvana (the veggie vendor who later commits suicide because of her shame over having become pregnant with Dickie/Jude's baby); watch Dickie/Jude and several other men playing bocci; greet Dickie/Jude with some banter about getting together at 7:00 pm; and later meet Dickie/Jude again for some clowning around with Silvana (ouch!) and a motor-scooter ride back to the jazz club in Naples, where we now ambi-diegetically watch what turns out to our surprise to be Tom/Matt himself *singing* just the last eight bars of his impressively accurate cinemusical impersonation of Chet Baker—with Dickie/Jude listening appreciatively and then playing an accompaniment on alto, rounded out by the muted Chet-like trumpet of Guy Barker.

OK, so maybe Ripley/Damon does not actually *look* exactly like Chet Baker. For one thing, unlike Tom/Matt, Chet never smiled—perhaps in part because he was such a gloomy guy but doubtless also partly because, as an important part of his embouchure, he was missing his left upper-front tooth due to a childhood accident (Gavin 2002, p. 18) and would have looked a little goofy if he had gone around grinning all the time in the way that Tom/Matt does even when he sings. For another, young Chet was a lot more beautiful to behold than even the good-looking Mr. Damon—right up there with James Dean in the eyes of his myriad female fans. But—all things considered and putting these minor quibbles aside—Ripley/Damon does a terrific job of mimicry, admirably capturing the pensive, sorrowful, effete, vulnerable, lyrical, edgy, slightly disturbed essence of the Baker persona (see also Gabbard 2007; Holbrook 2005e). Again, recall the full title of the film with its description of the *Mysterious-Yearning-Secretive-Sad-Lonely-Troubled-Confused-Loving-Musical-Gifted-Intelligent-Beautiful-Tender-Sensitive-Haunted-Passionate-Talented* Mr. Ripley. Recall, also, that the lyrics to "My Funny Valentine" were written by Larry Hart—"a gay man who is clearly suggesting that heterosexual romance is a joke" (Gabbard 2007, p. 269). "Among the film's less overt references to gayness is the film's fascination with jazz trumpeter/vocalist Chet Baker and the Richard Rodgers

/ Lorenz Hart song, 'My Funny Valentine,' that Baker performed throughout his career" (Gabbard 2007, p. 268) so that "When Tom uses his prodigious abilities as a mimic and sings in a Bakeresque voice . . . , he enjoys the homoerotic thrill of sharing an intense moment with Dickie" (Gabbard 2007, p. 269).

Here, Tom/Matt also manages to charm the pants off the appreciative Dickie/Jude—whom we soon encounter naked in the bathtub, playing chess with the more-and-more openly homoerotic Ripley/Damon (while Miles Davis performs "Nature Boy," nondiegetically and suggestively, in the background). Tom/Matt even asks if he can get in the tub—a thought that apparently fills Dickie/Jude with homophobic horror. But, blinded by passion, Ripley/Damon misinterprets these cues and—starting from such early misconceptions—develops a crush on Greenleaf/Law from which the rest of the film's intricately convoluted plot lines begin to unfold.

Briefly, Tom/Matt meets Dickie/Jude's overtly gay friend Freddie Miles (played over-the-top by Philip Seymour Hoffman), a legitimate jazz lover, whom he perceives as a competitor and loathes (especially when Dickie/Jude and Freddie/Philip whoop it up together at a jazz store in Rome and dismiss Tom/Matt to go back to the village alone). Later, Dickie/Jude returns home to find Tom/Matt playing around in his clothes closet, sort of like a little girl dressing up in her mother's party gowns. Meanwhile, things seem strained between Marge/Gwyneth and Dickie/Jude, who is preoccupied (perhaps somewhat anachronistically) with the need for "Marge Maintenance."

Tom/Matt incorrectly interprets all this as suggesting that he stands a chance with Dickie/Jude romantically. So when Dickie/Jude announces that he wants to break off their relationship, Tom/Matt is horrified. On a farewell trip to the jazz festival in San Remo, Dickie/Jude questions whether Tom/Matt really went to Princeton or even likes jazz. The two go out in a motorboat—ostensibly to look for a house to buy—and when Dickie/Jude professes his love for Marge/Gwyneth and his distaste for Tom/Matt as a leech who gives him the creeps, Ripley/Damon fulfills his role as spurned lover by bludgeoning Greenleaf/Law to death with an oar. He then lies with the object of his affections for a while before sinking the boat and swimming to shore.

From that point on, adding immeasurably to the complexity of the plot, Ripley/Damon begins to impersonate Dickie/Jude with some people while remaining Tom/Matt with others. This double identity involves all sorts of intricate duplicities, shameless lies, phony letters, forged signatures, purloined passports, cloak-and-dagger intrigues, and other elaborately creepy endeavors. As Dickie in Rome, Ripley/Damon accompanies Meredith/Cate to the opera where, as Tom, he encounters Marge/Gwyneth with her friend Peter Smith-Kingsley (Jack Davenport). Nearly trapped, he pulls off a brilliant maneuver wherein Meredith/Cate meets Marge/Gwyneth at the Café Dinelli, and the former tells the latter that Dickie still loves her. From a distance, Ripley/Damon watches until Meredith/Cate leaves and then shows up as Tom to greet Marge and Peter.

Interestingly enough, some of Ripley/Damon's deceptions parallel those of the original Joey in the Broadway production (starring Gene Kelly) but *not* in the Hollywood version of *Pal Joey* (featuring Frank Sinatra)—namely, the pretenses of coming from a wealthy family and of having gone to Princeton (Hyland 1995, p. 245). Contrasting the filmic Tom/Matt with the screen incarnation of Joey/Frank, it appears that a Baker-/Sinatra-like character could/couldn't appear to be fundamentally dishonest. In other words, the Baker-/Sinatra-related persona is/isn't sufficiently duplicitous to engage in deception at the level displayed by Matt-as-Tom. Chet (we must admit) fudges the truth, while Frank (we trust) tells it like it is.

Inevitably, the intertwined fabric of Ripley's deceptions gets increasingly ensnarled and more-and-more difficult to sustain. One evening, while sitting around and playing his magnificent new piano (Bach's "Italian Concerto," to which he has reverted now that he no longer needs to pretend to like jazz), Tom/Matt receives a visit from Freddie/Philip looking for Dickie/Jude. When Freddie figures out the hoax, Ripley has no choice but to brain him with an antique Roman bust he happens to have on hand and, then, to disguise the murder by driving Freddie into the country, faking an accident, and leaving him dead in his own red sports car.

The Roman police are suspicious. So Tom/Matt frames the long-deceased and now-fictitious Dickie by means of a forged letter and leaves Rome to visit Peter/Jack in Venice. Things grow increasingly intimate between Tom and Peter, who turns out to be a classically trained keyboard player (piano, harpsichord, organ) and therefore more-or-less Ripley's dream boy. Marge/Gwyneth and the elder Greenleaf/Rebhorn show up in Venice, and Tom/Matt nearly has to slash Marge/Gwyneth to death with his razor when she figures out his sordid little secret. But, as usual, Ripley bluffs his way out of this very awkward situation and eventually finds that he has convinced the elder Greenleaf not only that he has been loyal to Dickie but that he has been enough of a hero to deserve a substantial share of what would have been Dickie's inheritance, especially if he keeps his mouth shut about Dickie's embarrassing filial transgressions. Indeed, with heavy irony, Greenleaf/Rebhorn ends by actually *thanking* Ripley/Damon.

Tom/Matt and Peter/Jack depart on a celebratory cruise to Athens, momentarily appearing to have achieved happiness. But Meredith/Cate appears on board with her coterie of aunts and uncles—all of whom (mis)recognize Tom as Dickie. Tom-as-Dickie tries to improvise his way out of yet another crisis by giving Meredith/Cate a big kiss and promising to see her later. But, Peter/Jack—who knows Tom as Ripley—observes this exchange and questions him about it. Tom/Matt realizes that the jig is up and that, to escape yet again, he has no choice but to strangle his lover Peter/Jack. The movie ends with Ripley/Damon returning to his cabin while he replays in his head the sounds of this assassination. We hear Peter's soothing voice; then Peter's choking; then his death rattles accompanied by Tom telling Peter that he loves him.

This dismal stuff appears well-suited to a character drawn with the help of associations and identifications borrowed from the tragic image of the great lost soul Chet Baker. Obviously, unlike the fictitious Tom Ripley, Chet Baker was not a serial killer. Indeed, by all reports from various colleagues (Valk 1989; Wulff 1989, 1993; but cf. Gavin 2002) and as documented by such music videos as *Chet Baker: Live at Ronnie Scott's London* (1986) or *Chet Baker Trio: Sweden 1985* (2006), he was actually a fairly nice, gentle, and even sweet individual—well-liked, for example, by his acquaintances pictured in *Let's Get Lost* (1989)—as with other great jazz artists who have fallen into the abyss of drug addiction, more sinned against than sinning. Also (except when staging a scam to get himself discharged from the Army), as made abundantly clear in his salacious memoir (Baker 1997), the thrice-married and oft-attached Chet definitely was *not* gay or even bisexual, preferring to surround himself at every turn with a bevy of beautiful women—some of them wives, some girlfriends, some not. But the two personas—Tom Ripley and Chet Baker—do share many qualities of character in common. Both are basically vulnerable, fragile, introverted, self-destructive, androgynous, dishonest, manipulative, fraudulent, sociopathic misfits. Recall, for example, that Chet Baker served more than his fair share of time in jail—often for forgery when he signed doctors' names to phony drug prescriptions (Gavin 2002; Valk 1989)—forgery being a specialty that Ripley/Damon has also mastered. In *Live at Ronnie Scott's London*, Chet comments with ingratiating bemusement that he escaped an even longer prison sentence because the judge who tried one of his prescription-forgery cases happened to have been a trumpet player in college.

So Ripley/Damon's adroit impersonation—that is, his deadly accurate imitation of Chet Baker singing "My Funny Valentine"—builds a set of imaginative associations vital to conveying the complexity of his mysterious-yearning-secretive-sad-lonely-troubled-confused-loving-musical-gifted-intelligent-beautiful-tender-haunted but ever so "passionate," "sensitive," and "talented" nature. As noted earlier, in the film, the first 24 bars of Ripley/Damon's performance of "My Funny Valentine" serve as nondiegetic background music for a montage of interactions among the Gwyneth-Jude-and-Matt characters, with only the last eight bars appearing in the form of Damon's ambi-diegetic cinemusical performance at the Naples jazz club. I therefore consider it highly significant that—when preparing the trailer released by Sony Classical (www.sonyclassical.com/music/51337/multi media.html), linked to the film's official Website (www.talentedmrripley. com) and included on the DVD version of the film—Minghella and Co. covered the *whole performance* of the piece by Matt at the "Hot Jazz Vesuvio" with scattered snatches from the film intermixed in a re-edited version that favors the on-screen music. Viewed at this extended length, the fidelity of Matt Damon's ambi-diegetic impersonation of Chet Baker becomes more impressive than ever. Without actually achieving the purity of Baker's sound or the accuracy of his intonation, Damon has managed to capture the essence of his vocal mannerisms.

All this attains even greater significance if we contemplate for a moment the piece that serves as something of a theme song for *The Talented Mr.*

*Ripley*. Specifically, three times during the course of the film, we hear the meaning-laden tune "You Don't Know What Love Is" by Gene DePaul and Don Raye (1941). Dickie/Jude plays it on his alto sax just after he has witnessed the grim aftermath of Silvana's suicide, for which he is largely responsible. A lone tenor saxophonist intones the piece on a corner in Venice outside the café where Ripley/Damon meets the elder Greenleaf/Rebhorn, who—sick with grief and guilt over the loss of his son—says that he would pay the street musician $100 to be quiet. And the full lyrics appear over the film's closing credits in a rendition performed in an appropriately croaky voice by John Martyn.

Since its introduction by Carol Bruce in an Abbott-and-Costello film called *Keep 'Em Flying* (1941), DePaul-and-Raye's "You Don't Know What Love Is" has been recorded by countless singers in innumerable contexts. These include (among many others) Karrin Allyson, Tony Bennett (with and without accompaniment by Bill Evans), Ann Hampton Callaway, Chris Connor, Dena DeRose, Billy Eckstine, Ella Fitzgerald, Eydie Gorme, Dick Haymes, Billie Holiday (near the sad end of her tormented life), Etta James, Gloria Lynne, Helen Merrill, Anita O'Day, Dakota Staton, Sylvia Syms, Dinah Washington, Andy Williams, Cassandra Wilson, and Nancy Wilson—but, amazingly enough, *not* Frank Sinatra! However, the hands-down *classic* vocal *and* instrumental recording of this song—the superlatively intense, darkly brooding, tenderly lyrical, deeply depressed, nearly suicidal version; the one you hear ubiquitously today in bars, restaurants, nightclubs, and stage productions all over Los Angeles and New York City; the one that grabs you by the guts and won't let go—was recorded long ago by someone very close to the essence of *The Talented Mr. Ripley*. Specifically, in 1955. For Pacific Jazz. With Russ Freeman on piano, Carson Smith on bass, and Bob Neel on drums. By . . . none other than . . . Chet Baker.

Part III

# The Plot Thickens: Cinemusical Meanings in the Crime-Plus-Jazz Genre

# Introduction to Part III

Part III

Cinemusical Meanings in
the Crime-Plus-Jazz Genre

The three chapters in Part III further explore the role of film music in creating meanings of concern to those with an interest in consumption, markets, and culture. Specifically, Part III examines ways in which the significance of *ambi-diegetic cinemusical moments*—that is, music performed *on-screen* (diegetic) in a manner that advances the *dramatic development* of plot, character, and other themes (nondiegetic)—enrich our interpretation of three key exemplars from the crime-plus-jazz motion-picture genre: *Pete Kelly's Blues* (1955), *The Cotton Club* (1984), and *Kansas City* (1996). Key homologous parallels and contrasts among these three films touch on various consumption-, markets-, and culture-related themes in general and on the contrast or tension between commerce (crime) and art (jazz) in particular.

## BRIEF REVIEW: CONSUMPTION, MARKETS, AND THE CULTURE OF MUSIC IN FILMS

Before proceeding to our detailed illustrations, let us briefly review *four important ways* in which the role of *music in films* engages issues of relevance to various aspects of *consumption, markets, and culture*.

### (1) Product Placement

First, as noted earlier, the appearance of music in a movie represents a form of *product placement* in which the film music itself constitutes a viable cultural offering that competes for patronage in the marketplace and that often generates enviable sales when issued in the form of soundtrack albums or compilation recordings. As we shall see, all three films discussed in Part III earned those kinds of returns from the production of subsidiary offerings that recycled the music they contained.

### (2) Product Design

Second, film music contributes to the *product design* of a motion picture. As in any case of product design, the success of the overall offering depends on the manner in which its constituent features are combined into an effectively integrated composite—where the commercial viability of that composite invariably reflects the interactions among its elements in the manner of a gestalt for which the whole differs from the sum of its component parts. In this connection, as noted in earlier chapters, the present work continues to focus primarily on the role of *ambi-diegetic film music*. Here again, ambi-diegetic film music includes those types of cinemusical moments that are central to motion-picture design in that they are produced on-screen (dieget-ically) but play an important role (nondiegetically) in developing the film's dramatic meanings.

### (3) Symbolic Consumer Behavior

Third, we shall continue to regard film music in general and ambi-diegetic jazz in particular as an important special case of the phenomenon wherein *symbolic consumption*—how the actors in a novel, play, television pro-duction, or motion picture consume various products as part of their personae—contributes meanings to the development of character, plot, and other key dramatic themes (Holbrook and Hirschman 1993). The three films interpreted in Part III all treat music and especially jazz as a central type of product offering consumed and produced by their main characters.

### (4) Themes of Social Significance

Fourth, as also emphasized earlier, the deployment of film music in general and of ambi-diegetic jazz-based cinemusical meanings in particular may reflect, embody, and convey *themes of social significance* of the type that interest students of (macro)marketing and consumer-culture studies. For example, the chapters in Part III will treat the crime-plus-jazz genre as embodying a metaphor that contrasts the essence of art (jazz) with that of commerce (crime)—where art (jazz) emerges as the more socially desirable pursuit.

## THE ROLE OF FILM MUSIC IN THE CRIME-PLUS-JAZZ GENRE

The chapters in Part III pursue the viewpoint just elaborated as it applies to ambi-diegetic cinemusical meanings in a particular type of feature film— namely, *the crime-plus-jazz motion-picture genre*. Here, I shall emphasize that the role of music in general or of ambi-diegetic jazz in particular as a key aspect of meaning in an artistic offering such as a motion picture calls for an interpretive analysis of the *music itself*—that is, *not* merely the lyrics to songs; *not* just the non-musical screen personae of the performers; and *not* only the extra-musical aspects of costumes, props, or scenery; but *rather* the details of the actual musical compositions and performances. As already mentioned, this logic pursues the viewpoint offered in previous analyses of symbolic consumption in motion pictures, television programs, novels, and plays (Holbrook and Hirschman 1993) insofar as the interpretation of (say) clothing, automobiles, or furniture goes beyond the recognition of their roles as costumes (Prada, Vuitton), props (Rolex, Ferrari), décor (Victorian, contemporary), and so forth to embrace their special significance and deeper meaning as manifestations of symbolic consumer behaviors that work toward the dramatic development of plot, character, and other themes. In this connection, to repeat, the ambi-diegetic music that film characters choose for consumption in the form of playing-singing-listening-and-dancing contributes to advancing a film's significant meanings.

Describing this interpretive strategy in the abstract makes little progress toward demonstrating its potential applicability. For this reason, the interpretation of ambi-diegetic music in motion pictures will be illustrated by an analysis of cinemusically meaningful on-screen jazz performances in three key films from the crime-plus-jazz genre in general and by an appreciation of how these cinemusical moments illuminate the theme of commerce-versus-art in particular. Specifically, the three interpretive analyses in Part III will examine the meanings of cinemusical performances as these reflect the contrast or conflict between commerce (crime) and art (jazz) in *Pete Kelly's Blues* (1955), *The Cotton Club* (1984), and *Kansas City* (1996).

## PREVIEW: THREE ILLUSTRATIONS OF AMBI-DIEGETIC CINEMUSICAL MEANINGS IN THE CRIME-PLUS-JAZZ MOTION-PICTURE GENRE

For better or worse, jazz musicians—almost always in need of a night's work and a good day's sleep—often perform at expensive nightclubs, fancy grills, posh watering holes, brassy brasseries, comfortable taverns, dangerous roadside restaurants, boisterous beer halls, dank dives, sleazy bars, and any number of other establishments ranging from the most upscale and elite that money can buy to the most downscale and bedraggled that one might imagine where folks can go to have a drink, eat some peanuts, chew a steak, and listen to some good music. Most of the people who hang out in nightclubs, grills, taverns, bars, and other such places are doubtless perfectly decent nine-to-five workers who just want to have a little fun, toss back a couple of shots, snap their fingers to some hip sounds, or keep time by tapping with swizzle sticks on the rims of their glasses. But low-life gangsters, hoodlums, and felons also need a place to congregate. And it appears, especially in crime films, that jazz clubs often provide their typical meeting places of choice. For this reason—with a lot of help from the *film-noir* genre, from the movie or television scores of composers like Henry Mancini (the TV series *Peter Gunn* during the late-1950s), and from partially valid stereotypes that just won't die—jazz has become a sure-fire signifier for the premonition of robbery, blackmail, kidnapping, or murder.

Some day, an ambitious musical historian, with far more patience and way better funding than I, will trace this trend from (say) *After the Thin Man* (1936) to *The Pink Panther* (1964) to *Manhattan Murder Mystery* (1993) to *The Score* (2001) to *Inside Man* (2006). But, in the meantime, let us confine our attention to three particularly conspicuous and representative examples of the crime-plus-jazz genre—namely, *Pete Kelly's Blues* (1955), *The Cotton Club* (1984), and *Kansas City* (1996). Taken together, these three films span the last half of the past century and give us some clear insights into the ways in which the crime-plus-jazz motion-picture genre has deployed ambi-diegetic cinemusical meanings. In short, the three chapters in Part III explore how on-screen film music can function ambi-diegetically to advance the dramatic development of a motion picture in general and a crime-plus-jazz film in particular. We shall consider detailed illustrations based on our cinemusical interpretations of the three aforementioned examples. As a brief overview, consider the following set of parallel homologous comparisons among the three films of interest—shown here in Table 3 and developed more systematically in the three chapters that follow.

*Table 3* Comparisons of Three Films From the Crime-Plus-Jazz Genre

|  | Pete Kelly's Blues | The Cotton Club | Kansas City |
| --- | --- | --- | --- |
| Release Date | 1955 | 1984 | 1996 |
| Director | Jack Webb | Francis Ford Coppola | Robert Altman |
| Setting | Speakeasy | Nightclub | Nightclub |
| City | Kansas City | New York | Kansas City |
| Time | 1927 | 1930-ish | 1934 |
| Hero | Pete Kelly | Dixie Dwyer | ?Lester Young? |
| Actor | Jack Webb | Richard Gere | Joshua Redman |
| Instrument | Cornet | Cornet | Tenor Sax |
| Dubbing | Dick Cathcart | Richard Gere | N.A. |
| Synchronization | Excellent | Excellent | Real-Time |
| Heroine | Ivy Conrad | Vera Cicero | Honey O'Hara |
| Actress | Janet Leigh | Diane Lane | Jennifer Jason Leigh |
| Other Musicians | Al Gannaway; Joey Firestone | Duke Ellington; Cab Calloway | Charlie Parker |
| Actors | Lee Marvin; Martin Milner | Zane Mark; Larry Marshall | Albert J. Burnes |
| Dubbed By | Matty Matlock (cl); Nick Fatool (d) | Mark Shane (p); Larry Marshall (v) | N.A. N.A. |

*Table 3* Continued

|  | Pete Kelly's Blues | The Cotton Club | Kansas City |
|---|---|---|---|
| House Band | Matty Matlock (cl) | Bob Wilber (cl) | Don Byron (cl) |
|  | Dick Cathcart (tp) | Lew Soloff (tp) | Nicholas Payton (tp) |
|  | Eddie Miller (ts) | Joe Temperly (bs) | J. Redman, |
|  | Moe Schneider (tb) | Britt Woodman (tb) | Craig Handy, |
|  | Ray Sherman (p) | Mark Shane (p) | James Carter, |
|  | George Van Eps (g) | Mike Peters (g) | David Murray, & |
|  | Jud De Naut (b) | Chuck Riggs (d) | David Newman (ts) |
|  | Nick Fatool (d) |  | Geri Allen & |
|  |  |  | Cyrus Chestnut (p) |
|  |  |  | Russell Malone & |
|  |  |  | Mark Whitfield (g) |
|  |  |  | John Goldsby (b) |
|  |  |  | Ron Carter & |
|  |  |  | Christian McBride (b) |
|  |  |  | Victor Lewis (d) |
| Singing | Peggy Lee | Lonette McKee | Kevin Mahogany |
|  | Ella Fitzgerald |  |  |
| Ambi-Diegetic Jazz | Expresses Emotions; Reflects Stresses; Motivates Action | Recreates Color Barriers; Reflects Angst; Shows Integrity | Poor on Realistic Depiction; Good on Dramatic Development |
| Key Parallels | Crime : Jazz | Crime : Jazz | Crime : Jazz |
|  | Commerce : Art | Commerce : Art | Commerce : Art |

As indicated in Table 3, the three films of interest show key similarities and contrasts. More importantly, in their various ways, they reflect the manners in which the ambi-diegetic meanings of on-screen music contribute to a film's dramatic development in the crime-plus-jazz genre. All converge on a key homologous parallel between crime-versus-jazz and commerce-versus-art. These points provide the major focus for detailed illustrations in Chapters 4, 5, and 6.

# 4   *Pete Kelly's Blues* (1955)

*Pete Kelly's Blues* (1955)—starring its director Jack Webb in the role of Pete Kelly, a cornet-playing bandleader whose gig at a 1927 Kansas City speakeasy puts him in conflict with a gangster Fran McCarg (Edmond O'Brien) trying to extort money from the band—comes across as a cinematic disaster until you stop paying attention to its improbable plot, ignore its awkward acting, and regard it instead as a fine vehicle for the presentation of some excellent jazz. At the time he made this film, Webb was riding high on the success of his television show *Dragnet*, on which he played a tough, curt, macho, world-weary cop. So what does he play in *Pete Kelly's Blues*? Of course: A tough, curt, macho, world-weary cornet player.

The only problem is that this cinematic manifestation of socially-challenged interpersonal ineptitude also encompasses the development of a love story between Pete/Jack and the irresistibly attractive Ivy Conrad (Janet Leigh). In real life, Webb had been married to the lovely singer Julie London, but apparently had not learned much from experiencing this up-close encounter with an unsurpassed combination of talent and beauty. Instead, Pete/Jack's tendency to talk to Ivy/Janet in roughly the same manner that *Dragnet*'s Sergeant Joe Friday addresses his detective partner down at the Los Angeles police station renders the lovers' scenes deliciously comic, but leaves an uneasy feeling that Webb did not intentionally play them for laughs.

Further, the crime-related aspects of the story line go way over the top. When McCarg/O'Brien clumsily imposes his extortion racket on the musicians, the band's drummer Joey Firestone (enacted by the same Martin Milner who later starred, again with no trace of subtlety, as the guitar-playing hero in *Sweet Smell of Success* [1957]) goes bonkers and—very, very foolishly—insults the crime boss so flagrantly that Fran/Edmond has no choice but to gun Joey/Martin down like a mallard on the first day of duck-hunting season. This tends to make Kelly/Webb angry and disoriented to the point where the bandleader—also very, very foolishly—spends the rest of the movie ducking the romantic advances of Conrad/Leigh until the preposterous scene at the end in which she traps him in a dance to a hurdy-gurdy that happens to be playing an unbearably schmaltzy version of her leitmotivic theme song ("I Never Knew") in the very same ballroom where, at that very moment, Kelly/Webb is in the process of stealing McCarg/

O'Brien's personal papers for the purpose of incriminating him and thereby ending his reign of terror. When McCarg/O'Brien and his henchmen burst upon the scene—presumably attracted by the horrendous racket of the noisy calliope—Conrad/Leigh and Kelly/Webb take cover behind some overturned tables, fire off a few errant shots, and wait for the propitious moment when Kelly/Webb can hurl a chair at one of the henchmen, causing his gun to misfire and hit McCarg/O'Brien in the chest, dealing this loathsome hoodlum the happy-ending *coup de schmaltz* that he so richly deserves.

So—as an interpretive strategy—let us *forget* the story line and, instead, *go for the music*. In this connection, the film opens with a soulful rendition of "Just a Closer Walk with Thee," played by a mournful cornet with gospel-choir accompaniment around the grave at a burial service in New Orleans circa 1915. This dirge segues, in the manner of the old New Orleans funerals, into a happy version of "Oh, Didn't He Ramble" as joyful marching music for the traditional spirited procession back to town. On the way, the cornet of the deceased falls off the hearse wagon, to be kicked around in the mud, pawned, and passed down from hand to hand for a few years until Pete Kelly wins it in a craps game and ultimately, learns to play it well enough to become a bandleader. All this establishes the link of jazz with its African-American ancestry and sets the stage for the authenticity of Pete Kelly's commitment to his horn—quite consistent with that evinced by (say) Rick Martin (Kirk Douglas) and Bleek Gilliam (Denzel Washington) in such previous and subsequent productions as *Young Man with a Horn* (1950) and *Mo' Better Blues* (1990), respectively (Chapters 7, 9; Holbrook 2005b).

As we pick up the story of Pete Kelly, we find the cornetist playing a rousing version of "Smiles" in a small Kansas City speakeasy in 1927. The ambi-diegetic music in this scene bursts with light-hearted abandon provided by a real-life band put together by Matty Matlock (clarinet) and featuring Dick Cathcart (trumpet), Eddie Miller (tenor sax), Moe Schneider (trombone), Ray Sherman (piano), George Van Eps (guitar), Jud DeNaut (bass), and Nick Fatool (drums)—essentially the same group of jazz-oriented L.A. studio musicians who recorded together many times during the mid-1950s under the name of "The South Rampart Street Paraders." The full contents of five such albums have recently reappeared in a reissue set entitled *Classic Columbia Condon Mob Sessions* (Mosaic MD8-206) and might serve as the gold standard for happy-go-lucky Chicago-styled Dixieland-jazz revivalism at mid-century. I have loved this music since I first heard it as a young boy on a 1954 Paraders recording of "Chinatown, My Chinatown," especially the punchy trumpet work by Dick Cathcart or later Clyde Hurley and the boisterous clarinet counterpoints by Matty Matlock. Matlock—a vastly under-appreciated jazz giant who spent much time behind the scenes in such aggregations as the Bob Crosby Band—was a master of the New-Orleans-Chicago-Dixie-styled clarinet-obbligato flourishes and knew how to bend himself to perfection around the crisp lead horns of the trumpeters with whom he worked (including, besides Cathcart and Hurley, the formidable Red Nichols and the marvelous Wild Bill Davison).

Interestingly enough, the music from *Pete Kelly's Blues* found its way onto long-playing records in at least three different versions. First, the renditions of tunes from the movie recently reissued on Mosaic appeared under the name of *Matty Matlock and His Jazz Band* on Columbia (CL 690). The same group—calling itself *Pete Kelly's Big Seven*, with a narrative by Jack Webb—recorded essentially the same repertoire for RCA Victor (reissued on CD as BMG DRC12081 CCM-055-2). And songs performed in the film by Peggy Lee and Ella Fitzgerald also showed up on a record album entitled *Songs from Pete Kelly's Blues* released by Decca (reissued as MVCJ-19197).

In "Smiles" and in other ensemble pieces featured throughout the film, Jack Webb benefits from this hospitable musical setting with aplomb. Apparently, the actor was a major jazz fan—owner of over 6,000 recordings and an amateur cornet player who diligently practiced the horn. According to Richard Sudhalter's liner notes for Mosaic (MD8-206), Webb had worked before with Dick Cathcart in a short-lived radio version of *Pete Kelly's Blues* in mid-1951, and Meeker (1981) reports that Cathcart continued to perform for a 1959 television series based on the film. Undoubtedly, Webb's fondness for the music inspired his directorial and thespian efforts in the movie version of *Pete Kelly's Blues*. Certainly, his aptitude on the horn facilitated the near perfection Webb achieved in synchronizing his cornet miming with the trumpet sounds ghosted by Cathcart. The effect helps to preserve the aura of great jazz—its spontaneity amidst precision—and moves the story forward by revealing the Kelly character as a serious musician with a high level of bandstand charisma.

These personality characteristics qualify Kelly/Webb for the amorous advances of Conrad/Leigh, who invites him to a drunken party and performs a prophetic and unbelievably cute—not to mention *echt* flapper-based, realistic, and irresistible (to anyone but the dour Kelly/Webb)—rendition of "Gonna Meet My Sweetie Now." As the couple dances, ambi-diegetic music provided by an on-screen orchestra, plays "I Never Knew"—the tune that turns out to be Ivy/Janet's leitmotif—a lovely ballad that captures something of her gentle nature. When she later visits Pete/Jack to apologize for her tipsy behavior at the rowdy party—where she tried to grab his cornet and fell into the goldfish pool—the nondiegetic soundtrack again plays "I Never Knew" as they awkwardly work their way toward a first amorous embrace and passionate kiss. Usually, the "I Never Knew" theme appears in the score whenever images or thoughts of Ivy/Janet come into play—for example, on the aforementioned awful-sounding out-of-tune calliope in a scene at the Everglade Ballroom when Ivy/Janet wants to dance with Pete/Jack and, later, via a full orchestral treatment when Conrad/Leigh offers a charming marriage proposal to Kelly/Webb. Again, we hear this leitmotif non-diegetically when Conrad/Leigh waits for Pete/Jack in her car outside the speakeasy; they argue; she ends up telling him that he wouldn't really want to get married unless he found a girl who looks like a cornet; she adds that she is "three valves short"; they break off their engagement; and she drives away with the classic line, "Gosh, I'm sorry to see me go." Yet again, the theme appears in the background when Conrad/Leigh tries to make up with Kelly/Webb and to renew their relationship at the very moment when he is rushing off in search of McCarg/O'Brien's incriminating documents, too busy to talk with her, and in the mood to dismiss her brusquely. But, as the film approaches its end, we encounter two occasions when the Conrad/Leigh leitmotif shows up in dramatically important ambi-diegetic form.

First, in the suspenseful scene when Kelly/Webb breaks into McCarg/O'Brien's office and prepares to steal his incriminating papers, the calliope machine plays "I Never Knew" as a basis for Ivy/Janet again to ask Pete/Jack to dance—this time under circumstances fraught with imminent danger. The ludicrous sound of the hurdy-gurdy playing the old jazz/pop standard by Ted FioRito (music) and Gus Kahn (words) perfectly complements the wildly improbable nature of this dance episode—in which Conrad/Leigh just wants to twirl around in a romantic way while Kelly/Webb wrestles with a life-threatening crisis that she knows nothing about.

In a sense, the song "I Never Knew" deserves more respect than that. Recall that FioRito wrote the tunes to other such classics as "Toot Toot Tootsie," "When Lights Are Low," and—most estimably—"Laugh! Clown! Laugh!" As a lyricist, Kahn created an even longer line of masterpieces like "Dream a Little Dream of Me," "I'll See You in My Dreams," "It Had to Be You," "Liza," "Love Me or Leave Me," "Makin' Whoopee," "My Baby Just Cares For Me," "My Buddy," "The One I Love Belongs to Somebody Else," "Yes, Sir, That's My Baby," and "You Stepped Out of a Dream"—plus "Toot Toot Tootsie" and "When Lights Are Low" (both with FioRito). As one of the best and most widely circulated hits for both songwriters, FioRito-and-Kahn's "I Never Knew" (1925) has been performed and recorded by an endless list of musical heroes including Louis Armstrong, Charlie Barnet, Count Basie with Lester Young, Ruby Braff, Les Brown, Kenny Burrell, Charlie Christian, Nat "King" Cole, John Coltrane, Wild Bill Davison with Vic Dickenson, Tommy Dorsey, Duke Ellington, Benny Goodman, Coleman Hawkins, Glenn Miller, Zoot Sims, Frank Sinatra, Lennie Tristano with Warne Marsh, Warren Vaché, Bob Wilber with Scott Hamilton, Teddy Wilson, and Lester Young without Count Basie—plus Peggy Lee and George Van Eps (both of whom appear in *Pete Kelly's Blues*). In other words, the song has an impressive musical pedigree, is associated with the finest jazz artists, and carries amorous associations from an era evocative of the budding jazz-age romance between Kelly/Webb and Conrad/Leigh.

Hence, in the song's second crucial on-screen appearance, we experience a feeling of triumph when the ambi-diegetic music in the last scene turns out to be none other than "I Never Knew"—this time performed by Kelly/Webb himself, miming the music by Cathcart with Matty Matlock and Co., in the old speakeasy before an appreciative audience that includes Conrad/Leigh. This concluding performance sounds jubilant, recalling the atmosphere surrounding "Smiles" when the movie began and, again, at the Everglade Ballroom when things were temporarily going well for the band and for the Kelly-Conrad romance. In that earlier Ballroom scene, a voiceover by Webb (a la Joe Friday in *Dragnet*) tells us that, on its own merits, the Everglade is a pretty drab scene, *but* that the good thing about the place is Ivy/Janet. And—BAM!—we see and hear the start of a crackling version of "Smiles." At the end—with an authentic Chicago-style version of "I Never Knew," performed full-tilt by the Matlock band with Jack Webb and the guys doing their convincingly well-synchronized miming on-stage—things have returned to normal. McCarg/O'Brien, the wicked crime boss, is dead. Kelly/Webb and Conrad/Leigh have found true love. And all is well—both musically and socially.

But there is more ambi-diegetic jazz of (1) musical note and (2) dramatic substance in *Pete Kelly's Blues*.

In the first connection (musical note), Webb the director gives us two wonderful performances by Ella Fitzgerald playing the part of Maggie Johnson, the singer at Fat Annie's, a wayside roadhouse where the musicians meet for their secret rendezvous. In this capacity, Fitzgerald delivers her lines with a wide-eyed sort of wooden innocence that clashes violently against her role in the film and places her immediately in the category of great musicians who cannot act. Further, her presence does absolutely nothing to advance the movie's plot line. Her only function in the story itself is to tell Kelly/Webb that there are people waiting for him upstairs in the still—which, in both cases when it happens, he and we already know. So Ella Fitzgerald is there strictly for the transcendent touch of musical excellence that she so characteristically provides.

In this direction, Ella's singing presents us with a remarkable gift that we, as viewers, should take time to appreciate. When we first encounter her at Fat Annie's, Maggie/Ella is singing "Hard Hearted Hannah" in a joyfully Fitzgeraldesque rendition backed by a piano-bass-and-drums trio (Don Abney, Joe Mondragon, and Larry Bunker, respectively, on the soundtrack but played by black actors on-screen). The camera presents her in an up-close head shot, barely moving and seeming stiff (especially when compared with her relaxed in-person and television appearances), but filling the screen and looking way larger than life. In playing Maggie, Ella hits those pitch-perfect notes for which she is so justly famous with aplomb and with all her trademark glissandos and coloratura effects thrown in for good measure—working her way three times to the high note on the concluding phrase, a repeated D-natural on the words "*vamp* of Sava*n*nah, G . . . A." The first two times, she reliably nails the D-naturals with that enviably precise vocal instrument of hers. On the third, she leads us to the same moment in the song—at which point we fully expect to hear those two D-naturals one more time—but then lifts her voice up a half-step to produce two shining E-flats (in effect, a downward appoggiatura, from the fourth to the third of the tonic chord). In context, the effect of this little musical surprise—a phrase often found in gospel music and associated with a soul-jazz feeling—is *electrifying*.

Later, Kelly/Webb again visits the roadhouse and finds Maggie/Ella in the midst of singing "Pete Kelly's Blues" (with words by Sammy Cahn and music by Ray Heindorf written especially for the film). Until now, this tune has served as the film's principal nondiegetic music—supplying background effects whenever something particularly seedy needs to happen, such as Pete/Jack mixing a drink for an already-inebriated guest or arguing heatedly but fruitlessly with a gangster. In Maggie/Ella's ambi-diegetic version, we hear the piece for what it was apparently intended to be—a bluesy torch song sung as only Ella could sing it. Thus, Maggie/Ella's performance, however irrelevant to the main story line, carries an important part of the movie's meaning—anchored in the commerce-versus-art theme (paralleling the crime-plus-jazz genre)—namely, that there is great music out there, as performed by someone of Ella Fitzgerald's caliber (art in the form of jazz), to be treasured far beyond the sort of monetary gain that crooks and hoodlums covet as the sordid lucre from their larcenous capers and squalid shake-down schemes (commerce in the form of crime).

Notice that the account just presented departs significantly from the race-related reading offered by Gabbard (1996), who stresses the early scene where a cornet from a black funeral in New Orleans (1915) finds its way into the hands of Kelly/Webb in Kansas City (1927). In Gabbard's view, this circuitous treatment allows the film to perpetuate "the entrenched practice of denying black subjectivity" (p. 77). Gabbard could have viewed this scene as an attempt to honor the roots of the music but, instead, goes on to suggest that "black instrumentalists are absent from the film after the prologue" (p. 77). This reading accommodates Gabbard's tendency to play the interpretive race card whenever possible, but it entails the disadvantage of denying the reality of what actually happens in the film. Specifically, we have seen that, on at least two occasions and at considerable length, Ella Fitzgerald literally steals the show—accompanied by three musicians played by African-American actors in creating the *mise-en-scène*. Thus can the fight against racism, however well-motivated and worthwhile, potentially blind one to the events that actually transpire in a motion picture.

In the second connection referred to earlier (dramatic substance), the ambi-diegetic music provided by Peggy Lee—playing the part of McCarg's/O'Brien's girlfriend Rose Hopkins (for which she received an Academy-Award nomination as best supporting actress)—contrasts vividly in style and function with that provided by Ella Fitzgerald. Specifically, unlike Maggie/Ella's songs, Rose/Peggy's musical performances are crucial to the dramatic development of the film. Something has to get Kelly/Webb angry enough to resist McCarg/O'Brien's strong-arm tactics and to render him ready to make the move toward a gun-toting, breaking-and-entering mentality. That "something" turns out to be the way Fran/Edmond treats Pete/Jack's friend Rose/Peggy, whom the film portrays as a talented but frail songbird—deeply miserable (reasonably enough) in her abusive relationship with the gangster; profoundly wishing that she had settled down with a family and kids when she had the chance (before she reached the hopelessly advanced age of 35, which in 1955 seemed downright matronly, we gather); touchingly apologetic when McCarg/O'Brien tries to foist her talents on Kelly/Webb's band of Dixielanders (whose usual style does not really fit her somewhat anachronistic Billie-Holidayesque sensibilities); and pitiably prone to drowning her resulting sorrows in drink (especially during one alarming scene in which she guzzles enough whiskey to put most people into a coma). In short, Rose/Peggy contrasts with Maggie/Ella in almost every way imaginable:

| Maggie/Ella | Rose/Peggy |
| --- | --- |
| Blues | Swing |
| Dark | Light |
| Loud | Soft |
| Solid | Insecure |
| Strong | Fragile |
| Hot | Cool |
| Sober | Inebriated |
| Sane | Crazy |
| African American | Caucasian |

When she performs her "try out" number with Pete/Jack's band, Rose/Peggy sings "He Needs Me"—a song specially composed for the film by Arthur Hamilton and subsequently oft-recorded by such worthy female singers as Rebecca Gilgore, Cleo Laine, Gloria Lynne, Polly Podewell, Nina Simone, Frances Wayne, and Peggy Lee herself—in a really compelling performance that resembles nothing so much as a white distillation of the essence of Billie Holiday. In this scene, Hopkins/Lee stands at the far left-hand side of the stage—statuesque and virtually immobile, with her left hand resting on the piano and her right arm hanging loosely at her side—delivering the torchy lyrics in a husky but dead-on accurate voice, soft and sultry, but with perfect intonation and pellucid enunciation. She is terrific. And she follows this stunning performance by moving to center stage to sing "Sugar"—accompanied by fine obbligatos from Kelly/Webb—still standing stoically immobile but doing incredibly expressive things with her eyes and lips while looking as precariously alluring as a beautiful rose (her name) that is about to be hit by a terrible storm (her boyfriend). In subsequent stages of the film, "He Needs Me" serves as nondiegetic music to underscore scenes that portray the defoliation of this flowerlike singer.

Clearly, Kelly/Webb (no fool) is impressed by the formidable singing talents of this tragic songbird but—more important to the ambi-diegetic role of this music—her musical style and demeanor bring out a protectiveness in him that he has not shown in his other relationships (including that with his attractive soon-to-be fiancée Conrad/Leigh). These protective feelings stand their test in a parallel follow-up scene in which Hopkins/Lee—having drowned her sorrows in way too much booze—tries but fails to perform "Somebody Loves Me" with the band. Predictably enough, McCarg/O'Brien reacts with characteristic violence. He takes Rose/Peggy upstairs and beats her up. Semi-conscious, she falls down the stairs and suffers a head injury that reduces her to the mental capacity of a five-year-old and confines her to a state hospital for the insane.

Following the music rather than the verbal text, we should observe that—when playing drunk during a humiliating performance in front of a loud and hostile crowd—Peggy Lee acts her role as a debilitated lush by slurring and forgetting the words, *but she still sings perfectly in tune*! Even when playing the role of a brain-damaged patient, Rose/Peggy *still sings in tune*—this time, a forlornly childish song called "Sing a Rainbow," also written by Arthur Hamilton for this film but not (thank heavens) pursued by other singers (with the unfortunate exception of Astrud Gilberto)—when Pete/Jack visits her at the insane asylum. Here, Rose/Peggy spends her time playing with a limp rag doll and crooning this sad song about red-yellow-pink-and-green to herself in a demented state of perpetual regression to infancy. This scene, colored so strongly by Hopkins/Lee's distraught ambi-diegetic singing, furthers the dramatic development by revealing Kelly/Webb's decent side, highlighting his protectiveness toward Rose/Peggy, and arousing his righteous indignation to the point of taking action against McCarg/O'Brien.

So—to put it mildly—ambi-diegetic cinemusical meanings play a key role in *Pete Kelly's Blues*. In innumerable cases, on-screen performances of jazz pieces and songs sung by singers ranging from competent (Janet Leigh) to accomplished (Peggy Lee) to shimmering (Ella Fitzgerald) perform one or another function in advancing the development of plot, character, or thematic material—Ivy/Janet as a bit ditsy but lovable; Rose/Peggy as a tragic motivation for retribution; Maggie/Ella as a vivid contrast with Rose/Peggy. Further, much of the jazz in *Pete Kelly's Blues* enjoys the sort of *in-between* status (Chapter 1) celebrated by Kassabian (2001)—in the sense that it often begins as diegetic/nondiegetic music and then reappears as nondiegetic/ diegetic music, as in the mixed (non)diegetic scoring of such tunes as "I Never Knew," "He Needs Me," and "Pete Kelly's Blues." However, one especially deft use of this device appears to deserve special comment.

Specifically, early in the film, the Kelly/Webb band makes a record of the old Donaldson-and-Lyman chestnut "(What Can I Say) After I Say I'm Sorry?"—featuring a nice clarinet solo, taking the tune at an unusually slow tempo, and playing it for all its potential poignancy. True to character, this diegetic performance presages the imminent departure of the group's clarinetist Al Gannaway (Lee Marvin), who has been scared off by the intrusion of gangsters into their formerly carefree existence. As Gannaway/ Marvin says goodbye to Kelly/Webb outside the studio, we hear the replay of "What Can I Say?" from the recording session inside. The two exchange some references to the Jean Goldkette Orchestra—where Al hopes to find a job and where (we know) the trumpet chair is currently occupied by Bix Beiderbecke, the then-reigning white *enfant terrible* of the cornet. And then, as the band's newly waxed recording of "What Can I Say?" continues in the background, it's "Goodbye, Al."

Later, Gannaway/Marvin returns, full of rage at how Kelly/Web has caved in to the evil gangsters. The two quarrel. Gannaway/Marvin leaves, this time on a bitter note. But Kelly/Webb redeems himself by following in his car and offering Al/Lee a ride. A reconciliation ensues. Everybody smiles. In the background, we hear a performance of the formerly-diegetic-but-now-nondiegetic "(What Can I Say) After I Say I'm Sorry?"

# 5   *The Cotton Club* (1984)

Directed by Francis Ford Coppola and starring Richard Gere as the cornetist Dixie Dwyer, *The Cotton Club* (1984) might be characterized as a variation on *Pete Kelly's Blues* (1955) with the addition of numerous songs by Duke Ellington, a great deal of mediocre dancing, and an extra half-hour of tedium. In a nutshell, Dixie Dwyer (Richard Gere) recapitulates the role of Pete Kelly (Jack Webb) as a jazz-loving cornet player who gets embroiled in the evil machinations of the Prohibition-Era Mafioso types. Specifically, an especially nasty gangster named Dutch Schultz (James Remar) takes a "liking" to Dwyer/Gere because Dixie has saved his life in a barroom bomb attack. Dutch/James honors this debt by employing Dixie's brother Vincent (Nicholas Cage) and by hiring Dixie to escort his mistress, Vera Cicero (Diane Lane) with whom Dwyer/Gere has already had a brief romantic fling and toward whom he feels a strong sexual attraction. Much of the film's action hinges on the hoodlum-related activities of brother Vincent/Nicholas and the temptations presented to Dixie/Richard in trying to keep his nose clean, while accompanying the alluring Vera/Diane to her rendezvous with Dutch/James. Ultimately, Dixie/Richard and Vera/Diane find a way to (re)unite, while both Vincent/Nicholas and Dutch/James meet violent ends. Alas, in the most perfunctory of scripts—routinely concocted by Coppola with William Kennedy and Mario "Godfather" Puzo—the likelihood of a violent end can never recede too far from center stage.

Meanwhile, a subsidiary plot develops (accounting for much of the extra half-hour) in which Sandman Williams (Gregory Hines), working on-and-off with his (real life) brother Clay Williams (Maurice Hines), wins (1) a dancing job at the Cotton Club and (2) the affections of a silver-tonsiled Cotton Club performer named Lila Rose Oliver (Lonette McKee), who is light-skinned and can pass for white or, more importantly, for a jazz singer somewhat in the mold of Lena Horne. As described in what follows, the ramifications of Item (1) subject us to a great deal of rather undistinguished tap dancing, while the ramifications of Item (2) provide a love story to parallel that of Dwyer-and-Cicero (Gere-and-Lane) and to set the stage for some of the film's few distinguished musical moments.

In an apparently sincere effort to recreate the musical ambience of the 1930-ish Cotton Club—a famous locale in Harlem where Duke Ellington performed with his so-called "jungle style" orchestra from 1927 to 1932 and where black performers provided the scintillating shows but were not permitted to participate as members of the audience—Francis Ford Coppola has cluttered up his film with what we might regard as way too much celebrity-based local color. For example, we must endure gratuitous and unconvincing appearances by Diane Venora as Gloria Swanson, Gregory Rozakis as Charlie Chaplin, Vincent Jerosa as James Cagney, and Rosalind Harris as Fanny Brice. Worse, we are invited to believe that the gaping rictus of Zane Mark bears some resemblance to Duke Ellington's smile. Worst, we are forced to sit through the tormented efforts by Larry Marshall to recreate the offensive preenings of Cab Calloway on "Minnie the Moocher"— that supremely-dreary, obnoxiously-commercial, obsequiously-pandering, offensively-lowbrow song with the annoying refrain about "Hi-Di-Hi-Di-Hi-Di-Hi . . . Ho-Di-Ho-Di-Ho-Di-Ho."

But, beyond these celebrity touches that conspire to add so much needless weight to this production-heavy musical extravaganza, the film offers a great deal of diegetic music that comes across as a mixed blessing. With impressive accuracy as far as the real-life Cotton Club in the late-1920s and early-1930s is concerned, the film features a very large amount of material provided by a bunch of crackerjack studio musicians reproducing the sounds of the early Duke Ellington Orchestra. For example, the film's soundtrack album *The Cotton Club* (Geffen GEFD-24062)—produced by the movie's musical supervisor John Barry and displaying not (say) a saxophone but (rather) a machine gun on its cover—includes many tunes strongly associated with the Duke, masterfully transcribed and arranged for the film by Bob Wilber (with a little help from people like Sy Johnson, David Berger, Randy Sandke, and Al Woodbury): "The Mooche"; "Cotton Club Stomp #2"; "Drop Me Off in Harlem"; "Creole Love Call" (vocal by Priscilla Baskerville); "Ring Dem Bells" (vocal by Dave Brown); "East St. Louis Toodle-O"; "Cotton Club Stomp #1"; "Mood Indigo"; "Wall Street Wail"; "Slippery Horn"; and "High Life." These recreations benefit from the technically proficient contributions of ace studio musicians who do a masterful job of reproducing the famous Ellington sound.

Above all, Duke was a colorist—given to exercising his penchant for interesting musical textures. Thus, from the "jungle music" days in the 1920s until the end in the 1970s, the Ellington Orchestra specialized in a number of colorful and unusual sonic aberrations produced by trombones with plunger mutes (e.g., "Tricky" Sam Nanton); trumpets with wa-wa effects ("Bubber" Miley or "Cootie" Williams); squealing high-stratosphere brass pyrotechnics ("Cat" Anderson); syrupy saxophones (Johnny Hodges); and screeching violins (Ray Nance). Leonard Feather (1960) puts a positive spin on these extraneous intrusions of the "jungle style" by praising the Duke's "unique . . . tonal colors" created by "orchestral voicings that could never be duplicated because the individual timbre of each man in the orchestra was itself essential to the overall effect" (p. 191). But even Feather (1960) must admit that "Cat" Anderson "spoiled many of his performances with high note effects and poor musical taste" (p. 101) and that Ray Nance "has been known primarily as a comedy personality in the Ellington band [with] an excessive accent on grotesque visual mannerisms" (p. 347). *The Cotton Club* both benefits and suffers from these sorts of musical effects.

In this motion picture—often in ways that do not appear to contribute significant meanings to its dramatic development—hoofers hoof; tappers tap; and singers, sometimes with squealing incompetence, mercilessly sing. In the latter connection, I refer especially to the agonized faux-operatic excrescences of Priscilla Baskerville on "Creole Love Call"; the noisome delivery by Dave Brown of "Ring Dem Bells"; and the trying effusiveness of Gregory Hines on "Copper Colored Gal." However, it is the dancing in *The Cotton Club* that really bogs down beyond salvaging. The chorus-line numbers consist mostly of thick-legged beauties strutting their stuff, lovely to look at individually but painful to watch collectively as they shuffle around the stage in quasi-disarray. Even worse are the tap routines featuring the Williams Brothers (Gregory and Maurice Hines) and falling far below the standard expected from a film purporting to capture the great tradition of tapsters harking back to the likes of Bill "Bojangles" Robinson, the Berry Brothers, Sammy Davis and Family, or the nonpareil Nicholas Brothers (on whom the Williams/Hines characters appear to be loosely based). Quite unfortunately and rather inexplicably, the Hines style of tapping involves flicking your feet in a manner that makes clicks totally unrelated to the rhythm of the music to which you are dancing. Instead of beat-reinforcing taps or syncopated clicking, they give us random noises made by feet flailing with arms waving in oblivious self-indulgent excess. Losing contestants on Ted Mack's *Original Amateur Hour*—back in the days when people took tap dancing seriously—did a better job of synchronizing their tapping with the musical pulse (right before they lost to a seven-year-old ventriloquist or a three-foot-tall baton twirler) (but cf. Yanow 2004, p. 154).

As partial recompense for the painful experience of watching the Cotton Club chorus line dance out of step and the Williams/Hines team tap out of rhythm, the film does offer one nice moment of musical fallout from the romantic relationship that develops between Sandman Williams (Gregory Hines) and the light-skinned Lila Rose Oliver (Lonette McKee). Specifically, en route to a tryst at a sleazy hotel that will accept them as guests only if they offer reassurances that they are both "colored" (because Lila/Lonette looks light enough to pass for white), we find Lila/Lonette singing in an all-white nightclub run by Vera/Diane (her reward for shacking up with the evil club-owner, Dutch/James). In this strained setting—that is, passing for something she's not in an atmosphere clouded by corruption and potentially riddled with bullets—Lila/Lonette rears back and lets us have the magnificent "Ill Wind," written for a Cotton Club *Parade* show in 1934 by Ted Koehler (words) and Harold Arlen (music), who had composed "Stormy Weather" for the same venue in the previous year. The latter song—quite similar in feeling and very close in harmonic structure to the former—is indelibly associated with Lena Horne, who memorably performed the piece in the film

*Stormy Weather* (1943) and who also recorded "Ill Wind" at about the same time. Just in case we miss this association, the source music for *The Cotton Club* includes a snatch from "Stormy Weather" in the ambi-diegetic performance of "Ill Wind"—a direct quote, near the end, by trumpeter Lew Soloff in the back-up band—by which time, we cannot help but notice that Lila/Lonette bears a striking resemblance to the young Lena. Hence, "Ill Wind" serves as a perfect vehicle for her ambi-diegetic torch-song delivery—all the more because, in its explicit angst-ridden lyrics and its plentiful implicit musical associations with at least one other world-weary song, it sums up the emotional destructiveness and physical danger of the gangster-dominated scene in which Sandman/Gregory and Lila/Lonette seek to nurture a budding romance—thereby developing both Lila/Lonette's character and relevant aspects of the dramatic setting.

But the aspect of *The Cotton Club* that emerges as its only plausible commendation lies *not* in the spectacular diegetic musical extravaganzas described earlier—virtually all of which, with the exception of the ambi-diegetically meaningful "Ill Wind," deserve to be forgotten as fast as humanly possible—but *rather* in the quietly confident and little-celebrated way in which Richard Gere *plays his own cornet solos*. Historically, matinee idols have sometimes met with mixed success when trying to bring their musical talents to fruition on the silver screen. Recall, for example, Jimmy Stewart's ridiculously wobble-voiced rendition of Cole Porter's "Easy To Love" in *Born To Dance* (1936). Or the misplaced method acting of Marlon Brando in *Guys and Dolls* (1955)—proving beyond doubt that "the method" cannot help a person carry a tune. Or even the otherwise magnificent Fred Astaire—just about any time he opened his mouth to sing in a relentlessly off-key croak. But Richard Gere is something else!

Apparently, recalling Jack Webb, Gere played the trumpet in a band during his high-school years and retains enough technique to enable him to learn some simplified horn solos written out and taught to him note-for-note by the acclaimed mainstream jazz artist, Warren Vaché. Ultimately, Gere's virtual and virtuous cornet playing is the only taste of humanized reality in the whole film and is therefore much to be savored. Specifically, this ambi-diegetic jazz reveals the character of Dixie/Richard as at least serious about something (namely, his music) and as a person of enough integrity (in this case, artistic commitment) to make us care what happens to him (that is, a passable career as both musician and screen actor in gangster movies) and to help us believe that he deserves the love of an appealing woman (such as Vera/Diane). If Dwyer/Gere did not play the cornet so attractively, we would be hard-pressed to find any persuasive reason to like him at all. Hence, as an instantiation of the art-versus-commerce theme, his ambi-diegetic cine-musical performances contribute meaningfully to the dramatic development of the film.

Unfortunately, however, these performances are few and far between. Inexplicably, they make no appearance whatsoever on the aforementioned soundtrack album. However, a careful viewing of *The Cotton Club* suggests at least one occasion on which the cornet work by Dwyer/Gere deserves careful notice and more than a little admiration. Specifically, in a scene where Dutch/James meets with his fellow mobsters while Dixie/Richard and Vera/Diane wait impatiently in utter boredom, the gangster suddenly asks Dwyer/Gere to play "that piece" by Bix Beiderbecke. Dixie/Richard responds by tossing off Beiderbecke's cornet solo from "Singin' the Blues"— the legendary performance that Bix (cornet) recorded with, among others, Frank Trumbauer (C-melody sax), Miff Mole (trombone), Jimmy Dorsey (clarinet), and Eddie Lang (guitar) on February 4, 1927. The importance of this improvisation emerges in the liner notes provided by producer George Avakian for *The Bix Beiderbecke Story* (Columbia CL 845): "It is a solo of intense, brooding beauty, carefully built up to a typical tumbling break in the middle, with a surprise explosion after it." Avakian adds that band-leaders of the 1930s such as Fletcher Henderson scored the solo for large ensembles and that "There was hardly a contemporary white musician of jazz pretensions who didn't learn it by heart."

I also know this Beiderbecke solo by heart because—when I was a boy— my father used to play it verbatim on the piano. Speaking of fathers, years later, when searching one time for an apartment on New York's Upper West Side to be occupied by a visiting colleague during his stay in the City, I answered an anonymous ad in *The New York Times* for a sublet up on Riverside Drive and, when I got there, discovered that the whole place was filled with the most exquisite Oriental rugs I had ever seen. The owner had died, and his son gave a tour of the beautiful apartment with great courtesy and patience. At the end of this encounter, the son of the deceased mentioned that he used to be in the music industry but had taken a leave of absence to manage his Armenian father's rug-import business. He said he had been a record producer. When I asked him what sort of music he had recorded, he began, "Well, have you ever heard of Erroll Garner?" I knew at once that I had struck pay dirt. His name, it turned out, was . . . none other than . . . George Avakian. Such a nice man. So dedicated to this music. Besides his expertise on the subject of Bix Beiderbecke and contributions to the priceless Beiderbecke reissues, Avakian was a tireless producer for such artists as Duke Ellington, Louis Armstrong, Benny Goodman, Dave Brubeck, Paul Desmond, Miles Davis, Sonny Rollins, J. J. Johnson, Erroll Garner, Art Blakey, Keith Jarrett, Charles Lloyd, and Bill Evans. We might wonder what George Avakian—now over 90 years old—thinks of Richard Gere's performance in *The Cotton Club*. Most likely, he approves.

# 6 Kansas City (1996)

In approaching Robert Altman's *Kansas City* (1996), we might plausibly adopt the critical perspective often pursued by Gabbard (1996, 2000) and regard it as a film about race relations and/or gender issues. Gabbard (2000) himself, *comme d'habitude*, gets substantial mileage out of such a reading and, indeed, sheds considerable light on the film from the angle of this essentially postmodern cultural critique. *Kansas City* does in fact present issues of racial prejudices and gender-switching reversals that deserve attention. Further, Gabbard (2000) provides important details on key characters and events that might well pass under the radar of many viewers.

However, to extend the work of Gabbard (1996, 2000) past these issues of race and gender, I wish to interpret *Kansas City* from a somewhat different angle more consistent with our focus on the meaning of ambi-diegetic jazz—namely, as a continuation of the crime-plus-jazz genre in general with implications for the commerce-versus-art theme in particular. Thus, with reference to films of which Gabbard (1996, 2000) takes relatively little notice, my interpretation places *Kansas City* (1996) in the direct line of descent from *Pete Kelly's Blues* (1955) through *The Cotton Club* (1984) to the more recent cinematic scene. As suggested by the three-fold set of homologies developed as a table of parallel comparisons in the Introduction to Part III on crime-plus-jazz films, the problem is that *Kansas City* pursues the familiar themes but does so without the help of any real music-performing hero. Indeed, instead of a horn-playing protagonist such as Pete Kelly (Jack Webb) or Dixie Dwyer (Richard Gere) to occupy the film's central core, the always-quirky Altman gives us a gun-toting non-musical heroine.

This heroine—really a sort of anti-heroine—appears in the form of Blondie O'Hara (Jennifer Jason Leigh), whose major preoccupation is to rescue her ne'er-do-well husband Johnny O'Hara (Dermot Mulroney) from the evil clutches of the gangster boss, Seldom Seen (Harry Belafonte), who hangs out with all the other local Bad Boys at the Hey-Hey Club, where an exceedingly impressive roster of major jazz talent plays full-time 'round-the-clock jazz on a 24/7/365 basis in a kind of perpetual musical nirvana, more or less oblivious to the vile corruption that surrounds them on all sides.

That corruption includes the violent detainment of Johnny/Dermot who has infuriated Seldom/Harry via his part in a robbery hoax that involved mugging one of Seldom/Harry's out-of-town gambling customers. Betraying a grotesque degree of *customer orientation* and spouting absurdly carica-tured rhetoric that sounds like a reading from the textbook for *Marketing 101*, Seldom/Harry and his henchmen evince the link between commerce and crime while giving Johnny/Dermot a very hard time—asking him difficult questions, with typical Altmanesque irony, such as whether he likes the movies. Not really, it appears.

By contrast, Blondie/Jennifer loves motion pictures, idolizes movie stars, and has learned most of what she knows about both styling her peroxide-tortured hair and being a gun moll from watching old Jean Harlow films such as *Hold Your Man* (1933)—which, she brags, she has seen six times. Desperate to free Johnny/Dermot, she launches an elaborately convoluted scheme based on kidnapping one of her sister's manicure clients—Carolyn Stilton (Miranda Richardson), the wealthy but chain-smoking, laudanum-swilling, pharmacologically-challenged wife of an unloving presidential advisor to FDR named Henry Stilton (Michael Murphy)—in order to force Henry/Michael to persuade "Boss" Tom Pendergast to use the clout of his political machine in the service of forcing Seldom/Harry to let Johnny/Dermot go. Predictably, the upshot of all this—after two hours of agonizing—is that Carolyn/Miranda and Blondie/Jennifer have become sympathetic friends but that, in an unfortunate recapitulation of Clark Gable's and Jean Harlow's misadventures in *Hold Your Man*, Johnny/Dermot and Blondie/Jennifer are both . . . deceased.

This febrile, disjointed, gangster-laden story hovers like a lead balloon over the surface of the ambi-diegetic jazz that limns the atmosphere of the seedy Hey-Hey Club where much of the action takes place. Miscreants obsessed with filthy lucre and other ill-gotten monetary gain come there to lie, to cheat, to steal, and to kill each other, while the musicians—Altman seems to say—just behave like the true artists they are (the ones with whom Altman identifies and hopes we shall also identify). The guys in the band more or less ignore all the crime-related violence and mayhem, playing their music with total dedication and an air of detachment bordering on indif-ference to the degradation and vice that surround them. I think it makes sense to view this scenario as supporting the Altmanesque subtext that a jazz musician (that is, the true artist with creative integrity or the film director with a flair for spontaneity) must ignore the greed and corruption that run rampant through the inter-related worlds of business and crime (that is, the commercial pressures of the music industry or the profit motive of Hollywood). Better to remain detached, to do your own thing, and to create inspired improvisations than to become embroiled in the evils of commodi-fication.

In this connection, the illustrious house band at the Hey-Hey Club includes, among others, Don Byron (clarinet); Nicholas Payton (trumpet); Joshua Redman, Craig Handy, James Carter, David Murray, and David "Fathead" Newman (saxophones); Geri Allen and Cyrus Chestnut (piano); Russell Malone and Mark Whitfield (guitar); Ron Carter and Christian

McBride (bass); and Victor Lewis (drums). These musicians—all highly respected jazz masters, plus others too numerous to list here—play with total aplomb. The mood characterizing this scene is captured to telling effect by Oliver Stapleton's brooding cinematography—all in hues of black, brown, gray, and other somber colors. The club patrons wear the right clothing, adopt the right postures, and rightly signify their approval with loud vocal encouragement.

The legitimacy of this scene benefits from the fact that the ambi-diegetic cinemusical performances are filmed in real time—that is, we see the jazz musicians captured on film *while they are actually playing*, a stupendously worthwhile innovation in jazz filmology that harks back to the work of Bertrand Tavernier in *'Round Midnight* (1986, discussed in Chapter 15). Indeed, so good is the real-time ambi-diegetic music in *Kansas City* (1996) that Altman issued a 75-minute companion release entitled *Robert Altman's Jazz '34: Remembrances of Kansas City Swing* (1997), comprising full-length versions of tunes represented only by excerpts in the film. Altman's *Jazz '34* makes no pretense to dramatic content but ranks as one of the finest cinemusical presentations of jazz ever offered.

At many junctures in *Kansas City*, the on-screen presence of a musical group—jamming away on familiar tunes like "(Back Home Again In) Indiana," "I Surrender Dear," and "Lullaby of the Leaves"; swinging "Blues in the Dark," "St. Louis Blues," and "Harvard Blues"; or playing simple head arrangements of well-known Kansas City standards such as "Moten Swing," "Tickle Toe," and "Froggy Bottom"—adds an aura of authenticity to a *mise-en-scène* that depends heavily on Altman's use of diegetic jazz with the K.C. flavor. A potential problem arises, however, in that most of these musicians—generally in their twenties or thirties in 1996 and born 30 or 40 years after the heyday of the music they are called on to play—do not sound very much like their K.C. role models. Rather, they mostly sound like exactly what they are—namely, young modernists trying to emulate a relaxed, bluesy sort of style from days of yore. The Kansas City feeling is there, found in such details as Mark Whitfield's Freddie-Green-styled comping on guitar and the smoothly chugging rhythm section with Geri Allen (piano), Christian McBride (bass), and Victor Lewis (drums) that this chording supports—approximating, as it does, the famous Green-Basie-(Walter)Page-(Jo)Jones sound associated with the "Count" Basie Band. But the harmonic language that characterized the historical guys from Basieland is totally transformed. The note selections of Joshua Redman (as Lester Young), Craig Handy (as Coleman Hawkins), or James Carter (as Ben Webster) deviate sharply from anything that would ever have entered the head of the real Pres, Bean, or Ben. Young's ardent lyricism, Hawkins' busy arpeggios, and Webster's breathy gruffness—all quite old-fashioned by today's standards—are nowhere to be found. Instead, we hear three well-trained guys who sound as if they went to school on the Slonimsky thesaurus of scales, the Wayne Shorter transcriptions, and the Jamey Aebersold play-along recordings—which, mostly, they did.

The real question that we should ask ourselves is whether the manifest musical incongruities just described really matter. On this issue, we might anticipate a continuum of opinions ranging between two divergent extremes, each of which deserves exploration. Let us call these polar perspectives the *anti-Altman* and the *pro-Altman* positions, respectively.

The *Anti-Altman Position* places a high positive value on the role of *diegetic music* in the *realistic depiction* of the *mise-en-scène*. This realism-oriented perspective would argue along the following lines.

(1)  In order to achieve realistic depiction, a film must depict realistically.

(2)  To depict realistically, the film must use props, costumes, décor, scenery, settings, and other aspects of consumption symbolism appropriate to the time and place in which the action occurs.

(3)  Conversely, the appearance of consumption symbolism that is inappropriate to the time and place of the action tends to detract from the film's realistic depiction. For example, in the 1934 world of *Kansas City*, it would be unrealistic to have Blondie/Jennifer drive a Chrysler PT Cruiser; to have Johnny/Dermot wear a Tommy Hilfiger sweatshirt; to have Carolyn/Miranda addicted to Prozac; or to have Henry/Michael call Washington on his iPhone.

(4)  By the same logic, realistic depiction requires that a film's diegetic music match the time and place in which the action occurs. Musicians playing at the Hey-Hey Club in Kansas City circa 1934 should look, sound, and behave as much like Lester Young, Coleman Hawkins, Ben Webster, "Hot Lips" Page, Jo Jones, Freddie Green, Walter Page, "Count" Basie, Jay McShann, Mary Lou Williams, and the rest as humanly possible. Lester should hold his horn at a 90-degree angle; should play with spare melodic lyricism; should confine himself to notes that do not stray beyond the root, third, fifth, sixth, seventh, and ninth of the relevant chord; should wear a porkpie hat and a thin moustache; and should utter phrases like "I feel a draft," "I've got eyes," "Lady Ben," or one of his other patented expressions.

(5)  *Kansas City* gets the porkpie-hat part more or less right; but, in general, Lester Young (Joshua Redman), Coleman Hawkins (Craig Handy), Ben Webster (James Carter), Herschel Evans (David Murray), and the others come across as contemporary jazz players dressing up for a movie. In one scene, a saxophonist (James Carter as Ben Webster) plays a squealing passage that Ornette Coleman might be proud to create and then gives the others a look that comes more out of a Hip-Hop ethos than a Hey-Hey sensibility. In another, Cyrus Chestnut delivers a mock version of stride piano with a harmonic structure so far past Bill Basie that it sounds more like something from Bela Bartok. Similarly, Geri Allen captures the piano style of Mary Lou Williams about as much as Jackson Pollack resembles Rembrandt. Meanwhile, Victor Lewis on drums recalls Jo far less than "Philly" Joe Jones. Elsewhere, Ron Carter plays a pizzicato bass solo on "Solitude" in a manner not heard prior to

the 1950s and with a tone not found in jazz until his own post-Scott-LaFaro playing with Miles Davis in the 1960s. Both he and Christian McBride on bass produce sustained low notes as different from the thumpy sound of (say) Walter Page as it is possible to imagine. And if Kevin Mahogany bears any resemblance to Jimmy Rushing on "I Left My Baby"—other than a tendency to be somewhat rotund—this similarity remains a well-kept secret that *Kansas City* will do nothing to betray (especially given that Mahogany sings from behind the bar in the manner of Joe Turner).

(6) So every time we hear these musicians play—that is, often and for long periods throughout the entire film—we cannot help but think . . . *anachronism*.

(7) In this sense, we may conclude that Altman's choice of diegetic jazz clashes with the film's objectives of realistic depiction.

*But*, in response to this anti-Altman argument, the *Pro-Altman Position* places a high positive value on the role of *ambi-diegetic jazz* in the *dramatic development* of plot, character, and other key themes. This contrasting drama-oriented perspective would argue as follows.

(1) In order to achieve dramatic development, a film must develop dramatically.

(2) To develop dramatically, the film must use props, costumes, décor, scenery, settings, and other aspects of consumption symbolism that resonate with the emotions, identifications, and associations of leading characters, plot lines, and emerging themes.

(3) Conversely, the appearance of consumption symbolism that is inappropriate to the characters' emotions, plot-related identifications, or thematic associations tends to detract from the film's dramatic development. For example, in the sin-infested, crime-oriented, danger-filled, politically-corrupt world of *Kansas City*, it would be dramatically misdirected to have Blondie/Jennifer drive a convertible sports coupe; to have Johnny/Dermot wear tennis clothes; to have Carolyn/Miranda drink soda pop; or to have Henry/Michael travel to Washington in a pick-up truck.

(4) By the same logic, dramatic development requires that ambi-diegetic cinemusical meanings match the emotional tone, plot-related identifications, and thematic associations of the characters and events around which the action occurs. Musicians playing at the Hey-Hey Club in Kansas City should look, sound, and behave like guys at the periphery of a world embroiled in crime that they seek to escape by means of immersion in jazz. In this connection, consider the description of K.C. during the 1930s found on a website called "Club Kaycee," sponsored by The University of Missouri—Kansas City (www.umkc.edu/orgs/kcjazz). Viewing K.C as the "Paris of the Plains," this description emphasizes the roles of "bootlegging, gambling, and prostitution";

limns the town's "sin industry"; and notes that "the city's clubs never closed . . . their doors." The evocation of this scene found in Altman's *mise-en-scène* for the Hey-Hey Club—which appears to be a composite of the real-life Hey-Hay (different spelling), Cherry Blossom, and Reno Clubs—appears dramatically true to the emotions, identifications, and associations of importance. Specifically, the musicians drift in and out—talking, drinking, and even sleeping, but obviously coming to play. They take turns and trade choruses on the bandstand. For the most part, they maintain a laid-back K.C.-based rhythmic feeling in their performances to suggest "the 'flavor' of their predecessors' playing" (Gabbard 2000, p. 145). And, most importantly, the jazz artists provide the counterpart to the "sin industry" so rampant elsewhere in the film—the point of contrast that spells out the alternative lifestyle to which those of an Altmanesque persuasion are called—namely, immersion in your own creative integrity though the world around you may be going to hell in a hand basket. Here, the parallels with Altman-in-Hollywood suggest a strong and important art-versus-commerce subtext. Elsewhere, as revealed especially in the droll cynicism of *The Player* (1992), Altman finds the crass commercialism of the movie industry positively lethal. In reviewing *The Player*, Roger Ebert (1992) notes the "cold sardonic glee" with which Altman made this satiric "movie about today's Hollywood," after Hollywood had "cast him into the outer darkness in the 1980s, when his eclectic vision didn't fit with movies made from marketing studies": "Here is a movie that uses Hollywood as a metaphor for the avarice of the 1980s."

(5) *Kansas City* in general and its ambi-diegetic cinemusical meanings in particular get not only the porkpie-hat part pretty much right, but also a lot of the other emotions, identifications, and associations that surround the jazz community on the edge of a politically and ethically corrupt turmoil. In this film, the jazz musicians have no lines to recite. They do not interact with the criminals. They do not dirty their hands with political involvements. They do not get embroiled in the gambling, drug dealing, prostitution, kidnapping, larceny, or murders that flank them on all sides. They just sit there and play their instruments—a feat requiring an almost superhuman dedication to their art and a prodigious ability to focus on the creative process despite the most harrowing distractions from all directions at once. (To repeat, this situation significantly parallels the artistic struggles of Robert Altman in Hollywood). Some sense of the fidelity with which Altman has captured these aspects of the K.C. jazz scene comes to light in the descriptions offered by Russell (1973), who views Kansas City as "a honeycomb of night clubs that had been operating without interruption all through Prohibition, as if the Volstead Act did not exist, and all through the hard years of the early 1930s, as if there were no Depression either" and who reports that in many clubs "shifts of musicians relieved one another and entertainment continued around the clock" (p. 30). According to Russell, "A

remarkable feature of music in Kansas City was that nobody told the musicians what to play or how to play it [so that jazzmen] were free to create as the spirit moved them": "As the result of favoring conditions—steady work, isolation, a concentration of talent, and almost total lack of commercial pressures—Kansas City had developed a jazz style of its own" (p. 32). Once we abstract our way past the differences in musical style between the 1930s K.C. musicians and the young guys deployed in the ambi-diegetic jazz of *Kansas City*, it becomes clear that Altman has done a superb job of conveying the key thematic elements portrayed in the preceding quotations from Russell (1973)—namely, a fiercely competitive level of musicianship (e.g., Hawk versus Pres); an active club scene where the music never stops (e.g., clubs with names like Reno, Cherry Blossom, and Hey-Hay); a surrounding atmosphere of crime and corruption; and the *freedom* of the musicians to pursue *maximum creativity* unhindered by interference from the gangsters or by commercial pressures that might impede their *artistic integrity*. In this connection, Gabbard (2000) suggests that "*Kansas City* may have succeeded more than almost any other Hollywood film in folding jazz performances into a cinematic narrative" (p. 146).

(6) So every time we hear these musicians play—that is, gratifyingly often and for long periods throughout the entire film—we must focus on the relevance of this ambi-diegetic jazz to the evocation of the film's major characters, plot lines, and thematic ideas. In this connection—as also discussed by Gabbard (2000)—a particularly effective use of ambi-diegetic jazz appears in the scene featuring musicians at the Hey-Hey Club in which we witness a titanic tenor-saxophone battle between Coleman Hawkins (Craig Handy) and Lester Young (Joshua Redman). This frenetic *musical cutting contest* contrasts with the juxtaposed scene in which some of Seldom/Harry's henchmen drive an unfortunate victim to a distant and deserted location where, as the tenor battle concludes at 4:10 a.m. and as the two competing musicians shake hands triumphantly, the gangsters viciously knife their prey to death and leave him to the dogs. This disturbing demonstration of violently *homicidal cutting* contrasts with the parallel musical confrontation to telling effect. Here, we see a vivid opposition between the forces of rapacious criminality (that is, evil commercialism) and the voices of pure jazz (that is, artistic integrity). And lest we miss the point, the unfolding drama of the relevant homology is driven home by the *cinematic cutting* via which Altman presents both sides of the juxtaposition simultaneously. In short, we observe *cutting* from *three vantage points* that, in effect, compose a revelatory sort of *dialectic* consisting of a *thesis* ("cutting" via a sublime saxophone battle); an *antithesis* ("cutting" via a murder by stabbing); and a *synthesis* ("cutting" via a cinematic montage). Thus, in Altman's foreboding use of ambi-diegetic jazz to presage the counterposed forces of evil about to unfold, the on-screen music does its job of providing contrasting emotions, associations, and identifications to

perfection. The fact that Joshua Redman and Craig Handy sound more like each other than like either Lester Young or Coleman Hawkins becomes irrelevant.

(7) In this sense, we may conclude that Altman's choice of ambi-diegetic jazz fulfills the film's objectives of dramatic development.

In another passage from Russell (1973), we find a highly relevant account of the peripheral role played by Charlie Parker—the immortal "Bird"—on the Kansas City jazz scene circa 1934, where Bird "was very much a product of this vigorous grassroots musical culture" (p. 32): "Between 1928 and 1939 . . . , Charlie Parker underwent a metamorphosis from an unexceptional schoolboy studying at Crispus Attucks grammar school to one of the geniuses of American music" (p. 33). This aspect of Bird's background, it turns out, becomes a central metaphor in Altman's film—one that we notice only gradually and only if we pay very careful attention.

An early scene in *Kansas City* shows a young girl—14-year-old Pearl Cummings (Ajia Mignon Johnson) arriving at the train station where she expects to be met by some well-intentioned but incompetent white society ladies who have charitably brought her there for purposes of giving birth to her illegitimate baby but who have managed to be late for meeting the train. Returning from a trip with his high-school marching band—alto saxophone in hand—a youthful Charlie Parker (Albert J. Burnes) finds Pearl/Ajia sitting in the white section of the waiting-room seats, warns her that this is forbidden, and then—with common sense and protectiveness far beyond his years—takes her with him to the mezzanine of the Hey-Hey Club where, still holding his horn in case we have missed the point, Charlie/Albert proceeds to act as a sort of Greek Chorus by explaining to Pearl/Ajia, as well as to us viewers, the significance and identities of the musicians performing on the stage below in general and of Lester Young in particular.

Meanwhile, when Blondie/Jennifer kidnaps Carolyn/Miranda, she takes the wealthy politician's wife to the Western Union office for purposes of sending a telegram calling her husband back from his trip to Washington, D.C. There, we encounter the cleaning lady doing her evening chores. However improbably, this cleaning lady turns out to be Addie Parker (Jeff Feringa)—that is, Charlie's mother (who actually did have a job with Western Union in real life). But this is typical Altman—a director for whom all roads, no matter how disparate, tend always to lead toward convergence in the end. In this connection, recall (say) *Nashville* (1975) or *Short Cuts* (1993). In a similar spirit of convergence, the telegraph-office scene gives Blondie/Jennifer a chance to ask Addie/Jeff how her son Charlie/Albert is doing with his music. It transpires, in case we hadn't guessed, that Charlie Parker is doing just fine, thank you. Meanwhile, via his protectiveness toward Pearl/Ajia, Charlie/Albert is busy revealing himself to be one of the two estimable characters (not counting the ambi-diegetic musicians) to be found in the film—the other, in her own warped way, being Blondie (in one of Jennifer Jason Leigh's most surpassingly edgy roles).

Ultimately, it is really Parker/Burnes through whose eyes we see much of the film unfolding. He sits up there in the balcony while the musicians play their ambi-diegetic jazz and, also, while the gangsters carry Blondie/Jennifer screaming from the Hey-Hey Club. There he sits while all the musical beauty and criminal ugliness transpires. He of all people in the film appreciates the deep opposition between crime (commercial greed gone amuck) and jazz (artistic integrity held aloft). And, of course, he also seems to represent the sensibilities of the director Robert Altman (cf. Gabbard 2000, p. 151).

In this connection, notice that—like Charlie Parker—Robert Altman came from Kansas City. Like Parker in the film, Altman himself was 14 years old when Parker, as leader of Jay McShann's saxophone section, left town. It takes little imagination to envision Robert Altman, at age 14, sitting in the balcony and watching the heroic Charlie Parker perform in the same manner that Charlie Parker in Robert Altman's film sits and watches his own avowed hero Lester Young.

So, in the last analysis, maybe this film *does* have a real music-performing hero after all. Maybe its true cinemusical hero is Lester Young—through the eyes of Charlie Parker—via the sensibilities of Robert Altman. Charlie Parker was born in Kansas City on August 29, 1920. Robert Altman was born in Kansas City on February 20, 1925. But Bird has been dead for 50 years. Fortunately, Altman survived until 2006 to tell the tale.

## CODA

The interpretations found in Part III began with a table of homologous parallels among three major crime-plus-jazz films—*Pete Kelly's Blues*, *The Cotton Club*, and *Kansas City*. The specific analyses of these films in Chapters 4, 5, and 6 suggest that all three lend themselves to an understanding based on the contrast or conflict between commerce (as represented by the selfish, greedy, and/or tainted aspects of crime) and art (as represented by the creative, honest, pure aspects of jazz). Though this subtext remains mostly unstated—below the surface level—in all three motion pictures, it appears clearly to those willing to unfold the meanings implicit in the juxtaposition of crime and jazz that colors all three films and that speaks volumes about the underlying tension between commerce and art. Commerce—as mirrored by the persistently self-interested and resolutely evil activities of common criminals—comes across as inherently evil or at least highly suspicious. Art—by contrast, as mirrored by the bravely self-sacrificing and stubbornly courageous jazz performances of the true music-for-music's-sake heroes—emerges as a force that shines forth as a source of sweetness and light. Similar aspects of the art-versus-commerce theme will again concern us in Part IV. Meanwhile, it appears that, in the face of crime, *film noir* has a potential bright side. And its name is jazz.

# Jazz, Films, and Macromarketing Themes: Art versus Commerce in the Young Man-with-a-Horn Genre

# Introduction to Part IV

As music in film moved into the 1950s and beyond, a change gradually occurred in the way that the audience regarded jazz and, therefore, in the role that jazz as source music in motion pictures played in advancing the dramatic development of characters, plots, and related themes. Specifically, the stature of jazz shifted from that of America's commercially successful popular music (swing) to that of an esoteric, an elitist, and even an exclusionary artform (bebop and beyond). With this shift as a background, the three chapters in Part IV examine the theme of art-versus-commerce via a semiotic analysis of ambi-diegetic cinemusical moments in a trio of films from the young-man-with-a-horn genre: *Young Man with a Horn* (1950), *Paris Blues* (1961), and *Mo' Better Blues* (1990). Specifically, *Young Man with a Horn* deals with the first part of the before/after picture in which jazz shifts its position from the commercial to the hermetic side of the market-driven boundary. *Paris Blues* addresses the aftermath. And *Mo' Better Blues* brings the discussion up to date concerning the more recent cinemusical scene.

## THE ART-VERSUS-COMMERCE THEME IN MACROMARKETING

As anticipated by the three chapters in Part III, a theme of great importance to those with a scholarly interest in issues of relevance to macromarketing concerns the contrast between art and entertainment—that is, between cultural forms aspiring to creative integrity and those aimed at achieving commercial success through popular appeal. The nature of this contrast has inspired a centuries-long debate represented in the macromarketing literature by the sorts of works covered in some of my own various reviews and essays (Holbrook 1995b, 1995c, 1998b, 1999a, 1999c; Holbrook and Day 1994). The full scope of this debate extends beyond the purview of the present work. But the macromarketing-related role of commercialism in general and its manifestation in the tension between art and entertainment in particular nonetheless provide a telling background to the emergence of the art-versus-commerce theme that I wish to discuss here.

Better minds than mine (e.g., Bourdieu 1983, 1984, 1986, 1993) have suggested that, if anything, the relationship between critically-acclaimed aesthetic excellence and commercial appeal tends to be negative—that is, that ordinary consumers tend to enjoy what those endowed with highly educated critical sensibilities evaluate as low in artistic merit and that, conversely, the mass audience tends to dislike what expert critics judge as high in aesthetic value (see also Bloom 1987; Brantlinger 1983; Gans 1974; Henry 1994; Ross 1989; Twitchell 1992; Washburn and Thornton ed. 1996; Washburne 2004). Plenty of anecdotal evidence suggests that this negative relationship between mass popularity and artistic excellence appears—sometimes with almost excruciating insistence—in such arenas as reality television, TV game shows, sitcoms and soap operas (not to mention Oprahs), blockbuster adventure films, pulp fiction, or book-of-the-month clubs and tends especially to surface in the vivid contrast between popular and serious music (e.g., Bayles 1994; Gridley 1987; Hayakawa 1955, ed. 1957; Macdonald 1962; Ortega y Gassett 1932, ed. 1957; Pattison 1987; Washburne 2004). Nonetheless, the limited systematic empirical evidence has tended to find correlations between expert judgments and popular appeal that show detectable-but-small positive associations between the two (e.g., Holbrook 1999c, 2005f; Holbrook, Lacher, and LaTour 2006)—that is, a significant-but-weak correlations that we have labeled the "little taste" phenomenon (Holbrook and Addis 2007). Put simply, it seems that people like what they like—whether it happens to be good or bad in the eyes of professional critics—so that the efforts of the media-and-communications industries tend to cater to the masses, giving people what they want with little regard for its aesthetic excellence.

Pending further studies capable of providing definitive empirical answers, this debate concerning art-versus-commerce remains one of the most vexed and potentially inflammatory issues in the entire macromarketing literature—with those who fancy themselves connoisseurs ready to hurl accusations of philistinism at the plebian tastes of the *hoi polloi*, while those who support the dignity of the common man defensively attack their critics with charges of elitism. Rather than adding further fuel to the fires of this debate, the chapters in Part IV examine the art-versus-commerce issue for what it can contribute to our understanding of three films that depict the lives of jazz musicians over the past half-century.

## VIEWPOINT: ASK NOT. . . .

Perhaps understandably, most commentators who have examined the role of marketing imagery or consumption symbolism in motion pictures, novels, plays, songs, television programs, or other vehicles of popular culture have adopted a focus on the question of what art and entertainment can tell us about marketing, consumer behavior, business, or some other issue of concern to those with an interest in the bottom lines of profit-driven enterprises.

(For reviews and examples that extend beyond the scope of the present work, see Holbrook and Hirschman 1993.) In other words, as typically practiced by those addressing an audience devoted to the profit motive, the conventional business-oriented perspective inquires about how semiotics, hermeneutics, or some other interpretive approach—applied to entertainment and the arts—can glean insights into issues of potential relevance to consumer researchers or marketing strategists. Over the years, I have argued repeatedly—though without gaining many converts among those with a relentlessly managerial bent—that the diametrically opposed viewpoint also deserves our attention. Specifically, in my view, we should devote at least equal scholarly effort to asking how our understanding of consumption experiences and marketing strategy can shed light on the meanings of cultural objects from the worlds of art and entertainment.

It would seem that the audience of readers with an interest in *macro*marketing should be more sensitive than those with a more traditional marketing orientation to issues of broader relevance to society in general, to the not-necessarily-profitable aspects of art-for-art's-sake as opposed to art-for-mart's-sake in particular, and especially to the question of how the art-versus-commerce theme sheds light on the meanings of motion pictures or other cultural objects. Put differently, I would anticipate that—unlike our colleagues in the traditional marketing camp—those of us concerned with *macro*marketing would enjoy a healthy interest in how our discipline might illuminate issues pertinent to the interpretation of art and entertainment. Or—to paraphrase President John F. Kennedy's famous inaugural address—we might expect that, unlike conventional profit-driven marketers, *macro*marketers would embrace the logic: "Ask *not* what semiotics can do for (macro)marketing; *rather* ask what (macro)marketing can do for semiotics."

In that spirit, pursuing our focus on the meanings of ambi-diegetic jazz in motion pictures, I offer the analyses contained in Part IV—namely, illustrations of the macromarketing-oriented art-versus-commerce theme as it contributes to our understanding of jazz-based film music in three motion pictures drawn from what I shall call the *young-man-with-a-horn genre*.

## HISTORICAL BACKGROUND

In this connection, via a crucial discussion entitled "The Celebration of Popular Song" (p. 49), Feuer (1993) describes the situation that prevailed prior to 1950, as illustrated by the use of jazz in *The Hollywood Musical*. As she points out, during the 1930s and 1940s—and on into the early 1950s—the notion of "jazz" tended to evoke the bands of the swing era such as Benny Goodman, Artie Shaw, Count Basie, Duke Ellington, Tommy and Jimmy Dorsey, Harry James, Glenn Miller, Gene Krupa, Woody Herman, and the others: "For a period of time roughly coinciding with the heyday of the Hollywood musical, the so-called 'Swing Era' (*c*. 1935–55), popular music in America was very closely related to jazz" (p. 53). During this swing-oriented epoch, therefore, jazz stood for a type of music that had ethnic folk roots (especially Afro-American) and that depended on a high degree of improvisational spontaneity, thereby aligning this music with the popular accessibility that appealed to the masses and that distinguished jazz from the more stiff and formal aspects of European classical music or opera (p. 54; see also Levinson 1999, p. ix).

This situation inspires Feuer (1993) to describe "the war between elite and popular art" under the heading of a "standard plot" that she calls the "'opera *vs* swing' narrative" (p. 54). Harking all the way back to the first talkie—*The Jazz Singer* (1927)—this paradigmatic plot involves "a son who wants to sing swing and a father or matriarchal grandmother figure who prefers classical musicianship" (p. 54). Typically, this tension is resolved "by reconciling the generations through a merger of musical styles" (p. 54; see also Chapter 16; Gabbard 1996; Holbrook 2008a, 2009). According to Feuer (1993), this basic tension prevailed in the clash of styles between Jeanette MacDonald (operatic vocalizing) and Maurice Chevalier (music-hall singing) in the Paramount operettas during the late-1920s and early-1930s (p. 55). As noted earlier (Chapter 1), a similar dialectic characterized the progress of the relationship between Jeanette MacDonald (operatic style) and Nelson Eddy (popular style) in the operetta *Maytime* (1937) (see also Holbrook 2003a; Rodman 2000). Meanwhile, the contrast between (elitist, classical) ballet and (populist, jazz-inspired) tap dancing informed the sensibilities of such films as *Easy Go* (1930), *Shall We Dance* (1937), *Goldwyn Follies* (1938), *The Band Wagon* (1953), and *Silk Stockings* (1957).

This paradigmatic *opera-versus-swing* structure depended on the convention of catering to and thereby, validating audience tastes associated with mass popularity: "The particular syntax opposing popular and elite elements arises out of the genre's overall rhetoric of affirming itself by applauding popular forms" (Feuer 1993, pp. 55–56). Thus, in the classical/popular contrast, the jazz-oriented pop style emerged as triumphant in such films as *The Time, the Place and the Girl* (1946), *This Time for Keeps* (1947), and *It Happened in Brooklyn* (1947; see Chapter 1).

To review briefly, Feuer (1993) supports this discussion with detailed illustrations from the work of Judy Garland (swing over opera at MGM during the 1940s) and Fred Astaire (jazz dance over ballet at RKO during the 1930s and, subsequently, at MGM during the 1950s). For example, in *Every Sunday* (1936), *Babes in Arms* (1939), and *Presenting Lily Mars* (1943), we find Garland representing the virtues of jazz-oriented swing against the potentially constraining forces of serious opera and, of course, winning the contest every time. Similarly, in *Shall We Dance* (1937), *The Band Wagon* (1953), and *Silk Stockings* (1957), Fred Astaire plays roles in which his jazzy tap dancing privileges the virtues of spontaneous popular entertainment over the refinements of serious classical music and ballet (p. 62; see also Chapter 1; Holbrook 1985).

As we shall again see in Chapter 16, the same convention—that is, the *opera-versus-swing* or *classical-versus-jazzy* or *rigid-versus-free* paradigm—

---

can be found operating quite conspicuously in various swing-era jazz-star biopic films, typified by *The Fabulous Dorseys* (1947), *The Glenn Miller Story* (1954), and *The Benny Goodman Story* (1955). In each case, the traditional, serious, officially sanctioned side of music loses out to the triumphant ascendance of a more innovative, vigorous, light-hearted, popular brand of jazz (see also Gabbard 1996; Holbrook 2008a, 2009).

## KEY CONTRASTS

Though I do not wish to take sides in the often-acerbic contest between various interpretive approaches (new critical, structural, deconstructive, postmodern, ethnographic, consumer-culture, and others), but instead prefer a healthy degree of pluralism (Hirschman and Holbrook 1992), the arguments of Feuer (1993) and others might be summarized via a set of *homologies*—that is, paired contrasts or parallel bipolarities—between jazz-as-swing and classical-or-legitimate music. From an essentially structuralist perspective, these Lévi-Straussian *parallel binary oppositions* mirror the sort of sociological analysis associated with the Bourdieusian perspective (Bourdieu 1983, 1984, 1986, 1993), in which class membership, cultural capital, education or knowledge of the arts, and aesthetic tastes all follow inter-related systems of hierarchical organization. Specifically—during the 1930s, 1940s, and 1950s—the forces of jazz-as-swing in the Hollywood musical and other music-enriched motion pictures tend to win in the contest between the popular and the elite or between the fun and the serious. These pop/elite or fun/serious homologies would appear as follows:

> jazz-as-swing : classical-or-legitimate music
> popular : elite
> entertainment : art
> fun : serious
> light : heavy
> free : rigid
> spontaneous : stiff
> informal : formal
> hot : cold
> in-touch : out-of-touch
> new : antiquated
> future : past
> young : old
> American : European
> ordinary : esoteric
> commercial : artistic
> success : failure
> good : bad

To repeat, the purpose of the chapters in Part IV is *not* to analyze how films have worked to elucidate the theme of art-versus-commerce as it relates to the broader sort of societal issues mentioned in Part III (with reference to the crime-plus-jazz genre) and discussed elsewhere by a number of commentators (cited earlier), but *rather* to show how the macromarketing-related theme of art-versus-commerce helps to shape our understanding of key ambi-diegetic cinemusical moments in three films chosen to illustrate the development in our consciousness of jazz-related commercialism over time. This strategy of cinemusical interpretation asks not what semiotics can do for macromarketing, but rather what macromarketing can do for semiotics.

# 7  *Young Man with a Horn* (1950)

The tendency for American films during the 1930s, 1940s, and 1950s to affirm the left-hand side of the homologies listed in the Introduction to Part IV (jazz as popular entertainment) at the expense of the right-hand side (classical music as elite art)—as documented by Feuer (1993) for the case of Hollywood musicals—further manifests itself in the prototypical tale of an aspiring but troubled jazz artist, directed by Michael Curtiz and entitled *Young Man with a Horn* (1950). This film—which Yanow (2004) considers "greatly underrated" (p. 212)—stars Kirk Douglas in the role of a trumpet player named Rick Martin, torn between the disappointment of a failed marriage to a preposterously self-centered but beautiful socialite named Amy North (Lauren Bacall) and his attraction to a young fresh-faced singer named Jo Jordan (Doris Day). Though loosely and vaguely based on the saga of the renowned cornetist Bix Beiderbecke, this story departs so widely from the true biography of Bix that it seems best to ignore that particular aspect of the plot line. It happens that Hoagy Carmichael, who plays Rick/Kirk's pianist friend Willie "Smoke" Willoughby, was a real-life associate of Bix and that, like Martin/Douglas in *Young Man with a Horn*, Bix himself had a major alcohol-abuse problem. However, the similarities between the two men end right about there. The real-life Bix died at the tragically tender age of 28 years old, whereas Rick/Kirk survives his trials and tribulations to enjoy a successful career as a jazz-trumpet balladeer. Further, as strongly emphasized by musical performances throughout the film, Martin/Douglas plays in a style vastly different from that of Beiderbecke. The legendary Bix—the quintessential white Dixieland musician—developed a clean, sparse, compact, lean-toned, lyrical approach to playing the cornet that emphasized the middle register and favored the use of broken chords circling around ingenious melodic turns of phrase. By contrast, Rick/Kirk's trumpet parts are dubbed by the phenomenal Harry James—the ultimate master of the swing-era style and, apparently, no choir boy himself (Levinson 1999, p. x)—whose bravura trumpet technique features soaring pyrotechnic excursions into the highest reaches of the horn's upper range with a big fat juicy tone and plenty of impressively brassy flourishes.

These attributes of the Harry James sound plus a bit of his swaggering persona emerge clearly in the large amount of source music that appears in this film. We follow Rick Martin's progress from a small boy who sneaks out of the house to practice the piano at a local church; to a young trumpet student who receives generously helpful coaching from his friend-for-life Art Hazzard (an older black musician played poignantly, indeed magnificently, by Juano Hernandez miming the trumpet work of Jimmy Zito); to a young player seeking work in a straight-laced band that specializes in mickey-mouse arrangements (that is, stock-or-schlock versions of pop standards); to a living legend who earns a good salary in Phil Morrison's larger violin-filled orchestra (but who sneaks off for late-night jam sessions with Hazzard and the other authentic jazz musicians in a nightclub downtown); to a deeply troubled alcoholic trying to blow everybody else under the table (but failing to retain his steady gig due to his manifest unreliability and uneven temperament); to a broken-down has-been (who cannot hit a crucial high note at a recording session); to a recovered hero (who has scraped bottom and rebounded to play inspired obbligato parts behind Doris Day's stylish singing). At every stage of this progress, we hear ambi-diegetic jazz generated inside the film's narrative in ways that reflect the swing-oriented trumpet sound of Harry James, that express the shifting aspects of Rick/Kirk's character, and that thereby drive the storyline forward.

Perhaps the less-than-enthusiastic critical acceptance of *Young Man with a Horn* (Meeker 1981) might have been more enthusiastic had Kirk Douglas managed to do a more credible job of miming Harry James' estimable trumpet licks. Truth be told, despite coaching by James himself (Levinson 1999, p. 175), Douglas awkwardly places his knuckles (instead of his finger tips) on the trumpet valves, takes breaths during (rather than between) notes, and moves his fingerings during sustained tones (as opposed to waiting for the tones to change). In short, the visual impression of Kirk's playing ranges by varying degrees from fake . . . to phony . . . to fraudulent. And this glaringly visible flaw tends to disrupt the ambi-diegetic cinemusical effect whereby we infer Rick/Kirk's feelings and persona from the sounds we see and hear him making with his horn. If the music looks bogus, we irresistibly wonder, might not the implied character and emotions also be false?

However, if we can more or less close our eyes or at least squint so as to get past this difficulty with the cinemusical *mise-en-scène*, we shall find that the ambi-diegetic jazz performances pervasive in *Young Man with a Horn* do much to advance the film's dramatic development of character, plot, and key themes. When young Rick first encounters the vibrant sounds of the Art Hazzard band, their playing of "Chinatown, My Chinatown" conveys exactly the sort of joyous feeling that would plausibly win the heart of an impressionable fledgling musician. When Martin/Douglas takes his first job with Jack Chandler's mickey-mouse dance band where music is regarded as a business and nothing more, the tedium pervading the band's unimaginative stock arrangement of "The Very Thought of You" almost demands some sort of defiance, which Rick/Kirk supplies via musically brilliant but contextually inappropriate trumpet obbligatos. When Rick/Kirk jams with his mentor Art/Juano, the empathetic rapport and musical chemistry between these two men shines forth (exaggerated by their ability, without rehearsal, to toss off intricate choruses of virtuosic passages voiced in parallel thirds). When Martin/Douglas, Willoughby/Carmichael, and the guys in the band drive to New Jersey for an after-hours session, their music conveys the ferocity of Rick/Kirk's playing (as an apparent sublimation of the frustration and bitterness he feels over his cruel treatment by the nasty North/Bacall character). When the troubled Martin/Douglas fails to hit his high note on "With a Song in My Heart," we feel his pain (all the more when he plays further erratic notes that constitute a scream of anguish before smashing his trumpet to bits and breaking down in a fit of sobbing). When the rehabilitated Rick/Kirk successfully accompanies Jo/Doris in the same piece, we sense the new maturity and self-control in his playing (poised, lyrical, sweet-toned swing trumpet in what would, at the time, have been regarded as the best of taste for a jazz musician).

All this suggests that—if we overlook the clumsy finger wiggling by Kirk Douglas and focus on his otherwise fine acting—*Young Man with a Horn*'s source music does a near-perfect job of advancing its characterizations, plot lines, and themes in a manner well-suited to furthering the film's dramatic development. In this connection, the ambi-diegetic cinemusical fabric of *Young Man with a Horn* might help us resist two misconceptions encouraged by Gabbard (1996).

First, Gabbard (1996) repeatedly suggests (pp. 72, 148, 153) that—anticipating his immanent breakdown—Rick/Kirk's inability to hit his high note on "With a Song in My Heart" signals his loss of manliness, his emasculation, his symbolic castration, and/or his impotence stemming from the rather shabby treatment he has received from the unappreciative wife Amy/Lauren.

But I disagree.

True, Lauren Bacall's rendition of Amy North creates a veritable touchstone of bitchiness on film—coming across as one of the most selfishly egocentric, aggressively nasty, pathologically disturbed, generally maleficent characters ever to appear on the silver screen. She romances Martin/Douglas just out of self-centered boredom and the curious desire for an interesting experience. That North/Bacall has no soul is evidenced by her lack of feeling for music. She has paid for expensive piano lessons to learn to play a Chopin nocturne but can offer only the most unconvincing rendering of this piece. That she is cold and indifferent emerges from her patent disinterest in hearing the wonderful much-cherished 78-rpm records that Martin/Douglas has carefully crated and carried all over the country. When he tries to play a magnificent old recording by Art Hazzard for her, she succumbs to ennui and leaves the room while his back is turned. That Amy/Lauren personifies cruelty in the extreme appears most clearly when she smashes Rick/Kirk's prized collection of highly breakable shellac disks. To a devout record collector, this musical carnage—which leaves piles of priceless recordings broken into bits and lying all around the living room—is an act of irredeemable hostility.

For all these reasons, the loathsome North/Bacall deserves to be feared, hated, and avoided at all costs. In leaving her, Martin/Douglas acknowledges defeat but also shows himself to be the stronger of the two characters. In wrestling with his demons, he expresses his sorrow, but also bravely blames himself for his problems. When he curtly dismisses the helpful efforts of his trusted loyal friend Hazzard/Hernandez—just before the old fellow walks off in a confused daze, steps in front of a Studebaker, and gets killed—Martin/Douglas cannot forgive himself. But, in my view, this self-punishment does *not* show signs of impotence or emasculation. *Rather*, it represents an understandable and almost admirable if debilitating tendency to set high standards for himself and to judge himself harshly.

Symbolically, it is these high standards—metaphorically and literally—that cause Martin/Douglas to fluff that crucial note in "With a Song in My Heart." The note in question comes toward the end of an improvised chorus after the portion sung by Doris Day (whose excellence as a jazz singer, by the way, is one of the best-kept secrets in American pop culture). Early in the piece, Martin/Douglas has woven a beautifully inventive obbligato background behind the well-crafted singing by Jordan/Day. When he starts his solo, he tosses off some impressive phrases with his usual flair. But, as the solo builds, Rick/Kirk (miming a melodic progression brilliantly invented by Harry James) sets up a musical pattern that could be completed only by hitting a high note that lies above the comfort zone of virtually any trumpet player alive, including Harry James himself. As Jo/Doris correctly and reassuringly points out, Rick/Kirk should not feel bad because the note he tried for was beyond reach. Like a true Romantic, his reach has exceeded his grasp—not because he is weak, impotent, effeminate, or emasculated, but because he has set an impossibly lofty target for himself.

Second, Gabbard (1996) suggests that the denouement of *Young Man with a Horn* involves a willingness of Martin/Douglas to sell out and to settle for playing schlock music in a watered-down style, just for the sake of regaining his sanity and wooing the pretty-perky Jordan/Day. In Gabbard's view, the film pursues an "anti-jazz project" (p. 68), consigns Rick/Kirk to the demeaning "role of accompanist to a singer" (p. 73), displays "no real use for jazz" (p. 74), and views its hero as "being more than a jazz musician and, of course, less than a jazz musician" (p. 72): "We are told that he has renounced his desire to be 'an artist'" (p. 148).

Again, I disagree.

Such a view depends on ignoring the time-honored homologies suggested by our earlier reading of Feuer (1993) and hinges on a failure to appreciate the subtleties of the ambi-diegetic cinemusical clues that unfold from the beginning of the film to its end. Specifically, let us compare two pivotal cinemusical moments that serve as bookends to Rick/Kirk's musical career in the company of Jo/Doris.

In *Cinemusical Moment Number One*, early in the film, Martin/Douglas gets a job in Jack Chandler's hopelessly square mickey-mouse dance band for which the character Willie "Smoke" Willoughby (played by Hoagy

Carmichael, the real-life composer of such songs as "Stardust," "Skylark," "The Nearness of You," "Heart and Soul," and "Georgia on My Mind," among many others) is the pianist and in which the character Jo Jordan (played by Doris Day, a swing-oriented singer blessed with an innocently pretty face, perfectly accurate intonation, and a lot more musical hipness than she usually receives credit for) is the featured singer. After a few desultory greetings to its newest member, the band launches into a drab rehearsal of its sad, unimaginative, by-the-book, stock arrangement on "The Very Thought of You." As Jordan/Day sings the melody, Martin/Douglas feels irresistibly moved to introduce some uninvited but captivating trumpet obbligatos. Needless to say, the authoritarian bandleader Jack Chandler immediately calls him to task, puts him in his place, and orders him never to depart from the written script again. But Rick/Kirk's love of musical freedom and jazz-oriented improvisation is too strong to squelch in this manner. Before long, he and a few co-conspirators engage in a little impromptu jamming on an up-tempo version of "Get Happy," and Martin/Douglas promptly finds himself without a job.

More specifically, this interplay between the left and right sides of the aforementioned Feuerian homologies underlies the structure and meaning of this film. Martin/Douglas represents the free, spontaneous, young, hot, good side of the relevant binary oppositions. The stodgy dance bands in which he earns his living represent the rigid, stiff, old, cold, bad side against which this film rebels. We the audience are invited—by means of the ambi-diegetic cinemusical semiosis—to sympathize with the forces of light on the left-hand side of these contrasts, in opposition to the forces of heaviness or even of darkness on the right.

However, we note one key departure from the Feuerian homologies found in *Young Man with a Horn*. In this film, the pure spirit of jazz is portrayed as less rather than more commercial than the alternative—precisely because the alternative has come to embody traditional straight-laced dance music rather than classical music. Think of Guy Lombardo, Lester Lanin, Meyer Davis, Lawrence Welk, or any of the countless other society and mickey-mouse bands of the last century that would instantly make you want to puke if you were strapped to a chair, as in *A Clockwork Orange* (1971), and forced to listen to their music for more than ten seconds. In *Young Man with a Horn*, such schmaltzy bands are represented by the musical excrescences of Jack Chandler and Phil Morrison. The spirit of Martin/Douglas rebels against all of that—laudably, but in a way that the film recognizes as inherently anti-commercial. Specifically, the film draws the character of Rick/Kirk as a musician who refuses to sell out. As a man less concerned with the market than with the purity of his music. As a jazz player whose values are not for sale. As a genius who will not sacrifice his art on the altar of commerce.

Throughout all this, "Smoke"/Hoagy (the real-world composer of numerous popular standards and therefore no stranger to the market for music, who acts as the voice of reason through this motion picture) reminds

Martin/Douglas that he needs a job to put food on the table and that there is little money to be made from playing true jazz. From Willoughby/ Carmichael's perspective, the only people who buy records are young girls who want to learn the words. Anyone who confines himself to pure jazz will starve as a result. Hazzard/Hernandez (trusted teacher, mentor, and friend) offers similar warnings on the economic realities of the music business.

It happens that, in the context of the period (circa 1950), "Smoke"/ Hoagy's and Art/Juano's observations were quite accurate. Ten years later, they remained accurate and constituted the major reason—along with a conspicuous lack of talent—why I never seriously considered pursuing a career in music (Holbrook 1995a, 2007b). Today, they remain more accurate—and more depressing—than ever.

In 1950, the luster of the magnificent big bands from the swing era had faded, while horribly insipid popular dreck had gained the ascendancy. At Columbia Records, Mitch Miller forced Frank Sinatra to sing "Mama Will Bark" with a howling dog in the background. Before long, people would be vacantly swaying to the anaesthetized sounds of Teresa Brewer's "Music, Music, Music" (1950); Jo Stafford's "Shrimp Boats Are Comin'" (1951); Eddie Fisher's "Wish You Were Here" (1952) and please-save-us-from "Oh Mein Papa" (1953); Patti Page's "How Much Is That Doggy in the Window?" (1953); the Chordettes' "Mister Sandman" (1954); and Bill Hayes' "The Ballad of Davy Crockett" (1955). There are many more in the dark hole where those came from, but I shall be merciful and stop with these few sorry reminders. Henceforth, nobody would be listening to the likes of Rick Martin or, for that matter, Harry James—whose own brilliant career went into permanent eclipse about the time this film was made.

Thus, *Young Man with a Horn*—according to the Hollywood aesthetic described earlier—needs to find some way to let the free-spirited musical playfulness of Martin/Douglas triumph without condemning him to a life of everlasting penury. The film achieves exactly this sort of denouement by concluding with a scene that parallels Rick/Kirk's earlier disappointing rehearsal of "The Very Thought of You" with Jo/Doris while recuperating his disastrous note-fluffing experience on "With a Song in My Heart."

Specifically, in *Cinemusical Moment Number Two*, we find Jordan/Day again singing "With a Song in My Heart" and Martin/Douglas, now restored to his legendary musical prowess, playing an inspired obbligato part in a manner that recalls or even improves on his earlier performance behind Jo/Doris on "The Very Thought of You." But, this time, Rick/Kirk is a hero. And we, the great American music-loving public, have reason to celebrate the triumph of jazz-as-swing on the left-hand side of Feuer's contrasts (cf. Levinson 1999, p. 175).

In case we have been napping through the ambi-diegetic cinemusical semiosis, Hoagy-as-"Smoke" recapitulates the significance of this ending for us. He says that Martin/Douglas has succeeded in learning how to be a better person first and an artist second. This phraseology inspires Gabbard (1996) to develop his notion that Rick/Kirk has sold out. In Gabbard's view of

Rick/Kirk, "we are told he has renounced his desire to be 'an artist'" (p. 148). But this is emphatically *not* what we are told. *Rather*, we are told that Rick/Kirk has found success as (first) "a human being" and (second) "an artist" (p. 74). Contra Gabbard, Willoughby/Carmichael decisively adds the definitive statement made by this film: "*And what an artist!*"

That is the whole point—namely, that Martin/Douglas has not sold out but has found a way to integrate his fun, light, free, spontaneous, informal, hot, in-touch, youthful jazz-as-swing into the fabric of a more conventional dance-band arrangement in a manner that brilliantly accompanies and accommodates the very accomplished singing of Jordan/Day (which is pretty much what he wanted to do, but was forbidden to try, the first time he played with her). Anyone who questions my highly favorable appraisal of Doris Day's worthy-but-neglected talents as a songstress should consult her excellent reading of "I May Be Wrong" earlier in the film, which presciently anticipates the soon-to-be-ubiquitous jazz approach of the cool school by several years. Anyone who doubts the valorization of Rick Martin's trumpet mastery should listen, through the 1950-ish ears of a swing aficionado, to the magnificence of Harry James on the concluding "With a Song in My Heart." Pace Gabbard (1996), this is not some emasculated wimp who has sold out and settled for limping along in the secure setting of an insipid dance band. This is a fine swing trumpet player at the peak of his musical powers. This is the ambi-diegetic cinemusical evocation of the brilliant Harry James—trumpet legend—showing us the validity of Feuer's emphasis on the all-American Hollywood-endorsed era-exalted appeal of jazz-as-swing.


## SEGUE ONE

As jazz moved past 1950 into the post-swing era—with the ascendancy of bebop among jazz circles after World War II—the meanings associated with jazz in the minds of audience members began to shift so as to reflect a newly emerging sensibility in which jazz had become a complex, inaccessible, difficult, off-putting artform. In short, truth be told, jazz had taken on many of the perceived qualities formerly associated with classical music. Think, for example, of Charlie Parker and Dizzy Gillespie with their intricate up-tempo cascades of notes on self-composed tunes in improvisations of bewildering harmonic complexity. Contemplate the inscrutably solipsistic musings of Thelonious Monk; the epicene jazz-classical fusion espoused by such "third stream" artists as the Modern Jazz Quartet and composer Gunther Schuller; or the abstract, introverted, somewhat effete lyricism found in the work of such West-Coast masters as Chet Baker, Gerry Mulligan, Paul Desmond, Jimmy Giuffre, and Jim Hall. Or ponder the onslaught of anger in the music of Charles Mingus, the serene disengagement of the birth-of-the-cool Miles Davis, the fiery magnificence of Clifford Brown, the deep introspection of Bill Evans, the self-absorbed volubility of John Coltrane, and the way-out formlessness of Ornette Coleman's, Don Cherry's, or Eric Dolphy's experiments in free jazz. Different as they indubitably are, the one thing these post-WWII styles share in common is their uncompromising inaccessibility to the mass audience—their stubborn insistence on remaining intentionally hard to assimilate, purposely difficult to understand, and therefore . . . for better or worse . . . *not* commercial and *not* popular. It happens that I personally consider this to be the golden age of jazz and the musicians just listed, along with others of their ilk, to be the supreme masters of jazz as an artform. However, just as clearly to me, these tastes depart from those of the ordinary consumer in ways that bring new and changed meanings to any film made after 1950 in which jazz serves as the major form of cinemusical signification.

These points are well summarized in the authoritative book by Gabbard (1996), especially in his chapter entitled "Jazz Becomes Art" (p. 101). Though Gabbard overlays this theme with a pervasive concern for race- and gender-related overtones, I shall bypass these issues in favor of focusing on the crux of the matter for our present purposes—namely, the increased post-1950s positioning of jazz in motion pictures as a touchstone for artistic authenticity and highbrow seriousness. From this perspective, Gabbard (1996) clearly recognizes the post-bop image of jazz as an exalted form of creative expression—that is, "the notion that jazz is art . . . engaged in the creation of an art discourse" (p. 103). This move toward the sacralization of jazz as a serious artform has continued to the present day, as manifest in the high pretensions amidst small audiences to which the music currently aspires: "The bebop of the postwar era, which held immense appeal for jazz critics but practically none for audiences, has recently become the conventionalized, canonical style" (p. 105). Intimately associated with this sanctification of jazz-as-art, we find a concomitant tendency for the cult-like jazz cognoscenti to reject with the most venomous scorn any form of music that aspires to commercial success—thereby, strongly emphasizing the commercial/hermetic polarity mentioned earlier in which "The musicians most deserving of condemnation are the ones who 'sell out' or play music that is 'commercial'" (p. 107; see also Washburne 2004). A vivid instantiation of the tension between the newly aestheticized jazz-as-an-art-form and the dictates of popular music appears in a telling scene from Elvis Presley's *Jailhouse Rock* (1957) in which a caricature of the jazz cognoscenti serves to privilege "the authenticity of Elvis Presley over the effete pretensions of jazz lovers" (p. 124). After a parody of the typically pompous talk among post-bop jazz lovers (with references to the altered chords, dissonances, and atonality of musicians such as Brubeck, Desmond, and Tristano), Elvis proclaims that he doesn't know what they are talking about and storms out (p. 124). The Presley character's impatient dismissal of the pretentious jazz aficionados could serve as a prototype for the new sensibility in which jazz has shifted from one side of the aforementioned homologies to the other, to be replaced in the populist all-American left-hand column by rock-'n'-roll, rock, disco, rap, or whatever. Let's call the new left-hand pole "rock" to designate, with some imprecision, all these proto-populist sub-categories.

This new image of jazz—as encapsulated by Holmes (1958) in his novel *The Horn* and as contrasted with everything that we associate with rock music— portrays the jazz artist as a Julliard-trained composition student (like Miles Davis) who hangs around with Darius Milhaud (like Dave Brubeck), writes esoteric compositions using an occult tonal scheme (like George Russell), would prefer to live in Europe (like the many expatriates such as Bud Powell, Chet Baker, Art Farmer, Stan Getz, or Dexter Gordon who found a more hospitable jazz climate in Paris, Italy, Vienna, Holland, or Denmark), and performs in an inaccessibly alienating manner (like Thelonious Monk or Charles Mingus) (cf. Gabbard 1996, p. 132).

All this makes available a new signification for jazz, conditioned by the same set of homologies described in the Introduction to Part IV, *except* for the very important fact that jazz has now migrated from the left to the right side of the relevant binary oppositions:

old jazz (pre-1950) → new jazz (post-1950)
rock : jazz, classical, or traditional
popular : elite
entertainment : art
fun : serious
light : heavy
free : rigid
spontaneous : stiff
informal : formal
hot : cold
in-touch : out-of-touch
new : antiquated
future : past
young : old
American : European
ordinary : esoteric
commercial : artistic
success : failure
good?/bad? : bad?/good?

In short, jazz now emerges as a representation of elite, serious, artistic creativity dedicated to an anti-commercial, hermetic aesthetic that celebrates the music's integrity as an artform despite its lack of audience popularity. In the value system espoused by *Jailhouse Rock* (1957) and a vast number of other post-1950s popular films, this position for jazz is "bad." However, there are important senses—especially those identified with artistic integrity— in which the positioning of jazz as an art music might be construed as "good." Some of these surface in the two films that we shall consider in Chapters 8 and 9—namely, *Paris Blues* (1961) and *Mo' Better Blues* (1990).

# 8  *Paris Blues* (1961)

Directed by Martin Ritt with a score by Duke Ellington, *Paris Blues* (1961) depicts the story of Ram Bowen (played by Paul Newman)—a young expatriate jazz musician living in Paris and struggling to find himself or, in other words, to position himself vis-à-vis the aforementioned homologies in the gap that separates the popular, fun, commercial side as opposed to the elite, serious-minded, artistic side of jazz. To anticipate the film's denouement, *Paris Blues* concludes in favor of a life dedicated to artistic integrity— that is, the rigorous formal study of composition in Paris and a devotion to the European standard of professional creative endeavor rather than taking the easy way out by playing the trombone for a group that features pop-jazz standards appealing to the dumbed-down tastes of audiences in America. Clearly, this is a brave theme for a film to pursue, and its creators must enlist some powerful musical forces to help develop this story in a convincing way.

These powerful musical forces are provided by none other than Duke Ellington, working to an undeterminable degree with his regular but uncredited collaborator Billy Strayhorn (Ellington 1973, pp. 194, 512; Gabbard 1996, pp. 193–194). Let us pause to note that—whatever his early associations with "Jungle Music" in his period as leader of the house band at the Cotton Club during the 1920s (Chapter 5) and however often his name has appeared as a songwriter on an endless stream of pop standards such as (say) "Solitude" (1934), "Don't Get Around Much Anymore" (1942), "Just Squeeze Me" (1946), "Satin Doll" (1953), and the rest—Duke Ellington has also emerged as the canonical twentieth-century composer of serious jazz, world-renowned as an artist held in the highest esteem by virtue of his presidential appointments, State-Department tours, ambassadorial lectures, White House dinners, sacred concerts, and innumerable formal orchestral compositions that, as legitimate music, eclipse even the long list of popular songs with which he is also identified (Dance 1970; Ellington 1973).

We need not belabor Ellington's acclaimed credentials in this direction— well covered, for example, in the discussion by Gabbard (1996) in his chapter entitled "Duke's Place" (p. 160). On those grounds, Duke was probably the only conceivable American jazz musician who could plausibly knock George Gershwin's *Porgy and Bess* (p. 174); be angry that Benny Goodman got to Carnegie Hall before he did (p. 176); dismiss *Green*

*Pastures* (1936) in the Webster-and-Kuller lyrics to "Jump for Joy" as "just a Technicolor movie" (p. 184); and compose a film score to the court-room murder mystery in Otto Preminger's *Anatomy of a Murder* (1959) hailed by critics as "a vernacular American symphony" (p. 189). Suffice it to say that—despite my own personal disenchantment with Ellington's "jungle style" (Chapter 5)—most of the jazz intelligentsia regard Ellington's work as the *crème de la crème* of jazz professionalism. Thus, Ellington's concert-oriented oeuvre in general—say, such formal pieces as "Black, Brown and Beige" (1945), "Liberian Suite" (1947), "A Drum Is a Woman" (1956), "Shakespearean Suite (Such Sweet Thunder)" (1957), "Toot Suite" (1958), "Nutcracker Suite" (1960), "Peer Gynt Suites" (1962), "Perfume Suite" (1963), "Far East Suite" (1964), "The River" (1970), "New Orleans Suite" (1971), or "Togo Brava Suite" (1973)—and his film music in particular can serve as a prototype for the potential of jazz to achieve the stature of "serious" formal composition ordinarily accorded to "classical" music.

Perhaps the most conspicuous example of Ellington's serious film music appears in his jazz score for Otto Preminger's *Anatomy of a Murder* (1959). Here, interestingly enough, no background music accompanies the lengthy courtroom scenes that comprise the central core of the movie and that shape much of the film's dramatic tension. Rather, Ellington's score serves mostly to flesh out the local color (the Upper Peninsula of Michigan) and to limn such characters as Laura Manion (Lee Remick as a beautiful temptress whose seductive nature is captured by a theme significantly titled "Flirtibird") or Paul "Polly" Biegler (Jimmy Stewart as a delightfully eccentric and decep-tively cagey country lawyer with penchants for fly fishing and for every kind of jazz from Dixieland to Brubeck). On the ambi-diegetic jazz front, Polly/Jimmy spends his spare time noodling on the piano and, at one point, sitting in at a roadhouse with a small band led by "Pie Eye" (the great Duke himself) for some four-handed jamming. On the fishing front, Polly/Jimmy's fondness for escapist activities with his fly rod (resulting in a refrigerator crammed full of trout) are indelibly associated with a nondiegetic theme from Ellington's underscore that later became something of a pop/jazz classic (with lyrics by Peggy Lee) under the title "I'm Gonna Go Fishin'" (recorded by, among others, Ellington, Lee, Ella Fitzgerald, Mel Tormé, the Four Freshmen, Lambert-Hendricks-and-Ross, and Gerry Mulligan's Concert Jazz Band). In their notes for the booklet accompanying a reissue of the *Anatomy of a Murder* soundtrack album (Columbia/Legacy CK 65569), Wynton Marsalis terms Ellington's score "an incredible work of art, one of the most important ever in jazz" (p. 14), while Phil Schaap calls it a "classic breakthrough in Ellington's music and career" belonging to "the pantheon of Ellington repertoire" (p. 20).

Comparably complex Ellington-inspired meanings play a major role in the signification of his music for the film *Paris Blues* (1961). Gabbard (1996) covers the manner in which Ellington (probably working with Strayhorn) "succeeded to a remarkable degree in bringing unity to the story and enhancing the emotional expression of the characters" (p. 193). I shall summarize this accomplishment only briefly, with a couple of minor personal emendations, in favor of devoting my major attention to three pivotal cinemusical moments (the first two ambi-diegetic, the third nondiegetic) whose telling details—ultimately manifested in the significance of one note played by Johnny Hodges in the background score—develop a meaning that is, I believe, lost on Gabbard.

In *Paris Blues*, Ram Bowen (Paul Newman) plays trombone (dubbed by Murray McEachern) and leads a small band featuring a tenor saxophonist (dubbed by Paul Gonsalves) named Eddie Cook (Sidney Poitier) at a French nightclub—Club 33—where Ram/Paul carries on a rather tepid affair with the club owner and sometime singer Marie Séoul (Barbara Laage). Though never explicitly acknowledged, the band exclusively specializes in playing tunes associated with Duke Ellington—treating us to excellent on-screen performances of "Take the 'A' Train," "Mood Indigo," and "Sophisticated Lady" (sung by Marie/Barbara)—with fine work by actors Newman and Poitier in miming the trombone and tenor solos by McEachern and Gonsalves (Meeker 1981). (Again, on the importance of visual realism in such miming-and-dubbing efforts, see Karlin 1994, pp. 42–45.)

This lighter side of Ram/Paul's and Duke's ambi-diegetic music (leaning toward the left-hand poles of the revised homologies listed earlier) contrasts vividly with a heavier side (leaning toward the right-hand poles) in which Bowen/Newman seeks to compose a serious jazz-based concert piece entitled "Paris Blues," which Ellington-and-Strayhorn deploy nondiegetically in the form of musically accomplished background orchestrations throughout the film. As a composition, "Paris Blues" can stand on its own and, beyond its recording on the movie-soundtrack album, has reappeared in versions by the Ellington Orchestra featuring Paul Gonsalves on tenor sax in F major and by Duke's band with a vocal by Milt Grayson in Bb major—as well as in readings by, among others, the Count Basie Orchestra in D major and Wycliffe Gordon on trombone with Eric Reed on piano in D major. In *Paris Blues*, Ram/Paul works compulsively on this composition, but does not proceed as rapidly as he would like, especially not after he and Eddie/Sidney meet Lillian Corning (Joanne Woodward) and Connie Lampson (Diahann Carroll).

These two alluring tourists show up at the train station where Bowen/Newman has gone to consult with "Wild Man" Moore (Louis Armstrong) in hopes that Moore/Armstrong will show his fledgling blues composition to René Bernard (André Luguet), seen as "a grand old man of French classical music" (p. 199). After two early scenes in which Ram/Paul clearly finds Connie/Diahann the more appealing of the two traveling companions—which, to my mind (pace Gabbard), should dispel any issues of racial bias at the outset—Eddie/Sidney ends up courting Connie/Diahann while Ram/Paul gets "stuck" with Lillian/Joanne. The ironic spectacle of Paul Newman feeling put upon because he must escort his real-life wife Joanne Woodward enjoys a certain amount of comic potential, but foreshadows the ultimately doomed tenor of their relationship—the eventual outcome of which is sabotaged by Bowen/Newman's aspirations to the stature of a serious jazz composer as mirrored by the film score, featuring "Paris Blues," that unwinds in the background. The truth is that—in vivid contrast to Cook/Poitier and Lampson/Carrol—the moments of romantic chemistry between Bowen/Newman and Corning/Woodward are few and far between, primarily because the former pursues a rather obsessive preoccupation with his developing career as a composer of serious music (reflected by the oft-repeated recurrence of "Paris Blues" in the nondiegetic underscore).

From the viewpoint of semiotics—leaning toward the sorts of structural analyses that draw from a Lévi-Straussian emphasis on binary oppositions of the type emphasized in the series of homologies listed earlier (Lévi-Strauss 1963; see also Culler 1975; Saussure 1915, ed. 1966; Scholes 1974; also Holbrook and Hirschman 1993)—the dramatic tension in *Paris Blues* hinges on a related implicit set of parallel bipolarities evident in the two sides of Duke Ellington's work to which I have previously referred. As noted in *The Jazz Text* by Nanry with Berger (1979), "Jazz is marginal in the special sociological sense that it has always been on the cusp where serious and popular music interact" (p. 4). In other words, jazz occupies an indeterminate position on the art-versus-commerce continuum from which it can gravitate, more or less, toward one extreme or the other—that is, toward the more popular (commercial) or more serious (artistic) sides of the relevant bipolar contrasts. Thus, in *Paris Blues*, we find the usual set of homologies operating in full force. On one hand, we have the light, fun, popular, commercial side of Duke represented by such jazz standards as "Take the 'A' Train," "Mood Indigo," and "Sophisticated Lady." On the other, we have the heavy, serious, elite, artistic side of Ellington represented by his formal compositions (the suites and sacred music) and by his film scores (*Anatomy of a Murder* and *Paris Blues*). With special relevance to Duke Ellington, we might expand and summarize our earlier parallel homologous contrasts as follows:

Duke's Light Side : Ellington's Serious Side
light : heavy
fun : serious
popular : elite
commercial : artistic
talented : dedicated
informal : formal
ordinary : esoteric
improvised : composed
spontaneous : stiff
free : rigid
hot : cold
simple : advanced
easily accessible : difficult
American : European
Entertainment : Art
"Duke Lite" : "Serious Ellington"

In the relationship between Ram/Paul and Lillian/Joanne, she favors the "Duke Lite" side of his musical personality—greatly admiring the sensitivity and emotional intensity of his playing, as manifested in his band's nightclub repertoire, and wanting him to leave Paris in order to accompany her back to the United States (where she lives with two children from a former marriage). Connie/Diahann feels pretty much the same way about Eddie/Sidney. But the two musicians see this idea as a threat to their careers as dedicated jazz musicians. Especially, Bowen/Newman sees Corning/Woodward's wishes as counterposed to the "Serious Ellington" side of his aspirations toward formal musical composition—as manifested by the nondiegetic music found in the *Paris Blues* soundtrack. Indeed, early in the film, Eddie/Sidney comments that Ram/Paul's "Paris Blues" theme seems "heavy" and should be lightened up by being scored for oboe. As a demonstration of Ellington's compositional finesse, the piece does indeed sound ponderous, lacking in melodic grace, and heavy in the ways that Eddie/Sidney has indicated.

After a delightful session in which Moore/Armstrong visits the club and engages the Bowen/Newman ensemble in a joyous ambi-diegetic jam session (dominating the scene by virtue of both his charismatic stage presence and his habit of alternating choruses with each accompanying musician so that he plays fully half of the time), Ram/Paul gets his long-awaited audition with Bernard/Luguet—who tells him, in effect, that he is talented but not yet ready for prime time and who advises him explicitly that Paris is a great city for an artist wishing to work, to compose, and to study the theories of harmony and counterpoint.

I differ somewhat from Gabbard (1996) in my interpretation of this pivotal scene. Gabbard sees it as a repudiation of the potential for jazz as a serious form of music: "In *Paris Blues*, jazz . . . can be charming and melodic but not truly serious" (p. 200). I disagree with this under-nuanced reading of Bernard/Laguet's comments. I see Bernard/Laguet as suggesting that, thus far, Bowen/Newman has mastered only the lighter side of Duke, the side associated with Ram/Paul's ambi-diegetic on-screen performances of "'A' Train," "Indigo," and "Lady." He has not yet mastered the more serious side of Ellington, the universally acclaimed and respected side associated with the maestro's various orchestral compositions in general and with his nondiegetic background music for this film in particular. This comparative shortcoming in Ram/Paul's current musical stature is signified throughout the film by his struggles to compose and by his frustrations over orchestrating his concert piece (that is, Ellington's "Paris Blues") at the level of professional competence to which he aspires (as illustrated throughout by the Ellington-Strayhorn underscore).

At any rate, initially and Gabbardesquely, Bowen/Newman elects to interpret Bernard/Laguet's advice as a rejection, feels despondent, and resolves to drift toward the left-hand side of the aforementioned Duke-related homologies by departing for America with Corning/Woodward. Cook/Poitier makes essentially the same decision vis-à-vis Lampson/Carroll, thereby anticipating the denouement of Spike Lee's *Mo' Better Blues* (Chapter 9). But subsequently, Ram/Paul reconsiders, regains his orientation toward the right-hand side of the Ellingtonian bipolarities, and shows up at the train station to bid Lillian/Joanne farewell—telling her that he must follow Bernard/Laguet's advice, stay in Paris to study, and see how far his music can take him. Clearly, Gabbard's reading completely fails to account for this change of heart.

The film ends with a nondiegetic reprise of the "Paris Blues" theme in the background, obscured by additional serious-toned music of a much more discordant nature, which gradually drowns it out as workmen come to paper over a huge poster advertising the appearance of "Wild Man" Moore (Louis Armstrong)—a poster that has appeared repeatedly as a focal point throughout the film. This cinemusical conclusion—the erasure of Armstrong's on-screen image and its displacement by the nondiegetic Ellington score—appears rather clearly to signify the renunciation of Ram/Paul's lighter Armstrong-like Duke-lite side in favor of the more serious Ellington-inspired compositional ethos to which the young jazz musician now aspires. Thus, as Gabbard (1996) concedes,

> Bowen will . . . write music that will in a sense cover over the "charming" but "lightweight" jazz exemplified by Wild Man Moore/Louis Armstrong, whose image is erased [by an advertisement for Librarie Larousse] as Bowen sets off to become a "serious" artist.
>
> (Gabbard 1996, p. 202)

Here, we must interpret "jazz" in the last sentence to refer to the lighter Duke-derived side of Ram/Paul's nightclub repertoire—as opposed to his more serious Ellingtonian inclinations toward formal musical composition, associated with the *Paris Blues* score in general and with the "Paris Blues" theme in particular. Presumably, Eddie/Sidney will follow Connie/Diahann to America (where, he repeatedly insists, he does *not* wish to become involved in issues related to race relations), while Ram/Paul will return to Marie/Barbara at the club (which is *not* such a bad deal, by the way, insofar as the Séoul/Laage character appears considerably more attractive than the Corning/Woodward character and certainly more supportive of Bowen/Newman's aspirations to artistic stature). Early in the film, presciently, the appealing Marie/Barbara has told Ram/Paul that she wishes to keep him "untied" because, she knows, he needs his work . . . and her . . . or someone *like her*. To put it mildly, the overly-controlling high-maintenance Corning/Woodward has been *nothing* like her.

Gabbard (1996) believes that the discordant background music at the end of *Paris Blues* signals Ellington-and-Strayhorn's discomfort with various aspects of the storyline—especially the pronouncements by Bernard/Laguet. Gabbard sees these pronouncements as a dismissal of jazz in general. By contrast, from the perspective of the aforementioned homologies, I interpret Bernard/Laguet's comments as a critique of Ram/Paul's propensities toward Duke's lighter side (improvising new melodies on the changes of jazz/

pop standards in the manner associated with "Wild Man" Moore/Louis Armstrong) and an endorsement of his aspirations toward Ellington's more serious side (to be achieved only by dedicated study in the manner recommended by Bernard/Laguet).

We might, of course, wonder how Ellington himself would feel about all this. In his memoirs entitled *Music Is My Mistress*, Duke comments on how he regards music that panders to the extreme popular-light-accessible end of the art-versus-commerce spectrum, dismissing such "commercial" music as "*deliberately* bland . . . and elementary, so that the dullest ear could have no problem comprehending what (little) was going on" and adding that he "could not imagine" that any of his own musical associates would embrace "that kind of musical nadir" (Ellington 1973, p. 334). These comments resonate with the oft-noted distinction between "commercial values" and "jazz values"—as embodied, say, by the difference between "dance band musicians" and the true jazz "innovator" (Nanry with Berger 1979, pp. 246, 252; see also Becker 1963; Washburne 2004).

How Ellington might regard Bowen/Newman's decision to remain in Paris and to work studiously toward his dream of becoming a serious composer emerges in a passage from the autobiographical musings in which Duke frames the ultimate question as "have we been true to ourselves?" He answers by eschewing "compromise for the sake of monetary or material gain," by calling such commercialism "a form of prostitution," and by concluding that "Anyone who loves to make music knows that study is necessary" (Ellington 1973, pp. 298–299). That Duke Ellington put this art-over-commerce philosophy to practice in his own work emerges clearly in a description from *The World of Duke Ellington* by Dance (1970):

> As he repeatedly affirms, Ellington likes to hear his music performed as soon as possible after it has been composed, and when this does not coincide with the policies of the record companies, he goes ahead and records it at his own expense.
>
> (Dance 1970, p. xiii)

Conversely—reflecting the fact that there are two sides to Duke's persona (Serious Ellington versus Duke Lite)—Ellington could turn right around and question or blur the distinction between art and commerce: "But there's certainly nothing demeaning to my mind in playing music for dancing [because] there *is* a kind of relationship between art and popular taste" (quoted by Dance 1970, p. 16). Further, reflecting the two sides of Duke Ellington and echoing the major dramatic tension in *Paris Blues*, the maestro himself showed an unmistakable ambivalence toward formal musical education. Indeed, he appeared somewhat self-contradictory or even conflicted in considering the merits of academic training and worried about the "risk of . . . original thought being modified by scholastic training": "It's necessary for some people to study, but others don't have to go to school to learn how to think" (quoted by Dance 1970, p. 22).

So—with respect to the aforementioned homologous bipolarities—Duke Ellington himself was nothing if not ambivalent and equivocal.

Overall, from the perspective of the art-versus-commerce contrast, I concur with the broad interpretation of *Paris Blues* proposed by Gabbard (1996). My major reservation concerning Gabbard's approach stems from his tendency to neglect the film music itself (in favor of focusing on various gender- and race-related issues that arise in the storyline). In the case of Ellington-and-Strayhorn's film music, Gabbard refrains from systematically pursuing the ways in which the "Paris Blues" theme appears repeatedly as a leitmotif in the background score—shifting shape from scene to scene in the nondiegetic service of complementing the relevant mood or plot development from one episode to the next. Thus, the "Paris Blues" theme in the key of Eb major (with a trumpet scream from Cat Anderson) accompanies the scene in which Lillian/Joanne wakes up with Ram/Paul after their first night together and finds the city looking from his window like it does in every painting she has seen. Later, "Paris Blues" in F major (played in up-tempo three-quarter time by a saxophone section) sounds in the background while the two pairs of young lovers wander aimlessly but amorously around Paris in the rain. Then, at Ram/Paul's apartment, we hear a demo recording of "Paris Blues" in F major (at medium tempo in duple meter), which quickly becomes an underscore for the major lover's quarrel between Ram/Paul and Lillian/Joanne on the subject of his caring more for his music than he does for her. The theme reappears in C major (played slowly on guitar) in the scene where Ram/Paul learns that Bernard/Laguet wants to see him and, again, in G major (in a slow and mournful version) when Lillian/Joanne returns alone to her hotel after her quarrel with Ram/Paul.

Further—pursuing a focus on small-but-significant details of the cinemusical text—I would refine Gabbard's reading by calling attention to *three cinemusical moments* involving the "Paris Blues" theme that escape Gabbard's analysis but that appear central to the dramatic development of the film's characterizations, plotlines, and key themes. On casual inspection, these three detailed pieces of textual evidence might seem too trivial or too fleeting to merit our attention. Yet I shall argue that, taken together, they are charged with significance in a way that constitutes a tripartite Auerbachian *Ansatzpunkt* or *point of departure* from which unfolds much of the meaning in Bowen/Newman's character and in his plausible rejection of Corning/Woodward (Auerbach 1953). Ultimately, the cumulative significance of these three cinemusical moments manifests itself in one note played in the background score by Johnny Hodges on alto saxophone. In a sense—pushing the *Ansatzpunkt* to its limits—this one note embodies the meaning of the entire film.

*Cinemusical Moment Number One* occurs when Lillian/Joanne spends the night at Ram/Paul's apartment and rises early to fetch coffee and croissants for her new lover. As he wakes—on one of those occasions when the nondiegetic background music spills over into the ambi-diegetic on-screen *mise-en-scène*—she examines Ram/Paul's (Ellington's) score for "Paris

Blues," propped open on the piano's music stand. When Bowen/Newman sees Corning/Woodward silently fingering the notes to his music, he tells her to go ahead and play it. She plays the first few notes of the main melodic theme—C# up to B, followed by A, back down to C# again; then the same phrase repeated except that instead of dropping back down to C# at the end, she ascends to . . . D# a ninth higher: C#-↑B^-↓A; ↓C#^^^; C#-↑B^-↓A; ↑D#^^^. (As before and in what follows, in this notation, letters refer to the names of notes; "↑" and "↓" indicate upward and downward movement, respectively; "^" indicates the passage of one additional beat; and ";" or "." indicates the end of a measure.) But, in playing D-sharp, Lillian/Joanne has hit a wrong note. Ram/Paul scowls and corrects her, somewhat scornfully, telling her that she should have played *D-natural*. Specifically, the correct melody line and chord progression are:

> Melody: C# ↑B ^ ↓A ; ↓C# ^ ^ ^ ; C# ↑B ^ ↓A ; ↑D ^ ^ ^ .
> Chords: Dmaj7 D6 ; G7♭5 ; DMaj7 D6 ; Am7 D7 .

The misplaced note played by Lillian/Joanne—D-sharp instead of D-natural in the fourth bar—signifies the tension between Bowen/Newman and Corning/Woodward. On one hand, hers is an intelligent mistake. Not being a professional musician and not noting the key signature, she has started on C# and just naturally assumes that the piece is in a key with a lot of sharps in its signature—including D#, when she gets there a few notes later. This reflects her status as a jazz fan who does not know a lot about serious music but who appreciates the more entertaining Duke-Lite side of Bowen/Newman's style and loves him for the deep feelings that he projects through his playing and that he reveals via his ambi-diegetic performances in this more commercial and accessible vein. But the piece is actually written in the key of D major—its melody starting on the major seventh (C-sharp)—so that the correct note (D-natural) is the root of a D7 chord or an Am7-D7 transition that appears at the moment in the piece where Corning/Woodward hits her clinker. Ram/Paul's discomfort with this wrong note signals his similar reactions toward Lillian/Joanne's aspirations for him—which, from his perspective, imply renouncing the higher goal of perfecting his skills as an artistically-dedicated jazz composer (his more serious Ellingtonian musical side) and settling for a career as a more popularity-oriented crowd-pleasing jazz trombonist (his Duke-Lite as well as his Armstrongian musical side). Ram/Paul sees Lillian/Joanne's declaration of love as forcing him to make a choice between these two alternatives, the latter of which constitutes a sell-out to the more easily accessible, commercial end of the jazz spectrum (the left-hand poles of the aforementioned homologies). Vividly articulating this tension and expressing his inclination toward the "Serious Ellington" as opposed to the "Duke Lite" side of the art-versus-commerce opposition, Bowen/Newman tells Corning/Woodward emphatically that he lives his music, that he has no time for anything else (including, by implication, her), and that he is *not* on the *market*. The latter point carries the double message that Ram/Paul is, first, committed to pursuing the artistic rather than the commercial end of the jazz spectrum and, second, unavailable as a suitable candidate for an amorous relationship.

*Cinemusical Moment Number Two* occurs after Ram/Paul—disappointed by the response of Bernard/Laguet—has rather ruefully told Lillian/Joanne that he will accompany her to America. He sits pensively at the piano in the nightclub and noodles obsessively with his "Paris Blues" piece. This time, Bowen/Newman plays the piece in the key of C major (rather than D major, as before) and, when he gets to the fatal note that Corning/Woodward botched in the earlier scene, plays *not* C-natural (the correct note as it would be transposed to the new key) but *instead* . . . D-sharp . . . that is, the same note that Lillian had (incorrectly) played earlier (in the old key of D major). In the new key of C major, D# represents the augmented ninth in a C7#9 chord and violates our expectations in a manner crucial to the generation of cinemusical meaning (Meyer 1956, 1967):

Melody: B ↑A ^ ↓G ; ↓B ^ ^ ^ ; B ↑A ^ ↓G ; ↑D# ^ ^ ^ .
Chords: CMaj7 C6 ; F7♭5     ; CMaj7 C6 ; C7#9    .

From one perspective—especially from the vantage point of the mainstream pre-bop tradition in which Duke's light-sided jazz/pop standards were written and are played by Bowen/Newman's band—the D-sharp in the fourth measure sounds dissonant. Yet from another viewpoint—that of the formal approach to composition associated with Ellington's serious-sided film scores—the D-sharp jibes with an harmonic alteration frequently employed by post-bop jazz musicians and consistent with the rules of the contemporary jazz language (Holbrook 2007b). (In this context, it resolves potentially as a sort of appoggiatura to a C7b9 chord, implied earlier by Lillian/Joanne's interjection of D# or E♭ over an implied D7 chord in the key of D major.) Thus—now in the key of C major—D-sharp becomes an ambiguous or ambivalent note, dissonant from one viewpoint but fitting the norms of the frequently used augmented-ninth chord from another perspective. The newly indeterminate status of this note (D-sharp)—melodically wrong earlier, but now harmonically plausible—reflects Ram/Paul's indecision. On one hand, the note is jarring—in parallel with how Ram/Paul feels about the prospect of giving up his musical aspirations to the stature of serious composer. On the other, Ram/Paul has found a way to transform Lillian/Joanne's intrusively incorrect note (D-sharp in the key of D major) into one—the same note viewed in a different context (the new key of C major)—that now coheres with his musical vision (as part of an harmonically-advanced augmented-ninth chord). This cinemusical reconfiguration parallels his willingness to consider changing his stance (modulating to a new key) and returning to the United States (a different context), conceivably without sacrificing too much of his artistic integrity in the process (a gesture in accord with his romantic feelings for Lillian/Joanne).

But in the last analysis, Bowen/Newman's commitment to his more serious Ellingtonian side—the resolutely non-commercial or artistic side dedicated to creative integrity, the right-hand side of our parallel homologies—triumphs at the expense of his mixed feelings for Corning/Woodward. Via Ellington-and-Strayhorn's nondiegetic background music, **Cinemusical Moment Number Three** arrives when Ram/Paul visits the train station to bid farewell to Lillian/Joanne. As he tells her that he only came to say goodbye, we hear the Ellington Orchestra's performance of "Paris Blues" in the background with the melody now played in the original key of D major by the alto saxophonist Johnny Hodges. At the precise moment when Bowen/Newman says that he has decided to stay in Paris, to follow through with his music, and to study composition so as to find out how far he can go—in other words, at the precise moment when he definitely surrenders to the Serious Ellington side of his bipolar musical personality—Johnny Hodges hits a great big fat D natural, the satisfyingly correct note for which Ram/Paul has, in effect, been searching throughout most of the film.

> Melody: C# ↑B ^ ↓A ; ↓C# ^ ^ ^ ; C# ↑B ^ ↓A ; ↑D ^ ^ ^ .
> Chords: DMaj7 D6   ; G7♭5   ; DMaj7 D6   ; Am7 D7 .

Musically if not romantically, this single note—charged as it is with meaningful significance within the context of "Paris Blues" as the theme song for this motion picture—resolves the emotional conflict through which Bowen/Newman has suffered. All this eludes Corning/Woodward—precisely because she remains out of touch with this more serious Ellingtonian side of Bowen/Newman's musical temperament and, of course, does not hear "Paris Blues" playing in the background as a nondiegetic comment on Ram/Paul's feelings. Lillian/Joanne cannot resist a rather unattractively acerbic speech before departing. The "Paris Blues" theme in D major (played on trombone, Ram/Paul's instrument, supported by the full orchestra) continues in the background as she turns her back and walks away. We see—as the "Wild Man"/Louis poster is covered over and as dissonant music covers over the "Paris Blues" theme—that Ram/Paul's serious compositional ambitions have gained the ascendancy (manifested by Johnny Hodges' musically correct D natural) and that he can now pursue the artistic side of his persona (identified with the non-commercial, serious, elite, and artistically dedicated aspects of his character, as mirrored by the harmonic challenges of the concluding underscore). And besides, the very attractive and musically sophisticated Marie/Barbara awaits him back at Club 33, ready to cook him chicken the way he likes it and content to let him remain "untied" and free to pursue his "work." Corning-and-Bowen's loss is Marie-and-Ram's gain.

## SEGUE TWO

As jazz continued to grope its way toward the start of a new millennium, the initial rift—apparent in *Paris Blues*, between a serious aesthetic commitment to jazz as a creative artform and any chances for commercial success via popular appeal—grew steadily into a yawning chasm. Brands of jazz referred to as "crossover" or "fusion" occasionally dumbed down the music enough to reach a wider audience. Kenneth Gorelick—aka Kenny G.—thrived and prospered (Washburne 2004). At the time of his death in 1991, Miles Davis was working on a hip-hop album, *Do-Bop* (released posthumously). I think it killed him. But, my opinionated theory notwithstanding, the fate of Miles reminds us that—in the Clinton(s)-and-Bush(es) era of jazz—selling big has come to mean selling out.

Meanwhile, the racial tensions always lurking below the surface of the jazz genealogy, have emerged in countless ways and have often received more attention than the music itself—never more than when a commentator named Donald Bogle (1990) composed a "Foreword" to a volume by Spike Lee with Lisa Jones (1990) on the subject of another film toward which we are heading. In what can only be regarded as a masterpiece of "resistant reading"—a textbook example of how reader-response theory can embrace even the most wayward interpretation—Bogle (1990) suggests that "*Paris Blues* failed to tell its story from a Black perspective" (p. 22). According to Bogle, "the movie chooses to shift its focus from the compelling story of Eddie [Sidney Poitier] to that of the romance between Newman and Woodward, obviously making a concession to the large White movie audience (p. 21)": "The Black audience would have preferred that *Paris Blues* focus on Poitier's character; that it address his racial, personal, and professional tensions; that . . . he would be relating more with other Black musicians rather than bonding with a White buddy" (p. 22).

This reading might seem a bit bizarre in light of the energy with which *Paris Blues* chronicles the romance between Eddie Cook (Sidney Poitier) and Connie Lampson (Diahann Carroll) and the clarity with which the film represents the struggle of Ram Bowen (Paul Newman) to fulfill his creative aspirations toward aspects of Duke Ellington as an African-American composer of serious music with artistic integrity. But, bizarre or not, Bogle (1990) prophetically prepares the way for our third film on the theme of art-versus-commerce in the young-man-with-a-horn genre—namely, *Mo' Better Blues* (1990).

# 9   Mo' Better Blues (1990)

In 1990, Spike Lee released a film—*Mo' Better Blues*—intended to correct the often misleading and sometimes demeaning way that jazz had been presented in such blockbusters as *Lady Sings the Blues* (1972), *'Round Midnight* (1986), and *Bird* (1988) (Chapter 15). Lee's film—which Yanow (2004) regards as "one of the most accurate depictions of the jazz life" (p. 182)—stars Denzel Washington in the role of a young trumpet player, Bleek Gilliam, pursuing a career as a struggling jazz artist. Early in the film, we see little Bleek as a child, practicing his horn under the intrusive supervision of a tyrannical mother (Abbey Lincoln), who insists that he keep plugging away even while his friends stand outside the window and call out for him to come and play baseball. Soon, however, we observe the fruits of this musical training when we cut to a scene featuring Gilliam/Washington in a nightclub, now full-grown and playing an intricate and challenging arrangement of a complex and beautiful medium-tempo jazz piece scored for bass, drums, piano, tenor sax, and trumpet.

Here and elsewhere, Bleek/Denzel on trumpet and Shadow Henderson (Wesley Snipes) on tenor do an excellent job of synchronizing their finger movements and body language to the sounds of source music played by Terence Blanchard (trumpet) with a quartet led by Branford Marsalis (tenor). The painstaking efforts that produced such accuracy in the miming of this ambi-diegetic film music are described at length by Spike Lee with Lisa Jones (1990, pp. 92–93, 158–161). This on-screen music does indeed achieve a high degree of audiovisual realism, creating the sounds and atmosphere of an excellent contemporary jazz quintet playing to a largely African-American audience in a dark and elegant nightclub.

But soon it transpires that Gilliam/Washington has become something of a womanizing workaholic—obsessive about his rigid practicing regimen on the horn, yet insatiable in the sexual energy that he directs toward two women, Indigo Downes (Joie Lee, Spike's sister) and Clarke Bentancourt (Cynda Williams). Indeed, the sexual stamina that Bleek/Denzel reveals when rapidly alternating between making love to these two partners could qualify him as a clear winner in the humper-of-the-month contest or the frequency-of-banging sweepstakes.

Meanwhile, pressures and problems are building in several directions at once. The guys in Gilliam/Washington's band are restless because their inefficacious manager Giant (Spike Lee himself) cannot persuade the two white club owners—the brothers Moe and Josh Flatbush (played by Nicholas and John Turturro)—to give them a fair share of the business receipts. In addition, Henderson/Snipes is unhappy—both because of the financial shortfall and because of his frustrated aspirations to play a more commercially appealing brand of jazz. Further, Giant/Spike has amassed enormous gambling debts to his bookie Petey (Ruben Blades) and will soon be roughed up by Madlock (Samuel L. Jackson) and Rod (Leonard Thomas). And Bleek/Denzel's two girlfriends have grown impatient with his two-timing refusal to commit to either one of them, not to mention his disconcerting habit of getting their names confused during passionately climactic moments of coitus.

So, predictably, everything explodes. Gilliam/Washington's two girlfriends abandon him. He tries—rather clumsily (as we shall see)—to make his music more accessible, but the club owners still hold out, and Shadow/Wesley quits in frustration. The gangsters beat up Giant/Spike and, when Bleek/Denzel tries to help his friend, smash him in the mouth with his own trumpet, busting his chops and sending him on a long struggle toward only a partial restoration of his instrumental virtuosity. In the meantime, Shadow/Wesley and Clarke/Cynda have coupled, have formed their own group with Bleek/Denzel's former sidemen, and now prosper by performing some rather bland but commercially-appealing crossover jazz with Clarke/Cynda heavily featured in a pop-diva singing role. But, though Gilliam/Washington's ruined embouchure has sabotaged his otherwise promising career as a bandleader, he finds happiness with Indigo/Joie, who ultimately forgives his two-timing transgressions, bears him a son named Miles, and is seen at the end under a huge poster of John Coltrane (whose "A Love Supreme" fills the soundtrack), before trying to persuade Miles to continue with his trumpet lesson from Bleek/Denzel while the neighborhood kids stand outside the same old window and holler for the boy to come out for a baseball game. This time, the loving parents decide to let their son go out and play ball. Maybe the self-destructive pattern of obsessive workaholism in the pursuit of artistic integrity won't be repeated the second time around.

To me, expanding on the art-versus-commerce theme of *Young Man with a Horn* and *Paris Blues*, the major thrust of *Mo' Better Blues* is pretty obvious: Money-related problems of various shapes and sizes will get you in a whole lot of trouble. Greed (the Flatbush/Turturro brothers) will turn friend (Henderson/Snipes) against friend (Gilliam/Washington). Debts (Giant/Spike to Petey/Ruben) will precipitate disaster (Madlock/Samuel and Rod/Leonard). And, most important to our present concerns, *commercialism will corrupt artistic integrity, will turn jazz into pop, and—via cinemusical associations with greed and exploitation—will ruin a promising artistic career.*

Let us pause to consider the fact that Spike Lee's family struggled financially during his youth because his father—Bill Lee, a jazz musician who played the acoustic bass—remained true to his musical standards and lost gigs when he refused to compromise by taking up the electric bass guitar (Bill Lee 1990, p. 173; Lee with Jones 1990, p. 161). As Bill Lee (1990) puts it, "a jazz career . . . calls for a special dedication . . . a total commitment": "I believe that there are not many things that you can do along with it—the spirit may get up and find another place to dwell" (p. 179). Further consider that Bill Lee wrote the soundtrack score for *Mo' Better Blues*, as well as for previous Spike Lee films. Isn't the message pretty clear? Selling out is tempting financially but ultimately fatal to one's potential artistic creativity.

To put it mildly, no such clear message is apparent to Gabbard (1996), who—as elsewhere—pursues a postmodern focus heavily oriented toward a consideration of issues involving race, gender, and other proto-PoMo topics. Reminiscent of Johnny Cochran at the O. J. Simpson trial, Gabbard plays the "race card" at just about every turn. In addressing *Mo' Better Blues*, however, Gabbard focuses with equal insistence on questions concerning gender and sexuality. From this race-, gender-, and sex-preoccupied perspective, Gabbard (1996) offers at least seven interpretive conclusions concerning *Mo' Better Blues* that I would strongly question. Much of the support for my challenges comes from the *nature of the music* and how it is used in the film. In my view, this music provides *clues to interpretation* that Gabbard chooses to ignore.

Let us begin by considering *seven key points* that constitute the essence of Gabbard's reading.

(1) In a chapter entitled "Signifying the Phallus: Representations of the Jazz Trumpet," Gabbard (1996) makes the indisputable point that, since the days of Louis Armstrong in New Orleans, the trumpet in jazz has been used "to express phallic masculinity along with a great deal of . . . sexual innuendo" (p. 139). As Gabbard notes, Dizzy Gillespie bent the bell of his horn upwards—ostensibly, so that he could hear himself better on a crowded, noisy stage; but, also, with clear phallic implications concerning his potency on the horn.

(2) According to Gabbard (1996), against this stereotype of trumpet-as-sex-symbol, Spike Lee offers us a real-life "post-phallic" trumpeter (p. 139) in the form of Terence Blanchard—a relatively lyrical, soft-toned, and melodically-restrained stylist whose sound "undermines" the trumpet-as-phallic-empowerment image—so that Lee has inadvertently diluted the trumpet's machismo "without intending to do so" (p. 140). In Gabbard's view, the "phallicism" deriving from "pitch, speed, and emotional intensity" as well as how "the trumpeter displays himself" in the work of (say) Armstrong or Gillespie (p. 141) is loaded with "libidinal energy" (p. 143) where—recalling Gabbard's reading of *Young Man with a Horn*—an ability/failure to hit the right note, often a high note, symbolizes sexual potency/impotence (p. 144). By contrast,

the post-phallic style (Miles Davis, Art Farmer, Wynton Marsalis, . . . Terence Blanchard) involves "a retreat from phallic bravado" into "a frequently understated manner" more suitable for conveying "emotional depth and introspection, even vulnerability" (p. 144). Based on this dubious logic, Gabbard concludes that Denzel Washington's image as an empowered black stud might have come across more convincingly if Spike Lee had chosen a different trumpet player to dub the solos by Bleek Gilliam—for example, Jon Faddis (p. 145). Faddis is an unquestionably fine musician of the powerhouse school who plays very much in the manner of Dizzy Gillespie with plenty of fast, loud, pyrotechnic passages in the high register of the horn. In Gabbard's opinion, the sound of Faddis would have been more appropriate than that of Blanchard by virtue of the Faddis/Blanchard phallic/post-phallic homology. After all, when challenged about why he cannot commit to just one sexual partner, Gilliam/Washington replies that "it's a dick thing" (Gabbard 1996, p. 146; Lee with Jones 1990, pp. 228, 255). Doesn't that establish the need for a more macho and phallocentrically Gillespian voice on trumpet? Here, Gabbard (1996) regales us with an impressive list of other cinematic or televisual trumpet players whose inability to hit high notes has signaled emasculation—Rick Martin in *Young Man with a Horn* (1950), Red Nichols in *The Five Pennies* (1959), Jackie Gleason as Ralph Cramden, Jackie Vernon on the Ed Sullivan show, Ish Kabibble with Kay Kyser (pp. 148–150). The list is endless—so endless, in fact, that we might begin to suspect that fluffing high notes is an occupational hazard for trumpet players and not necessarily a demonstration of impotence.

(3) According to Gabbard (1996), when Gilliam/Washington's lip is ruined and he can no longer hit the "right notes" (that is, the high notes), we encounter "a metaphor for his sexual or masculine inadequacy" (that is, his inability to get it up) (p. 147). In Gabbard's surmise, there is nothing left for Bleek/Denzel but the emasculating act of "begging for salvation" from Indigo/Joie, giving up "the jazz life," and becoming "a bourgeois patriarch" (p. 146). From this perspective, Bleek/Denzel has suffered symbolic castration via damage to his embouchure (mouth) along with the loss of its prosthetic extension (the trumpet) and must now succumb to middle-class values (life with Indigo/Joie).

(4) Worse than his cop-out to bourgeois conventionality, according to Gabbard (1996), Gilliam/Washington fails to resolve his debate with Henderson/Snipes about "what kind of music the band ought to be playing" (p. 150). Shadow/Wesley favors a more crowd-pleasing, commercial sort of music that panders to the audience. Bleek/Denzel demands a more committed and personal but less listener-friendly level of artistry. Shadow/Wesley and Bleek/Denzel regard each other's postures as "grandiose" and "grandstanding," respectively (p. 150). Clearly, this contrast presents an important tension, ripe with implications concerning the conflict between true art and mere entertainment, as set forth by the

series of homologies listed earlier. Yet, in Gabbard's view, "None of these issues, however, are [sic] directly addressed at the film's conclusion" (p. 150).

(5) Gabbard (1996) sees the climactic scene in which Gilliam/Washington hands his horn to Giant/Spike and walks away in the rain as an example of "the 'perfectly overblown' qualities of classical Hollywood" (p. 151) —all the more because Giant/Spike melodramatically proclaims that he "won't sell" the trumpet (implying, in my view, that it will remain "permanently underblown" rather than "perfectly overblown") and because the scene shifts to an upbeat conclusion in which Bleek/ Denzel and Indigo/Joie live happily ever after to the sounds of John Coltrane's "A Love Supreme" (p. 151). In what Gabbard (1996) regards as "another film about a self-destructive jazz musician," Bleek/Denzel has "chosen the less sexual of his two women, given up his obsessive artistic aspirations, and become . . . saved by abandoning jazz" (p. 153).

(6) The ending, in which young Miles is allowed to play with his friends instead of practicing his horn, represents to Gabbard (1996) "the idealization of baseball in *Mo' Better Blues*" (p. 153). Somehow, rather circuitously, this leads Gabbard to play the "race card" by commenting that "In *Mo' Better Blues*, Spike Lee largely ignores the racist aspects of baseball history that correspond closely to the exploitation of black jazz artists portrayed in the film" (p. 154). Gabbard manages to position this as signaling a sell-out by Lee embodied by "the inevitable movement of an independent filmmaker toward familiar models of sexuality and cultural behavior as his budgets and audiences expand" (p. 154).

(7) Finally, Gabbard (1996) sees *Mo' Better Blues* as an expression of Spike Lee's tendency to gravitate "toward the highly representable codes of masculinity established for rap music" (p. 156). The evidence for this interpretation appears in a "most memorable performance scene" when Gilliam/Washington wears his baseball cap backwards and sings a rap-inflected tune called "Pop Top 40 R 'n' B Urban Contemporary Easy Listening Funk Love" (p. 156) and in the music behind the film's closing credits when a rap group called Gangstarr sings "Jazz Thing" in a way that positions jazz as "the revered but obsolete forerunner of more contemporary—and more provocative—forms of African American expression" (p. 156). Why go broke and be unhappy when there is rap to sing and baseball to watch?

I have lavished so much attention on the interpretation by Gabbard (1996) because—though I disagree with his conclusions concerning *Mo' Better Blues*—I would point to his work as the state-of-the-art in the cinemusical criticism of jazz on film. In general, Gabbard (1996) has provided the definitive historical and analytic account of the role played by jazz in motion pictures. Though he tends, in my view, to overemphasize issues concerning race and gender—on which he maintains something of a monomaniacal focus at the expense of both downplaying other potentially important themes and neglecting detailed aspects of the music itself—he does so with conviction and authority, making his case in a compelling fashion almost every time. The views of Gabbard (1996) therefore deserve our most serious attention. Nonetheless, with this in mind, I find his interpretation of *Mo' Better Blues* unpersuasive with respect to the seven points just enumerated—not because these arguments fail to make sense in the abstract, but because they *fly in the face of the film's narrative structure* and because they *disregard the actual music contained in the film.* By ignoring much of this narration/music in its dramatic context, I believe, Gabbard has failed to see/hear some of the meanings that lurk below the film's surface.

In this spirit, let us now reconsider the **seven key points** that comprise Gabbard's reading.

(1)  Only a fool could miss the phallic implications associated with the trumpet in general and with Gilliam/Washington's horn in particular. *Mo' Better Blues* opens with a long, loving pan shot that moves down the shank of Bleek/Denzel's vertically positioned instrument—from the flange of the upward-pointed mouthpiece descending toward the piston-like valves below. The visual identification with a large erect penis is unmistakable. *But,* I must insist, the trumpet imagery is a lot more complicated than that. The trumpet also embodies key aspects of femininity and of copulation with a woman. It contains various succulent, juicy, and pleasurable orifices—a mouthpiece, a spit valve, and a large, curved, open bell. It features three valves that work via an in-out push-pull action highly suggestive of sexual intercourse. The player, in effect, performs cunnilingus on the horn—kissing the mouthpiece with his lips, tonguing it, and spitting into it—while simultaneously fingering its coitus-associated private parts. At one juncture, Bleek/Denzel emphasizes this point while making love to Indigo—first performing a tonguing exercise on his own two separated fingers, then transferring this gesture to her mouth. So, yes, the trumpet is a phallic symbol. But it is *also* a symbol of femininity, *not* only *with* which but also *on* which the trumpeter performs an act highly suggestive of copulation. In this connection, recall Janet Leigh's sardonically suggestive comment in *Pete Kelly's Blues* that she is "three valves short" of being a cornet (Chapter 4). Thus, the iconography in *Mo' Better Blues* of Gilliam/Washington's horn—his horniness—parallels the ultimately successful development of his sex life. Early in the film, we find him cleaning and oiling his trumpet. In, very quickly, goes the first valve—paralleling his promiscuous relationship with Clarke/Cynda. Then, immediately, the second valve—paralleling his equally promiscuous early relationship with Indigo/Joie. Finally, after a noticeable delay, the third valve—paralleling the ultimate achievement of his more fulfilling relationship with Indigo/Joie. The pattern of Bleek/Denzel's sexual encounters follows the same timing scheme. We see him making love, first, with Clarke/Cynda; then, very soon, with Indigo/Joie during their initial fling; finally, only much later,

with Indigo/Joie in a more spiritual and permanent sort of way. This should tell us quite a bit about the success of Gilliam/Washington's sexual evolution and its relation to the iconography of the trumpet. But, just in case we have missed the point, the film ends with Bleek/Denzel lovingly giving his young son Miles a trumpet lesson and patiently showing him the first, the second, and . . . finally . . . the third valves of the horn.

(2) I strongly disagree that Jon Faddis, despite his formidable talents, might have served as a musician more appropriate than Terence Blanchard to dub Bleek Gilliam's trumpet parts—for two reasons. First, in the last scene during which Gilliam/Washington plays his horn before the gangsters beat him up, having had a partnership-ending argument with Henderson/Snipes, he watches with alarm from the bandstand as two hit men escort Giant/Spike out of the nightclub. Forcefully, he expresses his rage over the predicament of Giant/Spike and over his abandonment by Shadow/Wesley by means of a ferocious assault on the trumpet in which fast high notes from his instrument furiously reign down on the listener in an overpowering torrent of sound. No trumpet player—not even Jon Faddis at his most Dizzyesque—could have surpassed the stratospheric intensity of this musical onslaught in which the small but potent Terence Blanchard shows himself to be fully "up" to the task. Second, notwithstanding questions of pyrotechnics, the style of Jon Faddis would have fit very poorly with the fabric of this film's ambi-diegetic cinemusical approach. In the spirit of the Gillespie tradition, Faddis is primarily a big-band trumpet player, uniquely gifted at soaring high above the riffs played by a large ensemble performing behind him, as in the case of his justly famous work as leader of the Carnegie Hall Jazz Band. Our musical associations with his sound would struggle against the confines of a jazz quintet of the type deployed in the film, as shown performing for an intimate audience at a small nightclub in Brooklyn.

(3) Rather than an expression of impotence or emasculation, Gilliam/Washington's progress toward an eventual union with Indigo/Joie represents an achievement of maturity. Throughout, Clarke/Cynda has emerged as a good-looking and classy but inherently shallow concubine motivated in part by a desire to foster her own singing career and insensitive to Bleek/Denzel's need for physical and emotional time and space to practice his horn and to devote himself to his art. Clarke/Cynda constantly interrupts Bleek/Denzel's practice regimen, intrudes into his attempts to work out a new composition, and—most unforgivably, however playfully—bites him on the lip in a way that ominously threatens the integrity of his embouchure (with forebodings of the even more devastating destruction still to come); for, as Bleek/Denzel notes with alarm, he earns his living with his lips. When Bleek/Denzel makes love to Clarke/Cynda, in the background we hear "All Blues" by Miles Davis from the *Kind of Blue* album—the best-selling record in the history of jazz—in other words, an emblem for the commercial poten-

tial of this music. Clarke/Cynda is high-maintenance and pricey; she demands to be heard and—as a would-be vocalist—wants to make money by doing exactly that. By contrast, Indigo/Joie is quieter, less conventionally pretty but more real, a school teacher, and a person of substance who wants to be with Gilliam/Washington for himself rather than for the purpose of advancing her own career. The demands she makes on him are for commitment rather than for material success. When Downes/Lee and Gilliam/Washington make love, we hear a soft, romantic, lyrical but essentially anonymous trumpet accompanied by strings in the background. Also significant is the manner in which Spike Lee (Lee with Jones 1990) refers to his two principal female leads. He sees Clarke/Cynda as "a very attractive sister" (p. 230) but regards his real-life sibling Indigo/Joie as "a very beautiful sister" (p. 227). And when Bleek/Denzel returns to Indigo/Joie late in the film, we hear "Lonely Woman"—written by Ornette Coleman but played here by Branford Marsalis—as the background soundtrack, pregnant with nondiegetic meaning concerning her need to be with him and thereby proleptic regarding the success of his plea for salvation. Rather than succumbing to middle-class values, Gilliam/Washington has reached maturity and self-awareness in a way that suits his social situation. Anyone who doubts this should again consider the implications of Coltrane's "A Love Supreme" as the nondiegetic background music for the penultimate montage celebrating Bleek/Denzel's entrance into family life. The spiritual aspects of 'Trane's masterpiece run very deep.

(4) Most seriously, Gabbard (1996) misses or at least misplaces the main point of Mo' Better Blues—namely, its sustained outcry against the destructive forces of commercialism—which appear in the maleficent greed of the club managers; the menacing usury of the loan sharks; and (most of all, but beneath Gabbard's radar) the debate concerning musical standards between Gilliam/Washington (favoring allegiance to artistic integrity) and Henderson/Snipes (favoring concessions to popular appeal). Contrary to Gabbard's dismissal, the latter debate constitutes a—maybe the—main axis on which the meaning of the whole film rotates. Specifically, by catering to his audience with a silly parody performed in a rapper costume—namely, a backwards baseball cap—Bleek/Denzel has hinted at a form of pandering reminiscent of the old comedy routines for which (say) Louis Armstrong (poking fun at bebop in "The Whiffenpoof Song") and Dizzy Gillespie (satirizing rock-'n'-roll in "School Days") were so roundly criticized by the jazz cognoscenti (Holbrook 2007b). When Bleek/Denzel and Shadow/Wesley discuss this issue at a loud cocktail party in the aforementioned dialogue referred to by Gabbard (1996, p. 150)—wherein Shadow/Wesley tells Bleek/Denzel that if he played the "shit" that people like, they would come to listen—we hear "Mercy, Mercy, Mercy" by the Cannonball Adderley Quintet, never noticed by Gabbard but playing as background music for this crucial scene. During the 1950s and 1960s,

however unfairly, Cannonball with his recourse to such soul-jazz crowd pleasers as "This Here" and "Dat Dere" (both written by pianist Bobby Timmons) took a beating for his eminent role as what many critics considered the veritable embodiment of selling out—an image very much retained in his subsequent performances of the crowd-pleasing "Mercy, Mercy, Mercy" (by pianist Joe Zawinul). After the debate between Bleek/Denzel and Shadow/Wesley on the virtues of a commitment to artistic integrity versus the pursuit of an audience-oriented popularity, in the very next scene, we find Gilliam/Washington himself temporarily and momentarily *selling out* while the two greedy white club-owner brothers watch with approval. Specifically, Bleek/Denzel introduces the movie's *title tune* with a rap that strongly recalls the sorts of introductions voiced by Cannonball Adderley at his most obsequiously commercial moments. He follows this by performing "Mo' Better Blues"—an infectiously pleasant soul-jazz rip-off—in an aloof manner that suggests total emotional disengagement. Shadow/Wesley (miming Branford Marsalis) solos effectively on the piece—anticipating his later capitulation to commercialism—but Bleek/Denzel (miming Terence Blanchard) contents himself with mostly playing the highly accessible melody. The crowd loves it. This scene—pivotal to the film— thereby signals Gilliam/Washington's dawning realization that success as a jazz musician necessitates watering down his art, leveling it to the lowest common denominator, pandering to the interests of commercialism. Late in the film, when Bleek/Denzel visits a more prosperous venue (with Giant/Spike as its doorman) to sit in with Shadow/Wesley and Clarke/Cynda, he stands at the back of the room and endures Clarke/Cynda's painfully pop-oriented, intonationally-challenged, rhythmically-insecure performance of a song—enthusiastically received by a large and mostly white audience—on which, as even Gabbard (1996) admits, she sounds more like Joni Mitchell than Billie Holiday. During the easy-listening soprano-sax obbligatos by Shadow/Wesley— dubbed by Branford Marsalis but coming about as close as this talented man could manage to imitating Kenny G.—we have plenty of otherwise vacant time to reflect on the celebrated real-life clash between the Marsalis brothers when Wynton (the committed jazz artist) objected to Branford's work with various rock stars (such as Sting) and lamented Branford's acceptance of a day job in popular entertainment (via his appointment as leader of Jay Leno's *Tonight Show* orchestra). All this is anathema to the likes of Gilliam/Washington. During the performance and while mechanically clapping after its conclusion, he wears a dazed look on his face, as if he just cannot believe how vacuous Shadow/ Wesley's music has finally become in its quest for popularity. When Bleek/Denzel takes the stage and attempts with difficulty to play a ballad that we earlier saw him struggling to write amidst constant interruptions from Clarke/Cynda, he cannot satisfactorily perform the piece for two reasons—the first explicit, the second implicit. First, most obviously, his lip is injured—though, in time (we surmise), it might eventually heal. Second, he cannot stomach the implications of what he has just endured—namely, the warm reception (by an audience half composed of white people) of a pop-flavored musical atrocity that falls far beneath his own artistic standards—a wound that, given the dumbed-down temper of the times and the resolutely poor taste of the mass audience, can never heal.

(5) Thus—when Bleek/Denzel surrenders his horn to Giant/Spike and walks away—beyond the physical injury to his lip, his gesture of resignation represents disgust with the degradation of the jazz that he loves by the commercialism that he hates. Recall the aforementioned experiences of Spike Lee's own father, who wrote the background score for this film and who suffered financially for his refusal to compromise his own artistic integrity. In this context, the "melodramatic" proclamation by Giant/Spike—to the effect that he *won't sell* Bleek/Denzel's horn— comes as a trenchant commentary on the fate of the jazz ideal represented by Gilliam/Washington's abandoned trumpet. Symbolically and all-importantly, Bleek/Denzel has *not sold out*. Rather, he has gained a new maturity that permits him to seek salvation with Indigo/Joie (Spike's sister) while "Lonely Woman" segues into "A Love Supreme." To repeat, given that Bleek/Denzel's trumpet (in the hands of Giant/ Spike) will remain forever silent, this strikes me as an *under*blown rather than an *over*blown denouement. Thus, in contrast to the critique voiced by Gabbard (1996), this motion picture does *not* evolve into "another film about a self-destructive jazz musician" (p. 153). Rather, in purpose-fully walking away from the artistic corruption of a musical career in which nothing succeeds like self-abnegating distress in the face of aesthetically-abhorrent commercialism, Bleek/Denzel has taken a strong step in the direction of *self-preservation* through accepting a better way of life focused on family and on his new role as a teacher rather than a performer.

(6) In my view, pace Gabbard (1996), the metaphor of baseball as representing an openness to the fun-oriented, child-like side of life—an attitude of value in the parenting of small boys—does *not* represent a missed opportunity for the insertion of yet another commentary on the exploitation of black ballplayers prior to the days of Jackie Robinson and Willie Mays. Here, Spike Lee makes an important statement about people in general and about the raising of children in particular and *not* about the fretted area of race relations in pro ball.

(7) Finally, I agree that Spike Lee probably likes rap music and certainly uses it ubiquitously in his films. But that is not the point of *Mo' Better Blues*. Instead, the point is to move beyond the tragedepictorial *Lady Sings the Blues*, *'Round Midnight*, and *Bird* (Chapter 15) so as to portray the life of a realistic African-American jazz musician (Bogle 1990; Lee with Jones 1990, p. 39). Such a life, in Lee's vision, faces difficult choices premised on the conflict between art and entertainment.

Just as Spike Lee's own father and family suffered from this tension, Denzel Washington's enactment of Bleek Gilliam endures the various pressures of commercialism (stingy club owners, gambling debts, crowd-pleasing but vapid music) until the point at which his artistic integrity, with more than a little help from a lip injury (which has itself resulted from his strength of character in helping a defenseless friend), forces him to withdraw from the scene (rather than selling out to the quest for filthy lucre).

Other films have used such scenarios to play on the misfortunes of jazz performers by capitalizing cinematically on their self-destruction and ruin (Chapter 15). For the sake of audience appeal, we have seen these artists succumb to the ravages of alcohol, drugs, and other forms of self-abuse (*Lady Sings the Blues*; *Sweet Love, Bitter*; *'Round Midnight*; *Bird*; even *Sweet and Low Down*). Bogle (1990) accurately characterizes such films as "sad-eyed elegies that begin on one low note and end on another" (p. 24). Few such fallen heroes are redeemed (*Young Man with a Horn*; *The Man with a Golden Arm*; *The Gene Krupa Story*). In a sense, then, these films sacrifice their jazz heroes on the altar of public righteousness for the sake of commercial appeal to a Hollywood-trained audience.

But, to his credit, Spike Lee refuses to do that. Instead, he climbs into his own picture and stands there near the end, in the pouring rain, voicing its moral in perfectly clear language. Paraphrasing rather freely—but in a manner that I believe reflects Lee's viewpoint—he tells us, "Your horn stands for something important, Bleek." "It stands," still paraphrasing, "for artistic integrity and for a commitment to pure music that you will not sacrifice for the sake of popular appeal." And—no longer paraphrasing very much at all—he says, "I will not compromise this symbol of artistic commitment, Bleek; I will not sell your horn." And—unless we are blinded by ideological distractions or deaf to the subtleties of the film's music—for the first time in our experience of Giant/Lee's character, now forcefully overshadowed by the presence of the director himself standing there and talking to us directly, we must honor his claim that he *won't sell* it. We must recognize what this commitment means in the context of the endless battle between commerce and art. Or, as Spike Lee puts it in his book with Jones (1990), "All artists are driven by love for their art, and great artists are selfish in their devotion to it" (p. 31).

## CODA

One way to view the art-versus-commerce theme from a macromarketing perspective is to regard it as yet another example of a social trap or tragedy-of-the-commons problem (Shultz and Holbrook 1999) in which, this time, each member of society wants to hear music personally regarded as enjoyable or entertaining even though, collectively, this insistence ultimately throttles the creative integrity of an artform such as jazz, which has little commercial appeal to the lowest-common-denominator tastes of the mass-market multitudes. In this spirit, the theme of art-versus-commerce in three illustrative films from the young-man-with-a-horn genre reaches the same conclusion every time on the issue of primary interest to macromarketers. Specifically, selling out to commercialism is tempting to the struggling jazz musician but bad for the preservation of a socially valuable artform. Conversely, honoring creative integrity is good for society but potentially self-destructive to the starving artist. However, the ways in which this conclusion manifests itself evolve as jazz changes its meaning as a cine-musical signifier over time.

At mid-century, in *Young Man with a Horn* (1950), jazz still retains the rapidly-disappearing swing-era possibilities for artistic integrity rewarded by commercial success. The hero Rick Martin (Kirk Douglas) achieves equilibrium by finding a niche as a gifted performer of listenable swing based on fine musicianship.

A decade later, *Paris Blues* (1961) portrays a newly emerging choice in much starker terms—commercial success via an adherence to the old-style model of jazz as entertainment (the light side of Duke Ellington) versus artistic integrity via a commitment to the newer standard of jazz as an elite art music (the serious side). Ultimately, Ram Bowen (Paul Newman) opts for the latter as an artistically-dedicated but financially-challenged expatriate—a man without a country or, at least, without a commercially-viable market-based home in America.

Approaching the New Millennium, *Mo' Better Blues* (1990) shows that the sacrifice embraced by Ram/Paul may have disappeared as an option in the more "bleek" world of Bleek Gilliam (Denzel Washington), in which true jazz has grown so esoteric and out-of-touch with the marketplace that it cannot survive the test of economic viability. When Bleek/Denzel contemplates the enormity of the artistic compromises required to achieve commercial success, he has no choice but to lay down his horn and walk away.

From a macromarketing perspective, the potentially destructive force of market-driven economic realities has claimed yet another victim. And—as usual, figuratively speaking—those members of society who would have benefited from the creative integrity of artists who won't sell out to the remunerative allure of commercial success are left standing—like Spike Lee, at the end of his film—alone in the pouring rain.

Part V

# Ambi-Diegetic, Nondiegetic, and Diegetic Cinemusical Meanings in Motion Pictures: Commerce, Art, and Brando Loyalty . . . or . . . De Niro, My God, to Thee

# Introduction to Part V

As seen in Parts III and IV, the theme of art-versus-commerce has surfaced in many motion pictures in the crime-plus-jazz and young-man-with-a-horn genres. Here, while continuing to trace this art-versus-commerce theme, Part V will juxtapose three otherwise disparate films that draw on the power of *ambi-diegetic*, *nondiegetic*, and *diegetic jazz* as a force toward the dramatic development of character, plot, central themes, and other cinemusical meanings. Specifically and as described in Chapter 10, via the significance of its *ambi-diegetic* music, *New York, New York* (1977) shows the elevation of artistic integrity (Robert De Niro as Jimmy Doyle) over commercialism (Liza Minnelli as Francine Evans). In *Heart Beat* (1980), as interpreted in Chapter 11, the raw honesty of a committed-but-doomed creative genius (Art Pepper) provides *nondiegetic* music that signifies the self-destructive degradation of a key protagonist (Nick Nolte as Neal Cassady). Finally, as found in Chapter 12, the appealing nature of *diegetic* jazz in the cinemusically-enriched nightclub environment of *The Score* (2001) helps to explain why a soon-to-be-reformed criminal (Robert De Niro, again, as Nick Wells) would risk everything in collaboration with two bizarre partners (Marlon Brando as Max Baron and Ed Norton as Jack Teller) in hopes of a payoff big enough to allow him to retire from a lucrative but sordid career in crime in order to run his legitimate jazz venue and to settle down with his true love (Angela Bassett as Diane Boesman).

Thus, Part V examines the role of ambi-diegetic, nondiegetic, and diegetic film music in advancing the dramatic development of character, plot, and other cinematic content in general and in contributing jazz-based cinemusical meanings that reflect the socially significant art-versus-commerce theme in particular—as found in three illustrative motion pictures. In this connection, the broad relevance of film music for issues of concern to (macro)marketing and consumer researchers once again emerges in four main ways whereby cinemusical meanings relate to important aspects of consumption, markets, and the consumer culture. Let us briefly review these four key aspects—with special relevance to the three movies featured in Part V.

## (1) Product Placement: Movie-Soundtrack Albums

First, as mentioned earlier, music in films involves a kind of *product placement* in which various tunes, songs, compositions, or performances that appear in motion pictures become cultural artifacts in the form of movie-soundtrack recordings to compete for patronage in the marketplace for musical offerings. For example, at this writing, soundtrack albums for two of the films discussed in Part V are currently for sale on amazon.com—*New York, New York* (1977, customer reviews = five stars, sales rank = #56,401) and *The Score* (2001, two stars, #271,180)—whereas the soundtrack recording for the third film *Heart Beat* (1980) is apparently out-of-print but available as a vinyl LP on www.ebay.com for prices ranging from $4.00 to $59.99, all of which says something about the comparative commercial success of the three films and the ancillary material licensed therefrom.

## (2) Product Design: Diegetic, Nondiegetic, and Ambi-Diegetic Music in Films

Second, as also emphasized earlier, film music plays a role as one key component in the *product design* of a motion picture. Here, we shall continue to distinguish *three main types* of film music—namely, *diegetic source music* (on-screen performances that enhance the realism of the *mise-en-scène*); *nondiegetic film scores* (background music or underscoring performed off-screen to advance a film's dramatic development of character, plot, or some other cinematic theme); and *ambi-diegetic film music* (performed on-screen like diegetic music but designed to advance the dramatic development in a manner similar to nondiegetic music). To repeat—extending beyond our primary focus on ambi-diegetic jazz—the three chapters in Part V will deal with all three types of film music where they appear to be most relevant to key aspects of cinemusical meaning in the product design of the three films under consideration—namely, *ambi-diegetic* music in the case of *New York, New York* (1977); *nondiegetic* music in the case of *Heart Beat* (1980); and *diegetic* music in the case of *The Score* (2001).

## (3) Symbolic Consumer Behavior: Performing and Listening to Music as a Form of Consumption Symbolism

Third—to review briefly—when the characters in a film engage in various music-related consumption experiences, the relevant cinemusical meanings serve as one aspect of *symbolic consumer behavior* that works toward advancing the dramatic development of character, plot, and other cinematic themes. Here, as noted earlier, performing or listening to music constitutes just one more form of consumption symbolism that combines with clothing (Armani vs. Levi), accessories (Coach vs. Samsonite), jewelry (Tiffany vs. J. C. Penney), automobiles (Lamborghini vs. Chevrolet), furnishings (Maurice Villency vs. Jennifer Convertibles), and other opportunities for drawing on the significance of brand names or of product-related associations to limn the nature of a character's personality, to move the plot forward in some way, or to develop other relevant cinematic themes (Holbrook and Hirschman 1993). Thus, for the three films reviewed in Part V and comparable to other aspects of symbolic consumer behavior (props, costumes, décor, scenery, and so forth), we glean important meanings concerning the nature of various characters' motives, dispositions, or values from the ambi-diegetic musical performances by Liza Minnelli and Robert De Niro in *New York, New York* (1977); from the metaphorically jazz-enriched nondiegetic cinemusical context surrounding Nick Nolte, John Heard, and Sissy Spacek in *Heart Beat* (1980); and from the diegetic offerings by Cassandra Wilson and Mose Allison in *The Score* (2001).

## (4) Themes of Social Significance: Art versus Commerce

Fourth, the cinemusical meanings of ambi-diegetic, nondiegetic, or diegetic film music may again express, reflect, or signify various *themes of social significance* to students of (macro)marketing and consumer behavior. Such socially significant themes may concern issues of interest from the viewpoint of macromarketing theory, social marketing, public policy, human welfare, quality of life, ethics, or other broad aspects of the consumer culture. One such issue that has attracted attention in recent times and earlier in the present work involves the theme of art-versus-commerce as it pertains to the conflict between the need for artistic integrity and the demand for popular appeal in the production of *motion pictures* (Holbrook 1999c; Holbrook 2005f; Holbrook and Addis 2007); in the offerings of *professional musicians* (Bradshaw and Holbrook 2007; Bradshaw, McDonagh, and Marshall 2006a; Holbrook, Lacher, and LaTour 2006; Kubacki and Croft 2004); and in the *combined* focus on the cinemusical representation of *musicians in films* (Parts III and IV; see also Bradshaw, McDonagh, and Marshall 2006b; Holbrook 2005b, 2006c; 2007a).

## Review and Preview

In sum, the three chapters in Part V will examine the three major types of film music in general and ambi-diegetic/nondiegetic/diegetic cinemusical jazz performances in particular as related to the theme of art-versus-commerce in three motion pictures whose connections reflect an intricate web of associations. Specifically, the ancient and ubiquitous theme of art-versus-commerce serves to juxtapose three otherwise disparate films that draw on the power of jazz to generate meanings associated with the cinemusical aspects of semiosis or signification described previously. A synopsis of the relevant homologous comparisons—that is, a summary of the key parallels and contrasts to be explored in what follows—appears in Table 4.

*Table 4* Comparisons Among Three Films Presenting The Art-Vversus-Commerce Theme

|  | New York, New York (1977) | Heart Beat (1980) | The Score (2001) |
|---|---|---|---|
| Director | Martin Scorsese | John Byrum | Frank Oz |
| Cinematographer | László Kovács | László Kovács | Rob Hahn |
| Music Director or Composer | Ralph Burns | Jack Nitzsche | Howard Shore |
| Cinemusical Focus | Ambi-Diegetic | Nondiegetic | Diegetic |
| Representative of Art | Jimmy Doyle (Robert De Niro) | Neal Cassady (Nick Nolte) Jack Kerouac (John Heard) Carolyn Cassady (Sissy Spacek) | Nick Wells (Robert De Niro) |
| Artistic Manifestation | Georgie Auld's Post-Swing Tenor Sax Solos | Art Pepper's Alto-Saxophone Improvisations | Nick/Robert's Dedication to the NYC Jazz Club |
| Representative of Commerce | Francine Evans (Liza Minnelli) | N.Y.C. Publishers | N/R's Star Power as Heroic Safe-Cracker |
| Commercial Manifestation | Popularity of FE/LM's Singing | Market Success of *On the Road* | Huge $$$ Rewards for Risk and Skill |
| Role of Music | Ambi-Diegetic Contrast: JD/RD's Artistic Integrity Versus FE/LM's Commercialism | Nondiegetic Characterizations: NC/NN, JK/JH, and CC/SS | Diegetic Songs by Cassandra Wilson and Mose Allison to Show the NYC Club as Worth the Risk |
| Denouement | JD/RD as Happy Jazz Musician and Successful Nightclub Owner | CC/SS as a Compromising Conformist in Suburbia | NW/RD as a Domesticated Tax-Paying Jazz-Club Owner |

# 10 Commerce and *New York, New York* (1977)

## He's Delightful; He's Delicious; He's . . . De Niro

By now, it should have become pretty clear that jazz can serve and has served as a free-floating signifier to represent just about anything that a filmmaker wishes to incorporate into the meaning of a motion picture. We have observed and will later observe the use of cinemusical moments to represent jazz-as-pop, jazz-as-swing, jazz-as-bebop, jazz-as-commercial, jazz-as-elitist, jazz-as-phallic, jazz-as-emasculating, jazz-as-enabling, jazz-as-disabling, jazz-as-genius, jazz-as-destructive, jazz-as-good, jazz-as-bad—in short, you name it, and jazz can be used to evoke its essence. Think of a potential meaning for jazz, and—quite probably—some film has exploited that meaning . . . or will do so in the near future.

The one thing that we have not yet seen thus far (with the partial exception of *Paris Blues*), however, is a full-fledged anti-commercialistic paean in praise of a dedicated jazz musician who refuses to compromise the integrity of his art and stubbornly preserves the purity of his creative vision despite a price paid in the loss of loved ones or a resigned retreat from prospects for material success. In *Young Man with a Horn*, Rick Martin (Kirk Douglas) ends by wisely adjusting both his artistic vision (settling for an aesthetically valid role as musical accompanist) and his amorous excesses (wisely choosing the cute freckle-faced Doris Day over the beautiful but odious Lauren Bacall character). In *Paris Blues*, Eddie Cook (Sidney Poitier) sacrifices his art in order to chase his pretty girlfriend Connie Lampson (Diahann Carroll) back to the United States, while Ram Bowen (Paul Newman) does reject Lillian Corning (Joanne Woodward) to pursue concert music (the serious side of Duke Ellington) at the possible expense of his more playful jazz roots (Duke Lite) but probably salvages his more supportive and rewarding relationship with Marie Seoul (Barbara Laage). And in *Mo' Better Blues*, Bleek Gilliam (Denzel Washington) must renounce his devotion to jazz in order to enjoy the bliss of family life with Indigo Downes (Joie Lee). Later, we shall see that *The Fabulous Dorseys*, *The Glenn Miller Story*, and *The Benny Goodman Story* all have affirmative endings. At the end, the Dorseys (Tommy and Jimmy) don't win the hearts of any particular girls, but they do achieve material success and brotherly reconciliation. Glenn Miller (Jimmy Stewart) loses his life, but has previously won both popular acclaim and the love of a real heroine (June Allyson). And Benny Goodman (Steve Allen) gets it all—fame, fortune, artistic integrity, and a wealthy heiress (Donna Reed). Similar logic applies to Pete Kelly (Jack Webb) in *Pete Kelly's Blues*; to Dixie Dwyer (Richard Gere) in *The Cotton Club*; and—later—to Red Nichols in *The Five Pennies* and to Gene Krupa in *The Gene Krupa Story*. In sum, thus far, we find no central character (with, again, the partial exception of Paul Newman as Ram Bowen in *Paris Blues*) who *refuses to compromise the integrity of his art* and who *stubbornly preserves the purity of his creative vision* despite a price paid in the *loss of loved ones* or the cost of a *resigned retreat from prospects for material success*.

Martin Scorsese's *New York, New York* (1977) presents such a central character in the form of a dedicated jazz musician, played by Robert De Niro, who does indeed refuse to compromise the integrity of his art despite a price paid in the loss of a loved one. Specifically, this film offers us some scope for an interpretation of the De Niro character as a martyred jazz purist who remains true to his creative vision and whose refusal to compromise with the forces of commerce leaves him in a state of romantic loss, if not financial failure, or musical exile. This, it turns out, is just about where we want him if we happen to be a little bit idealistic or even slightly optimistic about the dubious prospects for the artistic integrity of jazz in films.

Admittedly, as developed in what follows, this interpretation involves a high level of subjectivism—akin to that celebrated by proponents of reader-response theory, by advocates of resistant readings, by supporters of auto-biographical criticism, and by those predisposed toward interpretive insights drawn from subjective personal introspection (Hirschman and Holbrook 1992; Holbrook 1995a; Holbrook and Hirschman 1993). In other words, I plan to offer a reading of *New York, New York* that cuts across the grain of conventional interpretations and that, in the tradition of reception studies, may indeed contradict—at least, partially—the avowed, publicly expressed intentions of the film's director Martin Scorsese. Hence, for the sake of balance, I shall begin with a brief account of what I would regard as the party line—the conventional wisdom, the received view—concerning the meaning of this film as found, for example, in the writings of Gabbard (1996).

Gabbard (1996) does an excellent job of summarizing the highlights of *New York, New York* and of placing it into the context of Scorsese's career as a director. Specifically, Gabbard sees this film as "a brief history of popular music" (p. 267) in general and as a "'love note' to the great musicals of classical Hollywood at the same time that [Scorsese] wanted to critique the genre" (p. 268) in particular. This latter somewhat ambivalent project invites a certain level of paradox, irony, or even self-contradiction. Indeed, listing a myriad of influences mentioned by Scorsese, Gabbard (1996) finds the film "extremely eclectic" (p. 275) to the point of being "stylistically incoherent" (p. 271). Scorsese himself is reputed to have called the film "a mess" and to have considered it "a miracle that the film makes any kind of sense" (pp. 271–272).

But what emerges from Gabbard's analysis—beneath all this browbeating over inconsistencies of style—positions the film as an evocation of "the art versus commerce dichotomy" (p. 268) as represented by the contrasting characters of Jimmy Doyle (Robert De Niro) and Francine Evans (Liza Minnelli). Jimmy/Robert is a dedicated post-WWII swing-rooted but bop-friendly jazz musician with a tough-arrogant-or-even-obnoxious attitude toward music, a penchant for improvisation (both as the musician Jimmy and as the actor Robert), and a fierce devotion to his art. Francine/Liza is a colorfully-costumed visually-stunning pop-oriented big-band singer with a sweet but assertive personality, a dependence on scripted-choreographed-and-rehearsed material (both as the singer Francine and as the actress Liza), and a flair for commercial success. And—despite a strong physical attraction between the two—never the twain shall meet.

The rather lumbering plot documents how the lives of Jimmy/Robert and Francine/Liza converge for a while but ultimately diverge—dragging on for anywhere from 137 to 164 minutes, depending on whether you are lucky enough to get hold of the early cut version or must endure the more recent full-length re-release. Along the way, we note that the film builds a carefully devised series of binary oppositions, as follows:

Jazz : Pop
Jimmy Doyle : Francine Evans
Art : Commerce
Robert De Niro : Liza Minnelli
Improvisatory : Scripted
Obnoxious : Sweet
Dedicated : Ambitious

Hence, this series of homologies does indeed establish key tensions in the film that demand some sort of resolution. The *debate* concerning *how* these conflicts are resolved seems to hinge on whether we focus on the *non-musical aspects* of the film (as does Gabbard) or on the *ambi-diegetic jazz* that (in my view) tells its story more definitively.

Gabbard (1996) seems to face something of a quandary regarding how to interpret this motion picture. Toward this end, he makes extensive use of biographical material on Scorsese and a heavy reliance on the film's visual narrative and verbal dialogue. Thus—even while acknowledging that Scorsese has expressed a great love for the music of the swing masters (the Dorseys, Goodman, Shaw, and so forth) (pp. 270, 280)—Gabbard pays more attention to the fact that, during the stages of film production, the director showed admiration both for the songwriters who composed the music and words featured in Francine/Liza's numbers (John Kander and Fred Ebb) and for the performances by Ms. Minnelli herself, whom Scorsese considered "a major talent" (p. 272). Gabbard also makes much of the fact that Scorsese worked again with Ms. Minnelli, briefly but abortively directing her in a play (*The Act*) from which he ultimately withdrew (due, he said, to lack of experience in the theater). But if such indices of revealed preference deserve credulity, surely we must also acknowledge the rather lengthy display of mutual compatibility between the director Martin Scorsese and the actor

Robert De Niro—a close association that has continued over the decades through no fewer than nine motion pictures such as *Mean Streets* (1973), *Taxi Driver* (1976), *New York, New York* (1977), *Raging Bull* (1980), *The King of Comedy* (1983), *Goodfellas* (1990), *Cape Fear* (1991), *Casino* (1995), and *I Heard You Paint Houses* (in progress as of 2010). Clearly, if Scorsese has demonstrated substantial long-term loyalties, we would have to credit them primarily to De Niro rather than to Minnelli.

Nonetheless, Gabbard (1996) interprets *New York, New York* as validating the right-hand Liza-dominated side of the aforementioned homologies at the expense of the left-hand Robert-centered side. He bases this judgment primarily on the film's visually commanding production numbers featuring Evans/Minnelli in what he considers her triumphal role as a pop diva: "Ultimately, the film, released at a moment when the fortunes of jazz were close to the nadir, seems to lose interest in the music, while celebrating the spectacle of Liza Minnelli in performance" (p. 268). Thus, in Gabbard's view, the ethos of the film deserts Jimmy/Robert's art-for-art's-sake jazz in favor of Francine/Liza's art-for-mart's-sake popular appeal as "a great entertainer" (p. 272): "Lavish attention to Minnelli's performances is often at the expense of the film's representation of jazz artists" (p. 272). Artistic integrity, in Gabbard's reading, loses out to commercial appeal and to the glitzy gloss typical of the Hollywood musical in full flower insofar as "Scorsese's real sympathies lie with the more accessible art of Liza Minnelli" (p. 276). Thus, Gabbard states repeatedly in various ways that "Francine is the decided winner over Jimmy" as part of the film's "obvious project of celebrating the talents of Liza Minnelli" (p. 278): "Scorsese has in effect handed his film to Liza Minnelli and asked audiences to lose themselves in her seamless presentations of the Kander and Ebb songs" (p. 282). In other words, Gabbard sees a valorization of the Pop-Francine-Commerce-Minnelli-Scripted-Sweet-Ambitious side of the aforementioned homologies at the expense of the Jazz-Jimmy-Art-De Niro-Improvisatory-Obnoxious-Dedicated side.

The main problem with Gabbard's interpretation of *New York, New York* is that it depends primarily on the glitzy visual impression made by the film and on attention to its snappy verbal dialogue rather than on a careful and critical audition of its ambi-diegetic music. For I would contend that the ambi-diegetic cinemusical meanings found in *New York, New York* develop Jimmy/Robert's and Francine/Liza's characterizations while elaborating the theme of art-versus-commerce in ways that belie the interpretation proposed by Gabbard (1996). In making this case, let us listen first to the jazz performances expertly mimed by Robert De Niro to enact tenor solos dubbed by the swing veteran Georgie Auld (who also doubles in the film, in an interesting example of reflexivity, as a clarinet-playing bandleader named Frankie Harte, himself miming clarinet parts dubbed by Abe Most) and then to the song stylings of Ms. Minnelli singing in her very own inimitable voice.

We first encounter Doyle/De Niro—minus his saxophone—at a celebration of V-J Day in 1945 during a huge dance party for enlisted personnel where Jimmy/Robert hits on almost every young woman in sight, including the conspicuously unattached Evans/Minnelli. Here, Francine/Liza resists Jimmy/Robert's advances—repeating "no" so often that this insistent line attains a sort of infectious comic gaiety—while Jimmy/Robert manages to be so aggressively obnoxious as to become almost endearingly funny. Behind this scene, from the stage, we hear the Tommy Dorsey Orchestra running through a major portion of its impressive repertoire ("I'm Getting Sentimental Over You," "Song of India," "Opus One," and the rest). This ambi-diegetic cinemusical environment establishes the swing-oriented origins for the slightly more bop-friendly tenor sounds of Jimmy/Robert (channeling Georgie Auld and miming his dubbed solos to perfection) that set the tone for jazz-as-art in the remainder of the film. Soon, at an audition, we find Doyle/De Niro playing "too loud" for the tastes of an audience-oriented club manager who wants to hear something I'm not familiar with, do not know how to spell, and cannot find on Google called "she-bang." Whatever it is, "she-bang" must be pretty awful because De Niro avoids it like the plague. Rather, as the film unfolds, he treats us to a jazz-purist, artistically-centered reading of "Once In a While" (via *a cappella* tenor, played slowly and mournfully, under a street lamp); fast-paced saxophone flourishes to nameless tunes (while auditioning for the Frankie Harte band and while touring with this rather conventional dance-oriented ensemble); a rehearsal of "Takin' a Chance on Love" (in which he shows a rather high-handed perfectionist's intolerance of the difficulties experienced by the band members in playing his overly ambitious arrangement); thoughtful, almost lugubrious, ballad-tempo versions on both tenor and piano of "New York, New York" (a song whose music he composes for Francine/Liza); an up-tempo blues played with a group of black musicians in Harlem (showing that he can hold his own with a front line of highly accomplished jazz instrumentalists); a set of tunes that includes "Honeysuckle Rose," "Just You, Just Me," and a very fast blues (performed impressively with a similar group of musicians in Harlem); and a recapitulation of the slow and thoughtful approach to playing "New York, New York" (at his own jazz club called "The Major Chord," where he has achieved financial success as a nightclub owner and where his artistically-dedicated critically-recognized music has earned him a feature story on the cover of *DownBeat* magazine). In short, Jimmy/Robert's long years of fidelity to his jazz-oriented artistic integrity have ultimately achieved something close to the "major chord" that he mentions early in the film as his personal emblem of success, where everything comes together in satisfying harmony—the only exception in Jimmy/Robert's life, the only dissonance in his major chord, being . . . Francine/Liza.

Without belaboring the trials and tribulations of Jimmy/Robert's and Francine/Liza's tempestuous love affair—where we find no lack of on-screen romantic chemistry—we can chart the lesson for our art-versus-commerce theme by briefly reviewing the nature of the Evans/Minnelli singing style. With the utmost clarity, *New York, New York* presents an unapologetic and very public manifestation of the way in which she routinely assassinates otherwise worthwhile songs in a manner for all to observe and deplore. At a minimum, an artistically viable singer must be able to carry a tune. But this, unfortunately, is a talent that Ms. Minnelli conspicuously lacks—as she has demonstrated throughout her career in one histrionically off-key perform- ance after another, usually with an air of breathless excitement that suggests she has every hope that at long last, this time, she will produce vocal sounds that correspond to some degree with the notes she is trying to sing. I do not believe that the significance of this point can be overemphasized in general and certainly not with reference to the cinemusical meanings of *New York, New York* in particular.

Arguably, the vast majority of successful pop singers—not to mention master jazz vocalists—sing in tune. In the area of pop, recall Bing Crosby, Lena Horne, Doris Day, Rosemary Clooney, Frank Sinatra, Perry Como, Barbra Streisand, Andy Williams, Aretha Franklin, Linda Ronstadt, Paul Simon, James Taylor, or Celine Dion. In the area of jazz, consider Nat Cole, Ella Fitzgerald, Sarah Vaughan, Anita O'Day, Chris Connor, June Christy, Mel Tormé, Carmen McRae, Julie London, Marlene VerPlanck, Meredith D'Ambrosio, Irene Kral, Diana Krall, Stacey Kent, Tierney Sutton, Jane Monheit, Roberta Gambarini, or Hilary Kole. Every one of these singers always sings in tune. Even those with raspy, hoarse, androgynous, or otherwise challenged voices usually manage to zero in on the notes they are trying to hit. In this connection, think of Louis Armstrong, Billie Holiday, Chet Baker, Matt Dennis, Ray Charles, Janice Joplin, Dr. John, Joe Cocker, Rod Stewart, Ricki Lee Jones, Willie Nelson, Tom Waits, Randy Newman, or David Frishberg. Very few singers achieve success without a firm sense of musical pitch. Such occasional exceptions to the general rule might include Fred Astaire, Johnny Cash, Bob Dylan, Madonna, Judy Garland, and most conspicuously—indeed, with spectacular conspicuity—Judy's own daughter . . . Liza Minnelli.

By virtue of her inveterate tendency to sing profoundly off-key, I per- sonally find it nearly impossible to listen to the song stylings of Liza Minnelli. Nonetheless—as a service to you, Dear Reader—I have done exactly that throughout the entire two-and-a-half-hour length of *New York, New York* and, after recuperating sufficiently to return to more worthwhile labors, have this to report: Put simply, Liza Minnelli *demolishes* the musical integrity of the songs she sings in this film. She *destroys* every tune on which she imposes her overbearing but hopelessly out-of-tune cinemusical persona.

Consider, first, her pushy intrusion into Jimmy/Robert's audition—where, uninvited, she launches into a shaky-voiced rendition of "You Brought a New Kind of Love To Me"—to which he plays obbligatos convincingly enough to get them a job as a boy-girl act. From one perspective, given the popularity of chick singers, she helps to get him some work. From another, she plunges him into a commercial gig from which it takes him years to recover musically. When we next see Francine/Liza performing "Once In a While" with the mickey-mouse Frankie Harte Orchestra behind her, the hallmarks of her singing style begin to emerge all too clearly. Intonationally challenged, she seldom hits a note dead-on but prefers to sneak up on it by sliding from below or to collapse into it by sinking from above to its general vicinity, relying on the width of her wobbly vibrato to cover the general range where, with luck, the correct pitch lies somewhere within her very broad margin of error. To a musician—such as, we infer, Jimmy/Robert— the effect resembles fingernails on a blackboard, starlings in a cherry tree, or a yard full of felines energetically engaged in caterwauling. Francine/Liza chokes off notes in short, painful paroxysms, even while pushing the volume level of her declamations way past the limit of her modest capabilities. Unfortunately, the louder Francine/Liza sings, the more off-key she gets. Further, Francine/Liza accompanies her distressing vocalizations with a repertoire of exaggerated body gestures that constantly annoy witnesses to the cinematic spectacle without managing to distract us from the musical carnage that transpires on the soundtrack.

Still with Frankie Harte's dance band, Francine/Liza again displays her outlandish cinemusical persona on "You Are My Lucky Star"—to which Jimmy/Robert responds, recalling Orson Welles in *Citizen Kane* (1941) with what can only be heavy irony, by awkwardly leading the reluctant applause of the understandably inattentive audience. More of the same follows in "The Man I Love"—at the conclusion of which, after a demonstration of arm-waving, hand-gesticulating, finger-wagging body language that would do credit to a cheerleader for the Dallas Cowboys, she manages to end on three notes representing the three key words in the song's title with each one resoundingly off-key in its own unique way that sets it apart from the others. She deals a similar deathblow to "Just You, Just Me," right before announcing to Jimmy/Robert that she is pregnant and wants to return to New York to have their baby.

So here come some of the film's heavy implications concerning the art-versus-commerce theme. Without the inexplicably popular, crowd-pleasing charms of Francine/Liza, the dancers dwindle to the vanishing point. Francine/Liza is replaced by Bernice Conrad—a devastating caricature of the Minnelli-type singer, hilariously enacted by Mary Kay Place. Bernice/Mary Kay treats us to comical versions of "Blue Moon" and "Do Nothin' Till You Hear From Me"—both of which illustrate the ludicrous extremes to which the commercialistic ethos can sink while simultaneously making the point that even the intentionally mocking absurdities of Conrad/Place are nowhere near as aurally painful as those routinely but unintentionally dispensed by Evans/Minnelli.

But, after Francine/Liza and Jimmy/Robert finally break up, Evans/Minnelli bounces back with a vengeance—sort of like one of those ghouls or zombies in a horror movie that won't go away no matter how many times you kill it. Thus, do we encounter Francine/Liza's hyper-dramatic and resolutely-mawkish exhibition of over-reaching on "But the World Goes 'Round" (and 'round and 'round and 'round, it seems). Thus, too, must we endure her ridiculously extravagant performance of "Happy Endings" (in a motion-picture scene that makes Busby Berkeley look subtle and restrained by comparison). Thus, three, are we subjected to her quintessentially hyperbolic reading of "New York, New York" (to which Francine herself has written some transcendentally corny lyrics)—which she performs "her way" amidst self-obsessed, wide-eyed, arm-swinging, torso-twisting, super-inflated excitement that propels her toward an appalling finale of almost sublimely excruciating exuberance. Though Jimmy/Robert claps politely, when he visits Francine/Liza's dressing room, he can only mutter that he saw "Sappy Endings"; that she has "found another way" of doing his song; and that he is proud of her "in a way." Recall that Jimmy/Robert wrote "New York, New York" as a tender ballad. By transforming it into a grotesque flag-waving monstrosity—one destined, ironically enough, for great popularity (in Frank Sinatra's version)—Francine/Liza has single-handedly destroyed it.

All this culminates a bit earlier in a crucial scene that represents the ambi-diegetic cinemusical pivot point for the entire film. In this scene, Francine/Liza goes up to Harlem to hear Jimmy/Robert and to meet with a Decca executive who wants her to sign a lucrative recording contract. Jimmy/Robert emerges from a cubicle in the men's room, where he has been smoking something suspicious with some other members of the mostly-black band. After a conversation about Francine/Liza's singing contract, Jimmy/Robert returns to the bandstand to accompany a fetching and musically hip version of "Honeysuckle Rose" by a beautiful African-American singer (the gorgeous Diahnne Abbott, who was De Niro's real-life wife at the time). In context, Diahnne Abbott is everything that Francine/Liza is not—statuesque, poised, ultra cool, musically expert, and artistically centered (not to mention, literally, married to De Niro). After this—while Francine/Liza sits there gulping a glass of wine despite her pregnancy and conspicuously not applauding the efforts of her cinemusically vibrant rival—Jimmy/Robert launches into a post-swing, proto-bop version of "Just You, Just Me." Francine/Liza misinterprets this choice of material as her cue to come forward to join her husband in song. But, as she makes her move toward the stage, we see Jimmy/Robert's eyes fill with horror. Clearly, he feels upset on several levels at once. First, he resents Francine/Liza's success, her recording contract, her sell-out to the forces of commercialism. Second, paradoxically, he feels jealous of the very popularity and commercial appeal that he disapproves so deeply. Third, he knows from bitter experience how she sings "Just You, Just Me"—as do we, Dear Reader—that is, extremely badly indeed. So, fourth, he worries with justification that he will be humiliated in front of his mostly black and very savvy musical friends (including the lovely and talented Diahnne Abbott). All this passes across the face of the great actor and converges to inspire Jimmy/Robert to make an abrupt switch to a mercurially rapid blues—something that Francine/Liza cannot possibly try to sing—as if to say, "Whatever you do, don't come up here on this bandstand." She is embarrassed and flees from the club. Metaphorically, at last, he has driven a stake through her misbegotten cinemusical heart.

Taken together, the dramatic development attributable to the ambi-diegetic cinemusical meanings in *New York, New York* does much to vindicate the left-hand side of the homologies listed earlier—that is, to support jazz over pop, to privilege art over commerce, to elevate impro-visation over scripting, and to exalt the obnoxious-but-dedicated Jimmy/Robert over the sweet-but-ambitious Francine/Liza. The evidence for this judgment comes from the on-screen music and the manner in which it raises artistic integrity over crowd-pleasing commercialism as a continuous theme and as a recurring characterization in this particular film. Robert/Jimmy stands for art, Francine/Liza for commerce. As I have tried to show, on ambi-diegetic cinemusical grounds, the former clearly wins the competition between the two.

Viewers and readers are left to wonder whether the arguments just advanced do or do not capture the intentions of the director Martin Scorsese. Clearly, our verdict on this point hinges on whether we do or do not imagine Mr. Scorsese to be tone deaf. On the tone-deaf hypothesis, implicitly held by Gabbard (1996), the director inserted elaborate production numbers featuring Liza Minnelli in order to celebrate the wonders of her entertaining stage presence as a popular song stylist. Indeed—in the exorbitant flourishes of "But the World Goes 'Round," "Happy Endings," and "New York, New York," which even Yanow (2004) considers "over-the-top" (p. 186)—she entertains us mercilessly, to within an inch of our lives. On the darker and more uncompromising interpretation that I favor, Scorsese knows perfectly well that Minnelli sings off-key and—though too polite to say so publicly—has evinced this sensibility by letting her create her own unintentionally self-parodic display of excruciatingly out-of-tune performances that comment reflexively on her own musical histrionics in a way that consistently advances the theme of anti-commercialism in this film.

By the way, I do not deny that—being a man of good musical taste—Gabbard (1996) himself also experiences considerable discomfort with the offerings of Ms. Minnelli. At one point, he explicitly refers to the "excesses" evinced by her "highly mannered style of singing" (p. 272). Later, he sees her "posturings" (p. 282) as "narcissistic" (p. 279) and, in an obscure foot-note, confesses his "dismay" at the film's "lavish attention to Liza Minnelli" (p. 314). But Gabbard (1996) does appear to give short shrift to this film's valorization of jazz as an artform. In this, he contrasts the spirit of Scorsese's movie and its saxophone-playing hero with that of the master saxophonist Art Pepper, who—in his autobiography (Pepper 1979), as quoted by the epigraph for Gabbard's chapter—voices a deep devotion to the rapturous ecstasies involved in jazz improvisation:

> I played way over my head . . . searched and found my own way . . . played myself . . . knew I was right . . . blew and . . . blew, and when I finally finished I was shaking all over; my heart was pounding; I was soaked in sweat. . . . And that was it.
>
> (Pepper 1979, p. 476)

As he concludes his critical discussion of Scorsese's film, Gabbard (1996) asks, "Why is there nothing in *New York, New York* like the passage from Art Pepper's autobiography that begins this chapter?" (p. 282). The world of motion pictures had to wait a couple of years for the answer. And herein lies the topic for Chapter 11.

# 11  Art and *Heart Beat* (1980)

## Stars Fell on Algolagnia

OK, let's get this straight, right up front. One of my greatest jazz heroes of all time is . . . Art Pepper. I place this great West Coast alto saxophonist—who first came to prominence in the 1950s and remained on the scene into the 1980s—right up there with Bird and Diz, Lester and Teddy, Tatum and Garner, Billie and Ella, Bud and Thelonious, Mulligan and Baker, Brubeck and Desmond, Farmer and Golson, Miles and 'Trane, Oscar-Ray-and-Herbie, the Modern Jazz Quartet, Bill Evans, Tal Farlow, Hampton Hawes, Jim Hall, Bud Shank, Zoot Sims, Gary Burton, Keith Jarrett, Joe Locke, and all the rest of the jazz luminaries that I hold in awe. To my ears, Pepper filled his playing with endless invention, a haunting melodic imagination, a matchless sense of rhythmic urgency, and a profound purity of conception. He owned a completely distinctive sound on the alto sax and stood out as one of the very few players instantly recognizable after only a few notes of soloing. Sticking mostly to jazz standards and tunes composed on the chord changes of familiar pop tunes, he played with a sense of passion and a depth of emotion seldom equaled by other players of his or any era. He expressed and inspired a feeling of ecstatic involvement in his music. Put simply, Arthur Edward Pepper was, as his name implied, the essence of . . . Art.

That's the good news. The bad news is that, throughout most of his adult life, Art Pepper was a hopeless junky—heroin being his preferred narcotic of choice—a self-destructive miscreant who devoted most of his energy to scoring his next fix; who wallowed in unrepentant masochism; whose addictive propensities toward self-destruction kept him constantly afoul of the law, often in prison, and ultimately a totally debilitated person; and who dedicated himself so single-mindedly to the pursuit of iniquity that he barely had any time left over to nurture his transcendent musical abilities. Documenting all these sordid details of his own squalid existence, Pepper (1979) wrote an autobiography that described his drug-induced status as a hardened criminal, that bitterly recounted all the myriad injustices perpetrated upon him by a long list of former friends and ex-partners, that left this reader with a deep sense of hopeless despondency over the possibility of his ever leading a productive life, and that revealed only one clearly estimable virtue in the man—namely, his complete and unshakeable commitment to . . . honesty.

Indeed, Art Pepper spared no pains in telling all about himself, however bad it could and did make him look to the eyes of the world. The same open honesty that filled his book also characterized his playing and was, perhaps, essential to his greatness as an artist. The same pain that pervaded his written pages also poured forth through his horn in an endless stream of wounded agony. One could not read . . . or listen . . . without seeing and hearing it. And all this appears—enigmatically, compellingly, as Art—in both his recordings and his autobiography (Pepper 1979).

Shortly before Pepper's death from a stroke in 1982, with plenty of help from Art's wife Laurie, Don McGlynn created a documentary entitled *Art Pepper: Notes From a Jazz Survivor* (1982). In this film, we find the jazz giant—somewhere between defiant and pathetic—raging at the world and expressing various paranoid feelings of persecution mixed with delusions of grandeur. Pepper declares himself to be a genius. And, seeing him immersed in the detritus of his daily surroundings, we are tempted to discount his claims as self-inflating hyperbole. But then, if we think about it, we realize that he is absolutely right. Few jazz performers have risen to the musical heights of Arthur Edward Pepper. Few musicians have attained such an exalted level of jazz as Art. And few stars have fallen so low, so deeply into a masochistic shambles, so far into Algolagnia.

Thus—through his life, career, and music—Art Pepper becomes available as a free-floating signifier linked to the meanings associated with a key protagonist from the *ménage a trois* portrayed in the film directed by John Byrum entitled *Heart Beat* (1980) (shot, incidentally, by László Kovács, the same cinematographer who filmed *New York, New York*). Based loosely on a vaguely autobiographical account by Carolyn Cassady (Sissy Spacek) of her relationship with Neal Cassady (Nick Nolte) and Jack Kerouac (John Heard) during the period when the latter was composing such stream-of-consciousness beat-generation treasures as *On the Road* (1957) and *The Subterraneans* (1958), *Heart Beat* manages quite powerfully to convey the general sleaziness and desperation of the poetic but perverse existence—in the service of art—pursued by its male anti-heroes (especially Neal/Nick, who was the model for Dean Moriarty in *On the Road*). In one scene, so repugnantly disgusting that it attains an almost exalted level of sick humor, we see Kerouac/Heard writing his deathless prose in a filthy latrine where his opium-dazed friends come to vomit into the mephitic toilet at his elbow. In another, we follow Cassady/Nolte as he does a drug fix in a men's room cubicle, rapturously participates in a torrid up-tempo jam session, and then wanders forlornly through the streets—begging for a piece of bread at the bakery and washing his face with ice at the fish monger's. When the film is not documenting the rampant nonconformity—bordering on squalor, verging on depravity—of these beat-generation luminaries, it devotes gleeful attention to satirizing the foibles of 1950s families who live in tract houses, raise 2.4 perfect children, plant-weed-mow-and-water their lawns, and watch totally mindless television programs. At one critical juncture, Cassady/Nolte sneaks into the back yard of such an establishment to smoke a joint while we see not one but two televisions in neighbors' windows—both simultaneously playing that masterpiece of dumbed-down mid-1950s conservatism, *The Ozzie and Harriet Show*. Later—after the Cassady-Kerouac-and-Cassady threesome has taken up residence as a *ménage a trois*, in a scene that seems more comical than dangerous—Neal/Nick and Jack/John plant large marijuana bushes in their garden.

So what kind of nondiegetic music do we need to represent such characters? Composer Jack Nitzsche offer us a pretty, innocent, lilting leitmotif to accompany Carolyn/Sissy whenever she makes one of her grand entrances, whenever she appears as a long-suffering but devoted spouse or friend, and whenever Neal/Nick or Jack/John thinks about her in her absence. This theme covers an octave and a half, via a soothingly pretty melodic sequence, in waltz time:

F^-↓F#; ↑G^^; ↑E^-↓G#; ↑A^^; ↑D^^; ↑C^-↓B; ↓G^^; ^^^.

For example, the first time we see Carolyn/Sissy—at a fancy restaurant where Neal, Jack, and Neal's current girlfriend Stevie (Ann Dusenberry) dine with an old friend of Neal's who has a lot of money and treats them to a lavish lunch—the diegetic music comes from a piano quietly playing in the huge dining area. Before a propitious pause, this piano builds a vertically ascending scale, just as the wealthy friend announces the arrival of his date. At the exact moment when we see Carolyn/Sissy enter, dressed all in white and looking ravishingly beautiful, the diegetic piano shifts to a full non-diegetic orchestra playing the F-F#-G-E-G#-A-D-C-B-G waltz. Early in the film, this leitmotif continues to accompany Carolyn/Sissy, in her comparatively liberated days as an art student, dressed like a fashion model from *Vogue*. Whenever Neal/Nick or Jack/John thinks about her longingly and lovingly, we hear F-F#-G . . . in the background score. After Carolyn/Sissy starts having babies—three by the movie's end—and Carolyn-Neal-and-Jack move into their tract house in the bowels of middle America, Carolyn/Sissy looks more like a Madonna, but the waltz theme remains the same. At the conclusion of the film, an estranged Neal/Nick drives around in a psychedelic school bus (during his Ken Kesey phase), and Jack/John rides off in a taxi cab to nowhere (perhaps a plane to St. Petersburg, where he dies in 1969 at age 47 in relative obscurity). Following a voiceover in which Carolyn/Sissy proclaims that they did nothing wrong (but just did it first) and muses philosophically that compromises are like dentist appointments (damned if you do, damned if you don't), she places a sprinkler on her lawn, right in front of the blue-and-white Nash Metropolitan that sits in the driveway of her quintessential 1950s tract house. The nondiegetic orchestral music swells to a reprise of the F-F#-G . . . theme.

So, if a pretty waltz provides the nondiegetic commentary on the sub-urbanization of Carolyn/Sissy, what kind of underscore do we need to contrast vividly with this sweet-sounding 3/4-time theme in ways that establish the dramatic departure from conventional norms represented by the two male characters? Here, the manners of treating Jack/John and Neal/Nick differ rather tellingly. Specifically, Jack/John is presented primarily *as music*, while Neal/Nick is represented primarily *by music* in general and especially *by Art Pepper* in particular.

Thus, early in the film, Carolyn/Sissy's voiceover introduces Jack/John as a "struggling novelist" who sits at his mother's kitchen table, tapping furiously on an old portable typewriter and creating "jazzed-up stories" about artists and musicians he knows in New York. In Carolyn/Sissy's description, Jack/John writes the words as if they are notes to a saxophone solo. At this point, cutting through a nondiegetic arrangement for big band by Shorty Rogers in the background score by Jack Nitzche, we hear the instantly recognizable saxophone of Art Pepper as the scene shifts to an encapsulated montage of Jack/John's and Neal/Nick's trip by car to the West Coast. Later in the film—at the decisive moment of artistic gestation when Jack/John slots a roll of paper towels into his typewriter and announces that, with the help of a few bennies, he will now finish his book so that, some day, he can have a house in the hills—he further proclaims that he will "play this thing" (the typewriter) like Charlie Parker (the jazz genius). Hence, the metaphor that constantly accompanies Jack/John's literary efforts is that of a jazz musician blowing the saxophone, a soloist wailing on his ax, Bird on a flight of brilliantly spontaneous improvisatory creation. Those who have read *On the Road*—the major book that resulted from this style of composition—know that Kerouac's convoluted, meandering, free-form, stream-of-consciousness prose does bear at least some resemblance to his self-congratulatory image of himself as a sax-playing jazz improviser.

Meanwhile, all this leaves us with the issue of what sort of background music, in this context, would best signify the debased debauchery of the Neal/Nick character. As already intimated, the answer is . . . Art Pepper! The saxophonist went into the studio to record his contributions to the sound-track for *Heart Beat* in March of 1979—close to the moment when his monstrously lamentable autobiography hit the bookstands. But, by that time, he had long since achieved the dubious distinction of iconicity as a paragon of drug-dependent self-punishment. He had established a solid reputation as a hardened criminal, willing to commit any felony to support his narcotics habit—including, for example, an armed robbery at a gas station, to which he cheerfully confesses. Whose music—loaded with such unsavory connotations—could possibly be a better match for the degradations of Neal/Nick?

As previously mentioned, *Heart Beat* begins with Art Pepper soloing over a big-band jazz score in the background as we watch scenes of Neal/Nick and Jack/John motoring from New York toward the West Coast. Nondiegetic flourishes from Art accompany their almost comical tactics for ripping off gas and supplies from a service station on a lonely country road. Art's clarion call signals the perversity of Jack/John fornicating with Neal/Nick's girlfriend Stevie/Ann in the back of their big stolen car while Neal/Nick watches from a few feet away. Later in the film, Art's alto in the underscore—this time, *a cappella*—sets the stage for a scene in the squalid apartment on Haight Street where Neal/Nick asks a pregnant Carolyn/Sissy to marry him. Still later—in a long scene in which Neal/Nick leaves a jazz club, begs for some bread, and wanders past a fish monger to a coffee shop where he sips coffee, smokes cigarettes, and thinks about his troubles—we hear the slow, mournful saxophone of Art Pepper with piano accompaniment in the background. This distressing nondiegetic music leads to a moment when Neal/Nick sees his old girlfriend Stevie/Ann going into an apartment building with a sailor, follows them, beats up the sailor, and begins an adulterous fling with Stevie/Ann (all the while protesting illogically that he loves Carolyn/Sissy). After this initial tryst, we again hear Art Pepper in the nondiegetic score—this time playing furiously at a frantic tempo as Neal/Nick drives at warp speed to catch the train for his day job as a conductor and continuing as Neal/Nick further pursues his two-timing affair with Stevie/Ann while Pepper's pungent solo surges in the background. Later still, when Jack/John's book achieves success and he travels to New York to appear on talk shows amidst a flurry of publicity for his heralding of the "beat generation," Neal/Nick (ironically, the very prototype of the beatnik via his thinly disguised role as Dean Moriarty in Kerouac's book) stumbles around the streets of San Francisco—drinking, smoking dope, and eventually getting busted by an undercover policeman—all to the tune of Art Pepper's symbolically significant alto saxophone in the underscore.

So, throughout *Heart Beat*, Art Pepper serves as a sort of running nondiegetic commentary on the sociopathic tendencies of the Neal/Nick character. This role for the off-screen Pepper reaches a kind of apotheosis and begins to bleed into the *mise-en-scène* in one vivid scene at a jazz club. The scene begins with noises coming out of a cubicle in the men's room (recalling Doyle/De Niro in *New York, New York*). Soon five guys who have been fixing in the toilet, including Neal/Nick, file out and head back into the club where they perform an extremely hot, sweaty, up-tempo jazz piece featuring in-tandem soloing by cornet and alto—the latter dubbed, of course, by Art Pepper, whose music now provides a meaningful ambi-diegetic cinemusical moment. This music—flashing by at 320 beats-per-minute—seems wild, perspiration-drenched, out-of-control (like Gabbard's epigraph, quoted near the end of Chapter 10). All this mirrors Neal/Nick's sensibilities, as echoed by the frenetic music. But maybe the most telling moment in the scene occurs as the five guys leave the toilet cubicle. After the first four have walked past the camera, the last man stops, turns, goes back, and re-emerges carrying . . . his alto saxophone. This man bears an undeniable—indeed, an alarming—resemblance to . . . Art Pepper.

# 12 Brando Loyalty and *The Score* (2001)

## How Do You Keep the Music Paying?

It might appear self-evident that convincingly realistic acting, whether on the stage or in a film, requires a commitment to delivering one's lines intelligibly in the language in which they were written—that is, to pronouncing them correctly and articulating them clearly in a manner suited to comprehension by the typical audience member. I realize, of course, that certain notable cinematic exceptions have appeared. Russell Rouse's *The Thief* (1952), starring Ray Milland, contains no spoken dialogue at all. In Jane Campion's *The Piano* (1993), the character played by Holly Hunter chooses not to speak. Woody Allen's *Sweet and Lowdown* (1999) features Samantha Morton in a superb performance as a mute woman in a romantic relationship with the 1930s jazz guitarist Emmet Ray (Sean Penn). In Steven Soderbergh's *Traffic* (2000) some of the dialogue involving Mexican characters, spoken in Spanish, appears with subtitles. And so forth. But—most of the time, as a general rule—we really do need to hear a movie star say something that we can decipher. Thus, even an actress such as Marlee Matlin—who is deaf and who delivers her lines mostly in sign language, usually with the help of an on-screen interpreter—successfully negotiates, often to striking effect, those occasional moments when it becomes necessary for her to speak out loud. While affecting a heavy speech impediment as Toulouse-Lautrec in Baz Luhrman's *Moulin Rouge* (2001), the actor John Leguizamo still manages to make himself understood. And who could forget those dramatic junctures when—in response to the command, "Lassie, speak"—the noble collie correctly pronounced the clearly recognizable word, "Woof!"?

Let us therefore devote some attention to a conspicuous exception that appears to prove the rule. In this spirit, let us ask ourselves what would happen to an American actor who is afflicted by a chronic inability or an inveterate unwillingness to speak clearly but who nonetheless perseveres. Let us imagine an almost charismatic fellow—manly, strong, athletic, and muscular in his youth—with darkly handsome good looks and with a repertoire of body language, physical gestures, and facial expressions that elevates him without question to the immortal pantheon of thespian greatness. But let us further suppose that when this gifted star opens his mouth to speak, what comes out is pure mush. That his voice—which, to fit his screen

persona, should sound macho—emerges as whiney, wimpy, and whimper-
ing. That his singing—which, in good conscience, should never have been
inflicted upon the movie-going public—is excruciatingly inept. That in one
Oscar-winning performance, he actually wears a dental prosthetic device to
help himself mumble better. That his enunciation—which, to our horror,
deteriorates over his lifetime in direct proportion to the magnitude of his
always-burgeoning box-office appeal and the size of his ever-mushrooming
paychecks, matched only by the vastness of his gargantuan ego and the
massiveness of his relentlessly expanding corporeal bulk—puts one in mind
of the famous efforts by the Greek Demosthenes to learn oratory by
practicing at the seashore with pebbles in his mouth. That his tortured
failures to make himself understood remind us inevitably of those legendary
silent-screen stars who had such offensive speaking voices that they could
not credibly manage the post-1927 transition to talkies. That his arrogance
or laziness in refusing to move beyond mumbling his lines invariably tempts
us to storm the box office in an effort to get our money back. And that—
until his recent passing—he diligently perfected this skill in the slurring of
words to the level of a high art. I refer, of course, to . . . none other than . . .
Marlon Brando—an actor of the most elevated celebrity to whom audiences
have steadfastly remained as inexplicably faithful or as "Brando loyal" as it
is possible to imagine.

To illustrate this sad case of an over-inflated ego corrupted by star power
via a recent film that draws on the telling use of diegetic jazz to develop the
theme of art-versus-commerce, I offer for consideration a motion picture
starring (again) Robert De Niro, co-starring Edward Norton, featuring
Marlon Brando, directed by Frank Oz, and entitled . . . *The Score* (2001).
Besides indicating the film's place in the great *score*-related tradition of heist-
based action-suspense movies, the title of *The Score* (2001) reminds us of the
considerable financially-remunerative star power invested in its production
by signaling the extent to which each actor *scored* in terms of monetary
compensation for appearing in the film—Marlon Brando (77 years old,
$10 million); Robert De Niro (57 years old, $15 million); Edward Norton
(32 years old, $6.5 million). Further, the title awakens our attention to the
film's *score*—a jazz-inflected post-fusion nondiegetic drone created by
Howard Shore in a spirit that one critic found evocative of Miles Davis but
that does not crackle with anything remotely resembling the energy of that
great trumpeter's work in (say) *Ascenseur Pour L'Échafaud* (1958; see also
Chapter 13; Holbrook 2008b). Fortunately, as we shall see, this background
music is amplified diegetically via various atmospheric jazz performances by
the likes of Cassandra Wilson and Mose Allison.

In *The Score*, we witness the enervating spectacle of one great actor
working at the peak of his powers (De Niro) playing opposite an over-paid
and bloated "superstar" who has sunk beneath the nadir of even his own
past public affronts to our cinematic sensibilities (Brando). Partly reading
and partly improvising his lines in a sort of grotesquely lisping and effetely
unintelligible pixie voice, Brando rolls his ponderous corporeal enormity

from one seated or sprawling position to the next, mauling his speaking part and putting one in mind of nothing so much as Jackie Gleason after several martinis, Orson Welles on Quaaludes, or Orca playing the role of a beached whale. Thus, one critic comments perceptively that "Brando . . . looks and sounds as if Truman Capote had swallowed Sydney Greenstreet whole" (Lou Lemenick in the *New York Post*, July 31, 2001, on-line @ www.ny post.com).

This cinematic disaster becomes all the more poignant when we recall that Robert De Niro's first great motion-picture success rewarded his Oscar-winning role as the young Don Vito Corleone in Francis Ford Coppola's *The Godfather Part II* (1974), playing a youthful version of the older character in *The Godfather* (1972) for which Brando had himself won an Academy Award two years earlier. Ironically, though Brando and De Niro both achieved acclaim by playing the same character in different films, *The Score* captures the first and last time that the two renowned actors appeared together on-screen. The singularity of this event makes it seem all the more regrettable that their one-and-only joint appearance represents such a star-crossed travesty.

In *The Score*, Robert De Niro plays the role of Nick Wells . . . the owner of a jazz club called "NYC" in Montreal, who balances a discreet affair with Diane Roesman (Angela Bassett) against his secret life as a master criminal who has developed his safe-cracking skills to a high art. Marlon Brando's ineffably pathetic character—Max Baron, who fences the jewels stolen by Nick/Robert and with whom Nick/Robert has been working for many years—needs a few million dollars to repay a debt to a ruthless gangster (Teddy Salida). Toward this financial end, working with the young and cocky Jack Teller (Edward Norton in an inspired performance that involves posing as a mentally retarded or autistic janitor named Brian), Max/Marlon has planned an intricately choreographed heist of an incalculably valuable seventeenth-century golden-and-jeweled French royal scepter from the vaults in the basement of the Montreal Customs House. If successful, Nick/Robert will get six million dollars for his efforts—more than enough to permit him to retire from his precarious secret life of crime, to repay the mortgage on his jazz club "NYC," to keep this legitimate business going, to clear the debts accumulated via his lavish consumption habits, and to marry the fetching Diane/Angela (who has made a law-abiding environment her prerequisite to matrimony). In return, all Nick/Robert has to do is . . . well . . . most of the work.

Nick/Robert badly wants to negotiate this lifestyle switch, to keep his nightclub open, and to wed Diane/Angela. However, Max/Marlon's plan to snatch the priceless scepter from the Montreal coffers in collaboration with Jack/Brian/Edward directly contradicts Nick/Robert's two self-imposed cardinal rules for safe-cracking decorum—namely, (1) always work alone and (2) never operate in the city where you live. Besides his NIMBY-inspired unwillingness to break-and-enter in his own neighborhood (not in my back yard), Nick/Robert feels an intuitive aversion toward the young, cocky, and potentially careless Jack/Brian/Edward—all the more, we suspect, because Jack/Edward has attained his insider position at the Customs House by pretending to be a mentally retarded assistant janitor named Brian. When Jack/Edward tries his Brian act on Nick/Robert, the latter becomes enraged. Thus, to convince Nick/Robert to risk everything in return for a chance to retire from his life of crime, Max/Marlon has a formidable job of persuasion to accomplish.

Notice the implicit parallel between Jack/Brian/Edward and Max/Marlon. Specifically, neither manages to make himself clearly understood. The irony is that, even at the heights of his most linguistically-challenged babbling, Jack/Brian/Edward is far easier to comprehend than Max/Marlon on even his best day. Thus, Max/Marlon's speaking part in the tense scene during which he must bring all his rhetorical powers to bear on the challenge of persuading Nick/Robert to participate in the dangerous scepter-snatching caper—that is, to convince him that undertaking this high-risk/high-reward opportunity in grand larceny promises a payoff that justifies the chances of being caught, sent to prison, and losing not only the jazz club but also his paramour Diane/Angela—consists entirely of unintelligible muttering and mumbling. Inexplicably inspired by this bizarre verbal exchange, Nick/ Robert sallies forth; snatches the scepter in one of the most intricately improbable capers ever captured on the silver screen; achieves righteous retribution over the insidious Jack/Brian/Edward via a nicely-prepared double-double-cross; and, implicitly blessed by a smile of satisfaction from Max/Marlon, happily subsides into the lifestyle-switching contentment of law-abiding domesticity with Diane/Angela.

Clearly, only one thing could save this otherwise preposterous movie from the problem of pushing its violations of verisimilitude past the breaking point—namely, the judicious deployment of first-class diegetic jazz. More specifically, to position Nick/Robert's participation in the dangerous scepter snatch as a remotely plausible possibility, he must want very badly to settle down to the crime-free lifestyle of a domesticated tax-paying jazz-club owner (as he refers to himself with evident satisfaction near the film's conclusion). The indubitable charms of Diane/Angela handle the domestically-related half of this problem. Solving the tax-paying half requires that the jazz club be a really cool place . . . with really good music.

Partly, this necessary effect is achieved by the décor of the NYC Club, owned and run by Nick/Robert as a legitimate front for his clandestine criminal activities. Like his well-appointed apartment, the nightclub exudes a deliciously opulent atmosphere (dark hues, plush seating, tasteful furnishings, subtle lighting, plentiful liquor bottles, and a classy bar that features an array of elegant blue glass). Who wouldn't want to quit the rat-race headaches of the safe-cracking business so he could hang out in a joint like this and, like Nick/Robert, start each day with a stiff Scotch-on-the-rocks while leafing absent-mindedly through the inconsequential daily mail?

But mostly, the positioning of the NYC Club hinges on the film's use of diegetic jazz to explain the efforts by Nick/Robert to make this really cool place—this soul-satisfying musicscape—the decorous and law-abiding epicenter of his reformed domesticity and reformulated lifestyle. The film achieves this effect through its diegetic deployment of jazz as part of a realistic *mise-en-scène* that justifies Nick/Robert's desire to remain a night-club owner. Toward this end, *The Score*—as might be suggested by at least one of its title's multiple meanings—offers some rather excellent scene-setting, ambience-defining, environment-establishing source music that deserves our attention for its role in elucidating what could possibly motivate Nick/Robert to undertake a criminal escapade of such enormously risky proportions. If successful, the heist will make it possible for Nick/Robert to relax into the life of a jazz-club owner who gets to sit around, sip Scotch, consort with Diane/Angela in connubial bliss, and listen to all this good music for free.

And what *is* this "good music"? Here, I bypass the functionally adequate nondiegetic score created by Howard Shore—a rather monotonous, moody, modish quasi-jazz background that features Tim Hagans on a Miles-like muted trumpet. Also, the compilation parts of the score revisit Miles from the late-1950s playing "Autumn Leaves" with Cannonball Adderley on the latter's classic album entitled *Somethin' Else* (Blue Note, 1958) as well as Thelonious Monk doing "'Round Midnight" (Blue Note, 1947) and Clifford Brown performing "Easy Living" (Blue Note, 1953). This proliferation of artists associated with Blue Note suggests that a compilation-based sound-track album might have originally been envisioned. But, unfortunately, it never materialized. Instead, what we get is a pure soundtrack recording that revisits only Howard Shore's repetitive background music (Varese Records 066267), also managing to omit Diana Krall's "I'll Make It Up As I Go" (which serves as a backdrop to the closing credits). At any rate, the non-diegetic underscore and compilation pieces give a sense of the cool, hip, dangerous environment surrounding the main plotlines. But it is the diegetic jazz performed at the NYC Club that convincingly establishes a music-enriched artistically-centered environment to explain the inclination of Nick/Robert toward retiring to a life of mellow listening as a law-abiding tax-paying jazz-club owner.

Specifically, I refer to cinemusically striking on-screen performances at the NYC Club by Cassandra Wilson and Mose Allison.

Early in the film, accompanied by a piano-bass-and-drums trio, Cassandra Wilson—the still-youthful darling of the jazz cognoscenti, who happens to bear a noticeable resemblance to Diane/Angela—performs a sultry version of "You're About To Give In" that sets the mood and establishes the luxuriant, musically hip feeling of Nick/Robert's jazz club. The camera quickly pans past Cassandra, wearing a sexy red dress with a plunging neckline, en route to finding Nick/Robert at the bar, where the main story-line continues.

Later, in a similar fashion, the camera rushes past the legendary Mose Allison—hunched over his keyboard, accompanied only by bass—singing "City Home." As the visual image finds Nick/Robert and Ed/Jack in conversation, the latter gesticulates in the general direction of the great Mose and subliminally mutters two words that can be gleaned only by resorting to the DVD's subtitling feature: "He's good."

Good Mose is, for sure. And so, likewise, is Cassandra. All this establishes art (in the form of jazz at the NYC Club) as a force that trumps commerce (in the shape of the hero's criminal activities). Indeed, this use of diegetic jazz-related source music would almost render the film worth seeing for its own sake if only these performances did not flash by so quickly—namely, in less than one minute for Cassandra-and-Mose combined (under 40 seconds and under 20 seconds, respectively) (see also Yanow 2004, p. 194). Via another DVD feature, wherein the director comments on the film as it unfolds, Frank Oz confesses that he would have liked to show more of Cassandra and Mose but that he was a "slave to the story." In other words, he needed to dispense with the diegetic jazz quickly in order to get back to Nick/Robert because, after all, that and not diegetic jazz is what the action-minded attention-deficited ticket-buying mass-market motion-picture audience wants to watch.

The latter consideration strikes me as somewhat unsettling, rather contradictory to the rationale for the film's denouement, and reflective of the real commercially-motivated rather than artistically-inspired response to the question, "How Do You Keep the Music Paying?" The answer is that you keep the story focused on the criminal adventures of Nick/Robert—where the real-life Robert gets three times the fee for playing this movie role (15 million 2001 American dollars) that the fictitious Nick demands for the risky job of stealing the scepter (6 million 2001 Canadian dollars). In this, paradoxically or ambivalently, you shape the diegetic cinemusical meanings to work partly in the service of art but also, as constrained by the limits of audience tastes, to fit the dictates of commerce as embodied by the star power of our central protagonist—always remembering that, hey, "He's Delightful; He's Delicious; He's . . . De Niro."

## CODA

The three chapters in Part V have examined the role of film music in advancing the development of cinemusical meanings such as the art-versus-commerce theme via the use of ambi-diegetic jazz in *New York, New York* (1977), nondiegetic jazz in *Heart Beat* (1980), and diegetic jazz in *The Score* (2001). In this connection, generally speaking, the inclusion of jazz in a motion picture (1) represents a form of product placement (leading to marketable offerings in the shape of soundtrack albums); (2) serves as a key element in the product design of a film (ambi-diegetic dramatic performances, nondiegetic background score, diegetic source music); (3) provides symbolic consumer experiences whereby characters reveal consumption-related aspects of their personalities (via the cinemusical meanings of their musical tastes); and (4) reflects the development of socially significant themes such as the dramatic tension between art (the drive toward creative integrity) and commerce (the quest for popular appeal or market success). Pursuing these perspectives, in particular, Part V draws on interpretive approaches (semiotics, hermeneutics) to surface jazz-related cinemusical meanings expressed in the form of subjective personal introspective essays (SPI or autoethnography). A formal presentation of this essentially impressionistic account appears in the homologous comparisons shown in Table 4 in the Introduction to Part V. From this formalization, the various uses of ambi-diegetic, nondiegetic, and diegetic jazz emerge in ways that share a common structure to convey the cinemusical tension between art (creative integrity) and commerce (popular entertainment) in the three illustrative films under consideration. Overall, as hinted by my various titles, commodification ("Brando Loyalty") fails to triumph over artistic integrity ("De Niro, My God, To Thee").

# Part VI
# God Is in the Details

# Introduction to Part VI

> I sing because I'm happy.
> I sing because I'm free.
> His eye is on the sparrow,
> And I know He watches me.
>
> (Traditional Gospel Spiritual)

We have seen at least one example—namely, *Paris Blues* in Chapter 8—in which a detail as small as the transformations of one note among three occasions when it appears in the jazz score engenders significant meanings in the dramatic development of characterizations, plotlines, and key themes of importance in conveying the film's major implications. Part VI will explore additional examples of films in which, as an interpretive strategy, we shall find that significant meanings emerge from seemingly trivial aspects of the text or, in other words, that "God Is in the Details."

Such an elevated attention to seemingly small textual elements has appeared as an accepted path toward discovery in a number of different kinds of interpretive analysis that have converged on the role of such subtleties in the understanding of otherwise difficult-to-interpret materials. Examples would include the following areas of investigation.

(1) First, during the middle years of the last century, literary proponents of the *new criticism* practiced *close reading* as the key to extracting every ounce of meaning from the novels of (say) Austin, Joyce, or Faulkner and the poems of (say) Yeats, Pound, or Eliot (e.g., Brooks 1947; Brooks and Warren ed. 1960; Empson 1949; Wimsatt and Beardsley 1946, 1954). The essence of close reading is that no detail is too small to deserve careful scrutiny as a potential key to connotations, associations, or other implications that lie below the surface of the text.

(2) Second, among social scientists, *content analysis* has placed an emphasis on the role played by *minor encoding habits* in detecting the authorship of texts with doubtful origins. For example, in identifying the authors of *The Federalist Papers* (James Madison or Alexander Hamilton), it proved less important to count their relative usages of words such as "Democracy" or "Freedom" (major encoding habits) and more import-

ant to chart the frequencies of such words as "and" or "the" (minor encoding habits) (e.g., Holsti 1969; Mosteller and Wallace 1964; Paisley 1964; see also Holbrook and Hirschman 1993). As described by Holsti (1969), it is "the 'minor encoding habits,' the apparently trivial details of style, which vary systematically within and between communicators' works" (p. 86). Holbrook and Grayson (1986) took this insight as a central argument for their use of consumption symbolism as a key to interpreting "fine-grained nuances of plot and character": "Interestingly, . . . the personal identity of an author often appears . . . in the . . . more minor encoding habits . . . the little linguistic habits that guide the consistent selection of seemingly trivial verbal units" (p. 374).

(3) Third, advocates of *psychoanalytic approaches* attach great importance to the unconscious desires and wishes that appear in disguised form via such otherwise unnoticed and seemingly innocent *surrogates* as slips of the tongue, jokes, dreams, or other forms of indirect expression (Freud 1900, ed. 1965; 1916, ed. 1977). Thus, no detail is too small to command the attention of a well-trained Freudian psychoanalyst.

(4) Fourth, the field of *hermeneutics* pursues interpretive approaches to understanding a text that receive their primary justification from what is often referred to as the *hermeneutic circle* (Bleicher 1980; Thompson 1981). As developed by Schleiermacher (1911, ed. 1978), Dilthey (1924, ed. 1972), and others, this Hermeneutic Circle concerns the relation between the interpretation of a whole text and the explication of its parts. Rather than comprising a "vicious" circle, the Hermeneutic Circle remains "virtuous" in the sense—developed by Gadamer (1975), Ricoeur (1976, 1981), and others—in which, via a sort of cybernetic feedback loop, it follows a *self-corrective process* wherein the reader adjusts prejudices concerning the larger meanings of a text via a confrontation with its details so as to engage in a continuous cycle of revision that moves toward ever-increasing validity. Ricoeur (1981) emphasizes that *any* meaningful activity can serve as a text suitable for such hermeneutic interpretation—literature, music, or painting, of course; but also consumer behavior, marketing practice, or any other aspect of business-related sign systems that appear in pieces of popular culture or works of art (Hirschman and Holbrook 1992; Holbrook and Hirschman 1993). It follows that the textual details of jazz in films appear ripe for this sort of hermeneutic analysis.

(5) Fifth, following the work of Charles Peirce, students of *semiotics* have argued for interpretive approaches based on what Peirce called *abductive inference* (Eco 1976, p. 131). Most of us are familiar with *deductive* and *inductive* inference. Thus—given a *rule* (e.g., all the beans in this bag are white), a *case* (e.g., these beans are from this bag), and a *result* (e.g., these beans are all white)—*deductive inference* moves from a rule and a case to a result (e.g., because all the beans in this bag are white and these beans are from this bag, it follows that all these beans are white), whereas *inductive inference* moves from a case and a result

to a rule (e.g., because these beans are from this bag and these beans are all white, it appears that all the beans from this bag are white). By contrast, *abductive inference* moves from a rule (e.g., all the beans from this bag are white) and a result (e.g., these beans are all white) to a case (e.g., these beans are from this bag) (Harrowitz 1983, p. 182; Sebeok 1983, p. 8). In the context of interpreting a film or other artwork, "abductive inference involves bringing *rules* from different contexts (e.g., elite people drive expensive cars) to bear on *results* found in the work of art (e.g., Mary drives a Cadillac) to infer something about *cases* at intermediate levels of generality (e.g., Mary is elite)" (Holbrook and Hirschman 1993, p. 240). In a brilliant series of essays edited by Eco and Sebeok (ed. 1983) and entitled *The Sign of Three: Dupin, Holmes, Peirce,* various semiologists have linked abductive inference with the logic of discovery practiced by such fictional characters as C. Auguste Dupin and Sherlock Holmes in detective stories by Edgar Allan Poe and Sir Arthur Conan Doyle. As exemplified by such writers of crime fiction, the abductive approaches of their heroes depend on the enlightened interpretation of minor facts and small pieces of information—that is, "apparently trivial fragments" (Carettini 1983, p. 139). For example, Sherlock Holmes based his inspired inferential leaps on "details," "trifles," the "infinitely little," "minute perceptions," or "the one little point" (Sebeok and Umiker-Sebeok 1983, *passim*) so as, via abduction, to gather "a great deal of information from a single object or event" (Truzzi 1983, p. 69). As noted by Truzzi (1983), for Holmes, "there is nothing so important as trifles" because "to a great mind . . . nothing is little" (p. 69). According to Sherlock, "the little things are infinitely the most important": "My method . . . is founded upon the observation of trifles" (p. 64; see also Holbrook and Hirschman 1993, p. 26). Quite importantly, inferences drawn from abduction (unlike deductive inferences) require some sort of validation in which they are tested against external criteria: "Abduction represents . . . a conjecture about reality which needs to be validated through testing" (Truzzi 1983, p. 70; see also Eco 1983; Harrowitz 1983; Holbrook and Hirschman 1993). In this, the abductive interpretation of a text—reminiscent of the Hermeneutic Circle—relies on beginning with a general interpretation, testing this against detailed textual evidence, and—if falsified—revising the general interpretation accordingly (Hirsch 1967; Ricoeur 1976): "Hence, evidentiary details from the text plus an understanding of its context provide the grounds for the validation of its own interpretation" (Holbrook and Hirschman 1993, p. 240).

(6) Sixth—though the traditional faith in aesthetic unity has increasingly been questioned in postmodern times (Flinn 1992, p. 51; but cf. her nuanced discussion, pp. 80–87, of Adorno 1967, 1991)—one application of this viewpoint appears in the concept of the *point of departure* or *Ansatzpunkt* (Auerbach 1953, 1969), in which an entire interpretive analysis of a literary creation or other work of art unfolds from just one

crucial passage, scene, or detail that (like a DNA molecule or a holo-gram) seems to contain the code for a meaning that extends throughout the entire work. Via this *Ansatzpunkt*, "such a point of departure . . . can radiate outward, shedding light on the overall work, in a way that helps to anchor the so-called Hermeneutic Circle based on the interaction between the parts and the whole" (Holbrook and Hirschman 1993, p. 239).

(7) Seventh and finally, those concerned with the visual arts have discovered that the *identification of artistic forgeries* often hinges on a careful *scrutiny of small details* (e.g., the background) as opposed to major content (e.g., the overall style of the painting itself). Thus, Ginzburg (1983) discusses Morelli's method of detecting artistic forgeries by focusing on "marginal and irrelevant details" (p. 86)—that is, the "characteristic trifles" through which the artist "gives himself away" (p. 82). Indeed, Ginzburg (1983) shows that Freud (e.g., 1900, ed. 1965) recognized the close analogy between this interpretive approach and his own psychoanalytic method, which "is accustomed to divine secret and concealed things from despised or unnoticed features": "Laying stress on the significance of minor details . . . which every artist executes in his own characteristic way . . . is closely related to the technique of psychoanalysis" (Freud, quoted by Ginzburg 1983, pp. 84–85; see also Holbrook and Hirschman 1993, p. 27). Here, Ginzburg (1983) draws intimate connections among the Freudian approach to psychoanalysis, the Sherlock Holmesian method of detection, and the Morellian inter-pretation of artworks insofar as "In all three cases tiny details provide the key to a deeper reality, inaccessible by other methods": "These details may be symptoms, for Freud, or clues, for Holmes, or features of paintings, for Morelli" (p. 87).

In short, from a variety of interpretive viewpoints, it appears that *significant meanings* emerge from a careful scrutiny of *seemingly small details* of the textual evidence. From this, it follows that we must approach a work of art (a text) as a kind of mystery that contains numerous clues in the form of ostensibly trivial details (consisting of the fine-grained aspects of the relevant textual evidence) whose meaning the reader, viewer, or listener must unravel like a detective trying to solve a crime (by inspecting fragmentary pieces that require integration into a significant whole). I believe that a similar con-clusion applies to the project of understanding the significant meanings of jazz in films—namely, that we benefit from interpreting the significance of pivotal cinemusical moments much as did the New Critics in ferreting out the meaning of a poem by means of close reading; content analysts in identifying the authors of the *Federalist Papers* via their minor encoding habits; Freud in penetrating the disguised nature of various repressed wishes or desires; hermeneuticists in understanding a text; Dupin or Holmes in seeking the solutions to puzzling crimes; Auerbach in unfolding the implications of an *Ansatzpunkt*; or Morelli in detecting an artistic forgery.

Accordingly, continuing the approach followed in our analysis of *Paris Blues* (Chapter 8), I shall illustrate this conviction in Chapter 13 with examples from the scores by Miles Davis for *Ascenseur Pour L'Échafaud* (1958) and by John Lewis for *Odds Against Tomorrow* (1959) and in Chapter 14 with the case of the film music by Elmer Bernstein and Chico Hamilton for *Sweet Smell of Success* (1957).

# 13 His Eye Is on the Sparrow
## Small-but-Significant Cinemusical Moments in Jazz Film Scores by Miles Davis and John Lewis

As a general proposition, any number of interpretive strategies present themselves as viable candidates for those wishing to examine the cinemusical role of jazz in films. These range from the most macroscopic approaches (sociological, historical, or cultural studies) to those in the middle range (hermeneutics or semiotics) to the most microscopic sources of insights (close readings or psychoanalysis). The present chapter supports and illustrates a combination of these interpretive approaches—namely, close readings of seemingly trivial cinemusical details in the service of achieving an integrated understanding of these otherwise minor musical moments within the overall interpretive context of the motion picture as a whole. After a brief overview of this theme and its relevance to the dialectical process that underlies the so-called Hermeneutic Circle, the chapter pursues some telling examples drawn from the jazz scores by Miles Davis and John Lewis for films that appeared 50 years ago, that influenced a trend toward jazz-related source and background music in motion pictures, and that stand high in artistic merit, but that have been seldom-viewed by mass-market audiences in recent years. These examples encourage a heightened awareness of how small-but-significant cinemusical moments in the jazz scores by Davis for *Ascenseur Pour L'Échafaud* or *Elevator to the Gallows* (1958) and by Lewis for *Odds Against Tomorrow* (1959) contribute significantly to the broader development of plot, character, and other themes in these two films.

## Hedgehog, Fox, and . . . Maine Coon Cat

In his essay on *The Hedgehog and the Fox*, echoing the Greek poet Archilochus, Sir Isaiah Berlin (1953, ed. 1993) draws a distinction between two kinds of worldview or artistic vision. The first characterizes the European hedgehog (American groundhog) who looks for his shadow on Candlemas Day (February 2), makes a global assessment, and plans his future actions accordingly. Such a unitary worldview appears in the work of (say) Plato or Dostoevsky. The second characterizes the fox who observes life in its smallest details, remains open to a wide variety of experiences, and adjusts his behavior in ways that reflect a keen sensitivity to tiny nuances and minute subtleties in the world around him. This latter particularistic

248 God Is *in the Details*

perspective appears in the work of (say) Shakespeare or Pushkin. In short, the hedgehog knows one big thing, whereas the fox knows many little things.

Berlin (1953, ed. 1993) takes this fundamental distinction in one particular direction by focusing on Tolstoy and suggesting that this literary giant was a fox by nature but believed in the desirability of being a hedgehog. According to Berlin, Tolstoy's lifelong inclination to go to the root of every matter—immersing himself in the concrete, empirical, intricate experience of everyday life—robbed him of the overarching grasp that he longed to achieve. Colloquially, Tolstoy suffered the fate of a man who wants to see the forest (a unifying principle) but can only observe various aspects of each tree such as its leaves-twigs-bark-and-acorns (the minute particles of the underlying reality)—a predicament even worse than that which afflicts the proverbial person who cannot see the forest for the trees.

On the vexing question of what constitutes insight, wisdom, or truth, we might expand Berlin's essay to suggest that true understanding emerges from a rapprochement between the more Erinaceinaean (hedgehog-like) and Vulpine (fox-like) sides of Tolstoy's dilemma. More colloquially, we might aspire *not* just to an all-encompassing view of the forest (a grand unifying principle) and also *not* merely to an intense scrutiny of each tree's leaves-twigs-bark-and-acorns (the particularistic properties) but *rather* to an integrated vision of a grove of trees in all its verdurous glory (a true understanding).

In sum, extending Berlin's focus, I wish to propose that, in the manner of a *dialectic*, the secret to insightful understanding often lies in combining, resolving, integrating, or reconciling the two opposing perspectives—that is, the *thesis* (all-encompassing overview) and *antithesis* (particularistic details)—in such a way that a satisfying *synthesis* occurs (in-depth comprehension). This rapprochement is something akin to what Rocky, my Maine Coon Cat, routinely accomplishes on a daily basis. Rocky studies the most minute details of his environment (sniff, sniff), reaches a global conclusion (approach, avoid), and thereby signifies his uniquely cat-like view of the world (the feline perspective). This dialectic process achieves the sort of vision that may lead to insight or truth. Thus: Thesis (Hedgehog) → Antithesis (Fox) → Synthesis (Maine Coon Cat).

## Regarding the Text of a Film Score

All this suggests that there exist different ways of regarding the text of a jazz score found in a film. One perspective—the Erinaceinaean thesis, devoted to the Big Picture and consistent with a broad sociological, historical, or cultural focus—might consider the film music in the larger context of the composer's other work, his or her authorial intentions, the work's historical background, its connections to pieces by other composers, or its societal implications. The opposing perspective—the Vulpine antithesis, obsessed with Minute Details and consistent with a close reading or a psychoanalytic interpretation—might analyze the subtleties of how a thematic leitmotif changes its modality from one scene to another, the connection between a particular character and some recurring musical theme, the intricacies of changes in orchestral timbre or dynamics as the plot unfolds, or the acceleration of tempo at certain pivotal moments. The integrative view—a Feline synthesis, pursued here and dedicated to finding meaning in the interplay between the Big Picture and its manifestation in Minute Details in the manner associated with hermeneutics or semiotics—might focus on showing how even the most subtle cinemusical nuances of the film score work to establish significant meanings within the context of its larger dramatic development.

## Analogy with Literary Texts

In literary studies, as noted in the Introduction to Part VI, pursuit of the third perspective just suggested is sometimes referred to as the *Hermeneutic Circle*—that is, as a form of interpretation that proceeds by tacking back and forth between an overall understanding of the text and substantiation of this view by means of a close reading of the textual evidence. An overarching conjecture leads to a testing of this hypothesis against the textual details, resulting in a modification of the overview that is then tested again against further evidence from subsequent close reading (Gadamer 1975; Hirsch 1967; Hirschman and Holbrook 1992; Holbrook and Hirschman 1993; Ricoeur 1976, 1981). Such a process may be envisioned as an expanded dialectic in which the current synthesis (integration) becomes a new thesis (overview) as the basis for further antitheses (details) followed by subsequent syntheses (integrations) and so on in the potentially endless regress of a self-corrective cycle.

Auerbach (1953, 1969) pushed this approach to its insightful limits by means of applying his concept of the *Ansatzpunkt* or *point of departure*. In this, he recognized that, in a great work of art, all parts are inter-related in an overall holistic gestalt such that each detail of the text reflects the whole essence of its larger meaning. In a sense, like a hologram, the work of art embodies a principle analogous to that from genetic biology in which each minute cell of a living organism contains its entire DNA code.

A similar attention to seemingly inconsequential minutiae characterizes what many regard as the greatest treatise on hermeneutic analysis of all time—namely, *The Interpretation of Dreams* (Freud 1900, ed. 1965). Here, as elsewhere in Freud's work (e.g., 1916, ed. 1977), no detail (slip of the tongue, pun, joke, tip-of-the-tongue problem, or other minuscule aspect of manifest content) is too tiny to shed light on the larger significance of potential repressed or latent meanings.

## The Hermeneutics of Film Music

In an essay on "Musical Hermeneutics Applied to Film Music," Rosar (2001) expresses some reservations concerning the prospects for validity in the interpretation of cinemusical meaning: "Critical thinking and a good measure of skeptical rigour are . . . desirable so as to curtail flights of fancy which may lead the hermeneutic process astray into unfounded speculation" (p. 103). One answer to such concerns emphasizes the importance of a close reading of textual details—musical or otherwise—as the basis for a sound interpretation along the lines of the Hermeneutic Circle.

Indeed, something like this self-corrective cycle happens in our interpretive analysis of a film score—especially if we accept the plausible premise that music is a sort of language (Berliner 1994; Bernstein 1981; Nanry with Berger 1979).

> ***Thesis***: We begin, perhaps, with an overall assessment—say, that a jazz composer has given us a gritty musical background befitting the seamy side of life as represented by a *film-noir* style or genre.
> ***Antithesis***: Consistent with this global view, we observe the details of a background theme that consists of a blues in B-flat played on a muted trumpet accompanied by just bass and drums—lean, sparse, almost impoverished in its limited use of orchestral resources.
> ***Synthesis***: We amplify our original reading by concluding that the hero is rugged and tough but a bit déclassé in his social standing.
> ***Subsequent Dialectic***: This refinement of our original hypothesis serves as the thesis for a further round of analysis—again proceeding through stages of the Hermeneutic Circle in what turns out to be a long iterative process that moves toward convergence on a final interpretation. *Notice that, usually, we do not report each stage in this iterative analysis; rather we report the ultimate overall interpretation, supported by various small-but-significant details.*

Rosar (2001) is particularly concerned that apparently significant cinemusical coincidences may be incorrectly attributed to authorial intention and thereby misconstrued as meaningful connections. In this spirit, Rosar suggests that some questions of musical interpretation (in his case, the issue of whether a motif used by Bernard Herrmann in *Citizen Kane* came from the *Dies Irae* or from Rachmaninov) can be resolved only by "comparing the details of each motif" or, in other words, by "close scrutiny" (p. 109). For example, Rosar argues, "The fact that both Rachmaninov's and Herrmann's motifs have identical phrase length and share a distinctive rhythm not belonging to the *Dies Irae* makes it hard to dismiss this resemblance as mere coincidence" (pp. 110–111).

As mentioned in Chapter 1, the emphasis on a close reading of detailed evidence from cinemusical moments also informs an analysis by Rodman (2000) of the film *Maytime* (1937). Here, Rodman focuses on the shift from C major (Nelson Eddy, popular song, lowbrow) to D major (Jeanette MacDonald, opera, highbrow) to Db major (the Eddy–MacDonald duet, operetta, middle ground) in Romberg-and-Young's song "Will You Remember?" where this "tonal dissolve" signals the "reconciliation of Paul and Marcia" (p. 202).

Along similar lines, the analysis in Chapter 8 focuses on the significance of transformations in just one note found in three successive versions of the theme song to *Paris Blues* (1961). This analysis thereby highlights the interpretive importance of "seemingly trivial but nonetheless significant textual details that cohere by virtue of the relevant thematic focus" (Holbrook 2006c, p. 85).

Though these exhortations to a detailed scrutiny of the musical text reflect a fairly standard conception of how interpretive analysis might beneficially proceed, the importance of close reading to problems of cinemusical interpretation, like so many other prescriptive desiderata, is probably most often honored in its breach. Put differently, in the interpretation of film music in general and of cinematic jazz in particular, we all too frequently fail to push our analysis down to the smallest level of detail that would justify a claim to having tested our overarching hypothetical interpretation against the closest possible reading of the textual evidence.

When I was a freshman in college, we were all virtually required to take an infuriating course called Humanities Six or Hum 6, the main point of which—inspired by the so-called "New Criticism" of Empson, Brooks, Wimsatt, Beardsley, and others—was that no textual detail is small enough to ignore. In one impressive lecture, Richard Poirier memorably advised us to read every word of every poem, novel, or play with the same attention to meanings lurking between the lines that we would invest in the interpretation of a love letter. This recommendation had little effect on my grasp of contemporary poetry or other challenging literature but proved quite beneficial to my subsequent understanding of love letters. Indeed, I believe that—by analogy—the same advice drawn from our approach to romantic epistles applies with equal force to our interpretation of small-but-significant cinemusical moments in a film score.

## Preview

In sum, no sooner do we make claims on behalf of attention to minute details in the analysis of film music than we realize that most of the interpretive work in the film-music field stops short of focusing on (say) the significance of one snatch of melody or one brief performative gesture at a pivotal moment of the film's dramatic development. Nonetheless—as just suggested—such an analysis of cinemusical minutiae, rooted in the dialectic logic of the self-corrective Hermeneutic Circle, may foster helpful insights into the meaning of a movie. In what follows, I shall pursue this point as the basis for my approach to illustrative interpretations of jazz-based film scores by Miles Davis for *Ascenseur Pour L'Échafaud* (1958) and by John Lewis for *Odds Against Tomorrow* (1959).

## JAZZ FILM SCORES BY MILES DAVIS AND JOHN LEWIS

Here, I shall illustrate the larger relevance of small-but-significant cinemusical moments by means of some telling examples drawn from the jazz scores by Miles Davis and John Lewis for important-but-neglected films that,

50 years ago, influenced a trend toward jazz-related source and background music in motion pictures. In addressing these illustrations, my purpose is to encourage a heightened awareness of how subtle-but-meaningful cine-musical details serve to deepen the viewing-and-listening experience. Specifically, I shall stress the ways in which short-but-pivotal cinemusical moments in *Ascenseur Pour L'Échafaud* and *Odds Against Tomorrow* contribute meanings that enhance the development of character and plot in these two motion pictures.

## Background

During the mid- to late-1950s—partly via the influence of various foreign films from outside the conventional Hollywood ambit—something of a vogue developed favoring the use in motion pictures of background music composed and/or played by such top jazz artists as John Lewis of the Modern Jazz Quartet, Miles Davis, Duke Ellington, Gerry Mulligan, Thelonious Monk, and Art Blakey. For example, Elmer Bernstein's score for Otto Preminger's *The Man With the Golden Arm* (1955) made heavy use of jazz-inflected backgrounds to limn the seedy, near-desperate decadence of the environment that surrounds Frankie Machine—played by Frank Sinatra in what Yanow (2004) regards as "one of his better roles" (p. 181)—as he struggles to kick his drug habit and launch a career as a jazz drummer. Further, during Frankie/Frank's audition on-screen (miming a drum part dubbed by Shelly Manne), we observe on-camera jazz performances by Shorty Rogers and a crew of top-flight West-Coast musicians including Pete Candoli (trumpet), Bud Shank (alto sax), Frank Rosolino (trombone), and Bob Cooper (tenor sax). Subsequently, Robert Wise's *I Want to Live!* (1958)—starring Susan Hayward in her Oscar-winning role as the doomed Barbara Graham—boasted a fine background score by Johnny Mandel with on-screen nightclub performances by Gerry Mulligan (baritone sax), Art Farmer (trumpet), Pete Jolly (piano), Red Mitchell (bass), and some of the other West-Coast stalwarts just mentioned (such as Shank, Rosolino, and Manne). Some of the same musicians (Mulligan, Farmer, Mitchell, and Manne) reappeared in André Previn's source music for *The Subterraneans* (1960)—with further contributions from Dave Bailey (drums), Chico Hamilton (drums), Buddy Clark (bass), Russ Freeman (piano), Art Pepper (alto sax), Bob Enevoldsen (trombone), Bill Perkins (tenor sax), and Carmen McRae (vocals). Meanwhile, Duke Ellington provided strong background music for Otto Preminger's *Anatomy of a Murder* (1959), appearing on-camera briefly in a small cameo role. Even a highly serious score such as that by Ernest Gold for Stanley Kramer's monumental *On the Beach* (1959) featured some music by the usual cast of West-Coast characters like Candoli, Mitchell, and Manne. And Thelonious Monk—with Charlie Rouse (tenor), Sam Jones (bass), and Art Taylor (drums)—did the underscore recordings for Roger Vadim's *Les Liaisons Dangereuses* (1959), whose source music for party and nightclub settings (mimed on-screen by Kenny Dorham on trumpet, Barney Wilen on tenor sax, Duke Jordan on piano, Paul Rovere on bass, and Kenny Clarke on drums) was composed by pianist Duke Jordan and performed on the soundtrack by drummer Art Blakey's Jazz Messengers featuring Lee Morgan (trumpet), Barney Wilen (tenor), Bobby Timmons (piano), and Jymie Merritt (bass).

As the next decade wore on, the presence of jazz scoring became something of a Hollywood cliché—found, for example, in the idiomatic work by Quincy Jones for Sidney Lumet's *The Pawnbroker* (1964) and for Norman Jewison's *In the Heat of the Night* (1967); by Johnny Mandel for Vincente Minnelli's *The Sandpiper* (1965); by Henry Mancini for Blake Edwards' *The Pink Panther* (1963); or by Michel Legrand for Norman Jewison's *The Thomas Crown Affair* (1968) and for Robert Mulligan's *Summer of '42* (1971). Were we to include jazz backgrounds for television shows—such as those by Henry Mancini for the late-1950s TV series *Peter Gunn* and *Mr. Lucky*, which spawned innumerable crime-plus-jazz imitators, including the work by Elmer Bernstein for *Johnny Staccato*—the list could be expanded almost without limit (including the 1989 remake of *Peter Gunn*, starring Peter Strauss in the title role and featuring Mancini's tried-but-true ambi-diegetic-jazz).

But the instances on which I wish to focus—namely, the work by Miles Davis for *Ascenseur Pour L'Échafaud* (1958) and by John Lewis for *Odds Against Tomorrow* (1959)—have something of a special flavor. In both cases—though the formidable talents of a master jazz musician are brought to bear on the composition and performance of nondiegetic background music—telling significance nonetheless attaches to brief-but-significant on-screen ambi-diegetic cinemusical moments. Each time, the relevant ambi-diegetic cinemusical moment of interest is fleeting and subtle but nonetheless pivotal in reflecting meanings of central importance to the film's dramatic development. Before turning to these two films, however, we must pause briefly to consider the intertextual origins of some key source material that plays an important role in the first illustration.

## Source Material: *Sait-On Jamais* or *No Sun In Venice* (1957)

The tradition for the specialized use of modern jazz as background music in films appears to have originated with the score composed by John Lewis for the film by Roger Vadim entitled *Sait-On Jamais* ("One Never Knows") or, in the English version, *No Sun in Venice* (1957). Though this legendary film is not available on video so that I must draw on recollections from a televised screening 30 years ago, we can at least appreciate the Modern Jazz Quartet's performance of the music from the motion picture, recorded on April 4 of 1957 and first played in concert at New York City's Town Hall on May 12 of the same year.

Gary Kramer's perceptive liner notes for this record album—*The Modern Jazz Quartet Plays* **One Never Knows** (Atlantic LP 1284 or CD-1284-2)—convey much of the strategy behind the nondiegetic underscoring approach pursued by *auteur* Vadim and composer Lewis for this film. Specifically, only one piece—entitled "Venice" for the record album—appears diegetically on-screen as part of a nightclub sequence and does not, in Kramer's view, contribute to the "dramatic development." Elsewhere, as evident in the soundtrack recording, Lewis composed a background score characterized by strong structural unity and careful internal organization, sensitively tuned to the range of emotions evoked by the film and the development of the story as the film progresses. Via the use of leitmotifs, "The Golden Striker" (a rousingly cheerful anthem-like celebration that opens the Atlantic recording) represents a character named Michel; "One Never Knows" (a pensive exercise in lyricism) captures the sweet personality of young Sophie; "The Rose Truc" (a blues-like piece) represents Sforzi's efforts to win her affections; and "Cortege" (a dirge in the spirit of a New Orleans funeral procession) connects with the persona of an old man named Baron Von Berger. As a demonstration of his brilliant scoring technique, Lewis managed to compose the Michel-, Sforzi-, and Berger-related pieces in such a manner that they fit together polyphonically into a fugal design wherein the three leading male characters intertwine contrapuntally to create a musical representation called "Three Windows."

One could not overstate the musical intricacy of these pieces composed by Lewis to complement the dramatic characterizations in Vadim's film—though, curiously, Jean Luc Godard (1972, ed. 1986) manages to review *Sait-On Jamais* without ever mentioning its jazz score (pp. 55–57). Lewis was justifiably proud of this work and, after its Town Hall debut in May, took the Quartet's concert version to a festival in Donaueschingen, Germany on October 20, followed by a highly acclaimed tour throughout the rest of Europe during the last two months of 1957. According to Kramer and of special significance to the present chapter, "No other modern jazz work has received such wide-spread acceptance in such a short time as the pieces now known everywhere as either *Sait-On Jamais* or *One Never Knows*."

In 1977, MPS records issued the Donaueschingen concert from 20 years earlier, with liner notes by Joachim Ernst Berendt and with featured performances of "Three Windows," "The Golden Striker," and "Cortege" (MPS 68.161). According to Berendt, this concert in general and the presentation of the film music by the Modern Jazz Quartet (MJQ) was *the* European cultural event of the year, earning extensive media coverage comparable to that surrounding Benny Goodman's Carnegie Hall concert in 1938.

Arguably, the high point of this performance and of the original film-music album is the MJQ's rendering of "Cortege"—a powerful dirge that accompanies the movie's funeral scene:

Eb-↓D-↓C^^^-C-↓Ab; ↑C-↑D-↑Eb-↑F-↑G^-G-↓Eb; ↑G^-G-↓Eb-↑G^-G-↓D; ↑G-↑C^^-↑Db-↓C-↓Bb-↑C; ↓Ab-↓G-↓F-↓D-↑F^-F-↑Bb; ↓G-↓F-↓Eb-↓C-↓Eb^-Eb-↑Ab; ↓F-↓Eb-↓D^^^-D-↓C; ↑D-↑G^^^. . . .

Specifically, this piece begins quietly with just Milt Jackson's vibraharp and Percy Heath's bass playing softly but then builds to a shattering climax with striking tympanic effects from drummer Connie Kay and resounding chords from John Lewis on piano. Lewis soon transformed "Cortege" into a version arranged for full orchestra and recorded under his direction by the Stuttgart Symphony Orchestra in February of 1958 for an album on RCA entitled *European Windows* (LPM-1742). This impressive recording—recently reissued on CD by American Jazz Classics (99004)—establishes "Cortege" as a major serious jazz composition.

### *Ascenseur Pour L'Échafaud* or *Elevator to the Gallows* (1958)

I shall return later to some further comments on "Cortege," which plays an important intertextual role in the present analysis. But let us simply note, for now, that this piece appeared on the American and European jazz scenes to great attention and acclaim just prior to the time when Miles Davis entered a recording studio in Paris on December 4–5 of 1957 to record his sound-track music for the first feature film by Louis Malle, entitled *Ascenseur Pour L'Échafaud* or *Elevator to the Gallows* (1958). This soundtrack by Miles Davis made an impact as revolutionary in its own way as that of the score composed by John Lewis only shortly earlier. Specifically—in a manner diametrically opposed to the meticulous control exercised by Lewis—Davis and a quintet composed of Barney Wilen (tenor sax), René Utreger (piano), Pierre Michelot (bass), and Kenny Clarke (drums) improvised background music to fit scenes from Malle's film while watching the cinematic images as they unfolded on-screen. The results appeared on an album entitled *Jazz Track* (Columbia CL 1268)—later re-released on compact disc, with all the out-takes from the original recording session included, as *Ascenseur Pour L'Échafaud* (Fontana CD 836-305-2). (For extended reflections on the use of music by Miles Davis in this and other films, see Gabbard 2004, 2007, 2008.)

In the *Ascenseur* soundtrack album—to accompany the scene in which Julien Tavernier (Maurice Ronet) acts in collaboration with his lover Florence Carala (Jeanne Moreau) to kill her husband—we hear the plaintive, foreboding "L'Assassinat de Carala," featuring the muted horn of Miles against a bleak piano-and-bass ostinato. During the chase scene in which Louis (the book-store clerk) and Veronica (the young florist) race with a Mercedes 300SL driven by an older German man, the quintet plays a high-speed improvisation based on the familiar chord changes to "Sweet Georgia Brown" and entitled "Sur L'Autoroute" on the soundtrack recording. While Tavernier/Ronet struggles in vain to escape from the elevator in which he is trapped, we hear "Julien Dans L'Ascenseur" with its ominous repeated bass-tone pedal point on "A" and the harmon-muted trumpet hauntingly impro-vising morose phrases in the key of D minor (basically a modal approach that anticipated the breakthroughs by Miles and Co. on the *Kind of Blue* album in 1959). As Florence/Jeanne futilely searches for Julien/Maurice through the streets of Paris, Davis plays "Florence Sur les Champs-Élysées" on an open horn, still improvising in D minor, but with a more ironically jaunty rhythmic feeling that belies Florence/Jeanne's sense of impending doom. While Louis, Veronica, and the German couple have dinner at a motel where Louis later shoots the Germans, the soundtrack provides very fast, free-form tenor and muted-trumpet passages as a background entitled "Diner au Motel." And when some incriminating photographs implicate Carala/Moreau and Tavernier/Ronet in the murder of her husband, the musicians play "Chez le Photographe du Motel"—still in D minor, but alternating between open and muted horn and now more mournful than ever.

Clearly, all this happens at the level of off-screen nondiegetic background music—indeed, in the shape of an underscore intended to complement the film's dramatic development, added by musicians watching and commenting musically on the cinematic action from their positions as creative artists in the recording studio. Thus, except for one brief scene in a bar while Florence/Jeanne tries to find Julien/Maurice, we search in vain for on-screen ambi-diegetic cinemusical moments provided by Miles and Co. to further the film's dramatic development. Brief snatches of ordinary diegetic source music do occur sporadically to flesh out the realism of the narrative action—as when Florence/Jeanne enters a restaurant where a piano is playing; when Veronica puts a classical record on her phonograph just before she and Louis make an unsuccessful suicide attempt; and when we hear a piano lesson in progress during Florence/Jeanne's visit to Veronica's apartment building. But I can find only one clear instance of a pure on-screen drama-enhancing ambi-diegetic cinemusical moment in *Ascenseur Pour L'Échafaud*. It is a small-but-meaningful, subtle-but-significant, ambi-diegetic cinemusical gesture that happens to be loaded with intertextual implications and charged with resonating associations for any viewer who pays enough attention to notice it.

Specifically, at a critical juncture early in the film, Tavernier/Ronet has fled the scene of his crime, has started the engine of his car, and has only then realized that he forgot to remove the rope with which he had climbed up to the balcony outside his victim's window. Clearly, he must return to retrieve this incriminating evidence. Rushing back to his building, he enters the elevator and begins the ascent to his office on one of the higher floors. But, just then, a security guard shuts off the electric power for the night, inadvertently trapping the doomed Tavernier/Ronet as a prisoner on the stalled elevator. We watch the guard leave the building, locking up behind himself. As the watchman closes and fastens the outside gate, we hear him whistling. With profoundly ominous implications, he whistles a fragment from . . . "Cortege":

E♭-↓D-↓C^^^-C-↓A♭; ↑C-↑D-↑E♭-↑F-↑G^-G-↓E♭; ↑G^-G-↓E♭-↑G^. . . .

This fleeting ambi-diegetic cinemusical moment—an intertextual allusion to the celebrated dirge from *Sait-On Jamais* whose score by John Lewis, as previously documented, was very much in the limelight at the time of the Davis/Malle collaboration—carries the meaning, of course, that Tavernier/Ronet's fate is sealed; his doom is assured; his goose is cooked. It takes another cinematic hour for this unhappy demise to unfold. Yet, early on,

Tarvernier/Ronet's ultimate downfall is signaled by that one portentous intertextual reference to a musical theme from the funeral procession in another then-recent French film. It requires some effort to recognize the funereal film music by John Lewis in the rather shaky off-hand out-of-tune whistling of the ironically unconcerned security guard. But, after listening appreciatively for almost five decades to the Lewis composition in various guises, I spotted its theme immediately when I recently revisited Louis Malle's *Ascenseur Pour L'Échafaud*. This epiphany serves as a foreboding signal to those who, recognizing "Cortege" as a vivid intertextual clue, realize very early in Malle's film that Tavernier/Ronet's ultimate defeat is a foregone conclusion. He will not manage to escape from that elevator to the gallows. Thus, the pregnant intertextual significance carried by this otherwise trivial snatch of ambi-diegetic whistling beautifully illustrates the potential power of a tiny detail in the cinemusical text to advance the development of character, plot, and other themes in a motion picture.

## Odds Against Tomorrow (1959)

A second illustration of a small-but-significant ambi-diegetic cinemusical moment comes from the jazz score by John Lewis for Robert Wise's *Odds Against Tomorrow* (1959). Starring Harry Belafonte, Robert Ryan, and Ed Begley as three incompetent robbers who, with tragic consequences, bungle their misbegotten attempt to hold up a bank—with Shelley Winters as Ryan's hapless live-in partner and Gloria Grahame as his temptress—this film provides one of those plots that, as so often noted by Gabbard (1996), hinges on the evils of racial prejudice. Specifically, because the (white) Ryan character is too bigoted to trust the (black) Belafonte character with the keys to the getaway vehicle, all three bandits end up dead. We care about their fate one way or the other only because we have grown to like the Belafonte character by virtue of his warm and protective feelings toward both his estranged wife and his adorable little daughter.

In making sense of the jazz score by John Lewis for this motion picture, we benefit from *both* a soundtrack recording of the background music for the film (**Odds Against Tomorrow: Original Music from the Motion Picture Sound Track**, United Artists UAS 5061, reissued on CD as Signature AK 47487) *and* an album of expanded versions played by the Modern Jazz Quartet itself (*Music From Odds Against Tomorrow*, United Artists UAS 5063, reissued on CD as Blue Note CDP 7 93415 2). The former presents the nondiegetic background music from the movie, scored for a large orchestra that includes a number of New York studio musicians as well as the MJQ members themselves plus Jim Hall on guitar and Bill Evans on piano. This nondiegetic underscore shows the flexibility of John Lewis as a composer and demonstrates his ability to complement a broad variety of characterizations, plot details, and other aspects of the dramatic development.

As quoted by Nat Hentoff's liner notes for the soundtrack album, the distinguished jazz educator Gunther Schuller sees this work as an advance over the Lewis pieces for *Sait-On Jamais* insofar as it constitutes "a full-fledged film score integrated dramatically with the action of the film." For example, when Belafonte takes his little girl to Central Park for a father-daughter outing, the poignant "Odds Against Tomorrow" theme appears as a charming calliope-like piece accompanying the painted horses on the carousel, but gradually fades to dissonant brass instruments when the hoodlums pursuing Belafonte to collect his gambling debts make their appearance. Shortly thereafter, we hear "Skating in Central Park," a skater's waltz built on the chord changes to "My Wild Irish Rose" and scored for some mellow celli, plus flute and vibraphone. Then "No Happiness for Slater" uses Jim Hall's guitar and some more dissonant brass on a blues-like piece of the type that Hall plays so convincingly to dramatize the scene in which the Ryan and Winters characters quarrel. Later, fulfilling these proleptic warnings of discord, "Social Call" deploys almost quizzical sounding pizzicato strings and French horns against a piano solo by Bill Evans to underscore the sultry seduction scene between the adulterous Ryan and Grahame characters.

When the MJQ got around to recording its own versions of these pieces from the film score, the Quartet revealed much about the contrast between the cinemusical function of the Lewis compositions in the motion picture as opposed to their concert potential away from the film. Most conspicuously, of course, John Lewis replaces Bill Evans at the piano, thereby bringing the composer's idiosyncratic pianism to the MJQ's group sound. But more important to my ears, the role of vibraharpist Milt Jackson—surprisingly subdued in the film itself—expands greatly to dominate the aura of the film music recontextualized as independent concert pieces. This expansion of Jackson's role looms especially large on "Skating in Central Park," where this master jazz artist plays one of the most intricately luminous solos of his career—building this simple skater's waltz to a multi-layered musical monument of shimmering solidity. Then, on the hauntingly beautiful title tune "Odds Against Tomorrow," Jackson attains a level of matchless musicianship that still impresses the listener 50 years after he recorded it, especially when he comes to the thematic phrase contained in the ascending melodic sequence—D^-↑E-↑G; ↑C^^^; ↓C^-↑D-↑F; B♭^^^—on which his vibes ring out in crystalline splendor with the pulse of the ethereal instrument's vibrato perfectly timed to create triplets against the duple meter in which the piece is played by the other musicians. Even with the most patient and persistent twirling of the speed control on a vibraphone, the synchronicity that Jackson attains here with such apparent ease and naturalness is impossibly difficult to duplicate. (Trust me; I have tried and tried, but have failed miserably.) Yet this felicitous rhythmic achievement seems to have resulted from the utmost professionalism rather than from any sort of luck. Indeed, Jackson produces essentially the same three-against-two tremolo effect in a live recording of "Odds Against Tomorrow" from a concert in Scandinavia during April of 1960 (*The Modern Jazz Quartet: European Concert*, Atlantic 1385, reissued on CD as Warner Pioneer Corporation 50XD-1013-4). To achieve this at a live concert strikes me as even more amazing than its earlier accomplishment in the recording studio.

So, with forces like that for John Lewis to work with, how does it happen that Milt Jackson plays such a relatively small role in the nondiegetic background score for *Odds Against Tomorrow?* The decision by Lewis largely to omit Jackson from the underscore appears to be a major mystery. The explanation for this otherwise curious disappearing act lies, I believe, in the use of on-screen ambi-diegetic jazz to portray the character of Johnny Ingram as enacted by Harry Belafonte.

In the dramatic development of the film, it is essential that we perceive Ingram/Belafonte as a sincere but incompetent loser—that is, one who endearingly loves his family, but who has piled up insurmountable gambling debts, will collaborate in a badly botched robbery attempt, and will ultimately perish as the result of his ineptitude. Toward this end, a pivotal smallbut-significant ambi-diegetic cinemusical moment in the motion picture appears about 25 minutes into the action when we see Ingram/Belafonte in his role as a nightclub performer, singing the blues and playing the vibraphone to backing by a piano-bass-and-drums trio, first without and later with a female vocalist. In this scene, Johnny/Harry must appear emotionally frustrated (by his gambling debts) and musically maladroit (as a less-thanjourneyman singer and worse-than-mediocre vibraharpist). Via his on-screen performance, Ingram/Belafonte accomplishes these dramatic goals with precision.

It happens that—in real life—Harry Belafonte could sing (quite well) and could play at least a little bit of vibes (with enough skill to make the vibraphone his instrument of choice in this particular film). Applying these talents in his role as Johnny Ingram, Belafonte begins with a blues in E minor called "When That Cold, Cold Sun Goes Down" on which he sings in a barely perceptible echo of the real-world Belafonte style and accompanies himself by means of some amateurishly rudimentary vibes playing—featuring some rather tasteless mallet pounding and a tremolo set at an annoyingly fast speed (an out-of-date anachronism that would have driven Milt Jackson crazy). Following this display of shaky musicianship, Johnny/Harry encounters a menacing mobster who, with the help of some brutal thugs serving as his savage henchman, strongly registers the message that unless Ingram/ Belafonte delivers $7,500 within the next twenty-four hours, the singervibist will be a dead man. Johnny/Harry reacts by getting drunk and by accompanying a heavy-set female singer on "All Men Are Evil"—another blues in E minor—in a most disturbing duet. Specifically, Johnny/Harry interjects off-key, out-of-synch, intentionally offensive intrusions during the female singer's choruses and follows this untoward display of bad taste with a catastrophic vibraphone solo in which he flails and hammers at his instrument in a manner calculated to produce a singularly unpleasant sound—a gratingly clunky and clanky noise with no apparent melodic, harmonic, or rhythmic grounding. He finishes this off with an *a cappella* flourish that is completely off-the-wall, sounds as if he is whacking the vibes with wooden kitchen spoons, and consists entirely of cacophonous banging at a level of aggressive assault that would doubtless damage the instrument irreparably if it were sustained for more than a few seconds. At the conclusion of this transparent display of frustration, one of the women at the bar opines, "That little boy's in big trouble." Indeed, as an expression of frustrated aggression and tormented self-destructiveness, Ingram/Belafonte's ambi-diegetic cinemusical vibraphonic onslaught seems more offensive, uncontrolled, and even sociopathic than anything we could have imagined so long before the days of funk, fusion, punk, and hip-hop.

Interestingly and mercifully enough, Ingram/Belafonte's ambi-diegetic performance on vibraphone is omitted from the soundtrack recording. But, for the remaining hour after it appears in the film, its nasty aural echoes seem to preclude the further use of the vibraphone for any remaining cinemusical purposes. The magisterial Milt Jackson, it appears, will have to wait for some other more sympathetic context in which to shine. As an expressive instrument, the vibraphone has been temporarily tainted by its sordid associations with Johnny/Harry's troubled character and, more important, vice versa: Johnny/Harry's role takes on the unsavory and dismal connotations of his inept singing and offensive vibes playing. To paraphrase the title of this chapter—not unlike the ignominious fate of the male protagonist foretold by the ominous whistling of the security guard in Louis Malle's earlier thriller—when coupled with the suicidal racism of the Robert Ryan character, Harry Belafonte's troubles as Johnny Ingram can be diagnosed according to the detailed nuances of a small-but-significant ambi-diegetic cinemusical moment.

## CONCLUSION

This chapter applies close readings—analogous to those associated with verbal or visual texts—to the case of music from motion pictures in general and to small-but-significant ambi-diegetic cinemusical moments in the jazz scores by Miles Davis and John Lewis in particular so as to show how seemingly trivial musical details carry meaningful implications that enhance the development of character and plot. Though this approach to detailed textual analysis has a long pedigree in the case of verbal and visual materials, it has less frequently appeared in the interpretation of film music. Nonetheless, the interpretive strategy based on a close reading of detailed textual evidence offers considerable promise of refinement in the study of jazz in films. In short, the interpretations offered here appear to demonstrate the usefulness of the approach proposed at the outset—namely, a dialectic synthesis based on the integration of a thesis (the big picture concerning the broad meanings of film music) with its antithesis (the minute details of a cinemusical text). As anticipated, short-but-meaningful cinemusical moments from *Ascenseur Pour L'Échafaud* and *Odds Against Tomorrow* do seem to illustrate how subtle nuances carry larger implications. Apparently, via minute-but-significant cinemusical meanings, a potential enrichment of understanding lies below the surface of film music, waiting to be discovered via a close reading of the cinemusical text. As reflected in the title of Part VI and as further illustrated in the chapter on *Sweet Smell of Success* that follows—recalling what Albert Einstein, Gustave Flaubert, Friedrich Nietzsche, Ludwig Mies Van Der Rohe, or some other smart person once said about the Deity and about the sanctity of attending to the smallest of subtleties or nuances—"God Is in the Details."

# 14 Small-But-Significant Implications of the Man Who Isn't There In *Sweet Smell of Success* (1957)

In the last chapter, we visited the meaning of a subtle-but-significant detail in the cinemusical design of *Odds Against Tomorrow*—namely, the simultaneous obtrusiveness of Harry Belafonte as an offensive on-screen ambi-diegetic vibraphone player and the concomitant absence of the magnificent vibraphonist Milt Jackson from the off-screen nondiegetic score. As a second illustration of the small-but-meaningful implications that can arise from someone-who or something-that is *missing* from the musical score—recalling the poem by William Hughes Mearns entitled "Antigonish" but often referred to as "The Little Man Who Wasn't There"—the present chapter will examine the role of ambi-diegetic music in *Sweet Smell of Success* (1957). This film attracts the interest of those concerned with (macro)marketing theory partly because—reflecting an issue of *social relevance*—it has been explicated as a text on the battle of artistic integrity against the forces of commercialism (Gabbard 1996, p. 128). Careful examination suggests, however, that a subtext of equally compelling interest to scholars concerned with (macro)marketing theory hinges on the manner in which ambi-diegetic cinemusical moments work to develop the characterization of a leading protagonist. Specifically, the identity as opposed to the misidentification of the real-life guitarist who dubs the source music that this character mimes on-screen turns out to carry important implications for our interpretation of the character's personality, disposition, and capabilities. Thus do the small-but-significant subtle-but-meaningful nuances of ambi-diegetic jazz play a key cinemusical role in the *product design* that creates a viable work of art.

Based on a novelette by Ernest Lehman and a screenplay by Lehman and Clifford Odets—the famous left-wing excoriator of American cultural excesses badly in need of excoriation—director Alexander Mackenrick's *Sweet Smell of Success* (1957) initially tended to escape the attention of both the industry pundits (earning no Oscar nominations) and the viewing public (performing poorly at the box office) but, in the ensuing years since its release, has accumulated something of an underground reputation as a classic *late-film-noir prototype*. Our interest in the music for this film stems from its jazz-flavored background score by Elmer Bernstein in general and, more importantly, from its ambi-diegetic jazz by the Chico Hamilton Quintet in particular.

The cinematic presence of a jazz quintet—real-life musicians with actual speaking parts—stems from the film's situation among scenes set in New York City's nightclub and late-night restaurant circuit. Briefly, the movie involves the evil machinations of a conniving publicity agent named Sidney Falco (Tony Curtis) whose career aspirations hinge on the willingness of a powerful but corrupt gossip columnist named J. J. Hunsecker (Burt Lancaster) to mention Sidney/Tony's clients in his daily newspaper feature. Lately, J.J./Burt has put Sidney/Tony's livelihood in jeopardy by withholding his publicity favors until Falco/Curtis can make good on his promise to break up a budding romance between Hunsecker's kid sister Susie (Susan Harrison) and a young musician named Steve Dallas (Martin Milner). Hunsecker/Lancaster seems to be motivated largely by some rather sordidly incestuous feelings for his sister Susie/Susan. Meanwhile, the main characteristics of Susie/Susan and Steve/Martin—needed dramatically to balance the fascinatingly evil natures of Hunsecker/Lancaster and Falco/Curtis—revolve around the innocent devotion of a young couple in love. Susie/Susan is delicate, shy, pretty but dependent and unsure of herself. Steve/Martin is likeable, upstanding, clean-cut, well-dressed, earnest, and brave but a little naïve, inarticulate, conventional, and—worse, far worse in the eyes of Hunsecker/Lancaster, than any of these other shortcomings—employed as the guitarist in a jazz quintet.

As far as the dramatic purposes of the film are concerned, Dallas/Milner could have been just about anybody likely to be found hanging out in New York bars and restaurants late at night—a bartender, a waiter, a club manager, a doorman. The essential attribute for Steve/Martin is that he must enjoy a station in life far enough down the status hierarchy that the wealthy and powerful Hunsecker/Lancaster would feel enough contempt for Dallas/Milner to escalate his pressure on the efforts by Falco/Curtis to break up the budding romance to the point where—avaricious and maleficent beyond belief—Sidney/Tony plants a bogus story about Steve/Martin being a marijuana-smoking communist (payback time for Clifford Odets, who was blacklisted as part of the McCarthy fiasco, I'm thinking) and later hides marijuana in Dallas/Milner's overcoat pocket, alerts the police, and thereby causes him to be arrested, beaten, and hospitalized. So—looking around for someone who would fit that particular job description—the writers, playing against social stereotypes, hit on the idea of casting Steve/Martin as an honorable, clean-living, kind-hearted, hard-working jazz musician.

Now, when most people think of the stereotypical jazz musician, they conjure up a socially maladroit, beret-wearing, zoot-suited ne'er-do-well who would indeed smoke pot and join the Communist Party except that he is too strung out on heroin, cocaine, or demon rum to care about such comparatively sober pastimes. But Steve/Martin needs to come across as just the opposite of all that. To repeat, the main character traits of this hero require that he must be vulnerable and attractive enough to win the heart of Susie/Susan but, on the whole, honorable and bordering on . . . well, to be polite . . . bland. So let's have him play guitar and lead a band of five guys all wearing coats and ties, sporting short haircuts, speaking politely, and performing an intellectualized brand of jazz typical of the 1950s West-Coast sound. (Though the film is set in New York City, the Hamilton Quintet was perhaps *the* prototypical Los Angeles jazz group during the late 1950s insofar as it enjoyed a reputation for being quiet, cool, soft, subtle, laid-back, cerebral, and all those other qualities associated, often pejoratively, with West Coast jazz at mid-century.)

Ordinarily, I would not have been curious enough to resurrect this neglected film from the tombs of cinematic obscurity, but the singularly favorable press given this movie by at least one jazz-in-film historian (Gabbard 1996) piqued my curiosity overpoweringly when, in an enticing description, he portrays *Sweet Smell of Success* as "one of the American cinema's most unrelentingly negative portraits of U.S. culture at the same time that it is one of the most flattering portraits ever of a jazz musician" (p. 128). Well, who—I ask you, Dear Reader—does not long to see our local culture trashed while thrilling to the adventures of a heroic jazz artist? Indeed, Gabbard (1996) enriches the already sweet-smelling pot further when he promises that this film depicts Steve/Martin as taking a stand "very much on the right side of the art versus commerce binarism" (p. 129). Not having seen the movie, we might well imagine that it might reflect a wholesome contest between the forces of creative integrity (aka art) and the appeal to mass popularity (aka commerce). And our temptation becomes irresistible when Gabbard (1996) further assures us that "Steve is shown performing with his group at several moments in the film" and adds, most enticingly, that "Jim Hall dubbed in the guitar solos for Martin Milner in the group that Chico Hamilton was leading at the time" (p. 128). Apparently, Gabbard (1996)—a focus on the actual music in films he critiques not being his major preoccupation—bases this attribution to the great guitarist Jim Hall on the work of Meeker (1981), who informs us that the film features "superb ghosting by **Jim Hall**" (#3174). Yanow (2004) dutifully repeats the same claim (p. 203).

Thus, the account by Gabbard (1996) implies that *Sweet Smell of Success* delves promisingly into one of *the* most fascinating and (until recently) under-researched regions of (macro)marketing theory—namely, the relationship between popular appeal (commercial success) and artistic excellence (creative integrity). As noted earlier in the Introduction to Part IV, this issue remains one of the most vexed and potentially inflammatory in the entire (macro)marketing literature. The hope that a film such as *Sweet Smell of Success* might shed light on such perplexing questions should be more than enough to inspire the curious (macro)marketing theoretician to pay attention.

We should therefore immediately dispense with the notion that *Sweet Smell of Success* offers reflections on the theme of art-versus-commerce in anything like the overt manner of other jazz-oriented movies discussed elsewhere in the present volume. Rather, in *Sweet Smell of Success*, "commerce" is represented by the greedy publicity agent Sidney/Tony, the supercilious gossip columnist J.J./Burt (said to have been modeled in part on the infamous Walter Winchell), and their disreputable cronies hanging around the tables and bars at "21" and Toots Shor's. This corrupt form of "commerce"—centered on the unsavory side of journalism in the service of a show-business mentality—contrasts with the innocence of pure "art" as represented by the untainted music and unsullied romantic love that characterize the guitarist Steve/Martin and his young girlfriend Susie/Susan. So don't go to *Sweet Smell of Success* in search of ammunition for the anti-commercialistic struggle against the manifest popularity of inferior art and mediocre entertainment. If you do, you will be disappointed to find that—thanks, no doubt, to the worthy efforts of score-composer Elmer Bernstein—the film is refreshingly free of bad music.

But who really cares about such niceties when we consider the enormity of the tantalizing prospect that we might listen at length to the 1957-ish guitar sounds of Jim Hall used ambi-diegetically to develop the character of a jazz-playing culture hero? In order to appreciate the attractiveness of this promise by Gabbard (1996), Meeker (1981), and Yanow (2004), I suppose one must have some familiarity with the uniquely subtle richness of the jazz style that this guitar genius unveiled in his earliest performances beginning on the West Coast in the mid-1950s. As merely one among countless examples, consider the work by Jim Hall on his 1957 recording for Pacific Jazz entitled *Jazz Guitar* (PJ-1227) and featuring a piano-bass-guitar trio with Carl Perkins on piano and Red Mitchell on bass. In his liner notes for this album, Jimmy Giuffre (the noted clarinetist, saxophonist, composer, arranger, and leader, in whose trio Jim Hall participated at about this time) describes Hall's playing as possessing "an original manner," a "devoted awareness to sound," a "high quality of lyricism," a "purity of feeling," and a flair for conveying "what music's all about." But those kind words amount to pale understatements of Jim Hall's gargantuan capabilities. Hall's playing in general and on this record in particular goes far beyond anything encapsulated by such meager language. Above all, his sound is absolutely unique, easily identifiable after hearing as few as three or four invariably well-timed and carefully-placed notes. It is a beautifully funky sound—earthy and bluesy, but at the same time thoughtful and spare, almost pensive in tone but still clear as a bell and punchy when needed. On this album, as elsewhere, Hall's solos are epigrammatic—seldom longer than a chorus or two—unfolding via a compelling logic that makes them sound almost as if they had been written out and memorized note-for-note (which, of course, they most definitely were not). In retrospect, they have the air of classic perfection—reminiscent of the carved-in-stone quality often achieved by (say) Bix Beiderbecke, Lester Young, Paul Desmond, Chet Baker, Art Farmer, Bill Evans, Milt Jackson, or the early Miles Davis. But, at the time when they first appeared, Jim Hall's marvelous contributions burst on the scene as a breath of fresh air from a musician of compelling individuality and artistic accomplishment.

So imagine my disappointment when I dutifully watched this film and encountered *not* the crystalline purity of Jim Hall's endlessly fascinating improvisations coming from the dubbed guitar of Dallas/Milner *but rather* some anonymously faceless guitar licks that could have been played by any one of a hundred competent jazz guitarists—most of them up to their ears in the lucrative business of the New York and Hollywood recording-and-film studios—who all played in the typical post-(Charlie)Christian style of the 1950s. Some diligent detective work—reminiscent of Sherlock Holmes obsessed by seemingly trivial details—pinpointed the source of the problem. Specifically, the videotape box identifies the dubbed guitar as that of John Pisano—a talented and technically proficient but (at the time) rather routine player who was two months younger than Jim Hall and who also appeared ubiquitously on the West-Coast jazz scene during the 1950s. In *The New Edition of the Encyclopedia of Jazz*, Feather (1960) also clearly identifies John Pisano's film credits as including *Sweet Smell of Success* (p. 383). Much of Pisano's post-1950s career—unlike that of Hall, who went on to increasingly greater glory—appears to have come to something of an artistic stand-still via long tours of duty with Herb Alpert's Tijuana Brass and with the back-up band for Peggy Lee.

The source for all this mystification arises from the evolving personnel of the Chico Hamilton Quintet during the years 1956–1957. As already mentioned—with the exception of the fictional guitarist/leader Dallas/Milner—the other real-life members of the Hamilton Quintet appear on-screen and are specifically identified by name: Chico Hamilton, drums; Fred Katz, cello; Carson Smith, bass; Paul Horn, flute and reeds. Hamilton and Katz both have minor speaking parts in the film and help to establish the authentic jazz-related feeling of the scene at the Elysian Room where they occupy the bandstand. But—unlike the real world in which this group worked under the leadership of drummer Chico Hamilton—the film puts the fictional guitarist Dallas/Milner in charge as the leader of the quintet (thereby leaving the identity of the real guitarist behind his sound, who never appears on-screen, in doubt). It happens that, prior to the spring of 1956, Chico Hamilton's group included Katz and Smith with Buddy Collette on flute-plus-reeds and with none other than Jim Hall on guitar. Obviously, for Hall fans, this was the "great" incarnation of the Chico Hamilton Quintet—one that recorded 36 tunes for Pacific Jazz, spread out over three albums and recently reissued by Mosaic in *The Complete Pacific Jazz Recordings of the Chico Hamilton Quintet* (Mosaic MD6-175). But in the fall of 1956, Jim Hall left the Hamilton Quintet to join the Jimmy Giuffre Trio (first with Ralph Peña and then Jim Atlas on bass, later with Bob Brookmeyer on trombone, as the third member). Hall was replaced in Hamilton's group by John Pisano, and Paul Horn assumed the position on flute-and-reeds formerly occupied by Buddy Collette. After that, according to the liner notes by Robert Gordon for the Mosaic set, the original Collette-Hall version of the Quintet never recorded together again, except for a two-day reunion in January of 1959 to perform 11 tunes associated with Duke Ellington (*Ellington Suite*, World Pacific WP-1258). Hence, if we still need further proof that Pisano plays on the *Sweet Smell of Success* soundtrack (as also mentioned in Gordon's liner notes for Mosaic MD6-175), we observe that the film appeared in 1957 (long after Hall's departure from the group) and that the flute parts on-stage are played by Paul Horn (Pisano's and not Hall's band mate).

But, more importantly, we need consult only the *playing* of the guitarist mimed by Dallas/Milner in *Sweet Smell of Success* to know that we are listening to John Pisano and *not* to Jim Hall. The playing that Steve/Martin mimes on-screen is fluid but flat, multi-noted but repetitive, competent but undifferentiated, energetic but unimaginative, appropriate but forgettable. That by Hall would have been mellow, varied, distinctive, ear-catching, and memorable. What we see/hear in the film music *has* to be Dallas/Milner/ *Pisano* and *cannot* be Dallas/Milner/*Hall*.

By now, the impatient reader may be wondering—in the wise words of William Wells (1993)—"So What?"

All this fuss about what might otherwise appear to be a trivial detail matters from the perspective of the present chapter, Dear Reader, because the ambi-diegetic guitar performances of John Pisano play a key role in the characterization of Dallas/Milner. Recall that Steve/Martin betrays a sincere but straight-laced personality. These qualities exactly match those brought by Pisano to his guitar playing in *Sweet Smell of Success*. When Dallas/ Milner solos, we hear some appropriate and competent but essentially routine journeyman-jazz guitar of a character lacking in uniqueness or individuality. The notes march along in lock-step, like little soldiers, without dynamic contrast or varied pacing. They move forward in smoothly predictable sequences with no clear articulation, no subtle shaping, and no complexities of phrasing. Further, when the actor Martin Milner mimes these notes, he does so with a sort of expressionlessly impassive visage and a rigid body language that signal his character's lack of real involvement with the music. Thus, Martin Milner miming John Pisano supplies exactly the ambi-diegetic cinemusical attributes needed to establish the character of Steve Dallas as . . . to repeat . . . rather *bland*.

For an instructive comparison, take a look at Jim Hall playing with the Jimmy Giuffre Trio in Aram Avakian and Ben Stern's documentary on the 1958 Newport Jazz festival entitled *Jazz on a Summer's Day* (1958). Here, Hall appears attentive, alert, alive—sympathetically responsive to the musical gestures of his compatriots, full of rich and challenging ideas—in short, . . . cinemusically . . . *on fire*.

Had an unfettered Jim Hall played the music in *Sweet Smell of Success*, things would have turned out quite differently. They would better have served the listening experience of the dedicated jazz aficionado, but they would less well have aided the ambi-diegetic cinemusical purposes of the scenes in the jazz club. Specifically, as always, Jim Hall would have brought an intense feeling of engaged involvement, stubborn uniqueness, and singular individuality to this music. He would have supplied solos with his usual understated complexity—intricate lines that break up their notes into irregular phrases, full of jagged surprises, strung together in meaningful clusters, with a ringing bell-like clarity of sound. Even if the film's director had explicitly instructed Jim Hall to be boring, he could not have played in the drab Dallas/Milner/Pisano style if had wanted to. Rather, by the irrepressible power of his indomitably creative musical personality, he would willy-nilly have commanded our attention and would perforce have rewarded it with his constantly catchy turns of phrase and his always enthralling harmonic subtleties.

That Jim Hall would have done this is not just some figment of my febrile jazz-fanatic imagination. I have already mentioned the evidence presented by his superb work in *Jazz on a Summer's Day* (1960). After the 1950s, Hall continued apace—contributing the indelible personal qualities mentioned earlier to performances, tours, and innumerable recordings made with countless stellar musicians who clambered to recruit him for their various musical projects. Following Jim Hall's stellar work in the sterling and stirring group led by Jimmy Giuffre (especially the version of this group that also featured Bob Brookmeyer), a short list of loyal Hall collaborators would include John Lewis and the Modern Jazz Quartet, Hampton Hawes, Paul Desmond, Lee Konitz, Zoot Sims, Sonny Rollins, Bill Evans, Art Farmer, Ron Carter, Gary Burton, Pat Metheny, and Bill Frisell (omitting a host of others too numerous to list here). Obviously, all these great names in jazz have heard those qualities in Jim Hall's playing that set him apart from such mere mortals as (the undeniably gifted) John Pisano. To pursue an example from film music of the nondiegetic type, when Hall appears briefly in the score by John Lewis for *Odds Against Tomorrow* (1959), his unique sound immediately catches our ear. His personal stamp of individuality distracts us momentarily from the film while we make a mental note, "O, there's Jim Hall." His playing has displayed that compelling sense of captivating originality for over 50 years and would have had exactly the same effect had it appeared in *Sweet Smell of Success*. Indeed, in *Sweet Smell of Success*, the use of Jim Hall as a source of ambi-diegetic music for Dallas/Milner—a seemingly small but ever so significant detail—would have completely altered our perception of the Steve/Martin character and would thereby have irreparably damaged the ability of the film to convey its intended meanings.

So in the last analysis, disappointed as I felt not to hear the inimitable sounds of Jim Hall (the little man who isn't there) emanating from the guitar of Steve Dallas (Martin Milner) in *Sweet Smell of Success*, I must admit that such a small-but-significant substitution for the ambi-diegetic dubbing by John Pisano would have sabotaged the film's dramatic development. In short, the greatest of guitarists would have been a poor choice for this particular ambi-diegetic cinemusical assignment. If dubbed by Hall instead of Pisano, Dallas/Milner would doubtless have come across as less naïve, less inarticulate, less conventional, less uninteresting, less straight-laced, less . . . bland. Hall's music is far too sophisticated, individualistic, intricate, fascinating, and unique to suggest those Dallas-like qualities. In the crucial scenes when Steve/Martin confronts first Sidney/Tony and then J.J./Burt, the Dallas/Milner/Pisano character more or less babbles with righteous indignation, powerless to cut through the conniving palaver of Falco/Curtis or the menacing treachery of Hunsecker/Lancaster. If the part had instead been played by a Dallas/Milner/Hall amalgam, I can easily imagine this character putting Sidney/Tony in his place with a well-aimed fusillade of esoteric language and skewering J.J./Burt with a sardonic accusation that he is (say) a "sister-loving incest-mongering gossip-grabbing hun-sucker."

Such an episode would have done the heart good but would have been entirely out of character for Steve/Martin. Better to let Dallas/Milner splutter with inarticulate rage and to let John Pisano lay down the musical foundation for his feckless blandness. Better to let Jim Hall go off and do his thing to better advantage with Giuffre and Brookmeyer, the MJQ, Hawes, Desmond, Rollins, Evans, Farmer, Cater, Burton, Metheny, Frisell, and that long line of Jim Hall admirers who really knew how to use his formidable talents—talents that, by virtue of their instantly recognizable uniqueness and individuality, would have been wasted on this film or even destructive to its dramatic integrity.

Meanwhile, today, Jim Hall remains luminously active on the New York jazz scene while John Pisano continues to play gigs in the Los Angeles area and has become one of the true dignitaries in the current West Coast jazz culture. Over the years, Pisano's style has matured, deepened, mellowed, ripened, and progressed to the point where his present level of musical refinement and sophistication bears little resemblance to the comparatively more callow and routine playing he offered during the 1950s. If they made *Sweet Smell of Success* again today—to find a guitarist appropriate for the ambi-diegetic cinemusical moments needed for the film's design—they would surely have to hire a different man.

Part VII

# Jazz Biopics as Tragedy and Comedy: Pivotal Ambi-Diegetic Cinemusical Moments in Tragedepictions and Comedepictions of Jazz Heroes

# Introduction to Part VII

Part VII addresses an aspect of film music in general and of cinematic jazz performances in particular in which *ambi-diegetic cinemusical moments* become, in a sense, the *whole point* of a motion picture. Here, I refer to the mini-genre of the *jazz-based biographical picture* or the *jazz biopic* wherein the life of some noteworthy jazz artist is refracted through the lens of an often-heavily-fictionalized historical dramatization or an all-too-frequently distorted romantic idealization. In this connection, I shall distinguish between *two contrasting types* of jazz biopics—namely, in Chapter 15, *tragedepictions* that emphasize the dark side of existence in which musicians begin with promise but eventually succumb to irresistible personal or societal demons; as opposed, in Chapter 16, to *comedepictions* that emphasize the bright side of life in which musicians struggle at first but eventually conquer the forces that resist them. The former jazz biopics feature downward spirals and operate in the realm of tragedy. The latter feature upward trajectories and operate in the realm of comedy. The tragedepictions lead toward death and destruction, the comedepictions toward success and happiness.

We shall deal first, in Chapter 15, with the jazz-oriented tragedepictions in general and with three important tragedy-oriented biopics in particular—namely, those portraying the tortured life of Billie Holiday in *Lady Sings the Blues* (1972); the sad end of a Lester-Young-and-Bud-Powell composite character in *'Round Midnight* (1986); and the misbegotten misadventures of Charlie Parker in *Bird* (1988). These three downbeat or even deadbeat jazz biopics share a thematic focus on how racial intolerance, social injustice, the demands of the marketplace toward the commercialization of artistic gifts, and other societal problems can confront creative geniuses with debilitating pressures so as to encourage dependencies on drugs and/or alcohol in ways that prove devastating to the central characters of interest. Chapter 3 explored similar themes in connection with the self-destructive habits of the famous singing and trumpet-playing jazz artist Chet Baker (Bradshaw and Holbrook 2007). In Chapter 15, the present work examines related issues in the context of their ambi-diegetic cinemusical settings in the three afore-mentioned jazz tragedepictions. In each case, I shall argue that the films in question achieve only partial success in their use of the sorts of pivotal ambi-diegetic cinemusical moments that we have adopted as our primary focus.

Nonetheless, I shall give a brief account of what I take to be the closest thing we can find to a pivotal ambi-diegetic cinemusical breakthrough in each of these three major tragedepictions.

Second, in Chapter 16, we shall deal with some more success-oriented jazz biopics in general and with five upbeat biopics in particular that focus on the bright side of life, that view the world as comedy, and that represent opportunities for fulfillment and possibilities for happiness. Especially in the years surrounding the mid-point of the last century, these kinds of jazz-oriented comedepictions appeared in great abundance and dedicated their ambi-diegetic cinemusical resources to celebrating the lives of such noted swing-era icons as Tommy and Jimmy Dorsey in *The Fabulous Dorseys* (1947); Glenn Miller in *The Glenn Miller Story* (1954); Benny Goodman in *The Benny Goodman Story* (1955); Red Nichols in *The Five Pennies* (1959); and Gene Krupa in *The Gene Krupa Story* (1959). As explained in perceptive depth by Gabbard (1996), the comedepictions represented by these particular jazz biopics hark back to the prototypical format provided by *The Jazz Singer* (1927)—what he calls "a uniquely American template" (p. 36)—a famous precursor that has proven decisive in its influence not only because it was the first feature-length talking movie but, even more, because it provided the dramatic model on which, as Gabbard (1996) convincingly shows, all subsequent success-story jazz biopics have based their fundamental structure. While acknowledging and building on Gabbard's viewpoint, I shall focus primarily on a recurrent aspect of each film that, I believe, has tended to get lost in the jazz-singer two-step shuffle. Specifically, I shall focus on how—in each jazz comedepiction—there comes a time when an old, corny, drab manner of playing gives way to a new, fresh, exciting style that characterizes the approach introduced by the main biopictorial protagonist(s)—the Dorseys, Miller, Goodman, Nichols, or Krupa. In each case, this watershed moment serves as the cinemusical pivot on which the purport of the entire film hinges. And, in each case, the comedepiction rises to the occasion by providing a vivid and compelling cinemusical recreation of the jazz style, musical charisma, and performance capabilities that transformed the relevant biopictorial hero into a legendary star. The ambi-diegetic cinemusical moment by which this revolutionary change is conveyed thus becomes a critical vehicle for the dramatic development of each film. The meaning and significance of the motion picture depend on the successful enactment of this pivotal ambi-diegetic cinemusical moment. In many ways, as we shall see, these comedepictions represent re-enactments of the American Dream—as portrayed, for example, in the old Horatio Alger stories. But, of course, there is a Dark Side to all this. And we conclude with a consideration of this Dark Side as it appears in the life and work of the great-but-tormented, successful-but-disillusioned, charismatic-but-reclusive, famous-but-misunderstood Artie Shaw.

# 15  When Bad Things Happen to Great Musicians

## The Troubled Role of Ambi-Diegetic Jazz in Three Tragedepictions of Artistic Genius on the Silver Screen

### INTRODUCTION

As we have seen repeatedly in earlier chapters, the judicious use of music plays a crucial role in the design of a successful motion picture. Previous chapters have provided abundant indications of ways in which music in general and ambi-diegetic jazz in particular can deepen the meanings of a cinematic experience; can enrich the development of character, plot, or other dramatic themes in a motion picture; and can contribute to various aspects of a film's significance. In this connection—with special relevance to jazz—the work by Gabbard (1996, 2000, 2001, 2003, 2004, 2007, 2008) and by Holbrook (2003a, 2004, 2005a, 2005b, 2005e, 2006c, 2007a, 2008a, 2008b, 2008c, 2009) has focused primarily on a large number of cinemusical success stories. Thus, we have seen numerous examples of cases involving the effective use of ambi-diegetic cinemusical moments produced when an on-screen musical performance sheds light on a character's motivations, advances aspects of the plot, contributes significant symbolic meanings, or signals key thematic ideas—an approach to cinemusical design that has achieved striking success in any number of jazz-related applications. Conversely, however, inadequacies or breakdowns in the use of music to develop character, plot, or other themes can lead to highly unsatisfactory or problematic cinemusical results—especially when dealing with the life of a great jazz musician. In Chapter 15, I shall focus on this latter possibility. Specifically—rather than continuing to celebrate the effective use of jazz to create or bolster important cinemusical meanings—the present chapter examines three cases of biographical motion pictures or biopics in which, partly due to failures in the cinemusical design process, bad things happen to great musicians.

### TRAGEDEPICTION AS A JAZZ GENRE

Clearly, the happy outcomes and upbeat story lines that typify jazz comedepictions in the chapter to follow contrast vividly with the darker-sided jazz tragedepictions of central interest in the present chapter. Here, we shall focus

mostly on anguish rather than triumph, on death rather than life, on mourning rather than celebration, on decline rather than ascent, on sorrow rather
than humor, on distress rather than happiness. Notice that, as Gabbard
(1996) would be quick to point out, all five jazz biopics under the heading
of comedepictions in Chapter 16 deal with white musicians as opposed to
black or other minority artists (Holbrook 2008a, 2009). By contrast—as
emphasized by Gabbard (1996) and with the recent partial exception of *Ray*
(2004)—films dealing with African-American jazz performers have tended
overwhelmingly to present a darker, more dismal side of the musical life in
a way that constitutes the very antithesis of the comedepictorial ethos.
Obvious examples of such racially-centered tragedepictions include our three
major illustrations in Chapter 15—namely, *Lady Sings the Blues* (1972),
*'Round Midnight* (1986), and *Bird* (1988).

These quasi-biographical tragedepictions present aspects of the jazz life
viewed as misfortune and depart strikingly from stories mirroring the Jazz-
Singer prototype that feature successful outcomes seen as comedy, as dis-
cussed in Chapter 16. Ironically enough, nobody has bothered to make an
upbeat jazz biopic on the life of an African-American artist such as (say)
Louis Armstrong, Duke Ellington, Earl Hines, Coleman Hawkins, Nat
"King" Cole, Erroll Garner, Dizzy Gillespie, Ella Fitzgerald, Sarah Vaughan,
Carmen McRae, Teddy Wilson, Oscar Peterson, Ray Brown, Art Farmer,
Sonny Rollins, Sonny Stitt, Cannonball Adderley, Hank Jones, Quincy
Jones, Ornette Coleman, Clark Terry, Milt Jackson, John Lewis, Wes
Montgomery, Herbie Hancock, Freddie Hubbard, Wayne Shorter, or
Wynton Marsalis—any of whom could be represented in ways consistent
with happy endings. Indeed, even the relatively optimistic biopic on Ray
Charles entitled simply *Ray* (2004) features the seamy-and-seedy side of this
great artist's early career—complete with narcotics addiction, drug busts, jail
time, and agonizing withdrawal symptoms—before heading in the direction
of a triumphantly redemptive denouement that celebrates the manner in
which this genius singer-pianist overcame his personal demons to achieve
artistic victories and commercial successes. Industry gossip suggests that
Miles Davis stands next in line for an analogous kind of inherently ambivalent biopictorial treatment. Thus, typically, black jazz musicians have been
portrayed—even exploited—for the sake of their potential to convey the
painful side of racial discrimination, the debilitating effects of poverty, the
agony of creation, the tyranny of the marketplace, the betrayal of artistic
integrity, the price of freedom, or the debasement of the human spirit by
drugs, booze, and psychological torment. Partly—as in the case of the white
artist Chet Baker (Chapter 3; Bradshaw and Holbrook 2007)—this is
because they are *jazz* musicians. But mostly—as in the three films examined
here—it is because they are *black* jazz musicians. As Atkinson (1995) puts
it, "jazz, in the contemporary biopic, is a frontier of racial spite and wholesale self-destruction . . . implying that like a poet's madness, smack-fueled
dissolution is the price you pay for jazz glory" (p. 28). This dark and bitter
side of the jazz world—suggestive of tragic dimensions that, as noted earlier

and developed in what follows, have not yet achieved full ambi-diegetic cinemusical realization—serves as the disquieting theme of interest in the present chapter.

## THE POTENTIALLY PIVOTAL ROLE OF AMBI-DIEGETIC CINEMUSICAL MOMENTS IN A JAZZ TRAGEDEPICTION

The *essence of tragedy*, as developed in literary examples ranging from *Oedipus Rex* to *King Lear* to *Paradise Lost* to *Faust* to *Moby-Dick*, hinges on a *fall from grace*—that is, a plunge from an exalted level to a lowly station, from prosperity to wretchedness, or from happiness to misery—precipitated by some sort of fatal mistake, character flaw, or reversal in fortune (Abrams 1988; Frye, Baker, and Perkins 1985). For such an event to become truly *tragic*—as opposed to merely *sad*—the plot and characterization must convey that a hero's greatness, eminence, or elevated stature has preceded some sort of self-destruction, twist of fate, or other untimely end. Thus, the story of a jazz musician who never fully develops his or her talent because of poverty or lack of education or racial prejudice would qualify as extremely sad, but not tragic. The accidental death of a fledgling trumpet player might bring tears of sorrow, but not the pathos of true tragedy. The murder of a marginally competent sideman—say, a drummer with a poor sense of time— might evoke deep sympathy but would not prompt the Aristotelean catharsis or purging of pity and fear associated with the classic tragedians. By contrast—from our present perspective—tragedy in the world of jazz occurs when a musician who has risen to the highest pinnacle of artistic achievement somehow perishes at an early age or self-destructs in a long, slow, ineluctable slide from the peak of creative supremacy into abject penury or hopeless debilitation. Here, we think irresistibly of (say) Clifford Brown—suddenly killed in an auto accident at the apex of his gigantic musical powers. We think of Scott LaFaro—similarly taken from us in a car crash at the highest moment of his ascendant mastery. We think of Lee Morgan—brutally gunned down while still a reigning titan of the trumpet. Or—recalling that depressingly long list of jazz geniuses who have perished through the use of drugs, booze, and other avenues of self-abuse—we irresistibly recall Buddy Bolden, Bix Beiderbecke, Bunny Berigan, Billie Holliday, Lester Young, Charlie Parker, Bud Powell, Thelonious Monk, Hampton Hawes, Bill Evans, Art Pepper, Chet Baker, and far too many other compatriot spirits (Bradshaw and Holbrook 2007; Gabbard 2008).

It follows that, for the biographical depiction of a jazz musician to qualify as true tragedy, this jazz biopic must manage to convey the elevated stature of its artistic hero or heroine before portraying that character's downfall or untimely end. Put differently, tragedy requires that the sense of exalted greatness must precede the recognition of ultimate doom.

From this viewpoint, I shall propose that (unlike the comedepictions considered in Chapter 16) the jazz tragedepictions explored here have tended to misfire in their deployment of ambi-diegetic cinemusical moments that should in theory—but often do not in practice—advance the dramatic development in a meaningful direction. Specifically, where cinemusical episodes should help to establish the exalted greatness of the relevant biopictorial protagonist, these tragedepictions have tended to fail in their use of ambi-diegetic jazz to portray musical genius. From this, as argued earlier, it follows that they have unsuccessfully conveyed the enormity of a great musician's decline from the elevated stature of artistic supremacy. And, failing that, they have fallen short of achieving the heroic proportions of true tragedy but have instead wallowed in the sordid squalor of self-destructive depravity, debility, and degradation. As flawed exemplars of cinemusical motion-picture design—in sharp contrast to the aforementioned cases of successful ambi-diegetic music in jazz comedepictions and elsewhere—these failures in the use of ambi-diegetic jazz have detracted considerably from the dramatic success of all three tragedepictions under consideration. In this connection, for each case, I shall give a brief account of what I take to be the closest thing we can find to a pivotal ambi-diegetic cinemusical breakthrough and shall indicate why I believe that cinemusical uses of ambi-diegetic jazz have failed to provide the needed dramatic effects in all three of the major tragedepictions portraying the undeniably sad lives of Billie Holiday, of a (Lester)Young-(Bud)Powell-(Dexter)Gordon composite character, and of Charlie Parker. (By the way, though not even remotely falling under the rubric of jazz, similar troubles afflict the recent Oscar- and other award-winning portrayal of Edith Piaf by Marion Cotillard in *La Vie en Rose* [2007].)

## THE CINEMUSICAL DARK SIDE OF AMBI-DIEGETIC JAZZ AND THE FAILURE TO CAPTURE ARTISTIC GENIUS IN THREE TRAGEDEPICTIONS

A number of broad generalizations appear to cover the genre that we refer to here as *jazz tragedepictions*.

First, the dark-sided jazz biopics have typically shown our greatest artistic heroes—Billie, Lester-Bud-Dexter, Bird—under the most sordid and squalid possible conditions. Generally speaking, aspiring toward tragedy, they seek (but, too often, fail) to dramatize the painful decline of a creative genius—a fall from greatness, a long slide from the pinnacle of artistic creativity toward degraded oblivion. Always, the principal agents of this destruction are drugs (Holiday), booze (Young), madness (Powell), illness (Gordon), or all of the above (Parker). And always, the story is almost unbearably painful to watch.

Second, such films follow a paradigm departing drastically from the Jazz-Singer template that characterizes the aforementioned jazz comedepictions (Chapter 16). Specifically—where the comedepiction climbs bravely upward toward success in the manner characteristic of the Dorseys, Glenn Miller, Benny Goodman, Red Nichols, and Gene Krupa—the tragedepiction spirals inexorably downward toward destruction in the manner characteristic of Lady Day, Pres, Bud, and Bird. Here, the relevant paradigm follows a structure that Bourjaily (1987) refers to as *The Story* in which

> a musician of genius, frustrated by the discrepancy between what he can achieve and the crummy life musicians lead (because of racial discrimination, or the demand that the music be made commercial, or because he has a potential he can't reach), goes mad or destroys himself with alcohol and drugs.
>
> (Bourjaily 1987, p. 44; cf. Gabbard 1996, p. 67)

Third, as I shall argue, the jazz-oriented tragedepictions place a more subdued, a miscalculated, or even a cinemusically counterproductive emphasis on the sorts of ambi-diegetic performances that have, by contrast, served as primary exemplars of excellent ambi-diegetic cinemusical design throughout this volume and that I regard as a key topic of interest in the present chapter—chiefly concerned, as it is, with the role of ambi-diegetic jazz in three cinemusical tragedepictions. In this connection, I shall give a brief account of what I take to be the closest thing we can find to a pivotal ambi-diegetic cinemusical breakthrough in each of the major tragedepictions that portray the sad lives of Billie Holiday, (Lester)Young–(Bud)Powell, and Charlie Parker, respectively. In each case, I shall explain why I believe that the relevant ambi-diegetic cinemusical moment fails to establish the protagonist as a credible tragic hero or heroine. Notice that these three films cover a span of two decades in which the Hollywood-style happy-ending comedepiction gave way to the grim-outcome tragedepiction. One might imagine that, during this period, the producers and directors of jazz tragedepictions would refine their craft to a high art. Yet, if anything, these offerings grew more dismal artistically and less successful commercially as the years marched forward. By the time we get to *Bird* (1988), many viewers—especially true jazz fans—might have difficulty forcing themselves to watch.

## Lady Sings the Blues (1972)

Directed by Sidney Furie and loaded with historical inaccuracies from start to finish—some of them encouraged in exaggerated self-reports by Lady Day herself (Gabbard 1996, p. 95; O'Meally 1991, p. 197)—*Lady Sings the Blues* (1972) begins and ends with its heroine Billie Holiday (Diana Ross) at death's door. For nearly two and a half hours, we see Holiday/Ross get raped as a young girl; work in a whore house scrubbing floors as a teenager; graduate to the role of turning tricks as an adolescent prostitute; sing under degrading conditions in a Harlem nightclub; go on the road with a band led by Reg Hanley (James Callahan), whose pianist Harry (Paul Hampton) turns her on to hard drugs; suffer, in America's rural South, the unspeakable indignities of racial discrimination, vicarious lynching, and attacks by the

Ku Klux Klan; struggle valiantly with the problems of drug addiction and substance abuse; cop and fix in the most sordid and squalid ways; sing while stoned, wasted, and otherwise spaced out; collapse on stage; crack up and crash; spend time in sanitariums; suffer from harassment by the police; go to jail and, in a straightjacket, endure horrific withdrawal symptoms; lose her cabaret card and, with it, her right to work in New York City; watch her best friend Piano Man (Richard Pryor, all too loosely modeled on the real-life Lester Young) get beaten to death by some drug dealers; and . . . via ominous anticipatory newspaper headlines . . . die. About every hour or so, Billie/Diana manages to snatch a brief, fleeting moment of happiness—smooching with her impossibly and fictitiously saint-like lover/husband Louis McKay (Billy Dee Williams) or clowning with the musicians on the bus. But, for the most part, she comes across as one of the most thoroughly miserable characters ever to parade across the silver screen. (If all this sounds way too similar to the depressing depiction of Edith Piaf in *La Vie en Rose* 35 years later, I would be the last to disagree.)

In the service of this totally dismal story, Diana Ross (not unlike Marion Cotillard as Piaf) turns in a stunning performance as the doomed singer. Ross does not literally mimic Holiday, but she captures enough of Billie's style—the laid-back rhythm, the reconstruction of melodies, the catch in her voice, the classic beauty, the white gardenia—to give us a faint inkling of the real Lady Day in action. However—for inexplicable reasons that sabotage the film's dramatic success—Holiday/Ross never once gets the opportunity to rear back and let loose with a pivotal ambi-diegetic cinemusical moment of the type that would establish her valid credentials as the greatest vocalist in the history of jazz. Thus—not surprisingly (again, with parallels to *La Vie en Rose*)—Gabbard (1996) concludes that the film does "little to clarify her real gifts as a singer" (p. 97).

Rather, virtually every time Billie/Diana sings, something or someone thwarts a full realization of her artistic powers. Early in the film, she performs as a gangly, awkward, insecure girl ("All of Me," "The Man I Love"). Sometimes her songs are interrupted by various cinematic distractions such as collecting monetary tips ("Them There Eyes"), time-compressing montages drawn from touring on the band bus ("I Cried For You"), or scenes based on moving from one headlining marquee to another ("Our Love Is Here To Stay"). Often, Holiday/Ross sings when she is stoned, wasted, or ill with withdrawal symptoms ("Mean To Me," "Good Morning, Heartache," "Ain't Nobody's Business," "Lover Man"). On "God Bless the Child," Piano Man/Pryor sacrilegiously toots his harmonica. Nor does it help that—at several crucial moments of trial and turmoil—a completely anachronistic soft-rock love theme by Michel Legrand suffuses the nondiegetic underscoring to sabotage the film's dramatic continuity.

In the closest thing we get to an early glimpse of Billie Holiday performing with anything remotely resembling her full command, Billie/Diana sings an emotionally devastating version of "Strange Fruit"—presented via a flash-forward to her older and sadder-but-wiser self at a later stage in her career.

But the majesty of Holiday/Ross on "Strange Fruit" is blurred, clouded, and interrupted by dissolves in which she relives the pain of seeing the body of a lynched black man hanging from a tree while she stares forlornly from the window of the band bus. This scene glaringly falsifies the manner in which "Strange Fruit" was written in 1939—with words and music by the poet Lewis Allan (pen name for Abel Meeropol, a Bronx high-school teacher). But the key point is that, here as elsewhere, the film's cinemusical trickery forces us to focus on the pain and suffering of Billie/Diana's life rather than on the genius of her music.

Later, in what might have provided an opportunity for some sort of elusive but nonetheless well-earned Jazz-Singer-type climax at the film's conclusion, we see Holiday/Ross performing at Carnegie Hall and singing the last few bars of "My Man" followed by a magnificent version of "God Bless the Child." Even though it has taken us 140 minutes to arrive at this point, this scene could have offered a long-delayed but pivotal ambi-diegetic cinemusical moment in the demonstration of Billie Holiday's supreme artistry. But, even while Billie/Diana sings her heart out to stunning effect, the film intentionally thwarts the possibility for such a pivotal ambi-diegetic revelation. Just as Holiday/Ross seems to reach the height of her vocal and interpretive powers, before a rapt audience of devoted admirers representing one of America's great cultural institutions, we see a sequence of distressing newspaper headlines float across the screen. These intrusive news clips tend to eclipse the impact of "God Bless the Child"—telling us that our heroine fails to win a reinstatement of her cabaret card; suffers further police harassment; does more jail time; and dies at the age of 44.

Based on true details from the real Billie Holiday's troubled existence and untimely demise, this finale does in fact make a profound impression. But this impression hinges less on Billie Holiday's gigantic greatness as a singer than on her manifold misfortunes as a person. The film has opted for a strong tragedepictorial effect—the irony of showing distressing news banners framing a moment of triumph—at the expense of failing to create a pivotal ambi-diegetic cinemusical turning point.

Some readers might be inclined to ask, "So what?" What's wrong with making a sad movie that reflects the unhappy life of a drug addict who got hounded to her death by an overzealous New York police force? Nothing, indeed, is wrong with that if all you want to do is make an endlessly pathetic movie about somebody who endures mental breakdowns, suffers from heroin addiction, unsuccessfully struggles with her problems, and perishes. As they say: Life's a bitch and then you die.

But if you want to establish the truly tragic proportions of Billie Holiday's story, you need to show her fall from greatness. You need to establish Holiday/Ross as the most sublime, most respected, and most influential female jazz singer who ever lived—a position of reigning musical supremacy that makes her downward spiral into darkness all the more conducive to the purging of pity and fear. You need to let her shine brightly before you mercilessly extinguish her blaze of glory.

To do that, you would need to take some account of Billie Holiday's actual career—the details of which, strange and puzzling as it might seem, make virtually no appearance in *Lady Sings the Blues*. For example, you might want to depict Billie's luminous work for Columbia Records with such fellow artists as Teddy Wilson, Lester Young, Buck Clayton, and Benny Goodman ("More Than You Know," "Pennies From Heaven," "When You're Smiling," "Back in Your Own Back Yard," and the rest). You might want to show the majesty of her recordings for Commodore ("I'll Get By," "I'll Be Seeing You," "Yesterdays," and so forth). You might even want to reveal the courage of her late-career efforts for Verve ("Trav'lin' Light," "Some Other Spring," "I Thought About You," "Willow Weep For Me," and others) or her final touchingly brave moments of public deterioration, depressingly captured in panoramic stereo by Columbia ("I'm a Fool to Want You," "You Don't Know What Love Is," "But Beautiful," and the like). But—whatever route you chose—you would certainly need to offer some pivotal ambi-diegetic cinemusical representation of Billie Holiday performing as a universally acclaimed artistic genius at the height of her vocal powers.

Such a representation—allowing us to experience the majesty of Billie Holiday as the greatest female jazz singer of all time—would be crucial to the intended dramatic impact of this film. We need to see, hear, and feel the glowing magnificence of (say) "When You're Smiling" with Lester Young before we can fully grasp the enormity of Billie Holiday's dismal decline. But *Lady Sings the Blues* never manages to do that. As a result, its tragic import is squandered on a series of scenes showing sequentially escalating squalor sans surcease.

Only at the very end of *Lady Sings the Blues*, in the concluding Carnegie Hall concert, do we catch a fleeting glimpse that might have qualified as a key pivotal ambi-diegetic cinemusical moment if only it had come about an hour and a half earlier in the film. Specifically, if presented in a straight-forward way, "God Bless the Child" could have served as the crucial ambi-diegetic pivot point. But even here, to repeat, the effect is obfuscated by the melodramatic dance of depressing newspaper headlines. Thus, this scene strikes us as offering much too little, way too late. To venture a comparison, it is as if they made a movie about the sinking of the Titanic in which they took us through three hours of watching the ship go down and then said to us at the very end, just before rolling the final credits, "Oh and by the way, you know, that was a really big boat."

## 'Round Midnight (1986)

Though Lester "Pres" Young—officially designated by Billie Holiday as the "President" of the tenor sax—may not be a household name chez many contemporary listeners (much less among current members of the more general audience for motion pictures), there is no doubt as to his mastery of jazz improvisation and his magisterial influence on succeeding generations of jazz musicians. By virtue of providing a learned dissection and, indeed, a data-driven analysis of Lester Young's style—which ultimately led to a whole school of "cool" saxophone playing (Stan Getz, Zoot Sims, Al Cohn, Jimmy Giuffre, Bill Perkins, Paul "The Vice Pres" Quinichette, Wardell Gray, Lee Konitz, Warne Marsh, Paul Desmond, and countless others too numerous to mention)—Porter (1985) substantiates his view of Pres as "one of the greatest artists in jazz" (p. vii): "It would be no exaggeration to say that the language of modern jazz developed out of the music of Lester Young" (p. xi; see also Delannoy 1993). Similar praise appears in the words (from Young's fellow musician Thad Jones) with which Büchmann-Møller (1990) concludes his comprehensive book on *The Story of Lester Young*: "The path he carved out is being walked on by many people of every instrument" (p. 220).

Yet—like Billie and Bird—Lester ended his days in a downward spiral of tragic proportions. Apparently, Pres abstained from hard drugs such as heroin; but he did consume a vast quantity of tobacco, marijuana, and alcohol—especially a rather disgusting-sounding "mixture of gin and sherry" (Porter 1985, p. 18; cf. Delannoy 1993, p. 191). Toward the end, these addictive habits mushroomed and rendered Lester a pathetic shadow of his former self—a frail and faded remnant of his former glory, who often appeared before audiences in a drunken stupor, unable to execute even the familiar tunes that had won him fame in his early years (Büchmann-Møller 1990). Büchmann-Møller chronicles Young's late-career vicious-cycle episodes involving drunkenness at concerts in general and at appearances for Jazz at the Philharmonic (JATP) in particular, quoting others who saw Pres perform at about this time to compile a relentlessly distressing description: "The minutes he spent on stage were among the most embarrassing I have experienced in large public gatherings . . . a pitiful parody of himself . . . absent-minded and incoherent . . . a shadow of himself" (1990, p. 188). Ultimately, at age 49—suffering from an escalating combination of illnesses including alcoholism, malnutrition, cirrhosis of the liver, syphilis, heart trouble, horrendous problems with his teeth (compounded by his refusal to see a dentist), maybe paranoia or agoraphobia, depression, schizophrenia, progressive paresis, sporadic epileptic seizures, ulcers, and bleeding esophageal varicoses—having just returned to the USA after a last engagement at the Blue Note in Paris, Pres stopped eating entirely and drank himself to death in his room at New York's Alvin Hotel (Büchmann-Møller 1990, pp. 195 ff.; Delannoy 1993, pp. 181 ff.; Porter 1985, pp. 23 ff.).

During 1956 and 1957, I attended two of the fabled Jazz at the Philharmonic (JATP) concerts that Norman Granz brought to Milwaukee, WI during the height of his activities as a world-beating jazz impresario. Being something of a packrat, I still have the programs from those concerts of a half-century ago—featuring wonderful cover art by David Stone Martin and listing casts of characters that were nothing short of amazing. For example, the 1957 JATP—which appeared in Milwaukee on the night of September 28 (Büchmann-Møller 1990, p. 249)—presented a roster of talent grouped into sets with the following components:

- Lester Young, Sonny Stitt, Illinois Jacquet, Flip Phillips (tenor saxophones); Oscar Peterson (piano); Ray Brown (bass); Herb Ellis (guitar); Jo Jones (drums)
- The Modern Jazz Quartet (MJQ)—John Lewis (piano); Percy Heath (bass); Connie Kay (drums); Milt Jackson (vibraphone)
- Coleman Hawkins (tenor sax); Roy Eldridge (trumpet); members of the MJQ
- The Oscar Peterson Trio (OPT)—Oscar Peterson (piano); Herb Ellis (guitar); Ray Brown (bass)
- Stan Getz (tenor sax); J. J. Johnson (trombone); Jo Jones (drums); members of the OPT
- Ella Fitzgerald—backed, as I recall, by Jo Jones plus the OPT

This, to put it mildly, was quite a line-up. It embraced at least 17 of the greatest musicians in the history of jazz—none greater, of course, than the genius of the tenor saxophone, Lester Young.

At age 14, although I had already worshipfully attended performances by many of the featured artists on the bill in 1957's JATP extravaganza (Phillips, Jacquet, Eldridge, Getz, Stitt, Fitzgerald, the Peterson Trio, and the MJQ), I had never seen Lester in person and therefore waited with eager anticipation for Pres to make his appearance. But what I saw when Young finally took his place on stage gave me something of a shock.

Lester Young emerged from the wings looking like a person at death's door. He walked with a sort of stumbling shuffle that seemed barely sufficient to propel him as far as the microphone located at stage center. When he finally got there, it became evident that he was playing with great difficulty—in a halting, rhythmically disjointed, melodically fractured, harmonically incoherent, tonally off-center manner. No one who saw this sad performance by one of the pioneering geniuses in jazz could have doubted that Pres was on his last legs.

The comparatively recent authoritative biography by Porter (1985) confirms my disillusioning childhood impressions that "His health was poor during the last American JATP" (p. 28): "Young's playing during his last period was inconsistent . . . fluffy and, at times, pathetic" (p. 55). Let's face it. Toward the end, Lester played out-of-tune—flat, as if he did not have the strength to get it up to concert pitch. With specific reference to the 1957 JATP tour that brought Pres to Milwaukee, Büchmann-Møller (1990) reports that "Right from the start . . . he was . . . so weak that he had to be helped out of the hotel into a car so as to be able to perform" (p. 199). Büchmann-Møller (1990) quotes a description of Lester Young at this time offered by the great tenor saxophonist Johnny Griffin: "Prez wasn't in good shape. He was in a very bad condition actually . . . a master deteriorating" (pp. 199–200).

Clearly, this sorrowful saga almost seems to beg for translation into the format of a jazz biopic. Indeed, the sad end of Lester Young in 1959 constitutes about a third of the story behind Bertrand Tavernier's *'Round*

*Midnight* (1986)—a resolutely dark-sided tragedepiction dealing with the demise of a decidedly Lesterian saxophonist named Dale Turner as played by the real-life jazz titan of the tenor sax Dexter Gordon. Many of the mannerisms affected by Gordon in his portrayal of Turner, as well as salient details from Turner/Gordon's life, come directly out of the Pres-related biographical folklore. These include Lester's later-life shuffling walk; his famous porkpie hat; his tendency to prepare meals on a hot plate in his hotel room; his habit of calling other men named X by the epithet "Lady X"; his insistence on the importance of knowing the lyrics to ballads before playing them; and even his early-career habit of holding his horn horizontally (mirrored in a gesture that Dexter makes when acknowledging the applause of an audience). Further, like the real Pres, Turner/Gordon in the film reports unhappy experiences in the U.S. Army (Delannoy 1993, Ch. 17; Porter 1985, pp. 23–25) and contends that his whole life is music (Porter 1985, p. ix). Like Pres, Dale/Dexter lives in the Alvin Hotel (across the street from Birdland) when in New York and returns there to die after an engagement at the Blue Note in Paris (Porter 1985, pp. xxi, 29; Büchmann-Møller 1990, p. 219).

A second major component of the Turner/Gordon character in *'Round Midnight* comes from the life of another great but tragic jazz musician, the influential pianist Bud Powell. Though he was a giant of the bop-piano idiom—in tandem with Thelonious Monk, another great but troubled jazz genius, whose life has been chronicled in a couple of hard-hitting documentary films entitled *Thelonious Monk: Straight No Chaser* (1989) and *Thelonious Monk: American Composer* (1991), respectively—Powell suffered from any number of physical and psychological infirmities, some of which may have resulted from a head injury received when a Philadelphia policeman beat him up in the mid-1940s. At various times in Bud's career and with increasingly debilitating effects as he grew older, these illnesses included mental problems diagnosed as autism or schizophrenia; ill effects from electroshock therapy, including impotence; epilepsy; chronic alcoholism and cirrhosis of the liver; tuberculosis; and, ultimately, fatal pneumonia. Apparently, Powell was intermittently incoherent, withdrawn into a shell, childlike or infantile, and constantly in a befuddled state. As reflected in Tavernier's film, Bud lived for a time during the 1950s with a universally disliked woman named Buttercup, who collected his money, kept him under tight reign, and sedated him with tranquilizers past the point of reason. As also shown cinematically, Powell's liver was so shot that even one or two glasses of wine could flip him over the edge into dementia and put him in the hospital; yet he would shamelessly beg or borrow money for the purpose of going on one of these psychosis-inducing benders. During this period, as further seen in the movie, Powell often could not even recognize his own playing on recordings that he had recently made.

But, on a brighter note that appears as the central focus of *'Round Midnight*, Bud Powell was for a time rescued from his sufferings by the ministrations of a real-life commercial artist and amateur pianist named

Francis Paudras (1998), represented in the film by the character Francis Borler (played by François Cluzet). In the motion picture, as in real life (modeled on Paudras), Borler/Cluzet liberates Turner/Gordon (modeled, in part, on Powell) from the clutches of Buttercup (played by Sandra Reaves-Phillips); moves into a larger apartment to make room for Dale/Dexter; gets the saxophonist back on his feet; helps to restore some of his lost musicianship; makes a comfortable life for him in Paris; returns with him to New York City for an engagement at Birdland; but then—fatefully—goes back to Paris, leaving Turner/Gordon surrounded by drug dealers and other unsavory characters in NYC, where he dies only a short time later. The real-life Bud Powell himself died in 1966 at age 42. Francis Paudras committed suicide in 1998 at age 62, around the time when a translation of his *Portrait of Bud Powell* appeared in America (Paudras 1998).

The third ingredient in the Dale Turner composite makes reference to the life of Dexter Gordon himself. Though not a movie actor by trade, Gordon had appeared previously as a musician in Jack Gelber's play *The Connection* on the West Coast and reappears strikingly in footage assembled for a posthumous documentary entitled *More Than You Know: Dexter Gordon* (1996). The imposing six-foot-five-inch Dexter plays the role of Dale Turner to perfection, partly because much of this role involves saxophone soloing in scenes that were filmed while the musicians were actually performing—making these solos, along with those in Robert Altman's *Kansas City* (1996), among the most realistic cinemusical examples of ambi-diegetic jazz ever created—and partly because Gordon was intimately acquainted with aspects of the composite character he portrays. Himself a major titan of the tenor saxophone during the period following the reign of Lester Young—when Gordon introduced a fusion of Lester's sound with that of such bebop masters as Charlie Parker, influencing the styles of followers like Sonny Rollins and John Coltrane—Dexter had encountered problems with drug abuse during the 1950s; had done some serious jail time that temporarily sidetracked his career; had become an expatriate, first in Paris and later in Denmark (where we heard him in 1964 at the Copenhagen's Club Monmartre); and had even made a celebrated recording called *Our Man in Paris* for Blue Note in 1963 (BST-84146) with none other than Bud Powell on piano and with Pierre Michelot on bass (who accompanied Lester Young during his last engagement at Le Blue Note in Paris and who actually appears as the bassist at the Blue Note during the scenes when Turner/Gordon plays there in the film) (Büchmann-Møller 1990, p. 214; Delannoy 1993, p. 113). Further, Gordon was an ardent admirer of Lester Young, reporting that "when Pres appeared, we all started listening to him alone": "Pres had an entirely new sound, one that we seemed to be waiting for" (quoted by Porter 1985, p. vii). As noted by Büchmann-Møller (1990), "Lester was . . . an inspiration for young saxophone players, one of his most important pupils being Dexter Gordon" (p. 90).

Clearly, Dexter Gordon felt a deep resonance with the character he plays in *'Round Midnight*—both because this character combines facets of musicians he admired and because it reflects aspects of his own life, including those related to drugs, illness, and a tendency to call people "Lady." At the time he made the film, Gordon suffered from a number of physical infirmities (kidney problems, diabetes, cancer), which are apparent in his cinematic persona and which cost him his life only four years later at age 67. It does not seem farfetched to view this motion picture as Dexter's own "Valediction: Forbidding Mourning." Allegedly, after watching *'Round Midnight*, Marlon Brando called Dexter Gordon to say this was the first film in 10 years that had taught him something about acting. We might interpret Brando's tribute as high praise for Gordon's portrayal of Dale Turner—which Yanow (2004) regards as "sincere and effective" (p. 192) and for which Dexter did in fact receive an Oscar nomination.

Though *'Round Midnight* certainly qualifies as a jazz tragedepiction, it differs from the other tragedepictions described here in that its arc temporarily bends ever so slightly upward rather than inexorably downward—until, of course, the ultimate death of its hero at the end, which we do not see on-screen and experience only second-hand via a telegram to Borler/Cluzot. In this, the film becomes—above all else—the story of a rather touching and ennobling friendship between a generous Parisian and the artistic genius he idolizes. Francis/François simply wants the world's greatest sax player to live decently. And the movie tells the tale of Dale/Dexter's limited progress in that direction.

Toward this end, it is important for the pre-Borler/pre-Cluzot enactment of Turner/Gordon to appear spaced-out almost past the point of no return. This he accomplishes in part via his everyday speech patterns (slurred words, hoarsely guttural delivery); his mannerisms (shuffling walk, heavy-lidded eyes); and his obsession with getting a drink (bumming beers from his neighbor "Lady" Ace, played by the vibraphonist Bobby Hutcherson, and trying to sneak a sip from the glass of his pianist Eddie Wayne, played by Herbie Hancock). Further, the impression of Dale/Dexter's initial decrepitude receives considerable strengthening from the ambi-diegetic music during this early portion of the film.

Specifically, in the initial scenes at the Blue Note in Paris (faithfully recreated for the motion picture), Turner/Gordon is accompanied by a quartet featuring Eddie Wayne on piano (Herbie Hancock), Billy Higgins on drums (who worked with Dexter Gordon frequently during the 1960s), Pierre Michelot on bass (frequent cohort of the real Bud Powell), and John McLaughlin on guitar (seeming rather out of place in this context)—to which are added, at different times, various musicians who sit in rather subliminally such as "Lady" Ace on vibes (Bobby Hutcherson), Wayne Shorter on saxophone (an illustrious younger player closely associated with Herbie Hancock), and Eric Le Lann on trumpet (a lesser-known white guy who might be viewed as a stand-in for Chet Baker, whose work appears diegetically on the phonograph in Dale/Dexter's room and who did play frequently in Paris circa the time represented by the film). The formidable rhythm section plus Dale/Dexter performs an agonizingly slow version of "As Time Goes

By"; a very laid-back rain-echoing rendition of an unidentified riff-based blues; a somber "I Love Paris"; the ending to a vibes-enhanced take on Charlie Parker's "Now's the Time"; a dueling- or at least sparring-tenors version of Bud Powell's Latin-flavored "Una Noche Con Francis"; a sad, painfully slow ballad by Herbie Hancock called "Still Time" that is played nondiegetically and during which Dale/Dexter nods off on the bandstand; a low-energy interpretation of "Autumn in New York"; and an intense, tough, endlessly sorrowful reading of "Body and Soul." As he comments on more than one occasion, Turner/Gordon is tired of everything except the music. But music is his life. And there is plenty of it in this film—indeed, plenty that relentlessly displays him to poor advantage as a wasted, burnt-out alcoholic.

Normally, as noted by Nat Hentoff in his liner notes for the *Our Man in Paris* album on Blue Note, Dexter Gordon's tone on ballads could be described as possessing a sort of "gruff lyricism"—that is, as characterized by a soft edge and a gentle but manly vibrato. But, slumped in a chair in his early scenes at the Blue Note and doing his acting through his horn, Dale/ Dexter hits the notes dead-on—giving them a harsh, biting quality hardened by a complete absence of vibrato. He sounds here like a personification of the emotions felt by a man staring with cold recognition into an abyss of futility and sorrow. In the cinemusical framework of this ambi-diegetic jazz, Turner/Gordon has reached rock bottom with nowhere to go but up.

This ascending progress—albeit, at best, to a limited degree—occurs as Turner/Gordon comes under the care of Borler/Cluzet. Slowly but surely, he takes up an interest in conversing, eating, drinking watered-down wine— ultimately giving up alcohol and ordering orange pressé at a café—and tenderly making friends with Francis/François's daughter (asking the young French girl, in a touching evocation of someone trying hard even though he has no clue what to say, if she likes basketball). Dale/Dexter transmogrifies into an immensely gentle towering bear of a man—somehow managing to look sensitive despite his corporeal bulk. His eyes begin to lose their haze. His speech becomes more clear. And, after Borler/Cluzot moves them into a larger apartment, Turner/Gordon sits at the piano composing tunes for his quintet to play.

One such tune provides the closest thing that this film offers to a pivotal ambi-diegetic cinemusical moment—not exactly Benny Goodman at Carnegie Hall, Glenn Miller creating "Moonlight Serenade," or Bing Crosby dueting with Louis Armstrong on "Now You Has Jazz," but at least a small step above ground zero. Specifically, after laboring diligently on Francis/François's piano, Dale/Dexter stands for the first time while he performs at the Blue Note, playing the higher-voiced soprano saxophone on a pretty Gordon-composed waltz called "Tivoli." When contrasted against his earlier dirge-like, seated, and besotted performances of creepingly slow ballads on tenor sax in the same context, the more buoyant and lighter soprano at a brighter tempo seems to float by comparison. So the effect of "Tivoli" is dramatic.

Interestingly, as revealed in Michael Cuscuna's liner notes on one of two soundtrack albums released from this film—entitled *The Other Side of*

*'Round Midnight* (Blue Note BT-85135), the other being *'Round Midnight: Original Motion Picture Soundtrack* (Columbia SC 40464)—this is the *only* ambi-diegetic performance in the film that was *not* recorded live *while* the musicians played. This change from playing to miming seems to detract ever so slightly from the impact of Turner/Gordon's ambi-diegetic performance. But the contrast with his earlier persona is still striking. The mood lifts. And Dale/Dexter seems temporarily to rise not only from his chair, but also from the dark depths of his personal depression.

Admittedly, Dale/Dexter does not rise very far or fly for very long. But he stays aloft just barely long enough to give us a fine performance of "How Long Has This Been Going On?" in Paris. Specifically, still standing but now on tenor in a scene that recalls the celebrated collaborations between Lester Young and Billie Holiday, Turner/Gordon plays supporting obbligatos to a rendition of "How Long?" by a beautiful young light-skinned singer named Darcey Leigh (Lonette McKee, who also appeared in *The Cotton Club*), who wears a white flower in her hair like Lady Day and with whom—like Pres with Billie—he enjoys a relationship that is deep without being physical (Büchmann-Møller 1990, p. 50; Porter 1985, p. 17). This cinematic incident is historically accurate in that Billie Holiday did visit Paris and sit in with Lester Young during his last engagement at the Blue Note (Büchmann-Møller 1990, p. 215). Later, Dale/Dexter masterfully plays the film's title tune, Thelonious Monk's "'Round Midnight," in a French recording studio. And after returning to New York—at a club that appears to be a recreation of the late-1950s Birdland, in a quintet that features Freddie Hubbard (trumpet), Cedar Walton (piano), Ron Carter (bass), and Tony Williams (drums)—Turner/Gordon plays a tender version of a pretty piece composed for his daughter called "Chan's Song" and a challenging brisker-tempo rendition of Monk's "Rhythm-A-Ning." The ability of Dale/Dexter to shine in an American venue in general and at Birdland in particular—however briefly—reflects the partially upbeat success intermittently enjoyed by Lester Young at the JATP concerts and by Bud Powell at Birdland itself. It also gives Turner/Gordon in *'Round Midnight* an evanescent taste of autumnal glory denied to the hero of the third major jazz tragedepiction that we shall consider—namely, *Bird* (1988).

## *Bird* (1988)

But before we address *Bird* (1988), another wannabe jazz tragedepiction requires brief attention—namely, the small-budget film under the direction of Hebert Danska entitled *Sweet Love, Bitter* (1967) that demands consideration as a fringe entry in the jazz-biopic sweepstakes, chiefly because its hero Richie Stokes (Dick Gregory) plays the alto saxophone and has the Bird-like nickname "Eagle." But if an "Eagle" were to a "Bird" as Stokes/ Gregory is to the real Charlie Parker, then an eagle would be about the size of a cockroach or maybe, more politely, a cricket. Put differently, *Sweet Love, Bitter* brings out all the degradation that we might associate with the life of a jazz musician such as Charlie Parker without managing to convey the tiniest smidgeon of the glory in his music. Further, the dramatic arc of *Sweet Love, Bitter* is essentially as flat as a pancake. We *start* with an out-of-work, impoverished, alcoholic, drug-addicted *struggling* jazz musician, and—after an hour and a half of drifting from one squalid scene to the next—we *end* with an out-of-work, impoverished, alcoholic, drug-addicted, *dead* jazz musician. We do not even really know what kills Richie/Dick, beyond the facts that Eagle's health regimen leaves a lot to be desired and that one of his friends says morosely that he died from "resisting reality." Reminiscent of Bud Powell, Richie/Dick gets battered on the head by a policeman. Reminiscent of Billie Holiday, he shoots up at every chance he gets. Reminiscent of Pres, he drinks to the point of oblivion whenever he has enough pocket change from pawning his sax or from hitting on all-too-willing girls who would gladly sleep with him if he took an interest in anything besides drugs. So, in essence, Stokes/Gregory becomes a lifestyle victim—which the film half-heartedly blames on racial discrimination, the only problem being that racial discrimination achieves no real embodiment in this particular film. Eagle's friend Keel Robinson (Robert Hooks) is black and doing quite nicely in running his own coffee house called Sadik's Café, his biggest race-related problem being that he suffers from impotence with his white girlfriend Della (Diane Varsi). By contrast, Eagle's other friend David Hillary (Don Murray) is white and almost as messed up with booze and destitution as Eagle himself. Hence, *Sweet Love, Bitter* fails to push the standard racial "hot buttons" that we usually associate with this type of film.

For us to care about any of this or, indeed, for us to regard Richie/Dick's demise as resulting from any sort of dramatic development, we need to feel that he was as great an artist as his friends—along with the "Eagle" posters that appear here and there on dingy walls—occasionally imply. For that to happen, we need to witness what we are calling a pivotal ambi-diegetic cinemusical moment—a scene that reveals Stokes/Gregory to be an inspired, accomplished, or otherwise gifted jazz musician. For that, we need to see him display his musical talents in a manner that absolutely blows us away. We need to see him demonstrate his artistic genius. We need to see him wail. But this simply does not happen in *Sweet Love, Bitter*—for at least two reasons.

First, the generally excellent film score—composed by the veteran pianist/composer Mal Waldron and played by an estimable cast of musicians that includes Charles McPherson (who ghosts for Dick Gregory on alto sax), Dave Burns (trumpet), Chick Corea (piano), Steve Swallow (bass), and Al Dreares (drums) (Meeker 1981, #3169)—consists almost entirely of non-diegetic background music. In other words, from off-screen, the music effectively reinforces the mood of a scene or highlights the emotional tone of an event, but seldom depicts Richie/Dick ambi-diegetically as an actual working musician. In the description by Gabbard (1996), "Mal Waldron wrote the score for *Sweet Love, Bitter*" where "The use of jazz to fulfill the emotive functions of the background score gives an authenticity . . . that more mainstream jazz films have lacked" (p. 93).

Second, the one ambi-diegetic performance that appears during the course of the film—namely, when Stokes/Gregory borrows a horn and sits in briefly at a local nightclub—utterly fails to establish that Eagle is anything more than a routine journeyman musician. Specifically, with very unrealistic miming by Gregory (who wears a beret, hides behind dark glasses, and looks as if he is somehow playing the saxophone without blowing air through the instrument), Eagle offers a brief solo on an up-tempo tune called "Smokin'" (whose chord changes lack a strong tonal center and therefore bear little resemblance to anything that, say, Charlie Parker would have ever played). So relatively unimpressive is Eagle's music here that various characters talk through the performance—mostly directing their attention to fears that the club will be busted for having a known junkie on its bandstand. At the end of this half-heartedly lackluster ambi-diegetic cinemusical moment, Richie/Dick makes a crack that people must be crazy if they think he'll blow all night as a freebie and walks off the bandstand without even bothering to finish the tune (a potential problem for the other musicians given that he was in charge of playing the dubiously coherent melody). The applause usually heard at the end of a jazz solo, particularly when a guest sits in, is almost imperceptible. Indeed, we do not find ourselves hoping that Eagle will give us more such ambi-diegetic cinemusical moments. And, mercifully, he does not.

How then can we account for the praise bestowed by Gabbard (1996) on the dubbing-and-miming of McPherson-and-Gregory? In this connection, Gabbard insists that "*Sweet Love Bitter* . . . makes excellent use of the alto saxophone of Charles McPherson, who dubs in the sound of Richie's horn": "McPherson's . . . fleet, lyrical dubbings for Dick Gregory . . . offer good reasons why the other two principal characters should be so devoted to keeping the saxophonist alive" (p. 93). But anyone who has watched and listened to this film will find it very difficult to agree with Gabbard's appraisal.

I certainly do agree that this is what we *wish* the ambi-diegetic jazz in *Sweet Love, Bitter* had accomplished. However, I believe that Gabbard's comments apply less to the aforementioned nightclub scene—the one true case of ambi-diegetic jazz in this film—than to the score behind the opening credits, which feature just the hands and fingers of a saxophonist playing some pretty strong musical extemporizations. Indeed, we are probably watching McPherson's fingers here, rather than Gregory's. But the promise of these opening moments never comes remotely close to fruition. And the background music for the credits—what Hagen (1971) or Atkins (1983) might have called "source scoring"—is never really integrated ambi-diegetically into the cinemusical progress of the film itself.

Meanwhile, in a manner reminiscent of *Sweet Love, Bitter* (1967), Clint Eastwood's openly biopictorial *Bird* (1988) presents its highly fictionalized story of Charlie Parker (Forest Whitaker) as one of such unremitting degradation in an atmosphere of such relentless gloom—mirrored to perfection by Jack Green's impenetrably murky cinematography—that we would be unwise or, indeed, foolhardy to show it to (say) a curious teenager as any indication of why Bird was perhaps the greatest musical genius of the Twentieth Century (Russell 1973). Rather, Parker/Whitaker staggers and stumbles his way from one depressing scene to the next—always drunk on alcohol or high on heroin or, most often, wrecked on both at the same time. Seldom does he speak coherently or even intelligibly.

When Parker/Whitaker does flash his impressively rich vocabulary, he talks with a slurred pronunciation. When he does execute a gallant gesture, it requires financing with money that he has obtained by pawning his horn. When he does crack a famously brilliant witticism—telling the doctor that he takes an occasional sherry before dinner—he dies from chronic drug- and alcohol-related pathologies only moments later.

True, Parker/Whitaker shows signs of being a loving father (to his three children); a considerate employer of the white trumpet player Red Rodney (Michael Zelniker); and a witty strategist (passing the russet-locked Rodney/ Zelniker off as a black member of the quintet by calling him "Albino Red"). Indeed, Charlie/Forest adopts a protective attitude toward Red/Michael— strongly discouraging him from trying drugs and becoming furious when the fledgling trumpet player gets hooked.

Gabbard (1996) makes much of the racial aspects of this episode, suggesting that "Parker . . . is more concerned about the white trumpeter's narcotics abuse than about the drug habits of any of his black acquaintances" (p. 89). But I would place less importance on Rodney/Zelniker's race and more emphasis on his age—the fact that, besides being the only white member of the band, he is also the youngest. Parker/Whitaker's concern for Rodney/Zelniker seems more paternally than racially motivated.

So Charlie/Forest shows some good qualities. But, counterbalancing those, he cheats on his faithful wife Chan (Diane Venora); shows up late for gigs in California with Dizzy Gillespie (Samuel E. Wright); collapses in a recording studio (after a heart-breaking rendition of "Lover Man"); gets busted often enough to lose his NYC cabaret card (making it impossible to work in New York); and generally tends to screw up just about everything just about everywhere he goes (even musically, as when he spaces out and vacant-mindedly plays "If I Should Lose You" after a string introduction for "Easy to Love"). Ultimately, Charlie/Forest presents the destitute spectacle of a fallen musical giant who cannot even perform legally in the club that was named after him—Birdland.

All that would be painful enough, but—far worse—the film's ambi-diegetic jazz performances provide precious little reason to attribute to Parker/Whitaker the reverence for genius that he so rightfully deserves.

Partly, this predicament results from some rather questionable editorial decisions—as when Bird's famous solo on "Now's the Time" is abruptly truncated at midpoint so that Charlie/Forest can clown around on a "blues" sung by the masquerading "Albino" Red/Michael. (And where in all this is Miles Davis, who played on the original recording of "Now's the Time"?)

Partly, the problem reflects the strange sound found on many of the classic Bird solos ("Lester Leaps In," "I Can't Believe That You're In Love With

Me," "Laura," "All of Me," "This Time the Dream's on Me," "Cool Blues," "April in Paris," "Parker's Mood")—where a fancy newfangled technology has been used to remove the original rhythm sections from the soundtrack and to replace them with digitally-recorded contemporary musicians—giving us, in essence, the scratchy low-fidelity original Bird accompanied by a high-tech studio sound supplied by, among others, Monty Alexander, Barry Harris, or Walter Davis, Jr. (piano); Ray Brown, Chuck Berghofer, or Ron Carter (bass); and John Guerin (drums). The result produces a disturbingly phony aural effect wherein the soundtrack captures an inevitably tinny-sounding guy recorded during the 1940s and 1950s in poor fidelity playing with a bunch of contemporary studio musicians presented in glorious 1990s digital stereophonic splendor. Further, as Gabbard (1996) points out, the musicians who accompany Bird on the soundtrack play in a "smoother" style than that of his real-life band mates so that "Parker's difficult music [is] tamed and made more accessible" (p. 88). Thus, the Parker performances appearing in *Bird* come across as distressingly bogus.

Partly, also, the ambi-diegetic jazz in this film suffers from the impression of falseness conveyed by Forest Whitaker's unsuccessful efforts to mime the Charlie Parker solos on alto saxophone. Probably no actor could visually match Bird's greased-lightening articulations in a convincing way—certainly not the actor on display here. Thus, Parker/Whitaker wiggles his fingers rapidly but out of synchronization with the music, takes breaths in the middle of musical phrases, blows where no sound is heard, and fails to show any apparent rhythmic involvement with the music he is supposedly playing so passionately. All this makes the music seem irretrievably dead and gone. Inexplicably, Yanow (2004) claims that "Forest Whitaker does an excellent job of portraying Charlie Parker in *Bird*, fingering his saxophone solos perfectly" (p. 146) with an effect that is "impeccable" (p. 147). I cannot think of a polite way to gloss over this rampant misperception. It is just plain wrong.

But, most of all, the ambi-diegetic jazz in *Bird* disappoints because it so conspicuously fails to convey the essence of Charlie Parker's genius—his path-breaking departures from the past that changed the face of music for all time to come. At one point near the end of the film, in a conversation with Rodney/Zelniker, Parker/Whitaker tries to put his contribution in perspective by mumbling something about finding his style when he started to play little figures that "fit with the song" but that seemed to go "inside [sic] the melody." Then, two days before Christmas 1939, he found a new way to play "Cherokee" by extending its chord changes so that it became a "whole new song," but in a manner that would "still fit." Charlie/Forest thinks of this as a wonderful "Christmas present."

Unfortunately, the closest the film comes to *showing* us the essence of this musical breakthrough—rather than just briefly talking about it in a semi-coherent fashion—comes from a loosely concatenated series of scenes involving a fictitious saxophonist named Buster Franklin (Keith David). As unusually patient viewers might perhaps glean through careful attention to a sequence of flashbacks and flashbacks-within-flashbacks, Franklin/David led the jam session back in Kansas City where a young Charlie Parker was publicly humiliated in a way he never forgets. Specifically, in a first-level flashback, Franklin/David (a musician in the Basie Band) shows up on Fifty-Second Street, where he says he remembers Charlie Parker from eight years ago in Kansas City when the young musician couldn't play even a simple church hymn like "Come To Jesus" in whole notes. Then, in a flashback within this flashback, we cut to the jam session in K.C. with Buster/Keith contemptuously introducing young Charlie Parker (Damon Whitaker) as "Charlie from Just Around." Charlie/Damon launches bravely into an improvised chorus on the chord changes to "I Got Rhythm" at a pretty brisk tempo of 240 beats per minute. He starts off strongly, but loses his harmonic bearings in the bridge. The musicians make faces and, before long, the drummer (Jo Jones in real life, but not identified in the film) picks up a cymbal and throws it at young Charlie/Damon. Buster/Keith, the other musicians, and eventually everyone in the club laugh at the unfortunate youth. Mental visions of this humiliating scene, with the cymbal flying through the air, reappear frequently throughout the movie—presumably, as a partial explanation for Parker/Whitaker's psychological problems.

Meanwhile, returning to the first-level flashback, the self-same Franklin/David walks into the club on Fifty-Second Street where the grown Parker/Whitaker now plays with Gillespie/Wright (who, in a strange casting blunder, bears not the slightest resemblance to the real-life Dizzy). As Buster/Keith enters, we find Bird in mid-flight on a furiously up-tempo version of "Lester Leaps In" in A major—based on the same "I Got Rhythm" chord changes that gave him trouble back in K.C. eight years earlier and that now flash by at a steaming 320 beats per minute with fresh melodic ideas over complex harmonies pouring forth in torrents. By the way, in real life—as represented on this film's CD soundtrack recording for CBS Records (Columbia CK44299)—Bird played the tune in Bb at an even faster 334 beats per minute. In other words, Bird is *cooking*. Unfortunately, Eastwood chooses this moment for some chitchat involving Buster/Keith and a voiceover reflecting the thoughts of Chan/Diane. Hence, the full effect of the degree to which Charlie/Forest shines forth ever so powerfully in this ambi-diegetic performance of "Lester Leaps In" is disrupted and thereby blunted for the film audience. At the conclusion of Parker/Whitaker's amazing solo flight, the onlookers applaud wildly. Buster/Keith gives him a standing ovation. Dizzy/Samuel comes to the microphone and asks the crowd what they think about "Yardbird."

After this episode, in apparent despair, a resoundingly demoralized Buster/Keith leaves the club, walks out onto the nearest bridge, takes his own horn out of its case, asks the instrument what it thinks about "Yardbird," and throws it into the river below. Symbolically, Buster/Keith has gone down in defeat via a cutting contest that has taken eight years to unfold. This complicated and cinemusically fractured scene is the closest we get to an ambi-diegetic pivot point in this particular film. But the effect is so fragmented and so confusingly clumsy that many or even most viewers will miss the point. I, for one, had to watch the film several times before I managed to sort out the significance of the Buster/Keith episode. Moreover, the clarity of the film's message concerning the Buster–Charlie relationship is further obscured when Parker/Whitaker talks to Rodney/Zelniker about getting lost on the bridge to "Cherokee" instead of "I Got Rhythm." Why the script confuses these two very different tunes is anybody's guess.

Many or most will also fail to get the moral when, late in the film, Charlie/Forest stops by the Paramount Theater to hear Buster/Keith play what turns out to be highly commercial but vapidly shrieking saxophone solos in a musically simple-minded pop-schlock band. Parker/Whitaker asks when Franklin/David started playing rhythm 'n' blues. The stage manager corrects him by insisting that Buster/Keith is performing "rock 'n' roll"— that is, the "music of today." While Buster/Keith signs autographs for his adoring fans, Charlie/Forest grabs his jewel-encrusted horn and begins to blow rapid-note Bird-styled improvisations just to see, in his whacked-out words, whether the instrument is capable of playing more than one note. Never, we infer, has Buster/Keith's ridiculous jewelry-studded alto sounded so good.

In short, Franklin/David has sold out; Parker/Whitaker remains true to his art. Buster/Keith is a popular success; Charlie/Forest is a commercial failure. The man who threw his horn in the river is a jerk; Bird is a genius. Buster Franklin is alive, well, and thriving on rock 'n' roll; Charlie Parker is derelict, despondent, and dying.

I conclude that these four interwoven scenes capture the ambi-diegetic cinemusical point of the whole film. But—via fuzzy photography, garbled sound, nonmusical distractions, intrusive voiceovers, convoluted time sequences, and fragmented presentations—they are connected in such a vague and casual way that few viewers will understand their meaning. Or care. Or glean from them any sense of the revolutionary role that Charlie Parker played—the immortal significance that Bird embodied—as a towering genius in the history of American music.

# 16  A Cinemusicaliterary Analysis of the American Dream as Represented By Biographical Jazz Comedepictions in the Golden Age of Hollywood Biopics

## Blow, Horatio, Blow; O, Jakie, O; Go, Tommy, Go; No, Artie, No

### INTRODUCTION

Numerous cultural commentators, social critics, behavioral scientists, business gurus, and other thinkers who guide our understanding of (macro)-marketing theory have portrayed the culture of consumption (Baudrillard 1988), the role of conspicuous consumption (Duesenberry 1949; Goffman 1959; Levine 1988; Packard 1959; Veblen 1899, ed. 1967), the capitalistic ethic (Weber 1930), the embrace of materialism (Holbrook 1999a, 2005d; Twitchell 1999), the equation of possessions with happiness (Lebergott 1993; Rosenblatt ed. 1999), the Romantic turn toward hedonic gratification (Campbell 1987; Hirschman and Holbrook 1982; Holbrook 1991, 1997b), the advertising-dominated consumer consciousness (Ewen 2001; Galbraith 1958), the appeal of luxury (Frank 1999), the exaltation of brand equity (Aaker 1991), the glorification of show business (Brown 2001; Holbrook 2002), the rise of experiential marketing (Berry, Carbone, and Haeckel 2002; Carbone and Haeckel 1994; Holbrook 2000, 2001a, b; 2006b; 2007c, d, e; Holbrook and Hirschman 1982; Milligan and Smith ed. 2002; Pine and Gilmore 1998, 1999; Schmitt 1999; Smith and Wheeler 2002), and other aspects of customer value (Holbrook 1994, 1999b) in ways that leave no doubt concerning the importance of *The American Dream*. The present chapter focuses on a *cinemusicaliterary analysis* of some ways in which this ubiquitous market-driven, capitalism-based, materialism-inspired, consumption-centered ethos in general and its rags-to-riches formulation in particular have intentionally informed or unconsciously shaped the creation of various cultural offerings over the last 150 years.

Specifically, I shall describe some *literary* antecedents in the works by Horatio Alger as a quintessential evocation of the values epitomized by the American Dream and encapsulated in the Horatian *rags-to-riches prototype*. I shall relate this prototype to a *cinematic genre* introduced by *The Jazz*

*Singer* (1927)—the earliest feature-length sound-enhanced motion picture and a vivid reminder of how the first words spoken by characters on the silver screen were embedded in the success-story scenario. Further, as a more sustained illustration, I shall show how this *cinematic ethos* infused the *narrative structure* and on-screen realization of the *musical texts* in comedepictorial jazz biographies in general and in five examples from the golden age of Hollywood biopics: *The Fabulous Dorseys* (1947), *The Glenn Miller Story* (1954), *The Benny Goodman Story* (1955), *The Five Pennies* (1959), and *The Gene Krupa Story* (1959). Finally, as an instructive counterexample, I shall discuss the *contrarian case* of Artie Shaw—an immensely successful bandleader who abandoned what he called "$ucce$$" in the music business to pursue artistic goals as a writer and who explained his reasons for this brave decision in his autobiographical account entitled *The Trouble With Cinderella* (1952).

## THE LITERARY BACKGROUND: BLOW, HORATIO, BLOW

Once upon a time, long before the days of biographical motion pictures on the lives of great jazz musicians, the Nineteenth Century author Horatio Alger (1832–1899) cranked out 135 bestselling dime novels that typically dealt with the rags-to-riches theme wherein—through persistence, patience, and perseverance—a down-and-out lad of humble origins attains the American Dream via the achievement of prosperity and a place of stature in society. After studying with Henry Wadsworth Longfellow at Harvard College, earning a degree from Harvard's Divinity School, and losing his job as minister at a Unitarian Church on Cape Cod due to some alleged pedophilia involving two teenage boys, the young Alger moved to New York, took an interest in the adventures of street urchins, and began to write his soon-to-be-famous virtue-inspiring character-building rags-to-riches sagas. By the time he was finished, his books had sold over 200 million copies (en.wikipedia.org/wiki/Horatio_ Alger,_Jr.; www.stefankanfer.org; www.lib.rochester.edu.).

### Blow, Horatio

Many or most of the Horatio Alger novels follow essentially the same formula wherein (*A*) a young boy languishes in *adversity and poverty*; (*B*) through some watershed act of courage or generosity, he achieves a *breakthrough moment*; and (*C*) this breakthrough results in his elevation to a position of *commendable stature in the community*. I shall call this tripartite structure at the center of the Horatio Stories the *ABC Paradigm*. As encapsulations of the ABC Paradigm, Horatio Alger's titles or subtitles tend to sound quaint or even bathetic by today's standards. For example:

• *Ragged Dick* (1866)
• *Mark the Match Boy* (1869)

- *Luck and Pluck* (1869)
- *Ben the Luggage Boy* (1870)
- *Tattered Tom* (1871)
- *The Telegraph Boy* (1879)
- *From Canal Boy to President . . . James A. Garfield* (1881)
- *From Farm Boy to Senator . . . Daniel Webster* (1882)
- *Abraham Lincoln: the Backwoods Boy* (1883)
- *The Adventures of a New York Telegraph Boy* (1887)
- *The Errand Boy* (1888)
- *The Chicago Newsboy* (1889)
- *The Fortunes of a New York Bootblack* (1890)
- *Jed, the Poor House Boy* (1899)
- *Nelson the Newsboy* (1901)
- *Jerry the Backwoods Boy* (1904)
- *The Story of a Shoe Factory Boy* (1905)
- *Tom, The Boot Black* (1908)
- *The Fortunes of a Young Janitor* (1909)

In one early example of the ABC Paradigm, (A) the hero of *Ragged Dick* (1866) begins ignominiously as an impoverished, ignorant, and semi-literate bootblack, who nonetheless harbors a desire to make himself respectable. One day, after already having begun a self-improvement regimen of learning to read and bathing more regularly, (B) Dick courageously and selflessly dives into the East River to save a small child from drowning. As fortune would have it, (C) the boy's appreciative father—a wealthy businessman— rewards Dick with an excellent job and a promising career such that "Ragged Dick" becomes "Richard Hunter, Esq." The immense popularity of *Ragged Dick* led to a long line of sequels, including those mentioned in the preceding list.

Of special relevance to our present concerns, we find two titles that bear directly on the rags-to-riches dream-fulfilling prosperity-achieving success stories of *specifically musical heroes*—namely, *Phil the Fiddler; or, The Story of a Young Street Musician* (1872) and *The Young Musician; or, Fighting His Way* (1906) (both available from Project Gutenberg @ www.gutenberg. org). Let us consider how these two music-related manifestations of the American Dream as a literary theme reflect the ABC Paradigm.

### *Phil the Fiddler;* or, *The Story of a Young Street Musician* (1872)

In a novel by Horatio Alger, kind-spirited folks are always good-looking; mean people are ugly; villains wear black; and bullies are cowards at heart. Plots unfold in a highly predictable formulaic march toward poetic justice according to the ABC Paradigm. Thus *Phil the Fiddler* proceeds as follows.

(A) **Adversity and Poverty.** Poor Filippo—an unfortunate but handsome 12-year-old Italian child with a smile of rare beauty—has been sold by his heartless father to a ruthless liquor-swilling *padrone* who brutally beats him and forces him to sing and play the violin on the streets of New York, wearing shabby ill-fitting clothes and toiling miserably for 16 hours a day with no pay except three cents for a frugal scrap of bread and a piece of cheese: "Can such things be permitted in the nineteenth century?" (p. 37).

(B) **Breakthrough Moment.** After a bully steals and smashes his fiddle beyond repair, Phil runs away from the tyrannical *padrone*. As Alger editorializes, "Evidently Phil had begun to think, and the essential injustice of laboring without proper compensation had impressed his youthful mind" (p. 39). Phil borrows money from a kind young man, Paul the Peddler, to buy a new violin from the pawnbroker for the laboriously negotiated price of $2.25. His generous benefactor predicts, "You won't be poor always, Phil": "You will be a great player, and give concerts at the Academy of Music" (p. 71). Phil escapes to Newark, NJ. Now he gets to keep the money he earns with his new violin and with "no master to account to" has become "his own employer" (p. 88). Though pursued in vain by the *padrone*'s nephew Pietro, Phil makes friends with an Irish couple and their three stout freckle-faced kids who protect him and who love his music as he plays "tune after tune, to the great delight of the children" (p. 100). Then, one day, Phil happens upon a rural schoolhouse where the attention of a kind teacher makes him ashamed of his ignorance and inspires him to pursue an education.

(C) **Commendable Stature in the Community.** Our hero is befriended and then adopted by a prosperous well-read doctor and his gentle wife, who have tragically lost their only son four years earlier and who save Phil from freezing to death in a snow bank: "We had a boy once, but he is dead. Will you stay with us and be our boy?" (p. 115). Thus, as the result of this fortuitous win-win situation, Phil gets an elegant new wardrobe and a chance to go to school where, making the best of this excellent opportunity, he quickly masters his lessons and learns to speak fluent English. Ultimately, he returns to New York to repay the money he borrowed from Paul the Peddler to buy his violin. By the end, Phil has acquired enough of an education to pass for American, has communicated with his long-lost mother back in Italy, and anticipates "a prosperous career" (p. 118). By contrast, after stabbing somebody in a barroom brawl, the *padrone* lands in Sing Sing.

*Go, Phil.* But, speaking of singing, we find no evidence that Phil ever touches his violin again. Indeed, it deserves notice that Phil the Fiddler—a self-taught violinist, at best, with a repertoire based mostly on popular ditties such as "Shoo Fly" and "Yankee Doodle," to which he seldom even knows the proper lyrics—does not rate as a real musician, even in the eyes of his creator, who views his musical activities as "devoted to a pursuit that did nothing to prepare . . . for the duties of life" (p. 33). Though Phil regards his fiddle as "all-important to him," this is less because of any real love of music and more because it provides "his livelihood" (p. 108) as his "stock in trade" (p. 114). In this bow to commercialism, he resembles Kenny G. more than Kenny Wheeler, Kenny Werner, or Kenny Washington. Phil's musical instrument, unlike that of the true jazz musician, is nothing more than a tool for making money.

## The Young Musician; or, Fighting His Way (1906)

(A) *Adversity and Poverty.* When we first meet young Philip Gray—recently orphaned and left a pauper—the 16-year-old lad is a candidate for the poorhouse. Though Philip is an honorable and popular fellow with a good education, excellent character, a cheerful disposition, and a firm desire to work for his living, Squire Pope—a *"portly"* man of self-approving "im*port*ance" and dignified "de*port*ment" (p. 5) in the rural village of Norton—rather *port*entously prepares to send the hapless boy to the town's residence for destitute derelicts. It happens that Philip is a "fine singer" and plays the violin with "considerable skill" (p. 8), these being talents that appear to be fairly easy to acquire in the Horatian world, though—unlike Phil the Fiddler, who apparently learned to play mostly by osmosis—Philip Gray has actually spent "many pleasant hours in practicing" his instrument (p. 10). Nick Holden—a nasty and therefore ugly fellow who has way too many freckles—seeks to take advantage of Philip's desperate situation by buying his violin for "a trifle" so that he can serenade the young ladies and thereby overcome some of his much-deserved unpopularity. Nick—who immodestly fancies himself "kinder [kind of] smart in business" though Philip knows him to be "a hopeless dunce in school duties" (p. 11), echoing the timeless clash between managerial practice and intellectual curiosity—reveals that his "business" involves the practical project of buying Philip's fiddle and offers him $1.64 for an instrument that originally cost $25.00. When Philip declines to sell his cherished fiddle and refuses to have it included in the auction to pay off his father's debts, having indefensibly declared Philip a pauper, Squire Pope now finds it ridiculous that the boy should own a violin and agrees to sell it to Nick for $2.50. Pay careful attention to these prices, Dear Reader. They matter greatly to the businesslike mind. For example, Squire Pope's willingness to sell a $25 violin for $2.50 brands him as a self-im*port*ant fool who was "surprised to learn that certain violins of celebrated make—such as the Cremonas [Stradivarius]—have sold for thousands of dollars" (p. 25). Impressed with this new knowledge of violin prices, Squire Pope reneges on his deal with Nick, to the great distress of the latter. But, stubbornly, Pope still insists on committing Philip to the poorhouse. As a prisoner in this "dingy-dirty-neglected-slipshod-squalid-unsavory-filthy" establishment, Philip's supper comprises two slices of dry bread, a skimpy piece of cold meat, and a barely sweetened cup of weak tea (pp. 40–41).

(B) **Breakthrough Moment.** With the help of a clothesline brought by his one loyal friend, Frank Dunbar, Philip escapes from his poorhouse prison, spends a comfortable night with Frank's generous parents, and skips town at 5:00 am the next morning to seek his fortune in more propitious climes. After a day's travel of about 40 miles—reduced to his last penny and just in the nick of time—Philip gets his first gig. In a little town that he passes through on weary feet and with a hungry belly, a local man named Abner Webb hires him to replace the fiddler—Paul Beck, an older local fixture who has taken sick—to play for a local dance at the Schoolhouse Hall. Clearly, this awakening to the commercial possibilities of his violinistic craft in the service of dance music represents a breakthrough moment for young Philip: "Philip didn't think it necessary to say that the idea of making money in this way had never occurred to him till this very day" (p. 67). Symptomatic of his new orientation, the view of music making as a "business" where the purpose is to provide customer "satisfaction" appears twice on one page (p. 68). Indeed, Philip practices all the harder as he realizes that his violin is "likely to prove a breadwinner" (p. 69). At Schoolhouse Hall, with his "animated style of playing," Philip demonstrates conclusively that he understands "his business" (p. 72). Earning his "entire capital" of three dollars in this way, he has now become "a professional player" (p. 73). His violin has become "a source of income" rather than "a source of amusement" (p. 74). Clearly, what matters to Alger is not art-for-art's-sake but rather music-as-a-craft and the violin as an instrument (the means) aimed at monetary gain (the end). No sooner does Philip complete his first musical engagement than he finds another "opportunity of earning some money through his faithful friend, the violin" (p. 75). When the 50-year-old violinist Paul Beck—whom Philip has again been hired to replace—rises from his sick bed and angrily bursts upon the scene, we are again reminded that the much younger Philip "understands his business" (p. 79). There ensues a cutting contest that resembles nothing so much as the confrontation portrayed by the Charlie Daniels Band in "The Devil Went Down to Georgia," with Paul Beck (cast as the Devil and clad entirely in black clothing) losing the contest to Philip Gray (playing the role of Johnny in the Daniels song): "When Philip began to play, . . . his delicate touch and evident perfect mastery of his instrument were immediately apparent" (p. 81). Beck—a good enough musician to know that he has been beaten—retires in disgrace. Philip is proclaimed "a genius," earns another three dollars for his trouble, and concludes with elation that he has embarked on a most profitable "money-making business" (p. 99).

(C) **Commendable Stature in the Community.** Philip travels on, gives further concerts, and receives additional adulation from appreciative audiences who greet his performances with "favor" and "applause" (p. 127). When he again encounters Squire Pope, Philip voices the definitive put-down: "You . . . wanted to sell my violin for a good deal less [$2.50] than I have earned in one evening [$10.00]" (p. 130). Interestingly and instructively, despite his success as a wandering fiddler, Philip entertains few aspirations as a professional musician but, rather, regards his violin as just a utilitarian source of income en route to pursuing a business career: "I have only been playing because I needed money, and my violin helped me to a living [but] I want to get a chance to enter upon some sort of business" (p. 133). Forget about any potential dedication to artistic integrity, a love for music, the pursuit of truth and beauty, or art-for-art's-sake. This lad expresses a desire for commercial success via a career that will lead straight into . . . business.

*Go, Philip.* So—like Phil the Fiddler before him—Philip the Young Musician abandons any avocation in the arts and turns instead to an enthusiastic embrace of the capitalistic ethos found in the pursuit of business enterprise. Why aspire to fame on the concert stage when you can seek a larger fortune in the more prosperous world of profit-seeking commerce? Thus, Philip heads toward New York where "there might be some opening for him in its multitude of business houses" (p. 134). Along the way, he meets Henry Taylor—a nice but foolish boy who has run away from home but, quite significantly, whose father is a broker on Wall Street. Recognizing a potential bonanza when he stumbles on it, Philip rescues Henry and escorts him back to New York where Henry's grateful father Alexander Taylor treats Philip as a favored guest in their "fine house on Madison Avenue" (p. 152). Alexander rewards Philip handsomely with both $100.00 and some elegant clothing made by his personal tailor. Moreover—impressed by Philip's excellent influence over his immature son Henry—Alexander sends both boys to school at Doctor Shelley's private academy in Elmwood, CT. Philip, it appears, has embarked on the first stage of a brilliant career.

## Horatio, Blow

As indicated by the two foregoing précis, the Horatio Alger novels were nothing if not cliché-ridden and predictable. Indeed, they have long served as the touchstone for what literary critics regard as formulaic pandering of the most simplistic order. Rarely does Alger rise above the level of what most contemporary readers would regard as bathetic drivel. And his writing style is worse than that—not one solitary spark in the whole lot of it. So, apparently, the Horatian ABC Paradigm needs some complexification and sophisticizing to render it ready for prime time. These further elaborations will appear in the prototype offered by the success story presented in *The Jazz Singer* (1927).

JAZZIN' THE PROTOTYPE OF *THE JAZZ SINGER* (1927):
O, JAKIE, O

## Interlude

Moving beyond Horatio Alger and the ABC Paradigm, as our main illustrations of the American Dream in action, we shall address the mini-genre of the *jazz-based biographical picture* or the *jazz biopic* where the life of some estimable real-life jazz artist is refracted through the lens of an often heavily fictionalized historical dramatization or an all-too-frequently distorted romantic idealization. In this connection, in the Introduction to Part 7, we have already distinguished between two contrasting types of jazz biopics—namely, *tragedepictions* emphasizing the dark side of life in which musicians begin with promise but eventually succumb to irresistible personal demons (Chapter 15), as opposed to *comedepictions* emphasizing the bright side of life in which musicians struggle at first but eventually conquer the forces that resist them (Chapter 16). As explored in the last chapter, the former jazz biopics feature downward spirals and operate in the realm of tragedy. As developed here, the latter jazz biopics—true to the ethos of the American Dream—celebrate upward trajectories and operate in the realm of comedy. Whereas the tragedepictions lead toward death and destruction, the comedepictions move toward success and happiness in a manner anticipated by Horatio Alger's Phil the Fiddler or his Philip the Young Musician.

## Preview

In turning to the success-oriented jazz biopics, we shall see that—especially in the years surrounding the mid-point of the last century—these jazz-based comedepictions appeared in great abundance and portrayed the lives of such noted swing-era icons as Tommy and Jimmy Dorsey, Glenn Miller, Benny Goodman, Red Nichols, and Gene Krupa. As explained in perceptive depth by Gabbard (1996), the comedepictions represented by these particular jazz biopics hark back to the prototypical format provided by *The Jazz Singer* (1927)—"a uniquely American template" (p. 36) that has proven decisive in its influence not only because it was the first feature-length movie with spoken dialogue (via the Vitaphone process) but, even more, because it provided the dramatic model as an "American fable of success" (Carringer 1979, p. 27) on which all subsequent success-story jazz biopics have based their fundamental structure.

## A Modified Précis of the Jazz-Singer Schema

In his insightful analysis, Gabbard (1996) presents an instructive chart that suggests the parallelism between *The Jazz Singer* (1927) and virtually all the other success-oriented jazz biopics or what I am calling comedepictions that have followed (p. 39). In this, he pursues an ideo-socio-political agenda rather different from our focus on the cinemusicaliterary aspects of the relevant ambi-diegetic jazz performances. Specifically, Gabbard (1996) insists that "It may be . . . accurate to think about jazz as *inseparable* from . . . displays of race [and] sexuality" (p. 1); that "race, gender, [and] sexuality . . . are central concerns" (p. 32); and that "In the *Jazz Singer* films . . . these issues dominate an important tradition of American cinema that can be traced into the various jazz biopics" (p. 32). In this connection, he proposes a reading of *The Jazz Singer* (1927) based on its race- and gender-related nuances wherein the film establishes "a set of conventions for narratives about race and Oedipal conflict in which the white hero transcends his ethnic background through success as a popular entertainer imitating African Americans" (p. 37).

I applaud these race- and gender-related insights. But, because my present theme pertains more to the cinemusicaliterary aspects of ambi-diegetic jazz in success-story biopics, I shall bypass some of the sociological (e.g., ethnic) and psychoanalytic (e.g., sexual) aspects and, recalling our earlier analysis of the Horatio Alger prototype, shall propose my own more streamlined précis of the *Jazz-Singer Schema*, as follows:

> As a child from a *downscale* social background *(D)*, a young *hero (H)* shows a precocious aptitude for some *opportunity (O)* such as a career in music. Contrary to these demonstrable gifts, his controlling *parents* or some other set of *pressures (P)* would dictate that the youngster follow a career in an *alternative area (A)*. But the force of *H*'s avocation is too strong. Against powerful opposition from *P*, he pursues his dedication to *O* as well as his devotion to a woman from a more *upscale* social milieu *(U)*, ultimately achieving fulfillment—fame, fortune, familial reconciliation, and romantic bliss—when he triumphs con- spicuously in a sensational display of *success (S)* such as a prosperous career, an impressive performance, or a happy life.

This modified Jazz-Singer Schema expands on the earlier Horatian ABC Paradigm in some key respects. Recall that, in the *ABC Paradigm* from the Horatio Alger novels, *(A)* a young boy languishes in *adversity and poverty*; *(B)* through some watershed act of courage or generosity, he achieves a *breakthrough moment*; and *(C)* this breakthrough results in his elevation to a position of *commendable stature* in the community. If we substitute *(D)* a *downscale* social background for *(A)* adversity and poverty, *(O)* some area of potential *opportunity* for *(B)* the breakthrough moment, and *(U)* a more *upscale* social milieu for *(C)* commendable stature and if we further complicate the picture slightly be expanding *D* to include *DH*, *O* to include *OPA*, and *U* to include *US*, we generate a *DHOPAUS Template* that has characterized the jazz-star biopic since the days of *The Jazz Singer* and that will inform our analysis of the five jazz-hero comedepictions addressed later.

Specifically—extending Gabbard (1996) and elaborating on Horatio Alger—the typical success-story prototype characterizing the American

Dream as presented in the various jazz comedepictions follows a *DHOPAUS Template* whose key elements usually take some form of the following values:

D = a *downscale* social background
H = our *hero*
O = some area of potential *opportunity* such as a career in music
P = a *parent* (authority figure) or some other set of *pressures* (constraints)
A = some *alternative* opportunity, profession, or job
U = a more *upscale* social milieu
S = an arena of *success* such as a prosperous career, an impressive performance, or a happy life

Given its resonance in the popular ethos of the rags-to-riches story—the instantiation of the American Dream—this Jazz-Singer Schema in general or my DHOPAUS Template in particular deserves careful consideration as a source for the mythos that lies behind Hollywood's typical revisionist reconstructions of the lives led by great jazz heroes.

## THE JAZZ SINGER (1927)

As directed by Alan Crosland with Al Jolson in its title role—all too loosely based on an understated and restrained story-and-play by Samson Raphaelson, who hated the melodramatically over-sentimentalized film version (Carringer 1979, p. 20)—*The Jazz Singer* (1927) uses the term "jazz" in ways that may sound somewhat strange to the contemporary ear. Gabbard (1996) rightly insists that the title may reflect norms prevailing in the white community at the time the film was made—namely, the so-called "Jazz Age" or "what was widely considered jazz in the 1920s" (p. 26). Fair enough. But, by the same token, this "Jazz Age" film has precious little to do with what we would today associate with jazz as a form of music (Stowe 1994, p. 132). Rather, Jack Robin (the Jolson character) is a minstrel-style singer who belts out such famous songs as "My Mammy" and "Toot Toot Tootsie, Goodbye." The term "jazz" is here thrown about with the same reckless abandon that permitted the spin-doctors of yesteryear to refer to Paul Whiteman as the "King of Jazz"; that allowed Theodor Adorno to attack a stereotype of "jazz" having everything to do with (say) Guy Lombardo or Lawrence Welk but virtually nothing whatsoever to do with (say) Louis Armstrong or Charlie Parker; and that encourages contemporary schools of dance to advertise something called "jazz dancing" that has no discernible connection with improvisational music or advanced harmonic, melodic, and rhythmic ingenuity. Nonetheless, the careless use of the term "jazz" made for good public relations at the time. And such misrepresentations of jazz for purposes of PR have continued down to the present day. Consider, for example, the otherwise inexplicably viable careers of such jazz-desecrating musicians as Kenny G. and George Winston.

*The Jazz Singer* (1927) itself inspired subsequent remakes (a) in 1953 (with Danny Thomas in the title role); (b) in 1959 (via a television production featuring Jerry Lewis as a clown); and (c) in 1980 (with Neil Diamond as the protagonist). I shall neglect these three follow-up versions— first, because they have little if anything to do with real jazz but everything to do with pop singing or musical comedy and, second, because they are widely regarded by film critics as, respectively, (a) not very good, (b) unavailable, and (c) wretched beyond contempt. For similar reasons, I shall omit discussions of some other biopic films that interest Gabbard (1996) because they reflect the Jazz-Singer Schema—namely, *The Jolson Story* (1946, vaudevillian minstrelsy of the title character personified); *St. Louis Blues* (1958, the composer W. C. Handy); and *La Bamba* (1987, the rock star Ritchie Valens). And with regrets, largely because I cannot find it on amazon.com, I shall even bypass the immortal Warner cartoon *I Love to Singa* (1937) about a family of strigiforms, featuring vocal performances by a just-hatched baby chick named "Owl Jolson."

Further, by contrast with the darker side of jazz-related tragedepictions (Chapter 15), our present focus deals with comedepictions that feature happy outcomes and that emphasize an upbeat rags-to-riches flavor typical of the American Dream—that is, success rather than anguish, life rather than death, celebration rather than mourning, and ascent rather than descent. Thus, as Gabbard (1996) would be quick to point out, it happens that all five of the jazz biopics under consideration here as comedepictions deal with white musicians as opposed to black or other minority artists. As emphasized by Gabbard (1996) and as documented in Chapter 15, films dealing with African-American jazz performers have tended overwhelmingly to present a darker, more tragic side of the musical life in a way that constitutes the very antithesis of the Jazz-Singer Schema. Thus, in general, black jazz musicians such as Billie, Lester-Bud, or Bird have typically been portrayed—even exploited—for the sake of their potential to convey the painful side of artistic integrity, the agony of creation, the price of freedom, or the debasement of the human spirit by drugs and hardship. This dark and bitter side of the jazz world contrasts vividly with the sweetness and light that characterize the five comedepictions of interest in connection with *The Jazz Singer*.

## O, Jakie

In *The Jazz Singer* (1927), reflecting life in a working-class Jewish family on the Lower East Side of New York City early in the last century, the basic aspiration of the father Cantor Rabinowitz (Warner Oland) for his young son Jakie Rabinowitz (Bobby Gordon) is really about as simple and traditional as it gets—namely, that Jakie/Bobby follow the family example by becoming a cantor. The boy's mother Sara (Eugenie Besserer) is more flexible, understanding, and wise. She suffers prodigiously while her inflexible husband throws his patriarchal weight around ponderously.

A family crisis occurs when a busybody neighbor named Moisha Yudelson (Otto Lederer)—also known as the *kibitzer*—sees young Jakie/Bobby pursuing his avocation as a "jazz" singer at the local bar-café. Yudelson/Lederer can't wait to tell old Rabinowitz/Oland, who rushes to the tavern just in time to catch "Ragtime" Jakie/Bobby happily doing a dance step that uncannily resembles the moonwalk while energetically belting out an uninhibited version of Muir-and-Gilbert's "Waiting for the Robert E. Lee" (1912). Furious, to put it mildly, the cantor grabs his kid, drags him home, and prepares to whip him—apparently a regular occurrence in the tyrannical Rabinowitz household. Being a high-spirited fellow, young Jakie/Bobby threatens that, if his father beats him, he'll run away and never return. Oblivious, the old fool whips the boy anyway. So—true to his word, amidst great lamentations from Sara/Eugenie—Jakie/Bobby keeps his promise and flees, taking only a framed photo of his dear old mom for comfort.

## Jackie, O

At this point, we flash forward about 20 years to find our hero as an adult with a new name—Jack Robin (Al Jolson)—trying to make it in San Francisco as a "jazz" singer (still using the term loosely). In a restaurant, Jack/Al sings Leslie-Clarke-Jolson-and-Monaco's "Dirty Hands, Dirty Face" (1923)—a transcendently bathetic song about a little kid who gets soiled in the yard but runs to greet his father returning home from work, as portrayed by the most awesomely pitiable gestures from Jack/Al and excused only slightly by our grudging recollection that the singer's relationship with his own dad is not so hot. The melodrama reaches such outrageous proportions that it prompts a sort of irresistible fascination as we watch a man who looks as if he is about to tear out his throbbing heart with his own bare hands.

Jack/Al follows this amazing spectacle with what, I surmise, are the first words ever audibly spoken in a feature-length motion picture—namely, the ironically appropriate phrase, "You ain't heard nothin' yet." Next, in a dramatic change of pace, he gives us Kahn-Erdman-Fiorito-and-King's "Toot Toot Tootsie" (1922) in what—raising the ante considerably—must surely be one of the funniest singing performances ever brought to the silver screen. We scarcely know whether to laugh or cry.

But the beautiful dancer Mary Dale (May McAvoy)—who arrives in the middle of all this and who apparently is stronger in maternal impulses than in musical taste—is powerfully impressed. There are lots of "jazz" singers, she says, via subtitles; but—putting it mildly—*he* has a *tear* in his voice. Notice that "tear"—printed rather than spoken—can mean both "crying" and "being torn by one's emotions." So it's love at first sight for Jack/Al and Mary/May, who obligingly offers to help him with his career.

Jack/Al begins to pursue this career as a "jazz" singer with a vengeance. He writes letters home to his Dear Mama Sara/Eugenie, who worries that he has fallen in love with a *shiksa*. When Mama shows these letters to Papa, the cantor insists that they now have no son.

After quite a few scenes showing Mary/May and Jack/Al doing their respective entertainment things on the road, Jack/Al gets his big chance to go to New York and star in a Broadway show called *April Follies*. Jack/Al arrives home on his father's sixtieth birthday and visits his mother—giving her a necklace with diamonds and then treating her to an incomparably hokey performance of Irving Berlin's "Blue Skies" (1927) invigorated by his inimitably corny "jazz" phrasing. It is hard not to admire the enormity of this musical desecration.

Unfortunately, the old ogre himself appears at this moment—so cold and looking about a 100 rather than 60 years old—quickly putting a stop to the festively "jazzy" ambi-diegetic musical proceedings. Jack/Al tries to humor his father with a birthday present—namely, a prayer shawl with loud gaudy stripes. However, Papa cannot be placated so easily and—shocked that his son will appear on Broadway—throws Jack/Al out of the house, saying that he never wants to see this "jazz singer" again.

As Jack/Al and Mary/May rehearse for the opening of *April Follies*, word comes that old Rabinowitz/Oland is ill and that Jack/Al is needed to sing the *Kol Nidre* at the synagogue for the Day of Atonement at exactly the same moment when he is scheduled to open on Broadway. This choice might sound like the proverbial no-brainer—especially after Jack/Al declares to Mary/May that *nothing* (not even Mary/May herself) means as much to him as his career (not a particularly clever romantic strategy, by the way, though Mary/May does not seem to mind as much as we might expect). But, despite everything, we are apparently intended to care about the old man. Accordingly, the old busybody kibitzer Yudelson/Lederer and the dear sweet mama Sara/Eugenie pile on the guilt until Jack/Al feels powerfully torn by the cruel dilemma he faces—honor his father and potentially damage his all-important career or adopt a show-must-go-on philosophy and abandon the old cantor in his hour of need.

At this moment of tormented indecision, Jack/Al puts on blackface in preparation for his minstrel-like performance in the dress rehearsal. We see him meticulously wiping the burnt cork onto his cheeks as the lily-white Mary/May watches and counsels him on his responsibility to his career. Gabbard (1996), of course, has a field day with the racist- and gender-related aspects of this scene. But I think he neglects the essential point, which emerges when Jack/Al stares into the mirror and sees his own blackened face dissolve into a vision of his father singing in the synagogue. The point here, I believe, is that—like the force exerted on (real) jazz musicians by the tradition of African-American music—Jack/Al feels powerfully drawn to the music from his own Jewish heritage. I cannot fathom how anyone could interpret this scene in any other way—especially when Jack/Al proceeds to take the stage to sing Silver-and-Clarke's "Mother of Mine, I Still Have You" (1927) and follows this extravagant exercise in filial sentimentality by returning home to comfort his ailing father.

Uncharacteristically—in his last act on this earth—old Rabinowitz/Oland sees the light, pats Jack/Al on his toupee, and tells his son that he loves him.

Thus inspired—amidst pressures from Mary/May and threats that if he does not appear for tonight's performance, he will "queer himself" on Broadway and never get another job—Jack/Al wrestles with the choice between potentially sabotaging his career and breaking an old man's heart. While his mother sits there, praying and lighting candles, Jack/Al lamely points out that he has not sung the *Kol Nidre* since he was a young boy. But in what strikes me as the funniest line in the film, Yudelson/Lederer quickly assures Jack/Al that—apparently, something like riding a bicycle—once one learns the *Kol Nidre*, one never forgets it. Thus, finally, Jack/Al—counting on his muscle memory—decides to sing at the synagogue for Yom Kippur. Thanks to a conveniently located window, his father hears the music, proclaims that they have their son again, and dies a happy man.

So does Jack/Al's career suffer the tiniest consequences from his failure to appear for the opening night of *April Follies*? No way. Rather, instead of contacting their lawyers and suing the derelict performer for every dime in his swollen savings account, the producers obligingly cancel the opening-night performance. The next time we see Jack/Al—in a Hollywood ending added to Raphaelson's original story and play (in which the protagonist chose to remain a cantor)—he has become the quintessential vaudevillian "jazz" singer. Specifically—with the kibitzer Yudelson/Lederer and his mother Sara/Eugenie in the front row of the audience at the Winter Garden—wearing blackface and falling to one knee in his trademark fashion, Jack/Al belts out Lewis-Young-and-Donaldson's "My Mammy" (1918). Mama Sara/Eugenie—flashing one of those million-mile smiles—looks about as happy as it is possible for an elderly Jewish Mammy to look. And Mary/May—apparently unconcerned that she is less important to our hero than his career and implying some sort of favorable romantic resolution—watches admiringly and amorously from the wings.

In sum, we could capture the key ingredients from our précis of *The Jazz Singer* via the basic DHOPAUS Template, as follows:

D = working class, Jewish, Lower East Side ghetto

H = Jakie Rabinowitz (Bobby Gordon) → Jack Robin (Al Jolson)

O = vaudevillian minstrel-style, musically-over-the-top, larger-than-life, in-your-face, down-on-one-knee, bathetically-sentimental belting

P = the domineering Papa Rabinowitz (Warner Oland), a cantor; the sympathetic Mama Sara Rabinowitz (Eugenie Besserer), a *mensch*

A = serving as a cantor

U = well-bred gentile girlfriend, the successful dancer Mary Dale (May McAvoy), who does not mind that Jack/Al's career means more to him than she does

S = father's deathbed blessing; performance by Jack/Al of *Kol Nidre* at the synagogue; triumph at the Winter Garden singing "My Mammy" on one knee while watched by mother Sara/Eugenie in the front row and girlfriend Mary/May in the wings

## THE PATTERN CONTINUES IN FIVE JAZZ BIOPICS: GO, TOMMY, GO

### Preview—Go, Tommy

With the success story of Jack Robin—né Jakie Rabinowitz—as a background, let us now turn to an examination of our five illustrative jazz biopics and inquire how the Jazz-Singer Schema or DHOPAUS Template plays itself out in the stories of Tommy-and-Jimmy Dorsey, Glenn Miller, Benny Goodman, Red Nichols, and Gene Krupa. Various jazz-oriented comede-pictions in general and our five jazz biopics in particular can be described according to this prototype, along lines comparable to what Gabbard (1996) calls "a paradigm for American success stories, regardless of what they are called" (p. 63). We shall briefly examine each film from that point of view.

### The Fabulous Dorseys (1947)

Directed by Alfred Green, *The Fabulous Dorseys* (1947) was something of a pioneer in converting the Jazz-Singer Schema to the world of true-story jazz icons. Perhaps for this reason, this film departs from the format more than any of the other four that we shall discuss subsequently—especially in its tendency to displace the romantic theme onto another otherwise extraneous character Bob Burton (William Lundigan), who woos the Dorseys' quasi-sisterly childhood friend Janey Howard (Janet Blair). This apparently fictitious fabrication complements the rather unsexy personae of the real-life Tommy-and-Jimmy Dorsey (TD and JD), playing themselves with admirable sincerity but with something-less-than-totally-charismatic stage presences.

As suggested by this film, young Tommy and Jimmy Dorsey grew up in a financially-challenged working-class environment in Shenandoah, PA. In the motion picture, their Irish father (Arthur Shields) works in a coal mine and gives music lessons on the side while their Irish mother (Sara Allgood) struggles to keep her stereotypically Irish-tempered family together in something approaching harmonious relations (a caricature cheerfully embraced by this particular film). Teaching young TD and JD the trombone and saxophone, respectively, Mr. Dorsey is a stern taskmaster. Hoping to give these boys the training needed for self-bettering careers in "serious" music so that they can enjoy livelihoods that he never had the opportunity to pursue, he forces his sons to practice their horns for four hours a day and takes away their shoes to make sure that they cannot escape this ordeal by going outside to play. We see TD and JD fitfully rehearsing dreary old hymns in two-part harmony. But, even here, Tommy has a tendency to cut loose with mischievously jazzy variations on the practice regimen. Arguments over this, as well as pent-up frustrations stemming from all sorts of sibling rivalries, cause the boys to fight incessantly while little Janey Howard struggles to keep the peace. Before long, rejecting their father's ambitions concerning "serious" music, TD and JD have embarked on careers in jazz.

With their childhood pal Janey/Janet in tow, TD and JD hit the road with their own band. They suffer the customary biopictorial indignities of poor public acceptance, a car that breaks down incessantly, and a discouraging lack of available gigs. When their pianist walks out, they find pianist-singer-composer Bob Burton (William Lundigan) playing behind silent films in a movie house and recruit him for the band. For Bob/William and Janey/Janet, it is love at first sight—a convenience that frees the film from needing to worry about the cinematically implausible love lives of TD and JD themselves.

When he is not busy wooing Janey/Janet, Bob/William tirelessly composes some truly sappy music—most intrusively, (1) "To Me" (whose exasperatingly sentimental lyrics Janey/Janet sings to ill effect and whose melody serves as the annoyingly insistent theme song for the film) and (2) "The Dorsey Concerto" (which represents Bob/William's classical aspirations, is scored for trombone-and-clarinet plus full orchestra, and commands the composer's diligent attention throughout most of the motion picture). When Bob/William tells Janey/Janet about the concerto, she says that she did not know he was interested in "serious" composition but that he does beautiful things with music and should continue doing them on this "higher plane" (implying that jazz occupies a "lower plane"). Meanwhile, strapped for funds, TD and JD give up the Dorsey Band and take a job with the Paul Whiteman Orchestra, vowing to regroup their own ensemble when conditions permit.

After a period of success with Whiteman, Tommy-and-Jimmy reform their band with Janey/Janet and Bob/William participating as singer and pianist, respectively. TD and JD still argue incessantly over such issues as the correct tempo for Harry Woods' "I'll Never Say 'Never Again' Again" (1935), but the Dorsey Band nonetheless begins to enjoy some commercial success. From afar, Mr. And Mrs. Dorsey are proud of the boys and listen to their records, though the elder Dorsey—stereotypical curmudgeon of an old Irishman that he is—cannot resist complaining that some parts are a little off and that his sons should resume practicing for at least four hours a day, just like the good old days. Meanwhile, Janey/Janet is torn between her sisterly concern for the constantly squabbling Dorsey Brothers and her budding romance with Bob/William.

One night, as cinematic coincidence would have it, the proud Dorsey parents come to hear the TD and JD Band at the Island Casino. This, of course, turns out to be the exact moment when all hell breaks loose. Things begin on a promising note when—proudly wearing her new engagement ring, looking great, and sounding wonderful—Janey/Janet performs a beautifully-sung big-band version of Tomlin-Poe-and-Grier's "The Object of My Affection" (1934). But when a customer requests "I'll Never Say 'Never Again' Again," you can feel trouble coming from a mile away. True to form, Tommy counts it off at what Jimmy regards as the wrong tempo; and, predictably, Jimmy throws a fit. The brothers erupt in yet another fight, to the dismay of Janey, the senior Dorseys, and all concerned.

Pretty soon, Tommy-and-Jimmy are fronting their own individual bands—albeit with smashing success as they rack up hits, win polls, earn newspaper headlines, and garnish praise wherever they go (all shown in the conventional biopictorial montage style). Janey/Janet and Bob/William have been forced to take sides and have gone their separate ways with Tommy's and Jimmy's respective bands. Everybody who loves TD and JD is miserable—especially Mr. and Mrs. Dorsey, who appreciate the success of their boys but who lament their break-up, which Mrs. Dorsey interprets as a symptom of their failure as a family. By contrast, we the viewers actually benefit from the split because we get to see and hear the JD Orchestra performing "Green Eyes" (with Bob Eberly singing a slow-tempo version to set the stage for the altogether irresistible Helen O'Connell doing her celebrated slur- and syncopation-filled up-tempo vocal) and the TD Orchestra playing "Marie" (with excellent trumpet, tenor, and trombone solos and with the famous obbligatos added by all the guys in the band singing together). Musically, both bands are wonderful. But everybody obsesses about trying to get the brothers to end their feud.

After the elder Dorseys fail in their efforts to achieve a reconciliation between their sons, Janey/Janet hatches an elaborate scheme of her own. She steals a copy of Bob/William's concerto and persuades Paul Whiteman to help out by inviting each brother to perform the piece without the other's knowledge. Both accept gladly. But when they arrive at rehearsal and see each other, they both withdraw. Just then, Mr. Dorsey dies—his last wish being to see the boys reconciled and playing together again. Of course, they agree, preparing the way for a closing scene featuring TD&JD in a tandem performance of Bob/William's "Dorsey Concerto" (actually written by Leo Shuken).

Unfortunately, the performance of the "Concerto" is one of the most unintentionally hilarious cinemusical scenes in all of biopicturedom. Specifically—while Bob/William, Janey/Janet, and Mrs. Dorsey watch from neighboring seats—Tommy on trombone, Jimmy on clarinet, and that jolly old "King of Jazz" Paul Whiteman himself with the world's most enormous faux-jazz orchestra on a gigantic stage in a humongous concert hall perform what turns out to be the millennium's shortest "concerto." I clocked the "Dorsey Concerto" at exactly three minutes and fifteen seconds—during which there is precious little time for anything much to happen musically. And precious little does. But a whole lot happens socially. Specifically, (1) the Brothers Dorsey are reunited in rather flatulent Hindemith-inspired harmony; (2) Janey/Janet and Bob/William are reconciled; and (3) Mrs. Dorsey is fulfilled as a mother to Tommy-and-Jimmy and as a friend to Janey/Janet.

Meanwhile, with apparently inadvertent humor, it takes Bob/William an amazingly long time to recognize the 3:15-minute piece on which he has labored for most of his life. Indeed, Bob/William delays until 1:10 to notice that the music sounds familiar and until 1:25 to realize that indeed it is his own composition. The viewer is left to wonder whether Janey/Janet—by far the brightest person in the film—might want to reconsider her commitment to marry this guy. On the evidence presented here, Bob/William appears to be at least a tutti or two short of a full-length symphony.

To summarize schematically in terms of the Jazz-Singer Schema or DHOPAUS Template:

D = working class, Irish
H = Tommy Dorsey (TD, trombone) and Jimmy Dorsey (JD, reeds)
O = first, Dixieland; then, Swing
P = a stern task-master music-teacher father; a doting family-oriented mother; self-imposed problems due to fights stemming from sibling rivalry
A = playing "serious" classical music
U = childhood sister-like playmate Janey/Janet, courted by pianist-singer-composer Bob/William, as a surrogate for a TD- or JD-related romance
S = a joint concert with the Paul Whiteman Orchestra in which, after Mr. D dies, (1) TD and JD are reunited; (2) J/J and B/W are reconciled; and (3) Mrs. D is fulfilled

However embarrassing to the Dorsey clan, the familial details surrounding the brothers' squabbling apparently mirror their real-world relationship with a high degree of historical accuracy. Thus, in his monumental *Lost Chords*, Richard Sudhalter (1999) offers a true-to-life account quite consistent with that found in the film: "Throughout their years as individual bandleaders the brothers maintained an uneasy, on-again, off-again truce; that's probably the only aspect of their story captured with any accuracy in Hollywood's otherwise fictionalized 1947 effort" (p. 380). Hokey as it might seem, the ending to the film actually carries the ring of truth: "After their fashion, they remained loyal to one another, and to their mother, who watched over both with concern—and outlived them both" (p. 381).

## The Glenn Miller Story (1954)

In the fraught-with-emotion world of Anthony Mann's *The Glenn Miller Story* (1954), the music often plays a backstage role in support of the romance between matinee idols Jimmy Stewart and June Allyson, playing the roles of Glenn and his wife Helen, respectively. Gabbard (1996) takes a dim view of Helen/June—characterizing her as "cloyingly wholesome" (p. 83). But I'm guessing that he is too young to remember the degree to which June Allyson was a heartthrob for countless movie fans prior to the days of (say) Kim Novak (my own personal favorite from the succeeding era). June had a sort of pretty, sweet, girl-next-door image that proved quite appealing through a long career (right up to her later-life days of doing television commercials for adult diapers). However, in the film, June's persona is accompanied by highly conventional nondiegetic background scoring that I *would* characterize as "cloying" and that seems to clash with the jazz-related aspects of the Miller career.

Unlike most of the other Jazz-Singer-derived biopics, *The Glenn Miller Story* portrays highly supportive parental figures from the start, though Glenn/Jimmy's father does show an inordinate interest in calculating the enormity of his son's ultimate wealth. Let's see: Revenue from "Moonlight Serenade" = 3 cents per copy multiplied by 800,000 copies sold = $24,000 (a lot of money in those days).

Yes, we see Glenn/Jimmy struggle at the outset—pawning his horn and all that. Yes, we encounter bumps along the road. Yes, we wait . . . and wait . . . for the musical breakthrough to come. But there is always that dreamy-eyed and oh-so-supportive Helen/June to fall back on—until the end, when the plane goes down and Glenn/Jimmy becomes a bona fide War Hero for the ages. Recently, some sensationalistic press coverage has suggested the rather improbable story that "Glenn Miller died of a heart attack in the arms of a French prostitute in 1944 and not, as officially reported, in a plane crash" (quoted and strongly disputed by Lees 1997, p. 2). Wherever the truth may lie, it is safe to say that music lovers of the 1940s and movie audiences of the 1950s would not have imagined such a possibility. Most of us still don't.

There is no need to rehearse every detail of the cinemusicaliterary progress through *The Glenn Miller Story* to that sad-but-proud and ultimately triumphant moment when Helen/June listens to the last radio broadcast. The correspondence to the Jazz-Singer Schema—or, more specifically, the DHOPAUS Template—should be clear for all to admire.

D = a middle-class family of modest means; college educated; but, when we meet him, so impoverished that he has to pawn his trombone and then work in a gas station to get his horn out of hock

H = Glenn Miller (Jimmy Stewart)

O = first, Dixieland; then, Swing

P = pressure to earn a decent living and support his young bride; conflicting pressure from the young bride to remain true to his calling as an "arranger"

A = job in a pit band; offers steady employment, but interferes with the search for his own "sound" via writing his own "arrangements"

U = wife, Helen Miller (June Allyson); icon of middle-American WASPish wholesomeness, though her maiden name is not necessarily that of a WASP (Helen Burger)

S = mass popularity during WWII; celebrated contribution to the morale of U.S. soldiers, followed by a premature heroic death

## *The Benny Goodman Story* (1955)

With respect to *The Benny Goodman Story* (1955), written and directed by Valentine Davies, Gabbard (1996) avows that "Once we accept a semantic change from singing to clarinet," this film "becomes an almost transparent reworking of *The Jazz Singer*" (p. 54). Specifically, we encounter the familiar themes of transcending a working-class ethnic background via a musical career and a romantic trajectory that initially meet with parental resistance but that ultimately lead toward liberating the hero from ethnically- and economically-related social constraints via commercial success, public acceptance, and a nuptial liaison with someone from a more upscale social milieu.

Young Benny's parents and music teacher are near-caricatures of immigrant Jews in Chicago. Benny's father has no formal schooling, works as a cutter in a pants factory, and wants his kids to benefit from the education-conferred opportunities that he never enjoyed. Benny's music teacher, Professor Schoepp, begs his pupil not to waste his gift, agreeing with the father that young Benny should "play Mozart." Meanwhile, Benny's mother Dora (Berta Gersten) shares her husband's traditional values concerning "good music" and marrying within one's own social circle.

In the latter connection, Dora/Berta feels that the socioeconomically upscale, ethnically WASPish Alice Hammond (Donna Reed) and the downscale Jewish Benny Goodman (Steve Allen) are like "caviar and bagels." Acting on this misguided conviction, Dora/Berta nearly manages to sabotage their budding romance with her well-meant but ill-timed intrusions. Further, because Benny/Steve's initially preferred type of hot Dixie-based small-group jazz seems to lack popular appeal, he faces strong financial pressures toward going commercial, selling out, and playing stock arrangements in mickey-mouse orchestras to earn a living.

Ironically, Alice/Donna is a bastion of strength through all this. She and her family show not a trace of prejudice toward Benny/Steve's discrepant social status. Moreover, though she comes from a background of wealth-facilitated appreciation of classical music (signified by an admiration of Mozart and a respect for Carnegie Hall), she admires Goodman/Allen's "strange" sort of artistic integrity, follows him around from gig to gig as his biggest fan, and aggressively plays her nurturing role as a sort of lovesick socialite groupie. Those of us who remember with discomfort the old *Donna Reed Show* as an almost embarrassing sop to 1950s television respectability may be surprised to see that the actress is hot as a pistol in this film. This characterization may perhaps subtly reflect the personality of the real-life Alice, who—unlike the Donna Reed character—was a divorcé with a couple of kids when she and Benny got together.

When Benny/Steve finally makes it to the famous 1938 Carnegie Hall Concert—with Alice/Donna arriving at the last minute in response to the belated urgings of Mrs. Goodman (who has finally seen the light)—the band opens with a tune whose title expresses Goodman/Allen's constant need to resist parental and other social pressures toward conformity ("Don't Be That Way"); Harry James solos brilliantly on trumpet ("Shine"); Benny and Co. perform a Dixieland number that evokes their musical roots ("Twenty Years of Jazz," with an image of Kid Ory floating in BG's mind as he plays); Ziggy Elman recalls *The Jazz Singer* by performing his immortal klezmer-inspired trademark ("And the Angels Sing"); Mr. Hammond (Wilton Graff), wearing formal attire, taps his foot appreciatively to the infectious beat laid down by

Gene Krupa ("Sing, Sing, Sing"); Benny/Steve "proposes" to Alice/Donna in front of a concert hall packed with well-dressed patrons by seductively playing "their song" ("Memories of You"); and she answers by eagerly nodding her head in acceptance.

Echoes of the Jazz-Singer Schema seem pretty obvious and not in need of much more elaboration. In the framework of our précis, the DHOPAUS Template:

D = working class, Jewish
H = Benny Goodman (Steve Allen)
O = first, Dixieland; then, Swing
P = a near-caricature of immigrant Jewish parents and teacher who favor good education, classical music, and marrying within the appropriate social milieu; financial pressures toward commercialization
A = getting a good education, playing classical music, and marrying a nice Jewish girl from the neighborhood; earning a decent living by playing stock arrangements in schlock dance bands
U = wealthy, gentile, WASPish Alice Hammond (Donna Reed)
S = the famous 1938 Carnegie Hall Concert—where Benny/Steve's mother watches approvingly (having finally seen the light); Alice/Donna's distinguished parents tap their feet appreciatively (to the infectious beat); and Alice/Donna agrees to wed Benny/Steve (in response to his musical proposal of marriage)

Notice, by the way, that—in real life, as indicated by Sudhalter (1999)—Benny Goodman's parents were considerably more supportive of his jazz career than this revisionist biopic would imply (pp. 557–558). Musicians whose actual parental conflicts bore a closer resemblance to those depicted in *The Benny Goodman Story* would include Ben Pollack (pp. 319–320), Bunny Berigan (p. 489), and Red Norvo (p. 655). All these musicians confronted a typical middle-class resistance to the idea of a son growing up to become a jazz musician—roughly comparable to what one would expect today in the case of a daughter who announces that she wants to be a prostitute or to pursue a career in pornography. On a personal note, I can empathize with this predicament because I experienced similar familial pressures as a young fellow with a strong interest in jazz. The sensible parental advice? Get your diploma(s) first and think about a musical career later. Fortunately, in my case, my music teachers convinced me of my demonstrable lack of talent as a jazz musician before I went too far off the deep end. By the time I had a few diplomas and a job offer in academia, it was too late to turn back (Holbrook 2007b).

## The Five Pennies (1959)

Beyond telling us that the hero's father and teacher is the greatest cornet player in his hometown of Ogden, Utah, Melville Shavelson's *The Five*

*Pennies* (1959) devotes relatively little attention to the family background of Red Nichols (Danny Kaye) and certainly gives no hint of parental hopes for a career outside music; indeed, if anything, we might infer just the opposite. Rather, the film conveys that Red/Danny has emerged from somewhat backward roots in a rural, unsophisticated part of the country and that the primary pressures he feels on his career are economic and family-related in nature. Specifically, he begins with the problem of scuffling to find remunerative and fulfilling work as a musician. Later, blaming himself for his daughter's crippling illness, he feels duty-bound to sacrifice his music career so that he can stay home and take care of her. Ultimately, Red/Danny's success story hinges on his ability to transcend these challenges and to return from his self-imposed exile to a triumphant jam session with . . . Louis Armstrong . . . before pursuing a deservedly successful career as a brilliant jazz musician.

Again, the conformity of *The Five Pennies* to the Jazz-Singer Schema in general and to the DHOPAUS Template in particular seems quite clear:

D = backward roots; rural, unsophisticated Ogden, UT
H = Red Nichols (Danny Kaye)
O = cornet-playing Dixieland pioneer (much-neglected leading trumpeter in early jazz, along with Louis Armstrong and Bix Beiderbecke)
P = at first, harsh economic realities; later, a guilty resolve to stay home and take care of his crippled daughter; self-imposed exile from music
A = at first, unfulfilling gigs in society bands, radio spots, and packaged-goods commercials; later, demeaning hard-hat work in a shipyard
U = attractive, blonde, WASPish Bobbie Meredith (Barbara Bel Geddes), though her real-life name is probably not that of a WASP (Willa Stutzman)
S = family reconciliation; daughter's recovery from her crippling illness; dramatic return to the music business after a frustrating absence; jamming triumphantly with Louis Armstrong

## The Gene Krupa Story (1959)

In *The Gene Krupa Story* (1959), directed by Don Weis, the young hero Gene Krupa (Sal Mineo) comes from a humble working-class Italian-Catholic background in Chicago and feels a deep love for a well-meaning but tyrannical father who wants his youngest son to become . . . a priest. Both the father (John Bleifer) and the mother (Celia Lovsky) disapprove of teenage Gene/Sal's innate affinity for the drums, badgering him mercilessly to give up this errant avocation in deference to his putative calling to the priesthood. Papa Krupa/Bleifer regards the drums as "noise" and viciously punches holes in Gene/Sal's snare and tom-tom.

Only the young, beautiful, well-to-do, Irish-Catholic Ethel Maguire (Susan Kohner) appreciates the inspiration with which Gene/Sal routinely beats the devil out of his drum kit. After hearing Gene/Sal play a smashing Dixie version of "Muskrat Ramble" with some of his pals from Austin High, hooked on his charismatic musical powers, Ethel/Susan courageously stands by him through thick and thin-thinner-thinnest. She always has a stick of gum when Gene/Sal badly needs one—which is surprisingly often. Ultimately—in vivid and ironic contrast to his pious parents—she proves to be his salvation.

Early in the film, young Gene/Sal remains shy, quiet, sweet, and innocent. When, at a rather free-spirited party, a flirtatious vixen tries to tempt him by dropping his gold neck chain down her abundant cleavage and daring him to come and get it, he picks her up, turns her upside down, and bounces her and her bulging breasts like a salt shaker until the chain falls out and onto the grass. Certainly, a provocative scene . . . albeit for mostly non-musical reasons.

When Papa Krupa/Bleifer dies, Gene/Sal promises on his father's deathbed that he will enter the priesthood. Big mistake . . . because, try as he might, Krupa/Mineo just cannot get those jungle rhythms out of his head. Nor, quite understandably, can he shake his attraction to the alluring Ethel/Susan. When Krupa/Mineo finally breaks the news to Mama Krupa/Lovsky that his plans are more musical and less ecclesiastical than she has hoped, his mother freaks out. She just doesn't have a clue. By contrast, Ethel/Susan understands perfectly and follows Gene/Sal to New York, helping to support him while he looks for gigs worthy of his formidable talents.

Gene/Sal's big break finally comes when he gets invited by an old Chicago chum, drummer Davey Tough (Shelly Manne), to a party where the guests of honor include Tommy Dorsey (Bobby Troup) and Red Nichols (as himself). Gene/Sal sits in with the guys just mentioned, blows them away, and begins an upwardly spiraling career as a jazz musician. We see Gene Krupa's well-known moments of success—records, concert posters, marquees, newspaper headlines—flash by in various rapid-fire montages.

But no matter how successful Krupa/Mineo becomes, his mother will not yield—refusing to visit her son and preferring to stay home and pray for him. At one point—during a drum solo on "Cherokee," with mounting resentment, as hundreds of people watch—Gene/Sal puts one of Mama Krupa's demeaning letters on his drum head and ferociously beats it to a pulp. The crowd cheers with wild approval.

All this culminates in an unintentionally hilarious scene at a new super-posh apartment that Gene/Sal has just rented where—anachronistically in the extreme—he simultaneously pursues his post-Goodman plans to launch his own big band (circa 1938) while he greets Bix Beiderbecke (who died in 1931), listens to a song performed by Anita O'Day (who was only 19 years old in 1938 and did not join Krupa's band until 1941), and hosts a small combo playing some progressive jazz (of a vintage common in the mid-1950s). We do not normally expect historical accuracy from Hollywood, but this particular festival of temporal mismatches pushes the fringes into the realm of absurdity (Yanow 2004, p. 162).

As his career ascends, Gene/Sal begins—ever so foolishly—to neglect his guardian angel Ethel/Susan. He dallies with a seductive but musically incompetent singer named Dorissa Dinell (deliciously played to sleazy perfection by Susan Oliver, who gives a superb impression of a songbird getting lost in the middle of "On the Sunny Side of the Street"); takes up the habit of drinking to excess; and—horror of horrors—tries a few puffs on . . . gasp . . . a reefer. Unlike our former president, he does inhale this toke(n) of depravity.

Eventually, Ethel/Susan grows tired of Gene/Sal's transgressions and leaves him. He goes out on his own with his wildly popular big band. But, while on the road, Gene/Sal starts to fall apart, drinking heavily and clumsily dropping his drum sticks at inopportune moments. Then somebody plants a stash of marijuana in Krupa/Mineo's coat pocket. Thus framed for a crime he never committed (Scott 2007, p. 3) and unwilling to plea bargain, he goes to jail, emerges from this ordeal with an undeserved reputation as a drug addict, and finds that no one will give him a decent job. At the nadir of this downward trajectory—while playing in a bedraggled band at a strip joint— he receives a visit from good-old always-angelic ever-loving Ethel/Susan, who persuades him to learn to read music and to apply for a job in a new band that Tommy Dorsey (Bobby Troup) is putting together.

After swallowing his pride and taking a crash course in musical literacy, Gene/Sal approaches Tommy/Bobby in search of a job. Dorsey/Troup has already hired Davey Tough (Shelly Manne) for the drum chair. But they arrange to have Krupa/Mineo join them for a featured spot involving a drum battle with Davey/Shelly.

On the night of the big performance, chomping on a stick of gum thoughtfully provided by the saintly Ethel/Susan, Gene/Sal ascends on a platform from the orchestra pit—like Lazarus rising from the dead—wailing away on "Hawaiian War Chant," which imperceptibly transmogrifies into "Cherokee." Though he nervously begins in a rocky fashion and actually drops one of his drum sticks at a crucial moment, Gene/Sal bounces back, mounts a stellar display of percussive wizardry, blows Davey/Shelly to smithereens (well, OK, this is fiction after all), and triumphantly regains both his public adoration and the affections of the seraphic Ethel/Susan.

Obvious parallels to the Jazz-Singer Schema or DHOPAUS Template appear in *The Gene Krupa Story* for all to behold:

D = working class, Italian Catholic
H = Gene Krupa (Sal Mineo)
O = first, Dixieland; then, Swing
P = devout Italian-Catholic parents; pressure to become a priest
A = entering the priesthood
U = well-to-do Irish-Catholic childhood sweetheart; prim-and-proper but gutsy Ethel Maguire (Susan Kohner)
S = triumphant comeback from his drug-related problems in a drum battle with the TD Orchestra's Davey Tough (Shelly Manne) and a concomitant reconciliation with the angelic Ethel/Susan

## Segue—Tommy, Go

Considering this sequence of five jazz biopics, we experience a satisfying sense—almost reminiscent of John Donne's "A Valediction: Forbidding Mourning"—of returning to the point from which we began. In our series of five comedepictions, young Tommy Dorsey is the first cinemusical hero to break with tradition by playing Dixie riffs on his father's boring etudes. At the end of this jazz-biopic era, Gene Krupa rounds out the picture with a triumphant comeback by playing in a drum battle opposite Davey Tough in front of—none other than—the Tommy Dorsey Orchestra.

Though one of the least assertive of all jazz instrumentalists, Tommy Dorsey has thereby become a cinemusical lightning rod for the jazz-biopic ethos. Meanwhile, *all* of the biopic heroes—Tommy-and-Jimmy Dorsey, Glenn Miller, Benny Goodman, Red Nichols, and Gene Krupa—have played together in various bands led by Red Nichols early in his career. In a sense, this hard-core coterie of jazz luminaries emerges as *the* cornucopia of American music in the first half of the last century. This comment becomes especially valid if we include Artie Shaw (discussed further at the end of the present chapter)—who did not inspire a biopic of his own but who played with Red Nichols, appeared prominently as himself with Fred Astaire in *Second Chorus* (1940), and served as the focus for an Oscar-winning documentary by Brigette Berman entitled *Artie Shaw: Time Is All You've Got* (1985) and the subsequent BBC special called *Artie Shaw—Quest for Perfection* (2003) (Nolan 2010).

With that as background, let us now turn our attention to an appreciation of the pivotal ambi-diegetic cinemusical moments at which each biopic hero displays the manner in which his personal creative style contrasts with what has gone before. Clearly, these dramatically-incisive watershed break-throughs stand as central turning points in each of the relevant films. They purport to show us—by ambi-diegetic cinemusical example—why the accomplishments of the jazz hero matter; why his contribution constitutes greatness; and why his music endures. In each case, this pivotal moment of reversal—this creative efflorescence, this adventurous break with the past—constitutes the musical life-force of the film in question. It therefore behooves us to inspect each with some care.

## PIVOTAL AMBI-DIEGETIC CINEMUSICAL MOMENTS IN FIVE JAZZ BIOPICS

In each jazz comedepiction, there comes a time when—as dramatized by *pivotal ambi-diegetic cinemusical moments*—an old, hackneyed, unimaginative, corny, dull, or otherwise drab style of music gives way to a new, fresh, creative, challenging, exciting, or otherwise brilliant manner of playing that characterizes the approach introduced by the main biopictorial protagonist(s). In each case, this pivotal ambi-diegetic cinemusical moment plays a crucial role in the film's dramatic development. Indeed, in such cases, the role of ambi-diegetic jazz and of its relevant cinemusical meanings becomes the whole point of a motion picture.

## *The Fabulous Dorseys* (1947)

*The Fabulous Dorseys* (1947) begins with an account of the brothers' childhood in which their father (Arthur Shields) browbeats young Tommy (Bobby Warde) and young Jimmy (Buz Buckley) into practicing their trombone and saxophone for hours at a time by taking away their shoes so that they cannot run outside for fraternal fistfights that later blossom into a long-running feud strong enough to thwart their ability to work together. Every so often, to the dismay of more serious-minded musicians (including his slightly older and comparatively straight-laced brother), young Tommy/Bobby takes off and plays syncopated variations on the regimen of scales, arpeggios, and duet exercises that their stern task-master father wants them to practice. This rebellious streak ultimately flowers into the brothers' full-blown jazz credentials.

The turning point arrives when the impecunious elder Dorsey/Shields—desperate for money after losing his job at the coal mine—has pressed young Tommy/Bobby and Jimmy/Buz into service as part of a Saturday-night dance band down at the local tavern, Gorman's Hall, where children would not ordinarily be expected to hang out. Steeped in the tradition of unbearably corny old-fashioned ballads such as the "Turkey Trot," this band plays the schmaltziest tunes in woebegone stock arrangements that sound as if they have been orchestrated by the same guy who wrote the four-voice harmony parts for the *1940 Hymnal*.

When the little Dorsey kids are brought into the tavern to play, some stalwart members of the local community object to the impropriety of allowing small boys to participate in the naughtiness of the dance-hall scene. Mrs. Dorsey (Sara Allgood) courageously defends the honor of her husband and children by means of a proactive attack on the nosiness of her neighbors. But the point becomes moot when young Tommy/Bobby and Jimmy/Buz suddenly cut loose with a pivotally jazzy ambi-diegetic cinemusical performance that rockets the otherwise sedate ensemble into a high-flying Dixieland orbit.

Specifically, "Waltz" begins as a sedate dance number in three-quarter time—with the adult patrons, including the senior Dorseys, wheeling around the room in dreamy oblivion. The stock arrangement of what turns out to be "When You and I Were Young, Maggie" grinds along in the most boring possible manner for one full chorus with Tommy/Bobby playing the saccharine melody on his sweet-sounding trombone. But at the start of the next chorus, Tommy/Bobby swings forth with a trombone break leading to an up-tempo version of the tune in four-four time, with smears and growls that soon egg Jimmy/Buz into a flurry of scintillating clarinet-like obbligatos. I say "clarinet-like" because, through the sonic haze of the poor-quality audio track, Jimmy/Buz *sounds* as if he is playing clarinet or possibly soprano sax even though he is *holding* a tenor saxophone (surely, a low point in the checkered history of dubbing-and-miming verisimilitude). Pretty soon, the whole band (sans Papa Dorsey, who remains on the dance floor) is swinging like crazy, while the audience bobs and bounces around the room in ecstasy.

The tune ends. A moment of suspenseful silence follows. Then, we hear . . . tumultuous applause. Though the boys are only in their pre-pubescent years, we have just watched their musical prospects adumbrated for all to see. Ambi-diegetically and figuratively, their incipient reign as future titans of the swing-band era has begun.

As the film makes clear via its coverage of the young Dorseys' early training and their subsequent breakthrough on this inspired performance of "Maggie," the musical credentials of the real-life Jimmy on reeds and Tommy on trombone—not to mention the excellence of their various big bands—have commanded respect from all observers. Foremost among these, the voluble Sudhalter (1999) finds many nice things to say about older brother Jimmy's work on saxophone: "Jimmy Dorsey . . . was by common agreement one of the most versatile and accomplished saxophonists of his time" (p. 140). Sudhalter (1999) waxes, if anything, even more effusive in his praise for younger brother Tommy Dorsey's performances on trombone: "His work on trombone, polished and consistent, seemed . . . an index of his professional musicianship. . . . The near-universal regard in which he was held throughout the '30s . . . attests to that" (p. 363). Sudhalter (1999) also heaps praise on the excellence of the Jimmy and Tommy Dorsey bands: "There's no disputing that between 1925 and '35 both of them *mattered* in jazz circles" (p. 380).

In this connection, the closest thing to a full-fledged realization of an unabashedly up-beat ambi-diegetic cinemusical jazz performance found in *The Fabulous Dorseys* occurs when the Dorsey-band cohorts—in search of a "real musician"—visit a nightclub where the great pianist Art Tatum is the featured attraction. After Art plays a solo piece, alternating between ad lib and stride tempos, he eases into a medium-tempo blues. Meanwhile, the guys in the Dorsey entourage leave Bob/William and Janey/Janet at their table and get up to join Tatum on the bandstand—TD on trombone; JD on clarinet; Charlie Barnet on tenor; Ziggy Elman on trumpet; Ray Bauduc on drums; plus an unidentifiable guitarist and bass player. After good but low-keyed blues solos by Barnet and Elman, Bauduc takes an eight-bar up-tempo drum break that launches the performance into a revved-up gear and that leads to high-energy solos by TD, Tatum, and JD—followed by a potent two-chorus N'Orleans-styled ensemble, a boisterous trading of two-bar stop-time phrases on the various instruments, and an exciting Dixie-type out-chorus.

In short, this upbeat ambi-diegetic performance fulfills the promise evinced long ago by the precocious Dorsey children in the pivotal cine-musical scene at Gorman's Hall. Beyond doubt, they swing. Besides exposing the audience to some very nice jazz, this elevating ambi-diegetic music echoes the mood established by the film's upward ratcheting of the romantic involvement between Bob/William and Janey/Janet. As the guys prepare to play their powerful blues, Bob/William proposes for the umpteenth time, trying a new spin based on his desire to dedicate his newly completed concerto to Janey/Janet as his wife. Consistent with the happy flavor of the cinemusical occasion that follows . . . Janey/Janet accepts.

## *The Glenn Miller Story* (1954)

*The Glenn Miller Story* (1954) presents a highly-fictionalized, overly-sentimental, Hollywood-style account of a musician more noted for his rather syrupy arranging, his immense popularity, his military heroics, and his tragic death during World War II than for his credentials as a jazz improviser. In my book, this motion picture could be subtitled *The Big Sell-Out* in the sense that Miller—a huge fan of Horatio Alger, by the way (Lees 2007a, p. 3)—forsakes his jazz roots as a Dixie-style trombonist, capable of holding his own with the likes of Louis Armstrong, to pursue a search for his own "sound" as a big-band "arranger" of tunes to which he ultimately learns how to impart a saccharine-but-danceable blandness that becomes wildly popular with the WWII servicemen and the anxious families they leave behind to sit at home, under the apple tree or not, and listen to Miller's morale-building radio broadcasts.

The story has two major themes—the first romantic, the second musical—each hinging on a pivotal scene that deploys an ambi-diegetic cinemusical moment for the purposes of dramatic development. The first involves an encounter with the magnificent Louis Armstrong. The second—of greater concern to our present focus—depicts the emergence of the famous Miller "sound." Let us consider each in turn.

First, though penniless, Glenn Miller (Jimmy Stewart) persuades Helen Burger (June Allyson) to come to New York via train from Colorado, to go straight to the marriage-license bureau, to move directly to a church for a hasty wedding, and—from there—to head to a Broadway show in which he has a job playing for the pit orchestra. It's been a long day for young Helen/June, to say the least. But when the newlyweds arrive back at their inexplicably palatial rooms in the Pennsylvania Hotel (dial PEnnsylvania 6-5000), they enter their suite—conveniently outfitted with such amenities as a grand piano—to find themselves the honorees of a surprise party attended by such luminaries as the great drummer Gene Krupa and the tenor saxophonist Babe Russin. The guests invite the couple to a party up at Connie's Inn in Harlem. Despite Glenn/Jimmy's concern that his bride must be very tired, Helen/June says that she wants to go and that it would be rude to disappoint their friends.

When they arrive at Connie's Inn, Louis Armstrong and his All Stars—Trummy Young on trombone, Barney Bigard on clarinet, Marty Napoleon on piano, Arvell Shaw on bass, Cozy Cole on drums—are holding forth with "Basin Street Blues." Louis plays and sings a couple of slow and soulful choruses and then begins inviting members of the Miller group to sit in. With a short drum solo—accompanied by all of his marvelously expressive facial gestures and impressively flamboyant body language—Gene Krupa (playing his charismatic self) picks up the tempo and propels the band into an up-tempo jam. Barney Bigard and Babe Russin play nice choruses of highly energized N'Orleans-style jazz. Then, Louis calls Glenn/Jimmy to the stand. He borrows Trummy Young's trombone and proceeds to play a fine solo—expertly mimed by Jimmy Stewart to sounds probably dubbed by Murray McEachern or Joe Yukl (Meeker 1981, #1218; Yanow 2004, p. 164). Then, Cozy Cole and Gene Krupa trade fours, duet briefly, and lead the band to a smashing finish.

In this pivotal ambi-diegetic cinemusical moment—via a process that repeats itself in *The Five Pennies* (discussed later), *High Society* (Chapter 2), and *Paris Blues* (Chapter 8)—the character of a white musician gains masculine legitimacy and sexual potency by being paired with the primordial creative energy of Louis Armstrong. Elsewhere in the film, Glenn/Jimmy seems a bit effete, timid, clumsy, stiff, reserved, or—in short—the ultimate WASP. But in this scene, he proves himself capable of sharing the bandstand with the big boys in general and with the great Satchmo in particular. As noted by Gabbard (1996), at this ambi-diegetic cinemusical pivot point, the Miller/Stewart persona gains a strong association with the powerful jazz-oriented masculine aura of Louis Armstrong: "Miller's acquisition of sexual maturity is associated with his acceptance by Armstrong at a Harlem nightclub" (p. 83) . . . "as if Armstrong were preparing him for the sexual initiation of his wedding night" (p. 225; see also Gabbard 2008). The next time we see Glenn/Jimmy, he is waking up in bed—looking very contented—at the Pennsylvania Hotel. Helen/June has been up for hours . . . since 7:00 am . . . doing the ironing.

The second pivotal cinemusical scene of major interest here concerns the discovery of the famous Glenn Miller "sound." Once we get past the endearing love story just described, this musical issue serves as arguably *the* major dramatic theme at stake in the film—certainly the theme of greatest concern to anyone interested in the significance of pivotal cinemusical moments involving ambi-diegetic jazz. Throughout the film, Miller/Stewart has been pursuing an ill-defined, vaguely sensed, tantalizingly-imminent artistic vision repeatedly presaged as the "sound" that he hopes to achieve by means of his "arrangements." From the start, at the pawn shop, we learn that Glenn/Jimmy plays his trombone to earn a living but, at heart, wants to write arrangements for his own band. He has this "idea" in his head that he seeks to realize on music paper. Finally, he manages to sell some arrange-ments to drummer and bandleader Ben Pollack (playing himself), tours on trombone with the Pollack band in the company of his friend and pianist Chummy MacGregor (Harry Morgan), and renews his acquaintance with Helen/June when the band makes a stop in Colorado.

Glenn/Jimmy dismisses Helen/June's tastes in music ("Little Brown Jug") as "tin-ear." She claims she can tell when something is good because she gets a funny feeling on the back of her neck as if her hair were standing on end.

He tells her that he wants to have his own band with its own "sound"—a "personality" that comes from his "arrangements."

When the Pollack band gets to New York, Glenn/Jimmy leaves on good terms and scuffles to make ends meet while still pursuing his arranging dream. After the romantic adventures already described, he supports his young bride by playing in a pit band at the Paramount Theater. Helen/June sees how awful this gig is and encourages him to resume his serious studies. Soon, we see Glenn/Jimmy searching with renewed vigor for "the sound" as he works out material for an arrangement on the piano in their new, little, more-modest-but-cute apartment. Helen/June says that his noodling sounds like a good song and suggests calling it "Moonlight Serenade."

Then, responding to Glenn/Jimmy's itch to do his own arrangements, Helen/June helps him start his own band with $1,842 that she has saved from his pocket change. Financially, the band experiences very tough times on the road—mirrored by the dreary ambi-diegetic music we see and hear them playing, such as a drab version of "Over the Rainbow," to which Helen/June responds by moping around and looking disappointed. Tin ear or not, she's not getting that telling frisson in the back of her neck. While Glenn/Jimmy still searches for the right "combination," the band collapses and Helen/June ends up in the hospital with a miscarriage that renders her incapable of having children.

Feeling guilty, the nice ballroom manager Si Schribman (George Tobias)—who has cancelled Glenn/Jimmy's engagement (because of some little old lady who owns the dance hall and needs to get paid)—offers to finance a new band. Glenn/Jimmy agrees, but only if he can try something "radical." However, "radical" turns out to be more elusive than he has anticipated. We next see him leading a huge aggregation, with four or five of every kind of reed and brass, through a pretty-sounding slow-tempo version of Gordon-and-Warren's "I Know Why (And So Do You)" (1941)—a song, incidentally, that the real Glenn Miller Band played with a vocal by Paula Kelly and the Modernaires in *Sun Valley Serenade* (1941). Glenn/Jimmy is busy bemoaning the fact that this performance still does not embody the "sound" he wants, when the lead trumpet player accidentally jambs his lip with his mouthpiece, cracking open the skin and rendering himself incapable of playing for at least a few weeks. This crisis is particularly serious because, apparently, (1) no other trumpet player exists on the face of the earth who could possibly play this musician's parts and (2) all the band's arrangements are written with a lead performed by this particular injured trumpeter. OK, so this is fiction. But the essential question is . . . what to do?

As with so many other great breakthroughs over the course of history— say, Archimedes in the Bath or Fleming and the Petri dish—an apparent accident leads to the Great Epiphany, a breakthrough moment of Creative Insight, a shattering Eureka Experience. With profound inspiration, Glenn/ Jimmy figures out that—wait a minute—Willie Schwartz could play those trumpet parts on clarinet. All Miller/Stewart has to do is rewrite all the arrangements with a clarinet lead in time to open at the ballroom tomorrow evening.

In a feverish rush of creative energy, Glenn/Jimmy stays up all night— drinking coffee, writing notes on paper, whirling around to try chords on the piano. By morning—after this ordeal of labor pangs—Miller/Stewart has given birth to . . . "The Sound." We now see and hear the Miller Band playing the full-fledged and oh-so-familiar version of "Moonlight Serenade" that served as Glenn's theme song for many years and that commands instant recognition as the hallmark of the Miller style. Success at last. (For a more accurate version of where the Glenn Miller "sound" really came from—which had a lot to do with the talents of Irving Fazola as a clar- inetist—see Lees 2007b, p. 6.)

The pivotal ambi-diegetic cinemusical moment that accompanies this transition to the Miller "sound" is brilliantly calculated to achieve the maximum possible dramatic effect. We begin with the performance of "I Know Why" by the full orchestra with an admirably melodic trumpet lead. We then segue into Miller/Stewart's febrile all-night vigil. As he whirls around like a dervish from paper to piano to paper to piano, we hear snatches of "Moonlight Serenade" in the off-screen background score, played by different sections of the orchestra—first, the rhythm section all alone; next, the trombones by themselves; after that, only the trumpets; then, just the saxophones—each heard separately to reflect what Glenn/Jimmy is thinking orchestrally as he plunks down ambi-diegetic chords on the piano to mirror the cinemusical progress of his thought. Ultimately, these disconnected nondiegetic/ambi-diegetic snippets begin to cohere and flower forth in a full-blown version of the piece as the camera dissolves to Miller/ Stewart leading the entire band in a completely realized performance of their immortal theme song at the rehearsal hall. As the band plays on, further dissolves take us to the ballroom that evening while Helen/June watches appreciatively. Full of justifiable self-satisfaction, Glenn/Jimmy smirks at Helen/June. She watches and listens intently; rubs the back of her neck; realizes what's happening; and . . . smiles. As the music builds to a climax on the last eight bars, the members of the band stand and are greeted by tumultuous applause from the audience of dancers who stop twirling long enough to clap enthusiastically. To which Helen/June replies by explaining that they are cheering "The Sound."

For the myriad devotees of the Glenn Miller Orchestra, I can imagine that this musical experience would be powerful indeed. When, after a night of intense labors, the full Miller Band blossoms forth with its immortal rendition of "Moonlight Serenade," I can understand that the frisson factor for a Miller fan would be pretty high—neck-tingling or possibly hair-raising for even the most tin-eared members of the popular audience *c.* 1954. To someone with a penchant for this style of dance music, the impact of the motion picture's ambi-diegetic cinemusical rendering must have been quite compelling.

Unfortunately for me, I do not share a great enthusiasm for the "sound" that Miller/Stewart has managed to attain by dint of his newly reorchestrated "arrangements." I happen to be a great admirer of Gordon-and-Warren's "I Know Why (And So Do You)" and think that the band sounded way better on "I Know Why" than on the comparatively syrupy "Moonlight Serenade" that follows from Glenn/Jimmy's night of impassioned creativity. Further, I note that for the rest of the film—including performances of relatively more upbeat numbers such as "String of Pearls," "Pennsylvania 6-5000," "Tuxedo Junction," "In the Mood," "Chattanooga Choo Choo," and so forth—Miller's saxophone section appears repeatedly with no hint of the celebrated clarinet lead. This lapse in ambi-diegetic cinemusical continuity dramatically falsifies the import of the much-touted discovery that imparts the dubiously satisfying sweetness to "Moonlight Serenade." Cinematically, it appears to the careful observer that Miller abandoned his musical innovation almost as soon as he discovered it, thereby contradicting the ambi-diegetic cinemusical point of Miller's nocturnal struggles.

The real-life arranging skills of Glenn Miller generate only mixed or subdued enthusiasm during the long course of the massive survey of pre-1950s jazz by Sudhalter (1999). An inventory of terms applied by Sudhalter to various Miller arrangements would include "textural clarity," "occasional clutter," "felicitous touches" (p. 324); "well crafted," "little of the sense of surprise and discovery" (p. 329); "never really takes off," "journeyman work," "nothing to elevate it above the level of a publisher's stock orchestration," "deeply sensitive to the demands of the marketplace" (p. 334); and "fussy . . . orchestration" (p. 497). Despite his book's extraordinary 890-page length, Sudhalter (1999) devotes no separate chapter to the Miller band. Presumably, Sudhalter agrees with the clear-headed assessment offered by a former Miller sideman, Al Klink that "We were all too scared to swing": "Glenn should have lived, and the music should have died" (quoted by Crow 1990, p. ix). To this, Artie Shaw (quoted by White 2004) adds a comment that Miller's band "was a mechanized version of what they call jazz music" (p. 73): "Musically, his was essentially ground-out music—ground out like so many sausages" (p. 180). As described by Stowe (1994), "Miller was above all a businessman, interested in bandleading primarily as a moneymaking venture": "At live engagements, members of the audience would request tunes that the band had broadcast but never recorded; Miller would keep track of such requests and record the most popular numbers" (pp. 120–121). Lees (2007a) agrees that "One thing never questioned is Miller's business acumen": "He was once described as the smartest businessman of any bandleader since John Phillip Sousa" (p. 2). Indeed, the aforementioned Willie Schwartz—a participant in the Miller "sound"—complains to Lees (2007b) that, like Lawrence Welk in later times, the band was "commercial" but "didn't really swing" and "became a bore" (p. 7).

Thus, ultimately, we tend to feel that we have been put through a very laborious process of discovery that leads—pivotal or not—to a rather minimal ambi-diegetic cinemusical payoff. At the end, the musical point of the film has sold out to marketing success and romantic adventure. Tragically, on a flight over war-torn Europe, Miller/Stewart's plane disappears. We watch Helen/June as she listens to the Christmas broadcast of the Miller radio show, with the now-leaderless band performing the program he had planned. As the broadcast begins, in an all-revealing close-up, Helen/June's eyes fill with tears. The announcer introduces a new arrangement done especially for this show by Major Glenn Miller himself. And, as the film ends on an emotionally draining note of quiet desperation, we hear . . . none other than . . . "Little Brown Jug." With a poignant smile of recognition, a misty-eyed Helen/June gazes at a picture of Glenn/Jimmy holding his trombone. She cocks her head, reaches with her hand, and feels the back of her neck.

## The Benny Goodman Story (1955)

In striking contrast to the saga of Glenn Miller, *The Benny Goodman Story* (1955) works hard to emphasize an anti-commercial impulse that fires Goodman's creative drive toward swinging immortality. I have discussed this theme at length elsewhere (Holbrook 1995a; Holbrook and Day 1994). For example, in two early scenes at the small Trombone Club (which features Teddy Wilson as its house pianist), Benny Goodman (Steve Allen) chats with the jazz patron John Hammond (Herbert Anderson), his sister Alice Hammond (Donna Reed), the manager Willard Alexander (Hy Averback), and especially his confreres Teddy Wilson and Gene Krupa (playing themselves) on the subject of the music business, the low popularity of their preferred style of Dixie-based jazz, the possibilities for hot dance music, and—in short—the musicological underpinnings of swing. The musicians puzzle aloud over how the energy of their small-group improvisations might be translated into a big-band format suitable for ballrooms and other dance gigs. These conversations lay the groundwork for the theme of com-mercialization versus artistic integrity that pervades the film—all the more when Alice/Donna says that she respects the latter quality in Benny/Steve.

In a scene that dramatizes the evil excesses of commercialism, we see Goodman/Allen at a fancy restaurant, dutifully playing clarinet in a large mickey-mouse band led by the highly unsympathetic Kel Murray—a symbol in this film for everything schlocky, schmaltzy, syrupy, soggy, or otherwise sappy in the music business and apparently an actual music-business figure whom most musicologists have mercifully forgotten (Sudhalter 1999, p. 561). Typical of this socioeconomically high-toned but musically low-grade supper club, the Kel Murray Orchestra plays a saprogenic waltz-time version of "Let's Dance" to which the dancers—including Alice/Donna in the company of a hopelessly square gentleman escort—twirl around the floor in a near-somnambulant torpor. In a conversation with Alice/Donna, Benny/ Steve expresses his disgust at having to play these putridly sweet arrange-ments. She chides him for not honoring his musical convictions—after which, goaded on by Maestro Murray, he impetuously quits the band, implicitly vowing to break free with his own style.

The ambi-diegetic cinemusical moment that signals this breakthrough comes when Goodman/Allen and Crew form a new swing band and win the audition for a gig on a nationally-broadcast NBC radio show called *Let's Dance* featuring three bands—the other two being Xaviar Cugat (not shown in the film) and Kel Murray (that vile purveyor of musical putrefaction himself). On the initial airing of this program, we see the Kel Murray Orchestra finishing up its segment on a revolving stage. As the announcer thanks Murray for his "fine music in an old tradition" and begins his segue into the next segment, Murray and Co. play their over-ripe rendition of "Let's Dance"—performed as a wilting waltz that features a dreary voicing for harp and celeste supported by a soporific slush of simpering strings.

The revolving stage rotates. Murray mercifully disappears, and the Benny Goodman Band rolls into view with many legendary musicians playing themselves (without much historical accuracy, but with a powerful dramatic impact on the jazz fan's sensibilities)—Buck Clayton, especially noted for his work with the Count Basie Band, on trumpet; Stan Getz, rather anachronistically, on tenor saxophone; Urbie Green, known for his work with Woody Herman, on trombone; Alan Reuss, an authentic Goodman member, on guitar; the musically immaculate Teddy Wilson, a member of the Goodman Trio and Quartet but not the band itself, on piano; and the endlessly energetic Gene Krupa on drums. And suddenly—without missing a beat, performing a bounce-tempo arrangement in the manner familiar to all fans as the classic Goodman rendition—Benny and Co. erupt with their immortal version of "Let's Dance."

Contrary to the usual practice after this tune became the Goodman Band's official theme song—as demonstrated later in the film in a recreation of their triumphant appearance at New York City's Paramount Theater—Benny/Steve and Co. play several choruses of "Let's Dance." Benny/Steve solos powerfully. Steve Allen—an accomplished pianist who studied the clarinet diligently and was coached by Sol Yaged in preparation for this role, thereby preparing himself for an unusually convincing performance—expertly mimes the music dubbed by Goodman himself (cf. Karlin 1994, pp. 42–45). The band's authentic aura shines forth.

Here, the contrast effect comes to the fore with a vengeance. Especially compared with what we have just heard from the woeful Kel Murray Orchestra—that is, a desiccated desecration of the piece—Benny Goodman's performance of "Let's Dance" . . . just . . . *roars*. It *rocks*. It *shakes* the airwaves, *rattles* the speakers in your home-entertainment system, and *rolls* out its sound in a powerful demonstration of quintessential swing. Dude, it *rules*. In short, the Goodman Band sounds as big as a house and projects a powerful ensemble impact that—even after all these years, way beyond tickling the back of your neck—will send shivers up your spine, Dear Reader, if you have but a tiny ounce of patience to experience this pivotal ambi-diegetic cinemusical moment for yourself.

In the film, this broadcast also appeals to Fletcher Henderson (played by Sammy Davis, Sr.), who drives around in a taxi for a while just so he can listen to the music on the car radio. The cab drops Henderson at the NBC studios. Fletcher/Sammy tells Benny/Steve that he likes the band because it plays with real feeling and offers to write some arrangements. This scene, of course, telescopes the history behind one of the more improbable but great musical liaisons in the history of jazz—leading to such celebrated arrangements by Henderson for Goodman as "Sometimes I'm Happy," "When Buddha Smiles," "King Porter Stomp," "Blue Skies," "Down South Camp Meeting," and "Wrapping It Up." According to Feather (1955), "The basic simplicity of [Henderson's] style involved such devices as the pitting of reed against brass section and the use of forthright, swinging block-voiced passages": "The style he popularized, which was virtually synonymous with swing and greatly responsible for the rise of swing music, was soon incorporated into the mainstream of popular music" (p. 158).

Goodman's ultimate commercial successes have sometimes distracted jazz devotees from his remarkable abilities as a musician—a passionate leader and virtuosic soloist in both the big-band and small-group formats (Stowe 1994, pp. 6–9). On this theme, consider the language used by Sudhalter (1999) to describe BG's abilities: "formidable technique" (p. 190); "lift, sharp attack, and an engaging brightness of tone," "formidable . . . talent," "poise, technical mastery, and fluency of expression" (p. 323); "flawless mastery of the clarinet," "a style which soon became an almost universal standard for his instrument" (p. 553); "a clarinet virtuoso," "blinding, seemingly flawless technique," "tone, control, pinpoint accuracy—yet the capacity to remain logical and melodically appealing even at roller-coaster tempos" (p. 555).

From that point forward in *The Benny Goodman Story*, the hero and his band of lusty musical confederates move steadily toward their ultimate triumph at Carnegie Hall. Along the way, they add Lionel Hampton to the mix and form the BG Quartet. Rather refreshingly, in a way, the film (which is all about breaking down ethnic barriers) does not even bother to mention that the BG Trio (with Krupa on drums and Wilson on piano)—later the BG Quartet (incorporating Hampton on vibraphone)—was the first racially integrated group to reach wide exposure in jazz. In a sense, the movie scores points by not making a Big Deal out of Goodman's lack of ethnic biases and freedom from bigotry.

Here, my reading differs somewhat from that of Gabbard (1996), who prefers to focus on Benny/Steve's embarrassingly awkward relationship with Kid Ory (playing himself). In an early encounter, the film implies that the young Benny—without benefit of any practicing or other relevant study— can pick up and flawlessly execute the complexities of Ory's New-Orleans- based style of spontaneity on the spot so that "Immediately, the young clarinetist becomes an accomplished improviser" (Gabbard 1996, p. 55). Even more improbably, the two perform impossibly intricate musical passages in tandem without ever having played together before. Gabbard concludes that "young Benny's easily acquired jazz competence in the scene with Kid Ory is only one of several racist fabrications in . . . the film" (p. 78). Admittedly, this scene is rather insulting to N'Orleans- or Dixie-style musicians who have spent a lifetime mastering an incredibly complex art form. And the film further compounds this offense in Gabbard's eyes when, later on, Ory visits the now-grown Goodman/Allen in Chicago to proclaim that "You have the best band I ever heard anyplace" (p. 55). After thanking Ory rather perfunctorily, Benny/Steve asks Fletcher/Sammy to hold his clarinet and quickly walks over to Alice/Donna, who has just entered. OK— a little rude maybe and, in Gabbard's view, loaded with all sorts of phallic associations concerning Goodman/Allen's "long black instrument" (p. 55). But I think that Gabbard (1996) overlooks several mitigating circumstances that obviate the need to attach an interpretation based on ethnic stereotyping or racist overtones.

First, the initial Ory incident typifies the sort of telescoping by which Hollywood customarily if inaccurately compresses otherwise long-winded and patience-exhausting rites of passage. A similar offense appears near the beginning of *Birth of the Blues* (1941) when the young lad who grows up to be the clarinet-playing protagonist (Bing Crosby) learns to play Dixieland by hanging around Basin Street with some African-American musicians who do not even know he is listening and, amazingly soon, outplays them at their own game (cf. Gabbard 1996, p. 78). Well, the Crosby character has to learn to play somehow or other, doesn't he? And we viewers do not have the patience to sit around and watch while he studies scales, harmony, and counterpoint, do we?

Second, the same sort of preposterously intricate musical rapport in a staggeringly complex arrangement reappears in reverse when the Goodman Trio (Benny, Teddy, and Gene) first sit in with Lionel Hampton to perform a dauntingly up-tempo version of "Avalon." Far beyond anything that could conceivably be accomplished in ordinary jamming, these musicians play an absurdly complicated three-part riff that in the real world would take hours of practice to work out successfully. But, this time, it is the African-American Lionel Hampton and not the white Benny Goodman who is the ridiculously quick study. So, in propounding the inherently insulting concept of jazz musicians as spontaneous cats who rely on sheer intuition to play together in flawless precision, this film is an equal opportunity offender.

Third—though Benny/Steve is inexcusably curt in responding to Kid Ory's warm greeting and effusive praise, perhaps also a little insensitive in asking Fletcher/Sammy to stand there and hold his clarinet for him—he here responds to raging hormones that have little if anything to do with race relations. The facts are that he is passionately devoted to Alice/Donna and that this is the first time he has laid eyes on her since she traveled all the way to Chicago from New York to visit him. What would you do, Dear Reader? Recall that Donna Reed playing Alice Hammond is uncharacteristically sexy in this particular movie. Personally, I would do exactly what Benny/Steve does. I would quickly but politely thank Kid Ory, hand my horn to Fletcher/Sammy, and hurry like mad over to the other side of the room to embrace Alice/Donna.

Fourth, as described in the authoritative study by Sudhalter (1999) with primary reference to New Orleans musicians of the type associated with Kid

Ory, "many early musicians of both races . . . couldn't read a note" (p. 9). Obviously, this did not stop many from playing in an extremely sophisticated manner.

Fifth, it happens that Benny Goodman did mature as a professional musician at an incredibly young age. Indeed, Goodman performed clarinet solos on recordings made by the Ben Pollack band when he was 16 or 17 years old (Sudhalter 1999, pp. 146, 320). Clearly, there is nothing inherently insulting in the notion that young Benny might have impressively jammed with Kid Ory at about this time.

Sixth—at a telling cinemusical moment in the film, when Benny/Steve performs "Twenty Years of Jazz" in a Dixie-style romp at Carnegie Hall— a camera-dissolve flashback shows what transpires in his mind as he plays. What transpires mentally is a vision of . . . Kid Ory. The film thereby acknowledges the profound influence that Kid Ory and other African-American musicians, some of whom are right up there on the stage with BG at Carnegie Hall, have had on the musical evolution of Benny Goodman.

Seventh—as noted earlier—Benny Goodman was the first jazz celebrity to form an inter-racial group (first, the Trio with Teddy Wilson and, later, the Quartet with the addition of Lionel Hampton). In a sense, to repeat, the movie scores points by not making a big deal out of Goodman's lack of ethnic biases and his freedom from bigotry. Clearly, this is just plain not a movie about race relations.

For all these reasons, I believe that trying to position Benny Goodman or his story as racist in intent is a thoroughly lost cause. Inept in a few musical details, yes. Silly in its portrayal of improvisation, certainly. But, I would argue, musicologically rather than politically incorrect.

But other inaccuracies do appear in *The Benny Goodman Story*.

As the film unfolds, Benny/Steve develops a few romantic problems with Alice/Donna having to do with—what else?—his intrusive mother's animadversions to her upscale, WASPish, fastidious, well-bred, prim, proper, patrician heritage. Actually, in real life, Alice was a swinging young divorcé with a couple of kids in tow. But never mind.

In the motion picture, by virtue of his charming personality, Benny/Steve coaxes golden music from the guys in the band. By contrast, the real-life BG was a domineering control freak, hated by virtually everyone who worked for him. But, hey, nobody's perfect. On this point, Sudhalter (1999) comments that "Goodman . . . had his quirks," one of them being "his treatment of his employees, his sidemen": "Since his death in 1986, the latter have come forward in ever greater numbers to tell bandroom tales about his parsimony, his sometimes cruel obliviousness to the feelings of others, his gaucherie" (p. 554). One such teller of bandroom tales is the marvelous jazz bassist and sometime Goodman sideman Bill Crow. In a book entitled *Jazz Anecdotes*, Crow (1990) assures us that "there are at least as many stories about Benny Goodman as there are ex-sidemen from his band" (p. vi): "Benny Goodman . . . was a superior instrumentalist and an extremely successful bandleader [but] was also absent-minded, inscrutable, ruthless, and often infuriating" (p. 255). But when we actually get to the backstage stories themselves, some of them actually seem fairly tame or even endearing. Consider, for example, the tale of woe offered by the great tenor saxophonist Zoot Sims. Apparently, Zoot brought a "big, beautiful apple" to rehearsal, planning to eat it on his lunch break; so Benny called for Zoot to take a long sax solo, during which BG grabbed the tempting apple and ate it himself (Crow 1990, p. 262). Who has such a resentful spirit as not to think that the Goodman prank was really pretty funny? Indeed, a careful reading of Crow (1990) suggests that the most damaging thing Goodman did to people involved a tendency to forget their names—certainly an "absent-minded" or even "infuriating" and pride-wounding insult to one's vanity, but not exactly a "ruthless" act of aggression—which is fortunate for many of us because, as we get older, we tend to do it ourselves. Crow (1992) drums up more ammunition in his sequel entitled *From Birdland to Broadway*. Herein, he describes his experiences on a tour to Russia with the Goodman band in 1962 and reports that Benny "was a little patronizing, . . . would get on different guys about inconsequential things . . . rarely expressed approval, undermined everyone's musical confidence, and rarely seemed to appreciate his best soloists": "Benny eventually made us all unhappy" (p. 195) and "generally made us all feel miserable onstage" (p. 197).

By the time Goodman and Co. arrive at their celebrated rendezvous with destiny in the 1938 Carnegie Hall Concert, he has added Harry James, Ziggy Elman, and Martha Tilton to the band. On film, these cats play and sing with the same fire that some of us remember from wearing out our old copies of the concert on Columbia records when we were kids. Harry James sizzles. Ziggy Elman cooks (miming a solo actually dubbed by Manny Klein based on Elman's own original conception). Gene Krupa does his visually stunning, exquisitely mesmerizing, inexplicably magical thing on drums. Teddy Wilson and Lionel Hampton wail. The band swings like blazes. And Benny/Steve charms Alice/Donna, who is impressed by seeing her man taking charge of such an admittedly distinguished musical event, with one more performance of "their song"—namely, Razaf-and-Blake's "Memories of You" (1930)—which she interprets as a marriage proposal and to which she responds by nodding her head seductively.

Ah, Benny. If only you could have been as charismatic as Steve Allen in your shoes. As noted earlier—in his only major acting role, if you don't count *College Confidential* (1960), and you shouldn't—Allen learned to play the clarinet and worked with Sol Yaged in order to impart the greatest possible verisimilitude to his miming of the solos dubbed by Goodman. In this, to repeat, he achieved near-perfect success, conveying just the right embouchure accompanied by highly believable finger movements. Bravo, Steve.

And, Ah, Benny. If only you could have been as nice to the guys in the band as you were to the members of your immediate family. Everybody agrees that—though, as a bandleader, the real-life Goodman was a jerk—as a family man, he was a loving and sweet guy. Forty-five years after I first saw

*The Benny Goodman Story*, I had a student in one of my classes who is the son of the daughter of the real Alice Hammond by a previous marriage—in other words, the step-grandson of Benny himself. My student's father happened to be the social psychologist Stanley Schachter—a distinguished member of the faculty at Columbia University. Besides a tendency to share loving recollections of his step-grandfather, my student told me a story that I believe the jaundiced members of Benny's band would have cherished.

Specifically, this family used to spend summers in the Hamptons on the East End of Long Island. One day, on the beach at East Hampton, Benny and Stanley were chatting peacefully and standing on the sand in the sun when they heard a voice from behind say, "O-My-God, I've always wanted to meet you and to shake your hand." Pleasingly flattered, Benny whirled around to greet yet another of his countless adoring fans, only to find that the stranger stood there with his hand extended to . . . Professor Schachter. Apparently, the individual in question was a lover of social psychology rather than swing bands.

But there were not many folks like that. During his day—as vividly evoked by the pivotal cinemusical moment featuring the rotating stage and the ambidiegetic performance of "Let's Dance"—Benny Goodman was, quite literally, the King of Swing. Personally, I find it easy to forgive Benny for going a bit overboard in whipping his sometimes recalcitrant band members into shape. If he had never done anything more than just play those amazing clarinet licks on his soaring theme song in *The Benny Goodman Story*, he would have made an indelible contribution to American music.

## The Five Pennies (1959)

During the mid-1950s—before my level of musical sophistication caught up with the challenging sounds of Parker, Gillespie, the Modern Jazz Quartet, Miles, Monk, Sonny, 'Trane, Max-and-Clifford, Mulligan-and-Baker, Brubeck-and-Desmond, Evans-and-Hall, Golson-and-Farmer, Peterson-Brown-and-Ellis, Al-and-Zoot, Shank-and-Almeida, Cannonball and Crew, and all the rest—there was a time when I was still exclusively enamored of the more harmonically accessible swing sounds of the Goodman Band and also some of the even more ancient N'Orleans styles evoked by such musicians as Red Nichols. It happened that my father, a doctor, had a grateful patient named Ewing Dunbar Nunn who ran a small record company in Milwaukee called Audiophile Records and who, when he was not making albums of thunderstorms and things like that to demonstrate the wonders of high fidelity, specialized in recording old Dixieland guys who happened to be traveling through the Midwest. Among these, Nunn's most illustrious visiting jazzman was . . . Red Nichols . . . who recorded two or three albums for Audiophile—one of which remains in my collection and features a superb rendition of "Row, Row, Row."

Now this was music that even somebody not hip enough to unravel the mysteries of the aforementioned bop, hard bop, or cool musicians could still manage to understand and appreciate. One day, riding around in my mother's big blue-and-white Oldsmobile 98 and listening to the car radio, I heard the agonizingly mournful sound of a pure sweet cornet playing the opening lines to "Battle Hymn of the Republic." What a drag, I thought, at first. Sounds as if they are burying somebody down by the levee. But then, in the manner of the old N'Orleans funeral processions, the mood lifted. A down-and-dirty clarinet began to hold forth in a considerably more earthy and scruffy medium-tempo version of the tune—something like what you might hear coming out of a dimly lit honky-tonk at two in the morning on Bourbon Street. Then the drummer suddenly erupted into a few percussive flourishes reminiscent of a marching band, followed by a romping-stomping up-tempo version of "Battle Hymn" that, in its joyously celebratory cornet-trombone-clarinet polyphony, brought an almost palpable elevation to my spirit, tears to my eyes, and tingles to my spine. The performance by Red Nichols and Co. on that "Battle Hymn of the Republic" record cut through me like a knife. I bought the 45-rpm version on Capitol Records and wore it out in endless, blissful, transcendent repetitions on my phonograph.

In retrospect, it seems likely that this recording of "Battle Hymn" was released in anticipation of the biopic called *The Five Pennies* (1959). Melville Shavelson directed this admittedly sentimental portrayal of the great cornetist, played by Danny Kaye with a little help from duets featuring the likes of Louis Armstrong. During the late-1950s, Red Nichols (1905–1965) and countless other traditional artists too numerous to mention were still relatively young men, operating at the peak of their musical powers. Fortunately, there still exist musical treasures out there—patiently awaiting rediscovery after a half-century of neglect—no farther away than the nearest dot.com seller and CD, VHS, or DVD player. Central to the magic of such long-eclipsed but potentially revelatory highlights in connection with Red Nichols is the ambi-diegetic cinemusical moment that plays a pivotal role in *The Five Pennies*.

The ambi-diegetic cinemusical pivot point in *The Five Pennies* occurs during a long sequence of inter-related scenes in which we see Nichols/Kaye perform the great traditional anthem "Indiana"—according to Yanow (2004, p. 1), the first jazz recording ever released (namely, in its version by the Original Dixieland Jazz Band in 1917)—in almost as many different ways as it is possible to play it (short of "Donna Lee," which came later, thanks to Miles Davis and Charlie Parker), culminating in a breathtaking ensemble chorus in which Red/Danny pulls out all the stops and soars on his horn into a state of polyphonic ecstasy. The glory of this concluding musical ensemble is that it retains the spontaneous polyphony—with trombone, clarinet, and trumpet or cornet working against each other in a kind of inspired improvisational counterpoint—that was more or less lost to succeeding generations of jazz musicians, starting with the swing bands (which relied heavily on complex written passages featuring reed and brass sections in riff-based call-and-response antiphony) and continuing right on through bebop or hard bop (with much emphasis on lines played homophonically by a trumpet and saxophone in unison) and beyond (where the fashion has increasingly favored a single soloist's monophony backed by an accompanying rhythm section of bass, drums, and piano or guitar). In other words, the history of jazz has tended to (d)evolve from polyphony (New Orleans) to antiphony (swing) to homophony (bop and hard bop) to monophony (post-bop or free jazz). This path of development does not necessarily represent an upward trajectory. Indeed, I would not blame those who might notice that "monophony" rhymes with "monotony."

In his empyreal *Lost Chords*, citing *Grove's Dictionary of Music and Musicians*, Sudhalter (1999) explains the essence of the *polyphony* or *counterpoint* or *polylinearity* found in the early New Orleans or Dixieland styles as the "interweaving of cornet, clarinet, and trombone" where "the chief interest lies in the various strands that make up the texture, and particularly in the combination of these strands and their relationship to each other and to the texture as a whole" (pp. 13–14). The point is that the glory of traditional jazz involves the symbiotic interweaving of melodic lines above a common harmonic framework—"like a piece of multicolored fabric, each strand easily discernible, but so finely woven together as to be inseparable one from another" (p. 283). The tonal fabric of this "loose, contrapuntally textured music" (p. 384) creates a Gestalt—that is, "a single consciousness compounded of many" (p. 383) and "dependent on the melodic parity of its components" (p. 389). Thus, the New Orleans or Dixieland style entails an interweaving of a strong melody line (usually played on the cornet or trumpet) with a higher obbligato part (most often supplied by the clarinet) and a lower harmonic foundation (generally emanating from the trombone)—perhaps with other harmonic complements filled in by one or two other instruments (such as a tenor or alto saxophone) (p. 732). Putting all this together in the inspired manner of the best New Orleans or Dixieland groups produces a brilliant musical texture—varied yet balanced, linearly interesting yet harmonically integrated—as satisfyingly complex in its own way as the counterpoint of such Baroque composers as J. S. Bach (with whom this style of early contrapuntal jazz is often compared).

By contrast with this polyphonic ideal, swing bands (say, Goodman, Shaw, or the Dorseys) performed in a style that we might describe as *antiphonal* in the sense that the writing involved a sort of call-and-response pattern with (say) the saxophone, trumpet, and trombone sections playing together as blocks of sound heard in juxtaposition via alternating riff-like passages (Stowe 1994, p. 10; Sudhalter 1999, p. 341). If one extends this principle to the even grander proportions of (say) the Duke Ellington or Paul Whiteman orchestras, the music becomes *symphonic* in texture.

Meanwhile, much ordinary music (say, an Episcopal hymn or barbershop quartet) is *homophonic* in texture (consisting of multiple parts moving together in parallel). Thus, bop tended to feature a couple of horns—say, saxophone and trumpet—playing melodic lines in unison or simple two-part harmony. With rare exceptions—found mostly in the West Coast groups of the 1950s (Gerry Mulligan, Chet Baker, Bob Brookmeyer, Jimmy Giuffre,

Jim Hall, Dave Brubeck, Paul Desmond, Dave Pell, John Graas, Shorty Rogers, and their ilk)—polyphonic jazz died when swing took over. And antiphonal jazz perished when bop gained ascendancy.

Then post-bop styles—such as free jazz—nailed the lid on the coffin, featuring mostly *monophonic* soloing in which one horn at a time plays at length over a supporting rhythm section. And fusion, funk, and rap put polyphony six feet under. Indeed—if one strips away both melody and harmony, in the manner of rap or hip-hop music—one creates a texture characterized by utter *monotony*.

But while it survived, polyphonic jazz shone forth in splendor. And never more so than in the work of the great New Orleans and Dixieland groups— King Oliver, Louis Armstrong, Kid Ory, Bix Beiderbecke, Red Nichols, Eddie Condon, Bob Crosby's Bobcats, Matty Matlock, and all the rest. Hence, in sum, we might recognize the following homologous hierarchy of polylinear complexity—with the New Orleans or Dixieland style ranking at or near the top of the musical spectrum in this connection:

New Orleans or Dixieland : Polyphony
Swing Bands : Antiphony
Orchestral Jazz : Symphony
Bebop and Hard Bop : Homophony
Post-Bop : Monophony
Rap : Monotony

MacDonald-and-Hanley's "Indiana" is a tune beloved to Dixie-type players and has been featured by almost every N'Orleans-inspired musician from Satchmo himself to Al Hirt. Alphabetically, a small sampling of the list would include Henry "Red" Allen, Louis Armstrong, Sidney Bechet, Wild Bill Davison, Pete Fountain, Al Hirt, Kid Ory, Bob Scobey, Joe Venuti, Dick Wellstood, and countless others too numerous to mention. And that's neglecting guys not associated with the style of traditional or "trad" jazz. Indeed, the modernists often substitute "Donna Lee," an inventively intricate melody written by Miles Davis and/or Charlie Parker with "Indiana" as its harmonic basis. After the first chorus of finger-numbing pyrotechnics, over the familiar chords burned into every jazz musician's central nervous system, "Donna Lee" becomes "Indiana" all over again. Interestingly, the remarkably poignant lyrics to the tune—almost tenderly evoking memories of the rural scene at the "Crossroads of America" and reminding me of nothing so much as Walter Pater's *Marius the Epicurean*—are hardly ever heard and are little known, even to natives of the song's eponymous state, many of whom I have quizzed on this topic to no avail in probing any sort of viable collective memory. To hear all about the gleaming candlelight, the sycamores, the new-mown hay, and the moonlight on the Wabash, try the version by the pianist-singer-composer Bobby Troup or the one by his lovely wife Julie London— by no coincidence, two of the rare recordings of the words to this song.

Meanwhile, contemplate the feat accomplished by Nichols/Kaye in the tour-de-force performance of "Indiana" that provides the pivotal ambi-diegetic cinemusical moment in *The Five Pennies*. The relevant sequence of scenes represents Red/Danny's demeaning and unsuccessful attempt to make a living by playing jobs on the radio for programs sponsored by various well-known brands. On the side, he writes his own musical arrangements in a Dixieland style that nobody wants to play. So, to make ends meet financially, he farms himself out to play essentially degrading commercial gigs.

On-camera, the ambi-diegetic cinemusical scenes place Red/Danny in a variety of settings. He begins with a broadcast for Cliquot Club over WEAF radio in which—performing "Indiana" while dressed as an Eskimo in a fur parka—he is called on to shake some faux sleigh bells and to make barking noises like a Siberian husky. Next, we see him broadcasting at WENW for the Sun-Flow Pineapple Company in the midst of hula-hula dancing girls and a grating steel guitar, doing a mock-Hawaiian luau-style version of "Indiana" while wearing a flowered hula-type skirt and noisily slurping an island drink with a lei draped around his neck. Next, for Samovar Tea, Red/Danny performs "Indiana" dressed like a Russian Cossack in a black fur hat and black boots with three similarly-attired Russian-looking guys singing vocal parts inspired by "The Volga Boatman" behind him before he segues into a Klezmer-inflected Ziggy-Elman-like version of the piece. Then, for Canada Dry, he appears as a Royal Mounted Policeman—sitting on a horse and tooting bugle-style obbligatos to an operatic performance of "Indiana" delivered by a grotesquely stagey soprano who wears a feathered Indian headdress and sings like an inept reincarnation of Jeanette MacDonald in a way that inspires the horse to rear up and throw Red/Danny to the ground. Not surprisingly, with Kaye's delicious comic effects, Red/Danny manages to screw up all these humiliating performing opportunities so that, we infer, he soon finds himself without employment and even more penniless than before.

As the sequence continues, Red/Danny's loving wife Bobbie (aka Willa) Nichols (Barbara Bel Geddes) enters a coffee shop in the rain and joins a table full of Red/Danny's musician friends—Tony Volari (Harry Guardino), Arthur Schutt (Bobby Troup), Jimmy Dorsey (Ray Anthony), Davey Tough (Shelly Manne), and Glenn Miller (Ray Daley). Notice that, in this assemblage, we have all the possible combinations covered—an obscure musician played by an obscure actor (Tony/Harry); an obscure musician played by well-known actor-musician (Arthur/Bobby); well-known musicians played by well-known actor-musicians (Jimmy/Ray, Davey/Shelly); and a well-known musician played by an obscure actor (Glenn/Ray). While they banter about Red/Danny's conspicuous lack of commercial success on the local music scene, Bobbie/Barbara hands them copies of his latest arrangement of . . . you guessed it . . . "Indiana." They pooh-pooh his efforts. But, when she retires to the ladies' room with a bad case of morning sickness (because Baby Dorothy is on the way at the most awkward possible time), the guys start singing their parts *a cappella* at a slow tempo. It sounds rather ragged but, of course, vastly superior to any of the woebegone versions that we have heard up to this point.

At precisely this moment, Red/Danny wanders into the coffee shop and overhears them. He is pleased, but tells them that they need to pick up the pace. He counts out a brisker tempo, and they all begin to scat a wonderfully complex polyphonic Dixie-style rendition of the tune. This scene segues to a shot of a 78-rpm phonograph record on the Celebration label by Red Nichols and His Five Pennies. This and other Nichols groups did, indeed, include at various times such stellar names as Jimmy Dorsey, Tommy Dorsey, Glenn Miller, Benny Goodman, Gene Krupa, and Artie Shaw (more or less the whole future of swing music a decade later and exactly the same prominent superstars represented by the list of jazz-biopic heroes reviewed in the present chapter) (Nolan 2010, p. 38). And we hear a superb Nicholsian version of "Indiana" that conveys the spirit of Red's historical greatness as a jazz cornetist. Further, through a series of dissolves from location to location, we follow the Five Pennies as they tour on the band bus from one town to another—always playing their steamy Dixieland music to wildly appreciative audiences. Newspaper headlines flash the message that the band is a "smash hit"—both in record sales and at college dances. Finally, Red/Danny and Bobbie/Barbara have embarked on the path to success, both artistically and commercially. In this film—not necessarily in correspondence to the real-life exigencies of the real-world marketplace— wonderful music elicits an enthusiastic audience response.

We might pause to notice that the scene just described telescopes a fair amount of historically accurate musical context into a rather compact cinematic montage. In particular—as already mentioned and as indicated at length by Sudhalter (1999), who follows this theme as a sort of leitmotif throughout his 890-page tome—Red Nichols did in fact operate as a frequent employer and source of livelihood for some of the greatest names in jazz (pp. 125, 142, 216, 237, 361, 385, 431, 712, 720). These included such illustrious heroes of our five jazz biopics as Tommy Dorsey (p. 134); Jimmy Dorsey (pp. 121, 123, 134, 365); Glenn Miller (pp. 125, 136, 334, 343, 720); Benny Goodman (pp. 125, 135, 143, 343, 555, 720); and Gene Krupa (pp. 125, 136, 143, 216, 343); not to mention Artie Shaw (pp. 570, 574). In this, Red's role parallels that of Ben Pollack (pp. 216, 332–333, 384–385), who also provided steady if artistically unrewarding employment for some of our biopic stalwarts such as Glenn Miller (pp. 146, 321, 325, 334) and Benny Goodman (pp. 146, 216, 243, 320–321, 325, 335, 555). Indeed, as noted earlier, we find the role of Ben Pollack in this capacity explicitly acknowledged in both *The Glenn Miller Story* and *The Benny Goodman Story*, whereas that of Red Nichols receives greater attention in *The Five Pennies* and *The Gene Krupa Story*. In a sense, Pollack and Nichols serve interchangeably to represent early career employers of swing-era super-stars who later went on to heights of fame and glory that vastly exceeded those of their erstwhile mentors. Partly because of this, we infer, Pollack's life ended tragically when the despondent former bandleader hung himself in the bathroom of his home in Palm Springs (p. 337). Red Nichols experienced a similar eclipse but managed to persevere long enough to die of natural causes (p. 131).

The real-life Red Nichols, consistent with his status as a commercially motivated employer-of-future-jazz-masters, garnered somewhat mixed reviews as an artist. In ways hinted at in *The Five Pennies* but not fully explored in the film (for obvious reasons), his music often struck critics as mechanical rather than expressive, routine rather than improvised, and synthetic rather than spontaneous. In other words, many regarded Red as more of a technically proficient and commercially well-connected bandleader than a gifted or inspired soloist. Sudhalter (1999)—himself an accomplished trumpeter—provides a balanced view of such criticisms juxtaposed with the opinions of those who held the playing of Nichols in higher regard (pp. 121, 131–137, 198, 343, 745). According to Sudhalter, "Nichols . . . recorded constantly, was widely listened to and emulated":

> If his hot solos lacked the depth and sheer beauty of Bix's [Beiderbecke's], he was undeniably a far more polished and versatile instrumentalist . . . fast, clean, and in tune; his attack was crisp, his tone light and controlled, impeccable in all registers.
>
> (Sudhalter 1999, p. 120)

So—serving as a major leitmotif in Sudhalter's book—Red Nichols impressed some favorably, others unfavorably, and still others with deep ambivalence. Nonetheless, consistent with its depiction in the film, Sudhalter makes a strong case for Red's performance of "Indiana" as a true-to-real-life Nicholsian masterpiece—recorded on April 18, 1929 with a band that included at least three of our biopic heroes—Benny Goodman, Glenn Miller, and Gene Krupa (p. 125). In Sudhalter's subsequent summary evaluation, "Red snaps out a crisp, Bix-like chorus in a derby" (p. 143). Later, Sudhalter returns to this theme for a third flurry of praise: "Two issued takes of 'Indiana' offer . . . a carefully devised Nichols chorus (played into a derby in the Bix manner)" (p. 720). What I find especially noteworthy here is Sudhalter's compulsion to return to this example for three separate discussions of its excellence. Clearly, "Indiana" means something special in the overall Nicholsian oeuvre.

Beyond the pivotal ambi-diegetic cinemusical moments provided by "Indiana," I must also say a few words about the striking and stirring way that "Battle Hymn of the Republic" functions ambi-diegetically in *The Five Pennies*. The first rendition of "Battle Hymn" appears quite early in the film. In New York, on their first date, Red/Danny and Bobbie/Barbara have gone uptown to hear Louis Armstrong, who plays and sings his inspired-as-usual versions of "After You've Gone" and "Won't You Come Home, Bill Bailey." (Notice that—unlike many professional actors playing musical roles—Armstrong is singularly unsuccessful at miming and lip-synching his own trumpet solos and vocal performances convincingly.)

Meanwhile, Bobbie/Barbara and Co. get Red/Danny roaring drunk on his first taste of Prohibition liquor. So drunk does he get that he wants to sit in with Louis, claiming that he is the second greatest trumpet player in Ogden,

Utah. Given the chance, he fluffs his notes and rushes to the men's room to be sick. Note the parallel with Bobbie/Barbara's aforementioned morning sickness later in the film; both augur the birth of an important ambi-diegetic cinemusical moment. In the present case, Red/Danny's nausea precedes his renewed resolve to make good on the horn.

After Louis concludes his next piece, Red/Danny begins to play "Battle Hymn of the Republic" from the back of the nightclub. First, he intones the mournful theme in the traditional funereal style. Next, moving toward the stage, he livens the tempo while Armstrong's band members join him in a rousing Dixieland ensemble chorus. Then, he picks up the pace another notch in a still more joyously rousing refrain that threatens to raise the roof to the heavens above. At this point, after a scintillating upward key change from C major to Eb major, Louis enters in a thrilling trumpet-cornet tandem. Again modulating up a notch from Eb to F major, the two play another soaring chorus before a triumphant ending.

Recalling my earlier comments on scenes from *The Benny Goodman Story* featuring Kid Ory and Lionel Hampton, the alert reader might wonder why I do not chastise *The Five Pennies* for implying that musicians who have never played together before could spontaneously execute fancy tempo changes and tricky modulations from C to Eb to F major. The reason is that—via an earlier exchange that escapes the attention of both Gabbard (1996, p. 85) and Yanow (2004, p. v)—Red/Danny has handed the members of Armstrong's All Stars copies of an arrangement that he has written of "Battle Hymn." This is why they can flawlessly follow the tempo shifts and key changes as the performance unfolds. They are expertly reading from a carefully arranged score. No other interpretation of the scene makes sense.

Louis rewards Red/Danny's transcendent performance with a flattering comment to the effect that somebody should get his license number as he and Bobbie/Barbara pause for a passionate kiss outside the club—forgetting that this is only their first date—before necking and petting in the back seat of a taxi cab all the way back to her home in Brooklyn. In the next scene, the two are already newlyweds. With a little help from Louis Armstrong and plenty of brassy bravura on the cornet, Red/Danny's romantic conquest is complete.

Notice that—again, as in *The Glenn Miller Story* (the present chapter), *High Society* (Chapter 2), and *Paris Blues* (Chapter 8)—a protagonist's character has gained strong identifications with powerful virility, sexual potency, and musical validity by virtue of his ambi-diegetic cinemusical association with Louis Armstrong, that inexhaustible fountain of artistic creativity. Again, the force of this masculinity-affirming and virtuosity-conferring juxtaposition prompts Gabbard (1996) to make an explicit link between Armstrong and "phallic power": "In the Red Nichols biopic, . . . the hero and his girlfriend go up to Harlem to hear Armstrong, and . . . the white musician gains sexual maturity after he plays with the black master" (p. 225; see also Gabbard 2001, 2008). Similar comments could and should be made about Danny/Red's stellar performance of "When the Saints Go

Marching In" with Louis Armstrong in a marvelous nightclub duet that appears later in *The Five Pennies* and that recalls something of the camaraderie evinced by Armstrong and Bing Crosby during their celebrated pairing in *High Society* (1956) on "Now You Has Jazz" (Chapter 2).

But Red/Danny and Co. have not yet finished with "Battle Hymn of the Republic." When their daughter Dorothy becomes ill and lapses into a coma, Red/Danny and Bobbie/Barbara sit despondently in the hospital while they await news of the little girl's prognosis. Feeling the need to pray but not knowing the words to any prayers, they instead recite the only religious text they know—namely, the lyrics to "Battle Hymn." Moments later, they receive news that Dorothy has regained consciousness and has called for them.

Later, after a lengthy self-imposed retirement during which he has renounced music in order to devote his full attention to nursing his crippled daughter back to health and has suffered the indignity of hearing the Glenn Miller Orchestra play "Indiana" while he listens from his position as a hardhat worker in the shipyards, Red/Danny returns to the bandstand to resume his musical career. In a virtual love fest at one of the Los Angeles nightclubs, Red/Danny stages his comeback. Suddenly, Glenn Miller (Ray Daley), Jimmy Dorsey (Ray Anthony), and Louis Armstrong (himself) enter, blasting away on "Won't You Come Home, Bill Bailey" and managing to work in some telling phrases from "Indiana" near the end.

After a touching reprisal of a family-related lullaby trio (written, incidentally by Danny Kaye's wife Sylvia Fine), Red/Danny picks up his horn and recapitulates his great rendition of "Battle Hymn." Again, the rafters shake with musical righteousness. And when Louis joins in on trumpet, as before, we hear a pair of striking upward modulations that again move the performance through two ascending key changes—from C to Eb major and from Eb to F major—as if toward the heavens . . . stirring our souls, warming our hearts, and firing our renewed appreciation for Dixieland jazz at its finest. Toward the end, on a glistening high note and with astonishing fidelity as an actor miming the gloriously authentic music dubbed by Red Nichols himself on cornet, Danny Kaye lifts his left leg in an almost ejaculatory moment of ecstasy that just about says it all. In an old Vitaphone clip from 1929 (available on youtube.com), while playing "China Boy," a young Red Nichols does in fact raise his leg (repeatedly) in the gesture faithfully mimicked by Kaye—the difference being that, as a savvy actor, Danny saves it for what is arguably the climax of the film.

## *The Gene Krupa Story* (1959)

Compared even with the sentimental excesses found in some of the jazz biopics visited thus far, *The Gene Krupa Story* (1959) comes on with the heavy-handed insistence of a Bible-thumping country preacher. The point of this film, I guess, is that you should watch out for booze, drugs, and evil women. You should keep your nose clean and hang in there with your cute little girlfriend from high school, who loves you and who supports you through all your careless indiscretions, understanding that you are a sweet genius of rhythm underneath that bad-boy exterior that you cultivate and flaunt every time you pick up a pair of drumsticks. If you don't follow these simple rules to happiness, you might antagonize people, get mixed up with a bogus marijuana-possession charge, and sidetrack your otherwise promising career—requiring an extensive rehabilitation project through the gentle auspices of said angelic girlfriend with a little help from the magnanimous Tommy Dorsey.

That said, we should recognize that—however bathetic it might seem—*The Gene Krupa Story* does actually bear a close resemblance to the truth and presents the drummer's saga with greater historical accuracy than one typically finds in a Hollywood biopic. As recounted in the excellent sourcebook by Bruce Klauber (1990), Krupa did marry a woman named Ethel in 1933, divorced her in 1941, and remarried her in 1944 (pp. 195–196). Rather than a childhood sweetheart, Ethel was a telephone operator at the Dixie Hotel on 42nd Street whom Gene met after coming to New York (p. 144). But in a touching account by Anita O'Day (pp. 144–147), we learn that—if anything—Ethel was even more saintly than indicated by the film. Apparently, when Gene divorced Ethel, he settled for $100,000. But Ethel didn't really need the money; so she saved it; and—later, when Gene was broke and in jail—she gave it back to him in a gesture of great generosity, which he honored by re-marrying her. The true story of Ethel, it seems, was even more astonishing than the little melodrama depicted by the film would imply. Hollywood had to tone down Ethel's real-life self-sacrifice to make it remotely plausible for the screen.

What kind of man, you might be wondering, deserves that kind of devotion? Apparently, a man like Krupa—who, if anything, was even nicer-kinder-and-gentler in real life than the image drawn by the motion picture might suggest. The excellence of Krupa's character and the warmth of his personality shine through in countless quotes offered by friends and fellow musicians scattered throughout the book by Klauber (1990). A brief sampling of comments to indicate how Gene was "universally loved as a human being" (p. 6) would include: "As much a gentleman as he was a musician" (Mel Tormé, p. 4); "a wonderful person" (Roy Haynes, p. 148); "Beautiful cat, great man" (Sonny Stitt, p. 148); "A gentle and wonderful human being" (Max Roach, p. 148); "a gentle man . . . a very likeable person" (Bobby Scott, p. 149); "all the other cats are nuts about him" (Norman Granz, p. 152); "probably the nicest man who ever lived" (Butch Miles, p. 153); "especially wonderful" (Roy Eldridge, p. 155); "one of the nicest men I ever met in my whole life . . . one of my very favorite people and one of the finest men I ever knew" (Teddy Wilson, pp. 160–161); "a very nice man . . . very religious . . . always very gracious and very good to people" (Marty Napoleon, p. 166); "as a human being . . . 100 percent, very spiritual . . . a very religious man . . . a good person" (Carmen Leggio, p. 171); "a wonderful human being" (Benny Goodman, p. 173). Too all this,

344 Jazz Biopics as Tragedy and Comedy

Bobby Scott (2007)—a pianist/composer/singer/songwriter who worked with Gene—characterizes Krupa as "a totally honest man" (p. 3) and "so sensitive to the sensitivities of others" (p. 9): "It is rare for an artist's personality to rank with his work" (p. 10).

So Gene Krupa probably deserved the almost reverential slant adopted by his biopic. But beyond the moralizing of this rather sanctimonious film, we encounter something that I never expected to see in a motion picture— namely, an absolutely riveting performance by none other than Sal Mineo, of all people, in the role of Gene Krupa. Indeed, this otherwise undistinguished actor manages to head-bob, gum-chew, and stick-twirl his way to an astonishingly life-like recreation of the great drummer. Mineo's thespian triumph succeeds on two fronts where other movie stars typically fail in enacting ambi-diegetic jazz.

First, Mineo has assimilated Krupa's idiosyncratic gestures and body language to perfection—expertly capturing that unique combination of facial grimaces, shoulder heaves, eye rolls, mouth chomps, foot kicks, arm waves, and stick flourishes with which Gene routinely enhanced his own accompaniments, even or maybe even especially when he was playing a slow-tempo ballad. The real-life Gene Krupa may well have been the most fun-to-watch musician who ever lived. Whereas a virtuosic drummer like Buddy Rich might sit there in stoic stillness while he pounded out impossibly rapid machine-gun patterns on his drum heads, Gene Krupa pantomimed every stroke of every beat as if it were the most important single rhythmic nuance ever conceived since the beginning of jazz drumming. In the quote-filled compendium by Klauber (1990), the most frequent descriptor applied to Krupa's stage presence is "showman" (pp. 8, 30, 43, 109, 110, 147, 154). Typical descriptions struggle against the limitations of the English language to evoke the indescribable Krupa charisma: "Krupa made a visual impact, what with his gum-chewing, frenetic movements, knocked-out expressions and grimaces, sweating and grunting, with hair flying and sticks twirling all the while under the light strobe" (p. 8). To this, Anita O'Day adds that "Gene was as magnetic as a movie star, filled with wild exuberance as his raven-colored hair, flashing brown eyes and black suit contrasted with the snow-white marine pearl drums that surrounded him": "His gum-chewing, facial gymnastics, tossing of broken sticks to the audience and general flamboyance visually complemented the Krupa sound" (quoted by Klauber 1990, p. 147). In short, Gene Krupa telegraphed his involvement and feelings with an arsenal of gesticulations never witnessed before or since. Never, that is, until Sal Mineo got hold of his role in The Gene Krupa Story. Mineo read Krupa's body language like a book and brought the fruits of these studies to bear on his admirably faithful impersonation of the great drummer. Watch Gene/Sal head-bob, shoulder-twitch, eye-roll, stick-twirl, and gum-chew his way through captivating performances of "Muskrat Ramble," "Way Down Yonder in New Orleans," "Cherokee," or "Hawaiian War Chant," and you'll almost forget that you are not watching the authentic original.

Second, more than any other actor I have seen on film, Sal Mineo manages to mime the music—in this case, the drum parts supplied by Gene Krupa himself—with the utmost fidelity. Apparently, Mineo literally learned to play the drums for his role in this film. And it shows. Every audible stroke of Krupa's sticks becomes visible in Mineo's meticulously synchronized performance. With perfectly matched timing, Sal follows Gene—tap for tap, bomb for bomb, cymbal crash for cymbal crash (Klauber 1990, pp. 129–131). Sal even manages, mostly, to keep his high-hat going on two and four, which is more than one can say for some real-life professional drummers. I know of no way to convey the perfection of Mineo's miming of Krupa in words other than to note how we constantly have the impression that if we were to put the soundtrack microphone on Sal instead of Gene, we would hear exactly what we hear in Krupa's dubbing of Mineo's ambi-diegetic cinemusical performances.

And what we hear is . . . sublime drumming. The power of Krupa/Mineo's musical statement emerges in a pivotal scene in which Gene/Sal's percussive gifts take wing before our eyes. This pivotal ambi-diegetic cinemusical moment transpires at a party given by the otherwise evil Dorissa Dinell (Susan Oliver) at which Tommy Dorsey (Bobby Troup), Jimmy Dorsey (an unidentified actor), and Red Nichols (playing himself) are holding forth on the bandstand when Krupa/Mineo—who has just recently arrived in New York and who has every reason to fear that he will be humiliated in public—sits down behind the drums and astonishes the more experienced musicians by setting a ferocious tempo on a tune that turns out, as they fall in one by one, to be . . . none other than . . . "Indiana."

Recall that "Indiana" was the tune that served to provide a pivotal ambi-diegetic cinemusical moment for Red Nichols (Danny Kaye) in *The Five Pennies* via a band that just happened to include the real-life Gene Krupa (playing himself) and that Gene had himself played on Red's immortal recording of the tune in 1929. Here, in *The Gene Krupa Story*, we find the same song used to carry Krupa/Mineo to the heights of jazzdom while, reciprocally, the real-life Red Nichols (this time, via a kind of reverse logic, playing himself) appears on-camera to help out.

As Gene/Sal wails away, Red Nichols leads the ensemble through a fiery rendition of "Indiana" with Sal Mineo delivering his whole repertoire of gum-chewing, head-bobbing, stick-twirling, eye-rolling, echt-Krupaesque mannerisms to a cinemusically satisfying fare-thee-well. At the conclusion of this stunning performance, Red tells Gene/Sal that he "kicks" a lot of drums and offers to hire him to play in the New York production of *Strike Up the Band*. Krupa/Mineo's career thereby receives its all-important jumpstart.

Later, "Indiana" reappears as the vehicle on which Krupa/Mineo solos in a feature with his own big band. Again, Mineo mimes Krupa to stupendous effect—at one point, walking around his drum kit while splashing away on the cymbals; next, playing the bass fiddle with his sticks while the bassist fingers the strings (a la Bob Haggart and Ray Bauduc on "Big Noise From Winnetka"); and, then, executing a completely authentic Krupa-synched solo in which Sal visually matches Gene in every audible detail with obvious gusto that must have made Krupa's heart swell with gratitude and pride. (Still later, "Indiana" makes one last brief appearance just before Gene/Sal gets arrested on a bogus drug-possession charge after he has manifestly given up smoking grass.)

Here, we experience the cinemusical reincarnation of the great Gene Krupa at the height of his glory. Of course, at the time, Krupa himself had appeared on-screen in *The Benny Goodman Story* just three years earlier and in *The Five Pennies* contemporaneously. But there is something about seeing Mineo mime Krupa that makes Gene's charisma seem even realer-than-real. If it can be copied so effectively—albeit with an amount of work that we mortals can scarcely begin to imagine—then it must be authentic in some otherwise indefinable sense.

In real life, Gene Krupa might have shown a shaky calling to the priesthood, but he was a famously wonderful drummer. As a percussionist, he lacked advanced technical facility (though he kept honing his craft, learning to read music proficiently and eventually opening a drum school in collaboration with Cozy Cole in New York during the late 1950s). But he deserves credit as the undisputed pioneer in developing the extended drum solo and in elevating this instrument to a starring role in front of the band. More important, his playing conveyed great emotional depth. These qualities emerge in numerous quotes from fellow musicians cited by Klauber (1990): "A highly musical drummer" (Mel Tormé, p. 4); "the best" (Benny Goodman, p. 5); "absolutely the first man when it comes to drums . . . the big inspiration for drummers" (Buddy Rich, p. 123); "a great master of the instrument" (Roy Haynes, p. 148); "a very musical drummer" (Don Osborne, p. 150); "a miracle drummer boy . . . a great musician and one of the world's greatest performing artists . . . always my favorite" (Lionel Hampton, p. 151); "the beginning and end of all jazz drummers . . . a great genius, a truly great genius of the drums" (Buddy Rich, p. 151); "the only man that would have that kind of quality to play drums like that" (Elvin Jones, p. 152); "a *feeling* for the tone of every one of his drums . . . and *each cymbal* . . . making the drum speak with *meaning*, and making every stroke say something" (Teddy Wilson, p. 160); "immaculate time and . . . a master of dynamics" (Carmen Leggio, p. 171); "charismatic; larger than life, and yes, magic" (Klauber 1990, p. 10). And, in his profound acting performance, Sal Mineo manages to capture this musical magic—quite literally—with his bare hands.

Somewhat surprisingly, both Sudhalter (1999) and Gabbard (1996) remain relatively silent, respectively, on the musical and cinematic aspects of the Krupa legend. Thus, the usually voluble Sudhalter (1999) provides the briefest of critical evaluations via just a small number of short phrases in only a few scattered places—characterizing Krupa's drumming as "aggressive" (p. 143), "enthusiastic and impulsive" (p. 198), "full and rhythmically powerful" (p. 199), but "erratic" (p. 540) and "often quite random" (p. 818)—adding that he was a "showman" (p. 564) and that, compared with other bosses, he led his band in "a rather gentler way" (p. 726). Gabbard (1996) pays still less attention to Krupa in general and to *The Gene Krupa Story* in particular—inexplicably seeing the drummer/bandleader as "almost devoid of stage presence" (p. 117) and casually dismissing the biopic as one more film best interpreted in juxtaposition to race- and gender-based issues in which Krupa emerges as "The archetypal white Negro" and in which his portrayal by Sal Mineo adds "a homoerotic subtext to the many subtexts already associated with his character" (p. 80). Here it appears to me that, for the sake of pursuing his favorite race- and gender-related themes (however briefly), Gabbard (1996) has constructed a very different movie from the one on which I have been commenting. From my perspective— when we contemplate how difficult it must have been to match every nuance of Gene Krupa's drum patterns, tap by tap and blow by blow—we cannot help but regard Sal Mineo's performance, whatever the nature of his largely irrelevant sexual preferences, as one of remarkable strength and courage. And, speaking of courage, that quality (surely not any sort of "homoerotic subtext") is exactly the characteristic—as conveyed forcefully in the film— that I would use to describe Gene Krupa himself.

On June 29 of 1973, 15 years after the filming of *The Gene Krupa Story*, we attended a reunion of the Benny Goodman Quartet at Carnegie Hall. The original quartet—Benny, Teddy, Lionel, and Gene—charged through a number of ancient masterpieces and warhorses from the old days ("Runnin' Wild," "Somebody Loves Me," "Avalon," "Memories of You," "Moonglow," and the rest).

The concert closed with a tremendous roof-raising solo from Krupa on "Sing, Sing, Sing." As many in the audience knew, Gene had for some time been suffering from both heart trouble and leukemia. And, as he played, music-inspired love seemed to pour out of him, reciprocated in kind by the immensely appreciative crowd of listeners.

On and on Krupa went, with powerful rhythmic thrusts balanced against novel tonal subtleties. With sweat pouring down his cheeks. With head bobbing and shoulder hunching and gum chewing at full tilt. And, as usual, with every stroke of each stick accompanied by a facial grimace or bodily gesture that meant . . . everything.

At the end, the applause was deafening. Goodman, Wilson, Hampton, and Krupa stood for a while—arm in arm, beaming—then left the spotlights. We all kept clapping. Waiting expectantly, even insistently. Hoping for one or two encores.

But there was no encore at Carnegie Hall that night. Gene Krupa, totally spent from his heroic exertions, had collapsed backstage. He managed to give a couple more performances that summer—one at the Singer Bowl on July 4th and another at Saratoga Springs on August 18th. But he died only a few weeks after that—on October 16, 1973—at age 64.

The Carnegie Hall Reunion was, in retrospect, the most courageous performance I have ever seen.

Thank God we were there.

## THE CINDERELLA SIDE OF THINGS: NO, ARTIE, NO

If *Horatio Blows* has served as the rallying cry for our thematic treatment of the American Dream, we must now end by recognizing another important sense—one that, in the context of (macro)marketing theory, we must not ignore—in which *Horatio Sucks*. In this connection, the astute reader will have noticed that one luminary genius of the Swing Era has escaped sustained attention in my chronicle of hero-worshipping jazz biopics—namely, the great but problematic Artie Shaw. Except for an obscure appearance with Lana Turner in *Dancing Co-Ed* (1939) and a cameo role with Fred Astaire in *Second Chorus* (1940), Shaw did not receive serious cinematic attention until the Oscar-winning documentary by Brigette Berman entitled *Artie Shaw: Time Is All You've Got* (1985, not available in DVD or VHS format) and the subsequent BBC special called *Artie Shaw—Quest for Perfection* (2003, currently posted in low-fidelity multi-part installments on youtube.com). Yet Shaw led one of the most popular swing bands of the 1930s–1940s, and many important jazz people (Barney Bigard, John Carter, Ray Charles, Buddy Collette, Buddy DeFranco, Paul Desmond, Benny Harris, Hank Jones, Lee Konitz, Teo Macero, Billy Mitchell, Gerry Mulligan, Charlie Parker, Dave Pell, Art Pepper, Jerome Richardson, Gunther Schuller, Bud Shank, Billy Taylor, Mel Tormé, and Phil Woods, among others) have regarded his musicianship as setting a standard surpassed by none (Nolan 2010). For example, Lees (1988, 2004) notes Shaw's "reputation for peerless musicianship," his "most beautifully polished and swinging of all the big bands," and his stature as "one of the finest jazz players America has produced" (1988, p. 61) and praises "his inventiveness, his harmonic sophistication . . . the long lines, the exquisite legato lyricism" (2004, p. 1). Nonetheless—reflecting a "dark side"—Artie Shaw chose to withdraw from the music business in 1954 at age 43, while at the peak of his powers, never to return again to pursuing this form of livelihood. He continued his reclusive retreat from music for 50 years, passing away in 2004 at age 93. Meanwhile, he had lived comfortably; had married eight times, including beauties like Lana Turner (1940), Ava Gardner (1945–1946), and Evelyn Keyes (1957–1985); had had affairs with Betty Grable, Lena Horne, Joan Crawford, and maybe Judy Garland; but, since dropping his musical career, had forever after refused to pander to the low-brow tastes of the mass audience that had insured his financial success (Nolan 2010; White 2004; en.wikipedia.org/wiki/Artie_Shaw; www.artie shaw.com/bio.html; www.musicianguide.com; www.nytimes.com). (For some interesting parallels in the career of film composer Paul Chihara, see Schelle 1999, pp. 130–133.)

Note that Artie Shaw appears to have revealed a somewhat schizoid personality—generally pleasant and kind, but sometimes capable of extreme anger or insensitivity. According to White (2004), "Shaw became—and remains—a controversial, contradictory, and enigmatic figure" (p. 10). For example, one acquaintance recalls "how generous he could be at one minute, and then cruel and unfeeling the next" (Arthur Gilbert, quoted by Lees 2004, p. 1). On the downside, the great guitarist Tal Farlow—a member of Shaw's last Gramercy Five—reports that "Artie . . . has no feelings. He is a block of ice . . . a cold fish" (quoted by Pacheco 2005, pp. 56–57). Shaw frequently disparaged former wives and remained estranged from his two sons, commenting that "I didn't get along with their mothers, so why should I get along with the kids?" (quoted by en.wikipedia.org/wiki/Artie_Shaw). One child, Jonathan, told Wadler (2005), "He was abusive, condescending, mean-spirited. . . . He died alone and miserable, as he chose to do." Lana Turner (1982) describes her marriage to Artie as unendurable: "By the third day of our marriage, I knew I was in trouble. . . . It was hell" (p. 47). But Artie put a rather different spin on the story of his relationship with Lana Turner: "I found that while Lana Turner was an industrial strength sex animal, the rest of the time she was an empty flower pot . . . shallow and vain as only an 18-year-old #1 starlet at MGM could be" (quoted by Pacheco 2005, p. 38). Shaw described wife number six Kathleen Winsor as "the most unmitigated b**** of a c*** I knew" and wife number seven Doris Dowling as "a multimillionaire ding bat" (p. 41). But, on the upside, Artie had much kinder things to say about Ava Gardner: "Ava was just as beautiful [as Lana], but she was funny and brainy" (pp. 38–39). And, reciprocally, Gardner (1990) speaks favorably and affectionately of Shaw: "Of my three husbands, I had the most admiration for Artie. He's impossible to live with . . . , but he is a worthwhile human being, an extraordinary man" (p. 98). According to Pacheco (2005), Ava and Artie "remained close friends her entire life" (p. 39). Similarly, Evelyn Keyes (1977) shows no restraint in recounting the difficulties of her marriage to Artie; but, apparently, these two also remained friends for life.

Shaw's clearly evident integrity and almost brutal honesty, especially in his self-assessments, endeared him to many. Thus, after calling him "snooty," Billie Holiday offered a generally favorable appraisal: "There aren't many people who fought harder than Artie against the vicious people in the music business or the crummy side of second-class citizenship which eats at the guts of so many musicians" (quoted by White 2004, p. 64). Lees (1988) comments that "one sees, behind all that rationalism and adamant logic, a hidden gentleness in Artie Shaw and a sense of brotherhood with all the world's musicians": "It is occasionally said that some of the musicians who worked for him hated him. . . . But I have never been able to find one of these detractors" (p. 65). One of Shaw's star trumpet players Billy Butterfield recalled that "Artie was a really good guy to work for. He treated you very well" (quoted by White 2004, p. 99). Mel Tormé (1988) recalls that "Artie was everything I had hoped he would be . . . someone worth looking up to" (pp. 88–89): "Highly intelligent, able to discuss a wide variety of engrossing subjects with insight and authority, Artie is someone with whom working was always a treat and often instructive" (p. 266). Pacheco (2005) concludes that "Everything he did had a perfectly sound reason. If not to the public, at least to Shaw" (p. 61). It could be that the apparently contradictory aspects of Artie Shaw's personality actually represented two sides of the same coin—namely, a commendable but inevitably abrasive candor, an incorruptibly ruthless honesty. Wadler (2005) describes this two-sided persona as follows: "Mr. Shaw . . . could be charming . . . , but he was . . . self-absorbed and brutally frank." In the words of *DownBeat*, Shaw displayed a "very human preference to be a good musician instead of a good businessman," earning praise for his "courage and honesty" (quoted by White 2004, p. 91).

Nowhere does this honesty appear more conspicuously than in Artie Shaw's admirably candid autobiographical revelations about his own character. Shortly before he fled the music business for good, Shaw (1952) seized upon a metaphor that recognizes the symmetry between the rags-to-riches fantasy of the American Dream and the much-celebrated Disney-elevated fairy tale of *Cinderella*. Just like a character from Horatio Alger, from the ABC Paradigm, from the Jazz-Singer Schema, or from the DHOPAUS Template, Cinderella begins in poverty and misery before rising to the lofty stature of a Princess Bride. But—drawing on his experiences in the music business and emphasizing the debasing aspects of catering to the dumbed-down lowest-common-denominator tastes of the low-brow audience members who alone can award the benefits of mass-market success based on popular appeal—Shaw (1952) penetratingly provides the definitive antidote to the poisonous aspects of the American Dream; a repudiation of the rags-to-riches success formula; and an unmasking of what he memorably calls *The Trouble With Cinderella*. Few self-respecting capitalists will agree with him. But we cannot dismiss his perspective without giving his voice its due.

Lees (1988) makes the connection between the American Dream, the Horatio Alger novels, and the Cinderella myth perfectly clear: "Shaw's book . . . was . . . not so much an autobiography as an unsparing and self-searching essay on the life of one troubled man living in a fame-crazed America" and victimized by "the myth . . . embodied in the nineteenth-century Horatio Alger novels" (p. 75). As a metaphor for the American Dream, for the Horatio Alger rags-to-riches story, for the Jazz-Singer success schema, or for the music-hero comedepictorial biopic, Shaw (1952) deploys the age-old paradigm for what he calls the *Cinderella Myth* with its focus on the project of living "happily ever after" (p. 6) in ways that achieve "a perfect blend of Success (that old thing again) and $ucce$$ (to spell it the way I think makes more sense in this context)" (p. 7). But, based on his own personal $ucce$$ story, Shaw proceeds to tell us that—in his experience—the life of Cinderella is not all that it's cracked up to be: "The trouble with Cinderella . . . is that nobody lives happily ever after" (pp. 6–7).

Shaw (1952) freely acknowledges his own "involvement with the Cinderella Myth" but maintains a deeply philosophical perspective on this theme (p. 13). A self-confessed beneficiary of Freudian psychoanalysis, he takes as his point of departure the period during which he suddenly found himself playing the lead role in this myth. Or as Shaw summarizes, "I got into the band business, and eventually shoved and climbed my way to the top of that little dung-heap" (p. 26).

Shaw (1952) himself is fascinated by his own metamorphosis from a shy and sensitive little Jewish kid (né Arthur Arshawsky)—discriminated against with almost obscene anti-Semitic prejudice by the other children in New Haven after his family moved there from the Lower East Side of New York City—to a prominent player in "a vortex of exhibitionism like the big band business" (p. 37). Amazingly well-read—especially for a high school dropout—Shaw entertains serious aspirations as a writer, takes extension courses at Columbia University, and even quits the music business at age 23 to pursue what he hopes will be a literary career.

Interesting though these literary aspirations might be, however, our main concerns focus on the reasons for Shaw's disillusionment with the music business, first and last. All this appears in Part II of his book, where he deals seriously with his Cinderella theme. Shaw (1952) sees his youthful self as motivated primarily by the rags-to-riches success story (p. 54). Artie takes up the saxophone and—after laboriously teaching himself to play some simple tunes and winning $5.00 in a talent contest—begins to see it as the key to his pursuit of success: "For this instrument was the first thing I had been able to discover that seemed to offer a way out of a life I hated" (p. 64). Here, the parallels with Horatio Alger's commercially inclined fiddlers—who regard their violins as tools of a lucrative trade—are too striking to ignore. But with this orientation toward business comes a loss in the joy of music. Indeed, we share a powerfully poignant moment when, from his current perspective, Shaw (1952) recognizes that—as a professional adult—he will never again capture the passion for playing that he felt as a 14-year-old boy in his first band: "For although I had no way of knowing it at the time, I was never going to have as much fun playing in any orchestra again" (p. 68).

As he continues on his way—playing in a variety of dance bands, largely self-taught, and always ready to acquire new knowledge based on life experiences in the band business—Artie moves from town to town, band to band, and task to task, constantly learning and continually growing as a musician. Even at this stage, he is well aware of the potential conflict between art and commerce, the tension between the creative integrity of the performer and a crowd-pleasing customer orientation, and the possibility that under such circumstances performers may adapt in ways that, some-what paradoxically, make them their own consumers by playing for themselves (Bradshaw and Holbrook 2007): "For since the average patron . . . hasn't the vaguest notion of what goes into the music . . . , what could be more natural than that the people who work seriously in this field should end up by playing or writing for themselves?"(Shaw 1952, p. 147). Artie's own choices—such as leaving his true love in Cleveland to advance his career by joining a band in Hollywood—stem mostly from the constant need to learn more about the music business (p. 180). Shaw comments ruefully on the "misery" that results from pursuing the "$ucce$$-Fame-Happiness-Cinderella constellation" (p. 180). Meanwhile, he openly admires musicians who play only for themselves—as in the case of clarinetist Frank Teschmacher who played so subtly that only another musician could understand it (p. 199).

As he begins a lifelong process of self-discovery, at age 20, Shaw's energetic pursuit of the American Dream (\$ucce\$\$, Cinderella) conflicts with his concomitant desire for self-improvement through education, reading, extension courses at Columbia, and other goals viewed as inherently "worthwhile" (p. 252). And here—as a preview, with profound relevance to the conflict between art and commerce or the tension between creative integrity and financial success in the big-band business—comes the answer that will steer the rest of Shaw's autobiographical musings and that serves as a resounding renunciation of the sunny optimism evinced by the comede-pictorial ethos of the Jazz-Singer Scenario as manifested by the DHOPAUS Template found in our five success-story biopics:

> To come back to the question of . . . whether it is or is not possible for a man to arrive at some kind of inner peace and self-understanding in order to do something truly worthwhile . . . and still have great public recognition and acclaim—my answer to all this is a definite No [because] it's safe enough to state categorically that the man *who deliberately sets out* to make money . . . is far more apt to turn out junk . . . than anything that might come under the heading of "worthwhile."
>
> (Shaw 1952, pp. 253–254)

These carefully chosen and deeply felt words encapsulate the heart of the art-versus-commerce problem—namely that, for any given artist, the push toward greater popular appeal or broader acceptance inevitably entails a compromise with creative integrity in the direction of dumbing-down the offering to make it more accessible to the low-brow tastes of the mass market. Here, Shaw emphasizes a consideration far too often neglected by cultural commentators—namely, that the point is *not* to compare (say) Kenny G. with (say) Phil Woods but *rather* to compare what Kenny (Phil) *could* (*might*) have become *if* he had chosen to pursue art (popularity) over commerce (creative integrity). Put differently, the point is *not* to compare apples with oranges but *rather* to compare fresh-juicy-delicious apples with rotten apples. The latter exemplars—by catering to the pressures of customer-oriented commerce—pander to the uneducated tastes of the mass market. And, elitist though it may seem to recognize this basic truth, the simple fact—as a matter of pure statistics, whether we like it or not—is that at least half the mass audience has below-average taste. From which it follows, ineluctably, that reaching those folks requires appealing to the lowest common denominator. Or—in the alleged words of the great sell-out artist Herbie Mann (famous for developing a near somnambulant form of "crossover" jazz of the suitable-for-elevators type that is now branded as "smoothjazz" or "chill")—"Never let your good taste get in the way of reaching a wider audience" (but cf. Washburne 2004).

Indeed, Artie Shaw frequently lashed out in undisguised contempt for his audiences—famously calling his jitterbugging fans "morons" (Nolan 2010; Wilson 2004)—in ways that reflected his deep sense of the conflict between art and commerce (Stowe 1994, p. 34). As quoted by White (2004), Shaw resisted any temptation to mince words in expressing his opinion of the typical swing fan and the customer-oriented degradation of the music business: "I hate the music business. I'm not interested in giving people what they want. I'm interested in making music" (p. 88). As early as 1939, Shaw wrote an article for *The Saturday Evening Post* in which he spelled out his reflections on the tension between art and commerce in detail, commenting that "popular music in America is 10 per cent art and 90 per cent business" (Shaw 1939, p. 15): "The mere fact that a piece is a hit means nothing. Enough hyping will make any song a hit" (p. 68). Later, he told Pacheco (2005), "I couldn't understand why kids paid for a ticket to hear the band, and then stood in front of it and yelled at the top of their voices for the whole night": "That's why I called all jitterbugs morons" (p. 45).

Note that Shaw was by no means alone in criticizing the jitterbug craze. Benny Goodman also directed negative comments toward these obtrusive audience members (Stowe 1994, p. 30). In the words of Stowe (1994), "If swing enjoyed a certain amount of cultural acceptance, its uninhibited cultists, known as jitterbugs or ickies, inspired alarm and derision among moralists and musicians alike": "Few observers of jitterbugs refrained from a tone of ridicule in describing them" (p. 30).

Toward the end of his life, Artie Shaw (with Sudhalter 2001) told a near-definitive story about the art-versus-commerce issues inherent in offering an artistic creation to a clueless audience. In 1949, he put together a new band that was praised by knowledgeable critics as "one of the finest bands anybody ever had" and potentially "the greatest modern band ever." But, ironically enough, "audiences absolutely *loathed* it." So Artie broke up that band and, as a sort of practical joke, put together "the *worst* band I'd ever had." To his disgust, "People thought it was the greatest band they'd ever heard!" One club manager told him, "Artie, . . . this is the best evening we've had since Blue Barron!" This was the last straw: "I decided then and there that no one in his right mind could remain in a business like that. So I quit, once and for all" (Shaw with Sudhalter 2001; see also Nolan 2010).

## No, Artie

The essence of Artie Shaw's complaint hinges on his unflattering appraisal of the musical taste demonstrated by the typical audience member. In this, Shaw (1952) will win no prizes for diplomacy or tact—though, in his forth-right musings on his own reciprocal role as a bandleader, he surely deserves high marks for self-awareness and honesty. Indeed—though Shaw (1952) shows no signs of drawing on the insights of such critical commentators as (say) Adorno (1984), Greenberg (1946, ed. 1957), Macdonald (1953, ed. 1957), or Ortega y Gasset (1932, ed. 1957), all of whose inherently high-brow viewpoints were very much in the air at the time of Shaw's writing (Stowe 1994, p. 183)—Artie's acute powers of observation appear to have enabled him to reach similarly incisive conclusions on the basis of his first-hand personal experience. (For further comments on the Adorno-type critiques, see Dahlhaus 2004; Frith 2004; Koehne 2004; Rodel 2004; Washburne 2004.)

In my interpretation, Shaw (1952) traces the abandonment of artistic integrity in the service of commercial opportunism in harrowing detail through a series of agonizing flashbacks. Thus, recalling the Horatio Alger characters portrayed earlier, he comes to regard music as "a way of earning a living . . . a *business* as well as a craft" (p. 256). In this connection, he now performs "purely for the money"—promising himself that, when he gets "enough money," he will "walk out of there and never come back" (p. 259). But the pursuit of "enough money" leads to an economically vicious cycle in the form of a kind of "mad treadmill" in which earning enough requires a lifestyle devoted to earning enough to support that lifestyle . . . and so on (p. 303).

Put differently, success in the music business depends on making money by catering to the paying customer in ways that—by sacrificing artistic integrity (beauty) to commercial gain (filthy lucre or musical crap)—can grow chillingly ugly or even obscene. Thus, complaining about Artie's small-sized audiences, one club manager tells him that "I don't give a good goddamn about music" and that "*Your* problem is to get people in here," adding that

> if you want to take your pants down on that goddamn bandstand every night and take a crap up there, and if people'll pay to come in here and see you do it—*I'll* pay you to take a crap up there every night.
>
> (Shaw 1952, pp. 305–306)

Artie Shaw responds to this vision from hell by vowing to give the (ignorant) people what they want (namely, musical crap disguised as meretricity) with a kind of "engine-turned, slick, flawless, shiny surface perfection" that will appeal to the "lowest common denominator" (pp. 308–309). Shaw's rather cynical response to these realities of the marketplace leads him to "give the public what it evidently wanted" by assembling "the loudest band in the whole goddamn world!" (pp. 310–311). Notice how Shaw's rhetoric at this point echoes the blasphemy of the untutored club manager in the beauty-versus-crap saga. The denigration of musical standards that he mentions seems to evoke such linguistic excesses. This completes his "metamorphosis" from true artist into "Cinderella Boy" (pp. 312–313).

## Artie, No

Nowhere, I believe, does there exist such an intimately detailed account-from-the-inside of the tension between art and commerce and how it unfolds in the pursuit of the American Dream. Nor, in my experience, has any other artist so vividly portrayed the poignantly painful clash that results when commercial considerations impinge on creative integrity. Obviously—as he freely acknowledges at every turn—Artie Shaw's willingness to participate in this degradation of his music reflected personal ambitions, flawed decisions, and infidelity to his own more worthwhile personal goals due to temptations that others, in theory (but probably not in practice), might possibly have managed to resist (albeit with unfavorable financial consequences). But, for our present purposes, it suffices to recognize that the public rags-to-riches success stories at the heart of the ABC Paradigm, the Jazz-Singer Schema, or the DHOPAUS Template may obscure various underlying private calamities that stem from a cost to human dignity paid in the betrayal of one's own artistic integrity.

We do not need an ethnographic study to support this recognition. All we need is a careful reading of Shaw (1952). Toward the end of his Cinderella story, he offers perhaps the clearest description of the art-versus-commerce dilemma available from the perspective of a true artist where, as he recognizes, "the bandleader is a musician trying to sell a mass commodity" so that "to do so successfully he must accommodate himself to mass standards" (p. 326). He goes on to complain that mass tastes turn out to be fickle, unpredictable, and even inscrutable because "You never know what [will] be acceptable to the public until after you've tried it" (p. 329). In response to this quandary, Shaw drops his relatively unsuccessful loudest-band format and builds a new library based on his analysis of the musical approach that makes for hit records—namely, crystal clear arrangements of popular standards by people like Kern, Gershwin, Berlin, Rodgers, and Porter. This strategy leads to what he calls "a kind of formula" (p. 330) where the music became so "simple" that "even a lay listener could (so to speak) see all the way through the surface" (p. 331). Artie's intentional adoption of this populist aesthetic results in his first big hit—namely, his blockbuster recording for RCA's Bluebird label of Cole Porter's "Begin the Beguine" (p. 334). By about 1940 at age 30, in the eyes of the public and the press, he becomes the King—if not of Swing (who, after all, was Benny Goodman), then of the Clarinet.

Actually, Artie Shaw would not have been comfortable with his designation as the King of the Clarinet. Indeed, in the implicit contest between himself and Benny Goodman, Shaw saw himself as aspiring to excellence on the side of pure music. Thus, he frequently told a story about a conversation between himself and Benny Goodman in which he wittily told BG that *Benny* played the *clarinet* but that *Artie* played *music*: "That was a new idea to him—that the clarinet was an instrument; you used it to play music" (interview on NPR with Renee Montague, broadcast March 8, 2002, on-line @ www.npr.org; see also Keepnews 2001; Nolan 2010, p. 49; Pacheco 2005, p. 26). Note Shaw's word play on both meanings of the term "instrument"— that is, a clarinet versus something that performs a function as a means to the end of playing music. Lees (1992) agrees that "While Goodman was the consummate jazz clarinet technician, Shaw was considered by many musicians the richer, the more inventive and certainly the more lyrical player." (p. 10). Balliett (1976, 1989) further corroborates this view of the Goodman–Shaw comparison, noting that "Shaw's clarinet playing [was] always admired more widely by musicians than Goodman's" (1976, p. 107): "Goodman, an arpeggio player, had great facility and passion . . . had a fine tone and was a first-class melodist. . . . Artie Shaw was cooler, narrower, and deeper . . . an even better melodist . . . more interesting harmonically" (1989, p. 191; see also Lees 1988, p. 60; Tormé 1988, p. 88). Given Benny's role as one of our comedepictorial heroes (embodying the rags-to-riches success-story Jazz-Singer Schema of the American Dream) and Artie's place on the dark side of the same coin (as revealed in his animadversions on the Cinderella Myth), it proves instructive to contrast these two bandleaders in detail, as shown in Table 5.

So—to paraphrase Shakespeare—uneasy lies or heavy hangs the head of King Artie, who wears the Clarinetist's Crown. Shaw (1952) begins to get frequent migraines, controlled with pills containing codeine, and even to entertain thoughts of suicide because, in his own mind, Artie remains Cinderella, with all of her troubling problems to contend with. For example, rather poignantly and even alarmingly, Shaw (1952) describes the unbearably sudden change in the way he is treated by others when "People began to point at me in the street, ask for my autograph, stare at me, and do all the nonsensical things" (p. 340) and when "there seem to be hundreds and thousands of crazy people . . . shrieking for no reason you can figure out" (p. 344). These intrusions render Artie "utterly miserable," paranoid, and suicidal. All this pain is intensified by Shaw's deep sense of having sold out artistically—as he expresses, again and again, with sardonic grimness—asking, "What's music got to do with all this stuff?" when "there just isn't time . . . left over for anything as vague and—well, immaterial, as music" (pp. 344–345).

In today's terminology, Artie Shaw was the victim of commodification: "I got miserable when I became a commodity" (quoted by Wilson 2004). Lees (1988) explains that "Artie . . . wasn't simply indifferent to fame" but "actively loathed it": "It is a very strange thing to realize you are no longer a person [but] have become a thing, an object, and the public thinks you belong to them" (p. 73). Given these intolerable pressures, only one thought sustains Shaw (1952) and forestalls his leanings toward suicide—namely, the realization that the money he is earning in this otherwise thankless and miserable existence will ultimately permit him to quit the business and to pursue something that he might actually enjoy—that is, to "walk right out of the whole shebang and start doing anything I felt like doing" (p. 346).

As we now know, the strategy just articulated is exactly the path that Artie Shaw ultimately decided to follow. For a decade, he pursued a sort of on-again off-again participation in the music business—periodically dropping out, then forming a band again, and then dismantling it in order to recuperate. As Shaw (1952) explains it, there is "only one basic reason why I went back into the band business again"—"I needed the money" (p. 359).

*Table 5* Comparisons Between Benny Goodman and Artie Shaw

|  | *Benny Goodman* | *Artie Shaw* |
| --- | --- | --- |
| Born | 1909 | 1910 |
| Childhood | Poor Jewish immigrant family with parents working in the garment industry in Chicago | Poor Jewish immigrant family with parents working in the garment industry in New York |
| Played | Clarinet only | Clarinet, but also alto sax |
| Assessment | Great clarinetist | Great musician |
| Early Instrumentation | Conventional | String section |
| Arrangements | Fletcher Henderson and others | Mostly his own |
| Good Leader? | No | Yes |
| Good Husband? | Yes | No |
| Main Repertoire | Jazz warhorses | Great American Songbook |
| Pioneering Racial Integration | Trio and Quartet (Teddy Wilson and Lionel Hampton) | Whole orchestra (Billie Holiday, "Hot Lips" Page, and Roy Eldridge) |
| Theme Song | "Let's Dance" (major key, upbeat) | "Nightmare" (minor key, dissonant) |
| Accepted Bebop? | Not so much | Yes |
| Played Classical Music? | Yes | Yes |
| Reputation | King of Swing | King of the Clarinet |
| Attitude Toward Fans | Grudging acceptance | Dismissive contempt |
| Success? | Yes and. . . . | Yes but. . . . |

Perhaps writing *The Trouble with Cinderella* gave Shaw (1952) the resolve he needed to quit for good. Two years later—in 1954 at age 43—Artie Shaw laid down his clarinet for the last time and never picked it up in public again. As a partial explanation for all this, Shaw (1952) paraphrases a line from the *Epistles* of Seneca. The stoic philosopher's words might well serve as a lesson to all of us: "From business, however, my dear Lucilius, it is easy to escape, if only you will despise the rewards of business" (Seneca, *Epistles*, Volume I, on-line @ www.stoics.com). Or, as Shaw told Lees (1988), to make a living "you must please a certain number of people so that they'll pay you the money you need": "When you get past that—that is, if you grow—you can then ask yourself, 'Now. What do I want to do?'" (p. 81). Inverting the old phrase, "If you're so wise, why ain't you poor?" (p. 81).

In concluding *The Trouble with Cinderella*, Shaw (1952) asks himself what kind of goal makes sense and answers, "Anything at all, providing it gives you a chance to go on growing and developing as a human being": "For if you ever do have to stop and tell yourself you're finished . . . you'll have stopped living" (p. 378). The impossibility of avoiding this terminal predicament constitutes Artie's major complaint against the music business—his very large gripe with the world of commercial entertainment (as opposed to creative art) in which the audience for a "mass commodity" demands that you stay the same and cease to grow: "Your audience says, in effect . . . don't go any further, because if you do we won't understand what you're trying to do and we won't pay to hear it" (p. 378). So—in the final analysis—Artie Shaw dismisses the music business as the Cinderella-creating apotheosis of commerce elevated over art, insisting that "I have nothing against the music business as a way of earning money" but that "there is far more business connected with it than there is music—or self-satisfaction": "Market-place values dominate to such an extent that musical ones finally cease to exist" (pp. 384–385). Put differently, Artie Shaw recognizes—and profoundly honors—the difference between entertainment and art, where pressures toward catering to the former cause him to despair of pursuing the latter. Thus, he tells Lees (1988), "Where the entertainer says, 'Give the people what they want,' the artist says, 'No, I'm gonna give the people what I want'": "If you cheat on your own ability, for instance by writing less than your best, in order to make money, you're doing something that'll vitiate your abilities forever" (pp. 80–81).

Ultimately, for those sorts of reasons, Shaw gravitated toward a career as a writer. He had already published *The Trouble with Cinderella*—which Lees (1988) regards as "an extremely well-written and literate book on an interesting subject" (p. 77). Balliett (1976) reports that *Cinderella* "was well received as a piece of scorching confessional writing" (p. 106). "Critics," Keepnews (2001) says, "have rated his published work as professional and richly talented." Sudhalter calls him "a writer of formidable, if occasionally idiosyncratic, strengths" (Shaw with Sudhalter 2001). After raising some questions about Shaw's egocentric style, White (2004) reports a series of favorable reviews—including one from *The New Yorker* that calls Shaw "an excellent writer" and praises his autobiography for being "as good as anything of the sort in print" (p. 146).

Artie Shaw followed the autobiographical memoirs in *Cinderella* with two more volumes: *I Love You, I Hate You, Drop Dead* (Shaw 1965) and *The Best of Intentions* (Shaw 1989). The first presents three novellas on the subject of marital problems—a topic on which, indubitably, Shaw ranks as a highly qualified expert. Here, White (2004) sees Shaw's writing as "much better than might have been anticipated" and reports that this "work of fiction received considerable critical acclaim" (p. 159). The second offers a collection of beautifully crafted short stories that clearly demonstrate the author's literary skill. Indeed, White (2004) finds that "Shaw's second collection of fiction is, in many ways, superior to his first" (p. 161). On a personal note, I was thrilled recently—while perusing my newly acquired copy of *The Best of Intentions*—to discover that it is signed, "Best Wishes, Artie Shaw, 9/19/89." I guess I am not much better than those autograph hounds whom the outspoken bandleader so despised. But, nonetheless, I found his signature loaded with all sorts of mystical nostalgic meaning. By now, it should be clear that Artie Shaw has been rising fast on my list of private heroes.

## Yes, Artie, Yes

Back in the day, during the early 1950s, my father had an enviably comprehensive collection of old 78-rpm black-colored shellac-covered highly-breakable scratchy-sounding records by the various jazz musicians featured in our discussion of the jazz-singer biopics—the Dorseys, Miller, Goodman, Nichols, Krupa, and the rest. Curiously, nestled among this treasure trove, I used to ponder a recording by Artie Shaw of an unfamiliar tune called "Adios, Marquita Linda." Much as I wanted to listen to this ancient disk, I could only get through the band's slightly corny statement of the main theme because—when the clarinet solo started—the music suddenly became inaudible. Careful examination showed that, through innumerable playings and replayings by my Dad, the grooves containing the clarinet solo had been worn down to a smooth white dusty surface. There was no more groove-encoded music for me to hear.

Decades went by before RCA got around to reissuing Shaw's recording of "Adios, Marquita Linda." But—when I finally got a chance to hear it on a CD compilation of Artie Shaw classics, 50 years after I had first seen the original and 65 years after Shaw had recorded it—I found good reason to regret Artie's decision, only a few years after giving this performance, to lay down his clarinet forever. Artie Shaw's solo on "Adios, Marquita Linda" is pure magic—the sort of transcendental moment in jazz that puts the attentive listener into a state of total rapture. Departing from the tedium of the orchestra's first chorus, Shaw launches into a flight of fancy that liberates his playing from all terrestrial concerns. This ecstatic glimpse of musical immortality somewhat belies Shaw's most pessimistic view of the Cinderella Myth. Though he did not enjoy a sense of it during his own celebrity-level success story, it now appears clear—from the perspective of an appreciative posterity—that, while at the height of his fame and fortune and while living so conspicuously as the very embodiment of the American Dream, Artie Shaw produced shining masterpieces that will live forever as a touchstone of musical greatness. Perhaps he laid down his clarinet, in part, because there was very little left to say.

Indeed, referring to his decision to quit show business, Artie Shaw himself told a reporter that he was driven by his inability to fulfill his own sense of perfectionism: "In the world we live in, compulsive perfectionists finish last" (quoted by en.wikipedia.org/wiki/Artie_Shaw). Apparently, Artie would rather play not at all than play less than perfectly—obviously a painfully self-defeating habit of mind for a musical performer. In this connection, he commented ruefully that "The closer an artist gets to perfection, . . . the further up his idea of perfection is, so he's chasing a receding horizon" (quoted by Rob Nagel @ www.musicianguide.com). Thus—in the interview with Renee Montague on NPR in March of 2002—Shaw explained a bit more of his deeply ambivalent on-again/off-again love/hate relationship with music in general and with the clarinet in particular, insisting that "he doesn't wish to play the clarinet again, though he still describes the experience with awe." In Shaw's words,

> the clarinet . . . it's just a piece of wood, you know, with holes in it and they put these clumsy keys on it and you're supposed to try to take that and manipulate it with throat muscles and chops . . . and try to make something happen that never happened before. . . . And when you do, you never forget it. It beats sex, it beats anything.
>
> (on-line @ www.npr.org)

## CADENZA

I leave you, Dear Reader, with these wise words from my hero Artie Shaw—namely, his assertion that "it beats anything." Shaw knew that the most successful musical experiences—as performers, but also as listeners—transcend all (well, almost all) other forms of human engagement. When this happens in a concert hall, the effect is magical. When it happens in a film—as part of an ambi-diegetic cinemusical moment—it contributes to the dramatic development of plot, character, and other themes in ways that profoundly enrich the viewer's appreciation. This book has sought to explore such aspects of music, movies, meanings, and markets in general—with special attention in particular to how ambi-diegetic jazz works in films to shape audience understandings of their most profound truths as part of the cinemajazzamatazz experience.

# References

Aaker, David A. (1991), *Managing Brand Equity: Capitalizing on the Value of a Brand Name*, New York, NY: Free Press.

Aaron, Michele (2000), "Hardly Chazans: *Yentl* and the Singing Jew," in *Musicals: Hollywood and Beyond*, ed. Bill Marshall and Robynn Stilwell, Exeter, UK: Intellect, 125–131.

Abrams, M. H. (1988), *A Glossary of Literary Terms*, New York, NY: Holt, Rinehart and Winston.

Adorno, Theodor W. (1967), *Prisms*, trans. Samuel Weber and Shierry Weber, Cambridge, MA: The MIT Press.

Adorno, Theodor W. (1984), *Aesthetic Theory*, trans. C. Lenhardt, London, UK: Routledge & Kegan Paul.

Adorno, Theodor W. (1991), *The Culture Industry: Selected Essays in Mass Culture*, ed. J. M. Bernstein, London, UK: Routledge.

Adorno, Theodor W. and Hanns Eisler (1947 with Adorno as anonymous, ed. 1994), *Composing for the Films*, London, UK: Athlone.

Adorno, Theodor and Hans Eisler (2003), "Prejudices and Bad Habits," in *Movie Music, The Film Reader*, ed. Kay Dickinson, London, UK: Routledge, 25–35.

Altman, Rick (1987), *The American Film Musical*, Bloomington, IN: Indiana University Press.

Altman, Rick (2001), "Cinema and Popular Song: The Lost Tradition," in *Soundtrack Available: Essays on Film and Popular Music*, ed. Pamela Robertson Wojcik and Arthur Knight, Durham, NC: Duke University Press, 19–30.

Altman, Rick (2002), "The American Film Musical as Dual-Focus Narrative," in *Hollywood Musicals: The Film Reader*, ed. Steven Cohan, London, UK: Routledge, 40–51.

Altman, Rick (2007), "Early Film Theories: Roxy, Adorno, and the Problem of Cultural Capital," in *Beyond the Soundtrack: Representing Music in Cinema*, ed. Daniel Goldmark, Lawrence Kramer, and Richard Leppert, Berkeley, CA: University of California Press, 205–224.

Arbuthnot, Lucie and Gail Seneca (2002), "Pre-Text and Text in *Gentlemen Prefer Blondes*," in *Hollywood Musicals: The Film Reader*, ed. Steven Cohan, London, UK: Routledge, 77–85.

Arnheim, Rudolf (1957), *Film As Art*, Berkeley, CA: University of California Press.

Arroyo, José (2000), "Queering the Folklore: Genre and the Re-presentation of Homosexual and National Identities in *Las cosas del querer*," in *Musicals: Hollywood and Beyond*, ed. Bill Marshall and Robynn Stilwell, Exeter, UK: Intellect, 70–78.

Atkins, Irene Kahn (1983), *Source Music in Motion Pictures*, East Brunswick, NJ: Associated University Press.

Atkinson, Michael (1995), "Long Black Limousine: Pop Biopics," in *Celluloid Jukebox: Popular Music and the Movies Since the 50s*, ed. Jonathan Romney and Adrian Wootton, London, UK: British Film Institute, 20–31.

Auerbach, Erich (1953), *Mimesis: The Representation of Reality in Western Literature*, trans. Willard R. Trask, Princeton, NJ: Princeton University Press.

Auerbach, Erich (1969), "Philology and *Weltliteratur*," *The Centennial Review*, 13, 1–17.

Babington, Bruce (2000), "Jumping on the Band Wagon Again: Oedipus Backstage in the Father and Mother of all Musicals," in *Musicals: Hollywood and Beyond*, ed. Bill Marshall and Robynn Stilwell, Exeter, UK: Intellect, 31–39.

Baker, Chet (1997), *As Though I Had Wings: The Lost Memoir*, New York, NY: St. Martin's Press.

Balliett, Whitney (1976), *New York Notes: A Journal of Jazz, 1972–1975*, Boston, MA: Houghton Mifflin Company.

Balliett, Whitney (1982, ed. 1995), "King Again," *The New Yorker*, in *The Sinatra Reader*, ed. Steven Petkov and Leonard Mustazza, New York, NY: Oxford University Press, 184–186.

Balliett, Whitney (1989), *Barney, Bradley, and Max: 16 Portraits in Jazz*, New York, NY: Oxford University Press.

Baudrillard, Jean (1988), *Selected Writings*, ed. Mark Poster, Stanford, CA: Stanford University Press.

Bayles, Martha (1994), *Hole In Our Soul: The Loss of Beauty and Meaning in America's Popular Music*, New York, NY: The Free Press.

Becker, Howard S. (1963), *Outsiders: Studies in the Sociology of Deviance*, New York, NY: Free Press.

Bergfelder, Tim (2000), "Between Nostalgia and Amnesia: Musical Genres in 1950s German Cinema," in *Musicals: Hollywood and Beyond*, ed. Bill Marshall and Robynn Stilwell, Exeter, UK: Intellect, 80–88.

Berlin, Isaiah (1953, ed. 1993), *The Hedgehog and the Fox: An Essay on Tolstoy's View of History*, Chicago, IL: Elephant Paperbacks.

Berliner, Paul F. (1994), *Thinking in Jazz: The Infinite Art of Improvisation*, Chicago, IL: University of Chicago Press.

Bernstein, Leonard (1981), *The Unanswered Question: Six Talks at Harvard*, Cambridge, MA: Harvard University Press.

Berry, Leonard L., Lewis P. Carbone, and Stephan H. Haeckel (2002), "Managing the Total Customer Experience," *Sloan Management Review*, 43 (3, Spring), 85–89.

Biancorosso, Giorgio (2001), "Beginning Credits and Beyond: Music and the Cinematic Imagination," *ECHO*, 3 (1, Spring), on-line @ www.humnet.ucla.edu/echo/volume3-issue1/biancorosso/biancorosso.html

Biancorosso, Giorgio (2004), "Film, Music, and the Redemption of the Mundane," in *Bad Music: The Music We Love to Hate*, ed. Christopher Washburne and Maiken Derno, New York, NY: Routledge, 190–211.

Bleicher, Josef (1980), *Contemporary Hermeneutics: Hermeneutics As Method, Philosophy, and Critique*, London, UK: Routledge & Kegan Paul.

Bloom, Allan (1987), *The Closing of the American Mind: How Higher Education Has Failed Democracy and Impoverished the Souls of Today's Students*, New York, NY: Simon & Schuster.

Bogle, Donald (1990), "Mo' Better Foreword," in *Mo' Better Blues*, by Spike Lee with Lisa Jones, New York, NY: Simon & Schuster, 15–30.

Bordwell, David (1985), *Narration in the Fiction Film*, Madison, WI: University of Wisconsin Press.

Bourdieu, Pierre (1983), "The Field of Cultural Production, Or: The Economic World Reversed," *Poetics*, 12, 311–356.

Bourdieu, Pierre (1984), *Distinction: A Social Critique of the Judgement of Taste*, Cambridge, MA: Harvard University Press.

Bourdieu, Pierre (1986), "The Production of Belief: Contribution to an Economy of Symbolic Goods," in *Media, Culture and Society: A Critical Reader*, ed. Richard Collins, James Curran, Nicholas Garnham, Paddy Scannell, Philip Schlesinger, and Colin Sparks, London, UK: Sage Publications, 131–163.

Bourdieu, Pierre (1993), *The Field of Cultural Production: Essays on Art and Literature*, ed. Randal Johnson, New York, NY: Columbia University Press.

Bourjaily, Vance (1987), "In and Out of Storyville: Jazz and Fiction," *New York Times*, Book Review Section, (December 13), 1, 44–45.

Bradshaw, Alan and Morris B. Holbrook (2007), "Remembering Chet: Theorising the Mythology of the Self-Destructive Bohemian Artist as Self-Producer and Self-Consumer in the Market for Romanticism," *Marketing Theory*, 7 (2, June), 115–136.

Bradshaw, Alan, Pierre McDonagh, and David Marshall (2006a), "No Space— New Blood and the Production of Brand Culture Colonies," *Journal of Marketing Management*, 22 (5/6, July), 579–599.

Bradshaw, Alan, Pierre McDonagh, and David Marshall (2006b), "Response to 'Art versus Commerce as a Macromarketing Theme,'" *Journal of Macromarketing*, 26 (1, June), 81–83.

Brantlinger, Patrick (1983), *Bread & Circuses: Theories of Mass Culture As Social Decay*, Ithaca, NY: Cornell University Press.

Brennan, Don (1990, ed. 1995), "Singing and Swinging by the Sea," *The News Gleaner*, 17 (October), 3–4, in *The Frank Sinatra Reader*, ed. Steven Petkov and Leonard Mustazza, New York, NY: Oxford University Press, 212–215.

Brooks, Cleanth (1947), *The Well-Wrought Urn: Studies in the Structure of Poetry*, New York, NY: Harcourt Brace.

Brooks, Cleanth and Robert Penn Warren (ed. 1960), *Understanding Poetry: An Anthology for College Students*, New York, NY: Holt, Rinehart and Winston.

Brown, Royal S. (1994), *Overtones and Undertones*, Berkeley, CA: University of California Press.

Brown, Stephen (2001), *Marketing—the Retro Revolution*, London, UK: Sage Publications.

Büchmann-Møller, Frank (1990), *You Just Fight For Your Life: The Story of Lester Young*, New York, NY: Praeger.

Buhler, James (2000), "*Star Wars*, Music, and Myth," in *Music and Cinema*, ed. James Buhler, Caryl Flinn, and David Neumeyer, Hanover, NH: Wesleyan University Press, 33–57.

Buhler, James (2001), "Analytical and Interpretive Approaches to Film Music (II): Analysing Interactions of Music and Film," in *Film Music: Critical Approaches*, ed. K. J. Donnelly, New York, NY: The Continuum International Publishing Group, 39–61.

Buhler, James, Caryl Flinn, and David Neumeyer (ed. 2000), *Music and Cinema*, Hanover, NH: Wesleyan University Press.

Burch, Noel (1979), *To the Distant Observer: Form and Meaning in the Japanese Cinema*, Berkeley, CA: University of California Press.

Burt, George (1994), *The Art of Film Music*, Boston, MA: Northeastern University Press.

Caley, Matthew (2005), "Heavy Rotation," in *Pop Fiction: The Song in Cinema*, ed. Steve Lannin and Matthew Caley, Bristol, UK: Intellect, 29–39.

Campbell, Colin (1987), *The Romantic Ethic and the Spirit of Modern Capitalism*, Oxford, UK: Basil Blackwell.

Carbone, Lewis P. and Stephan H. Haeckel (1994), "Engineering Customer Experiences," *Marketing Management*, 3 (3, Winter): 8–19.

Carettini, Gian Paolo (1983), "Peirce, Holmes, Popper," in *The Sign of Three: Dupin, Holmes, Peirce*, ed. Umberto Eco and Thomas A. Sebeok, Bloomington, IN: Indiana University Press, 135–153.

Carr, Roy, Brian Case, and Fred Dellar (1986), *The Hip: Hipsters, Jazz and the Beat Generation*, London, UK: Faber and Faber.

Carringer, Robert L. (1979), "Introduction: *History of a Popular Culture Classic*," in *The Jazz Singer*, Madison, WI: University of Wisconsin Press.

Carroll, Nöel (1988), *Mystifying Movies: Fads and Fallacies in Contemporary Film Theory*, New York, NY: Columbia University Press.

Chion, Michel (1994), *Audio-Vision: Sound on Screen*, ed. and trans. Claudia Gorbman, New York, NY: Columbia University Press.

Citron, Stephen (1992), *Noel and Cole: The Sophisticates*, London, UK: Sinclair-Stevenson.

Claxton, William (1993), *Young Chet*, London, UK: Schirmer Art Books.

Clover, Carol J. (2002), "Dancin' in the Rain," in *Hollywood Musicals: The Film Reader*, ed. Steven Cohan, London, UK: Routledge, 157–173.

Cohan, Steven (2002a), "'Feminizing' the Song-and-Dance Man: Fred Astaire and the Spectacle of Masculinity in the Hollywood Musical," in *Hollywood Musicals: The Film Reader*, ed. Steven Cohan, London, UK: Routledge, 87–101.

Cohan, Steven (2002b), "Introduction—Hollywood Musicals: The Film Reader," in *Hollywood Musicals: The Film Reader*, ed. Steven Cohan, London, UK: Routledge, 1–15.

Cohan, Steven (ed. 2002), *Hollywood Musicals: The Film Reader*, London, UK: Routledge.

Cohen, Annabel J. (2000), "Film Music: Perspectives from Cognitive Psychology," in *Music and Cinema*, ed. James Buhler, Caryl Flinn, and David Neumeyer, Hanover, NH: Wesleyan University Press, 360–377.

Connick, Harry, Jr. (1990, ed. 1995), "A Perfect Singer, Ever Since He Began the Beguine," *New York Times*, (December 9), H26, in *The Sinatra Reader*, ed. Steven Petkov and Leonard Mustazza, New York, NY: Oxford University Press, 253–254.

Conrich, Ian (2000), "Merry Melodies: The Marx Brothers' Musical Moments," in *Musicals: Hollywood and Beyond*, ed. Bill Marshall and Robynn Stilwell, Exeter, UK: Intellect, 47–54.

Conway, Kelley (2001), "Flower of the Asphalt: The *Chanteuse Réaliste* in 1930s French Cinema," in *Soundtrack Available: Essays on Film and Popular Music*, ed. Pamela Robertson Wojcik and Arthur Knight, Durham, NC: Duke University Press, 134–160.

Copland, Aaron (1957), *What to Listen For in Music*, Second Edition, New York, NY: McGraw-Hill.

Corliss, Richard (2001), "The Book on Bing Crosby," *Time* (May 17), on-line @ www.time.com/time/sampler/article/0,8599,99731-3,00.html

Creekmur, Corey K. (2001), "Picturizing American Cinema: Hindi Film Songs and the Last Days of Genre," in *Soundtrack Available: Essays on Film and Popular Music*, ed. Pamela Robertson Wojcik and Arthur Knight, Durham, NC: Duke University Press, 375–406.

Crosby, Gary and Ross Firestone (1983), *Going My Own Way*, New York, NY: Fawcett Crest.

Crow, Bill (1990), *Jazz Anecdotes*, New York, NY: Oxford University Press.

Crow, Bill (1992), *From Birdland to Broadway: Scenes from a Jazz Life*, New York, NY: Oxford University Press.

Culler, Jonathan (1975), *Structuralist Poetics: Structuralism, Linguistics and the Study of Literature*, Ithaca, NY: Cornell University Press.

Dahlhaus, Carl (2004), "Trivial Music (Trivialmusik): 'Preface' and 'Trivial Music and Aesthetic Judgment,'" in *Bad Music: The Music We Love to Hate*, ed. Christopher Washburne and Maiken Derno, New York, NY: Routledge, 333–362.

Dance, Stanley (1970), *The World of Duke Ellington*, New York, NY: Charles Scribner's Sons.

Delannoy, Luc (1993), *Pres: The Story of Lester Young*, trans. Elena B. Odio, Fayetteville: The University of Arkansas Press.

Dickinson, Kay (2003a), "General Introduction: Movie Music, The Film Reader," in *Movie Music, The Film Reader*, ed. Kay Dickinson, London, UK: Routledge, 1–11.

Dickinson, Kay (2003b), "Pop, Speed, Teenagers and the 'MTV Aesthetic,'" in *Movie Music, The Film Reader*, ed. Kay Dickinson, London, UK: Routledge, 143–154.

Dickinson, Kay (ed. 2003), *Movie Music, The Film Reader*, London, UK: Routledge.

Dilthey, Wilhelm (1924, ed. 1972), "The Rise of Hermeneutics," trans. Frederick Jameson, *New Literary History*, 3 (Winter), 229–244.

Doane, Mary Anne (1987), *The Desire to Desire: The Woman's Film of the 1940s*, Bloomington, IN: Indiana University Press.

Donnelly, K. J. (2001a), "Introduction—The Hidden Heritage of Film Music: History and Scholarship," in *Film Music: Critical Approaches*, ed. K. J. Donnelly, New York, NY: The Continuum International Publishing Group, 1–15.

Donnelly, K. J. (2001b), "*Performance* and the Composite Film Score," in *Film Music: Critical Approaches*, ed. K. J. Donnelly, New York, NY: The Continuum International Publishing Group, 152–166.

Donnelly, K. J. (ed. 2001), *Film Music: Critical Approaches*, New York, NY: The Continuum International Publishing Group.

Duesenberry, James S. (1949), *Income, Saving and the Theory of Consumer Behavior*, Cambridge, MA: Harvard University Press.

Dyer, Richard (2000), "The Colour of Entertainment," in *Musicals: Hollywood and Beyond*, ed. Bill Marshall and Robynn Stilwell, Exeter, UK: Intellect, 23–30.

Dyer, Richard (2002a), "Entertainment and Utopia," in *Hollywood Musicals: The Film Reader*, ed. Steven Cohan, London, UK: Routledge, 19–30.

Dyer, Richard (2002b), "Judy Garland and Camp," in *Hollywood Musicals: The Film Reader*, ed. Steven Cohan, London, UK: Routledge, 107–113.

Dyer, Richard (2007), "Side by Side: Nino Rota, Music, and Film," in *Beyond the Soundtrack: Representing Music in Cinema*, ed. Daniel Goldmark, Lawrence

Kramer, and Richard Leppert, Berkeley, CA: University of California Press, 246–259.

Ebert, Roger (1992), "The Player," *Chicago Sun Times* (April 24), on-line @ rogerebert.suntimes.com

Eco, Umberto (1976), *A Theory of Semiotics*, Bloomington, IN: Indiana University Press.

Eco, Umberto (1983), "Horns, Hooves, Insteps: Some Hypotheses on Three Types of Abduction," in *The Sign of Three: Dupin, Holmes, Peirce*, ed. Umberto Eco and Thomas A. Sebeok, Bloomington, IN: Indiana University Press, 198–220.

Eco, Umberto and Thomas A. Sebeok (ed. 1983), *The Sign of Three: Dupin, Holmes, Peirce*, Bloomington, IN: Indiana University Press.

Ellington, Edward Kennedy (1973), *Music Is My Mistress*, Garden City, NY: Doubleday & Company.

Empson, William (1949), *Seven Types of Ambiguity*, New York, NY: New Directions.

Everett, Wendy (2000), "Songlines: Alternative Journeys in Contemporary European Cinema," in *Music and Cinema*, ed. James Buhler, Caryl Flinn, and David Neumeyer, Hanover, NH: Wesleyan University Press, 99–117.

Everett, William A. and Paul R. Laird (2002), "Preface," in *The Cambridge Companion to the Musical*, ed. William A. Everett and Paul R. Laird, Cambridge, UK: Cambridge University Press, xv–xvii.

Everett, William A. and Paul R. Laird (ed. 2002), *The Cambridge Companion to the Musical*, Cambridge, UK: Cambridge University Press.

Ewen, Stuart (2001), *Captains of Consciousness: Advertising and the Social Roots of the Consumer Culture*, New York, NY: Basic Books.

Feather, Leonard (1955), *The Encyclopedia of Jazz*, New York, NY: Horizon Press.

Feather, Leonard (1960), *The New Edition of the Encyclopedia of Jazz*, New York, NY: Bonanza Books.

Feuer, Jane (1993), *The Hollywood Musical*, Bloomington, IN: Indiana University Press.

Feuer, Jane (2002), "The Self-Reflective Musical and the Myth of Entertainment," in *Hollywood Musicals: The Film Reader*, ed. Steven Cohan, London, UK: Routledge, 31–40.

Fish, Stanley (1980), *Is There a Text in This Class?: The Authority of Interpretive Communities*, Cambridge, MA: Harvard University Press.

Fiske, John (1982), *Introduction to Communication Studies*, New York, NY: Methuen.

Flinn, Caryl (1992), *Strains of Utopia: Gender, Nostalgia, and Hollywood Film Music*, Princeton, NJ: Princeton University Press.

Flinn, Caryl (2000), "Strategies of Remembrance: Music and History in the New German Cinema," in *Music and Cinema*, ed. James Buhler, Caryl Flinn, and David Neumeyer, Hanover, NH: Wesleyan University Press, 118–141.

Fowler, Cathy (2000), "Harnessing Visibility: The Attractions of Chantal Akerman's *Golden Eighties*," in *Musicals: Hollywood and Beyond*, ed. Bill Marshall and Robynn Stilwell, Exeter, UK: Intellect, 107–116.

Frank, Alan (1978), *Sinatra*, New York, NY: Leon Amiel Publisher.

Frank, Robert H. (1999), *Luxury Fever: Why Money Fails to Satisfy in an Era of Excess*, New York, NY: The Free Press.

Freud, Sigmund (1900, ed. 1965), *The Interpretation of Dreams*, trans. James Strachey, New York, NY: Avon.

Freud, Sigmund (1916, ed. 1977), *Introductory Lectures on Psychoanalysis*, trans. James Strachey, New York, NY: Norton.

Friedwald, Will (1990), *Jazz Singing: America's Great Voices from Bessie Smith to Bebop and Beyond*, New York, NY: Charles Scribner's Sons.

Friedwald, Will (1995), *Sinatra! The Song Is You: A Singer's Art*, New York, NY: Scribner.

Friedwald, Will (2002), *Stardust Melodies: The Biography of Twelve of America's Most Popular Songs*, New York, NY: Pantheon Books.

Frith, Simon (2004), "What Is Bad Music?" in *Bad Music: The Music We Love to Hate*, ed. Christopher Washburne and Maiken Derno, New York, NY: Routledge, 15–36.

Frye, Northrop, Sheridan Baker, and George Perkins (1985), *The Harper Handbook to Literature*, New York, NY: Harper & Row.

Furia, Philip (1992), *The Poets of Tin Pan Alley: A History of America's Great Lyricists*, New York, NY: Oxford University Press.

Gabbard, Krin (1996), *Jammin' at the Margins: Jazz and the American Cinema*, Chicago, IL: The University of Chicago Press.

Gabbard, Krin (2000), "Kansas City Dreamin': Robert Altman's Jazz History Lesson," in *Music and Cinema*, ed. James Buhler, Caryl Flinn, and David Neumeyer, Hanover, NH: Wesleyan University Press, 142–157.

Gabbard, Krin (2001), "Borrowing Black Masculinity: The Role of Johnny Hartman in *Bridges of Madison County*," in *Soundtrack Available: Essays on Film and Popular Music*, ed. Pamela Robertson Wojcik and Arthur Knight, Durham, NC: Duke University Press, 295–316.

Gabbard, Krin (2003), "Whose Jazz, Whose Cinema?," in *Movie Music, The Film Reader*, ed. Kay Dickinson, London, UK: Routledge, 121–132.

Gabbard, Krin (2004), "Miles From Home: Miles Davis and the Movies," *The Source*, 1, 27–42.

Gabbard, Krin (2007), "White Face, Black Noise: Miles Davis and the Soundtrack," in *Beyond the Soundtrack: Representing Music in Cinema*, ed. Daniel Goldmark, Lawrence Kramer, and Richard Leppert, Berkeley, CA: University of California Press, 260–276.

Gabbard, Krin (2008), *Hotter Than That: The Trumpet, Jazz, and American Culture*, New York, NY: Faber and Faber.

Gadamer, Hans-Georg (1975), *Truth and Method*, ed. Barrett Barden and John Cumming, New York, NY: Crossroad.

Galbraith, John Kenneth (1958), *The Affluent Society*, New York, NY: Houghton Mifflin.

Gans, Herbert J. (1974), *Popular Culture and High Culture: An Analysis and Evaluation of Taste*, New York, NY: Basic Books.

Gardner, Ava (1990), *Ava: My Story*, New York, NY: Bantam Books.

Garner, Ken (2000), "I've Heard that Song Before: Woody Allen's Films as Studies in Popular Musical Form," in *Musicals: Hollywood and Beyond*, ed. Bill Marshall and Robynn Stilwell, Exeter, UK: Intellect, 14–22.

Garner, Ken (2001), "'Would You Like to Hear Some Music?' Music in-and-out-of-control in the Films of Quentin Tarantino," in *Film Music: Critical Approaches*, ed. K. J. Donnelly, New York, NY: The Continuum International Publishing Group, 188–205.

Garwood, Ian (2003), "Must You Remember This? Orchestrating the 'Standard' Pop Song in *Sleepless in Seattle*," in *Movie Music, The Film Reader*, ed. Kay Dickinson, London, UK: Routledge, 109–117.

Gavin, James (2002), *Deep in a Dream: The Long Night of Chet Baker*, New York, NY: Alfred A. Knopf.

Giddins, Gary (2001), *Bing Crosby: A Pocketful of Dreams, the Early Years, 1903–1940*, Boston, MA: Little, Brown and Company.

Gill, Jonathan (2001), "'Hollywood Has Taken on a New Color': The Yiddish Blackface of Samuel Goldwyn's *Porgy and Bess*," in *Soundtrack Available: Essays on Film and Popular Music*, ed. Pamela Robertson Wojcik and Arthur Knight, Durham, NC: Duke University Press, 347–371.

Ginzburg, Carlo (1983), "Morelli, Freud, and Sherlock Holmes: Clues and Scientific Method," in *The Sign of Three: Dupin, Holmes, Peirce*, ed. Umberto Eco and Thomas A. Sebeok, Bloomington, IN: Indiana University Press, 81–118.

Gioia, Ted (1992), *West Coast Jazz: Modern Jazz in California, 1945–1960*, New York, NY: Oxford University Press.

Gleason, Ralph J. (1974, ed. 1995), "Frank: Then and Now," *Rolling Stone*, (June 6), in *The Sinatra Reader*, ed. Steven Petkov and Leonard Mustazza, New York, NY: Oxford University Press, 225–227.

Godard, Jean Luc (1972, ed. 1986), *Godard on Godard*, ed. and trans. Tom Milne, Cambridge, MA: DaCapo Press.

Goffman, Erving (1959), *The Presentation of Self in Everyday Life*, New York, NY: Anchor Books.

Goldmark, Daniel (2007), "Before *Willie*: Reconsidering Music and the Animated Cartoon of the 1920s," in *Beyond the Soundtrack: Representing Music in Cinema*, ed. Daniel Goldmark, Lawrence Kramer, and Richard Leppert, Berkeley, CA: University of California Press, 225–245.

Goldmark, Daniel, Lawrence Kramer, and Richard Leppert (2007), "Introduction—Phonoplay: Recasting Film Music," in *Beyond the Soundtrack: Representing Music in Cinema*, ed. Daniel Goldmark, Lawrence Kramer, and Richard Leppert, Berkeley, CA: University of California Press, 1–9.

Goldmark, Daniel, Lawrence Kramer, and Richard Leppert (ed. 2007), *Beyond the Soundtrack: Representing Music in Cinema*, Berkeley, CA: University of California Press.

Gorbman, Claudia (1987), *Unheard Melodies: Narrative Film Music*, Bloomington, IN: Indiana University Press.

Gorbman, Claudia (2007), "Auteur Music," in *Beyond the Soundtrack: Representing Music in Cinema*, ed. Daniel Goldmark, Lawrence Kramer, and Richard Leppert, Berkeley, CA: University of California Press, 149–162.

Gordon, Joanne (1990), *Art Isn't Easy: The Achievement of Stephen Sondheim*, Carbondale, IL: Southern Illinois University Press.

Gordon, Robert (1986), *Jazz West Coast: The Los Angeles Jazz Scene of the 1950s*, London, UK: Quartet Books.

Green, Benny (1989), *Let's Face the Music: The Golden Age of Popular Song*, London, UK: Pavilion Books.

Greenberg, Clement (1946, ed. 1957), "Avant-Garde and Kitsch," in *Mass Culture: The Popular Arts in America*, ed. Bernard Rosenberg and David Manning White, Glencoe, IL: The Free Press, 98–107.

Gridley, Mark C. (1987), "Is Jazz Popular Music?" *The Instrumentalist*, 41 (March), 18-26, 85.

Grossberg, Lawrence (2003), "Cinema, Postmodernity and Authenticity," in *Movie Music, The Film Reader*, ed. Kay Dickinson, London, UK: Routledge, 83–97.

Hagen, Earle (1971), *Scoring for Films*, Emeryville, CA: MixBooks.

Hamill, Pete (1980, ed. 1995), "Sinatra: The Legend lives," *New York*, 28 April 1980, 30–35, in *The Sinatra Reader*, ed. Steven Petkov and Leonard Mustazza, New York, NY: Oxford University Press, 227–239.

Harrowitz, Nancy (1983), "The Body of the Detective Model: Charles S. Peirce and Edgar Allan Poe," in *The Sign of Three: Dupin, Holmes, Peirce*, ed. Umberto Eco and Thomas A. Sebeok, Bloomington, IN: Indiana University Press, 179–197.

Hayakawa, S. I. (1955, ed. 1957), "Popular Songs vs. The Facts of Life," in *Mass Culture: The Popular Arts in America*, ed. Bernard Rosenberg and David Manning White, Glencoe, IL: The Free Press, 393–403.

Henry, William A., III (1994), *In Defense of Elitism*, New York, NY: Doubleday.

Hirsch, E. D., Jr. (1967), *Validity in Interpretation*, New Haven, CT: Yale University Press.

Hirschman, Elizabeth C. (ed. 1989), *Interpretive Consumer Research*, Provo, UT: Association for Consumer Research.

Hirschman, Elizabeth C. and Morris B. Holbrook (1982), "Hedonic Consumption: Emerging Concepts, Methods and Propositions," *Journal of Marketing*, 46 (Summer), 92–101.

Hirschman, Elizabeth C. and Morris B. Holbrook (1992), *Postmodern Consumer Research: The Study of Consumption as Text*, Newbury Park, CA: Sage Publications.

Hoeckner, Berthold (2007), "Transport and Transportation in Audiovisual Memory," in *Beyond the Soundtrack: Representing Music in Cinema*, ed. Daniel Goldmark, Lawrence Kramer, and Richard Leppert, Berkeley, CA: University of California Press, 163–183.

Holbrook, Morris B. (1985), "The Consumer Researcher Visits Radio City: Dancing in the Dark," in *Advances in Consumer Research*, Vol. 12, ed. Elizabeth C. Hirschman and Morris B. Holbrook, Provo, Utah: Association for Consumer Research, 28–31.

Holbrook, Morris B. (1986), "I'm Hip: An Autobiographical Account of Some Consumption Experiences," in *Advances in Consumer Research*, Vol. 13, ed. Richard J. Lutz, Provo, Utah: Association for Consumer Research, 614–618.

Holbrook, Morris B. (1991), "Romanticism and Sentimentality in Consumer Behavior: A Literary Approach to the Joys and Sorrows of Consumption," *Research in Consumer Behavior*, 5, 105–180.

Holbrook, Morris B. (1993), *Daytime Television Game Shows and The Celebration of Merchandise: The Price is Right*, Bowling Green, OH: Bowling Green State University Popular Press.

Holbrook, Morris B. (1994), "The Nature of Customer Value: An Axiology of Services in the Consumption Experience," in *Service Quality: New Directions in Theory and Practice*, ed. Roland T. Rust and Richard L. Oliver, Thousand Oaks, CA: Sage Publications, 21–71.

Holbrook, Morris B. (1995a), *Consumer Research: Introspective Essays on the Study of Consumption*, Thousand Oaks, CA: Sage Publications.

Holbrook, Morris B. (1995b), "The Four Faces of Commodification in the Development of Marketing Knowledge," *Journal of Marketing Management*, 11, 641–654.

Holbrook, Morris B. (1995c), "The Three Faces of Elitism: Postmodernism, Political Correctness, and Popular Culture," *Journal of Macromarketing*, 15 (Fall), 128–165.

Holbrook, Morris B. (1996), "Reflections on Rocky," *Society & Animals: Social Scientific Studies of the Human Experience of Other Animals*, 4 (2), 147–168.

Holbrook, Morris B. (1997a), "Borders, Creativity, and the State of the Art at the Leading Edge," *Journal of Macromarketing*, 17 (Fall), 96–112.

Holbrook, Morris B. (1997b), "Romanticism, Introspection, and the Roots of Experiential Consumption: Morris the Epicurean," *Consumption, Markets & Culture*, 1 (2), 97–163.

Holbrook, Morris B. (1998a), "Journey to Kroywen: An Ethnoscopic Auto-Auto-Auto-Driven Stereographic Photo Essay," in *Representing Consumers: Voices, Views, and Visions*, ed. Barbara B. Stern, London, UK: Routledge, 231–263.

Holbrook, Morris B. (1998b), "The Dangers of Educational and Cultural Populism: Three Vignettes on the Problems of Aesthetic Insensitivity, the Pitfalls of Pandering, and the Virtues of Artistic Integrity," *Journal of Consumer Affairs*, 32 (Winter), 394–423.

Holbrook, Morris B. (1998c), "The Katarche of Catology in Research on Marketing: *Breakfast At Tiffany's*, Stereography, Subjective Personal Introspection, and Cat," *Irish Marketing Review*, 11 (2), 29–38.

Holbrook, Morris B. (1999a), "Higher Than the Bottom Line: Reflections on Some Recent Macromarketing Literature," *Journal of Macromarketing*, 19 (June), 48–74.

Holbrook, Morris B. (1999b), "Introduction To Consumer Value," in *Consumer Value: A Framework For Analysis and Research*, ed. Morris B. Holbrook, London, UK: Routledge, 1–28.

Holbrook, Morris B. (1999c), "Popular Appeal versus Expert Judgments of Motion Pictures," *Journal of Consumer Research*, 26 (September), 144–155.

Holbrook, Morris B. (2000), "The Millennial Consumer in the Texts of Our Times: Experience and Entertainment," *Journal of Macromarketing*, 20 (December), 178–192.

Holbrook, Morris B. (2001a), "The Millennial Consumer in the Texts of Our Times: Exhibitionism," *Journal of Macromarketing*, 21 (June), 81–95.

Holbrook, Morris B. (2001b), "The Millennial Consumer in the Texts of Our Times: Evangelizing," *Journal of Macromarketing*, 21 (December), 181–198.

Holbrook, Morris B. (2002), "Book Review: *Marketing—The Retro Revolution* by Stephen Brown," *Journal of the Academy of Marketing Science*, 30 (3, Summer), 262–267.

Holbrook, Morris B. (2003a), "A Book-Review Essay on the Role of Ambi-Diegetic Film Music in the Product Design of Hollywood Movies: Macromarketing in La-La-Land," *Consumption, Markets & Culture*, 6 (3, September), 207–230.

Holbrook, Morris B. (2003b), "Adventures in Complexity: An Essay on Dynamic Open Complex Adaptive Systems, Butterfly Effects, Self-Organizing Order, Coevolution, the Ecological Perspective, Fitness Landscapes, Market Spaces, Emergent Beauty at the Edge of Chaos, and All That Jazz," *Academy of Marketing Science Review*, book-length monograph, on-line @ www.amsreview.org

Holbrook, Morris B. (2004), "Ambi-Diegetic Music in Films as a Product-Design and -Placement Strategy: The *Sweet Smell of Success*," *Marketing Theory*, 4 (3, September), 171–185.

Holbrook, Morris B. (2005a), "Ambi-Diegetic Music in the Movies: The Crosby Duets in *High Society*," *Consumption, Markets & Culture*, 8 (2, June), 153–182.

Holbrook, Morris B. (2005b), "Art versus Commerce as a Macromarketing Theme in Three Films from the Young-Man-with-a-Horn Genre," *Journal of Macromarketing*, 25 (1, June), 22–31.

Holbrook, Morris B. (2005c), "Customer Value and Autoethnography: Subjective Personal Introspection and the Meanings of a Photograph Collection," *Journal of Business Research*, 58 (1, January), 45–61.

Holbrook, Morris B. (2005d), "Living It Up in Twitchell's Branded Nation: Which Way to the Egress?" *Journal of Macromarketing*, 25 (2, December), 233–241.

Holbrook, Morris B. (2005e), "The Ambi-Diegesis of 'My Funny Valentine,'" in *Pop Fiction—The Song in Cinema*, ed. Steve Lannin and Matthew Caley, Bristol, UK: Intellect, 48–62.

Holbrook, Morris B. (2005f), "The Role of Ordinary Evaluations in the Market for Popular Culture: Do Consumers Have 'Good Taste'?" *Marketing Letters*, 16 (2, April), 75–86.

Holbrook, Morris B. (2006a), "Consumption Experience, Customer Value, and Subjective Personal Introspection: An Illustrative Photographic Essay," *Journal of Business Research*, 59 (6, June), 714–725.

Holbrook, Morris B. (2006b), "Photo Essays and the Mining of Minutiae in Consumer Research: 'Bout the Time I Got to Phoenix," in *Handbook of Qualitative Research Methods in Marketing*, ed. Russell W. Belk, Northampton, MA: Edward Elgar, 476–493.

Holbrook, Morris B. (2006c), "Reply to Bradshaw, McDonagh, and Marshall: Turn off the Bubble Machine," *Journal of Macromarketing*, 26 (1, June), 84–87.

Holbrook, Morris B. (2006d), "ROSEPEKICECIVECI Vs. CCV—The Resource-Operant, Skills-Exchanging, Performance-Experiencing, Knowledge-Informed, Competence-Enacting, Coproducer-Involved, Value-Emerging, Customer-Interactive View of Marketing Versus the Concept of Customer Value: 'I Can Get It For You Wholesale,'" in *Toward a Service-Dominant Logic of Marketing: Continuing the Discussion, Debate, and Dialog*, ed. Robert F. Lusch and Stephen L. Vargo, Armonk, NY: M. E. Sharpe, 208–223.

Holbrook, Morris B. (2007a), "Cinemusical Meanings in Motion Pictures: Commerce, Art, and Brando Loyalty . . . Or . . . De Niro, My God, To Thee," *Journal of Consumer Behaviour*, 6 (November-December), 398–418.

Holbrook, Morris B. (2007b), *Playing the Changes on the Jazz Metaphor: An Expanded Conceptualization of Music-, Management-, and Marketing-Related Themes, Foundations and Trends in Marketing*, 2 (3-4), 185–442, Book-Length Monograph, Now Publishers: Hanover, MA.

Holbrook, Morris B. (2007c), "The Consumption Experience—Something New, Something Old, Something Borrowed, Something Sold—Part 2," *Journal of Macromarketing*, 27 (1, March), 86–96.

Holbrook, Morris B. (2007d), "The Consumption Experience—Something New, Something Old, Something Borrowed, Something Sold—Part 3," *Journal of Macromarketing*, 27 (2, June), 173–183.

Holbrook, Morris B. (2007e), "The Consumption Experience—Something New, Something Old, Something Borrowed, Something Sold—Part 4," *Journal of Macromarketing*, 27 (3, September), 303–319.

Holbrook, Morris B. (2007f), "When Bad Things Happen to Great Musicians: The Role of Ambi-Diegetic Jazz in Three Tragedepictions of Artistic Genius on the Silver Screen," *Jazz Research Journal*, 1 (1, May), 99–128.

Holbrook, Morris B. (2008a), "A Cinemusicaliterary Analysis of the American Dream as Represented by Biographical Jazz Comedepictions in the Golden Age of Hollywood Biopics: Blow, Horatio, Blow; O, Jakie, O; Go, Tommy, Go; No, Artie, No," Working Paper, Graduate School of Business, Columbia University.

Holbrook, Morris B. (2008b), "God Is in the Details: Small But Meaningful Cinemusical Moments in Jazz Film Scores by Miles Davis and John Lewis," Working Paper, Graduate School of Business, Columbia University.

Holbrook, Morris B. (2008c), "Musical Meanings in Movies: The Case of the Crime-Plus-Jazz Genre," *Consumption, Markets & Culture*, 11 (4, December), 307–327.

Holbrook, Morris B. (2008d), "Pets and People: Companions in Commerce?" *Journal of Business Research*, 61 (5, May), 546–552.

Holbrook, Morris B. (2009), "A Cinemusicaliterary Analysis of the American Dream as Represented by Biographical Jazz Comedepictions in the Golden Age of Hollywood Biopics: Blow, Horatio, Blow; O, Jakie, O; Go, Tommy, Go; No, Artie, No," *Marketing Theory*, 9 (3, September), 259–313.

Holbrook, Morris B. and Michela Addis (2007), "Taste Versus the Market: An Extension of Research on the Consumption of Popular Culture," *Journal of Consumer Research*, 34 (October), 415–424.

Holbrook, Morris B. and Ellen Day (1994), "Reflections on Jazz and Teaching: Benny and Gene, Woody and We," *European Journal of Marketing*, 28 (8/9), 133–144.

Holbrook, Morris B. and Mark W. Grayson (1986), "The Semiology of Cinematic Consumption: Symbolic Consumer Behavior in *Out of Africa*," *Journal of Consumer Research*, 13 (December), 374–381.

Holbrook, Morris B. and Elizabeth C. Hirschman (1982), "The Experiential Aspects of Consumption: Consumer Fantasies, Feelings, and Fun," *Journal of Consumer Research*, 9 (September), 132–140.

Holbrook, Morris B. and Elizabeth C. Hirschman (1993), *The Semiotics of Consumption: Interpreting Symbolic Consumer Behavior in Popular Culture and Works of Art*, Berlin / New York, NY: Mouton De Gruyter.

Holbrook, Morris B., Kathleen T. Lacher, and Michael S. LaTour (2006), "Audience Judgments as the Potential Missing Link Between Expert Judgments and Audience Appeal: An Illustration Based on Musical Recordings of 'My Funny Valentine,'" *Journal of the Academy of Marketing Science*, 34 (1, Winter), 8–18.

Holbrook, Morris B. and John O'Shaughnessy (1988), "On the Scientific Status of Consumer Research and the Need for an Interpretive Approach to Studying Consumption Behavior," *Journal of Consumer Research*, 15 (December), 398–402.

Holden, Stephen (1984, ed. 1995), "Guide to Middle Age," *The Atlantic* (January), 84–87, in *The Sinatra Reader*, ed. Steven Petkov and Leonard Mustazza, New York, NY: Oxford University Press, 64–69.

Holden, Stephen (1990, ed. 1995), "Frank Sinatra Opens and Then Cancels," *New York Times*, (May 17), C21, in *The Sinatra Reader*, ed. Steven Petkov and Leonard Mustazza, New York, NY: Oxford University Press, 188–189.

Holmes, John Clellon (1958), *The Horn*, New York, NY: Thunder's Mouth Press.

Holsti, Ole R. (1969), *Content Analysis for the Social Sciences and Humanities*, Reading, MA: Addison-Wesley Publishing Company.

Hyland , William G. (1995), *The Song Is Ended: Songwriters and American Music, 1900–1950*, New York, NY: Oxford University Press.

Jewell (1985, ed. 1995), *Frank Sinatra: A Celebration*, Pavilion Books. Excerpt in *The Sinatra Reader*, ed. Steven Petkov and Leonard Mustazza, New York, NY: Oxford University Press, 53–55.

Kael, Pauline (1989), "Fascination," *The New Yorker*, May 1, on-line @ home.ica. net/~blooms/vol2no4.htm

Kalinak, Kathryn (1992), *Settling the Score: Music and the Classical Hollywood Film*, Madison, WI: University of Wisconsin Press.

Kalinak, Kathryn (2000), "Disciplining Josephine Baker: Gender, Race, and the Limits of Disciplinarity," in *Music and Cinema*, ed. James Buhler, Caryl Flinn, and David Neumeyer, Hanover, NH: Wesleyan University Press, 316–335.

Karlin, Fred (1994), *Listening to Movies: The Film Lover's Guide to Film Music*, New York, NY: Schirmer Books.

Kassabian, Anahid (2001), *Hearing Film: Tracking Identifications in Contemporary Hollywood Film Music*, New York, NY: Routledge.

Keepnews, Orrin (2001), "Reissue Producer's Note," *Self-Portrait*, New York, NY: BMG Entertainment.

Keightley, Keir (2003), "Manufacturing Authenticity: Imagining the Music Industry in Anglo-American Cinema, 1956–62," in *Movie Music, The Film Reader*, ed. Kay Dickinson, London, UK: Routledge, 165–180.

Kennedy, William (1993, ed. 1995), "Frank Sinatra: Pluperfect Music," from *Riding the Yellow Trolley Car*, New York, NY: Penguin Books, in *The Sinatra Reader*, ed. Steven Petkov and Leonard Mustazza, New York, NY: Oxford University Press, 254–258.

Kermode, Mark (1995), "Twisting the Knife," in *Celluloid Jukebox: Popular Music and the Movies Since the 50s*, ed. Jonathan Romney and Adrian Wootton, London, UK: British Film Institute, 8–19.

Kerrison, Ray (1993, ed. 1995), "Ol' Blue Eyes Still Has the Magic," *New York Post*, (August 25), 14, in *The Sinatra Reader*, ed. Steven Petkov and Leonard Mustazza, New York, NY: Oxford University Press, 191–193.

Keyes, Evelyn (1977), *Scarlett O'Hara's Younger Sister: My Lively Life In and Out of Hollywood*, Secaucus, NJ: Lyle Stuart Inc.

Killick, Andrew P. (2001), "Music as Ethnic Marker in Film: The 'Jewish' Case," in *Soundtrack Available: Essays on Film and Popular Music*, ed. Pamela Robertson Wojcik and Arthur Knight, Durham, NC: Duke University Press, 185–201.

Klauber, Bruce H. (1990), *The World of Gene Krupa: That Legendary Drummin' Man*, Ventura, CA: Pathfinder Publishing of California.

Knee, Adam (2001), "Class Swings: Music, Race, and Social Mobility in *Broken Strings*," in *Soundtrack Available: Essays on Film and Popular Music*, ed. Pamela Robertson Wojcik and Arthur Knight, Durham, NC: Duke University Press, 269–294.

Knight, Arthur (2001), "'It Ain't Necessarily So That It Ain't Necessarily So': African American Recordings of *Porgy and Bess* as Film and Cultural Criticism," in *Soundtrack Available: Essays on Film and Popular Music*, ed. Pamela Robertson Wojcik and Arthur Knight, Durham, NC: Duke University Press, 319–346.

Knight, Arthur and Pamela Robertson Wojcik (2001), "Overture," in *Soundtrack Available: Essays on Film and Popular Music*, ed. Pamela Robertson Wojcik and Arthur Knight, Durham, NC: Duke University Press, 1–15.

Koehne, James (2004), "The Flight from Banality," in *Bad Music: The Music We Love to Hate*, ed. Christopher Washburne and Maiken Derno, New York, NY: Routledge, 148–172.

Krämer, Peter (2000), "'A Cutie With More Than Beauty': Audrey Hepburn, the Hollywood Musical and *Funny Face*," in *Musicals: Hollywood and Beyond*, ed. Bill Marshall and Robynn Stilwell, Exeter, UK: Intellect, 62–69.

Kripke, Saul (1980), *Naming and Necessity*, Second Edition, Cambridge, MA: Harvard University Press.

Kubacki, Krzysztof and Robin Croft (2004), "Mass Marketing, Music, and Morality," *Journal of Marketing Management*, 20 (5/6, July), 577–590.

Laing, Heather (2000), "Emotion By Numbers: Music, Song and the Musical," in *Musicals: Hollywood and Beyond*, ed. Bill Marshall and Robynn Stilwell, Exeter, UK: Intellect, 5–13.

Lannin, Steve (2005), "Fluid Figures: How to see Ghost[s]," in *Pop Fiction: The Song in Cinema*, ed. Steve Lannin and Matthew Caley, Bristol, UK: Intellect, 71–84.

Lannin, Steve and Matthew Caley (2005), "Introduction," in *Pop Fiction: The Song in Cinema*, ed. Steve Lannin and Matthew Caley, Bristol, UK: Intellect, 9–14.

Lannin, Steve and Matthew Caley (ed. 2005), *Pop Fiction: The Song in Cinema*, Bristol, UK: Intellect.

Lear, Martha Weinman (1974, ed. 1995), "The Bobby Sox Have Wilted, but the Memory Remains Fresh," *New York Times*, Section 2 (October 13), 1, 12, in *The Sinatra Reader*, ed. Steven Petkov and Leonard Mustazza, New York, NY: Oxford University Press, 47–50.

Lebergott, Stanley (1993), *Pursuing Happiness: American Consumers in the Twentieth Century*, Princeton, NJ: Princeton University Press.

Lee, Bill (1990), "Eight Bars In," in *Mo' Better Blues*, by Spike Lee with Lisa Jones, New York, NY: Simon & Schuster, 165–179.

Lee, Spike with Lisa Jones (1990), *Mo' Better Blues*, New York, NY: Simon & Schuster, Inc.

Leeper, Jill (2001), "Crossing Musical Borders: The Soundtrack for *Touch of Evil*," in *Soundtrack Available: Essays on Film and Popular Music*, ed. Pamela Robertson Wojcik and Arthur Knight, Durham, NC: Duke University Press, 226–243.

Lees, Gene (1985), "Frank Sinatra," booklet/essay for *Frank Sinatra*, Time-Life Music Series on Legendary Singers, New York, NY: Time-Life Books.

Lees, Gene (1987), *Singers and the Song*, New York, NY: Oxford University Press.

Lees, Gene (1988), *Meet Me at Jim & Andy's: Jazz Musicians and Their World*, New York, NY: Oxford University Press.

Lees, Gene (1992), *Jazz Lives*, Buffalo, NY: Firefly Books.

Lees, Gene (1997), "The Death of Glenn Miller," *Jazzletter*, 16 (9, September), 2–3.

Lees, Gene (1998), *Singers and the Song II*, New York, NY: Oxford University Press.

Lees, Gene (2004) "Exchanges," *Jazzletter*, 23 (11, November), 1–8.

Lees, Gene (2007a), "The Glenn Miller Years I," *Jazzletter*, 24 (6, June), 1–8.

Lees, Gene (2007b), "The Glenn Miller Years IV," *Jazzletter*, 24 (9, September), 1–8.

Levine, Lawrence W. (1988), *Highbrow/Lowbrow: The Emergence of Cultural Hierarchy in America*, Cambridge, MA: Harvard University Press.

Levinson, Peter J. 1999. *Trumpet Blues: The Life of Harry James*. New York, NY: Oxford University Press.

Lévi-Strauss, Claude (1963), *Structural Anthropology*, trans. Claire Jacobson and Brooke Grundfest Schoepf, New York, NY: Basic Books.

Lindeperg, Sylvie and Bill Marshall (2000), "Time, History and Memory in *Les Parapluies de Cherbourg*," in *Musicals: Hollywood and Beyond*, ed. Bill Marshall and Robynn Stilwell, Exeter, UK: Intellect, 98–106.

London, Justin (2000), "Leitmotifs and Musical Reference in the Classical Film Score," in *Music and Cinema*, ed. James Buhler, Caryl Flinn, and David Neumeyer, Hanover, NH: Wesleyan University Press, 85–96.

Lovensheimer, Jim (2002), "Stephen Sondheim and the Musical of the Outsider," in *The Cambridge Companion to the Musical*, ed. William A. Everett and Paul R. Laird, Cambridge, UK: Cambridge University Press, 181–196.

Lusch, Robert F. and Stephen L. Vargo (ed. 2006), *Toward a Service-Dominant Logic of Marketing: Continuing the Discussion, Debate, and Dialog*, Armonk, NY: M. E. Sharpe.

Macdonald, Dwight (1953, ed. 1957), "A Theory of Mass Culture," in *Mass Culture: The Popular Arts in America*, eds. Bernard Rosenberg and David Manning White, Glencoe, IL: The Free Press, 59–73.

Macdonald, Dwight (1962), *Against the American Grain*, New York, NY: Da Capo Press.

MacKinnon, Kenneth (2000), "'I Keep Wishing I Were Somewhere Else': Space and Fantasies of Freedom in the Hollywood Musical," in *Musicals: Hollywood and Beyond*, ed. Bill Marshall and Robynn Stilwell, Exeter, UK: Intellect, 40–46.

Majumdar, Neepa (2001), "The Embodied Voice: Song Sequences and Stardom in Popular Hindi Cinema," in *Soundtrack Available: Essays on Film and Popular Music*, ed. Pamela Robertson Wojcik and Arthur Knight, Durham, NC: Duke University Press, 161–181.

Marks, Martin (2000), "Music, Drama, Warner Brothers: The Case of *Casablanca* and *The Maltese Falcon*," in *Music and Cinema*, ed. James Buhler, Caryl Flinn, and David Neumeyer, Hanover, NH: Wesleyan University Press, 161–186.

Marshall, Bill and Robynn Stilwell (2000), "Introduction," in *Musicals: Hollywood and Beyond*, ed. Bill Marshall and Robynn Stilwell, Exeter, UK: Intellect, 1–4.

Marshall, Bill and Robynn Stilwell (ed. 2000), *Musicals: Hollywood and Beyond*, Exeter, UK: Intellect Press.

McBrien, William (1998), *Cole Porter: A Biography*, New York, NY: Vintage Books.

McClary, Susan (2007), "Minima Romantica," in *Beyond the Soundtrack: Representing Music in Cinema*, ed. Daniel Goldmark, Lawrence Kramer, and Richard Leppert, Berkeley, CA: University of California Press, 48–65.

McClung, Bruce D. and Paul R. Laird (2002), "Musical Sophistication on Broadway: Kurt Weill and Leonard Bernstein," in *The Cambridge Companion to the Musical*, ed. William A. Everett and Paul R. Laird, Cambridge, UK: Cambridge University Press, 167–178.

McCracken, Allison (2001), "Real Men Don't Sing Ballads: The Radio Crooner in Hollywood, 1929–1933," in *Soundtrack Available: Essays on Film and Popular Music*, ed. Pamela Robertson Wojcik and Arthur Knight, Durham, NC: Duke University Press, 105–133.

Meeker, David (1981), *Jazz in the Movies*, New York, NY: Da Capo Press.

Mellencamp, Patricia (2002), "Sexual Economics: *Gold Diggers of 1933*," in *Hollywood Musicals: The Film Reader*, ed. Steven Cohan, London, UK: Routledge, 65–76.

Merriam-Webster (2001), *Collegiate Dictionary*, Tenth Edition, Springfield, MA: Merriam-Webster, Incorporated.

Metz, Christian (1974), *Film Language: A Semiotics of the Cinema*, New York, NY: Oxford University Press.

Meyer, Leonard B. (1956), *Emotion and Meaning in Music*, Chicago, IL: The University of Chicago Press.

Meyer, Leonard B. (1967), *Music, the Arts, and Ideas: Patterns and Predictions in Twentieth-Century Culture*, Chicago, IL: The University of Chicago Press.

Milligan, Andy and Shaun Smith (ed. 2002), *Uncommon Practice: People Who Deliver a Great Brand Experience*, London, UK: Pearson Education Limited.

Mizejewski, Linda (2002), "Beautiful White Bodies," in *Hollywood Musicals: The Film Reader*, ed. Steven Cohan, London, UK: Routledge, 182–193.

Monaco, James (1981), *How to Read a Film: The Art, Technology, Language, History, and Theory of Film and Media*, Revised Edition, New York, NY: Oxford University Press.

Moody, Bill (2002), *Looking For Chet Baker: An Evan Horne Mystery*, New York, NY: Walker & Co.

Mosteller, Frederick and David L. Wallace (1964), *Inference and Disputed Authorship: The Federalist*, Reading, MA: Addison-Wesley Publishing Company.

Mustazza, Leonard (1995), "Introduction—Sinatra's Enduring Appeal: Art and Heart," in *The Sinatra Reader*, ed. Steven Petkov and Leonard Mustazza, New York, NY: Oxford University Press, 3–10.

Nanry, Charles with Edward Berger (1979), *The Jazz Text*, New York, NY: D. Van Nostrand Company.

Neumeyer, David and James Buhler (2001), "Analytical and Interpretive Approaches to Film Music (I): Analysing the Music," in *Film Music: Critical Approaches*, ed. K. J. Donnelly, New York, NY: The Continuum International Publishing Group, 16–38.

Neumeyer, David, with Caryl Flinn and James Buhler (2000), "Introduction," in *Music and Cinema*, ed. James Buhler, Caryl Flinn, and David Neumeyer, Hanover, NH: Wesleyan University Press, 1–29.

Newquist, Roy (1968, ed. 1995), "Sinatra Power," *McCall's*, (July), 79, 120–122, in *The Sinatra Reader*, ed. Steven Petkov and Leonard Mustazza, New York, NY: Oxford University Press, 130–137.

*Newsweek* (1965, ed. 1995), "Sinatra: Where the Action Is," *Newsweek*, (September 6), 39–42, in *The Sinatra Reader*, ed. Steven Petkov and Leonard Mustazza, New York, NY: Oxford University Press, 90–98.

Nolan, Frederick (1994), *Lorenz Hart: A Poet on Broadway*, New York, NY: Oxford University Press.

Nolan, Tom (2010), *Three Chords For Beauty's Sake: The Life of Artie Shaw*, New York, NY: W. W. Norton & Company.

O'Meally, Robert (1991), *Lady Day: The Many Faces of Billie Holiday*, Boston, MA: Little, Brown.

Ortega y Gasset, José (1932, ed. 1957), *The Revolt of the Masses*, New York, NY: W. W. Norton & Company.

Osgerby, Bill (2000), "Beach Bound: Exotica, Leisure Style and Popular Culture in Post-War America from *South Pacific* to *Beach Blanket Bingo*," in *Musicals: Hollywood and Beyond*, ed. Bill Marshall and Robynn Stilwell, Exeter, UK: Intellect, 132–140.

Pacheco, Ferdie (2005), *Who Is Artie Shaw ... and Why Is He Following Me?*, Bloomington, IN: AuthorHouse.

Packard, Vance (1959), *The Status Seekers*, New York, NY: D. McKay.

Paisley, William J. (1964), "Identifying the Unknown Communicator in Painting, Literature, and Music: The Significance of Minor Encoding Habits," *Journal of Communication*, 14 (4, December), 219–237.

Pattison, Robert (1987), *The Triumph of Vulgarity: Rock Music in the Mirror of Romanticism*, New York, NY: Oxford University Press.

Paudras, Francis (1998), *Dance of the Infidels: A Portrait of Bud Powell*, trans. Rubye Money, New York, NY: Da Capo Press.

Paulin, Scott D. (2000), "Richard Wagner and the Fantasy of Cinematic Unity: The Idea of *Gesamtkunstwerk* in the History of Film Music," in *Music and Cinema*, ed. James Buhler, Caryl Flinn, and David Neumeyer, Hanover, NH: Wesleyan University Press, 58–84.

Pepper, Art (1979), *Straight Life: The Story of Art Pepper*, New York, NY: Schirmer Books.

Petkov, Steven (1995), "Ol' Blue Eyes and the Golden Age of the American Song: The Capitol years," in *The Sinatra Reader*, ed. Steven Petkov and Leonard Mustazza, New York, NY: Oxford University Press, 74–84.

Petkov, Steven and Leonard Mustazza (ed. 1995), *The Sinatra Reader*, New York, NY: Oxford University Press.

Pine, B. Joseph, II and James H. Gilmore (1998), "Welcome to the Experience Economy," *Harvard Business Review*, 76 (4, July–August). 97–105.

Pine, B. Joseph, II and James H. Gilmore (1999), *The Experience Economy: Work Is Theatre & Every Business a Stage*, Boston, MA: Harvard Business School Press.

Pleasants, Henry (1974), *The Great American Popular Singers*, New York, NY: Simon & Schuster.

Pomerance, Murray (2000), "Finding Release: 'Storm Clouds' and *The Man Who Knew Too Much*," in *Music and Cinema*, ed. James Buhler, Caryl Flinn, and David Neumeyer, Hanover, NH: Wesleyan University Press, 207–246.

Pomerance, Murray (2001), "'The Future's Not Ours to See': Song, Singer, Labyrinth in Hitchcock's *The Man Who Knew Too* Much," in *Soundtrack Available: Essays on Film and Popular Music*, ed. Pamela Robertson Wojcik and Arthur Knight, Durham, NC: Duke University Press, 53–73.

Porter, Lewis (1985), *Lester Young*, Boston, MA: Twayne Publishers.

Prendergast, Roy M. (1992), *Film Music—A Neglected Art: A Critical Study of Music in Films*, Second Edition, New York, NY: W. W. Norton & Company.

Previn, André (1991), *No Minor Chords: My Days in Hollywood*, New York, NY: Doubleday.

Ramaeker, Paul B. (2001), "'You Think They Call Us Plastic Now . . . ': The Monkees and *Head*," in *Soundtrack Available: Essays on Film and Popular Music*, ed. Pamela Robertson Wojcik and Arthur Knight, Durham, NC: Duke University Press, 74–102.

Ricoeur, Paul (1976), *Interpretation Theory: Discourse and the Surplus of Meaning*, Fort Worth, TX: The Texas Christian University Press.

Ricoeur, Paul (1981), *Hermeneutics and the Human Sciences: Essays on Language, Action and Interpretation*, ed. and trans. John B. Thompson, Cambridge, UK: Cambridge University Press.

Riis, Thomas L. and Ann Sears with William A. Everett (2002), "The Successors of Rodgers and Hammerstein from the 1940s to the 1960s," in *The Cambridge Companion to the Musical*, ed. William A. Everett and Paul R. Laird, Cambridge, UK: Cambridge University Press, 137–166.

Roberts, John (2005), "Always Blue: Chet Baker's Voice," in *Pop Fiction: The Song in Cinema*, ed. Steve Lannin and Matthew Caley, Bristol, UK: Intellect, 121–127.

Roberts, Shari (2002), "'The Lady in the Tutti-Frutti Hat': Carmen Miranda, a Spectacle of Ethnicity," in *Hollywood Musicals: The Film Reader*, ed. Steven Cohan, London, UK: Routledge, 143–153.

Robertson, Pamela (2002), "Feminist Camp in *Gold Diggers of 1933*," in *Hollywood Musicals: The Film Reader*, ed. Steven Cohan, London, UK: Routledge, 129–142.

Rockwell, John (1974, ed. 1995), "Sinatra at the Garden Is Superb TV as Well," *New York Times*, (October 14), 42, in *The Sinatra Reader*, ed. Steven Petkov and Leonard Mustazza, New York, NY: Oxford University Press, 166–167.

Rockwell, John (1984), *Sinatra: An American Classic*, New York, NY: Random House.

Rodel, Angela (2004), "Extreme Noise Terror: Punk Rock and the Aesthetics of Badness," in *Bad Music: The Music We Love to Hate*, ed. Christopher Washburne and Maiken Derno, New York, NY: Routledge, 235–256.

Rodman, Ronald (2000), "Tonal Design and the Aesthetic of Pastiche in Herbert Stothart's *Maytime*," in *Music and Cinema*, ed. James Buhler, Caryl Flinn, and David Neumeyer, Hanover, NH: Wesleyan University Press, 187–206.

Rogin, Michael (2002), "New Deal Blackface," in *Hollywood Musicals: The Film Reader*, ed. Steven Cohan, London, UK: Routledge, 175–182.

Romney, Jonathan and Adrian Wootton (1995), "Introduction," in *Celluloid Jukebox: Popular Music and the Movies Since the 50s*, ed. Jonathan Romney and Adrian Wootton, London, UK: British Film Institute, 2–7.

Romney, Jonathan and Adrian Wootton (ed. 1995), *Celluloid Jukebox: Popular Music and the Movies Since the 50s*, London, UK: British Film Institute.

Rosar, William H. (2001), "The *Dies Irae* in *Citizen Kane*: Musical Hermeneutics Applied to Film Music," in *Film Music: Critical Approaches*, ed. K. J. Donnelly, Edinburgh, UK: Edinburgh University Press, 103–116.

Rosar, William H. (2002), "Film Music—What's in a Name?" *Journal of Film Music*, 1 (1), 1–18.

Rosenblatt, Roger (ed. 1999), *Consuming Desires: Consumption, Culture, and the Pursuit Of Happiness*, Washington, D.C.: Island Press.

Ross, Andrew (1989), *No Respect: Intellectuals & Popular Culture*, New York, NY: Routledge.

Rubin, Martin (2002), "Busby Berkeley and the Backstage Musical," in *Hollywood Musicals: The Film Reader*, ed. Steven Cohan, London, UK: Routledge, 53–61.

Russell, Rosalind (1973, ed. 1995), "Sinatra: An American Classic," *Ladies' Home Journal*, in *The Sinatra Reader*, ed. Steven Petkov and Leonard Mustazza, New York, NY: Oxford University Press, 147–150.

Russell, Ross (1973), *Bird Lives! The High Life and Hard Times of Charlie (Yardbird) Parker*, New York, NY: Charterhouse.

Saussure, Ferdinand de (1915, ed. 1966), *Course in General Linguistics*, trans. Wade Baskin, New York, NY: McGraw-Hill.

Schaeffer, Pierre (1967), *Traité des Objets Musicaux*, Paris, France: Seuil.

Schelle, Michael (1999), *The Score: Interviews with Film Composers*, Los Angeles, CA: Silman-James Press.

Schleiermacher, Fr. D. E. (1911, ed. 1978), "*The Hermeneutics*: Outline of the 1819 Lectures," trans. Jan Wojik and Roland Haas, *New Literary History*, 10 (1), 1–16.

Schmitt, Bernd H. (1999), *Experiential Marketing: How to Get Customers to Sense, Feel, Think, Act, and Relate to Your Company and Brands*, New York, NY: The Free Press.

Scholes, Robert (1974), *Structuralism in Literature*, New Haven, CT: Yale University Press.

Schwartz, Jonathan (1989, ed. 1995), "Sinatra: In the Wee Small Hours," *GQ* (June), 228–231, in *The Sinatra Reader*, ed. Steven Petkov and Leonard Mustazza, New York, NY: Oxford University Press, 245–252.

Scorsese, Martin (1995), "Preface," in *Celluloid Jukebox: Popular Music and the Movies Since the 50s*, ed. Jonathan Romney and Adrian Wootton, London, UK: British Film Institute, 1.

Scott, Bobby (2007), "Gene Remembered," *Jazzletter*, 24 (4, April), 3–10.

Sears, Ann (2002), "The Coming of the Musical Play: Rodgers and Hammerstein," in *The Cambridge Companion to the Musical*, ed. William A. Everett and Paul R. Laird, Cambridge, UK: Cambridge University Press, 120–136.

Sebeok, Thomas A. (1983), "One, two, three spells UBERTY," in *The Sign of Three: Dupin, Holmes, Peirce*, ed. Umberto Eco and Thomas A. Sebeok, Bloomington, IN: Indiana University Press, 1–10.

Sebeok, Thomas A. and Jean Umiker-Sebeok (1983), "'You Know My Method': A Juxtaposition of Charles S. Peirce and Sherlock Holmes," in *The Sign of Three: Dupin, Holmes, Peirce*, ed. Umberto Eco and Thomas A. Sebeok, Bloomington, IN: Indiana University Press, 11–54.

Shaw, Arnold (1968), *Sinatra: Twentieth-Century Romantic*, New York, NY: Holt, Rinehart and Winston.

Shaw, Artie (1939), "Music Is a Business," *The Saturday Evening Post*, 214 (December 2), 14-15, 66–68.

Shaw, Artie (1952), *The Trouble With Cinderella: An Outline of Identity*, New York, NY: Farrar, Straus and Young.

Shaw, Artie (1965), *I Love You, I Hate You, Drop Dead!*, New York, NY: Fleet Publishing Corporation.

Shaw, Artie (1989), *The Best of Intentions*, Santa Barbara, CA: John Daniel and Company.

Shaw, Artie with Richard M. Sudhalter (2001), "Good Enough Ain't Good Enough: Artie Shaw Looks Back, Reflects and Sums Up," *Self-Portrait*, New York, NY: BMG Entertainment.

Shepherd, Donald and Robert F. Slatzer (1981), *Bing Crosby: The Hollow Man*, New York, NY: St. Martin's Press.

Sherry, John F., Jr. (1991), "Postmodern Alternatives: The Interpretive Turn in Consumer Research," in *Handbook of Consumer Behavior*, ed. Thomas S. Robertson and Harold H. Kassarjian, Englewood Cliffs, NJ: Prentice Hall, 548–591.

Shultz, Clifford J., II and Morris B. Holbrook (1999), "Marketing and the Tragedy of the Commons: A Synthesis, Commentary, and Analysis for Action," *Journal of Public Policy & Marketing*, 18 (Fall), 218–229.

Sinatra, Nancy (1985), *Frank Sinatra: My Father*, Garden City, NY: Doubleday & Company.

Sinker, Mark (1995), "Music As Film," in *Celluloid Jukebox: Popular Music and the Movies Since the 50s*, ed. Jonathan Romney and Adrian Wootton, London, UK: British Film Institute, 106–117.

Smith, Jeff (1998), *The Sounds of Commerce: Marketing Popular Film Music*, New York, NY: Columbia University Press.

Smith, Jeff (2000), "That Money-Making 'Moon River' Sound: Thematic Organization and Orchestration in the Film Music of Henry Mancini," in *Music and Cinema*, ed. James Buhler, Caryl Flinn, and David Neumeyer, Hanover, NH: Wesleyan University Press, 247–271.

Smith, Jeff (2001), "Popular Songs and Comic Allusion in Contemporary Cinema," in *Soundtrack Available: Essays on Film and Popular Music*, ed. Pamela Robertson Wojcik and Arthur Knight, Durham, NC: Duke University Press, 407–430.

Smith, Jeff (2003), "Banking on Film Music: Structural Interactions of the Film and Record Industries," in *Movie Music, The Film Reader*, ed. Kay Dickinson, London, UK: Routledge, 63–81.

Smith, Jeff (2005), "From Bond to Blank," in *Pop Fiction: The Song in Cinema*, ed. Steve Lannin and Matthew Caley, Bristol, UK: Intellect, 129–137.

Smith, Shaun and Joe Wheeler (2002), *Managing the Customer Experience: Turning Customers Into Advocates*. London, UK: Prentice Hall.

Stanfield, Peter (2000), "From the Vulgar to the Refined: American Vernacular and Blackface Minstrelsy in *Showboat*," in *Musicals: Hollywood and Beyond*, ed. Bill Marshall and Robynn Stilwell, Exeter, UK: Intellect, 147–156.

Stilwell, Robynn J. (2001), "Sound and Empathy: Subjectivity, Gender and the Cinematic Soundscape," in *Film Music: Critical Approaches*, ed. K. J. Donnelly, New York, NY: The Continuum International Publishing Group, 167–187.

Stilwell, Robynn J. (2002), "Music in Films: A Critical Review of Literature, 1980–1996," *Journal of Film Music*, 1 (1), 19–61.

Stilwell, Robynn J. (2005), "Clean Reading: The Problematics of 'In the Air Tonight' in Risky Business," in *Pop Fiction: The Song in Cinema*, ed. Steve Lannin and Matthew Caley, Bristol, UK: Intellect, 139–154.

Stilwell, Robynn J. (2007), "The Fantastical Gap between Diegetic and Nondiegetic," in *Beyond the Soundtrack: Representing Music in Cinema*, ed. Daniel Goldmark, Lawrence Kramer, and Richard Leppert, Los Angeles: University of California Press, 184–202.

Stowe, David W. (1994), *Swing Changes: Big-Band Jazz in New Deal America*, Cambridge, MA: Harvard University Press.

Sudhalter, Richard M. (1999), *Lost Chords: White Musicians and Their Contribution to Jazz, 1915–1945*, New York, NY: Oxford University Press.

Talese, Gay (1966 [1993], ed. 1995), "Frank Sinatra Has a Cold," from *Fame and Obscurity*, Ivy Books, in *The Sinatra Reader*, ed. Steven Petkov and Leonard Mustazza, New York, NY: Oxford University Press, 99–129.

Tan, Ed S. (1996), *Emotion and the Structure of Narrative Film: Film as an Emotion Machine*, trans. Barbara Fasting, Mahwah, NJ: Lawrence Erlbaum.

Thomas, Gary C. (2007), "Men at the Keyboard: Liminal Spaces and the Heterotopian Function of Music," in *Beyond the Soundtrack: Representing Music in Cinema*, ed. Daniel Goldmark, Lawrence Kramer, and Richard Leppert, Berkeley, CA: University of California Press, 277–291.

Thompson, John B. (1981), *Critical Hermeneutics: A Study in the Thought of Paul Ricoeur and Jurgen Habermas*, Cambridge, UK: Cambridge University Press.

Thompson, Thomas (1971, ed. 1995), "Frank Sinatra's Swan Song," *Life*, 25 June 1971, 70A–74, in *The Sinatra Reader*, ed. Steven Petkov and Leonard Mustazza, New York, NY: Oxford University Press, 142–147.

Tinkcom, Matthew (2002), "'Working Like a Homosexual': Camp Visual Codes and the Labor of Gay Subjects in the MGM Freed Unit," in *Hollywood Musicals: The Film Reader*, ed. Steven Cohan, London, UK: Routledge, 115–128.

Toop, David (1995), "Rock Musicians and Film Soundtracks," in *Celluloid Jukebox: Popular Music and the Movies Since the 50s*, ed. Jonathan Romney and Adrian Wootton, London, UK: British Film Institute, 72–81.

Tormé, Mel (1988), *It Wasn't All Velvet*, New York, NY: Viking.

Tormé, Mel (1994), *My Singing Teachers*, New York, NY: Oxford University Press.

Truzzi, Marcello (1983), "Sherlock Holmes: Applied Social Psychologist," in *The Sign of Three: Dupin, Holmes, Peirce*, ed. Umberto Eco and Thomas A. Sebeok, Bloomington, IN: Indiana University Press, 55–80.

Turner, Lana (1982), *Lana: The Lady, the Legend, the Truth*, New York, NY: Pocket Books.

Twitchell, James B. (1992), *Carnival Culture: The Trashing of Taste in America*, New York, NY: Columbia University Press.

Twitchell, James B. (1999), *Lead Us Into Temptation: The Triumph of American Materialism*, New York, NY: Columbia University Press.

Valk, Jeroen de (1989), *Chet Baker: His Life and Music*, Berkeley, CA: Berkeley Hills Books.

Vargo, Stephen L. and Robert F. Lusch (2004), "Evolving to a New Dominant Logic for Marketing," *Journal of Marketing*, 68 (January), 1–17.

Veblen, Thorstein (1899, ed. 1967), *The Theory of the Leisure Class*, New York, NY: Penguin.

Veeser, H. Aram (ed. 1996), *Confessions of the Critics*, New York, NY: Routledge.

Wadler, Joyce (2005), "Artie Shaw, Without Music," *New York Times*, (January 5), on-line @ www.nytimes.com

Warfield, Scott (2002), "From *Hair* to *Rent*: Is 'Rock' a Four-Letter Word on Broadway?" in *The Cambridge Companion to the Musical*, ed. William A. Everett and Paul R. Laird, Cambridge, UK: Cambridge University Press, 231–245.

Washburn, Katharine and John Thornton (ed. 1996), *Dumbing Down: Essays on the Strip Mining of American Culture*, New York, NY: W. W. Norton & Company.

Washburne, Christopher (2004), "Does Kenny G Play Bad Jazz?: A Case Study," in *Bad Music: The Music We Love to Hate*, ed. Christopher Washburne and Maiken Derno, New York, NY: Routledge, 123–147.

Weber, Max (1930), *The Protestant Ethic and the Spirit of Capitalism*, trans. Talcott Parsons and Anthony Giddens, Boston, MA: Unwin Hyman.

Wells, William D. (1993), "Discovery-Oriented Consumer Research," *Journal of Consumer Research*, 19 (March), 489–504.

White, John (2004), *Artie Shaw: His Life and Music*, New York, NY: Continuum.

Wilder, Alec (1972), *American Popular Song: The Great Innovators, 1900–1950*, London, UK: Oxford University Press.

Wilson, Earl (1976), *Sinatra: An Unauthorized Biography*, New York, NY: New American Library.

Wilson, John S. (2004), "Artie Shaw, Big Band Leader, Dies at 94," *New York Times*, (December 30), on-line @ www. nytimes.com

Wimsatt, William K., Jr. and Monroe C. Beardsley (1946), "The Intentional Fallacy," *Sewanee Review*, 54 (Summer), 468–488.

Wimsatt, William K., Jr. with Monroe Beardsley (1954), *The Verbal Icon: Studies in the Meaning of Poetry*, Lexington, KY: University of Kentucky Press.

Wohlfeil, Markus and Susan Whelan (2006), "Confessions of a Movie-Fan: Introspection into the Experiential Consumption of '*Pride & Prejudice*,'" Working Paper, Waterford Institute of Technology, Waterford, Ireland.

Wojcik, Pamela Robertson (2001), "The Girl and the Phonograph; or the Vamp and the Machine Revisited," in *Soundtrack Available: Essays on Film and*

*Popular Music*, ed. Pamela Robertson Wojcik and Arthur Knight, Durham, NC: Duke University Press, 433–454.

Wojcik, Pamela Robertson and Arthur Knight (ed. 2001), *Soundtrack Available: Essays on Film and Popular Music*, Durham, NC: Duke University Press.

Wood, Graham (2002), "Distant Cousin or Fraternal Twin? Analytical Approaches to the Film Musical," in *The Cambridge Companion to the Musical*, ed. William A. Everett and Paul R. Laird, Cambridge, UK: Cambridge University Press, 212–230.

Wootton, Adrian (1995), "The Do's and Don'ts of Rock Documentaries," in *Celluloid Jukebox: Popular Music and the Movies Since the 50s*, ed. Jonathan Romney and Adrian Wootton, London, UK: British Film Institute, 94–105.

Wulff, Ingo (1989), *Chet Baker: In Concert*, Bremen, Germany: Nieswand Verlag.

Wulff, Ingo (1993), *Chet Baker in Europe: 1975–1988*, Bremen, Germany: Nieswand Verlag.

Yanow, Scott (2004), *Jazz on Film: The Complete Story of the Musicians & Music Onscreen*, San Francisco, CA: Backbeat Books.

Zwerin, Mike (1981), "The Tender Trumpet of Chet Baker," *The International Herald Tribune*, (November 12), on-line @ home.ica.net/~blooms/premier.htm